Business Fluctuations

Forecasting Techniques and Applications

Second Edition

Dale G. Bails
Public Interest Institute

Larry C. Peppers
Washington and Lee University

Prentice Hall, Englewood Cliffs, New Jersey 07632

Library of Congress Cataloging-in-Publication Data

Bails, Dale.
  Business fluctuations : forecasting techniques and applications /
Dale G. Bails, Larry C. Peppers.—2nd ed.
    p.   cm.
  Includes bibliographical references and index.
  ISBN 0-13-093394-5
  1. Business cycles—Forecasting. 2. Business forecasting.
I. Peppers, Larry C. II. Title.
HB3711.B325 1993
338.5′442—dc20
                                                    92–22926
                                                         CIP

Acquisitions editor: Stephen Dietrich
Editorial/production supervision and
   interior design: Brian Hatch and Barbara Grasso
Cover design: Mike Fender
Copy editor: Patricia Daly
Prepress buyer: Trudy Pisciotti
Manufacturing buyer: Patrice Fraccio
Supplements editor: David Shea

 © 1993, 1982 by Prentice-Hall, Inc.
A Simon & Schuster Company
Englewood Cliffs, New Jersey 07632

Printed in the United States of America

10 9 8 7 6 5 4 3 2 1

ISBN 0-13-093394-5

Prentice-Hall International (UK) Limited, *London*
Prentice-Hall of Australia Pty. Limited, *Sydney*
Prentice-Hall Canada Inc., *Toronto*
Prentice-Hall Hispanoamericana, S.A., *Mexico*
Prentice-Hall of India Private Limited, *New Delhi*
Prentice-Hall of Japan, Inc., *Tokyo*
Simon & Schuster Asia Pte. Ltd., *Singapore*
Editora Prentice-Hall do Brasil, Ltda., *Rio de Janeiro*

Contents

Chapter 6   *Multiple Regression Models*   *216*

Chapter 7   *Advanced Topics in Regression Analysis*   *289*

PART IV   *TIME SERIES MODELS*

Chapter 8   **Time Series Models**   **346**

Chapter 9 Advanced Time Series Models   *420*

PART V MONITORING AND REVISING FORECASTS

Chapter 10 Monitoring and Revising Forecasts   *483*

PART VI COMMUNICATING FORECASTS TO MANAGEMENT

Chapter 11 Communicating the Forecast to Management   *516*

APPENDICES

Preface

Ten years have passed since the first edition of *Business Fluctuations* was published, and the ensuing decade has witnessed a number of major events which have served to permanently alter the practice of business forecasting. The birth and rapid evolution of the microcomputer industry has led to the decentralization of forecasting activity. Forecasters can now process vast quantities of data at their home or office without being dependent on large mainframe computers. Advances in software and hardware (statistical packages, spreadsheets, desktop publishing, and CD data storage systems) have resulted in a need for fewer people to carry out a given business forecasting assignment. At the same time, the globalization of the U.S. economy has meant that all forecasts are international in scope and that almost all firms are subject to greater competition. The decade of the 1980s witnessed a reduction in the size of corporate staffs, and forecasters were also forced to downsize their operations due to economic circumstances. Fortunately, the technological advances outlined above made such shifts possible without a significant reduction in quality. In contrast to the recession of a decade earlier, the recession which began in the summer of 1990 found business forecasters coping with an economy which was much more highly integrated with international economic forces and global shifts in political alliances. In other words, the task of forecasting has become more challenging in the past decade.

As with the first edition of *Business Fluctuations,* we assume that students must become well acquainted with the broad institutional environment surrounding the business sector, that forecasting skills are best developed and retained by repeated exposure to real (as opposed to contrived) forecasting models, and that techniques and applications must accurately reflect the process of forecasting as actually carried out in the business community. While new books on forecasting have been published in the past decade, we believe that our comparative advantage is in assisting students in understanding the activity of forecasting as performed by practicing business professionals. The second edition includes expanded coverage of data analysis, forecast monitoring systems, and Box-Jenkins modelling techniques. Data disks are available for professors so that students can easily replicate the models in the book.

The typical master's level student (or upper-level undergraduate) will have had at least two semesters of economics and two or more semesters of statistical techniques and quantitative methods, and this is the background we assume in presenting the material. In Chapter 1, an overview of forecasting issues and concepts is presented in order to outline a general road map for the remainder of the book and to stimulate students to start thinking again about macroeconomic concepts such as recession and growth, about forecasting topics such as disaggregation and interdependence, about the forecasting process itself, and about the role the company forecaster plays in providing management with the information needed to make decisions. Early in the book, we emphasize the functional division of labor that exists between commercial vendors that sell output from their large-scale econometric models and company-level forecasters who build statistical models designed to link the company's economic fortunes to national and international trends. The questions at the end of Chapter 1 are meant to familiarize students with basic data sources, such as the *Survey of Current Business,* which are to be found in the government documents section of most college libraries.

Although an elaborate review of macroeconomic theory is not presented in the book, Chapter 2 offers students a statistical and institutional profile of the business cycle that builds upon the historical legacies of Wesley Mitchell, Arthur Burns, and the National Bureau of Economic Research. The indicator approach is studied and documented, but the primary purpose of Chapter 2 is to heighten the student's awareness of the endogenous nature of cyclical forces.

Chapters 3 and 4 cover data collection and analysis and the process of decomposing a time series, as well as presenting a general overview of the various methods of evaluating forecast reliability. Through a series of simple examples and problems, the student is guided through the basic steps involved in isolating and measuring the trend, cyclical, seasonal, and irregular components of a time series. Once the time series model is understood, the next step is to integrate these components within a forecasting system. This is accomplished in Chapter 4 where the strategies and factors which influence technique selection are presented.

Chapters 5, 6, and 7 can be viewed as an integrated block of statistical methodology, empirical examples, and questions built around the least-squares regression model. Starting with the simple-regression model in Chapter 5, students are repeatedly taken through the steps involved in formulation and estimation of regression equations. Voluminous appendices contain the data used in the models, and students are permitted, by Chapter 7, to follow the step-by-step development and testing of multiple-regression models. The material draws heavily upon the authors' own experiences as business forecasters and economic consultants for a number of Fortune 500 companies, nonprofit agencies and government bureaus. The principal objectives of Chapter 5 are to present the theoretical foundations of the least-squares regression model and to illustrate how the model is adapted to the forecasting environment.

Chapter 6 introduces the complete multiple-regression model and investigates potential problem areas—nonlinearity, multicollinearity, heteroscedasticity, and autocorrelation. Chapter 7 focuses on a series of special topics, such as proxy and dummy variables, linear transformations, stepwise regression, and lagged and distributed lag models. The main purpose of Chapter 7 is to illustrate, through a series of applied examples, how forecasters work through the time-consuming task of developing a model.

Chapters 8 and 9 offer a two-chapter introduction to a variety of time-series (autoregressive) models such as single-moving-average techniques, exponential smoothing models, trend models, and Box-Jenkins models. Again, the models are presented in a sequential fashion from simple to complex and are illustrated with extended examples drawn from a wide range of situations and industries. Our approach to Box-Jenkins is decidedly nonmathematical and does not resort to complex formulations.

While the first nine chapters provide the bulk of material on the development and evaluation of forecasts, Chapter 10 provides the student with numerous procedures for identifying the source of forecast error, for tracking the reliability of previous forecasts, and for revising forecasts. The majority of the examples and information in this chapter have been drawn from the authors' experiences in developing forecasting models for corporations. We end the chapter with a discussion of how the forecast preparer can assist management in dealing with changing economic conditions by introducing the forecasting audit and control cycle.

Chapter 11, the last chapter in the book, does not, in our view, contain optional material. Rather, we focus on several topics that are usually neglected in forecasting textbooks: how to interpret a request for a forecast; how to respond to a request with a series of questions that will identify the user's level of technical literacy and actual information needs; and how to translate a statistical outlook into a format that allows decision makers to fully integrate the forecaster's projections with other information flows and with other plans which are developed by most business firms. Stated differently, Chapter 11 focuses on the nonquantitative skills a forecaster must possess in order to bridge the gap from forecaster to advisor. The authors' experiences in business suggest that many forecasters misallocate their time by spending too many hours perfecting inherently fragile statistical models and too little time on the interpersonal skills needed to *sell* the forecast to management. The vast majority of this textbook is devoted to the critical job of learning how to forecast. Chapter 11 addresses the equally important tasks of communicating the forecast to management and of understanding the inherent conflicts between forecast users and forecast preparers.

This book is oriented toward applications and not theory. The most obvious example of this perspective is the utilization of extended examples in which actual forecasting situations are studied. These extended examples are used not so much to get answers as to illustrate the process by which actual forecasts are generated. In adopting this perspective, we have had to sacrifice coverage of advanced topics in macroeconomic theory and econometric modelling. This choice reflects our experience as corporate forecasters and our philosophy that people can become successful forecasters without becoming macroeconomic or statistical theoreticians.

As always, many people have contributed to the final version of this book, and to all of them we express our sincere gratitude. For our editor, Stephen Dietrich, and our production editor, Brian Hatch, we extend our thanks for their high degree of professionalism. To our wives, Fran and Marcia, and to our families we direct special praise for tolerating countless late night conversations and endless hours spent in front of the microcomputer.

Larry C. Peppers   Dale G. Bails
Washington and Lee University   Public Interest Institute
Lexington, Virginia   Mt. Pleasant, Iowa

June 1992

1

Business Forecasting

INTRODUCTION

Starting in the late 1950s, both business firms and not-for-profit organizations began to display a much greater interest in forecasting. As organizations of all types have become more complex, managerial decision makers have been forced to develop a broader and more systematic view of the future that incorporates both the dynamics of the domestic marketplace and the expanding importance of global economic activity.

This chapter serves as an introduction to the world of business forecasting—an interesting and sometimes confusing arena that simultaneously entails a high degree of technical specialization and, hopefully, a large dose of common sense. The business forecaster combines expertise in business and economics with statistical training to analyze the behavior of a company or an industry over the course of the business cycle. To become a forecaster, a person must possess a solid grounding in economics, statistics, and business, a basic understanding of postwar business cycles and related concepts such as peaks and troughs in economic activity, recession versus depression and prosperity, exogenous versus endogenous cycles, and macroeconomic or economy-wide cycles versus microeconomic or company-level cycles. It is also important to grasp the broad range of activities actually performed by members of the forecasting profession—commercial forecasting companies that sell the output from their econometric models, business analysts responsible for translating general economic projections into specific sales estimates for their companies, industry and financial analysts making investment recommendations, and government forecasters trying to predict the course of prices and employment.

Although the prerequisites of forecasting can be neatly catalogued, the only sure way to develop the necessary skills is to become involved in repeated forecasting applications. This chapter provides a general overview of forecasting by examining the process of forecasting and the relationship between forecasting and decision making.

FORECASTING AS AN ART

Forecasting is as much an art as it is a science. Although in this chapter we focus initially on the mechanical steps in the preparation of forecasts, we would be remiss if we did not suggest at the outset that the preparation of a forecast entails more than plugging historical data into mathematical models to predict the future. At virtually all stages in the forecasting process, forecasters and managers must make informed judgments.

All forecasts require assumptions (some relating to factors internal to the firm or industry, others to the behavior of external agents such as the Federal Reserve). These assumptions are based in large part on the beliefs and knowledge of the forecaster and management. Judgment is required in the actual construction of the forecasting model and in interpreting the results generated by mathematical models. Rarely does a forecaster accept at face value the forecasts generated from a mathematical model. Rather, judgmental questions always arise: Is this forecast reasonable given the most recent experience? Do these results build in enough flexibility to account for changes by our rivals? Alternatively, it can be argued that the preparation of a forecast involves more than simply using historical data and statistical formulas. An integral part of forecasting is the inclusion of managerial judgment and intuition in the methodological framework. As a unifying thread throughout this book, we continually examine practical forecasting problems drawn from the authors' experiences to illustrate the range of judgmental decisions that are routinely required for the development of reliable forecasts.

DECISION MAKERS: THE NEED FOR FORECAST INFORMATION

Before we become immersed in the details of forecasting, it is worthwhile to discuss the purpose of forecasting from the perspective of a business organization. The goal of a business forecaster is to provide management with information that will facilitate the decision-making process. Although not always translatable into profit or loss, a forecast, to be usable, must relate directly to the decisions facing management. This blunt appraisal of a forecast's worth is the standard for every projection presented to management. Forecasters do not know what will happen in the future, but they can work to reduce the range of uncertainty surrounding a business decision. Although surprises such as a natural calamity or an international political incident can overwhelm a well-conceived projection, the forecaster's task remains one of analyzing historical data and institutional trends, studying the information needs of management, and generating detailed reports that focus on the de-cisions management must make.

Table 1-1 provides a sampling of the forecast users within a corporation, with specific forecast needs subdivided by functional responsibility. In essence, the categories listed in Table 1-1 represent general information requirements that are, in turn, linked to pending management decisions. For example, the production department has to schedule employment needs and raw-material orders for the next 60 days. Similarly, the finance department is required to arrange short-term financing for the next quarter to offset volatile cash-flow patterns. Key company executives must make capital-expenditure decisions to ensure that production capacity is adequate to meet projected market growth in the coming decade. Even traditional management support areas such as the law department are increasingly dependent on long-term projections related to social trends and environmental considerations. The demand for forecasts is, therefore, a derived demand based on management's constant decision-mak-ing activities. Although decision makers may be preoccupied with the im-mediate business environment, a forecaster's environment encompasses the broad social and political forces that shape the company's economic fortunes.

Practicing forecasters quickly come to realize that managers in each of the functional areas perceive their individual situations and decisions as re-quiring a unique approach to forecasting. While it is true that each specific situation has certain distinctive characteristics, virtually all of the situations depicted in Table 1-1 have at least three elements in common. The first element is time. Specifically, all decision-making situations deal with the future. A second element is uncertainty. If decision makers were certain of future out-comes, then the preparation of forecasts would be superfluous. Finally, deci-sions based on forecasts rely on statistical analysis to identify forecastable patterns in historical data.

While forecasting techniques are used to answer a wide range of man-agerial questions, managers at different levels require different types of fore-casts. For example, while we would not dispute the importance of controlling inventory costs, forecasting inventory demand for items that are available with a very short lead time requires little managerial input and can usually be handled with relatively mechanistic approaches. Alternatively, when a deci-sion involves a major financial commitment (for example, the construction of a new manufacturing facility), the relationship between the forecaster and the decision maker becomes more critical and necessitates a more rigorous state-ment of information requirements on the part of management.

A word of warning: Forecasting is not a substitute for planning. While it is true that forecasting plays an important role in every functional area of business management, it is only one aspect of the planning process. To use forecasting as a surrogate for planning is extremely dangerous. It removes much of the resourcefulness, vitality, and ingenuity from managerial decision making and, more importantly, leads to a situation in which management tends to react to changes in its environment rather than developing long-term

TABLE 1-1 Forecast Users Within the Corporate Structure and Their Forecast Needs*

			Business Areas			
Personnel	Finance	Marketing	Production	Law	Purchasing	Top Management
General economic conditions	General economic conditions	General economic conditions	General economic conditions	General economic conditions	General economic conditions	General economic conditions
Labor demand	Total dollar sales	Total dollar sales	Labor demand	Environmental constraints	Labor demand	Total sales and cost
Wage rates	Production costs	Unit sales by product and region	Unit sales by product and region	Social trends	Product demand by region and customer	Environmental constraints
Economic trends and turning points	Economic trends and turning points	Economic trends and turning points	Plant production	Economic trends Social trends	Raw-materials demand	Social trends
Personnel projections	Product inventory	Product prices	Product inventory	New-product technology	Product backlog	Economic trends and turning points
Fringe benefits	Cash flow	Consumer preferences	Equipment expenditure		Economic trends and turning points	Capital expenditures
	Interest rates	New-product technology	Plant expansion		Interest rates	New-product technology
	Capital expenditures	Product inventory	Environmental constraints New-product technology		Product prices	
					Capital expenditures Environmental constraints	

* These are merely generalizations about the most obvious forecast needs of each functional area. Although the law department is not ordinarily seen as a user of personnel projections, such information could become very useful if a new pension law was being analyzed.

**FIGURE 1-1   Managerial Alternatives when a Decline
in Sales is Forecasted**

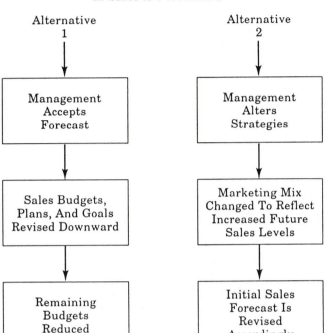

strategies to deal with these changes. Proper utilization of forecasts requires
that planning and forecasting be complementary. To provide a simple illustration of the complementarity of planning and forecasting, suppose that the
current forecast indicates a near-term decline in sales. Figure 1-1 depicts the
alternative scenarios facing management as a result of the predicted decline
in sales. When viewed in this light, forecasts become an input to the planning
and decision-making process. Forecasting leads to predictions of what will
happen under a given set of circumstances. Conversely, planning entails the
use of forecasts to assist decision makers in selecting the most attractive alternative. That is, a forecast attempts to predict what will happen, while a
plan is based on the supposition that decision makers can affect subsequent
results by altering strategic variables (such as the advertising budget).

THE FORECASTING PROCESS

For forecasts to be valuable to management, they should be regarded as one
step in a systemic process. That is, a forecast should not be considered as being
permanent or static. The dynamic nature of the marketplace dictates that the

forecast be subject to review, revision, and discussion. Thus, forecasting should be viewed as a multi-step process:

1. Determine the purpose and objective of the forecast.
2. Select the relevant theory.
3. Collect data.
4. Analyze data.
5. Estimate the initial model.
6. Evaluate the model and make revisions.
7. Present initial forecasts to management.
8. Make the final revision.
9. Distribute the forecast.
10. Establish monitoring procedures.

PURPOSE AND OBJECTIVE OF THE FORECAST

The objectives of each forecast should be formally and explicitly stated in writing. First and foremost in this stage of the forecasting process should be an answer to these questions: Why is the forecast needed, and how will the results be used? Forecasts are prepared so management can make decisions regarding current resource allocation, and, therefore, the forecaster needs to understand the intended managerial uses of the projections. For example, many organizations develop separate forecasts for different time periods (2-month inventory-control forecasts; 6-month personnel forecasts; 18-month sales forecasts), and the forecaster must ensure that there is consistency within and among forecasts.

The purpose of the forecast dictates the length of the forecast period and determines the frequency of revision. For example, capital budget forecasts are normally long term (two to five years) while production forecasts are immediate term (weekly or monthly). In the case of long-term forecasts, revisions are typically made on an annual basis; production forecasts, however, may be revised daily or weekly, while sales forecasts are revised monthly or quarterly.

THE RELEVANT THEORETICAL MODEL

Once the objective and purpose of the forecast have been specified, the next step is to outline the theoretical relationships that determine movements in the forecast variable. While the selection of a sound theoretical model does not automatically guarantee a reliable forecast, a failure to understand theoretical relationships will, most certainly, lead to unreliable forecasts.

A statement of the appropriate theory will also assist the forecaster in identifying any applicable constraints that need to be addressed and incorporated into the forecasting process. For example,

- Do we have the plant capacity to meet the predicted increase in sales?
- Are raw materials available at a price that is compatible with profit expectations?
- If a sales decline is projected, can we legally (ethically) reduce our labor costs?
- If a sales increase is projected, can we obtain the required personnel?
- What impact will existing or proposed laws have on future performance?
- What are the likely competitive reactions to any changes that we might make?

A theoretical model frequently assists in segregating influences into either internal or external factors. Those factors over which management has direct control are referred to as the internal factors. Among the most commonly mentioned internal factors are price, advertising expenditures, product quality, product characteristics (warranties, rebates, etc.), and distribution facilities. The external factors include all factors beyond the control of management, such as consumer income, rates of inflation, unemployment rates, and actions by competitors.

Finally, the process of developing a sound theoretical framework forces the forecaster to understand factors such as trade channels, historical trends, end-use patterns, market shares, geographical dispersion of customers, political and social factors, and the dynamic nature of the competitive marketplace—in other words, all of the variables that make up the fabric of the market under study.

COLLECTION OF DATA

The necessity of this stage in the forecasting process is largely self-explanatory, and chapter 3 outlines the task of data collection. The only additional point we need to make here is that the forecast preparer should make certain to document both the sources of data as well as the specific definitions of all variables that are used in developing the forecasts.

DATA ANALYSIS

The primary objective in this phase of the forecasting process is to ascertain whether or not anything can be learned from an analysis of historical data. The goal is to identify and measure long-run, trend, cyclical, and seasonal patterns. While data analysis is largely a mechanical process, a thorough understanding of the industry and the firm may be the most important first step in developing reliable forecasts. Your credibility as a forecaster is largely tied to how thoroughly you understand the idiosyncrasies of your employer's business.

MODEL ESTIMATION

Once the objectives have been specified, the theory identified, and the data collected and analyzed, a forecaster is in the position to develop the initial forecast model and prepare the preliminary forecasts. The majority of the time spent in this step revolves around technique selection. Much of what we learned in the preceding stages of the forecasting process will assist us in selecting the initial group of models to be tested. For example, if management has told us that their primary interest is in developing long-term trend forecasts, trend and regression models might be most appropriate. Conversely, if the production manager has made the request and his interest is in having weekly forecasts, moving average, exponential smoothing, or Box-Jenkins models would be investigated. Once the technique(s) has been selected, we would then proceed to estimate the specific models and test their reasonableness.

MODEL EVALUATION AND REVISION

Prior to actual application, a model should be tested to determine its expected accuracy, validity, and reliability. As various reliability and accuracy tests are applied to the model(s), revisions may be called for. These revisions might necessitate the inclusion of other causal factors in the model, require a different time frame, or change the periodicity of the data.

PRESENTATION OF INITIAL FORECASTS TO MANAGEMENT

For forecasting to be successful, managerial input is required. There are numerous questions that should be addressed by both the forecast user and the forecast preparer at this stage:

1. Does the forecast satisfy managerial requirements?
2. Is management going to accept the initial forecasts as final?
3. Are there any managerial strategies—price changes, special promotions, additional work shift—that need to be incorporated into the forecast?
4. Are the historical forecast errors acceptable to management?
5. Are the assumptions of the forecast and the forecast technique acceptable to management?

It is at this juncture of forecasting that judgmental adjustments will be made to reflect factors such as the likelihood of a national recession, the impact of inflationary price changes, the probability of a labor strike, or changes in governmental policies.

FINAL REVISIONS

To reemphasize a point made previously, no forecast should be treated as static. Depending on the answers to the questions posed in the preceding step, new forecasts may have to be prepared, another evaluation may be conducted, and we may even have to initiate another round of discussions with management. As each of these changes is made, it must be documented so the underlying forecast assumptions remain clear.

DISTRIBUTION OF THE FORECAST

Unless the forecast is delivered to management in a timely fashion and in a consistent format, its value to decision makers will be diminished. The forecaster must determine who should receive the forecast, the level of detail required by each of the users, and how frequently users need to be provided with updates. Having set up a distribution network, there is a continuing need to talk to users about the usefulness of the forecast information.

ESTABLISHMENT OF MONITORING PROCEDURES

A successful forecasting program requires the establishment of procedures for evaluating forecasts on an ongoing basis and of monitoring procedures that allow the forecaster to respond to unexpected surprises. Forecasts must be compared with actual results to assess the accuracy of the methodology that has been applied. Evaluation at this stage should be viewed as a control process and is a necessary step in maintaining reliable future estimates. When a forecast has missed the mark by a wide margin, the forecaster must strive to find out why and correct the problem. Even if the forecast fell within the error range specified by management, the forecast must still be updated. Monitoring procedures (for example, an analysis of monthly sales volume) provide a multitude of warning signals (some useful, some misleading) for forecasters to interpret. For example, did monthly sales drop because of a regional strike or because of a rival's price cut? The development of monitoring procedures thus involves a combination of statistical, graphical, and judgmental aids.

THE BUSINESS CYCLE: PAST AND PRESENT

More than 80 years ago, Wesley Clair Mitchell brought forth his classic study, *Business Cycles and Their Causes*, which was designed both to describe the dynamic internal forces propelling the economy and to develop a comprehensive business-cycle theory.

> Much would be gained for the conduct of individual affairs and the guidance of legislation could we single out from the maze of such sequences among business

phenomena a few that are substantially uniform. For, with a degree of confidence that depends upon the regularity with which they recur, these sequences could be used as guides in forecasting the immediate business future.[1]

Although Mitchell regarded every business cycle as the product of a unique series of historical events, his quest was the development of a theory comprehensive enough to describe how one set of business conditions (for example, those to be found during a period of economic prosperity) transforms itself into another set (such as the economic conditions prevailing during a recession). Mitchell was searching for an endogenous theory of the cycle—that is, a theory that would explain the rhythmical ups and downs in the economy solely as a function of the internal workings of the free-enterprise or capitalist system. He felt that, although exogenous forces or propitious events such as bad weather, bumper crops, or labor strikes might retard or speed up these endogenous forces, exogenous factors were not by themselves sufficient to explain the cumulative processes that are at the heart of the business cycle.

Judged from a contemporary perspective, we can summarize Mitchell's achievements by saying that he succeeded admirably in finding a number of uniform patterns or sequences in business-cycle activity, but that he failed in his attempt to develop an endogenous theory of the cycle that could be used to forecast accurately the likely course of the economy. Mitchell was writing in 1913, and yet the following quotation from the *Wall Street Journal* in 1979 vividly illustrates the timelessness of his quest for an answer to the riddle of the business cycle:

> Will lights flash? Bells ring? Sirens wail? How will we know when the economy has entered a recession? We won't. Certainly not for many, many months. Probably not until any recession that comes along is more than half over. . . . Recessions are difficult to see arriving and can prove hard to detect long after they are firmly established.[2]

To illustrate the difficulty of diagnosing when a recession has occurred (which is different from forecasting when a recession will occur), consider Figure 1-2, which summarizes the movement of disposable personal income and civilian employment since World War II. Can you spot the recessions that took place over this period? Economists call the onset of a recession the peak or upper turning point, and the end of a recession the trough or lower turning point. The turning points for the most recent recessions are as follows:[3]

[1] Wesley C. Mitchell, *Business Cycles and Their Causes* (Los Angeles: University of California Press, 1963), p. x. Copyright © 1941 The Regents of the University of California.

[2] *Wall Street Journal*, "If a Recession Does Come, Experience Shows Its Arrival May Go Undetected for Months," May 16, 1979, p. 48. Reprinted by permission of the *Wall Street Journal*, © 1979 Dow Jones & Company, Inc. All Rights Reserved Worldwide.

[3] U.S. Department of Commerce, Economics and Statistics Administration/Bureau of Economic Analysis, *Survey of Current Business* (Washington, D.C.: U.S. Government Printing Office, April 1991).

Peak	*Trough*
August 1957	April 1958
April 1960	February 1961
December 1969	November 1970
November 1973	March 1975
January 1980	July 1980
July 1981	November 1982
July 1990	May 1991*

* Many business forecasters felt (by late 1991) that
the economy bottomed out in the second quarter of
1991. As of July 1, 1992, however, the official date
of the trough had not been set by the National Bureau of Economic Research. We have listed the mid-
point of the second quarter of 1991 as a "probable"
turning point.

As outlined in Figure 1-2, the recession of 1973–1975 was the most dramatic.
Even in its January 1974 report to Congress (two months after the peak),
however, the president's prestigious Council of Economic Advisers was still
citing ". . . a number of factors tending to support the expansion of the economy . . ." in the remaining months of 1974.[4] The stock market crash in October
of 1987 led many to predict the immediate onset of a recession, while others

FIGURE 1-2   Income and Employment Growth

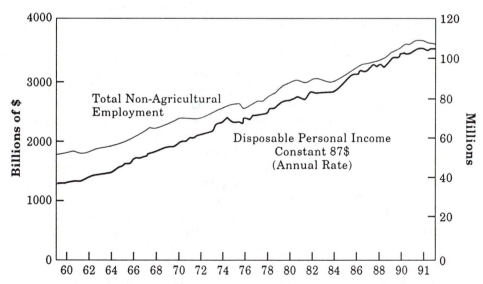

Source: U.S. Department of Commerce, *Survey of Current Business*, various issues

[4] *Economic Report of the President* (Washington, D.C.: U.S. Government Printing Office,
January 1974), p. 23.

felt that while a slowdown was imminent a recession was not likely. The actual peak in the economy took place in July 1990 and is visible in Figure 1-2. As noted above, the economy began to grow again in 1991, and many forecasters were, by the end of 1991, willing to argue that the recession had ended in May 1991. In fact, the economy experienced growth in the second half of 1991 and the beginning of 1992. The economy was growing so slowly, however, that unemployment actually rose. Jobs were not being created fast enough to absorb the new entrants into the labor force. The renewed strength of the stock market in 1991 and early 1992 seemed to suggest a revival in economic growth, but sagging consumer confidence reflected growing unease about the future. All of this serves to indicate that one of the most difficult tasks for forecasters is to correctly predict turning points in the economy.

MEASURING ECONOMIC ACTIVITY FROM PEAK TO TROUGH

Since the problems associated with pinpointing economic fluctuations are still present, an attempt must be made to analyze the ebb and flow of economic activity in the economy. As an alternative to the two measures presented in Figure 1-2, we might have chosen micro (partial) measures for, say, income and employment in Chicago or Pittsburgh over the same 25-year period. Such micro series often display different patterns of volatility from those of their macro counterparts.

Up to this point, we have introduced a number of terms—recession, prosperity, income, employment, business cycles, and so on—with which you have some general familiarity. However, it is likely that the meanings you ascribe to these terms are not the same as the technical definitions accepted by the business-conditions analyst. For example, the concept of profit has a general meaning to the public, but it has a much more specific meaning to a team of accountants who have labored to prepare General Motors' income statement. And what, precisely, is the economic measure in Figure 1-2 labeled "Disposable Personal Income in 1987 Dollars"? The complete answer to this question can be found by consulting the *Survey of Current Business*. However, a less technical definition will serve to highlight the necessity of mastering a host of terms and concepts before moving on to the task of business-conditions analysis. First, this series is better described as real disposable personal income in constant 1987 dollars. Because prices change from year to year, $100 of income in 1989 did not provide the same purchasing power as $100 in 1979. Thus, the income series shown in Figure 1-2 has been adjusted through a statistical procedure that holds prices constant at the level prevailing in 1987. But what is disposable personal income? Stated roughly, it is the amount of income a person has to spend after deducting personal income tax payments.[5] If this measure is aggregated across all the people in the economy, we arrive

---

[5] For a more precise definition of the exact process whereby the personal income figures are derived, consult a recent issue of *Survey of Current Business*.

at total disposable personal income—a basic indicator of consumers' ability to buy goods and services.

One would, in fact, expect a high degree of correlation between employment and income—a fact that is supported by Figure 1-2. You may be surprised, however, by how little employment fell in the 1973–1975 recession and in 1990–1991, or, alternatively, how much it declined relative to income during the 1981–1982 recession. Does that mean we were incorrect in labeling the 1973–1975 downturn as a severe recession or the most recent recession as a mild downturn? Not really. A glance at Figure 1-3 illustrates that the un-

FIGURE 1-3   Comparative Analysis of Labor Force Movements

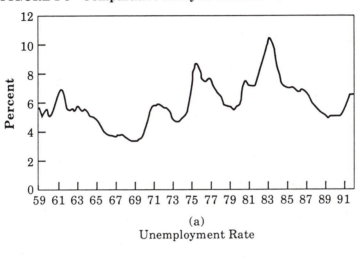

(a)
Unemployment Rate

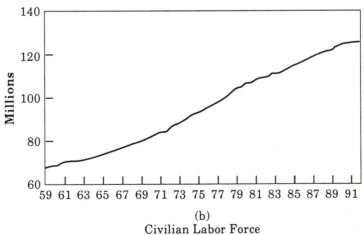

(b)
Civilian Labor Force

Source: U.S. Department of Commerce, *Survey of Current Business,* various issues

employment rate reached 9 percent in 1975, 11 percent in 1981, and 7.1 percent by the end of 1991.

Thus, if we gauge the severity of a recession by the level of unemployment, the 1980–1981 recession was clearly the most damaging to the work force. The recession that began in 1990 was unique in terms of its impact on previously untouched service sector jobs in areas such as banking, real estate and law. Furthermore, although people are laid off or put on shorter work hours during all recessions, the usual reason for the climbing unemployment rate is that the growth in the number of new job seekers entering the civilian labor force (see Figure 1-3) outpaces the number of new jobs generated by the economy. This dichotomy between employment and unemployment statistics points out one of the pitfalls associated with aggregate economic data.

ABSOLUTE VERSUS RELATIVE MEASURES OF ECONOMIC ACTIVITY

Of the many economic reports published each day concerning the health of the economy, no set of statistics is more widely heralded than the estimates for gross domestic product (GDP)—the dollar value of all the final goods and services produced in the domestic economy for a specific period. The GDP is the broadest single measure of the economy's output of goods and services. Figure 1-4 contains a graphical summary of postwar GDP movements. To the untrained eye, chart (a) contains two relatively straight lines, whereas chart (b) displays an obviously erratic series. In fact, both portions of the figure illustrate the same economic phenomena using different graphical techniques.

Look at chart (a) of Figure 1-4. Along the vertical axis, we have billions of dollars of GDP. Note that a ratio scale is used so the distance from $10 to $100 equals the distance from $100 to $1,000 and from $1,000 to $10,000—in other words, equal vertical distances measure equal percentage changes (this is known as semilogarithmic graph paper). Two quarterly GDP series are presented at seasonally adjusted annual rates (SAAR). The solid line measures GDP in actual prices, whereas the dotted line measures GDP in constant 1987 prices. Just as the dotted line has been statistically adjusted to eliminate the effect of changing prices, so both GDP series have been seasonally adjusted to statistically neutralize the normal ups and downs in the economy that are due to such seasonal GDP patterns as the pre-Christmas surge, the post-holiday winter decline, and numerous other institutional holidays, such as Labor Day and Memorial Day, which regularly affect the production of goods and services.

Finally, the quarterly data have been annualized by multiplying the quarterly figures by a factor of 4. Just as you can report your earnings as $5 per hour, $200 per 40-hour week, or $10,400 per year, we can say that a GDP of $200 billion in this quarter is equivalent to an annualized rate of $800 billion. You must therefore internalize all the aforementioned concepts—ratio scale, current versus constant dollars, seasonal adjustment, annualization—before you can attempt to answer the most basic of questions: What is the

**FIGURE 1-4 Aggregate Versus Incremental Fluctuations
in Gross Domestic Product**

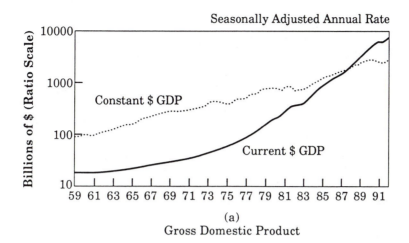

(a)
Gross Domestic Product

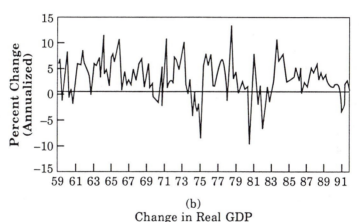

(b)
Change in Real GDP

Source: U.S. Department of Commerce, *Survey of Current Business*, various issues

secular or long-run pattern for postwar growth in GDP? By its nature, chart
(a) of Figure 1-4 is designed to emphasize long-run movements (say, five or
more years) as opposed to short-run fluctuations. When graphed using a ratio
scale on the vertical axis, the slope of the line is a measure of relative or
percentage change in GDP. Thus, the fact that the dotted line is nearly linear
tells us that real GDP (GDP in 1987 dollars) has been growing at a steady
percentage trend rate (roughly 3 percent). Note that the slope of the current-
dollar GDP line is steeper than the dashed line and that the differential has
been growing since 1970 due to inflation.

Your focus should not be on the total or absolute level of GDP or company
sales, but on quarter-to-quarter fluctuations; analysts work on the margin,

dealing with the relative or percentage changes typified by chart (b) of Figure 1-4. Just as micro theory centers on marginal revenue, marginal cost, and marginal productivity, so forecasters dwell on rates of change rather than absolute levels. As compared to chart (a), the emphasis in chart (b) of Figure 1-4 is on the annualized, quarter-to-quarter percentage change in real, seasonally adjusted GDP (1987 dollars). In other words, the absolute or aggregate data embodied in the dashed line in chart (a) has been translated into a relative or percentage change in chart (b). Notice how much easier it is now to identify the recessions beginning in August 1957, April 1960, December 1969, November 1973, January 1980, July 1981, and July 1990. Investigators of past business fluctuations are often asked to synthesize the long-run or trend rates in the economy with short-run business-cycle movements. Whereas it is a comparatively easy task to predict next year's real GDP, it is much more demanding (and monetarily rewarding) to forecast monthly or quarterly GDP movements and translate these into disaggregated projections of rates of change for industry and company unit sales, dollar sales, and profit.

DISAGGREGATION

There is a fundamental trade-off between the desire to disaggregate or decompose series into their subcomponents and the need to minimize the cost of the economic resources required to produce a given industry- or company-level forecast. For example, producers of consumer products such as automobiles and beer could make, at best, crude industry forecasts if they were forced to rely on the aggregate projections for the quarterly employment and income series shown in Figure 1-2. Since there is variation in consumer purchasing patterns for automobiles and beer based on age, race, and sex differentials, General Motors and Miller Brewing Company would be much more interested in having disaggregated unemployment (and income) projections. The payoff from disaggregation is the increased forecasting precision stemming from the ability to predict more accurately how many automobiles and gallons of beer will be purchased by males versus females, the over-35 age group versus the under-35 segment, and minority versus nonminority consumers.

As the end users of business projections demand more disaggregation, a host of new questions arises. Where has the most rapid growth come from in the personal-income series in Figure 1-2? As shown in Figure 1-5, much of the recent growth in personal income has come from transfer payments (non-wage payments by the government to individuals), which include unemployment compensation, Social Security benefits, welfare payments, and other income redistribution schemes.

A billion-dollar increase in personal income arising from augmented transfer payments does not have the same effect on beer and automobile sales that a billion-dollar increment from wage and salary disbursements does. If you overlook this structural shift in the composition of personal income, you

FIGURE 1-5   Components of Personal Income

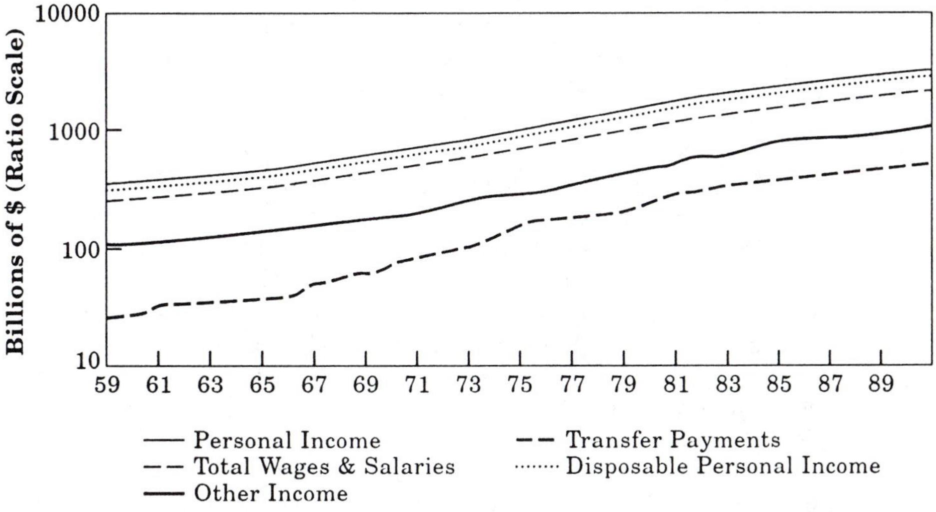

Source: U.S. Department of Commerce, *Survey of Current Business*, various issues

are likely to overestimate automobile sales and underestimate beer sales. Beer sales appear to be countercyclical; as the economy moves into a recession, unemployment rises, transfer payments increase, consumers switch from high-priced liquor to cheaper substitutes such as beer, and people devote more time to leisure activities such as beer consumption. In the case of automobiles, however, increases in transfer payments are not as likely to expand new-car sales.

The very process of disaggregation will lead to a series of follow-up questions: Which component of the GDP was responsible for the decline? Which group in the economy bore the greatest burden of the increase in unemployment? What part of the increase in personal income was simply due to higher Social Security benefits? Which automobile producer experienced the smallest relative decline in unit sales? Which region of the country has the fastest growth rate? Which company in the beer industry is predicted to have the sharpest increase in market share? The questions are innumerable, but they all lead in the direction of more and more disaggregation. The movement from aggregate demand for goods and services to sector-by-sector industry demand is one such form of disaggregation.

INTERDEPENDENCE

The need for forecasters who can put together cogent analyses of economic conditions is tied to the complex maze of interdependent problems facing businesses, the nonprofit sector, and government. The underlying forces producing this heightened sense of interdependence (simultaneous business peaks in numerous Western economies, inflation, uncertainty arising from government policies, the trend toward deregulation and heightened competition, and many other factors) have made the task of business-conditions analysis more challenging (some would even say hazardous).

Interdependence is not a new phenomenon. In Wesley Mitchell's classic study of cycles, he saw the diffusion of economic activity as proceeding along the "lines of interconnection among business enterprises" that lead backward to industries providing raw materials and forward to enterprises such as railroads that handle the increased output.[6] As pointed out earlier, however, Mitchell subscribed to an endogenous or internal theory of the business cycle. Exogenous or external factors could speed or slow cyclical movements, but it was the basic profit motive that propelled Mitchell's economy from recession to prosperity and back to recession. For Mitchell, therefore, interdependence was primarily manifested in the linkages within the economic system—that is, endogenous forces.

You may or may not support the extended role of government in today's economy, but government policies (both domestic and foreign) are themselves a response to the public's growing awareness of interdependence. Perhaps the most visible example of this lies in the increased demands by the populace for action on a number of broad social goals in the energy and environmental arenas. In turn, this increase in external or exogenous instability has modified the endogenous or internal transmission mechanism of the economy outlined by Mitchell, and at the same time it has significantly altered the task of the business-conditions analyst. In the Mitchellian world of endogenous cycles, the analyst's energy is devoted primarily to interpreting the signals of the marketplace—data on unit production costs, wage rates, interest rates, credit availability, product demand and company capacity, and other measures that quantify present and expected profitability. Today, however, you must construct a vast array of social and political assumptions dealing with the degree of government intervention in the economy. For example, will the Environmental Protection Agency (EPA) continue to close high-pollution plants, or will it make allowances for likely cyclical fluctuations in the economy? If it sticks to targeted long-run goals and ignores the consequences, it may exacerbate employment conditions during a recession. On the other hand, a number of manufacturers will already have made substantial capital investments under the assumption that the output will be needed to make up for the anticipated void caused by the closing of high-pollution factories. Whether the EPA does or does not alter its prior time schedule, there will be economy-wide ripples spreading backward and forward via the lines of interconnection among businesses.

Just as business analysts must have access to a complete forecast of the

---

[6] Mitchell, *Business Cycles*, p. 3.

economy before attempting an industry or company forecast, they must also have a thorough understanding of the governmental and societal forces that shape the exogenous parameters. In addition to being well-informed observers of social and political trends, forecasters need an analytical framework capable of translating these exogenous assumptions into concrete recommendations that will serve as the basis for decisions by the users of the business-conditions output. It is the task of the next section, therefore, to illuminate how forecasters can keep abreast of economic, social, and political shifts and mold this information into a business outlook.

COMMERCIAL FORECAST VENDORS

Having read or heard numerous statements by business-conditions forecasters, one is quickly struck by the probabilistic nature of their projections. Rather than making absolute assertions concerning the likely course of GDP, corporate profits, the profitability of selected industries, the prime rate, domestic automobile sales, or the labor costs associated with a strike, the projections are usually hedged with references to alternative scenarios that are possible but less likely than the business forecasters' best guess. Thus, even though economic forecasters may argue that the most likely outcome for the coming year is 3 percent real GDP growth and 4 percent inflation, they will admit that there is an outside chance of 1 percent real growth and 6 percent inflation. Whether they are in the political or business sectors, all economic forecasters produce contingency projections based on a subjective probability assessment of likely exogenous assumptions: How rapidly will the Federal Reserve expand the money supply in the next 12 months? Will the federal government be able to get a handle on the problems associated with the budget deficit? What is the domestic impact of a recession in the European Common Market countries? Will an unstable foreign government nationalize the assets of a U.S. subsidiary supplying critical raw materials to the U.S. economy? All these questions require subjective probability assessments. The outlook for a particular company's economic fortunes over the next four quarters is summarized, in Table 1-2 as best guess, optimistic, and pessimistic.

The best guess (or base case) is literally an estimate of the most likely

TABLE 1-2 The Company Outlook: A Probabilistic Assessment

Scenario	Best Guess	Optimistic	Pessimistic
Probability	50%	30%	20%
Company Sales (thousands of units)	125	150	95
Labor Requirements	10,000	13,000	7,000
Profit (millions of $)	1.2	1.8	−0.4

outlook for this company after the state of the economy and the host of exogenous variables have been considered. In this case, there is a 50 percent chance that company sales will reach 125,000 units. The worst possible outlook—perhaps based on the assumption of a severe recession—entails company sales of only 95,000 units. This range of possible outcomes allows the company to formulate a contingency plan in the event that the best guess proves to be incorrect. Thus, instead of a single-point forecast, a forecast range is compiled covering the entire spectrum from boom to bust for both the economy and disaggregated subcomponents, such as company sales.

Forecasters are not able to devote a large percentage of their time to the task of forecasting macro measures such as GDP, industrial production, the consumer price index, or the prime interest rate. Instead, they buy economic projections from forecast vendors in much the same way that businesses buy labor or other needed raw materials and services. Having selected the macroeconomic projections that best fit their economic outlook, forecasters are then able to construct linkages between their company and the macroeconomy, thereby permitting them to translate macro projections into an economic outlook that can serve as input to the internal decision-making process. At first, this division of labor may appear to be an abdication of responsibility, or even worse, a gross plagiarization of other forecasters' work. In reality, not even the largest corporation should attempt to produce a complete macroeconomic forecast. Anyone can make a guess of next year's real GDP and other key support measures such as industrial production, but this does not adequately meet the needs of today's interdependent economy.

To gain a better appreciation of the range and depth of the information produced by commercial forecast vendors, consider the format illustrated in Table 1-3. Each month commercial forecast vendors send to their subscribers interpretations of the most recent economic statistics and provide projected patterns of growth in various economic sectors. Table 1-3 provides a summary of important forecast variables compiled by a typical forecast vendor. Forecasts become obsolete almost overnight, so it should be obvious that these projections for 1993 (made in January 1992) are of little current use. These forecasts do provide, however, a sense of the types of information which can be obtained from commercial services. As you can see from perusing the table, the projections are grouped into major categories dealing with gross national product (GNP) and GDP, prices and wages, production, money and interest rates, and various income-related measures.[7] A forecast vendor first provides the best

---

[7] The National Income and Product Accounts (NIPA) are published monthly by the United States Department of Commerce in the *Survey of Current Business*. The December 1991 issue details the most recent of the major revisions made in the NIPA. In particular, the base year for real (inflation adjusted) magnitudes was switched from 1982 to 1987. While students of previous generations referred to Gross National Product (GNP), the broadest macroeconomic measure in the NIPA is now the Gross Domestic Product (GDP). GNP equals GDP plus net receipts of factor income from the rest of the world. Empirically, the two measures differ, at the present time, by less than one-half of one percent. The reader should, however, be aware of the distinction between GNP and GDP.

TABLE 1-3   Economic Outlook, January 1992

Economic Variable	1993			
	I	*II*	*III*	*IV*
GNP and its Components—Billions of Dollars, SAAR				
Gross National Product (GNP)	$6,016.6	$6,102.8	$6,199.3	$6,290.2
Consumption Expenditures	$4,139.4	$4,206.2	$4,276.2	$4,345.5
Durable Goods	$465.6	$477.5	$487.8	$503.7
Non-Durable Goods	$1,198.2	$1,202.6	$1,229.1	$1,240.3
Services	$2,475.6	$2,526.1	$2,559.3	$2,601.5
Gross Private Domestic Investment	$793.1	$810.3	$823.5	$844.2
Fixed Investment	$778.3	$799.4	$819.6	$832.8
Change in Business Inventories	$11.0	$11.0	$8.0	$11.4
Net Exports	($27.8)	($28.4)	($28.4)	($33.6)
Exports	$658.5	$674.3	$687.1	$699.0
Imports	$686.4	$702.7	$715.5	$732.6
Government Purchases of Goods and Services	$1,112.0	$1,114.7	$1,127.9	$1,134.1
Real Gross National Product (1987$)	$5,022.3	$5,070.6	$5,111.6	$5,137.9
Gross Domestic Product	$6,017.9	$6,105.2	$6,202.7	$6,295.2
Real Gross Domestic Product (1987$)	$5,027.8	$5,067.3	$5,104.0	$5,141.7
Prices and Wages—Annual Rates of Change				
Implicit Price Deflator	2.4	2.7	3.5	3.4
CPI—All Urban Consumers	3.0	3.1	3.4	3.2
Producer Price Index	3.0	3.9	3.9	3.3
Compensation Per Hour	4.0	4.9	4.8	3.8
Production and Other Key Measures				
Industrial Production (1987 = 100)	116.1	118.5	120.8	124.0
Annual Rate of Change	6.4	8.5	8.0	11.0
Paper & Products	−1.5	2.5	11.0	5.5
Printing & Publishing	7.1	3.1	−3.4	7.1
Appliances	36.4	−3.9	4.5	13.6
Electronic Components	4.7	10.1	9.2	8.9
Computers	18.2	14.1	8.8	13.9
Housing Starts (mil. units)	1.38	1.40	1.40	1.41
Retail Unit Car Sales (mil. units)	9.9	10.3	10.5	10.5
Unemployment Rate (%)	6.9	6.7	6.5	6.2
Total Employment—Annual Rate of Change	2.0	2.1	2.1	2.2
Money and Interest Rates				
Money Supply (M1) (Billions of $)	$967.3	$977.3	$984.7	$999.0
Annual Rate of Change	5.3	4.2	3.1	5.9
Effective Mortgage Rate	8.6	8.9	9.2	9.3
New High Grade Corp. Bond Rate (%)	8.60	8.69	8.77	8.85
Federal Funds Rate (%)	4.83	5.08	5.25	5.59
Prime Rate (%)	7.10	7.70	8.00	8.00
Incomes—Billions of Dollars				
Personal Income	$5,194.2	$5,285.6	$5,358.4	$5,427.4
Disposable Personal Income	$4,647.1	$4,710.2	$4,770.1	$4,845.9
Real Disposable Income (1987$)	$3,727.6	$3,746.7	$3,759.4	$3,783.1
Personal Tax Payments	$664.5	$674.4	$683.9	$695.7
Savings Rate (%)	5.1	4.9	4.6	4.5

guess for the outlook in the economy. Thus the vendor might decide that there was a 70 percent probability associated with the baseline forecast and the underlying assumptions contained in Table 1-3. Next, the forecast vendor provides his users with a series of alternative economic scenarios. For example, the baseline forecast could assume a moderate recovery (70 percent probability), while alternative projections could incorporate a weak recovery (20 percent probability), a strong recovery (5 percent), or a resumption of conflicts in the Middle East (5 percent).

Each of the summary forecast categories in Table 1-3 would, in turn, be supported by disaggregated analysis contained within the body of the monthly review or outlook. For example, in addition to forecasting expenditures for durable goods, for non-durable goods, and for services, forecasts would be provided for such disaggregated categories as expenditures on clothing, on food, on new automobiles, on used automobiles, and on health services. Several aspects of Table 1-3 merit additional attention:

- While the forecasts are revised each month, virtually all of the forecasts are presented on an annualized basis—for example, annualized car sales, annualized GDP, and annualized steel production.
- Some of the variables are measured in dollar terms (for example, all of the components of gross national or gross domestic product), while others are measured as annual rates of change (for example, price and wage forecasts).
- Many of the variables are measured in both current prices (gross domestic product) and inflation-adjusted prices (real gross domestic product in 1987 prices). This allows firm- and industry-level forecasters to separate real shifts (volume movements) from inflationary movements in the economy.
- Forecasts are made for both flow variables (such as income earned per period of time) and stock variables (such as the stock of housing units on June 1992).
- There are also many different measures of what may appear to be the same economic variable (but which, in fact, mask subtle differences). For example, there are at least three different measures of the price level: the implicit price deflator, the producer price index, and the consumer price index.
- An examination of the production section of Table 1-3 documents a common phenomenon that is extremely useful to business analysts who rely on commercial vendors for macroeconomic forecasts. A comparison of the quarter-to-quarter growth patterns indicates that there is significant variation in cyclical patterns across industries. Consider the comparative quarterly growth rates for 1993: I (the first quarter of 1993). The aggregate industrial production index is projected to grow at a 6.4 percent annual rate. However, this aggregate measure masks the fact that the computer industry is predicted to record an annualized gain of 18.2 per-

cent, while the paper and products industry is projected to decline at an annualized rate of 1.5 percent.

IS THE ECONOMY NEARING A TURNING POINT?

No matter how voluminous and disaggregated the forecast output provided by commercial vendors, there still remains a complex series of tasks for you, as forecast analyst, to complete. First, given the vendor's best guess, optimistic outlook, and pessimistic outlook, what forecast alternatives should be integrated within the set of recommendations to top management? This is not a simple question, and it is not a task for those who wish to avoid taking a hard stand: Do you, or do you not, foresee a near-term recession (or, alternatively, recovery) in the economy? If you choose to assume that your industry faces a recession, you must quantify the transmission of this recession into the company's outlook. Such an outlook presumes that you have already carried out elaborate historical analyses of past recessions and have developed, through either statistical or qualitative means, an in-depth knowledge of how the company fares during a recession: Does the company lead or lag the economy? Does it rise or fall more or less sharply than the economy? Do all regional segments of the company move sequentially? These and other historical and cyclical insights provide invaluable background when the next recession looms on the horizon. Although many unique factors surround each recession, researchers still rely on the pioneering work of Mitchell and his disciples at the National Bureau of Economic Research, which has shown that even with an exogenous business cycle, there remains a basic continuity in the endogenous or internal patterns of economic activity within the business cycle.

There is no better way for you to grasp actual forecasting issues than to select a past period of economic uncertainty and read through historical accounts of leading business publications. Think back to July 1990 (which has since been designated as the upper turning point of 1990). The 1983–1990 business expansion had already proved to be one of the more durable and strongest recoveries of the postwar period. However, as early as October 1987 (following the stock market crash), many of the leading economists and business forecasters had been embarrassingly premature in calling for a recession. Other prominent forecasters had wavered between predicting a continuation of the current expansion, slower growth, or a recession. Predicting when a turning point will occur is clearly a tricky business and is no easier today than it was 20 years ago.

Consider the range of fundamental macroeconomic questions faced by the forecaster in July 1990. Would a recession occur in 1990 or in 1991? If it did occur, would it affect all sectors equally? Would it be mild or severe? If an actual decline in real GNP did not happen, would there be a reduction in the rate of growth? What was the likelihood of a war breaking out in the Middle East, and what would be the ramifications? All these questions were paralleled by a similar set of industry and company forecasting issues. As a business-conditions analyst searching for a predictor of future economic conditions, you could have found a host of conflicting signals in July 1990 on which to base your own projections. With hindsight, we know that these uncertainties were heightened by Iraq's invasion of Kuwait in August 1990, and it was not until November or December 1990 that the forecasting community reached unanimity on the proximity of a recession.

PREPARING THE FORECAST

You may have done a thorough job of studying the outlook, selecting the appropriate economic scenario, translating this into total industry demand, and, finally, forecasting the company's total unit sales, but you cannot simply confront managers with a detailed computer printout. Ultimately, you will be asked to prepare a report that effectively focuses on the issues facing decision makers. The credibility of your projections will, most likely, be appraised by these decision makers. Thus, an equally important task for forecasters revolves around the presentation of a forecast to a nontechnical management team. You must be able to translate the results of your statistical estimations, your computer runs, your assumptions, and your judgmental adjustments into an understandable forecast.

In a broad sense, the framework of this book is designed to accomplish this translation process. Just as you must master a host of technical terms and concepts, so you will be required to provide forecast summaries that integrate these concepts in a clear manner. As you work through the successive chapters in this book dealing with the tools utilized by the business-conditions analyst, and as you become immersed in the application of these tools to actual forecasting topics, you should also keep in mind some broader normative questions: What tasks ought (ought not) business forecasters be doing? What are their professional limitations? What standards or norms should be used to evaluate the business forecaster's output? How does the business-conditions analyst fit into the broader corporate planning system? In general, how has the business-conditions analyst's role been modified by the events of the postwar era? These are important issues that may otherwise tend to be pushed aside as you attempt to master the technical side of forecasting. They cannot, however, be sidestepped when you attempt to carry out the day-to-day functions of the business-conditions analyst.

SOME FINAL FORECASTING TIPS

Here are some useful tips about forecasting:
1. Beware of consensus forecasts, which are nothing more than averages. Being near the mean or average does not guarantee accuracy.
2. There is something to be gained from an understanding of extremely optimistic or pessimistic forecasts. While you may not accept either ex-

treme, they may contain some elements that you have failed to account for in your forecasts.

3. Recognize that all forecasts (especially yours) will be wrong and that you are responsible for explaining why you were wrong.

4. In reporting forecasts, focus on a forecast range rather than a single set of numbers which represent your "best forecast."

5. Develop tools with which you can monitor the reliability of your forecasts over time.

6. Simple models are preferred over complex models.

7. As a forecaster, you must understand the process by which a given model generates forecasts. If you do not understand it, you will not be able to explain it to management.

8. All forecasting models are based on historical data patterns. These patterns can and do change, sometimes dramatically. Witness the oil embargo in 1973–1975, or the aftermath of the stock market crash of 1987 versus the 1929 crash.

9. Remember that the purpose of forecasting is to improve managerial decision making. It is not an end in itself.

10. Economists and forecasters have been criticized (justifiably, in many cases) in the last decade for missing turning points in the economy. Few foresaw the rapid growth that occurred after the 1982 recession. Even fewer forecasters accurately predicted the upper turning point of 1990. Despite this rather suspect record, economists continue to issue highly detailed forecasts with respect to what will happen to interest rates during the next 12 months; what will happen to the growth rate in real GDP; and how much the unemployment figure will change (down to a tenth of a percent). The problem is not solely with economic theory, but also with the application of this theory. Too often, economic forecasters are tempted to make projections for, say, GDP or some other economic measure months (or worse yet, many years) into the future. This temptation is furthered by the advances that have been made in empirical research methods. As long as (1) the economic environment is controlled by individual decision makers each pursuing their own self-interest, (2) individual expectations are subject to rapid and dramatic changes, and (3) unforeseeable events (such as the OPEC oil embargo in the mid-1970s or Iraq's invasion of Kuwait in 1990) occur, the best that we can do is to suggest what the likely or probable results are going to be. Until we recognize this limitation of our economic models, we will continue to be subject to intense (and warranted) criticism.

QUESTIONS FOR DISCUSSION AND ANALYSIS

1. "Subjective judgment has no place in forecasting." Evaluate the validity of this statement.

2. Distinguish between macro and micro forecasts; between top-down and bottom-up forecasting.

3. "Forecasting reduces the necessity for planning." True or false? Explain.

4. What is meant by the forecasting process?

5. What is meant by each of the following components of the forecasting process?
   a. The objective and purpose of the forecast
   b. Analyzing data
   c. Monitoring the forecast
   d. Presentation of the forecast to management
   e. Revising the initial forecast

6. Do you think that the forecast should be the goal that the firm should strive for? Why or why not?

7. Go to the library, locate the monthly Department of Commerce publication entitled *Survey of Current Business*, copy the GDP estimates in current and constant dollars for each of the last 16 quarters, calculate the quarter-to-quarter percentage change in both series, and write a short summary describing the behavior of the GDP over the last four years.

8. How would you describe the economy during the four-year span analyzed in question 7? Was there a recession? If not, did the economy grow steadily or erratically? Did inflation improve or worsen during this period? When is it better to use the quarterly percentage change in constant-dollar GDP than the quarterly percentage change in current-dollar GDP?

9. Compare the predicted performance of the macroeconomic variables in Table 1-3 with the actual performance. What explanations can you offer for the divergence between actual and predicted?

10. When did the most recent recession appear to have started? Based on an investigation of such publications as the *Wall Street Journal, Fortune,* and *Forbes,* when did the economists for these publications begin to predict the onset of a recession as compared to when the recession actually began?

11. Write a short paragraph for the textile, automobile, banking, computer production, and chemicals industries describing their economic fortunes during the years 1990, 1991, and 1992.
    a. Which of the industries suffered the most during this time?
    b. How did the performance in these industries compare to aggregate industrial production?
    c. Which industries appear to have been least (most) affected by the performance of the economy?
    d. Which industries turned down before the decline in the economy, after the decline in the economy, and at the same time?

12. Locate the annual *Economic Report of the President* published in January 1990 (and 1991) and *Fortune* magazine for the months of January through March 1990 (and 1991). What were the predictions regarding the turning point (onset of a recession)? Why would there be a difference in the outlooks of these two publications? Do either or both of these sources have a clear bias?

13. Do you know how many people there are in the U.S. economy, how many civilians are working, and how many are unemployed? You can get the answer to these and other

employment-related questions by looking in the section labeled "Labor Force, Employment, and Earnings" in the *Survey of Current Business*. Put together a summary for the last two years that illustrates the total population, the size of the civilian labor force, the number of people unemployed, the aggregate unemployment rate, and the disaggregated unemployment rates for males 20 years and over, females 20 years and over, both sexes 16 to 19 years old, whites, blacks, and other racial minorities, and white-collar and blue-collar workers. As a business-conditions analyst, what conclusions can you draw about the incidence of unemployment in the U.S. economy?

14. The most widely recognized measure of the increase (or decrease) in the cost of living is the consumer price index (CPI), which is calculated by the U.S. Department of Labor and is reproduced in the *Survey of Current Business*. Locate the section on prices, collect data for the last two years, and analyze which of the major components—food, housing, apparel, transportation, and medical care—experienced the greatest and smallest changes over this period. Would this disaggregation prove useful to a practicing forecaster? Why or why not?

15. Forecasts of the economy inevitably incorporate discussions about the stock market. What groups are represented on the supply and demand sides of the stock market? As a business-conditions analyst interested in future price movements of oil-company stocks, present a qualitative assessment of the factors that you would wish to incorporate in your forecast.

16. Explain how economic analysis and forecasting are related in the determination of business objectives.

17. Describe the relationship between forecasting and business planning.

REFERENCES FOR FURTHER STUDY

Adams, F. Gerard, *The Business Forecasting Revolution*. New York: Oxford University Press, Inc., 1986.

Armstrong, J. Scott, *Long-Range Forecasting*. 2nd ed. New York: John Wiley & Sons, 1985.

Ascher, W., *Forecasting: An Appraisal for Policy-Makers and Planners*. Baltimore: Johns Hopkins University Press, 1978.

Burns, Arthur F. and Wesley C. Mitchell, *Measuring Business Cycles*. New York: NBER, 1946.

"Business Roundup" in *Fortune*.

Clark, J. R., Clifford F. Thies, J. Holton Wilson, and Saul Z. Barr, *Macroeconomics for Managers*. Boston: Allyn and Bacon, 1990.

Closs, G. W., "How Good are the National Bureau's Reference Dates?" *Journal of Business,* January 1963.

Economic Report of the President. Washington, D.C.: U.S. Government Printing Office.

Fels, Rendigs and C. Elton Hinshaw, *Forecasting and Recognizing Business Cycle Turning Points*. New York: NBER, 1968.

Klein, L. R., *An Essay on the Theory of Economic Prediction*. Chicago: Markham, 1971.

Magliaro, A. and C. L. Jain, *An Executive's Guide to Econometric Forecasting*, rev. ed. Flushing, N.Y.: Graceway Publishing Co., 1987.

Moore, Geoffrey H., ed., *Business Cycle Indicators*. Princeton: NBER, 1961.

Moore, Geoffrey H., *Business Cycles, Inflation, and Forecasting*, 2nd ed. Cambridge, Mass.: NBER, 1983.

"The Outlook" in the *Wall Street Journal*.

Valentine, Lloyd M. and Dennis F. Ellis, *Business Cycles and Forecasting*, 8th ed. Cincinnati, Ohio: Southwestern Publishing Co., 1991.

"What Businessmen Expect," *Dun's Review*.

2

Macroeconomic Forces Shaping the Environment of the Business Sector

INTRODUCTION

Because business decision making takes place in a macroeconomic or economy-wide setting, it is important to understand the forces that shape the business environment at the national, regional, industrial, and company levels. Long-term trends, seasonal patterns, cyclical movements, and irregular factors combine to generate widely divergent growth paths for the industries and companies within the economy. This chapter traces the cyclical linkages that bind the economy together during a typical business cycle. The business-cycle research of the National Bureau of Economic Research is studied to develop an understanding of the endogenous nature of cycles. Finally, a review of economic fluctuations during the entire span of the 1900s provides a historical perspective and offers a clearer picture of the ongoing evolution of the institutional framework that plays such a critical role in altering the trend, seasonal, cyclical, and irregular forces at work in the economy.

THE BUSINESS CYCLE: AN OVERVIEW

In their seminal work, Arthur Burns and Wesley Mitchell introduced the most widely accepted definition of business cycles:

> Business cycles are a type of fluctuation found in the aggregate activity of nations that organize their work mainly in business enterprises; a cycle consists of expansions occurring at about the same time in many economic activities, followed by similarly general recessions, contractions and revivals which merge into the expansion phase of the next cycle; this sequence of changes is recurrent but not

periodic; in duration business cycles vary from more than one year to ten or twelve years; they are not divisible into shorter cycles of similar character with amplitudes approximating their own. . . .[1]

This definition highlights several important characteristics of business cycles. The business cycle refers to fluctuations in aggregate economic activity rather than fluctuations in particular industries or sectors of the economy. They occur only after an economic system has developed sufficiently to organize its activity into business units. The recurring sequence of changes that constitute a business cycle—expansion, downturn, contraction, and recovery—is not periodic. Although the phases of business cycles repeat themselves, their duration (time span), intensity (rate of change), and scope vary considerably. Expansions and contractions occur at approximately the same time in many phases of economic activity. Finally, these cycles cannot be further subdivided into shorter cycles that have similar characteristics.

Although business cycles are generally found only in modern industrialized nations whose economic activities are organized through market-oriented business enterprises, this does not necessarily imply that the market system is the sole or even a contributing cause of business cycles. Indeed, even a cursory examination of the literature on business cycles reveals a diversity of opinion as to their cause(s).[2] Business-cycle theories vary widely and encompass explanations such as random external events (sunspots), financial readjustments (stock market declines), or efficiency adjustments (elimination of inefficient firms). Additionally, there are underconsumption theories, psychological theories, monetary theories, overinvestment theories, and a host of ad hoc explanations.

While business-cycle theories are diverse in terms of detail and emphasis, the majority of them assume that the internal dynamics of a market economy inevitably lead (sometimes due to external shocks and other times due to inherent internal forces) to the observed regularity of fluctuations in aggregate economic activity. In particular, these theories focus on the excesses and imbalances that are thought to develop after prolonged periods of economic growth. For example, after a sustained expansionary period, wages and other costs eventually begin to increase faster than final prices for goods and services, which in turn leads to pressures on profit margins. Following a decline in profit margins, there is typically a cutback in business investment, particularly in those sectors where there has been abnormally rapid growth during the up-

---

[1] Arthur Burns and Wesley Mitchell, *Measuring Business Cycles* (New York: NBER, 1947), p. 3.

[2] See, for example, Lloyd M. Valentine and Dennis F. Ellis, *Business Cycles and Forecasting*, 8th ed. (Cincinnati, Ohio: Southwestern Publishing Company, 1991), pp. 262–304; or Gabish, Gunter, and Hans-Walter Lorenz, *Business Cycle Theory: A Survey of Methods and Concepts* (New York: Springer-Verlag Publishers, 1989).

swing of the economy. These interconnections between financial and real variables lead, finally, to the end of expansion and the onset of contraction in the economy.

Table 2-1 provides a chronology of business cycles in the United States from 1900 to 1990 that vividly documents the lack of cyclical conformity. Published in the Commerce Department's *Survey of Current Business*, these reference dates reflect the consensus reached by experts at the National Bureau of Economic Research (NBER) concerning the upper and lower turning points (called peaks and troughs, respectively) in economic activity. A peak is des-

TABLE 2-1   Chronology of Business Cycles in the United States, 1900–1990

Business-Cycle Reference Dates				Duration in Months of		
Trough		*Peak*		*Expansion*	*Contraction*	*Full Cycle*
December	1900	September	1902	21	23	44
August	1904	May	1907	33	13	46
June	1908	January	1910	19	24	43
January	1912	January	1913	12	23	35
December	1914	August	1918	44	7	51
March	1919	January	1920	10	18	28
July	1921	May	1923	22	14	36
July	1924	October	1926	27	13	40
November	1927	August	1929	21	43	64
March	1933	May	1937	50	13	63
June	1938	February	1945	80	8	88
October	1945	November	1948	37	11	48
October	1949	July	1953	45	10	55
May	1954	August	1957	39	8	47
April	1958	April	1960	24	10	34
February	1961	December	1969	106	11	117
November	1970	November	1973	36	16	52
March	1975	January	1980	58	6	64
July	1980	July	1981	12	16	28
November	1982	July	1990	92	10	102
May	1991*					
Average, all cycles:						
20 cycles, 1900–1990				39	15	54
8 cycles, 1948–1990				51	11	62

* As explained in chapter 1, the May 1991 date for the trough is a probable date, but this had not been confirmed (as of July 1992) by the NBER.

Source: Survey of Current Business, April 1991, p. c-25.

ignated by the NBER as the month that marks the end of an economic expansion and the beginning of a recession, whereas just the reverse is true of a trough.

An examination of the information in Table 2-1 indicates that business cycles vary widely in duration. The cycle in 1980–1982 lasted only 28 months (from a trough in July 1980 to a trough in November 1982). By contrast, the decade of the 1960s witnessed a 117-month cycle from the trough in February 1961 to the trough in November 1970. The 20 cycles presented in Table 2-1 contained an average expansionary period of 39 months and a contractionary period of 15 months, for a total average cycle length of 54 months. Starting from the trough in 1948 (following World War II), however, the eight expansionary periods ending in July 1990 averaged 51.5 months, while the contractionary phases averaged just 11 months. Over the course of this century, therefore, expansions have lengthened and contractions have shortened. Note that the expansionary period from November 1982 to July 1990 lasted 92 months and continued the trend toward longer upswings in the economy.

Business cycles are not merely fluctuations in aggregate activity; they are widely diffused throughout the economy and produce cyclical movements that may be designated as industry and company cycles. Although related to and influenced by aggregate cycles, they have their own distinctive features. Some industrial activities—beer production, for example—appear to bear little relation in time to cycles in aggregate activity, while others—automobile production, for example—have turning points similar to those exhibited by aggregate cycles.

Figure 2-1 illustrates the cyclical pattern of beer production over the period from 1960 to 1990. While the peak in aggregate economic activity occurred in the third quarter of 1969, the beer industry did not reach its peak until the second quarter of 1972. Even more striking, although the economy peaked in the fourth quarter of 1973, the beer industry exhibited sustained growth throughout the 1974–1975 recession and did not reach its peak until the fourth quarter of 1975. Following the peak in economic activity in July 1990, beer production actually surged in the last two quarters of 1990. Thus, the production of beer occurs in an environment in which expansions and recessions do not parallel aggregate cyclical movements in the economy. In addition, one has to recognize the existence of long-run demographic trends that have lowered the percentage of the population in the prime beer-drinking age groups (say, from 18 to 35 years old). In the final analysis, these long-run or trend forces exert a much more profound impact on production and sales of beer than do cyclical fluctuations in economic activity.

Other economic sectors also display unique cyclical patterns. The growth in the production of computers, illustrated in Figure 2-2, indicates that this industry has been able to expand despite national recessions. An examination of Figure 2-2 indicates that during the recessions of 1980 and 1981–1982, as well as the first two quarters of the 1990 recession, the computer industry not

FIGURE 2-1   Comparative Cyclical Performance: Beer Index and Industrial Production Index, 1960–1990

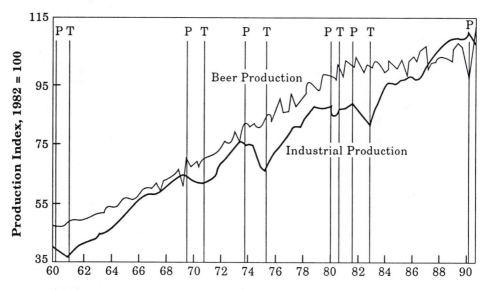

Source: Survey of Current Business

FIGURE 2-2   Business Cycles and Computer Production, 1977–1990

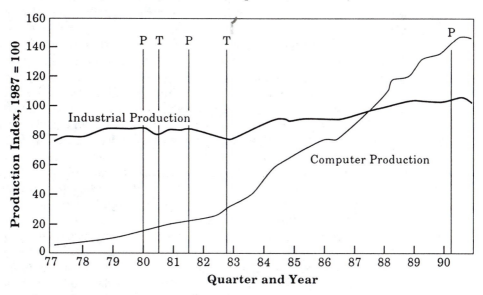

Source: Survey of Current Business

FIGURE 2-3   **Volatility of Communication Equipment Production, 1960–1990**

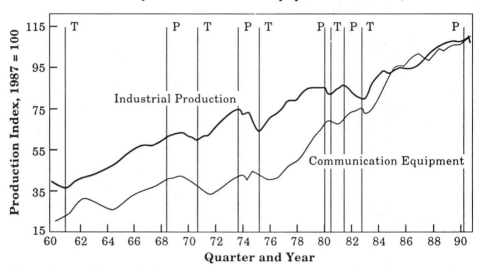

Source: Survey of Current Business

only continued to expand but to some degree experienced even faster growth. As with the beer industry, the computer industry is battered by trend forces that overwhelm cyclical factors. By 1990, for example, it was becoming clear that microcomputers produced by leading companies (such as IBM) and new competitors (such as Dell) were quickly becoming, in the minds of many consumers, interchangeable commodities rather than highly differentiated products. The downward price spiral for microcomputers in the early 1990s reflected technological forces (rather than cyclical) at work in this industry. Economic forecasting during such a period of turmoil is fraught with obstacles.

Figure 2-3 presents a comparison of the production of communication equipment versus aggregate industrial production. The unique characteristic of this industry is that its cyclical fluctuations bear little resemblance to the aggregate level of output. For example, the communication equipment industry skipped the 1960–1961 recession; experienced a decline from 1962 to 1964 while the national economy was growing; and reached a peak in the third quarter of 1969 at the same time as the national economy but declined for a much longer period. Similarly, following the 1974 recession, the communication equipment sector lagged behind the economy. The industry's performance from 1980 to 1990 does not parallel the economy, but it is clearly buffeted by cyclical factors. Again, trend factors such as international competition are likely to overwhelm short-term cyclical movements in this industry.

The cyclical performance of the beer, computer, and communication equipment sectors emphasizes the need to carry out detailed statistical analyses to segregate the unique factors affecting industries and individual firms from the general forces propelling GDP and employment. While this is not an easy task, it lies at the heart of the business forecaster's contribution to the business community.

As will be seen in chapter 3, time series (such as monthly computer production, daily stock prices, weekly automobile sales, or quarterly consumer borrowing) are the product of four forces (seasonal, cyclical, trend, and irregular factors). Seasonal patterns and long-run trends in the economy are comparatively easy to analyze and predict because of their relative consistency and stability. Some cyclical forces are endogenous (that is, generated internally by the private sector), and these endogenous forces may be partially or entirely responsible for the upper and lower turning points in business activity. Irregular factors (such as the 1991 war against Iraq) are exogenous (outside the internal workings of the economy) and are literally unpredictable. An explanation of when and why a firm's sales or production will stop declining (or expanding) must incorporate all endogenous seasonal, cyclical, and trend factors, as well as a host of external or exogenous variables.

The diversity of movement in various sectors of the economy means that expansion in some firms and industries is concurrent with contraction in others. This phenomenon occurs whether business as a whole is depressed or prospering. Turning points in industrial activity are not, however, randomly distributed. They come in clusters. Table 2-2 summarizes the industrial production expansion data centered around the peaks of July 1981 and July 1990. In particular, Table 2-2 reports the number of industries (out of a group of 20 that is monitored by the Commerce Department) that experienced production decreases in a given month. While seven industries experienced a decline in production in May 1990, the 13 others were either stable or experiencing an increase. Since both the 1981 and 1990 peaks occurred in July, it is easy to carry out a month-by-month comparison. While the results are not identical,

TABLE 2-2 A Cyclical Comparison of Production Decreases, 1981 Versus 1990

	Cyclical Peak			*Cyclical Peak*		
	July 1981			*July 1990*		
Number of industries experiencing	April	1981	9	April	1990	11
a decrease in production over	May	1981	7	May	1990	7
the prior month*	June	1981	9	June	1990	7
	July	1981	5	July	1990	8
	August	1981	15	August	1990	10
	September	1981	13	September	1990	12

* Out of the 20 manufacturing industries that are included in the index of industrial production.
Source: Survey of Current Business, April 1991.

the patterns are very close. Watching these month-to-month movements unfold in 1990, and knowing that the recession in 1981 was relatively mild, a forecaster might have predicted that the 1990 recession would not be severe.

When used in cyclical analysis, the term *diffusion* refers to the extent to which the cycle *spreads outward* to affect some or all phases of the production and consumption network (both by industry and by region) of business activity. Widespread expansions or contractions are apt to have a greater percentage change from trough to peak or peak to trough—that is, greater amplitude.

The index of industrial production is often monitored as both an aggregate measure of economic activity and as a measure of diffusion of cyclical forces. The index stood at 107.5 in January 1990 (relative to the base year of 1987 = 100), rose steadily to 110.4 in July 1991, stayed relatively flat in August and September, and then declined steadily until it reached 107.2 in December 1990. Interestingly, however, when one looks inside the index and asks what percentage of the 20 production components that make up the index were increasing in any given month, it turns out that 65 percent were increasing in January 1990, roughly 40 percent were increasing in March and April, 60 percent in July, 50 percent in August, 30 percent in October, and only 20 percent in December. In other words, the diffusion statistics that focus on percentage change within the index provided quicker and clearer evidence of the sharp slide in the second half of 1990.[3]

THE ANATOMY OF THE 1970–1975 CYCLE

The economic crosscurrents that are present in all phases of the cycle serve as a reminder of the problems involved in speaking of a typical business cycle. The degree of clustering and the precise sequence of the cyclical turns of individual sectors vary from one cycle to the next. Nevertheless, there is enough uniformity to warrant sketching what characteristically happens during the successive phases of a business cycle. This description will focus on the endogenous facets of the cycle during the 1970–1975 period as presented in Table 2-3 on pages 38–39.

The impetus for the 1974–1975 recession was, in fact, largely the product of external or exogenous shocks that not only destabilized the economy but dictated that some structural changes would continue even after the contraction had ended. To illustrate the interrelationships that bring about a business cycle and to get started, assume that the economy is stimulated by an appreciable increase in spending on automobiles. The catalyst for this increase may have been either endogenous (say, an increase in consumer incomes) or exogenous (say, a shift in the relative price of American automobiles vis-à-vis

---

[3] These statistics on industrial production are taken from Table 2-6, which appears later in this chapter. In addition, Table 2-6 also includes very detailed production information on the 20 industries that make up the index of industrial production.

imported automobiles). An example of this substantial increase in automobile sales occurred when retail sales of automobiles increased from an annual rate of 8.40 million units in 1970 to 10.23 and 10.87 million units in 1971 and 1972, respectively. This stimulus set in motion a chain reaction. To satisfy increasing demands, automobile producers increased employment by 10.5 percent in the first quarter of 1971 relative to the fourth quarter of 1970. Industrial production of automobiles increased from 59.4 in 1970 to 81.4 in 1971 to 84.7 during 1972. Manufacturers' inventories declined from 1.60 million units in 1971 to 1.48 million units in 1972. Clearly, part of the increase in sales was met by expanding productive capabilities and part was satisfied by running down inventories. As more workers were added in the automobile industry, wages and income of automobile workers increased.

With automobile workers spending their larger incomes on various commodities, retail sales increased (see lines 1 and 2 in Table 2-3). Thus, the initial expansion in the automobile industry spread slowly throughout the entire economy. The balance between expanding and contracting enterprises shifted (see line 3 in Table 2-3) toward aggregate expansion, and the index of industrial production (line 4 in Table 2-3) began to rise in the first quarter of 1971. This diffusion in growth across the majority of industries (seen by the fact that the diffusion index on line 3 in Table 2-3 exceeded 50 percent) caused secondary firms (suppliers to these expanding industries) to revise their production plans, which in turn led to production and employment gains in tertiary firms (see lines 3, 4, and 5 in Table 2-3). Each expanding firm and industry stimulated activity elsewhere. With the scope of the expansion gradually becoming wider, retailers, wholesalers, and manufacturers augmented orders from their suppliers. Indeed, all the way through 1972, net new orders (line 7, Table 2-3) rose. Although business viewed in the aggregate was still operating below capacity (line 8, Table 2-3), businesses were operating at close to full capacity throughout the second half of 1972. Moreover, as production expanded, profits climbed (line 9, Table 2-3). With profits and consumer incomes climbing, with capacity levels being pressed (line 8, Table 2-3), with delivery periods lengthening (line 12, Table 2-3), and with interest rates, machinery, and equipment prices and factor costs still relatively favorable (line 15, Table 2-3), expenditures for plant and equipment and capital goods began to rise consistently in the fourth quarter of 1971, fully one year after the trough. Finally, as the expansion spread, it generated a feeling of confidence about the future (line 10, Table 2-3), new firms began operations (line 11, Table 2-3), and even marginal firms remained in business as they were pulled along by the overall surge in prosperity.

As the expansion widened in scope (line 3, Table 2-3), the slack in the economy was reduced. Idle or excess capacity diminished in a growing number of industries (line 8, Table 2-3) and firms. Delivery time, as measured by vendor performance (line 12, Table 2-3), began to stretch out. As the 1973 peak approached, fully 93 percent of the reporting firms felt the pinch of slower service.

TABLE 2-3   Aggregate Economic Activity During the 1970–1975 Cycle (Data Seasonally Adjusted)

	1970 Trough		1971				1972				1973			Peak	1974				1975 Trough	
	Q3	Q4	Q1	Q2	Q3	Q4	Q1	Q2	Q3	Q4	Q1	Q2	Q3	Q4	Q1	Q2	Q3	Q4	Q1	Q2
1. Retail sales, current 82 dollars (billions)	207270	206099	212571	215891	219169	225414	226982	233187	237398	245576	252103	247899	246573	243363	235570	236740	238179	226916	229862	234796
2. Retail sales, constant dollars (billions)	94791	95219	99413	101902	104252	107748	108802	112475	115537	120417	126137	126841	128463	130014	130816	135256	139642	136215	139829	144567
3. Diffusion Index of Production, 24 industries	45.8	43.8	52.8	73.6	65.3	78.5	77.1	62.5	77.1	76.4	65.3	66.7	63.9	50.1	42.4	54.8	43.8	15.3	21.6	57.6
4. Industrial Production Index, manufacturing (1987 = 1.000)	61.500	60.200	61.367	61.900	62.133	63.533	66.033	67.600	68.433	71.000	72.467	73.433	74.533	74.800	72.900	73.567	73.567	70.800	65.233	64.833
5. Employees on payrolls of nonagricultural establishments (millions)	70.83	70.44	70.74	71.08	71.28	71.73	72.58	73.35	73.86	74.87	75.87	76.51	76.96	77.77	78.13	78.35	78.52	78.12	76.77	76.40
6. Expenditures for plant and equipment, constant dollars (billions)	295.4	286.4	289.0	292.6	292.6	296.0	302.6	306.4	310.2	327.2	343.2	357.6	363.6	364.9	364.0	363.3	354.9	343.7	320.7	312.4
7. New orders, net total (billions 82$)	286.3	274.6	305.3	292.9	300.7	307.5	326.1	336.3	348.6	371.3	401.3	404.5	405.0	413.7	414.0	415.9	420.8	362.8	324.4	323.1
8. Rate of capacity utilization, manufacturing	79.4	76.6	77.8	77.9	77.7	79.4	81.9	83.2	83.6	86.2	87.6	88.0	88.5	88.2	85.3	85.1	84.5	80.2	72.5	71.5
9. Net profit after taxes, all industries (billions)	44.9	42.1	48.8	50.7	54.2	55.7	59.4	60.1	62.8	68.3	79.1	81.2	81.3	85.0	89.0	91.2	97.1	86.8	75.8	81.0

TABLE 2-3 *(Continued)*

	1970 Trough		1971				1972				1973			Peak	1974				1975 Trough	
	Q3	Q4	Q1	Q2	Q3	Q4	Q1	Q2	Q3	Q4	Q1	Q2	Q3	Q4	Q1	Q2	Q3	Q4	Q1	Q2
10. Index of Consumer Sentiment (1966:I = 100)	77.600	72.400	78.100	80.200	82.100	82.000	92.800	88.600	95.200	90.700	81.900	77.000	72.000	76.500	61.800	72.100	64.400	59.500	57.600	72.800
11. New business incorporations	65591	66201	66480	71255	73312	76500	76585	79075	80322	81462	85512	84807	80406	78408	80025	82418	80598	75962	74816	79647
12. Percent of companies reporting slower deliveries, vendor performance	47.5	38.1	43.0	48.7	48.7	51.7	55.0	56.3	63.4	76.1	85.5	86.3	87.3	92.8	89.8	76.6	62.4	34.2	17.6	23.1
13. Unfilled orders, all industries (billions)	102.68	100.28	102.05	100.33	98.71	99.91	101.33	103.21	106.59	111.22	118.82	128.96	136.97	146.26	157.19	168.35	181.80	183.36	176.56	168.65
14. Implicit Price Deflator (1987 = 100)	35.3	35.7	36.3	36.8	37.3	37.6	38.2	38.6	39.0	39.6	40.1	40.8	41.6	42.6	43.3	44.2	45.5	46.6	48.0	48.6
15. Index of labor cost per unit of output, manufacturing (1982 = 100)	53.7	53.8	54.1	54.1	54.1	53.5	53.5	53.8	53.9	53.9	54.8	55.6	55.8	57.2	59.5	60.5	62.0	64.6	68.2	69.1
16. Index of labor unit cost, business sector (1982 = 100)	42.2	42.9	42.8	43.4	43.8	44.3	44.9	44.8	45.2	45.2	46.0	47.3	48.6	49.3	50.8	52.7	54.7	56.0	57.3	57.2
17. Index of net business formation (1967 = 100)	105.8	106.5	106.7	110.2	112.9	114.6	116.4	118.8	119.8	122.2	121.7	120.3	118.2	116.3	113.6	116.3	116.7	106.3	102.5	106.4
18. Claims for unemployment insurance (thousands)	293	317	291	287	306	281	261	269	254	242	225	235	240	260	304	299	339	462	530	503
19. Composite index of four coincident indicators (1982 = 100)	82.2	80.1	81.4	82.1	82.2	83.4	85.9	87.6	89.3	92.9	94.9	95.4	96.2	97.7	95.7	95.0	94.6	91.3	85.8	84.9

Source: Business Conditions Digest and Business Statistics

Analyzing the change in unfilled orders (line 13, Table 2-3), we find the percentage rate increasing despite the fact that employment levels and overall industrial production were climbing. Clearly, the demands placed on the producing sectors in 1972 and 1973 could not be fully satisfied. Rising sales in particular firms and industries released forces of expansion elsewhere, but their effects were negated since an ever-increasing number of firms had to contend with production bottlenecks—supply-side constraints. The monetary expression of these bottlenecks was an acceleration of price changes. In the first six quarters of the 1970–1972 expansion, while overall prices were increasing, the rate of increase was declining. However, as the supply-side constraints became more and more significant, this process reversed itself and the rate of inflation increased (line 14, Table 2-3).

The foregoing description of the expansionary phase following the trough in 1970 was meant to emphasize the cyclical variation between various sectors in a highly interdependent economy. Although postwar business forecasters tend to emphasize exogenous shocks—monetary policy, fiscal policy, weather, or international political turmoil—when explaining *why* an expansion or contraction took place, this description of the 1970–1973 expansion examines *how* changes spread throughout the economy. That is, regardless of whether the cycle is endogenously or exogenously determined, the economy's internal transmission mechanisms need to been understood.

As the expansion in economic activity advanced, declining productivity, rising labor costs, and falling profit margins became of increasing concern to investors (lines 15 and 16, Table 2-3). Even though these cost increases were offset by increased selling prices, there were some firms whose prices failed to rise enough to maintain desired profit margins. Further, the number of firms in this category grew as the expansion continued to the point of saturation. Other industries had overestimated future sales, and as a result more output led to higher inventories. New businesses were constantly being formed, but marginal firms, which were previously being pulled along by the overall prosperity, began to fail. Thus, in late 1973 the number of failures exceeded new formations; hence net business formations began to decline (line 17, Table 2-3).

These developments—the rise in labor costs, financing costs, and the cost of capital goods; the spread of these cost increases throughout the economy; falling profit margins and expected profits; and the decline in the number of business firms experiencing growth—were all present when the economy peaked in the fourth quarter of 1973. With retail sales falling (line 1, Table 2-3), businesses attempted to reduce inventories, and as a result materials orders (line 7, Table 2-3) softened. Unit production costs (line 16, Table 2-3) still increased as overhead costs were adjusted to lower sales levels. Further pressures were put on already-tight profit margins. Given these developments, many firms and consumers became concerned about future prospects (line 10, Table 2-3). New capital commitments (line 6, Table 2-3) became less prevalent.

As the decline was transmitted to other sectors, the economy entered into the contractionary phase of the business cycle.

Normally, a contraction does not cumulate in the same manner as an expansion. In the United States, the factors causing a contraction are countered by institutionalized forces of growth and by government policies designed to diminish the scope of any recession, even though other government policies may have been initially responsible for the contraction. Businesspeople and consumers are accustomed to economic growth, and they expect the government to undertake specific countercyclical programs—increase transfer payments, cut taxes, augment expenditure programs, provide more job-training funds—in the event of a recession. Consumers themselves are reluctant to lower their living standards, and they reduce spending less than they would if recession was seen as permanent. As a result, consumer spending is maintained in the face of declines in income that are judged to be transitory. An examination of retail sales in constant dollars (line 1, Table 2-3) reveals that from the peak, fourth quarter 1973, to the trough, first quarter 1975, the decline in retail sales was a modest 5.5 percent in real terms; current-dollar retail sales continued to expand. Further, both interfirm and interindustry competition intensify as profit margins are squeezed. Successful enterprises are able to expand their markets, and hence their sales, even while aggregate activity is declining. This expansion comes at the expense of less efficient firms and industries. Some of these less efficient firms are apt to move rapidly to counteract their ever-declining market shares. This involves purchasing new equipment, modernizing plants, and developing new and improved products as businesses operating at or close to capacity expand in anticipation of the upcoming recession.

The endogenous developments that naturally grow out of a recession help to moderate most downturns. As the recession proceeds, these endogenous factors cause interest rates to fall, credit to become more readily available, inventories to come into better alignment with sales, and unit costs (line 16, Table 2-3) to moderate even prior to the trough in economic activity. Thus, even before the trough in March 1975, an ever-increasing number of firms found their profit margins improving. With the prospect of profits looming brighter, existing firms expanded and new companies were formed (line 11, Table 2-3). Investment projects that had been postponed were now undertaken, and unwanted inventories continued to lessen as the recovery of aggregate production (line 4, Table 2-3) got underway.

The foregoing summary of the cycle from the trough in 1970 to the trough in 1975 was meant to reveal the general patterns operating during a business cycle. The cyclical process is full of economic crosscurrents. While some firms are failing, new companies are entering the same industry. While the economy is expanding, the pace of advance differs from company to company. Average industry performance may be a poor indicator of individual company achievement. Furthermore, we would be remiss if we did not explicitly indicate that the preceding discussion does not attempt to explain the actual cause of the 1973–1975 recession; rather, we have described the cyclical variations that comprise the business cycle.

BUSINESS CYCLES SINCE 1970

THE 1973–1975 RECESSION

The recession that began in late 1973 was by many standards the longest and most severe of the post-World War II contractions. Over the course of the 16-month recession, real GNP declined by 3.6 percent and industrial production declined by over 13 percent. Like all severe recessions, the recession of 1973–1975 had numerous causes. The major proximate cause of this contraction was severe and unprecedented rates of inflation. In part this inflation was attributable to the relatively easy monetary policies and excessive spending levels via fiscal policy in the years preceding 1973.[4] Moreover, this was generally true not only in the United States but in all major industrialized countries.

While governmental policies were the major cause of the historically high levels of inflation, there were other contributing causes. Poor crops in many parts of the world drove food prices up rapidly; oil prices rose dramatically as a result of the actions of OPEC (Organization of Petroleum Exporting Countries). Additionally, there was an increase in raw-materials prices as worldwide demand outraced existing supply. The exceedingly high inflation rates not only had adverse effects on financial markets, but consumption patterns were altered significantly. Increased prices for food and oil-related products left consumers with smaller levels of discretionary income for other items. The impact of inflation on wages led to bracket creep, whereby after-tax real income was lower than would have otherwise been the case.

Another contributing factor to the severity of the 1973–1975 recession was an excessive inventory build-up. Exceptionally strong levels of demand in preceding periods had led many businesses to build up their inventory levels despite the increasing likelihood of a contraction. When inventories had to be liquidated, workers were laid off, demand was further reduced, and the recession intensified. Real estate speculation and the resulting difficulties also contributed to the length and severity of this recession.

As the recession deepened, inflation slowed with the result that consumer spending, especially on nondurables, began to expand. As the previously excessive inventory levels were drawn down in the face of increased sales, it

---

[4] Many countries responded to the oil-price shocks during this time by relying on demand-stimulus policies. The result of these demand-stimulus policies was world-wide inflation. Thus, while it is true that the oil-price shocks led to a one-time contraction of aggregate supply, it is also true that the combination of expansionary monetary and fiscal policies led to the continuation of price increases.

FIGURE 2-4   Change in Real GDP

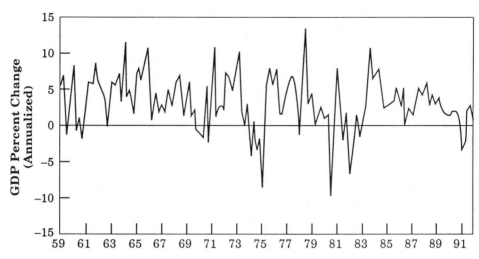

Source: Survey of Current Business, various issues

became apparent as early as the third quarter of 1975 that productive capabilities would have to be expanded. Economic activity continued to expand throughout 1976 and into 1977. Despite the remaining economic problems of historically high inflation and unemployment rates, it became clear that the economy was well on the way to a healthy and sustainable recovery in 1977.[5]

THE RECESSIONS OF 1980 AND 1981–1982

Following a relatively long period of stagnation and slow economic growth during 1979, the NBER in June 1980 indicated that a recession had begun in January 1980. While the housing and manufacturing industries had recorded losses as early as 1979, services and business fixed investment held up relatively well. However, even growth in these sectors could not sustain the economy, and beginning in early 1980 virtually all major macroeconomic indicators began to decline. The declines in the personal saving rate and low real interest rates, which had helped prop up the economy during the preceding year, began to reverse themselves, so the decline in economic activity accelerated rapidly during the spring quarter. As can be seen in Figure 2-4, real GDP fell at a record annual rate of 9.7 percent during the second quarter of 1980.

In mid-March, restrictive monetary policies of unprecedented severity in peacetime were suddenly imposed by the Federal Reserve. The reactions to this unanticipated monetary policy were disastrous, as private borrowing fell over 50 percent during the second quarter of 1980. At the same time, growth

---

[5] Alan L. Sorkin, *Monetary and Fiscal Policy and Business Cycles in the Modern Era* (Lexington, Mass.: Macmillan Publishing Company, 1988), pp. 64–69.

in monetary aggregates declined sharply, with the result that interest rates rose to the unheard-of levels of between 14 and 20 percent in March and April, and then fell abruptly to between 7 and 12 percent in June and July.

The excessively restrictive monetary policies were eliminated in early July 1980. Private borrowing increased strongly during the remainder of 1980. Reduced rates of increases in consumer prices and the previously noted declines in interest rates served to bolster consumer expectations, and consumers began increasing their spending levels. Although the 1980 recession was short by historical standards, the decline in real GNP made it one of the most severe postwar recessions.

The recovery that had begun in August 1980 was one of the shortest expansions on record, lasting only 12 months. Because it was a relatively weak and short-lived recovery, unemployment barely declined from the recession peak. Inflation remained at double-digit levels during 1980 and into 1981. The high inflationary rates led to relatively tight monetary policies. This combination of a restrictive monetary policy and high inflation rates pushed nominal interest rates to record levels. By the spring of 1981, the prime interest rate was nearly 20 percent compared to slightly more than 11 percent in mid-1980.

The historically high interest rates led to sharp declines in purchases of new homes, automobiles, household furniture, and other interest-rate-sensitive purchases. Declines in consumer purchases on durables declined by over 10 percent over the course of these two recessions. Thus, we can say that the proximate cause of the recession that began in 1981 was a decline in consumer spending, but the drop in consumer spending was, in turn, linked to the lagged effects of tight monetary policies.

Major tax cuts were enacted in 1981 that, when accompanied by substantial increases in government purchases of goods and services and transfer payments, led to significant increases in disposable income. This, together with lower interest rates, led the economy out of the recession, and by 1983 the economy was in the initial phases of one of the longest postwar recoveries and expansions.[6]

THE EXPANSION OF 1982–1990

The expansion that began with the lower turning point in November 1982 finally ran its course after 92 months, and the economy peaked in July 1990 (see Figure 2-4). Following the recession that ended in November 1982, real GNP enjoyed uninterrupted growth for every quarter of the remainder of the 1980s, except for the second quarter of 1986 (1986:II). Other measures of aggregate economic activity, such as industrial production, nonagricultural employment, real personal income, and sales, also demonstrated a pattern of virtually uninterrupted growth during this 92-month upswing in the U.S.

---

[6] Alan L. Sorkin, pp. 69–74.

economy. As is always the case, not all industries or regions flourished equally during this period of sustained growth. In the early- to mid-1980s, many segments of the manufacturing sector (steel, automobiles, etc.) experienced severe competition from foreign competitors, a process that was reinforced by the general appreciation of the dollar. The sharp decline in the price of oil in 1986 depressed the economies of the oil-producing states and contributed to the overall slowdown in 1985–1986.

In 1989, a second period of relatively slow growth occurred. This stagnation was concentrated in some segments of the manufacturing and construction sectors and led many forecasters to foresee a recession. In fact, predictions of a recession began surfacing as early as 1988. Even while forecasts of impending recession became more prevalent in 1988 and 1989, the export sector of the economy became more competitive due to the lagged effect of the depreciated dollar, a leaner cost structure arising from earlier worker and management layoffs, and the jettisoning of unwanted manufacturing capacity during the early and mid-1980s.

As opposed to the collapse and retrenchment of the manufacturing sector that highlighted the two recessions in 1980 and 1981, it was the financial sector of the economy that became increasingly unstable during the remainder of the 1980s. The collapse of the savings and loan industry is a complex story, but the breakdown was clearly linked to the ending of the inflationary spiral that had come to haunt the economy during the 1970s. Without the continuing presence of rapid inflation to rationalize the unwise expansion of commercial and residential real estate, many loans were not repayable. Greed and corruption and ineffective government regulation captured the headlines of the popular press and did, indeed, play an important part in this financial collapse. It can be argued, however, that the relative demise of the savings and loan industry was due, in larger part, to an economy shifting from double-digit inflation (linked, primarily, to escalating oil prices and an ineffective and accommodative monetary policy) to single-digit inflation (due to plunging oil prices and tighter monetary policy).

Public recognition of the deteriorating quality of bank portfolios lagged behind the publicity surrounding the savings and loan industry. The unprecedented surge of bank lending in the 1980s, however, left an economy in 1990 with a legacy of too many vacant office buildings (an excess supply equal to five to ten years of normal construction in some cities) and the need for massive bank loan write-offs. It was argued by many in 1989 and 1990 that the Federal Reserve's tight credit policy (or, as it was referred to by the popular press, "credit crunch") drained economic vitality from the household and corporate sectors. The financial pressures that preceded the 1990 recession must, however, be viewed in light of the banking excesses during the 1980s. That is, because so many major banks found themselves holding nonperforming loans (loans that were not being repaid according to the original terms of the contract), their need (demand) for liquidity (bank reserves provided by the Federal

Reserve) was extremely high relative to past recessions. Following the liberal lending policy of the 1980s, therefore, the switch by the banking sector to a more conservative lending policy was clearly a negative factor in terms of business optimism as the economy approached the summer of 1990.

In addition to the savings and loan and banking industries, the financial excesses generated by Wall Street yielded a corporate sector that was highly leveraged (dependent on debt), and, as a result, increasingly vulnerable to cyclical downturns in the economy. Businesses that rely to a greater degree on debt financing rather than equity financing through the stock market must continue to repay principle and interest in the face of the declining profits that accompany recessions. Similar trends were evident in the private or household sector, which found debt repayment to be an increasing percentage of disposable income as the 1980s came to a close. It remains for future economic historians to analyze thoroughly the root causes of the 1990 downturn, but the imbalances in the financial sector must surely have played a major role in causing the July 1990 peak in aggregate economic activity.

With the benefit of hindsight, we know that the NBER officially dated the business cycle peak as July 1990 (this official pronouncement came in April 1991, or nine months after the peak). While the official peak was dated as occurring one month before Iraq's invasion of Kuwait, it was not until the fourth quarter of 1990 that the economy actually experienced negative real growth in GNP. During the interim between July 1990 and November 1990, economists, politicians, and the public debated whether a recession was in process, whether it was caused by Iraq's invasion of Kuwait, and whether economic conditions would worsen if the United States became involved in the hostilities.[7]

Professor Victor Zarnowitz of the University of Chicago and a member of the NBER's business-cycle dating committee responded in April 1991 to the criticism that, by dating the peak in July, the committee was disparaging the Bush administration's view that the invasion of Kuwait caused the recession:[8]

> This [the NBER's determination that July 1990 was the upper turning point] isn't a refutation or confirmation of any hypothesis about what would have happened without the invasion. If there had been a sharp drop in the economy before the invasion, you could argue that the invasion wasn't the cause. But that wasn't the case here. We'll never know what would have happened if the invasion didn't occur.

FORECASTING A RECOVERY: THE RECESSION OF 1990–1991?

In May 1991, the U.S. economy experienced an increase in nonfarm employment of 59,000, the first increase since the summer of 1990.[9] While the popular

---

[7] Victor Zarnowitz, "A Guide to What is Known About Business Cycles," *Business Economics*, July 1990, pp. 5–13.

[8] Victor Zarnowitz, "Recession Began Before Gulf Crisis, Researchers Assert," *Wall Street Journal*, April 26, 1991.

[9] "U.S. Payrolls Grown by 59,000 Workers," *Washington Post*, June 8, 1991.

press was focused on the question of whether the recession was coming to an end, Sam Kahan, chief economist for Fuji Securities Co. in Chicago, felt (in June 1991) that this focus on the turning point was misplaced:[10]

> Everyone keeps looking for the turning point for the economy, but this is not the issue. The issue is whether it is going to be a normal recovery or rather anemic. . . . I think it will be anemic because of continuing problems such as the huge number of empty office buildings and problems with many financial institutions.

Following negative growth of − 2.5 percent for GDP (see Figure 2-4) in the first quarter of 1991, the U.S. economy experienced positive GDP growth of 1.4, 1.8, and 0.3 percent, respectively, in the last three quarters of 1991–a pattern very consistent with Kahan's projection of an anemic recovery. But was this a recovery? The *Economic Report of the President*, submitted in February 1992 by President George Bush's Council of Economic Advisers, speaks of the *1990–91 recession* and points out that a ". . . majority of the Blue Chip forecasters [an informal group of prominent business forecasters] surveyed in January 1992 placed it [the trough of the recession] in the second quarter of 1991."[11] When the first quarter of 1992 was completed, the GDP had grown at an annual rate of 2.7 percent, and this lent support to the Council's belief that the recovery was in full swing.

As of July 1, 1992, however, the National Bureau of Economic Research (the private, nonprofit research organization which officially dates peaks and troughs in the economy) had not been moved to date the trough in the economy. By July 1992, two years after the peak in July of 1990, the economy had experienced over a year of positive real growth in the GDP, but the unemployment rate had risen to 7.8 percent. As the economy entered the summer of 1992 and the prelude to the 1992 presidential campaign, a debate was raging among presidential contenders as to whether the economy had stalled on an anemic growth plateau rather than a sustainable recovery.

It is not surprising that so much controversy surrounds the dating of the upper and lower turning points in the economy. A popular, but simplistic, view of the economy is that all economic forces tend to move together in a parallel fashion, and, if this is so, turning points should be easy to recognize. A realistic view of economic activity is that literally trillions of economic crosscurrents (each individual business decision to expand or contract output, each consumer decision to buy or forego another major consumer durable, or each foreigner's decision to buy an American product rather than a domestic good) are at work at any moment. The net outcome of all of these actions produces an upward or downward movement in the economy. As the economy nears a peak or trough, many important barometers will be moving in opposite directions, and

---

[10] Ibid.

[11] *Economic Report of the President* (Washington, D.C.: U.S. Government Printing Office, February 1992), p. 54.

therefore the task of recognizing the coming or passing of a recession remains complicated.

THE CONTINUING PUZZLE OF BUSINESS-CYCLE TIMING

Many of the premature predictions that called for recessions in 1987, 1988, 1989, and 1990 were based on the presumption that the longer an expansion continues, the more likely that a contraction becomes inevitable. Numerous studies have shed some doubt on the belief that expansions die of old age. A study by Neftci found that more severe recessions tend to be followed by larger cumulative increases in output.[12] Thus, based on the severity of the 1981–1982 recession, the expansion of the 1980s should have been expected to last longer than average. Additionally, a recent study by Diebold and Rudebusch found no evidence that the probability of a recession rises as the length of an economic expansion increases.[13] All of these studies reinforce the earlier conclusion that the task of calling turning points in aggregate economic activity remains extremely complex.[14]

IS THE BUSINESS CYCLE DISAPPEARING?

The issue of the disappearing business cycle was raised in the 1960s, when some economists argued that we had learned how to fine-tune the economy. The recessions of 1969–1970 and 1973–1975 terminated this debate for decades. The recent decision by the Commerce Department to terminate publication of the *Business Conditions Digest* might also be taken as an indirect indicator of lessening interest in business cycles. No less an authority than Mike Evans speculated in a 1989 article entitled "Endless Expansion—Impossible Dream?" in *Industry Week* about the possibility of the economy growing indefinitely.[15] This theme was pursued in a more systematic way in 1990 by Garner and Wurtz, economists at the Federal Reserve Bank of Kansas City.[16] In particular, Garner and Wurtz document the structural changes in the economy (for example, the larger role played by the government, the relative increase in the service sector, and the growth of international trade) that

[12] Salih H. Neftci, "Is There a Cyclical Time Unit?" in *The National Bureau Method, International Capital Mobility, and Other Essays*, Carnegie-Rochester Conference Series on Public Policy, vol. 24 (North-Holland, spring 1986).

[13] Francis X. Diebold and Glenn D. Rudebusch, "A Nonparametric Investigation of Duration Dependence in the American Business Cycle," *Journal of Political Economy*, Vol. 98, 1990, pp. 596–616.

[14] Bryon Higgins, "Is a Recession Inevitable This Year?" *Economic Review*, Federal Reserve Bank of Kansas City, January 1988, pp. 3–16.

[15] Mike Evans, "Endless Expansion—Impossible Dream?" *Industry Week*, October 2, 1989.

[16] C. Alan Garner and Richard E. Wurtz, "Is the Business Cycle Disappearing?" *Economic Review*, Federal Reserve Bank of Kansas City, May/June 1990, pp. 25–39.

has resulted in moderation of the severity of postwar business cycles. Garner and Wurtz conclude, however, that the business cycle will not disappear in the foreseeable future:

> ... The U.S. economy remains subject to unpredictable disturbances. ... A drought in U.S. agricultural regions, for example, can depress farm output and real GNP growth. ... Other examples of domestic disturbances are a sudden change in the tax laws or an unexpected shift in the willingness of U.S. firms to invest in new plant and equipment. ... A sudden tightening of Japanese fiscal policy, for example, could reduce Japanese purchases of U.S. products, thereby lowering U.S. employment and income. ... Recent changes in the economic system also may have worsened the economy's response to unexpected disturbances. The most notable change is the higher level of corporate and personal debt.[17]

In the end, Garner and Wurtz argue for moderation in the economy's cyclical sensitivity, but they see still an economy that is susceptible to internal or external disturbances. There is no final word in such a debate. The important point is that forecasters must assume that secular changes in the economy will continue to alter the relationship of the U.S. economy to its trading partners, as well as the relationships within and among key industrial, financial, and commercial sectors in the United States.

STATISTICAL MEASUREMENT: THE NATIONAL BUREAU OF ECONOMIC RESEARCH

The National Bureau of Economic Research (NBER)—a private, nonprofit research organization—has served as the leading source of information related to the tracking and measurement of business cycles since its inception in 1920. Its expressed purpose is ". . . to ascertain and to present to the public important economic facts and their interpretation in a scientific and impartial manner."[18]

The NBER's pioneering business-cycle studies date back to the 1850s. By common consent of government and private economists, the NBER performs the task of dating business-cycle turning points (peaks and troughs) and provides the official definition of contractionary and expansionary periods. In addition to many NBER publications dealing with cycles, the *Survey of Current Business*, published by the Department of Commerce, Bureau of Economic Analysis, contains a monthly update of the NBER's work and offers a wealth of quarterly and monthly time series.[19]

---

[17] Ibid., p. 35.

[18] National Bureau of Economic Research, Inc., *55th Annual Report* (New York: NBER, September 1975).

[19] U.S. Department of Commerce, Bureau of Economic Analysis, *Business Conditions Digest* (Washington, D.C.: U.S. Government Printing Office, January 1979), pp. 1–5.

In 1938, 25 years after Wesley Mitchell had put forth his classic treatise, the NBER, under the guidance of Mitchell and Arthur Burns, published its first list of business-cycle indicators.[20] Updated in 1950, 1960, 1966, 1975, and 1983, these barometers are among the most heralded and misunderstood statistics published by the popular news media.[21]

INDICATORS AND TURNING POINTS

The continuous evolution of business conditions necessitated the development of both a consistent method of isolating and dating business cycles and measuring cyclical activity and a rigorous basis for defining a myriad of forecasting-related terms such as *trough, recovery, peak,* and *recession.* Earlier in this chapter, you were introduced to the peaks and troughs in economic activity as they have been recorded by the NBER (see Table 2-1). These turning points mirror, as closely as possible, the cycle in aggregate economic activity. However, because no single measure captures the economy's diverse movements, the NBER analyzed many areas of economic activity before developing the reference dates shown in Table 2-1. Figure 2-5 contains an idealized conception of a simplified cyclical pattern in which you can readily identify the initial trough (T), the upper turning point or peak (P), and the terminal trough (TT). As stated in the *Survey of Current Business,*

> There are three composite indices of particular significance: Thus there is an index of leading indicators, series which historically reached their cyclical peaks and troughs earlier than the corresponding business cycle turns. There is an index of roughly coincident indicators, consisting of series which historically reached their turning points at about the same time as the general economy, and an index of lagging indicators, which includes series that typically reached their peaks and troughs later than the corresponding business cycle turns.[22]

The composite index of 11 leading indicators includes the following series (NBER identification number in parentheses): average weekly hours of pro-

[20] See Wesley C. Mitchell and Arthur Burns, *Statistical Indicators of Cyclical Revivals,* Bulletin 69 (New York: NBER, May 28, 1938); Geoffrey H. Moore, *Statistical Indicators of Cyclical Revivals and Recessions,* Occasional Paper 31 (New York: NBER, 1950); Julius Shiskin, *Indicators of Business Expansions and Contractions,* Occasional Paper 103 (New York: Columbia University Press for NBER, 1967).

[21] Victor Zarnowitz and Charlotte Boschan, "Cyclical Indicators: An Evaluation and New Leading Indexes," *Business Conditions Digest,* May 1975; V. Zarnowitz and C. Boschan, "New Composite Indexes of Coincident and Lagging Indicators," *Business Conditions Digest,* November 1975; Arthur Burns, "Causes of the 1973–1975 Recession," *Federal Reserve Bulletin,* May 1975, pp. 273–79; Victor Zarnowitz and Geoffrey Moore, "The Timing and Severity of the 1980 Recession," in *Business Cycles, Inflation and Forecasting,* 2nd ed., Geoffrey Moore, National Bureau of Economic Research, Studies in Business Cycles, no. 24 (Cambridge, Mass.: Ballinger Publishing Co., 1983).

[22] *Survey of Current Business,* April 1991.

FIGURE 2-5 Simplified Cyclical Pattern

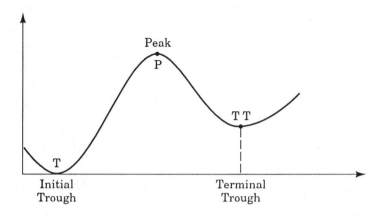

duction workers (1); average weekly initial claims for unemployment insurance (5); manufacturers' new orders in 1982 dollars, consumer goods, and materials industries (8); vendor performance—slower deliveries, diffusion index (32); contracts and orders for plant and equipment in 1982 dollars (20); new private housing units authorized by local building permits (29); change in manufacturers' unfilled orders in 1982 dollars, durable goods (92); change in sensitive materials prices (99); stock prices, 500 common stocks (19); money supply, M2, in 1982 dollars (106); and the index of consumer expectations (83).

The composite index of coincident indicators is comprised of four roughly coincident indicators: employees of nonagricultural payrolls (41); personal income less transfer payments in 1982 dollars (51); index of industrial production (47); and manufacturing and trade sales in 1982 dollars (57).

The composite index of lagging indicators is for those activities that respond only slowly to changing business conditions or that reflect the pressures created during the immediately preceding expansion or contraction. This index has six components: average duration of unemployment (91); the ratio of manufacturing and trade inventories to sales in 1982 dollars (77); change in index of labor cost per unit of output in manufacturing (62); average prime rate charged by banks (109); commercial and industrial loans outstanding in 1982 dollars (101); ratio, consumer installment credit outstanding to personal income (95); and the change in consumer price index for services (120).

The composites have variable leads and lags at the turning points. Additionally, the forecaster must be aware of the limitations of these indices. Specifically, these aggregates have a propensity to generate false signals.[23]

[23] For detailed discussions, see D. J. Daly, "Forecasting with Statistical Indicators," in B. G. Hickman, ed., *Econometric Models of Cyclical Behavior*, vol. 2 (New York: Columbia University Press, 1971), pp. 1159–94; and S. H. Hymans, "On the Use of Leading Indicators to Predict Cyclical Turning Points" and "Comments and Discussion," *Brookings Papers on Economic Activity* (Washington, D.C.: The Brookings Institution, 1973), Vol. 2, pp. 389–94.

For example, the leading index fell for seven months in 1984, five months in 1987, and two months in 1989, but in no case did a national recession follow immediately. Consider a point made by Geoffrey Moore:

> It is important to be clear what these results do not mean as well as what they do mean. They do not mean that one can get much advance notice that a general business contraction is beginning or is coming to an end. They do help to recognize these events at about the time they occur. Even then there is some risk of error.[24]

Additionally, in a 1982 study Zarnowitz and Moore propose some modifications to make the indicator series more applicable and useful to policy makers.[25]

MACROECONOMIC MODELS AND FORECASTING

Macroeconomics is concerned with the behavior of the economy in the aggregate. Macroeconomic theories and hypotheses describe how factors of production are converted into output (aggregate supply), and how this output is distributed among the various sectors (aggregate demand). Macroeconomic models integrate the commodities or product market, the factor market, the money and credit markets, and the government and international sectors.

Economic model building at the macroeconomic level may be thought of as an attempt to construct a general equilibrium model of the economy. Macroeconomic forecasters combine economic theory, mathematics, and statistical techniques as a means of constructing empirical models of the economy. The solution values or forecasts yielded by these models are simultaneous; that is, the forecast magnitudes are jointly determined at the same time rather than being individually or independently estimated.

Macroeconomic models came into vogue at approximately the same time that Keynesian macroeconomic theory began to dominate the economics profession. The first of the American macroeconomic models was the Klein-Goldberger (K/G) model.[26] The K/G model is a Keynesian real aggregate demand model in which the major components of both the output and income sides of the income and product accounts are endogenously determined. There is no attempt to model the behavior of the financial institutions. The short-run interest rate is determined by exogenous policy and banking conditions. The long-term interest rate, which is determined by a term structure rela-

---

[24] G. H. Moore, *Business Cycle Indicators*, Vol. I (Princeton, N.J.: Princeton University Press, 1961), p. 79. Copyright © 1961 by Princeton University Press. Reprinted by permission of Princeton University Press.

[25] For detailed discussions, see Victor Zarnowitz and Geoffrey H. Moore, "Sequential Signals of Recession and Recovery," in Geoffrey H. Moore, ed., *Business Cycles, Inflation and Forecasting*, 2nd ed. (Cambridge, Mass.: Ballinger Publishing Company, 1983), pp. 23–59.

[26] L. R. Klein and A. S. Goldberger, *An Econometric Model of the United States, 1929–1952* (Amsterdam: North-Holland), 1955.

tionship, is linked to the real sector because it affects investment. The Klein-Goldberger model, which appeared in 1955, contained approximately two dozen equations.

The Klein-Goldberger model set the pattern for later modeling efforts, such as those at the University of Michigan by Daniel Suits, at the Wharton School of the University of Pennsylvania by Lawrence Klein, and at the Office of Business Economics of the Department of Commerce. These first-generation quarterly econometric models appeared in the 1960s and are all similar to some extent.

Consider the following model, put forth by Daniel Suits in 1962 to explain to the economics profession the nature and use of econometric models:[27]

$$C = 20 + 0.7(Y - T) \tag{2-1}$$

$$I = 2 + 0.1Y_{t-1} \tag{2-2}$$

$$T = 0.2Y \tag{2-3}$$

$$Y = C + I + G \tag{2-4}$$

where

$$
\begin{aligned}
C &= \text{personal consumption expenditures by households} \\
Y &= \text{personal income, which in turn equals GDP} \\
T &= \text{taxes} \\
I &= \text{business investment} \\
Y - T &= \text{disposable income} \\
G &= \text{government expenditures} \\
Y_{t-1} &= \text{lagged income.}
\end{aligned}
$$

Suits provided the following concise summary:

> This econometric model approximates the economy by a system of equations in which the unknowns are those variables—income, consumption, investment, and tax yield—whose behavior is to be analyzed. The *knowns* are government expenditures and lagged income. When projected values for the knowns are inserted in the equations, the system can be solved to forecast the values of the unknowns.

By current standards, Suits's model appears to be excessively simple. However, we should remember that even this simple model taxed existing computer technology.

The key characteristic of many of these early first-generation models was

---

[27] Daniel B. Suits, "Forecasting and Analysis with an Econometric Model," *American Economic Review*, March 1962, pp. 104–32.

that there was very little emphasis on the interrelationships between the financial and real sectors. The second-generation models make an effort to rectify this problem by expanding the financial sector. Additionally, these models were expanded to mesh with such techniques as input-output analysis. Second-generation models would include the FRB-MIT model (1968), which is named after its sponsors, the Federal Reserve Board and the Massachusetts Institute of Technology, the Brookings model, and the Wharton Mark III model (1972).[28] At approximately the same time, the commercial econometric forecasting services began to deliver their services to paying clients. Among those that began operations at about this time were Chase Econometrics, started by Michael Evans, who had worked on the Wharton model; and Data Resources Inc. (DRI), started by Otto Eckstein, who had worked on the Brookings model project. Virtually all of these models were much larger than the first-generation models in that they contained more complete models of the financial sector, linkages between the real and financial sectors, and disaggregated detail on output and prices.

LINKING MACROECONOMIC MODELS
TO INDUSTRY- AND FIRM-LEVEL MODELS

Figure 2-6 provides us with a simplified version of a top-down relationship among macroeconomic models, industry models, and firm-level models. Exogenous factors determine the environment in which all economic activity takes place. As shown in Figure 2-6, these include monetary and fiscal policy in the United States and in foreign countries, as well as a wide range of factors such as oil shocks (for example, the creation of OPEC and the war in Iraq), abnormal weather, and other forces which are beyond the control of society to regulate. Just below the exogenous factors in Figure 2-6 we have depicted the macroenvironment within which the industry and firm must operate. In essence, consumers and businesses in the United States and around the world comprise the endogenous forces which propel the economy. For purposes of illustration in Figure 2-6, we show industry models for two sectors—consumer goods and machine tools—which are linked to the macroeconomic model of the economy. Beneath the industry models are, of course, the individual firms which comprise these two industries. Exogenous forces impact both the macroeconomic and the industry models. While it is true that macroeconomic fluctuations influence industries and firms, it is also true that the performance of industries and firms influences the achievements of the macroeconomy. That

---

[28] Published references are F. de Leeuw and E. Gramlich, "The Federal Reserve—MIT Econometric Model," *Federal Reserve Bulletin*, January 1968; J. S. Deusenberry, G. Fromm, L. R. Klein, and E. Kuh, eds., *The Brookings Quarterly Econometric Model of the United States* (Amsterdam: North-Holland, 1965); and M. McCarthy, *The Wharton Quarterly Econometric Forecasting Model Mark III*, Wharton School, University of Pennsylvania, 1972.

FIGURE 2-6 Linkages Among Macroeconomic, Industry, and Firm Models

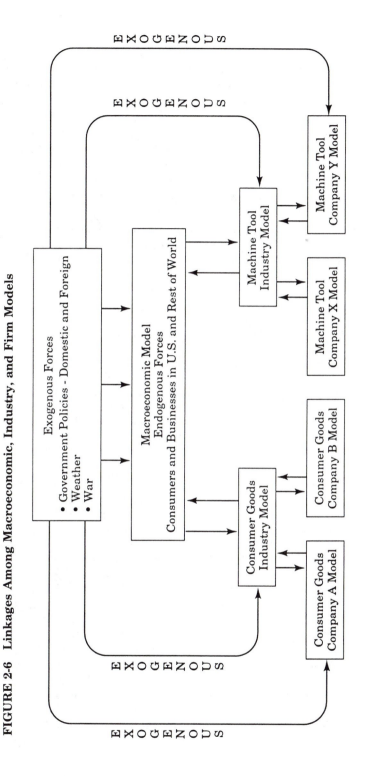

is, there are ripple effects from the company models to the industry models and from the industry models to the macroeconomic model.

For macroeconomic models to be most useful to forecasters who must prepare industry- and firm-level projections, the macro models must serve as a "driver" for models at lower levels of disaggregation. That is, the forecasted variables generated by the macro model must be useable as independent variables in the microeconomic models of the firm and industry. The availability of timely and well-documented output from the macroeconomic variables is, in the end, of utmost importance to customers of commercial forecast vendors. Macroeconomic forecasts are quickly made obsolete by changing endogenous and exogenous conditions. Forecasting, at the microeconomic and macroeconomic level, is a process of continuous revision. Judged in this light, macroeconomic models are extremely valuable to the forecaster putting together the outlook for his or her company.

QUESTIONS FOR DISCUSSION AND ANALYSIS

1. Among the many ways to quantify the severity of a recession, three closely monitored statistics are the percentage change in the GDP deflator, the percentage drop in industrial output, and the peak jobless rate. Using the *Survey of Current Business*, estimate the peak-to-trough magnitudes for the deflator, output, and unemployment for the last three recessions. For example, how much did industrial output fall between July 1981 and November 1982? How did the recession that followed the 1990 downturn compare to earlier declines?

2. Pick two industries of particular interest to you and analyze their cyclical experiences over the peak-to-trough period following the downturn of 1990. For example, what happened to unit sales, dollar sales, and employment? Did these industries lead or lag?

3. Identify a local company in your city and collect sales or production data (ideally, in nonmonetary units or in real, inflation-adjusted units over the one-year period following the peak in July 1990). Did this company seem to be affected by the recession, and did its sales performance match the decline in real GNP?

4. Consult a private or public company in your city, interview the person(s) who prepares the company's annual budget, and write a report discussing how this company incorporates forecasts of short-term business conditions in its budgetary review. For example, does it monitor the leading, coincident, and lagging indicators? Does it reestimate the budget monthly to incorporate changing economic conditions? Does it know whether the company or its industry leads or lags cyclical turning points? Does it subscribe to commercial forecasting services?

5. Analyze the 11 subcomponent series that make up the index of leading indicators during the period from January 1988 to January 1992. How soon before the downturn in July 1990 would you have been willing to predict that a recession was forthcoming? When would you have predicted an upturn?

6. Using the latest available issue of the *Survey of Current Business*, prepare an indicator outlook for the economy. Are there any unique circumstances dominating the current outlook? Is the economy mainly responding to endogenous forces, or are exogenous forces playing an unusually large role? Do you foresee a turning point?

7. What are the strengths and weaknesses of the indicator approach to forecasting?

8. Consult several local and regional publications (such as newspapers) concerning the leading and coincident indicators. Did they interpret the information correctly? How might both the local and national news media improve their coverage of movements in the composite index of leading indicators?

9. Prepare a two-page summary of the current outlook of the economy over the next 12 months, based on analysis of the information contained in the latest issues of business-oriented publications such as the *Wall Street Journal, Fortune, Business Week*, and *Forbes*. A reference librarian can help you compile a complete listing of such publications. Take the most optimistic and the most pessimistic appraisals of the outlook and try to explain why experts could have such varying interpretations concerning the future course of the economy.

10. Consult a publication such as *The Journal of Business Forecasting* for its consensus forecasts for the past 12 months. What is the difference between the most optimistic and the most pessimistic outlook? How has the outlook changed over the course of this 12-month period?

11. Using the latest issue of the *Economic Report of the President*, analyze how its appraisal of the economy differs from those of the optimists and pessimists. Is the President's Council of Economic Advisors likely to be optimistic or pessimistic?

12. An important characteristic of the free-market system is business freedom to enter and exit an industry, with business formation and failure being the most common method of exit for those eager or unable to earn a profit. Using the section labeled "Industrial and Commercial Failures and Formations" in the *Survey of Current Business*, locate the monthly series that identifies formations and failures. How would these various measures be interrelated and interpreted? Do these various measures lead or lag behind turning points? When might a business-conditions analyst be interested in forecasting the business failure rate? The business formation rate? How could this information be used by decision makers?

13. Business-conditions analysts often discuss countercyclical stabilization actions that can be taken by the federal government. How are these related to fiscal and monetary policy? What position concerning the proper degree of countercyclical economic intervention is taken by the neo-Keynesians and by the monetarists?

14. Explain why business fluctuations and cycles in a market economy such as ours, where consumer choice is predominant, differ from a controlled economy, where the planning board decides what will be produced and how it will be produced.

15. How does the 1973–1975 recession compare with the recession which began in July 1990?

16. Why would the 1973–1975 recession be characterized as an exogenous recession while 1980–1981 was more correctly classified as an endogenous recession? How should we characterize the latest recession?

17. What has been the average length of business cycles in the United States? Is an average meaningful?
18. What advantages would commercial forecast vendors have vis-à-vis industry- or firm-level forecasters relative to macroeconomic forecasting?
19. Why do you think that judgmental factors would play a major role in explaining differences in macroeconomic forecasts?
20. Why do you think that forecasters distinguish between macroeconomic and microeconomic forecasting?
21. Discuss two major areas in which macroeconomic forecasting has an impact on managerial decisions in the private sector and how it affects each area.

REFERENCES FOR FURTHER STUDY

Adams, F. Gerard, *The Business Forecasting Revolution.* New York: Oxford University Press, 1986.

Auerbach, Alan, "The Index of Leading Economic Indicators: Measurement without Theory, Thirty-Five Years Later," *Review of Economics and Statistics*, vol. 64, no. 4, November 1982, pp. 589–595.

Brayton, Flint and Eileen Mauskopf, "Structure and Uses of the MPS Quarterly Econometric Model of the United States," *Federal Reserve Bulletin*, February 1987.

Burns, Arthur F. and Wesley C. Mitchell, *Measuring Business Cycles.* New York: National Bureau of Economic Research, 1946.

Clark, J. R., Clifford F. Thies, J. Holton Wilson, and Saul Z. Barr, *Macroeconomics for Managers.* Boston: Allyn and Bacon, 1990.

Clark, Peter K., "The Cyclical Component of U.S. Economic Activity," *Quarterly Journal of Economics*, November 1987.

DeLong, J. Bradford and Lawrence H. Summers, "The Changing Cyclical Variability of Economic Activity in the United States," in Robert J. Gordon, ed., *The American Business Cycle*, Chicago: University of Chicago Press, 1986.

Eckstein, Otto, *The DRI Model of the U.S. Economy.* New York: McGraw-Hill, 1983.

Fabricant, Solomon, *Recent Economic Changes and the Agenda of Business Cycle Research.* New York: National Bureau of Economic Research, Inc., 1971.

Feldstein, Martin, *The American Economy in Transition.* Chicago: University of Chicago Press, 1980.

Glassman, James E. and Ronald A. Sage, "The Recent Inflation Experience," *Federal Reserve Bulletin*, May 1981.

Hafer, R. W., ed., *The Monetary versus Fiscal Policy Debate: Lessons from Two Decades.* Totowa, N.J.: Rowman and Allanheld, 1986.

Klein, Lawrence and Richard Young, *Introduction to Econometric Forecasting Models.* Lexington, Mass.: Lexington Books, 1980.

Long, J. B., Jr. and C. I. Plosser, "Real Business Cycles," *Journal of Political Economy*, vol. 91, 1983, pp. 39–69.

Lucas, R. E., Jr., "An Equilibrium Model of the Business Cycle," *Journal of Political Economy*, vol. 83, 1975, pp. 1113–1144.

McNees, Stephen K., "Consensus Forecasts: Tyranny of the Majority?," *New England Economic Review*, Federal Reserve Bank of Boston, November/December 1987.

McNees, Stephen K., "How Accurate are Macroeconomic Forecasts?," *New England Economic Review*, Federal Reserve Bank of Boston, July/August 1988.

McNees, Stephen K., "Man vs. Model? The Role of Judgment in Forecasting," *New England Economic Review*, Federal Reserve Bank of Boston, July/August 1990.

McNees, Stephen K., "Why Do Forecasts Differ?," *New England Economic Review*, Federal Reserve Bank of Boston, January/February 1989.

Miernyk, W. H., *Elements of Input-Output Economics.* New York: Random House, 1965.

Moore, Geoffrey, ed., *Business Cycle Indicators,* vols. I and II. Princeton, N.J.: Princeton University Press, 1961.

Moore, Geoffrey H., *Business Cycles, Inflation, and Forecasting.* Cambridge, Mass.: Published for the National Bureau of Economic Research, Inc., by Ballinger Publishing Company, 1983.

Myers, Henry F., "The Long Expansion May Keep Rolling On," *Wall Street Journal*, March 19, 1990.

Niemira, Michael P., "Sequential Signs of Recession and Recovery: Revisited," *Business Economics*, January 1983, pp. 51–53.

Palash, Carl J. and Lawrence J. Radecki, "Using Monetary and Financial Variables to Predict Cyclical Downturns," *Federal Reserve Bank of New York Quarterly Review*, New York, summer 1985, pp. 36–45.

Rush, Mark, "Real Business Cycles," *Economic Review*, Federal Reserve Bank of Kansas City, February 1987.

Sheffrin, Steven M., "Have Economic Fluctuations Been Dampened?" *Journal of Monetary Economics*, January 1988.

Silverman, L. and M. Bettayeb, "Policy Analysis with Econometric Models," *Brookings Papers on Econometric Activity*, no. 1, 1982, pp. 107–152.

Sims, C. A., "Comparison of Interwar and Postwar Business Cycles: Monetarism Reconsidered," *American Economic Review*, vol. 70, 1980, pp. 250–257.

Spivey, W. Allen and William J. Wrobleski, *Econometric Model Performance in Forecasting and Policy Assessment.* Washington, D.C.: American Enterprise Institute for Public Policy Research, 1979.

Stekler, O. and M. Schepsman, "Forecasting with an Index of Leading Indicators," *Journal of the American Statistical Association*, vol. 68, 1973, pp. 291–295.

Valentine, Lloyd M. and Dennis F. Ellis, *Business Cycles and Forecasting.* 8th ed. Cincinnati: South-Western Publishing Co., 1991.

Wachtel, Paul, *Macroeconomics: From Theory to Practice.* New York: McGraw-Hill, 1989.

Wecker, William E., "Predicting the Turning Points of a Time Series," *Journal of Business*, vol. 52, no. 1, January 1979, pp. 57–85.

Weir, David R., "The Reliability of Historical Macroeconomic Data for Comparing Cyclical Stability," *Journal of Economic History*, June 1986.

Zarnowitz, Victor, "Facts and Figures in the Recent Evolution of Business Cycles in the United States," Working Paper no. 2865, National Bureau of Economic Research, February 1989.

Zarnowitz, Victor, "A Guide to What is Known About Business Cycles," *Business Economics*, July 1990, pp. 5–22.

3

Data Collection and Analysis

INTRODUCTION

One of the earliest lessons that forecasters learn is that they should be skeptical users of data collected by others, which often comprises the bulk of the data that a forecaster uses. Each data series should be examined to determine its source and the circumstances under which it was collected. For example, a variable (monthly data on the number of people who are unemployed in the United States) may appear to be unchanged but may, in fact, be different due to a definitional change in the number of weeks a person must be laid off before being counted as unemployed.

This chapter explores and identifies those data characteristics that are relevant for a wide variety of forecasting methods. The first sections of the chapter describe the preliminary adjustments and transformations that are commonly made to business and economic data. Data adjustments and transformations, while not widely understood, are an integral part of data analysis and constitute the first step of the forecasting process.

The final sections of the chapter involve the identification and decomposition of patterns in time series data. These four patterns—trend, cycle, seasonal, and irregular—must be carefully identified before the task of forecasting can begin. In short, exploratory data analysis involves studying the data series, developing a sense for the information that the data contains, and then using various summary measures to classify the data.

PRELIMINARY ADJUSTMENTS TO DATA

Time series data are frequently collected in a form that is not directly related to the needs of management. For example, the most common method of recording data is in current-dollar values. These data series reflect changes in both physical levels of activity and in prices. Alternatively, data are generally reported in aggregate form. For example, when a firm sells to both final consumers and to industrial consumers, the data that are published are equal to the sum of these two groups. In developing forecasting models, accuracy will be improved by analyzing separately the different ways that these two markets react to changes in the business environment. Three adjustments arise frequently enough to warrant our consideration: (1) trading-day adjustments; (2) adjustments for price changes; and (3) adjustments for changes in population.

TRADING-DAY ADJUSTMENTS

The number of days in successive months can vary by as much as 10 percent, with January to February or February to March being the most dramatic examples. Consider the case of a retail outlet that derives a large portion of its business from sales on weekends. Clearly, the number of Saturdays and Sundays in a month can influence the recorded monthly sales figures. Conversely, the number of working days in a month affects the total volume of checks written for firms such as banks and savings and loans that derive the main portion of their business during the traditional five workdays of the week. The important aspect of these two examples is that the data that are recorded will be significantly different from month to month even though actual levels of activity may not have changed.

In these situations, the raw or actual data need to be corrected for the number of trading or working days in a month. There are two acceptable procedures for adjusting for the variation in active working days in a month. The first method involves taking the recorded monthly aggregate figure and dividing it by the number of working days in a month, with the resulting figure being referred to as an *average daily figure*. For example, suppose that in the months of February and March of 1987, The First Federal Bank processed 14 million and 16.5 million checks, respectively. On first glance it appears that there has been a substantial increase (17.9 percent) in check volume. However, both of these figures are influenced by the number of working days in the respective months. If we adjust for the number of working days in each of the months, we would find that average daily checks for February would be 700,000 (14 million divided by 20) and 750,000 (16.5 million divided by 22) for March. Thus, while the volume is 7 percent higher in March, this is significantly different from the first calculation of 17.9 percent.

The second method of adjusting for differences in trading days is only slightly more elaborate. Suppose that we have collected the information on trading days shown in Table 3-1. An examination of the trading-day data in the first block of Table 3-1 highlights that a given month, say, March, can vary from year to year. Once the number of trading days is known, a set of monthly averages is computed. This average is then used as a divisor to adjust

TABLE 3-1 Calculation of Trading-Day Adjustment

Year	Jan.	Feb.	Mar.	Apr.	May	June	July	Aug.	Sept.	Oct.	Nov.	Dec.
					Trading Days							
1986	22	20	21	22	21	21	22	21	21	23	19	22
1987	21	20	22	22	20	22	23	21	21	22	20	22
1988	20	21	23	21	21	22	20	23	21	21	21	21

Average Trading Days for Each Month

Month	Average
Jan.	21.00
Feb.	20.33
Mar.	22.00
Apr.	21.67
May	20.67
June	21.67
July	21.67
Aug.	21.67
Sept.	20.67
Oct.	22.00
Nov.	20.00
Dec.	21.67

Actual Demand Deposit Volume

Year	Jan.	Feb.	Mar.	Apr.	May	June	July	Aug.	Sept.	Oct.	Nov.	Dec.
1986	801	805	811	819	830	841	856	873	891	912	933	956
1987	981	1,006	1,026	1,040	1,051	1,065	1,082	1,101	1,117	1,127	1,132	1,134
1988	1,136	1,141	1,152	1,171	1,192	1,211	1,224	1,229	1,231	1,233	1,236	1,240

Trading-Day Computations for March

Year	Trading Days	Trading-Day Coefficient	Actual Data	Adjusted Data
1986	21	21/22 = 0.95454	811	850
1987	22	22/22 = 1.00000	1,026	1,026
1988	23	23/22 = 1.04545	1,152	1,102

the actual data for trading days. To illustrate this procedure, consider the month of March. The average number of trading days in March is 22: (21 + 22 + 23)/3. This average is then used to compute the trading-day coefficients. The adjusted value for 1984 of 850 is derived by dividing 811 by the trading-day coefficient (811 ÷ 0.95454), yielding an adjusted value of 850. The remaining adjusted values are computed via a similar procedure. These adjusted values would then be used in all future analysis.

ADJUSTMENTS FOR CHANGES IN PRICES

One of the most frequently made adjustments is to convert time series that are expressed in monetary units (dollars, francs, etc.) into series that reflect changes in physical volume or activity levels. This process is known as converting to *constant dollars* or deflating a time series. Conceptually, the process is accomplished by dividing each observation measured in dollars by the appropriate price index.

To illustrate this process, consider the information in Table 3-2. The data in column 3 represent the actual retail sales on an annual basis and contains both price-level changes and increases in sales volumes. To eliminate the effect of changes in the price level, we divide this actual data by the price-level data in column 2. For example, the value in 1988 of $7,522 is derived by dividing $8,131 by 1.081. In this instance the constant-dollar series could be referred to as retail sales in 1982 dollars, since 1982 is the base year for the price index.

TABLE 3-2 Retail Sales, Population, and Price Index in Memphis, 1970–1988

| | | | Retail Sales | | |
| | | | Current Dollars | Constant Dollars | |
Year	Population (thousands) (1)	Price Level (1982 = 1.00) (2)	(millions of dollars) (3)	(4)	Per Capita (dollars) (5)
1970	836	0.456	1,721	3,774	4,514
1971	845	0.474	2,077	4,382	5,186
1972	857	0.485	2,345	4,835	5,642
1973	859	0.517	2,619	5,066	5,898
1974	869	0.579	2,822	4,874	5,609
1975	872	0.623	2,977	4,778	5,479
1976	878	0.652	3,201	4,910	5,592
1977	884	0.687	3,489	5,079	5,745
1978	891	0.735	3,903	5,310	5,960
1979	904	0.807	4,272	5,294	5,856
1980	914	0.895	4,625	5,168	5,654
1981	921	0.967	4,881	5,048	5,481
1982	925	1.000	5,151	5,151	5,569
1983	929	1.021	5,838	5,718	6,155
1984	935	1.051	6,715	6,389	6,833
1985	945	1.070	7,108	6,643	7,030
1986	957	1.072	7,639	7,126	7,446
1987	971	1.076	7,878	7,322	7,541
1988	984	1.081	8,131	7,522	7,644

FIGURE 3-1   Retail Sales

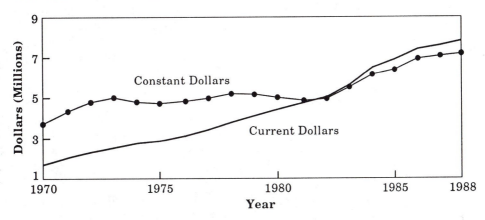

To show the impact of separating the effects of price-level changes, columns 3 and 4 are depicted graphically in Figure 3-1. With virtually no exceptions, retail sales in current dollars have shown a consistent upward trend since 1970. When this series is adjusted for changes in the price level, the picture is quite different. Retail sales expressed in constant 1982 dollars show the effect of the 1974–1975 and 1979–1981 recessions. Thus, even though the constant-dollar time series generally exhibits an upward trend, the business cycles can be seen clearly. Note also that the two series have equal values in 1982, reflecting that the base year for purposes of comparison is 1982.

ADJUSTMENTS FOR CHANGES IN POPULATION

A third preliminary adjustment that is often made to time series data is adjusting for population growth. This process is similar to that used in adjusting for price changes, except that instead of dividing by the price level we divide by population. For example, to adjust for growth in population and its effect on retail sales, we might adjust the constant-dollar retail sales figures noted in Table 3-2 by dividing the data in column 4 by the data in column 1. The resulting figures, which are presented in column 5, would then be referred to as per capita constant-dollar retail sales. In many instances this is the type of information that management is most interested in, as it represents both growth in real volume and, since population growth is eliminated, gains in the drawing power of the Memphis market. Alternatively, if the data in column 5 measured per capita sales for a single firm, this per capita figure could indicate that the firm's market share was increasing.

In the preceding example, the adjustment for population was based on total population. It is also possible to convert these figures to a per-household or a per-family figure by using either the number of households or the number of families as the divisor. For example, in the commercial banking industry, growth in the number of households is much more significant than is growth in total population. In other instances (for example, sales of compact discs), the appropriate population base might be the age group of 15 to 25.

DATA TRANSFORMATIONS

While the primary purpose of preliminary adjustments is to make the data more representative of the process being studied, there are occasions where the actual or raw data need to be transformed into a completely different time series. The two most common transformations are growth rate and linear transformations. A transformation is a process whereby the relative magnitude of the numbers is changed while the essential characteristics of the data patterns remain constant.

GROWTH RATE TRANSFORMATION

In many instances, management finds forecasted growth rates of an economic variable to be of more interest than forecasts of absolute levels. Growth can be stated in either unit or percentage terms. Table 3-3 presents the actual raw data for constant-dollar retail sales, with the data then transformed into unit growth and percentage growth.

The data on unit growth (column 2) or percentage growth (column 3) can now be used in developing forecasts. The advantage of the growth rate transformation lies in its neutrality with respect to the units of measurement for the original series. Furthermore, growth rate conversions tend to focus attention on marginal changes rather than absolute levels. This type of transformation is especially useful when we are developing forecasts with multiple economic variables measured in different units. For example, if we are interested in generating a forecast for interest rates (measured in percentage terms), one of the factors that we might consider would be the money supply (recorded in billions of dollars). We might find it more useful to convert the raw money supply data to a percentage growth format similar to column 3 in Table 3-3 for the selected measure in the money supply.

LINEAR TRANSFORMATION

Linear transformations are especially useful when applying regression analysis to forecasting problems. Specifically, regression analysis begins by assuming that the relationship between variables is linear. While we present this process in more detail in our discussion of regression techniques in chapter 7, a simple example of this transformation can be presented here.

TABLE 3-3 Growth Rate Analysis of Constant-Dollar Retail Sales

Year	Retail Sales in 82$ (1)	Unit Growth (2)	Percentage Growth (3)
1970	3,774		
1971	4,382	608	16.1
1972	4,835	453	10.3
1973	5,066	231	4.8
1974	4,874	− 192	− 3.8
1975	4,778	− 96	− 2.0
1976	4,910	132	2.8
1977	5,079	169	3.4
1978	5,310	231	4.5
1979	5,294	− 16	− 0.3
1980	5,168	− 126	− 2.4
1981	5,048	− 120	− 2.3
1982	5,151	103	2.0
1983	5,718	567	11.0
1984	6,389	671	11.7
1985	6,643	254	4.0
1986	7,126	483	7.3
1987	7,322	196	2.8
1988	7,522	200	2.7

Suppose that the original data can be represented by equation (3-1):

$$Y = aX^b. \tag{3-1}$$

The fact that the variable X is raised to the b power indicates that the relationship between X and Y is nonlinear in its original form. However, it is also true that with a straightforward logarithmic transformation, the model presented in equation (3-1) can be converted to that noted in equation (3-2):

$$\log Y = \log a + b \log X \tag{3-2}$$

or

$$W = c + bZ \tag{3-3}$$

where

$$W = \log y \text{ and } z = \log X.$$

TABLE 3-4   Logarithmic Transformation

Year	Actual Copier Shipments	Logarithmic Transformation
1975	19,888	4.30
1976	22,054	4.34
1977	24,256	4.38
1978	29,300	4.47
1979	37,836	4.58
1980	49,447	4.69
1981	60,334	4.78
1982	68,637	4.84
1983	84,609	4.93
1984	108,352	5.03
1985	117,950	5.07
1986	140,167	5.15
1987	159,511	5.20
1988	191,611	5.28

The advantage of this type of conversion is that we have been able to take a relationship (equation 3-1) that does not satisfy the requirements of linearity and transform the data (into the form of equation 3-3). Consider the information on copier shipments that is depicted in Table 3-4 and in Figure 3-2. When the actual operating revenue data is plotted, the growth pattern is clearly not linear. However, if the actual data is transformed logarithmically

FIGURE 3-2   Logarithmic Transformations

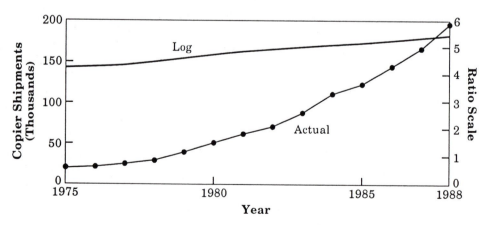

TABLE 3-5 Sales of Wingos and the Square Root Transformation

Year	Actual Sales	Square Root of Actual Sales
1979	16.8	4.1
1980	37.2	6.1
1981	67.6	8.2
1982	102.0	10.1
1983	146.4	12.1
1984	197.7	14.1
1985	248.2	15.8
1986	338.6	18.4
1987	405.1	20.1
1988	479.2	21.9

and then plotted, the relationship more closely approximates a linear growth pattern. In this case, the original data on copier shipments displayed a geometric or exponential growth pattern, while the transformed data is linear.

Another common transformation is the square root transformation. Consider the data presented in Table 3-5. A visual inspection of the original data as presented in Figure 3-3 clearly indicates a curvilinear growth pattern. However, if we take the square root of each of these original values and plot these values, we end up with a linear growth pattern. Note that we are not necessarily trying to interpret the meaning of the square root of wingo sales, or the

FIGURE 3-3 Square Root Transformations

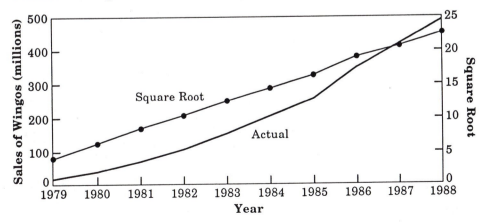

TABLE 3-6   Transformations to Achieve Linearity

Quadrant	Appropriate Transformation
a	square root or logarithmic or reciprocal in the dependent variable. $\sqrt{Y}$, log Y, $1/Y$
b	square root or logarithmic or reciprocal in the independent variable, $\sqrt{X}$, log X, $1/X$
c	square root or logarithmic or reciprocal in either the dependent or independent variable
d	reciprocal: $+(1/X)$ for top and $-(1/X)$ for the bottom
e	log reciprocal

FIGURE 3-4   Time Series Patterns of Raw Data Prior to Data Transformations

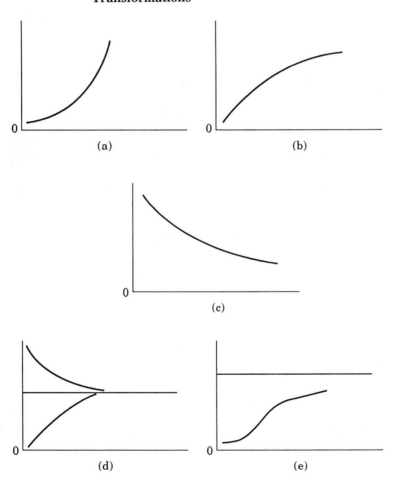

(a)

(b)

(c)

(d)

(e)

logarithm of operating revenues. Rather, we are simply trying to generate a growth pattern that is linear and, therefore, easier to handle with standard forecasting models.

Other types of transformations are illustrated in Figure 3-4, with the appropriate mathematical form presented in Table 3-6. The specific transformation applicable to each of the quadrants in Figure 3-4 are noted in Table 3-6.

At this point, the question is which transformation is appropriate. There are basically two approaches that can be suggested. The first of these is a visual inspection of the pattern of change in the variable over time. This is the approach that is suggested in Figure 3-4. The second approach would be to rely on the pragmatic notion that whichever transformation works best is the most appropriate. We would be remiss if we did not indicate that in some instances there is an a priori reason for believing that one functional form is most appropriate. For example, in the case of cost forecasting, it seems reasonable to suppose that the average cost curve would be more closely approximated by the curve noted in the top portion of quadrant (d) in Figure 3-4. Alternatively, in the case of a product sales life-cycle curve, quadrant (e) might be most likely. To reiterate, the primary purpose of these transformations is to convert data so linear statistical procedures (for example, linear regression) can be applied without any loss of statistical accuracy.

PATTERNS IN TIME SERIES DATA

INTRODUCTION

Prior to applying forecasting techniques to time series data, the analyst should be cognizant of the systematic patterns that historical data can take. Business analysts must be aware of changes that occur in variables such as sales, unemployment, and industrial production. Moreover, interest frequently centers on change over specific time periods, such as month to month, quarter to quarter, or year to year. In many instances, these changes occur with a regularity that permits them to be quantified and forecasted. In this section we begin to consider techniques of identifying and measuring the various types of patterns that characterize time series data.[1] The primary purpose is to identify and measure regularities in the data without attempting to explain the possible causes of the patterns observed. This process is often referred to as

---

[1] The identification of patterns in historical time series data can be regarded as a subset of the broad area of data analysis. For an excellent overview of the process of data analysis, see Frank M. Andrews et al., *A Guide for Selecting Techniques for Analyzing Social Science Data*, 2nd ed. (University of Michigan: Survey Research Center, Institute for Social Research, 1981).

descriptive analysis, since the objective, at this stage, is not so much to explain time patterns and changes as it is to identify and estimate them.

The three basic types of patterns that we want to consider are trend, cyclical, and seasonal fluctuations. While we will also discuss the irregular factor, this component is not predictable. In examining each of these patterns or components, we begin with annual data. This allows us to focus our attention on trend and cyclical patterns. Once we have introduced the procedures for analyzing trend and cyclical patterns, we discuss both seasonal patterns and the irregular or random factor. As we examine each of the individual patterns, we use a different time series to illustrate the points of interest. In the final section of this chapter, we present the entire process for one time series. This analysis of all of the components of one time series is referred to as the decomposition of a time series.

GENERAL TIME SERIES MODEL

We can begin our discussion by examining a company's production data for cameras. Recently, production has been approaching capacity, and the question facing management is: Should the production facilities be expanded? The engineering department has provided the figures in Table 3-7.

The distinguishing feature of the observations in Table 3-7 is that they consist of a sequence or ordering of observations on a particular variable, camera production, recorded over successive increments of time. Given this data,

TABLE 3-7 Production of Cameras

Year	Quarter	Camera Production (millions)
1987	1	0.740
	2	0.959
	3	0.841
	4	1.131
1988	1	1.242
	2	1.368
	3	0.976
	4	1.306
1989	1	1.373
	2	1.534
	3	1.092
	4	1.228

management might be interested in answers to some or all of the following questions:

1. When can we expect the demands on production to be highest or lowest?
2. Under what economic circumstances will these highs and lows occur?
3. Are we going to have sufficient working capital to finance finished inventories, work-in-process, and accounts receivable during peak periods?
4. What contingency plans must be made in the case of a prolonged shutdown of one of our plants?
5. What is our estimate of the likely occurrence, timing, and severity of a recession?

The observations recorded in Table 3-7 are, in reality, a composite of a number of factors that must be disentangled prior to the development of meaningful forecasts. Classical time series analysis attempts to segregate and analyze these factors in a systematic fashion. This process involves not only decomposition into component parts but also an analysis of the manner in which these forces interact.

The model most relied on for time series data is as follows:

$$Y_t = T_t \cdot C_t \cdot S_t \cdot I_t. \tag{3-4}$$

The practical significance of this model is that it identifies the integral components of many economic time series. Further, equation (3-4) illustrates that these components interact in a multiplicative fashion. The components of this model are

Y_t = the observed or actual value of the series in time period t
T_t = trend component in time period t
C_t = cyclical component in time period t
S_t = seasonal component in time period t
I_t = irregular component in time period t.

Implicit in the multiplicative model is the assumption that percentage changes best describe the observed fluctuations and level in the data, a fact that approximates reality in a great number of economic activities. In addition to the multiplicative model, an alternative additive formulation is available:

$$Y_t = T_t + C_t + S_t + I_t. \tag{3-5}$$

The trend component, T_t, is the general upward or downward tendency that characterizes all economic activity in a dynamic economy and represents long-run growth or decline in time-measured economic phenomena.

Cyclical fluctuations, C_t, in time series data are nonperiodic, recurring variations around the long-run trend growth pattern. As noted in later chapters, these fluctuations arise from endogenous forces and exogenous shocks.

Seasonal variation, S_t, occurs within a year and repeats, although not necessarily in an exact manner, in the following year. Seasonal variation may be related to noneconomic factors such as customs (spring purchases), holidays, and weather, or to institutional factors such as model-year changes in the automobile industry and inventory sales in anticipation of tax deadlines.

Irregular or random variation, I_t, is the erratic and irregular movement in time series data that is left over after we have isolated the seasonal, cyclical, and trend components. It is the residual effect of a myriad of unpredictable disturbances, such as strikes, hurricanes, or foreign government actions.

In this chapter, we are primarily interested in isolating and measuring the trend (T), cyclical (C), and seasonal (S) components. We focus on the statistical process involved in constructing stationary (detrended) data and the steps involved in moving from raw (original) to seasonally adjusted data. Although this decomposition process is somewhat tedious, an understanding of the historical movements of a time series is a necessary prerequisite to forecasting. In fact, an understanding of why a specific activity behaved as it did sharpens our insight into its future behavior.

TREND PATTERNS

ESTIMATION OF TREND PATTERNS

As previously noted, the trend component is the general upward or downward tendency that characterizes all economic activity in a dynamic economy and represents the long-run growth or decline in time-measured economic and business data. From a theoretical standpoint, this growth or decline reflects permanent shifts in either supply-side factors or demand-side determinants. A representative listing of these factors is as follows:

Changes in consumer preferences
Changes in income
Population shifts or demographic changes
Technological advances and constraints
Industrial expansion
Changes in tax policies.

There are three major reasons for studying trend patterns in time series data. First, a study of trend allows us to describe a historical pattern in the data. In many situations, we can use this information in evaluating the success of previous managerial policies. Second, a study of trend patterns permits us to project past patterns or trends into the future. Information from the past can frequently tell us a great deal regarding future changes. Finally, by studying the trend pattern of a time series data, we may be able to isolate or remove the trend component from the actual (Y_t) data. This removal of the trend component simplifies the study of the remaining components of a time series.

There are a number of trend patterns that occur frequently in time series data. The more common patterns are illustrated in Figure 3-5. The trend pattern illustrated in Figure 3-5(a) is linear. Figure 3-5(b) illustrates a growth curve, whereas the S-curve in Figure 3-5(c) corresponds to many industry or firm growth paths in which rapid initial growth is followed by a slowing as the industry or firm matures—the product life cycle. The familiar parabolic or second-degree trend pattern is noted in Figure 3-5(d). An identification of the specific trend pattern that dominates and characterizes time series data is deferred until later. For the present, we focus our attention on linear trend estimation.

FIGURE 3-5 Alternative Trend Patterns

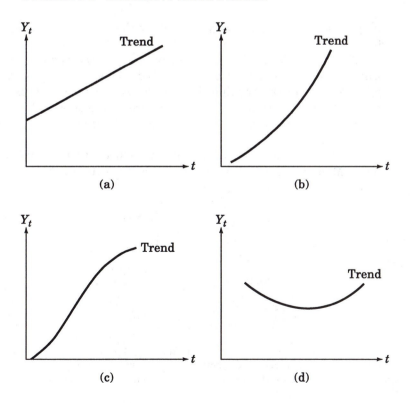

A linear trend pattern is best described with the following model:

$$Y_t = a + bT \qquad\qquad (3\text{-}6)$$

where

Y_t = value of the dependent variable in time period t

T = time variable, $T = 1$ in the first time period. T is incremented by 1 in each succeeding time period, hence in the second time period $T = 2$.[2]

a, b = coefficients to be derived.

The coefficients, a and b, are obtained via the method of least squares, which yields the following normal equations that must be solved (the bar above T and Y indicates the mean or average value):[3]

$$a = \overline{Y}_t - bT \qquad\qquad (3\text{-}7)$$

$$b = \frac{\sum TY_t - n\overline{T}\,\overline{Y}_t}{\sum T^2 - n\overline{T}^2}. \qquad\qquad (3\text{-}8)$$

This process of measuring and estimating the trend component is generally referred to as fitting a curve to the data.

Strictly speaking, this method implies that the passage of time causes the observed trend pattern, a claim that is dubious. Nonetheless, this approach can be rationalized by arguing that we are using time as a proxy variable for other determining variables (income, preferences, economic growth, or similar phenomena) and that our interest here is in identification rather than explanation of trend.

For purposes of illustrating this procedure, suppose that we use retail sales in Memphis as our Y variable (Table 3-2, column 4) with the results as follows:

$$\overline{Y}_t = \$5,494$$

$$n = 19 \text{ years}$$

$$\sum TY_t = 1,138,495$$

$$\overline{T} = 10$$

$$\sum T^2 = 2,470.$$

[2] The starting value of $T = 1$ is arbitrary. Indeed many software programs use a value of 0 as the starting value. As is seen shortly, the choice of 0 or 1 has no effect on the results.

[3] The proof and exact derivation of these definitional equations is presented in chapter 5.

FIGURE 3-6 Retail Sales in Memphis

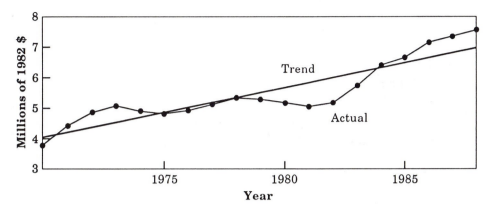

Therefore,

$$a = 3{,}833.7$$

$$b = 166$$

$$Y_t = 3{,}833.7 + 166T \qquad\qquad\text{(3-9)}$$

$$T = 1 \text{ in 1970, the first year.}$$

The trend value for 1970 (the first year) is $3,999.7 (3,833.7 + 166 · 1), and retail sales adjusted for inflation, Y_t, increase, on the average, by $166 million per year.[4] Figure 3-6 presents a comparison of the actual data with the trend line.

Once the equation is derived and the origin for T is specified, annual trend values for retail sales are obtained by simply plugging in the appropriate value for T. For example, the trend estimate of retail sales in 1988 equals $6,988 million (3,833.7 + 166 · 19). A comparison of the two lines in Figure 3-6 suggests that while there are time periods when the linear trend model overestimates and underestimates retail sales, the overall growth pattern exhibited by retail sales appears to approximate a linear trend.

Not all time series are characterized by linear trend patterns. In many time series, Y_t changes at an increasing or a decreasing rate. Industries or firms that are expanding rapidly will typically have exponential trend lines, as shown in Figure 3-5(b). In this case, the trend value of Y_t will be increasing

---

[4] If we had assigned a value of 0 to the initial time period, the trend equation would have been $Y_t = 3{,}999.7 + 166T$, with the result that the trend value for retail sales in the first time period would have equalled $3,999.7, the same value as in the text.

FIGURE 3-7 Copier Shipments and Growth Rate Model

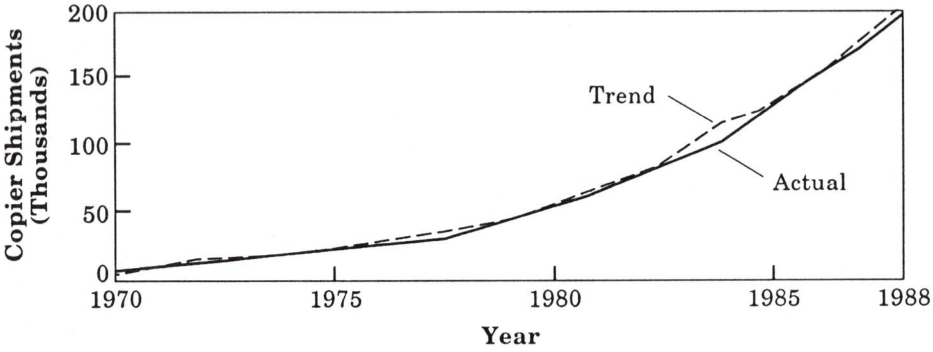

at an increasing rate. Figure 3-7 presents a graphical picture of annual copier shipments for a major supplier of copiers.

For these data, a more suitable trend equation is

$$Y_t = ab^T. \tag{3-10}$$

Here, b is a positive constant raised to the power T, which measures the number of time periods beyond the base year; and a is a constant multiple. Whenever the series has a negative exponential pattern, the appropriate equation will be

$$Y_t = ab^{-T} \tag{3-11}$$

where the minus sign indicates that Y_t is decreasing over time.

Taking the logarithm of both sides of equation (3-10), the result is

$$\log Y_t = \log a + T \log b. \tag{3-12}$$

The advantage of this log transformation is that the equation is now linear and can be estimated in the following fashion:

$$\log a = (\textstyle\sum \log Y_t/n) - \overline{T} \log b \tag{3-13}$$

$$\log b = \frac{\sum T \log Y_t - \overline{T}\sum \log Y_t}{\sum T^2 - n\overline{T}^2} \tag{3-14}$$

The procedure for copier shipments is illustrated in Table 3-8.

TABLE 3-8 Exponential Trend Line Computations: Copier Shipments

Year	Years beyond Base Period T (1)	Copier Shipments Y_t (2)	log Y_t (3)	T log Y_t (4)	T^2 (5)	Trend Value (6)
1970	1	7,032	3.487080	3.487080	1	8,241
1971	2	10,718	4.030114	8.060228	4	9,829
1972	3	14,033	4.147150	12.441452	9	11,723
1973	4	15,582	4.192623	16.770493	16	13,982
1974	5	16,835	4.226213	21.131066	25	16,678
1975	6	19,888	4.298591	25.791547	36	19,892
1976	7	22,054	4.343487	30.404412	49	23,726
1977	8	24,256	4.384819	35.078553	64	28,299
1978	9	29,300	4.466868	40.201809	81	33,753
1979	10	37,836	4.577905	45.779052	100	40,258
1980	11	49,447	4.694140	51.635539	121	48,017
1981	12	60,334	4.780562	57.366745	144	57,271
1982	13	68,637	4.836558	62.875258	169	68,309
1983	14	84,609	4.927417	68.983832	196	81,474
1984	15	108,352	5.034837	75.522554	225	97,177
1985	16	117,950	5.071698	81.147167	256	115,905
1986	17	140,167	5.146646	87.492978	289	138,244
1987	18	159,511	5.202791	93.650231	324	164,887
1988	19	191,611	5.282420	100.365988	361	196,644

$n = 19$
$T = 10$

$\sum T = 190$
$\sum T \cdot \log Y_t = 918.545982$

$\sum \log Y_t = 87.491919$
$\sum T^2 = 2,470$

Substituting the relevant values into equations (3-13) and (3-14),

$$\log b = 918.545982 - (10)(87.491919)\ 2470 - (19)(10)^2$$

$$= 0.0765382 \tag{3-15}$$

$$\log a = (87.491919/19) - (10)(0.0765382)$$

$$= 3.8394558.$$

The logarithmic trend line becomes

$$\log Y_t = 3.8394558 + 0.0765382T. \tag{3-16}$$

The values for a and b may be obtained by taking the antilogs of these coefficients:

$$a = \text{antilog } 3.8394558 \approx 6,910$$

$$b = \text{antilog } 0.0765382 \approx 1.192719.$$

Thus, the exponential trend line may be expressed as

$$Y_t = 6,910(1.192719)^T \qquad \textbf{(3-17)}$$

$$T = 1 \text{ in } 1970.$$

In computing trend values, equation (3-16) is commonly used because of computational ease. For example, to find the trend value for 1988, plug $T = 19$ into equation (3-16):

$$\log Y_{18} = 3.8394558 + 0.0765382(19)$$

$$= 5.29368816 \qquad \textbf{(3-18)}$$

$$Y_{18} = 196{,}644.$$

This exponential trend line is plotted alongside the actual line in Figure 3-6. Since equation (3-17) assumes a constant growth rate, the value of b, 1.192719, furnishes the rate of growth. That is, if we subtract 1.00 from this value and convert it to a percentage, it yields a growth rate of 19.27 percent. Copier shipments are growing at an average long-run trend rate of 19.27 percent.

Another common, although less frequent, trend line is a second-degree polynomial of the form

$$Y_t = a + bT + cT^2. \qquad \textbf{(3-19)}$$

The graph of such an equation takes a shape similar to that in Figure 3-5(d). Since T increases by one unit for each successive time period, the T values can be transformed by subtracting the mean value from each observation. That is, $t = T - \overline{T}$. This simplifies the computations when we simultaneously solve the following three definitional equations for a, b, and c:

$$\Sigma Y_t = na + c\Sigma t^2$$

$$\Sigma t^2 Y_t = a\Sigma t^2 + c\Sigma t^4 \qquad \textbf{(3-20)}$$

$$b = \frac{\Sigma t Y_t}{\Sigma t^2}.$$

**TABLE 3-9 Operating Revenues
(millions of dollars)**

Year	Operating Revenues
1977	$ 11,649
1978	15,701
1979	23,455
1980	40,099
1981	59,125
1982	76,317
1983	100,921
1984	116,720
1985	149,834
1986	202,466
1987	241,949
1988	272,415

The specific computations for this process will not be illustrated, but, suppose that we have collected the information on operating revenues noted in Table 3-9 and depicted in Figure 3-8.

The actual estimated trend line for the data presented in Table 3-9 is

$$Y_t = 11,097 - 1,052.40T + 1,937.82T^2. \tag{3-21}$$

A comparison of the actual and estimated operating revenue lines in Figure 3-8 indicates that the second-degree trend line provides a close approximation of actual growth.

FIGURE 3-8 Operating Revenues and Parabolic Trend Model

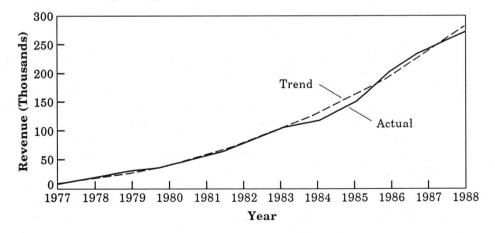

IDENTIFICATION OF TREND PATTERNS

In selecting the appropriate trend lines in the preceding three examples, we relied on visual inspection of a scatter diagram. There are, however, two more sophisticated methods for determining the most appropriate trend line for a given set of data: differencing and autocorrelation analysis.

The technique of differencing allows for a determination of whether a linear equation, a second-degree polynomial, or a higher-degree equation should be selected. When using the process of differencing, we are essentially looking at the trend pattern in terms of a pattern of changes. First-order differences are defined as

$$\Delta Y_t = Y_t - Y_{t-1}. \tag{3-22}$$

If the difference between successive observations is relatively constant, a linear trend is appropriate. That is, there is no change in the changes. This concept of a stationary time series can best be seen by deriving the first differences of the simple time series: 2, 4, 6, 8, 10. The first differences are 2, 2, 2, and 2. (This new series is sometimes called detrended.) The fact that there is no change in the differenced time series is indicative of a linear trend pattern. It is, however, highly unlikely that an actual time series will correspond to this ideal pattern of changes. Rather, it is more likely that some judgment will be required.

The first differences for printer production are tabulated in Table 3-10. Although the differenced series shown in the last column contains some minor variations, the change from one year to the next falls within the relatively narrow range of 1,123 to 1,246 for the entire time period. Whenever the pattern of changes in the original data exhibits this relative stability in the first differences, it is indicative of a linear trend.

The second difference of a time series is

$$\Delta^2 Y_t = \Delta Y_t - \Delta Y_{t-1}. \tag{3-23}$$

Alternatively, a second difference can be defined as the first difference of the first differences. Calculation of second differences is illustrated in Table 3-11. In this instance, the second differences are stationary, indicating that a second-degree polynomial best describes the trend pattern in the actual data. As was noted in the discussion of first differences, one would rarely find this idealized pattern. Nonetheless, the concept to be remembered is that if the second differences of a time series are relatively constant, this is indicative of a second-degree polynomial trend pattern.

While the process of differencing could be continued indefinitely, the other common trend pattern, the growth pattern noted in the package shipments example, would be identified by examining the first difference of the

TABLE 3-10   First Differences of Printer Production

Year	Printers Produced	First Differences
1970	6,024	
1971	7,270	1,246
1972	8,408	1,138
1973	9,531	1,123
1974	10,775	1,244
1975	11,925	1,150
1976	13,100	1,175
1977	14,302	1,202
1978	15,449	1,147
1979	16,638	1,189
1980	17,850	1,212
1981	19,017	1,167
1982	20,207	1,190
1983	21,408	1,201
1984	22,602	1,194
1985	23,785	1,183
1986	24,995	1,210

log values. If the first difference of the logs is linear, it would be indicative of a growth curve. To illustrate this process, consider the information presented in Table 3-12. The fact that the first difference of the logs is constant indicates that the actual data are characterized by a constant growth rate pattern.

In summary,

1. When the first differences are stationary, the underlying trend pattern in the actual data is linear.
2. When the second differences are stationary, the underlying trend pattern in the actual data is best modeled by a parabola.

TABLE 3-11   Computation of Second Differences

Y_t	First Differences	Second Differences
16		
29	13	
46	17	4
67	21	4
92	25	4
121	29	4

TABLE 3-12 First Differences of Growth Series

| | | | First Difference | |
Year	Actual Data	Log Value of Actual	Actual	Log
1982	1,000	3.0000		
1983	1,100	3.0414	100	0.0414
1984	1,210	3.0828	110	0.0414
1985	1,331	3.1242	121	0.0414
1986	1,464.1	3.1656	133.1	0.0414
1987	1,610.51	3.2070	146.41	0.0414

3. If the second differences are still not stationary, the next step should be to try differencing the logarithms of the actual data to permit identification of the growth curve.

A word regarding terminology may be in order. Trend patterns are frequently described in terms of degrees. A first-degree trend indicates a linear trend. Alternatively, a second-degree trend is depicted by a curved line, where the variable is growing (or declining) at either a decreasing rate or an increasing rate. A third-degree trend is also known as a cubic trend. The number of degrees, in reality, describes the number of changes in the general direction of the trend line. In the case of a first-degree or linear trend pattern, only one general direction is involved. With a second-degree trend pattern, the pattern changes once; and in a third-degree trend, the pattern changes twice. For this reason, practitioners rarely rely on trend patterns beyond the third degree. Once you get past this level, you are virtually forced to guess when the next turn or change in pattern will occur.

Once the trend pattern has been identified and estimated, it can be removed from the original data. This process of removing the trend pattern from the actual data is commonly referred to as detrending, and the resulting data are referred to as detrended or as a stationary time series. The concept of a stationary time series becomes important in our discussions of advanced autoregressive forecasting techniques such as Box-Jenkins models (discussed in chapter 9). Figure 3-9 illustrates the concept of a stationary time series.

Figure 3-9(a) depicts the original series (Y_t) and the trend line (T) that has been estimated. Removing the trend (detrending the data) may be thought of as rotating T to a horizontal position, as shown by the 0 axis in Figure 3-9(b). Since in Figure 3-9(b) we are interested only in the deviations from trend (that is, the trend pattern has been removed), the vertical axis can be set at zero and the deviations expressed in terms of plus or minus quantities.

FIGURE 3-9 Creating a Stationary Time Series

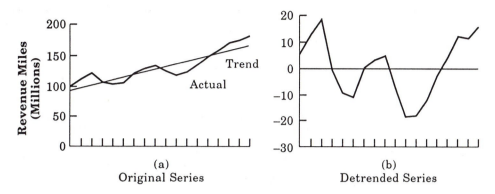

(a)
Original Series

(b)
Detrended Series

IRREGULARITIES IN TREND ESTIMATION AND IDENTIFICATION

There are two situations that frequently arise that may complicate the identification of a specific trend pattern: (1) major turning points (a permanent change), and (2) a major isolated or random shock.

A comparison of the actual and fitted retail sales (Table 3-2, column 3) lines in Figure 3-10 provides an opportunity to discuss the first of these points, a major turning point. A visual examination of the actual growth pattern suggests that during the period from 1970 to 1981 one trend pattern dominates, while during the period from 1982 to 1988 a distinctly different trend pattern

FIGURE 3-10 Permanent Change in Trend Patterns

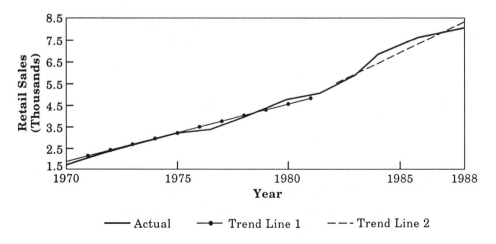

FIGURE 3-11   Short-Term Shock

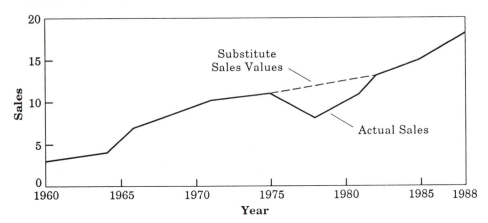

prevails. These two distinct trend patterns are shown by the two lines super-imposed on the actual data.

Situations such as those illustrated in Figure 3-10 can be analyzed by estimating two distinct trend lines.[5] To investigate the possibility that there has been a change in the underlying trend pattern, suppose that we estimate three trend lines, one for each of the time periods.[6]

$$Y_t = 944.2 + 365.535T$$
$$\text{Time Frame:} \quad 1970\text{--}1988 \tag{3-24}$$

$$Y_t = 1,430 + 279.112T$$
$$\text{Time Frame:} \quad 1970\text{--}1981 \tag{3-25}$$

$$Y_t = 4,930 + 498.000T$$
$$\text{Time Frame:} \quad 1982\text{--}1988 \tag{3-26}$$

A comparison of the trend coefficients for the two subperiods (279.112 versus 498.000) clearly indicates that the rate of change in retail sales has changed dramatically and that at least two different trend lines are needed to describe this set of time series data.

---

[5] In chapter 7 we present the use of dummy variables to account for such changes in un-derlying patterns. There are also more sophisticated statistical techniques that can be used in dealing with structural changes that occur in time series data. See, for example, Richard D. Marcus, "How to Deal with Structural Changes in the Data," *The Journal of Business Forecasting*, winter 1987–1988, pp. 14–16.

[6] While there are complex statistical procedures for selecting the precise point of change (if this precise point must be known), as a general rule the objective of trend analysis is usually to capture broad patterns. Hence, a visual inspection is an acceptable expedient.

Another frequent occurrence with time series data is that a major change in economic activity has taken place but that this change was relatively short-lived. For example, the introduction of rebates for automobile purchases may affect sales for a very short period of time. Suppose that we were to observe the situation noted in Figure 3-11. As long as the forecaster has a logical explanation for a major deviation from trend and believes that it will not recur, values that are more in line with the normal trend pattern can be substituted for the unusual decline noted in Figure 3-11.

CYCLICAL PATTERNS

One of the primary reasons that we are interested in isolating and removing the trend pattern from a time series is that it enables us to identify other patterns in the data. Thus, we would generally find that cyclical fluctuations show up much more clearly when the trend component has been isolated. Cyclical fluctuations in time series data are nonperiodic, recurring variations around a long-run trend. To repeat a point that was previously made, at this juncture we are primarily interested in identifying and isolating rather than explaining cyclical patterns.

To illustrate this process, suppose that we consider the situation as depicted in Table 3-13 and Figure 3-12.[7]

FIGURE 3-12 Isolating the Cyclical Component

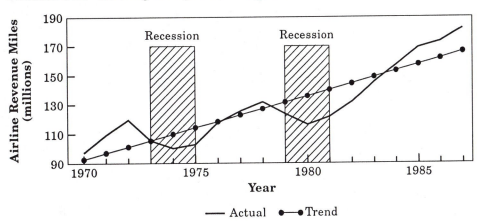

--- Actual •—•Trend

[7] The following example is specifically included to illustrate the process of isolating and measuring the cyclical component. As seen in our discussion of regression techniques in chapters 6 and 7, there are other approaches that tend to work better with respect to capturing the cyclical component. Our purpose here is to provide you with a conceptual understanding of the component patterns in a time series.

TABLE 3-13   Revenue Miles (millions of miles)

Year	Revenue Miles Y (1)	Trend Y_{tr} (2)	Cyclical Component (3)	Detrended Data (4)	$Y - Y_{tr}/Y_{tr} \cdot 100$ (5)
1970	98.22	93.75	104.8	4.47	4.8
1971	110.22	97.99	112.5	12.23	12.5
1972	120.37	102.22	117.8	18.15	17.8
1973	106.22	106.46	99.8	-0.24	-0.2
1974	101.01	110.69	91.3	-9.68	-8.7
1975	103.51	114.92	90.1	-11.41	-9.9
1976	118.37	119.16	99.3	-0.79	-0.7
1977	126.14	123.39	102.2	2.75	2.2
1978	132.16	127.63	103.5	4.53	3.5
1979	124.86	131.86	94.7	-7.00	-5.3
1980	116.64	136.09	85.7	-19.45	-14.3
1981	121.82	140.33	86.8	-18.51	-13.2
1982	131.66	144.56	91.1	-12.90	-8.9
1983	145.29	148.80	97.6	-3.51	-2.4
1984	156.67	153.03	102.4	3.64	2.4
1985	168.53	157.26	107.2	11.27	7.2
1986	172.53	161.50	106.8	11.03	6.8
1987	181.16	165.73	109.3	15.43	9.3

Trend Line: $Y_t = 89.521 + 4.234T$

The first of the methods used to identify cyclical variation is called the residual method. Mathematically, the residual can be expressed as

$$\text{Percent of Trend} = (Y/Y_{\text{trend}}) \cdot 100. \qquad (3\text{-}27)$$

The results of applying this formula provide measures of cyclical variation as a percent of trend. For example, for 1987, the cyclical variation index is computed as $(181.16/165.73) \cdot 100$, which yields 109.3.

The 1973–1975 and 1979–1981 recessions are shown by the fact that the cyclical factors are less than 100. Conversely, the time periods in which the cyclical factor exceeds 100 indicate periods of expansion. Thus, for example, the value of 109.3 in 1987 implies that the expansionary phase of the business cycle is causing growth to be higher than the trend (average) rate of growth by 9.3 percentage points. Conversely, the value of 86.8, the cyclical factor, indicates that because of the recession, actual growth is 13.2 (100.0 − 86.8) percentage points below the average or trend growth rate.[8]

[8] There are numerous other methods that can be used to isolate the cyclical component of a time series. Among these would be smoothing with moving averages, smoothing with medians, and smoothing of first differences. The limitation of all of these methods is the presumption that the length of the cycle is known. For a more detailed discussion of these approaches, see Paul F. Honing and David C. Hoaglin, *Applications, Basics and Computing of Exploratory Data Analysis* (Boston: Duxbury Press, 1981), especially chapter 6.

Another method used to measure the cyclical variation is the relative cyclical residual method. In this method, the percentage deviation from the trend is found for each value. The mathematical formula for determining the relative cyclical residuals is given by

$$\text{Relative Cyclical Residual} = \frac{Y - Y_{tr}}{Y_{tr}} \cdot 100. \qquad (3\text{-}28)$$

The results of applying equation (3-28) to the revenue miles data are depicted in column 5 of Table 3-13. Negative values indicate that the trend value is being pulled down by a recession, whereas positive values indicate that the trend value is higher than average because of an expansion. For example, the 1970 value of 4.8 indicates that actual growth exceeds that expected by trend patterns by 4.8 percent because of an expansion, whereas the -14.3 value in 1980 suggests that the actual value is lower than trend patterns because of a recession.

From the perspective of a decision maker, these cyclical factors can be used to gauge the impact of future business-cycle fluctuations. If management feels that the next recession will be similar to the 1979–1983 recession, the trend forecasts can be adjusted according to these factors. For example, if management felt, in 1987, that 1988 would be the first year of the next recession, the trend forecast of 169.967 ($89.521 + 4.234 \cdot 19$) revenue miles would be adjusted downward to 160.96 ($169.967 \cdot .947$).

An alterative way to view the cyclical fluctuations is to analyze the detrended data presented in column 4 of Table 3-13. Each of these values is derived by subtracting the trend estimate (column 2) from the actual values (column 1). Figure 3-13 illustrates the value of estimating trend patterns and then detrending the data.

An examination of Figure 3-13 reveals that the plot of detrended values closely parallels the national business cycle, as noted by the two periods of recession. Business analysts do not always attempt to isolate the trend pattern. Rather, forecasting models may be constructed to account for both the trend and the cyclical components inherent in time series data.

SEASONAL VARIATION

Seasonal variation occurs within a year and repeats, although not necessarily in an identical magnitude, in the following year. That is, seasonal patterns are fluctuations that recur over a specific calendar period—a day, a week, a year. Most frequently, when the term *seasonal pattern* is used by itself, it refers to consistent fluctuations in either monthly or quarterly economic time series data. Seasonal variation may be related to noneconomic factors such as customs (spring purchases), holidays (Christmas sales), and weather (sales of sleds in winter), or to institutional factors such as model-year changes in the auto-

FIGURE 3-13 **Detrended Data and the Cyclical Component**

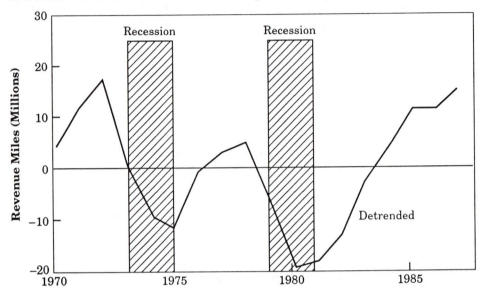

mobile industry, inventory sales in anticipation of tax deadlines, or sales of textbooks as school starts.

In general, the procedures used for monthly and quarterly time series data are virtually identical. When working with weekly data, special problems arise because there is not a whole number of weeks in the year, nor is there the same number of full weeks in a month.

There are at least three different reasons why forecasters are interested in seasonal fluctuations. First, in many actual business situations, seasonality is second only to trend forces as the most prominent component of time series data. As a result of this dominance, seasonal variation can mask cyclical movements and cyclical turning points. Thus, prior to using data in developing forecasts, it is necessary to remove seasonal variation. Most time series released by the federal government are reported as seasonally adjusted or deseasonalized. Since seasonal patterns remain relatively constant from one year to the next, the removal of this pattern simplifies the forecasting process. Specifically, once the seasonal pattern has been removed from the actual data, the task of estimating a forecasting model is made much more manageable.

Second, from a short-term perspective (less than one year), an understanding of seasonal variation is essential since the largest element in period-to-period (e.g., month-to-month) fluctuations is seasonal variation. In forecasting such items as inventories, work force, cash flow, or material requirements, an understanding of seasonal changes can dramatically improve forecast accuracy.

Finally, an understanding of seasonal patterns can be an important element of long-range planning. For example, in developing a long-range plan, management may be interested in products that have seasonal patterns distinctly different from currently produced products. For example, a firm that has lawn care products as its primary line of business is likely to experience idle capacity during the winter season. Thus, it may be particularly desirable to develop a line of products that experience a seasonal sales peak during the winter.

There are two commonly accepted approaches to removing or modeling the seasonal pattern in data. The first approach involves the use of seasonal differencing. This process is illustrated in the discussion of Box-Jenkins methodology in chapter 9. The more common approach to understanding and removing seasonal patterns entails the development of seasonal ratios or index numbers. As a first step toward forming these seasonal index numbers, consider the graphical approach for time series shown in Figure 3-14.

Figure 3-14 depicts the data contained in Table 3-14 and is similar to other time series graphs, except that the horizontal axis lists only the quarters of the year and each year is plotted as a separate line on the graph. The trend pattern in the data is illustrated by the gradual upward shift in the lines over time, while the cyclical component appears as a change in the spacing of the lines. (Note, for example, the closeness of the lines during the period 1980–1981 as compared to the spread between the lines during the period 1981–1982, or the decline noted in the 1984 line versus the 1985 line.) The advantage of this type of ladder graph is that the seasonal pattern becomes the dominant visual component. An examination of Figure 3-14 indicates a repeating pat-

FIGURE 3-14 Seasonal Patterns

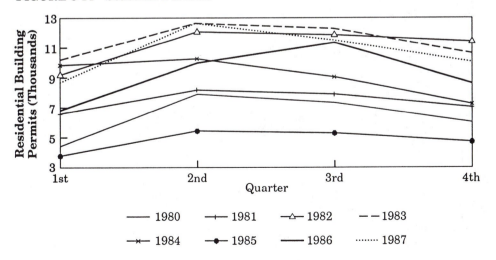

TABLE 3-14 Ratio-to-Moving-Average and Seasonal Adjustment for Quarterly Residential Building Permits

Date	Building Permits (1)	Four-Quarter Moving Total (2)	Sum of Two Successive Four-Quarter Totals (3)	Four-Quarter Moving Average (4)	Original Series As % of Moving Average (5)	Seasonal Index (6)	Deseasonalized Series (7)
1980: I	4,424	—	—	—	—	89.96	4,918
II	7,832	24,966	—	—	—	113.51	6,900
III	7,086	27,191	52,157	6,520	108.69	108.26	6,545
IV	5,624	27,458	54,649	6,831	82.33	88.27	6,371
1981: I	6,649	28,002	55,460	6,933	95.91	89.96	7,391
II	8,099	29,112	57,114	7,139	113.44	113.51	7,135
III	7,630	31,650	60,762	7,595	100.46	108.26	7,048
IV	6,734	35,523	67,173	8,397	80.20	88.27	7,629
1982: I	9,187	39,519	75,042	9,380	97.94	89.96	10,212
II	11,972	43,775	83,294	10,412	114.99	113.51	10,547
III	11,626	44,815	88,590	11,074	104.99	108.26	10,739
IV	10,990	45,332	90,147	11,268	97.53	88.27	12,450
1983: I	10,227	45,849	91,181	11,398	89.73	89.96	11,368
II	12,489	45,201	91,050	11,681	109.73	113.51	11,003
III	12,143	44,847	90,048	11,256	107.88	108.26	11,217
IV	10,342	42,542	87,389	10,924	94.68	88.27	11,716
1984: I	9,873	39,206	81,748	10,219	96.62	89.96	10,975
II	10,184	35,752	74,958	9,370	108.69	113.51	8,972
III	8,807	29,676	65,428	8,179	107.68	108.26	8,135
IV	6,888	24,775	54,451	6,806	101.20	88.27	7,803
1985: I	3,797	21,129	45,904	5,738	66.17	89.96	4,221
II	5,283	18,627	39,756	4,970	106.31	113.51	4,654
III	5,161	21,676	40,303	5,038	102.44	108.26	4,767
IV	4,386	26,253	47,929	5,991	73.21	88.27	4,969
1986: I	6,846	32,251	58,504	7,313	93.61	89.96	7,610
II	9,860	36,167	68,418	8,552	115.29	113.51	8,686
III	11,159	38,020	74,187	9,273	120.33	108.26	10,308
IV	8,302	40,693	78,713	9,839	84.38	88.27	9,405
1987: I	8,699	40,889	81,582	10,198	85.30	89.96	9,670
II	12,533	42,293	83,182	10,398	120.54	113.51	11,041
III	11,355	—	—	—	—	108.26	10,489
IV	9,706	—	—	—	—	88.27	10,996

tern—a relatively low first quarter; a strong peak in the second quarter; and a decline in the fourth quarter.

There are many alternative approaches to measuring the seasonality exhibited by the data in Figure 3-14. The method most relied on has been developed by the Census Bureau and is known as the Census II or X11 method.[9] Our purpose here is to illustrate the basic concepts involved in developing these seasonal indices.

The basic assumption underlying isolation of seasonal forces is that there is a repetitive pattern in the data. Further, isolation assumes that this pattern repeats in cycles, each of which is the same number of periods (quarters, months, weeks). If an extended time series of, say, quarterly data exhibits a seasonal pattern, the series value in each quarter will be inflated or deflated by this factor. For example, retail sales are typically very high in the fourth quarter due to the Christmas rush, and very low in the first quarter.

Patterns similar to those depicted in Figure 3-14 are estimated via a set of index numbers. These index numbers measure the percentage of the average value that typically occurs in that period. Thus, if the seasonal cycle repeats every four periods (a quarterly time series), seasonal analysis will generate four index numbers. Each of these numbers measures the relation between a specific quarter and the average quarter. A value of 100 implies that this quarter tends to be equal to the average quarter (no seasonality is present); a value of 115 (1.15) implies that this quarter is typically 15 percent above average (due to seasonality); and conversely, a value of 90 percent (0.90) implies that the quarter under consideration is 10 percent below the average quarter (due to the downward tug of seasonal forces). Thus, a forecaster attempts to compensate for the effect of seasonality (that is, seasonally adjust the data) by removing the seasonality from the raw data.

The seasonal patterns in residential building permits are illustrated in Figure 3-15 and Table 3-14. Looking at the original or raw data, notice that fourth-quarter permits are lower than that in the other quarters of the same year, and that the second quarter is consistently the highest-volume quarter within a given year. This, along with the pattern exhibited in Figure 3-14, is certainly suggestive of a strong seasonal pattern. Although seasonal patterns can occur within a week or day (for example, weekly utility demand or peak demand within a day for electricity), this chapter concentrates on seasonal cycles over a one-year span. The techniques presented here can be extended to any time period. Thus, the goal is to illustrate a procedure whereby a time series similar to that pictured in Figure 3-14 can be seasonally adjusted.

One of the most popular seasonal techniques is the ratio-to-moving-average method. The raw data in column 1 of Table 3-14 contain all four com-

---

[9] For a detailed explanation of this procedure, consult the U.S. Department of Commerce, Bureau of the Census, "The X11 Variant of the Census Method II Seasonal Adjustment Program," Technical Paper no. 15, 1967 revision (Washington, D.C.: U.S. Government Printing Office, 1967).

FIGURE 3-15   Residential Building Permits

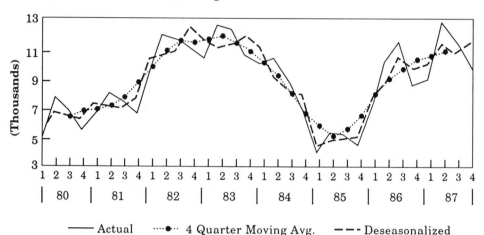

ponents of a time series: trend (T), cyclical (C), seasonal (S), and irregular (I). To isolate the first two components (T and C), calculate the four-quarter moving average shown in column 4. Columns 2 and 3 are simply intermediate steps in the derivation of the moving average. Since each moving average spans an entire year, the seasonal and irregular (S and I) factors have been averaged or smoothed out of the data. If we now divide the raw data (column 1) by the moving average (column 4) and multiply by 100, we obtain the seasonal and irregular factors (column 5) inherent in the series. To obtain the first-quarter seasonal index in column 6, average all first-quarter raw seasonals in column 5. The final seasonal index values are listed in column 6 of Table 3-14.

A specific illustration will clarify this seemingly complex process. Let us focus our attention on the first quarter of 1981. Actual building permits (column 1) were 6,649, whereas the four-quarter moving average (column 4) was 6,933.

An alternative, one-step procedure (circumventing columns 2 and 3) can be used:

Moving average for 1981:I

$$= \{[(1/2)(1980\text{:III})] + (1980\text{:IV}) + (1981\text{:I}) + (1981\text{:II}) + [(1/2)(1981\text{:III})]\}/4$$

$$= \{[(.5)(7086)] + (5624) + (6649) + (8099) + [(.5)(3815)]\}/4 \qquad \textbf{(3-29)}$$

$$= 6{,}932.5 = 6{,}933 \text{ Permits.}$$

The four-quarter moving averages are plotted along with the actual data in Figure 3-15. Since the moving average eliminates the seasonal and irregular components, these factors (S and I) were responsible for the fact that the actual value (6,449) was below the four-quarter moving average. Similarly, when we divide the actual value of 6,449 (T, C, S, and I) by 6,933 (T and C) and multiply by 100, the resulting value of 95.91 percent tells us that seasonal and irregular forces were depressing first-quarter air miles by 4.09 percent (100.00 − 95.91). Table 3-15 contains the raw seasonals taken from column 5 of Table 3-14. The value of 95.91 for the first quarter of 1981 reappears as the 1981 entry in the column labeled "I" in Table 3-15.

The irregular component contained in these raw seasonals is averaged out by calculating the means for each quarter. These means—89.33, 112.71, 107.50, and 87.65—are shown at the bottom of each column in Table 3-15. Since these figures total 397.18, rather than 400.00, the following adjustment for the winter quarter must be made:

$$(400/397.18)(89.33) = 89.96. \tag{3-30}$$

Similar calculations are made for the remaining three quarters. These figures then become the final seasonal factors illustrated in the last row of Table 3-15 and column 6 of Table 3-14. In place of actual residential building permits of 6,649, the seasonally adjusted or deseasonalized magnitude is 7,391 permits.

Seasonally adjusted figures are listed in column 7 of Table 3-14. Conceptually,

$$\text{Deseasonalized Value} = (Y_t)/(\text{Seasonal Index}/100) \tag{3-31}$$

For example,

$$\text{Deseasonalized Value: 1979:II} = (8099)/1.1351 = 7,135 \text{ Permits} \tag{3-32}$$

TABLE 3-15 Seasonal Indices for Residential Building Permits

Year	I	II	III	IV	
			Quarter		
	I	*II*	*III*	*IV*	
1980			108.69	82.33	
1981	95.91	113.44	100.46	80.2	
1982	97.94	114.99	104.99	97.53	
1983	89.73	109.73	107.88	94.68	
1984	96.62	108.69	107.68	101.2	
1985	66.17	106.31	102.44	73.21	
1986	93.61	115.29	120.33	84.38	
1987	85.3	120.54			
Mean	89.33	112.71	107.5	87.65	397.1812
Final Seasonals	89.96	113.51	108.26	88.27	400

or

Deseasonalized Value for 1987:IV = (9706/0.8827) = 10,996 Permits.   **(3-33)**

Thus, the final column in Table 3-14 contains the seasonally adjusted series for residential building permits. As before, this series is graphically illustrated in Figure 3-15. The line based on this series contains only the trend, cyclical, and irregular components of the time series.

In reporting these figures to management, it is common practice to use one of two approaches. The first method would state the following: Residential building permits for the fourth quarter of 1987 were 10,996 on a seasonally adjusted basis.

The second approach uses the concept of a seasonally adjusted annualized rate (SAAR). To obtain the SAAR, simply take the seasonally adjusted quarterly figure and multiply it by a factor of 4. Thus, for the fourth quarter of 1987, the SAAR is 43,984 (10,996 · 4). In other words, building activity was running at an annualized rate of 43,984 permits. Alternatively, if building permits are issued at the same rate as they were in the fourth quarter, the annual total will be 43,984. With a monthly series, take the seasonally adjusted monthly value and multiply by 12 to obtain the seasonally adjusted annualized rate. Alternatively, if you were given an SAAR for a specific quarter, you would derive the quarterly figure by dividing the SAAR by 4. Thus, if SAAR equals 43,984, the quarterly value is 10,996 (43,984/4).

EXAMPLE 3-1   Methods of Summarizing Data

While it is true that our primary interest here is in the development of forecasts, it is also true that the major source of the data to be used in generating these forecasts is the past. Thus, it can be said that respected forecasters are historians who begin their forecasting process by exploring the past for clues that will assist them in predicting what will happen and why it is likely to happen. In undertaking this endeavor, practitioners begin their work by summarizing the massive amounts of data with which they are frequently required to work.

Table 3-16 (pages 98–99), column 1, contains information on termite leads (inquiries from home owners wishing a termite inspection) on a quarterly basis for the years 1979 through 1988. As a first method of summarizing this data set, there are a number of quantitative measures that prove to be valuable. Table 3-17 (page 100) presents the most common of these quantitative measures.

The fact that the mean and the median are similar suggests that there are no significant outliers or extreme values present in the data. The geometric mean provides a measure of the growth of termite leads over time. The remaining four measures provide us with various measures of the dispersion exhibited by the series over time.

The remaining columns in Table 3-16 depict the results of using the Census X-11 methodology to decompose the actual termite lead data into its various components. A comparison of each of the quarterly seasonal factors, column 2 indicates that there have been some subtle shifts in seasonal patterns over time. Specifically, it appears that the second quarter is diminishing in relative importance over time. This can be seen by noting that the seasonal factor for the second quarter in 1979 was 100.6 while in 1988 it was 98.6, a decline of 2.0 percentage points. Conversely, the fourth quarter is increasing in relative importance, as the seasonal factor for this quarter has increased from 97.1 in 1979 to 99.4 in 1988, a net gain of 2.3 percentage points. While it appears that this type of analysis is rudimentary, it can and does provide management with useful information. For example, the changing seasonality might assist management in better scheduling labor time or planning capital expansions.

The primary difference between the seasonally adjusted termite lead column, column 4, and the trend-cycle column, column 5, is that the seasonally adjusted termite leads have not been adjusted for any irregular variations while the trend-cycle values have been adjusted to compensate for these random fluctuations. In developing forecasting models, you will use the data in either column 4 or 5. As long as the irregular factor is relatively small, the seasonally adjusted values in column 4 are to be preferred. One of the consequences of using the trend-cycle values is that they may be oversmoothed.[10] In the case of the termite leads, in an examination of the random or irregular factors (column 6), the only values that appear to be significantly different from 100.00 (recall that a value of 100.00 indicates no irregular variation present) are the values that occur in the first quarters of 1980 and 1983 and the second quarter of 1988. Thus, at first glance we would use the seasonally adjusted values, column 4, in our forecasting models with the qualification that we might substitute the trend-cycle values for the first quarters of 1980 and 1983 and the second quarter of 1988. Alternatively, we might attempt to identify the reasons for the irregular variations noted in these periods and adjust the values accordingly.

In many respects, graphical forms of data display and summary are easier and more functional than are either tabular forms or quantitative measures. Perhaps one of the primary differences between practicing forecasters and academicians is that the former tend to rely heavily on graphical devices. This reliance stems from the extraordinary amounts of information that can be gleaned from examining graphical displays.

---

[10] This oversmoothing follows from the repeated application of a series of moving averages.

TABLE 3-16 Decomposition Analysis of Termite Leads

Date	Actual (thousands) (1)	Seasonal Factors (percent) (2)	Deviation from Average (3)	Seasonally Adjusted (thousands) (4)	Trend-Cycle Values (thousands) (5)	Irregular Factors (percent) (6)	Deviation from Average (7)	Trend (thousands) (8)	Cyclical Factors (percent) (9)	Deviation from Average (10)
1979: I	125.3	98.81	-1.19	126.8	127.6	99.36	-0.64	118.7	107.47	7.47
II	129.8	100.63	0.63	129.0	128.1	100.73	0.73	119.7	107.01	7.01
III	131.4	103.43	3.43	127.0	127.2	99.90	-0.10	120.6	105.44	5.44
IV	121.6	97.09	-2.91	125.2	125.7	99.63	-0.37	121.5	103.44	3.44
1980: I	127.1	98.87	-1.13	128.6	125.0	102.84	2.84	122.5	102.09	2.09
II	125.0	100.52	0.52	124.3	124.9	99.55	-0.45	123.4	101.24	1.24
III	131.0	103.48	3.48	126.6	126.5	100.03	0.03	124.3	101.80	1.80
IV	126.6	97.22	-2.78	130.2	130.0	100.15	0.15	125.2	103.82	3.82
1981: I	132.1	98.86	-1.14	133.6	134.2	99.54	-0.46	126.2	106.40	6.40
II	138.2	100.25	0.25	137.9	137.0	100.60	0.60	127.1	107.82	7.82
III	140.3	103.62	3.62	135.4	135.2	100.12	0.12	128.0	105.63	5.63
IV	126.4	97.57	-2.43	129.5	130.5	99.26	-0.74	129.0	101.21	1.21
1982: I	125.0	98.62	-1.38	126.7	125.4	101.04	1.04	129.9	96.58	-3.42
II	119.6	99.98	-0.02	119.6	120.1	99.61	-0.39	130.8	91.81	-8.19
III	119.9	103.72	3.72	115.6	115.7	99.92	-0.08	131.7	87.82	-12.18
IV	111.2	97.84	-2.16	113.7	113.2	100.39	0.39	132.7	85.34	-14.66
1983: I	108.3	98.56	-1.44	109.9	112.4	97.80	-2.20	133.6	84.10	-15.90
II	114.3	99.64	-0.36	114.7	114.9	99.85	-0.15	134.5	85.40	-14.60
III	125.6	103.84	3.84	120.9	120.7	100.21	0.21	135.5	89.10	-10.90
IV	125.2	98.23	-1.77	127.5	127.6	99.90	-0.10	136.4	93.55	-6.45

TABLE 3-16 (*Continued*)

Date	Actual (thousands) (1)	Seasonal Factors (percent) (2)	Deviation from Average (3)	Seasonally Adjusted (thousands) (4)	Trend-Cycle Values (thousands) (5)	Irregular Factors (percent) (6)	Deviation from Average (7)	Trend (thousands) (8)	Cyclical Factors (percent) (9)	Deviation from Average (10)
1984: I	132.3	98.34	-1.66	134.5	134.5	100.03	0.03	137.3	97.96	-2.04
II	139.9	99.39	-0.61	140.8	140.8	99.99	-0.01	138.2	101.84	1.84
III	150.8	103.92	3.92	145.1	144.9	100.16	0.16	139.2	104.11	4.11
IV	144.2	98.58	-1.42	146.3	146.2	100.06	0.06	140.1	104.35	4.35
1985: I	142.7	98.23	-1.77	145.3	146.6	99.11	-0.89	141.0	103.95	3.95
II	146.2	99.08	-0.92	147.6	146.6	100.63	0.63	141.9	103.30	3.30
III	151.4	103.96	3.96	145.6	146.2	99.61	-0.39	142.9	102.32	2.32
IV	144.5	98.89	-1.11	146.1	146.1	99.99	-0.01	143.8	101.62	1.62
1986: I	143.7	98.11	-1.89	146.5	145.8	100.43	0.43	144.7	100.76	0.76
II	142.4	98.92	-1.08	143.9	144.9	99.37	-0.63	145.7	99.45	-0.55
III	150.7	103.98	3.98	144.9	144.3	100.42	0.42	146.6	98.46	-1.54
IV	143.2	99.20	-0.80	144.4	144.5	99.90	-0.10	147.5	97.95	-2.05
1987: I	143.0	98.01	-1.99	145.9	146.4	99.66	-0.34	148.4	98.62	-1.38
II	149.3	98.71	-1.29	151.2	150.8	100.28	0.28	149.4	100.97	0.97
III	161.5	103.99	3.99	155.3	155.6	99.82	-0.18	150.3	103.52	3.52
IV	157.8	99.37	-0.63	158.8	158.5	100.21	0.21	151.2	104.79	4.79
1988: I	156.0	97.98	-2.02	159.2	158.4	100.54	0.54	152.2	104.08	4.08
II	150.5	98.61	-1.39	152.6	156.7	97.38	-2.62	153.1	102.38	2.38
III	162.8	103.98	3.98	156.6	156.6	99.99	-0.01	154.0	101.67	1.67
IV	156.7	99.40	-0.60	157.6	157.3	100.21	0.21	154.9	101.53	1.53

**TABLE 3-17   Quantitative Summary Measures:
Termite Leads**

Median	139.1	Minimum	108.3
Mean	136.8	Maximum	162.8
Geometric Mean	9.2	Range	54.5
Standard Deviation	14.1		

FIGURE 3-16   Graphical Analysis of Time Series Components of Termite Leads

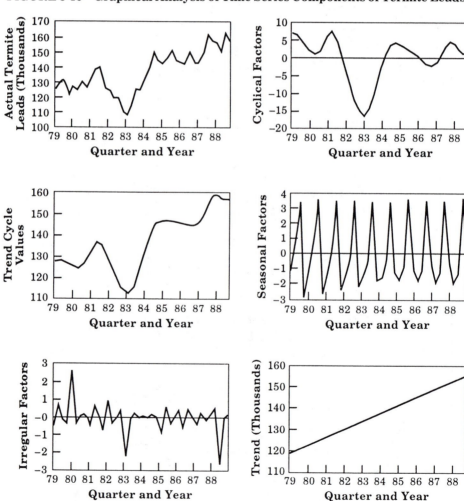

Furthermore, practitioners are universally called on to present their results to nontechnically oriented management, thereby further enhancing the use of graphical displays.[11]

Figure 3-16 presents the results of the decomposition of termite leads in a graphical format. All of these displays are simple time plots. A time plot is merely a graph in which the data values are arranged sequentially in time. The advantage of these time plots is that it becomes less difficult to note some of the preceding points. For example, the large spikes or bars associated with the first quarters of 1980 and 1983 and the second quarter of 1988 serve to identify the irregular variations previously noted. An additional advantage of this type of graphical analysis is that the cyclical fluctuations become much easier to identify than was the case with the original data series.

SUMMARY

While our primary purpose is the development of forecasting models, a necessary first step revolves around developing an understanding of the data. Thus, in this chapter we have provided a basic set of procedures for identifying and measuring the various components that comprise time series data. Specifically, a forecaster will learn which forecasting techniques are likely to be successful by understanding the significance of trend, cyclical, and seasonal components in explaining the pattern of changes exhibited by the actual historical data.

QUESTIONS FOR DISCUSSION AND ANALYSIS

1. Collect time series on a subject in which you are interested. Present the data in graphical format. Determine exactly what the data measure, how the data were obtained, what revisions are made, when revisions are normally made, and any other pertinent information.

2. Suppose that you had collected retail sales data for a department store located in Phoenix, a furniture manufacturer in North Carolina, and an apple grower in Washington State. Categorize the trend, seasonal, cyclical, and irregular forces you would expect to affect sales or production for each of these businesses. For example, what are the trend forces affecting apple sales or furniture sales?

3. Using current and past issues of the *Survey of Current Business*, collect monthly data for the production of electric power (millions of kilowatt hours) for the last 10 years,

---

[11] In this discussion we do not attempt to introduce all of the possible graphical displays used in developing forecasting models. Several other graphical displays (for example, scatter plots, actual versus fitted, and turning-point diagrams) are introduced at appropriate times in subsequent chapters. We have introduced various other graphical displays throughout this chapter.

convert to a quarterly series, and estimate the final seasonal factors for each quarter using the techniques illustrated in Tables 3-14 and 3-15. Explain precisely the meaning of each quarterly index. Focusing on just the seasonality of power production, by what percentage does the third quarter differ from the first quarter?

4. Fit a linear trend to electric power data, as illustrated by equations (3-7) and (3-8). Reestimate your trend equation using the logarithmic transformation shown in equations (3-13) and (3-14). Graph the two trend equations against the raw data. Which appears to fit best?

5. Set up a table in which column 1 contains the actual or raw data for power production for the last eight quarters, column 2 contains the appropriate seasonal factors, column 3 the seasonally adjusted series, column 4 the quarterly trend forecast, column 5 the cyclical component, and column 6 the irregular component. Explain your findings concerning the relative contributions of trend, seasonal, cyclical, and irregular components over this period.

6. Suppose that you have collected the following production data. Graph the data, and, based on a visual examination of the data, estimate the trend line that you feel is most appropriate.

Period	Production (in millions of units)
1	8.76
2	7.99
3	10.40
4	13.06
5	10.83
6	11.08
7	11.26
8	14.78
9	14.05
10	12.66
11	14.05

7. Suppose that you have collected the following information on the volume of checks written on a major urban bank.

Year	Check Volume	Year	Check Volume
1973	144,764	1981	398,982
1974	154,146	1982	446,416
1975	172,664	1983	462,502
1976	191,379	1984	547,573
1977	234,642	1985	584,179
1978	270,736	1986	609,332
1979	302,054	1987	646,820
1980	339,947	1988	692,710

a. Estimate an exponential trend line.
b. Interpret the meaning of the slope coefficient.
c. Estimate a second-degree trend line.
d. Which of the two trend lines appears to fit the data best?
e. Based on your choice in part d, compute and plot the detrended values. Do they indicate any pattern? If so, what pattern?

8. Given the following information on the production of Dalene Dolls, compute the first and second differences. What do these differences suggest about the underlying trend pattern in the data? Estimate the appropriate trend line.

Period	Production	Period	Production
1	14,348	16	34,584
2	14,307	17	36,366
3	15,197	18	37,865
4	16,715	19	39,173
5	18,476	20	40,119
6	19,404	21	39,626
7	20,173	22	39,107
8	20,645	23	39,796
9	20,937	24	41,567
10	21,501	25	43,646
11	22,788	26	43,534
12	23,579	27	44,157
13	25,319	28	44,551
14	28,250	29	45,572
15	32,191	30	47,221

After you have estimated the trend line, compute the detrended values. Do these detrended values suggest any cyclical pattern in the historical data?

9. Explain the conceptual difference between making preliminary adjustments to data and transforming data.

10. Suppose that you were given the following information:

Seasonally Adjusted Value = 52.6

Seasonal Factor = 95.4.

If this were monthly data, compute the seasonally adjusted annualized rate (SAAR).

11. If the actual level of sales is 2,036 and the seasonal factor is 105.6, what is the seasonally adjusted level of sales? What is the exact interpretation of a seasonal factor of 105.6?

12. Since seasonal variation is a recurring pattern, why are forecasters interested in isolating and measuring its impact on time series data?

13. In equation form, illustrate the process of decomposing a time series (ignore the trading-day adjustment).

14. What is the economic significance of the multiplicative time series model suggested by equation (3-4)?

15. Are the following statements true or false? If false, why?
    a. *Trend* refers to a systematic pattern in a particular direction that persists over a substantial period of time.
    b. Trends are always linear.
    c. Theory provides us with a guideline to the appropriate trend line.
    d. Cycles last longer than one year and repeat themselves in a consistent fashion.
16. The quarterly data on outstanding consumer loans are as follows:

Year	Quarter			
	I	II	III	IV
1985	211	214	218	216
1986	234	219	223	226
1987	224	229	240	241
1988	241	240	241	249

   a. Using the ratio-to-moving-average method, compute the seasonal indices.
   b. Estimate a linear trend line based on these seasonally adjusted values.
   c. Estimate the cyclical variation using both the residual and relative cyclical residual method.

17. A linear trend was fitted to the monthly sales of automobiles, and the equation was found to be

$$Y_t = 500 + 22T$$

where T equals 0 on January 1981 and is measured in monthly increments. From this trend line, what is the trend value for June 1981 and for January 1986? If the seasonal index for January was 110, what would be the cyclical value for January 1986?

18. What is the difference between a stock variable and a flow variable? Why is an understanding of this distinction important in using time series data in a forecasting model?

19. What is meant by trends in economic activity? What factors account for changes in trend patterns?

20. Describe the concept of a business cycle and the process of isolating the cyclical component.

21. Describe the seasonal variation that characterizes business activity.

22. Give some examples of random fluctuations as they influence the observed level of economic and business activity.

23. Explain the ratio-to-moving-average method of computing seasonal factors.

24. Describe the residual method of isolating the cyclical factor.

25. The following tables provide information on housing starts, total retail sales, and total employment. For each of these time series, carry out the following operations:
    a. Seasonally adjust each time series.
    b. Identify the most appropriate trend pattern.
    c. Based on your analysis in part b, conduct a cyclical analysis similar to that presented in the text.

Sample Data Sets for Time Series Analysis

Date	Housing Starts (thousands)	Total Retail Sales (millions)	Total Employment (thousands)
1970: Jan.	33.4	99,365	70,104
Feb.	41.4	101,479	70,208
Mar.	61.9	108,016	70,658
Apr.	73.8	107,002	70,972
May	74.8	109,239	70,995
June	83.0	113,502	71,636
July	75.5	106,067	70,873
Aug.	77.3	107,282	70,775
Sept.	76.0	111,049	71,134
Oct.	79.4	111,858	70,899
Nov.	67.4	106,223	70,859
Dec.	69.0	115,064	71,436
1971: Jan.	54.9	101,957	69,799
Feb.	58.3	106,171	69,720
Mar.	91.6	116,084	70,084
Apr.	116.0	116,078	70,672
May	115.6	117,021	71,165
June	116.9	123,256	71,879
July	107.7	113,267	71,066
Aug.	111.7	116,157	71,173
Sept.	102.1	120,606	71,809
Oct.	102.9	121,285	72,056
Nov.	92.9	121,433	72,357
Dec.	80.4	126,804	72,755
1972: Jan.	76.2	112,463	71,359
Feb.	76.3	118,145	71,546
Mar.	111.4	129,055	72,138
Apr.	119.8	125,753	72,770
May	135.2	131,427	73,402
June	131.9	135,557	74,383
July	119.1	123,010	73,377
Aug.	131.3	132,928	73,929
Sept.	120.5	136,638	74,491
Oct.	117.0	140,177	75,169
Nov.	97.4	140,609	75,581
Dec.	73.2	144,082	75,955
1973: Jan.	77.1	133,833	74,491
Feb.	73.6	138,683	74,869
Mar.	105.1	152,857	75,422
Apr.	120.5	149,730	76,008
May	131.6	155,752	76,591

Sample Data Sets for Time Series Analysis (*Continued*)

Date	Housing Starts (thousands)	Total Retail Sales (millions)	Total Employment (thousands)
June	114.8	158,573	77,508
July	114.7	147,893	76,568
Aug.	106.8	156,069	76,971
Sept.	84.5	154,951	77,562
Oct.	86.0	165,208	78,185
Nov.	70.5	165,211	78,587
Dec.	46.8	164,476	78,715
1974: Jan.	43.3	154,500	76,922
Feb.	57.6	159,132	77,039
Mar.	76.9	175,053	77,362
Apr.	102.2	175,978	77,911
May	96.3	181,785	78,513
June	99.3	182,686	79,210
July	90.7	176,156	78,311
Aug.	79.8	186,009	78,459
Sept.	73.4	184,777	78,959
Oct.	69.5	190,875	79,258
Nov.	57.9	183,884	78,937
Dec.	41.0	181,623	78,295
1975: Jan.	39.8	166,953	76,066
Feb.	40.0	169,014	75,641
Mar.	62.5	177,132	75,686
Apr.	77.8	178,894	76,018
May	92.8	182,295	76,649
June	90.3	185,287	77,143
July	92.8	177,807	76,466
Aug.	90.7	185,000	76,993
Sept.	84.5	189,782	77,602
Oct.	93.8	195,666	78,158
Nov.	71.6	185,875	78,312
Dec.	55.6	195,121	78,600
1976: Jan.	54.0	179,656	77,252
Feb.	72.6	186,681	77,482
Mar.	92.4	204,819	78,092
Apr.	107.8	204,551	78,919
May	112.2	202,989	79,414
June	119.6	213,116	80,043
July	112.8	198,755	79,272
Aug.	112.8	205,407	79,537
Sept.	108.0	211,563	80,244
Oct.	109.1	210,805	80,479

Sample Data Sets for Time Series Analysis (*Continued*)

Date	Housing Starts (thousands)	Total Retail Sales (millions)	Total Employment (thousands)
Nov.	89.4	210,977	80,839
Dec.	71.6	223,248	81,016
1977: Jan.	55.7	196,800	79,427
Feb.	87.2	208,929	79,636
Mar.	125.8	234,616	80,493
Apr.	138.8	229,899	81,418
May	152.2	231,268	82,252
June	149.1	239,745	83,210
July	138.2	219,010	82,551
Aug.	140.5	232,419	82,845
Sept.	131.6	237,068	83,798
Oct.	135.4	240,247	84,298
Nov.	109.3	238,820	84,744
Dec.	87.1	248,454	84,980
1978: Jan.	63.3	215,733	83,318
Feb.	72.7	230,822	83,614
Mar.	121.4	259,126	84,607
Apr.	139.9	256,484	85,910
May	154.9	265,245	86,715
June	154.3	273,000	87,701
July	139.3	246,894	86,872
Aug.	140.0	268,453	87,174
Sept.	124.6	270,042	87,801
Oct.	131.1	280,737	88,417
Nov.	110.4	277,053	88,965
Dec.	81.4	283,509	89,272
1979: Jan.	57.5	256,973	87,514
Feb.	59.3	266,305	87,751
Mar.	109.8	303,412	88,654
Apr.	121.2	287,107	89,183
May	131.2	304,512	90,012
June	134.5	306,049	90,857
July	117.8	286,343	89,869
Aug.	119.4	306,802	89,969
Sept.	105.7	305,441	90,521
Oct.	107.9	320,963	91,000
Nov.	72.0	314,098	91,204
Dec.	57.8	319,728	91,335
1980: Jan.	49.3	299,698	89,553
Feb.	49.9	313,806	89,691
Mar.	51.7	328,161	90,253

Sample Data Sets for Time Series Analysis (*Continued*)

Date	Housing Starts (thousands)	Total Retail Sales (millions)	Total Employment (thousands)
Apr.	61.5	315,965	90,603
May	64.9	317,178	90,623
June	76.9	319,774	90,778
July	85.6	309,942	89,436
Aug.	92.0	323,900	89,723
Sept.	95.0	339,921	90,390
Oct.	97.5	358,465	90,985
Nov.	71.2	343,593	91,329
Dec.	56.6	364,087	91,513
1981: Jan.	48.0	331,247	89,688
Feb.	48.0	338,126	89,833
Mar.	70.5	368,914	90,371
Apr.	83.6	362,612	91,027
May	73.8	360,961	91,514
June	72.5	372,840	92,158
July	69.5	347,914	91,237
Aug.	57.0	356,047	91,238
Sept.	58.3	363,921	91,739
Oct.	49.9	364,861	91,913
Nov.	40.1	348,919	91,745
Dec.	34.1	364,040	91,141
1982: Jan.	29.3	317,547	89,184
Feb.	32.5	332,584	89,273
Mar.	51.8	366,306	89,566
Apr.	55.8	352,073	89,878
May	58.9	356,967	90,361
June	63.5	365,604	90,554
July	61.4	337,955	89,221
Aug.	62.0	345,815	89,091
Sept.	63.3	354,202	89,516
Oct.	66.3	348,542	89,484
Nov.	66.0	346,127	89,381
Dec.	51.8	361,342	89,283
1983: Jan.	56.3	318,372	87,614
Feb.	60.4	326,559	87,621
Mar.	86.2	367,553	88,232
Apr.	93.2	351,902	89,095
May	114.9	367,958	89,925
June	114.2	389,208	90,751
July	100.4	355,658	90,179
Aug.	109.9	378,409	89,907

Sample Data Sets for Time Series Analysis (*Continued*)

Date	Housing Starts (thousands)	Total Retail Sales (millions)	Total Employment (thousands)
Sept.	97.2	390,019	91,634
Oct.	91.9	392,489	92,148
Nov.	81.9	392,100	92,506
Dec.	61.0	415,065	92,783
1984: Jan.	67.7	369,311	91,298
Feb.	81.0	385,608	91,867
Mar.	87.8	419,333	92,587
Apr.	106.4	404,333	93,548
May	115.2	425,259	94,430
June	111.0	431,887	95,250
July	97.9	395,215	94,554
Aug.	91.9	417,007	94,842
Sept.	90.5	411,810	95,769
Oct.	91.9	425,855	96,328
Nov.	80.0	419,874	96,707
Dec.	62.8	431,198	96,767
1985: Jan.	59.3	385,683	95,029
Feb.	63.4	391,489	95,242
Mar.	92.6	430,014	96,042
Apr.	108.7	423,098	96,851
May	107.5	440,501	97,708
June	101.7	431,155	98,258
July	105.6	407,120	97,402
Aug.	99.5	429,810	97,655
Sept.	89.9	430,462	98,468
Oct.	104.7	438,037	98,984
Nov.	73.4	429,696	99,238
Dec.	66.0	448,604	99,355
1986: Jan.	72.0	401,725	97,405
Feb.	65.1	399,421	97,598
Mar.	97.0	429,612	98,150
Apr.	118.4	428,705	98,989
May	126.1	435,552	99,687
June	124.9	443,069	99,994
July	113.5	414,536	99,248
Aug.	109.4	427,284	99,425
Sept.	102.5	450,744	100,352
Oct.	100.9	450,545	100,924
Nov.	77.5	428,790	101,184
Dec.	72.2	470,028	101,342
1987: Jan.	69.2	396,910	99,383

Sample Data Sets for Time Series Analysis (*Continued*)

Date	Housing Starts (thousands)	Total Retail Sales (millions)	Total Employment (thousands)
Feb.	71.8	421,206	99,711
Mar.	100.4	461,405	100,427
Apr.	118.3	455,025	101,440
May	114.1	459,897	102,214
June	114.1	477,979	102,821
July	111.5	447,414	102,075
Aug.	100.7	460,886	102,314
Sept.	109.1	479,670	103,087
Oct.	96.6	483,690	103,998
Nov.	79.3	465,129	104,345
Dec.	61.2	499,842	104,587
1988: Jan.	55.8	427,390	102,494
Feb.	64.0	455,013	103,077
Mar.	99.9	503,878	103,834
Apr.	106.1	484,586	104,737
May	104.0	496,236	105,497
June	113.6	519,859	106,378
July	100.3	471,827	105,496
Aug.	101.4	506,832	105,663
Sept.	91.7	516,377	106,525
Oct.	97.7	517,756	107,196
Nov.	81.2	512,060	107,670
Dec.	65.7	544,054	107,869
1989: Jan.	69.9	475,425	105,953
Feb.	59.3	485,093	106,370
Mar.	83.5	538,177	107,026
Apr.	100.4	519,736	107,845
May	101.4	541,066	108,545
June	100.3	549,920	109,226
July	98.0	492,856	108,162
Aug.	91.7	542,378	108,248
Sept.	82.4	539,917	109,053
Oct.	91.2	539,784	109,547
Nov.	71.9	533,121	109,990
Dec.	53.4	552,598	109,997
1990: Jan.	67.9	487,561	107,949
Feb.	65.9	501,624	108,449
Mar.	83.2	558,887	109,114
Apr.	90.0	531,298	109,774
May	92.4	556,157	110,721
June	88.9	565,762	111,405

Sample Data Sets for Time Series Analysis (*Continued*)

Date	Housing Starts (thousands)	Total Retail Sales (millions)	Total Employment (thousands)
July	85.5	515,266	110,045
Aug.	75.6	565,322	109,900
Sept.	71.9	554,011	110,478
Oct.	75.6	573,259	110,721
Nov.	54.9	549,639	110,691
Dec.	43.1	556,219	110,409
1991: Jan	39.2	485,259	107,979
Feb.	46.1	491,129	107,887
Mar.	61.4	532,805	108,147

26. Based on an analysis of the following service sector employment figures, carry out a differencing analysis and estimate the most appropriate trend pattern.

Employment in the Service Industry (thousands)

Date*	Employment	Date	Employment	Date	Employment	Date	Employment
		1988: 1	18,827	1989: 1	19,086	1990: 1	20,014
		2	18,865	2	19,141	2	20,082
		3	18,896	3	19,167	3	20,185
1987: 4	18,352	4	18,948	4	19,220	4	20,261
5	18,931	5	18,962	5	19,232	5	20,379
6	18,491	6	18,973	6	19,355	6	20,469
7	18,489	7	18,967	7	19,462	7	20,576
8	18,530	8	18,998	8	19,528	8	20,682
9	18,581	9	19,011	9	19,652	9	20,672
10	18,629	10	19,045	10	19,762	10	20,819
11	18,688	11	19,055	11	19,850	11	20,872
12	18,751	12	19,068	12	19,956	12	21,030
						1991: 1	21,139
						2	21,233
						3	21,320

* Year and month

27. Suppose that you have collected the following information on the sales of hard disks for personal computers and are interested in measuring the average rate of growth over the time period provided. How would you begin your analysis? What measure would you use based on an analysis of the specific numbers provided?

Sales of Hard Disks by Dalene Softhouse (thousands)

Date*	Sales	Date	Sales	Date	Sales	Date	Sales
1980: 1	475.7	1983: 1	578.7	1986: 1	721.2	1989: 1	864.8
2	478.6	2	581.5	2	723.8	2	867.8
3	483.5	3	585.9	3	725.5	3	874.4
4	485.6	4	587.3	4	728.4	4	875.1
5	490.8	5	588.4	5	734.7	5	875.6
6	504.7	6	612.5	6	761.5	6	905.6
7	512.3	7	618.5	7	769.0	7	907.6
8	505.7	8	614.2	8	767.0	8	904.2
9	501.7	9	608.3	9	757.5	9	887.0
10	508.0	10	613.6	10	765.2	10	892.9
11	514.1	11	619.7	11	768.1	11	896.6
12	516.4	12	620.0	12	771.3	12	900.0
1981: 1	514.9	1984: 1	620.0	1987: 1	777.1	1990: 1	899.8
2	515.8	2	627.0	2	780.7	2	903.2
3	517.6	3	631.7	3	784.0	3	906.7
4	519.8	4	634.8	4	786.4	4	905.6
5	521.9	5	635.6	5	791.0	5	909.7
6	543.1	6	660.7	6	819.2	6	941.2
7	547.2	7	662.0	7	824.5	7	940.6
8	544.4	8	660.9	8	820.9	8	933.7
9	536.5	9	648.9	9	807.3	9	915.7
10	540.8	10	654.5	10	818.4	10	920.4
11	544.9	11	660.2	11	822.6	11	924.0
12	542.1	12	662.0	12	825.1	12	923.9
1982: 1	544.6	1985: 1	663.9	1988: 1	829.9	1991: 1	920.6
2	547.4	2	666.6	2	831.9	2	920.1
3	551.3	3	671.9	3	832.3	3	921.9
4	550.6	4	674.8	4	835.5		
5	554.8	5	682.8	5	833.4		
6	575.9	6	709.4	6	867.6		
7	582.9	7	711.5	7	867.9		
8	577.5	8	709.4	8	863.0		
9	570.2	9	699.4	9	849.7		
10	573.9	10	708.5	10	856.7		
11	578.2	11	715.7	11	863.2		
12	580.2	12	715.4	12	866.6		

* Year and month

28. Based on the sample data sets provided in the following table, determine which trend pattern is the most appropriate.

Sample Data Sets for Trend Analysis

Year	Memphis Retail Sales (millions of dollars)	Sales of Wrist Watches (thousands of units)
1970	1,721	
1971	2,077	
1972	2,345	
1973	2,619	
1974	2,822	
1975	2,977	18,247
1976	3,201	21,452
1977	3,489	27,654
1978	3,903	35,589
1979	4,272	46,123
1980	4,625	58,075
1981	4,881	73,713
1982	5,151	89,449
1983	5,838	169,167
1984	6,715	222,719
1985	7,108	367,624
1986	7,639	739,942
1987	7,878	1,014,825
1988	8,131	1,443,869
1989	8,526	1,642,730
1990	8,392	1,998,237

29. As a forecaster for a major southern utility, one of your primary responsibilities is to provide forecasts of the consumption of electricity. As a first step, you collect the quarterly data depicted in the following table. Your assignment, is to seasonally adjust the data, identify the most applicable trend pattern, and conduct a cyclical analysis of the data. How would this cyclical analysis be helpful in the future?

Electricity Consumption (millions of kilowatt hours)

Date	Consumption	Date*	Consumption
1970: I	14,337	1980: I	20,710
II	13,682	II	19,768
III	19,710	III	30,755
IV	14,179	IV	19,728
1971: I	14,700	1981: I	20,202
II	15,378	II	19,518
III	21,698	III	27,213
IV	16,447	IV	18,729

Electricity Consumption (millions of kilowatt hours) (*Continued*)

Date	Consumption	Date*	Consumption
1972: I	16,038	1982: I	20,263
II	17,251	II	19,755
III	23,867	III	27,266
IV	18,301	IV	19,159
1973: I	18,019	1983: I	19,680
II	17,755	II	18,750
III	25,290	III	29,644
IV	18,608	IV	19,770
1974: I	17,424	1984: I	22,005
II	18,117	II	20,131
III	24,372	III	28,417
IV	17,037	IV	20,770
1975: I	17,437	1985: I	22,042
II	18,243	II	21,821
III	24,948	III	29,706
IV	17,655	IV	20,929
1976: I	18,691	1986: I	21,835
II	17,874	II	22,349
III	25,624	III	32,258
IV	19,505	IV	22,512
1977: I	20,538	1987: I	23,153
II	20,939	II	23,698
III	28,644	III	34,205
IV	19,802	IV	23,871
1978: I	21,649	1988: I	24,552
II	20,391	II	25,001
III	28,109	III	36,086
IV	20,001	IV	25,283
1979: I	22,271	1989: I	25,902
II	19,956	II	26,137
III	27,100	III	37,728
IV	19,995	IV	27,327
		1990: I	26,077
		II	25,109
		III	35,730
		IV	25,354

* Year and quarter

30. As a stock analyst for a major firm, one of your primary responsibilities is to conduct an analysis of the manufacturing sector. To understand the pattern of changes in this sector, you are required to seasonally adjust the data provided in the following table.

When you have completed the first step, identify the most appropriate trend pattern for the sales data.

Total Sales of Manufactured Goods
(millions of dollars)

Date*	Sales	Date	Sales
1974: I	242,043	1983: I	490,836
II	269,390	II	527,084
III	272,098	III	534,711
IV	277,029	IV	561,633
1975: I	247,134	1984: I	566,089
II	265,773	II	597,854
III	270,967	III	577,085
IV	281,340	IV	594,019
1976: I	284,189	1985: I	565,349
II	307,603	II	594,081
III	301,605	III	578,023
IV	309,833	IV	593,935
1977: I	311,510	1986: I	543,986
II	338,604	II	566,162
III	331,711	III	546,326
IV	346,236	IV	564,457
1978: I	340,330	1987: I	556,770
II	377,462	II	596,091
III	376,858	III	597,669
IV	401,781	IV	627,683
1979: I	406,566	1988: I	614,176
II	436,422	II	655,508
III	437,545	III	646,271
IV	461,215	IV	680,244
1980: I	465,677	1989: I	665,974
II	466,294	II	707,490
III	464,215	III	681,263
IV	516,639	IV	690,340
1981: I	520,813	1990: I	671,404
II	549,582	II	706,867
III	539,934	III	705,120
IV	534,369	IV	727,932
1982: I	502,897	1991: I	653,662
II	521,907		
III	507,952		
IV	506,580		

* Year and quarter

REFERENCES FOR FURTHER STUDY

Afifi, A. A. and S. P. Azen, *Statistical Analysis—A Computer Oriented Approach,* 2nd ed. New York: Academic Press, 1979.

Box, G. E. P. and D. R. Cox, "An Analysis of Transformations," *Journal of the Royal Statistical Society,* series B, no. 26, 1964, pp. 211–52.

Chambers, J. M., W. S. Cleveland, B. Kleiner, and P. A. Tukey, *Graphical Methods for Data Analysis.* Boston: Duxbury Press, 1983.

Cleveland, W. S. and G. C. Taio, "Decomposition of Seasonal Time Series: A Model for the Census X11 Program," *Journal of the American Statistical Association,* vol. 71, 1976, pp. 581–87.

Croxton, Frederick et al., *Applied General Statistics,* 3rd ed. Englewood Cliffs, N.J.: Prentice Hall, 1967, chapters 4 and 5.

Erickson, B. H. and T. A. Nosanchuk, *Understanding Data.* New York: McGraw-Hill-Ryerson Ltd., 1977.

Everitt, B. S., *Graphical Techniques for Multivariant Data.* New York: North-Holland Publishing Co., 1978.

Hartwig, Frederick and Brian E. Dearing, *Exploratory Data Analysis.* Beverly Hills, Calif.: Sage Publications, 1979.

Hoaglin, D. C., F. Mosteller, and J. W. Tukey, eds., *Understanding Robust and Exploratory Data Analysis.* New York: John Wiley & Sons, 1983.

Honing, Paul F. and David C. Hoaglin, *Applications, Basics and Computing of Exploratory Data Analysis.* Boston: Duxbury Press, 1981.

Kuznets, Simon, *Seasonal Variations in Industry and Trade.* New York: National Bureau of Economic Research, 1933.

McNeil, D. R., *Interactive Data Analysis.* New York: John Wiley & Sons, 1977.

Pack, D. J., "Revealing Time Series Interrelationships," *Decision Sciences,* vol. 8, 1977, pp. 377–402.

Thompson, H. E. and G. C. Tiao, "Analysis of Telephone Data: A Case Study of Forecasting Seasonal Time Series," *Bell Journal of Economics and Management Science,* vol. 2, no. 2, autumn 1971.

Tukey, John W., *Exploratory Data Analysis.* Reading, Mass.: Addison-Wesley, 1977.

4

Forecasting and Forecast Evaluation

INTRODUCTION

Given the macroeconomic overview in chapters 1 and 2 of the forces shaping the environment of the business sector and the basics of data analysis presented in chapter 3, it is now time to turn to the actual techniques forecasters use to select and evaluate various forecasting models. While managers who are concerned with the application of forecasting models and the use of forecast output will argue that their situation is unique, there is a clear body of forecasting techniques that cuts across all applications and that must be mastered before delving into the unique aspects of each industry or firm model.

FORECASTING AND FORECASTING TECHNIQUES

OBJECTIVES OF FORECASTING MODELS

Successful forecasting is much more than the simple extrapolation of historical patterns into the future. At virtually each stage of the forecasting process, managerial input and judgmental decisions are required. Business analysts must always keep in mind that a forecast is not an end product. It is one of many inputs needed by top managers to plan for the future of the business.

The first objective in constructing forecasting models is to reduce (not eliminate) the uncertainties facing a business. Second, a forecasting model must be capable of simulating the consequences of uncertain future events and quantifying the effects of alternative management decisions. Thus, the central problem facing the practicing forecaster is how most effectively to provide projections to managers who are faced with decision alternatives that will shape the future profitability of the company. Finally, forecasts are useful as control mechanisms for management. That is, forecasts provide users and preparers with standards or criteria of performance and procedures for comparing actual performance with projected performance.

Forecasting models represent a simplified version of reality that will, if the model is developed properly, provide an estimate of what is likely to happen under a given set of conditions. For example, a common approach is to develop a forecast for one or more variables under the assumption that "business continues as usual." This business-as-usual scenario is sometimes referred to as the base case forecast from which alternative scenarios are derived. In each of these alternative scenarios, different assumptions must be made and documented.

GROWTH IN FORECASTING

The demand for detailed forecast information has grown steadily for the past 25 years. As organizations and their external environments have become more complex, decision makers find it increasingly important to weigh or consider a wide range of factors (such as changing exchange rates) that could previously be ignored. In addition, forecasting models provide a convenient method for simulating alternative business strategies prior to implementation. Finally, the widespread availability of personal or microcomputers has led to the spread of sophisticated forecasting techniques by an increasing number of users.

FORECASTING STRATEGIES

There are three basic forecasting strategies: the *deterministic strategy*, the *symptomatic strategy*, and the *systematic strategy*. The deterministic strategy assumes that the present bears a close causal relationship with the future. For example, we might predict construction expenditures next year on the basis of construction contract awards already made.

The symptomatic strategy is based on the assumption that present signs and patterns provide a picture of how the future is developing. These signs do not determine the future outlook but reveal the process of change that is already taking place. Just as a falling barometer suggests that a storm is on the horizon, so a decrease in, say, the growth rate of the money supply may be viewed by some analysts as signifying a decline in the future growth rate of the economy. When applied to business and economic forecasting, this symptomatic strategy has led to the identification of leading indicators—time series (such as the growth rate of the money supply) whose movements foreshadow increases or decreases in the level of interest rates.

The systematic strategy assumes the existence of certain underlying regularities (consumer spending will rise in a stable fashion when household disposable income increases) that can be formulated as principles, theories, or laws. Thus, an observation (theory)—the demand for a commodity is (other things being equal) inversely related to price—can be used as the basis for a forecasting model. The test of the soundness of these theories or models is how well their predictions match with observed outcomes in the economy.[1]

CLASSIFICATION OF FORECASTING TECHNIQUES

The seemingly endless variety of situations in which forecasts are prepared has dictated the evolution of an equally divergent collection of techniques, which can be grouped into three general categories: *qualitative techniques*, *quantitative techniques*, and *technological methods*. Qualitative techniques, sometimes referred to as judgmental, nonstatistical, or nonscientific methods, generally rely on expert opinion or intuitive or informed judgments. These techniques are primarily used when historical data are scarce—for example, when a product is first introduced. The common feature of virtually all of these techniques is that they use human judgment and/or rating schemes to translate qualitative assessments into quantitative estimates. The underlying objective of these methods is to assemble in a logical and unbiased fashion all information and judgments that relate to the question at hand. Since there is little or no statistical analysis of historical data, "experts" are called on to present intuitive judgments and to assign subjective probabilities to the alternative scenarios. The more common of these approaches make use of the Delphi method, market research, panel consensus, historical analogy, naive extrapolation, sales force composite forecasts, and the jury of executive opinion. Perhaps the primary limitation of these methods is that we have no objective procedure whereby we can assign probabilities to the likelihood of the forecast's accuracy. This is not meant to suggest that the forecasts generated via qualitative methods are less accurate than those generated from the other two categories, for it is relatively easy to find some "expert forecasters" who seem consistently able to outperform most quantitative methods.

This textbook concentrates on the second of these forecasting classifications—namely, the quantitative or statistical approach—because the basic techniques are more readily learned, and because the qualitative approach cannot be formalized into a systematic series of steps that are widely applicable to a number of situations. Although expert opinion and judgment are invaluable, they represent the end result of years of study and on-the-job training, which cannot be replicated in a textbook. More importantly, most forecasters who are categorized as experts have started with the quantitative approach and developed, over time, qualitative techniques to supplement those portions of the quantitative projections that they believe to be inadequate.

---

[1] David M. Georgoff and Robert G. Murdick, "Manager's Guide to Forecasting," *Harvard Business Review*, January–February 1986, pp. 110–120.

Fortunately, the quantitative approach can be grasped quickly and provides the forecaster with an objective starting point for further refinement. To use this approach, you must have a historical data bank that furnishes a "chronological snapshot" of economic activity in the form of time series data. No matter how complex or sophisticated, all quantitative techniques are based on the assumption of constancy or historical continuity. The underlying economic patterns in the historical data must continue into the future. This need not imply that economic activity is static or unchanging, but it does assume that the pattern or structure of institutional relationships that exists in the historical data continues into the future. This process of projecting historical patterns is referred to as extrapolation.

We can further subdivide the various quantitative forecasting methods into time series and regression. This choice of titles, while commonplace, is unfortunate since it seems to imply that only the former category uses time series data. In fact, both techniques rely on time series data when used for purposes of forecasting. Time series models, or, more precisely, autoregressive models, forecast future values of a variable based entirely on the historical observations of that variable. As presented in this textbook, autoregressive techniques include moving averages, exponential smoothing models, adaptive filtering, time series decomposition, trend extrapolation, and Box-Jenkins.

For example, a simple time series model for retail sales might be formulated as

$$RS_{t+1} = c_0 + c_1 RS_t + c_2 RS_{t-1} \qquad (4\text{-}1)$$

where RS refers to retail sales in the current period, RS_{t-1} to last period's sales, and RS_{t+1} to sales one time period into the future. All autoregressive time series models, from simple trend extrapolations to advanced multivariate Box-Jenkins techniques, are extensions of equation (4-1). Since the forecast of retail sales is based solely on historical observations, this type of model is most satisfactory when cyclical turning points are not expected. Our simple model may indeed provide a reliable forecast of retail sales; however, it is of little value in predicting the impact of alternative prices, management policies, or advertising schemes. Thus, the principal limitation of autoregressive models is that they do not incorporate the impact of alternative marketing mix scenarios.

Regression or causal models are based on insights from economic theory. For example, in place of the autoregressive model for retail sales in equation (4-1), a regression model might take the form

$$RS_t = b_0 + b_1 DI_t + b_2 CPI_t. \qquad (4\text{-}2)$$

Here, retail sales in the current period (RS_t) is linked to disposable income (DI_t) and the current value of the consumer price index (CPI_t). The goal in fitting a regression equation is to find the exact form of the relationship between sales, income, and prices—that is, we want to derive estimates of the regression coefficients (b_0, b_1, b_2) that embody the historical or structural relationship among the three variables. A retail sales model similar to equation (4-2) can be used to provide management with an estimate of the change in sales resulting from a change in prices. The variable to be estimated, retail sales, is referred to as the dependent variable, and the other variables (disposable income and prices) are called independent or causal variables. Regression or causal techniques encompass correlation procedures, regression models, leading-indicator procedures, econometric models, and input-output models.

The third general category of forecasting models—technological methods—attempts to address long-term forecasting issues. These issues could be of a technological, societal, economic, or political nature. In many respects technological forecasting methods combine aspects of the preceding two categories. For example, in assessing the future impact of technological change on worker productivity (a key determinant of the growth rate of the gross national product), we would need to incorporate not only past data on productivity changes but expert opinion about the likely incorporation of future technological breakthroughs that are, as yet, unknown. As was the case with the qualitative or judgmental approach, technological forecasting is beyond the scope of this book. Here, too, quantitative forecasting may be seen as a necessary first step before one can move to technological forecasting.

TECHNIQUE SELECTION

To select a forecasting technique, one must have a working knowledge of the available forecast methodologies as well as an appreciation of the ways in which the following factors complement each technique:

1. The time frame
2. Data patterns
3. Costs
4. Desired accuracy
5. Availability of data
6. Ease of implementation and understanding
7. Accuracy and reliability.

The time frame or time horizon refers to the length of time into the future for which the forecast is desired. Typically, the forecaster is interested in one of the following time frames:

Immediate term: less than one month

Short term: one to six months
Intermediate term: six months to two years
Long term: longer than two years.

While these categories are generally applicable to all businesses, the precise duration of each category is not fixed. For example, a manufacturer of fax machines (which face rapid technological changes) may consider a two-year period to be the long term. On the other hand, a railroad company may view a two-year period as the short term. Additionally, the meaning of these time frames depends on the individual decision maker's position in the firm. Thus, to a production-line supervisor, immediate-term planning may mean an hour or day and long-term a six-month time horizon. Conversely, for the board of directors or the chief executive officer, six-month forecasts may be immediate term. Some models can be appropriately used for immediate- to short-term forecasts while other techniques are more applicable for intermediate- to long-term time frames. For example, moving average and exponential smoothing models are generally more applicable for immediate and short-term forecasts; decomposition models and Box-Jenkins models perform better in generating short-term forecasts; while regression and econometric models tend to perform best with intermediate- to long-term time frames.

Long-term forecasts tend to be related to trend factors such as the demand for the product, the general economic and political environment, technological change, and the competitive structure of the industry. Thus, one might develop a 10-year projection of regional demand patterns that is to be used to determine regional warehouse construction sites. Intermediate-term forecasts are tied to the cyclical factor and might, for example, focus on the allocation of resources among the competing product lines within a firm; alternatively, intermediate projections are used to revise long-term plans in light of cyclical developments. Thus, the marketing department's focus might be on the cyclical nature of sales and proper pricing strategy, while the production department's needs may be cost estimates, budget allocations, and cyclical employment forecasts. Similarly, the financial department will need cash-flow estimates over the course of the business cycle.

Short-term forecasts are tied to seasonality and minor cyclical variations. Within a six-month period turning points can occur, but monthly projections are dominated by seasonal characteristics. Short-term marketing forecasts might involve the evaluation of a promotional campaign or a price change. Production departments must have forecasts of seasonal demand patterns to schedule work shifts. Immediate-term forecasts are generally concerned with the irregular variations in time series data. Thus, in the immediate term, management might be interested in forecasting daily inventory levels or in allocating its fleet of trucks to various regions of its market area.

In general, the longer the time frame, the more useful regression and other causal models become, and the less valuable autoregressive schemes become. In part, this is due to the much more critical role that the assumption of constancy plays in autoregressive models. As the time horizon lengthens, uncertainty increases, as does the need for a theoretical foundation based on structural relationships.

Technique selection is affected by the pattern of the data. Frequently, this pattern is representative of characteristics inherent in the activity being studied. The relation between the data pattern and the time frame becomes obvious when one notes that trend patterns are long-term tendencies, while seasonal variation represents data patterns that repeat themselves within one year. Regression methods can deal with virtually all patterns that can be identified, while autoregressive schemes are better applied to time series that exhibit few turning points. In evaluating alternative techniques relative to data patterns, there is also the possibility that more than one procedure will be applicable to the same set of data. For example, certain techniques may be more accurate in predicting turning points, while others prove to be more reliable in forecasting stable patterns of change. Alternatively, some models may overestimate or underestimate in given situations. Further, it may be the case that the short-term predictions of one model are superior to those of another model, whose long-term prediction powers are more accurate. These examples serve to highlight an important principle in model selection: The technique should be selected so the underlying assumptions match the characteristics of the data. This principle frequently leads to the estimation of more than one forecasting model and has the advantage of avoiding biases that may be inherent in using a single technique.

Technique selection is also influenced by the costs associated with each of the forecasting alternatives. For example, there is the cost associated with formulating and developing the forecasting model. Included in this category would be items such as the labor cost for expert advice in model building, the costs of writing and testing the necessary computer programs, and the cost of internal data generation for use in the model. Regression models must be constructed by people who have expertise in the areas of economic or business theory and statistical estimation. Further, firm- and industry-level regression models must often be augmented by commercial forecast services. The development costs of autoregressive schemes range from less than a hundred dollars for simple moving averages and exponential smoothing methods to several hundred dollars for Box-Jenkins and adaptive filtering techniques.

The costs of collecting and storing the necessary data must be recognized. The major items here are the costs of storing the model and the data. On balance, autoregressive schemes result in larger data-storage costs. Additionally, program-storage costs tend to range from minimal in the simple schemes to extensive in the case of Box-Jenkins. Regression models involve somewhat more sophisticated computer programs and, therefore, higher costs. Data-storage costs for regression models depend on the complexity of the system being constructed.

The third cost component is related to the computer time needed to simulate alternative scenarios, update the model, and select the appropriate parameters. Regression models tend to have the advantage here, because autoregressive techniques require constant updating and experimentation prior to selection of the best smoothing parameters.

Technique selection is related to the level of desired accuracy, but it is difficult to ascertain the level of accuracy until one has closely evaluated the project under consideration. For example, in many situations a rough approximation of future trend patterns will provide sufficiently accurate projections. When a major television network negotiates an advertising contract for a future sporting event, the company purchasing the advertising contract may be satisfied with a judgmental estimate accurate to within ± 20 percent. Similarly, when faced with a location decision for warehouses, management is primarily interested in a reasonable estimation of long-term trends. At the other extreme, a forecast of future demand for electricity must be very refined since the cost of building an excessively large nuclear plant will be borne by utility customers. Likewise, an underestimate of electrical demand will result in inadequate capacity and a potential power shortage. For a utility, therefore, the desired degree of accuracy is tied directly to the negative consequences arising from both underestimates and overestimates.

FORECASTS AND FORECAST ACCURACY

CONCEPT OF A FORECAST

A forecast can be defined as a probabilistic statement concerning future events. Forecasts are made because organizations must have information regarding the occurrence of future events. Even though these future events are unknown, explicit assumptions about future activity levels or changes in current trends enter into present resource allocation decisions. For example, a manager at an electronic components factory may be interested in obtaining personal computer sales forecasts for the next six months to plan for the needed volume of computer boards and other accessories. A government planner wants to determine the potential effect of a policy shift (a lowering of the capital gains tax) on the economy and the budget deficit prior to its actual implementation. Financial managers require cash-flow forecasts to make certain that short-term cash requirements can be met with available internal funds and borrowed external funds. The president of a university needs enrollment projections to plan staffing requirements.

FORECASTING NOTATION

In preparing a forecast based on a statistical model, we customarily begin with a number of observed or actual historical values. Because these observations vary over time, we will use a variable designated by the letter Y. Thus, Y could represent the number of units sold, the interest rate, total volume, or any other similar measure of business activity. Because the majority of forecasting projects are based on time series data, Y takes on different values depending on the time period under investigation. To permit us to monitor the time period of interest, we need a method of identifying the specific period. Following standard notational procedures, we assign consecutive numbers to consecutive time periods. For example, the 12-month period beginning with January 1990 and ending with December 1990 would be referred to as time periods 1, 2, 3, . . . , 12. This permits us to refer to the July 1990 value as Y_7 while the value of Y in December 1990 would be Y_{12}.

While Y_t will be used to represent the actual observation of Y in time period t, $\hat{Y}_t$ will refer to the forecast value. As forecasts are generated, they will be denoted by $\hat{Y}_{t+1}$, $\hat{Y}_{t+2}$, etc., where the $t + 1$ refers to one time period into the future, $t + 2$ to two time periods into the future, and so on. The forecast or prediction error in time period t can be defined as the actual value less the predicted or forecast value:

$$e_t = Y_t - \hat{Y}_t. \tag{4-3}$$

There is an error term associated with each pair of actual and predicted forecast values. For purposes of simplicity, we will have occasion to use the summation sign ($\sum$) to refer to the addition of a number of error terms. The formulation suggested in equation (4-3), while commonplace in computer programs and in statistical writings, presents a problem. When defined as in equation (4-3), a positive value implies that the predicted value fell short of the actual observation (an underestimation) while a negative value suggests that the predicted value exceeded actual performance (an overestimation). To avoid problems when presenting forecasts to management, we therefore suggest that the process of defining the error term be reversed such that positive errors indicate an overestimation while a negative error suggests an underestimate. Mechanically, this simply means that we take the error terms that are produced by the computer program and reverse the signs.[2]

ERROR ANALYSIS

The ultimate test of any forecasting model is how well it forecasts. Specifically, an examination of forecast errors can frequently help us to choose the method that produces the smallest error. An evaluation of the reliability of any technique would, hopefully, be based on the best measure of accuracy. Unfortunately, the method that produces the "smallest" error depends on how the error

---

[2] Formally, the implication of reversing the signs is that we have defined the error term as follows:

$$e_t = \hat{Y}_t - Y_t.$$

is measured and how that measure is interpreted. The good news is that there are innumerable ways of computing error patterns, but the bad news is that the sheer number of alternative measures often leads to confusion. Our approach is to introduce these measures gradually throughout the text. The reason for adopting this approach is that some evaluation techniques are more applicable to certain types of forecast models than to others.

The process of measuring the accuracy of alternative models begins by computing the difference (e_t) between actual or observed values (Y_t) for specific time periods and the model's forecast $(\hat{Y}_t)$ for those periods. There are three general approaches that can be used in making this comparison:

1. The forecast model can be applied to the entire set of data points and the distribution of error terms (e_t) analyzed.
2. The model can be estimated from a subset (for example, the first 10 years of data rather than the entire set of 15 years) of actual data and then tested on the more recent observations that were omitted in the estimation process.
3. The most useful approach is to develop the model based on the entire data set and then evaluate forecasts against each new observation.

MODEL EVALUATION USING ERROR TERMS

Suppose that we have collected the actual sales figures presented in column 1 of Table 4-1. Typically, the analyst is faced with choosing among several forecasting techniques. Columns 2, 6, 10, and 14 of Table 4-1 contain predicted sales values $(\hat{Y}_t)$ generated by models 1, 2, 3, and 4, respectively. The predicted values from these four models are used to derive error terms (e_t) in columns 3, 7, 11, and 15. At this juncture, we are not interested in the specific models that were tested for consideration; rather, our sole purpose here is to illustrate the process of model evaluation by use of error analyses. The remaining columns in Table 4-1 present the error terms—in both real and percentage and cumulative terms—for each of the models.[3]

GRAPHICAL METHODS OF MODEL EVALUATION

Graphical displays of actual values, predicted values, and forecast errors can be a powerful tool in evaluating a model's performance and in identifying potential problems. Graphical methods allow forecasters to quickly and easily evaluate the reliability of any given technique, and they help to identify systematic error patterns. Figure 4-1 provides a comparison of actual versus fitted (predicted) values for each of the four models presented in Table 4-1.

---

[3] The reasons for the time periods in which there are no forecast values will become apparent when the specific types of forecasting models are presented in succeeding chapters.

TABLE 4-1 Historical Performance of Alternative Forecasting Models (sales in thousands)

Date*	Actual Sales (1)	Model 1 Predicted (2)	Model 1 Error (3)	Cumulative Error (4)	Model 1 Percent Error (5)	Model 2 Predicted (6)	Model 2 Error (7)	Cumulative Error (8)	Model 2 Percent Error (9)	Model 3 Predicted (10)	Model 3 Error (11)	Cumulative Error (12)	Model 3 Percent Error (13)	Model 4 Predicted (14)	Model 4 Error (15)	Cumulative Error (16)	Model 4 Percent Error (17)
1979: I	127.6													128.3	0.7	0.7	0.55
II	128.1													127.7	-0.4	0.3	-0.31
III	127.2	128.6	1.4	1.4	1.10					128.2	1.0	1.0	0.79	127.2	0.0	0.3	0.00
IV	125.7	127.0	1.3	2.7	1.03					126.8	1.1	2.1	0.88	126.8	1.1	1.4	0.88
1980: I	125.0	125.1	0.1	2.8	0.08					124.7	-0.3	1.8	-0.24	126.4	1.4	2.8	1.12
II	124.9	124.4	-0.5	2.3	-0.40					124.1	-0.8	1.0	-0.64	126.1	1.2	4.0	0.96
III	126.5	124.4	-2.1	0.2	-1.66					124.4	-2.1	-1.1	-1.66	126.0	-0.5	3.5	-0.40
IV	130.0	126.3	-3.7	-3.5	-2.85	124.4	-5.6	-5.6	-4.31	127.1	-2.9	-4.0	-2.23	125.9	-4.1	-0.6	-3.15
1981: I	134.2	130.3	-3.9	-7.4	-2.91	127.5	-6.7	-12.3	-4.99	132.2	-2.0	-6.0	-1.49	125.8	-8.4	-9.0	-6.26
II	137.0	135.0	-2.0	-9.4	-1.46	132.6	-4.4	-16.7	-3.21	137.6	0.6	-5.4	0.44	125.9	-11.1	-20.1	-8.10
III	135.2	138.0	2.8	-6.6	2.07	138.1	2.9	-13.8	2.14	140.2	5.0	-0.4	3.70	126.1	-9.1	-29.2	-6.73
IV	130.5	136.0	5.5	-1.1	4.21	140.3	9.8	-4.0	7.51	135.9	5.4	5.0	4.14	126.3	-4.2	-33.4	-3.22
1982: I	125.4	130.8	5.4	4.3	4.31	137.5	12.1	8.1	9.65	128.2	2.8	7.8	2.23	126.6	1.2	-32.2	0.96
II	120.1	125.2	5.1	9.4	4.25	130.3	10.2	18.3	8.49	121.4	1.3	9.1	1.08	127.0	6.9	-25.3	5.75
III	115.7	119.5	3.8	13.2	3.28	120.7	5.0	23.3	4.32	115.3	-0.4	8.7	-0.35	127.5	11.8	-13.5	10.20
IV	113.2	114.9	1.7	14.9	1.50	112.4	-0.8	22.5	-0.71	111.0	-2.2	6.5	-1.94	128.1	14.9	1.4	13.16
1983: I	112.4	112.2	-0.2	14.7	-0.18	107.4	-5.0	17.5	-4.45	109.6	-2.8	3.7	-2.49	128.7	16.3	17.7	14.50
II	114.9	111.5	-3.4	11.3	-2.96	105.7	-9.2	8.3	-8.01	110.4	-4.5	-0.8	-3.92	129.5	14.6	32.3	12.71
III	120.7	114.2	-6.5	4.8	-5.39	107.9	-12.8	-4.5	-10.60	115.3	-5.4	-6.2	-4.47	130.3	9.6	41.9	7.95
IV	127.6	120.3	-7.3	-2.5	-5.72	114.4	-13.2	-17.7	-10.34	124.1	-3.5	-9.7	-2.74	131.2	3.6	45.5	2.82
1984: I	134.5	127.6	-6.9	-9.4	-5.13	123.9	-10.6	-28.3	-7.88	133.1	-1.4	-11.1	-1.04	132.2	-2.3	43.2	-1.71
II	140.8	134.9	-5.9	-15.3	-4.19	134.9	-5.9	-34.2	-4.19	140.9	0.1	-11.0	0.07	133.3	-7.5	35.7	-5.33
III	144.9	141.4	-3.5	-18.8	-2.42	145.1	0.2	-34.0	0.14	147.2	2.3	-8.7	1.59	134.4	-10.5	25.2	-7.25
IV	146.2	145.7	-0.5	-19.3	-0.34	152.2	6.0	-28.0	4.10	150.2	4.0	-4.7	2.74	135.7	-10.5	14.7	-7.18
1985: I	146.6	147.0	0.4	-18.9	0.27	155.2	8.6	-19.4	5.87	149.3	2.7	-2.0	1.84	137.0	-9.6	5.1	-6.55
II	146.6	147.4	0.8	-18.1	0.55	154.8	8.2	-11.2	5.59	148.1	1.5	-0.5	1.02	138.4	-8.2	-3.1	-5.59
III	146.2	147.4	1.2	-16.9	0.82	152.3	6.1	-5.1	4.17	147.2	1.0	0.5	0.68	139.9	-6.3	-9.4	-4.31
IV	146.1	146.9	0.8	-16.1	0.55	149.3	3.2	-1.9	2.19	146.2	0.1	0.6	0.07	141.5	-4.6	-14.0	-3.15
1986: I	145.8	146.8	1.0	-15.1	0.69	147.2	1.4	-0.5	0.96	146.0	0.2	0.8	0.14	143.1	-2.7	-16.7	-1.85
II	144.9	146.5	1.6	-13.5	1.10	146.0	1.1	0.6	0.76	145.6	0.7	1.5	0.48	144.9	0.0	-16.7	0.00
III	144.3	145.5	1.2	-12.3	0.83	145.0	0.7	1.3	0.49	144.3	0.0	1.5	0.00	146.7	2.4	-14.3	1.66
IV	144.5	144.9	0.4	-11.9	0.28	144.2	-0.3	1.0	-0.21	143.7	-0.8	0.7	-0.55	148.6	4.1	-10.2	2.84
1987: I	146.4	145.0	-1.4	-13.3	-0.96	143.8	-2.6	-1.6	-1.78	144.3	-2.1	-1.4	-1.43	150.6	4.2	-6.0	2.87
II	150.8	147.0	-3.8	-17.1	-2.52	144.7	-6.1	-7.7	-4.05	147.3	-3.5	-4.9	-2.32	152.7	1.9	-4.1	1.26
III	155.6	151.5	-4.1	-21.2	-2.63	148.3	-7.3	-15.0	-4.69	153.6	-2.0	-6.9	-1.29	154.9	-0.7	-4.8	-0.45
IV	158.5	156.4	-2.1	-23.3	-1.32	154.1	-4.4	-19.4	-2.78	159.6	1.1	-5.8	0.69	157.1	-1.4	-6.2	-0.88
1988: I	158.4	159.3	0.9	-22.4	0.57	160.2	1.8	-17.6	1.14	162.1	3.7	-2.1	2.34	159.5	1.1	-5.1	0.69
II	156.7	159.3	2.6	-19.8	1.66	163.7	7.0	-10.6	4.47	160.1	3.4	1.3	2.17	161.9	5.2	0.1	3.32

* Year and quarter

127

FIGURE 4-1   Graphical Analysis of Fitted versus Actual Sales

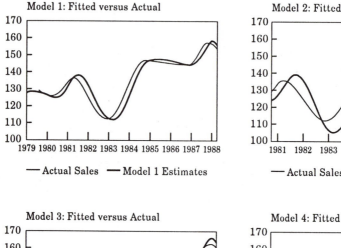

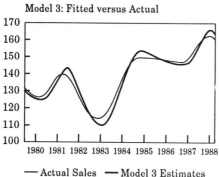

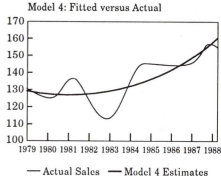

An examination of the four data plots in Figure 4-1 indicates that the historical simulations (predicted values) from models 1 and 3 most closely parallel the pattern exhibited by the actual sales data. Model 1 appears to match the level of actual sales more closely, while model 3 appears to capture the turning points more accurately. Model 2 generates forecasts that are subject to large period errors and overestimates the changes that occur at turning points. Model 4 captures none of the turning points that occurred in actual sales. After a quick appraisal of Figure 4-1, it is clear that models 1 and 3 are worthy of additional consideration while models 2 and 4 can be excluded.

A second graphical approach for determining the reliability of a specific forecasting technique focuses on an inspection of the error terms themselves. Thus, while the preceding approach permitted us to compare the simulated performance of a model with the actual data, it can mask the over- or underestimates that occur in each time period. A plot of the error terms themselves serves to overcome this limitation. If a particular technique forecasts accurately, the error terms should be randomly dispersed about a zero-error line.

FIGURE 4-2   Diagnosing Error Patterns

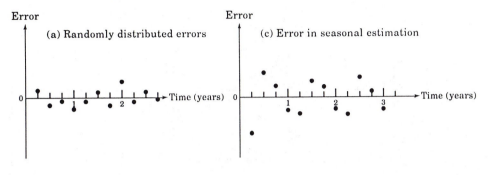

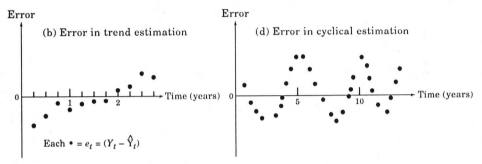

This random distribution corresponds to the irregular component of time series data and is illustrated in Figure 4-2(a). Quadrants (b), (c), and (d) contain nonrandom error patterns. Frequently, when the forecasting technique does not fit the data pattern, the error terms themselves will follow a systematic pattern. In Figure 4-2(b), the error terms appear to lie about an upward-sloping linear trend, and in Figure 4-2(c) the quarterly error terms suggest that the seasonal pattern has not been properly eliminated or accounted for. Finally, the graph illustrated in Figure 4-2(d) suggests that the cyclical pattern in the actual data has not been captured by the model.[4]

Figure 4-3 provides a portrait of the error plots for each of the four models estimated in Table 4-1, and all four exhibit systematic error patterns. When contrasted with the graph provided in Figure 4-2(d), we can conclude that all of the error plots associated with model 4 exhibit a cyclical pattern, but model 4 is the worst in terms of capturing turning points. The next stage would be to compare the absolute size of the error terms associated with each of the remaining three models. Remember, however, that error plots such as those presented in Figure 4-3 are subject to misinterpretation because of the scale

[4] As we see in chapters 5 and 6, a pattern in the error terms similar to that presented in Figure 4-2(d) can also be indicative of a statistical problem referred to as autocorrelation.

FIGURE 4-3   Error Plots for Alternative Forecasting Models

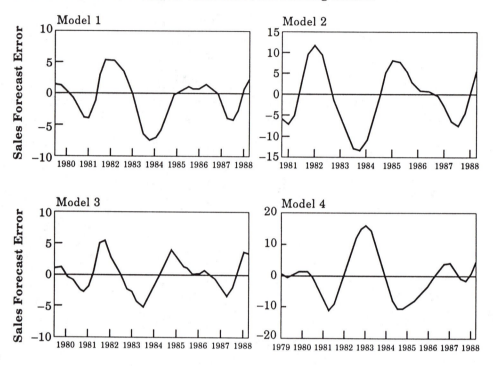

that is used on the vertical axis. That is, both the size and pattern of the error terms are sensitive to the scale that is selected. While it appears that the error patterns of models 1, 2, and 3 are similar, an examination of the vertical scale indicates that model 2 generates much larger errors than do the other two models. We are, therefore, left with the same conclusion that we obtained from Figure 4-1—the two most satisfactory models are models 1 and 3.

Control charts can be regarded as a third graphical means used in gauging a model's reliability.[5] To construct a control chart, forecast error and cumulative forecast error must be computed. The error and cumulative error terms for model 1 are presented in columns 3 and 4 of Table 4-1, respectively; for model 2, refer to columns 7 and 8; for model 3, refer to columns 11 and 12; and for model 4, refer to columns 15 and 16. The cumulative errors used in the control charts presented here are based on a two-period summation of forecast errors. For example, the second cumulative error term for model 1, 2.7, is the sum of the forecast error in the third quarter of 1979 (1.4) and the forecast error in the fourth quarter of 1979 (1.3). The remaining cumulative

---

[5] Control charts are also used as monitoring devices. This process is illustrated in chapter 11, where we discuss monitoring tools and techniques.

FIGURE 4-4   Control Chart for Alternative Forecasting Models

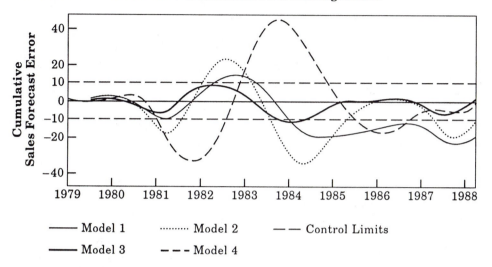

errors are derived by adding the last cumulative value and the forecast error in the most recent time period.[6] If there is no bias in the forecasting model, the cumulative errors should be randomly disbursed around and close to zero. A pattern of cumulative errors moving systematically away from zero in either direction is a signal that the model is generating biased forecasts. A bias toward overestimation is depicted by significant deviations above zero, while a bias toward overestimation produces a pattern below the zero line.

There is one additional aspect of control charts that requires judgment on the part of either management or the forecaster: A decision establishing the upper and lower control limits must be made. As a practical matter, there are many guidelines that are suggested for establishing these control limits. For example, one fairly common rule of thumb is that the control limits are equal to two or three times the standard error (a statistical average of all errors), while another rule would be based on the forecasting error that management is willing to accept. Suppose that management tells us that they are not willing to accept a forecast error in excess of ±10,000 units. With this as a guideline, the control limits are plotted in Figure 4-4. An examination of the cumulative error plots for the four models indicates that only model 3 generated historical forecasts that fell within this guideline. Thus, based on the control chart, we would conclude that model 3 was providing the most reliable forecasts. Alternatively, each of the other three models produced forecasts that contained either a bias toward over- or underestimation.

---

[6] When used as a control chart, these summations can include more than one preceding time period.

FIGURE 4-5   Turning-Point Error Diagram

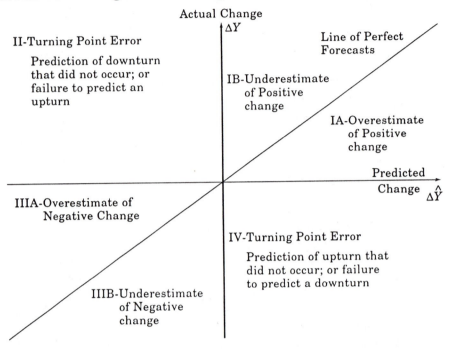

The final graphical device that is used in model evaluation is known as a turning-point diagram or a prediction-realization (P/R) diagram. This approach focuses specifically on the reliability of estimated models to capture turning points in the actual data and the model's tendency to generate false turning points. In Figure 4-5, actual changes in the data are measured along the vertical axis, and forecast changes are measured along the horizontal axis. To obtain the values required for construction of a P/R diagram, we begin by computing the actual and forecast changes. Forecast or predicted change is defined as

$$\Delta \hat{Y}_t = \hat{Y}_t - \hat{Y}_{t-1}. \tag{4-4}$$

Conversely, changes in the actual data—the vertical axis—are defined as

$$\Delta Y_t = Y_t - Y_{t-1}. \tag{4-5}$$

The diagonal line represents perfect forecasts in that a set of absolutely accurate forecasts will be represented by points along this line.

There are six types of errors that can be generated with forecasting models. Four error categories represent overestimates or underestimates,

FIGURE 4-6   Turning-Point Analysis for Model 4

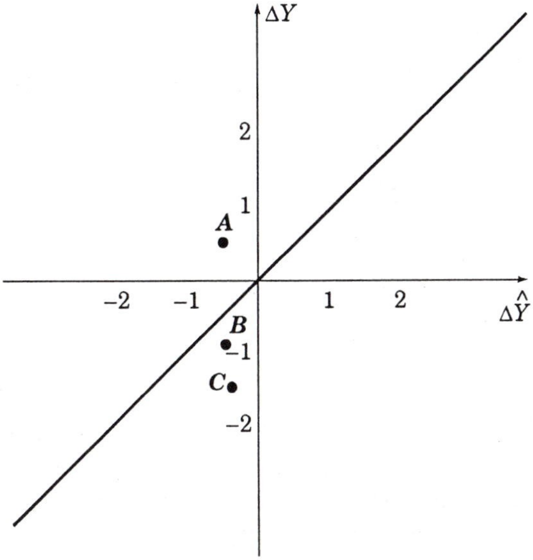

while two represent turning-point error (prediction of a positive change when a negative change occurred or prediction of a negative change when a positive change occurred). Explicit consideration of the types of errors associated with any specific forecasting model can be extremely critical to management since, in many instances, managers are more interested in having some information regarding potential turning points than they are in trend patterns. For example, a model that frequently generates turning-point errors is probably missing the cyclical component of the data, or it may be overly sensitive to changes in the explanatory variables. In Figure 4-5, zones IIIA and IA represent, respectively, zones of overestimation for an actual decline (IIIA) or gain (IA); zones IB and IIIB represent, respectively, zones of underestimation for an actual gain (IB) or decline (IIIB). Zones II and IV are turning-point error zones; that is, the model predicted a downturn that did not occur (zone II) or failed to predict an upturn (zone II); or an upturn was predicted and failed to materialize, or a downturn was not predicted (zone IV). If there is a large number of points in quadrants II and IV, the estimated model has either misspecified the structural relationship or is missing the cyclical variations.[7]

To illustrate the process of computing the actual and predicted changes, suppose that we focus on the first four quarters of 1979 and use model 4 as our example. Table 4-2 and Figure 4-6 present the changes that are necessary

---

[7] As was the case with control charts, prediction-realization diagrams can be used as monitoring devices.

TABLE 4-2   Actual and Predicted Changes in Sales (Model 4)

Date[a]	Y Actual Value	$\hat{Y}$ Predicted Value	ΔY Actual Change	$\Delta \hat{Y}$ Predicted Change
1979:I	127.6	128.3		
1979:II	128.1	127.7	0.5	−0.6 **A**[b]
1979:III	127.2	127.2	−0.9	−0.5 **B**
1979:IV	125.7	126.8	−1.5	−0.4 **C**

[a] Year and quarter
[b] Each of these sets of ordered pairs (denoted by the boldface letters) is plotted in Figure 4-6 and is labeled accordingly.

for a turning-point diagram. Similarly, Figures 4-7(a), 4-7(b), 4-7(c), and 4-7(d) present the turning-point diagrams for each of the four models presented in Table 4-1. An examination of the four components of this diagram reveals that the smallest number of turning-point errors occurred with models 2 and 3 (one turning-point error); model 1 has the next fewest turning-point errors (three); while model 4 generated six turning-point errors.

Although the graphical approach to model evaluation has merit, it also has certain disadvantages, since a scatter diagram may exhibit no discernible pattern despite the fact that the model is generating unreliable forecasts. Second, it may be difficult to make the final model selection via the graphical approach. For example, in our situation, we have been able to narrow the reliable models to numbers 1 and 3. Third, when there is a large number of data points, the graphical approach requires access to relatively sophisticated computer graphics. Finally, as is the case with all graphical methods, the interpretation of a model's performance can be influenced by the scale that is chosen for presentation. For these reasons, numerous quantitative criteria are used in conjunction with the graphical tools.

STATISTICAL METHODS

As was true with the graphical tools that are used in model evaluation, all of the statistical or quantitative tools that are available are based on an analysis of the error terms associated with the historical simulation. Before defining each of these statistical measures, there are three general guidelines. First, unless otherwise noted, the smaller the value of the statistic the more indicative it is of a reliable model. Second, the statistics are most meaningful when used to compare the relative performance of alternative models. When used to gauge the reliability of only one model, it becomes difficult to interpret their relative size. For example, if a model has an error of 5 percent, the analyst

FIGURE 4-7 Turning-Point Analysis of Alternative Forecasting Models

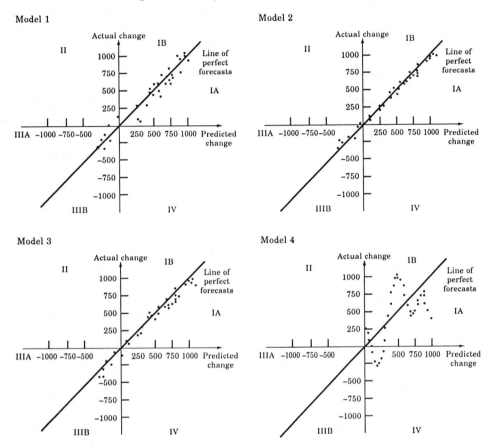

must arbitrarily decide whether or not this is a large error. Third, since the quantitative statistics are based on the historical simulation, they serve only as a guideline to the model's reliability in generating future forecasts.

The first measure of accuracy is the consistency of performance coefficient, which quantifies the frequency with which a forecasting method produces an error that is equal to or smaller than a desired limit set by management. Typically, this limit is based on the lead time required by managers to adjust the underlying business activities (financing, shipping, assembly-line production, purchasing) of the company. Each manager specifies the maximum error with which he or she can cope without adversely affecting company objectives. The shorter the lead time that a manager has, the lower error tolerance will tend to be. Once this limit is specified, we count the number of periods in which the percentage difference between the historically simulated forecast and the actual observation falls within this limit and divide this number by the total number of periods in the model. This quotient is then multiplied by 100 to obtain the percentage frequency. Assuming an error limit of ±5 percent, the results for the four models in Table 4-1 are as follows:

1. Model 1 has 36 periods in which a forecast value is available, and there were 29 periods in which the forecast error was less than or equal to the limit of 5 percent. This translates to a consistency of performance coefficient of 80.6 and means that model 1 generated acceptable forecasts 80.6 percent of the time.
2. Using the same process for model 2, there are 12 periods out of 31 in which the forecast falls within the limits and yields a consistency of performance coefficient of 38.7 percent.
3. For models 3 and 4, the consistency of performance coefficients were 91.7 and 63.2 percent, respectively.

The range of error statistics supply us with an indication of the spread between the largest overestimation and the largest underestimation. Model 1 overestimated actual sales by 4.3 percent in the first quarter of 1982 and underestimated actual sales by 5.7 percent in the fourth quarter of 1983; for model 2, the range went from an overestimate of 9.6 percent to an underestimate of 10.6 percent; for model 3, the range was from 4.1 percent over to 4.5 percent under; for model 4 it was from 14.5 percent above to 8.1 percent under.

Another widely used test is a variant of the turning-point diagram, and it uses a comparison of the signs of the predicted changes and actual changes to evaluate the model's ability to correctly predict turning points. For example, suppose we have a series that rises, declines, and then rises again in three successive periods. Furthermore, suppose that the forecast method predicts three increases. In this situation, we have missed one turning point; thus we have made one turning-point error. The pattern in the actual series was + − +, whereas in the predicted series it was + + +. We have missed the directional change between periods 1 and 2. Further, quoting Zarnowitz,

> In evaluating turning point errors, two questions must be asked: (1) How often do turning points occur that have not been predicted? (2) How often do predicted turns actually occur? Accordingly, there are two basic types of error: missed turns and false signals.[8]

False signals would be exemplified by a pattern of + + + for actual values, as opposed to a predicted pattern of + − +.

In contrast, there are two types of correct forecasts. In one, a turning

---

[8] Victor Zarnowitz, *An Appraisal of Short Term Economic Forecasts* (New York: National Bureau of Economic Research, 1967), pp. 51–59.

point was predicted and it actually occurred; in the other, no turning point was predicted and none occurred. Again, quoting Zarnowitz,

> Thus there are four basic possibilities, which can be arranged in a 2 × 2 table as follows. (N refers to the absence, T to the presence of a turning point. The first letter refers to actual values, the second to forecasts.)

| | *Forecast* | |
Actual	*No TP*	*TP*
No TP	NN	NT
TP	TN	TT

> The number of correct forecasts is the sum of the diagonal frequencies: NN + TT. False signals are represented by NT and missed turns by TN.[9]

To compute the proportion of false signals, we use the ratio

$$\overline{E}_{T1} = \frac{NT}{NT + TT} \qquad \text{(4-6)}$$

whereas the missed signals are given by

$$\overline{E}_{T2} = \frac{TN}{TN + TT}. \qquad \text{(4-7)}$$

For example, when applied to model 1, we find that NN equals 25; NT equals 4; TN equals 4; and TT equals 2. Model 1, therefore, generated false signals 67 percent of the time (that is, 67 percent of the time when the model predicted a change in direction, it was incorrect):

$$\overline{E}_{T1} = \frac{4}{4 + 2} = 67\%. \qquad \text{(4-8)}$$

Conversely, model 1 missed turning points 67 percent of the time:

$$\overline{E}_{T2} = \frac{4}{4 + 2} = 67\%. \qquad \text{(4-9)}$$

Computations for the missed and false signals for the remaining models would be derived in an identical fashion and are summarized in Table 4-3.

[9] Ibid., p. 52.

TABLE 4-3   Statistical Measures of Reliability

Statistic	Model Number			
	1	2	3	4
Consistency of Performance	80.6	38.7	**91.7**	63.2
Range of Error				
Largest Overestimate—Percent	4.3	9.6	**4.1**	14.5
Largest Underestimate—Percent	5.7	10.6	**4.5**	8.1
Turning-Point Performance				
False Signals	67%	100%	50%	100%
Missed Signals	67%	100%	50%	100%
Mean Square Error	11.3	47.4	**6.7**	49.9
Mean Absolute Deviation	2.66	5.78	**2.08**	5.38
Mean Absolute Percentage Error	2.00	4.33	**1.56**	4.12
Mean Error: Bias	−0.56	−0.35	**−0.03**	N/A*
Mean Percent Error: Bias	−0.39	−0.33	**−0.05**	N/A

* N/A = not applicable

The remaining evaluation statistics are based on various summations and interpretations of the error-term columns presented in Table 4-1. For this reason, our objectives in presenting these statistics are to (1) present the formulas that are required to compute the statistics, (2) provide an interpretation of the various statistics using model 1 as the illustration, and (3) detail the limitations of each of the statistics.

Another of the accuracy statistics is the mean square error, or MSE:

$$\text{MSE} = \frac{\sum\limits_{t=1}^{n} (e_t^2)}{n} .$$

(4-10)

An examination of Table 4-3 indicates that for model 1, the mean square error is 11.3. This statistic is most useful if management is not overly concerned with consistent small errors but rather wants to minimize the occurrence of a major error. The MSE satisfies this requirement because it severely penalizes a technique that generates large forecasting errors. For example, if we have a model that generates errors of 10, 1, 1, 1, 1, the MSE is 20.8. Applying a different model to the same data set yields errors of 5, 5, 5, 7, 7, or an MSE of 45.6. The principal limitation of this statistic is that it is difficult to provide management with a straightforward interpretation of the mean square error. In addition, the MSE measure may be overly sensitive to an error pattern that displays a small number of large errors (for example, in the preceding example, it is likely that a model with the 10, 1, 1, 1, 1 error pattern will prove to be more reliable on the average than a model with the error pattern of 5, 5, 5, 7, 7). Finally, the MSE does not provide information as to whether or not a model is systematically over- or underestimating relative to actual values.

To overcome the problem of overpenalizing a technique for a few large errors, the mean absolute deviation, MAD, is used. The mean absolute deviation is given by

$$\text{MAD} = \frac{\sum\limits_{t=1}^{n} |e_t|}{n}. \tag{4-11}$$

For model 1, the mean absolute deviation is 2.66, which implies that the average error when measured in units is 2.66 thousand units (2,660 units). The principal advantages of this statistic are its ease of interpretation and the fact that each error term is assigned the same weight. Due to the fact that we have taken the absolute value of the error terms, this statistic ignores the importance of systematic over- or underestimations.

The third measure is the mean absolute percentage error, MAPE. Conceptually, this measure is similar to the MAD except that it is expressed in percentage terms. Percentage error measures prove to be especially useful when the units of measurement of Y are relatively large. It may be difficult to decide whether an error of 500,000 units is large or small without some reference point. For example, if Y is measured in billions of units, then 500,000 is a relatively small average error, whereas if Y is measured in thousands of units it is a large average error. Thus, the advantage of the mean absolute percentage error is that it implicitly relates the size of the error term to actual observations:

$$\text{MAPE} = \sum\limits_{t=1}^{n} \frac{|(e_t/Y_t)\cdot 100|}{n}. \tag{4-12}$$

When applied to the forecasts from model 1, the MAPE is 2 percent, which implies that the historical simulation has an average error of 2 percent. The most significant limitation of this statistic is that it fails to take systematic over- or underestimations into consideration.

The mean error (bias) and the mean percent error (percent bias) attempt to take into consideration a model's tendency to over- or underestimate relative to actual observations. The formulas for these two statistics are as follows:

$$\text{Mean Error (Bias)} = \frac{\sum\limits_{t=1}^{n} e_t}{n} \tag{4-13}$$

and

$$\text{Mean Percent Error (Percent Bias)} = \frac{\sum\limits_{t=1}^{n} (e_t/Y_t)}{n}. \qquad \textbf{(4-14)}$$

If the error terms are randomly dispersed about zero, their average should be zero or close to zero. If the mean error is significantly greater or less than zero, it implies that the model exhibits a tendency either to over- or underestimate, respectively. When viewed from a managerial perspective, this over- or underestimating tendency of a model may carry significant implications. For example, an overestimate of sales may have significant inventory cost implications, while an underestimate, although costly in terms of lost sales, minimizes the negative cash flow associated with purchasing inventories. For this reason, management might indicate that overestimates of sales have much more serious implications than do underestimates. When this situation prevails, the analyst might rely on either of these two bias measures.

When applied to the forecasts generated by model 1, the mean error is -0.56 and the mean percentage error is -0.39 percent. Interpreting these statistics is relatively easy, as the value of the bias measures for model 1 implies that, on average, the forecasts have underestimated actual volumes by 0.56 thousand units (560 units) or have underestimated by 0.39 percent. The principal limitation of these two measures is that the mathematical characteristics of some of the forecasting models to be presented in this text do not lend themselves to calculation of the mean error and mean percent error statistics. For example, because of their mathematical formulation, regression models will generate errors that sum to zero.

The models that perform best according to the various statistical measures are highlighted in boldface. An examination of Table 4-3 indicates that, for all error measurements, model 3 performs best. Additionally, Table 4-3 spotlights the advantage of using these statistics to compare the relative performance of alternative models rather than using them to evaluate only one model's performance. The drawback of these statistics is that the models are being benchmarked against the same data set from which the model is derived. To overcome this problem, there is also a series of *ex post* evaluation techniques that can be applied to alternative models. To derive these statistics, the following steps are necessary:

1. The model is estimated based on a truncated sample period (i.e., the entire data base is not used). A common practice is to omit from 6 to 18 months so you have enough data points to compute the statistics and, at the same time, provide the forecaster with a meaningful interpretation. The models presented in Table 4-1 were estimated through the second quarter of 1988, and we have omitted the last six quarters through the end of 1989.

2. The model is then used to generate forecasts for the six omitted quarters.
3. The ex post forecasts are then compared with the actual values.
4. Once the superior model(s) are identified, they are then reestimated using all available data.

When ex post forecasts are used, the error terms measure the difference between the ex post forecasts and the actual values which were excluded from the original model. The statistics used for error evaluation in ex post forecasts are as follows:

1. Root Mean Square Error (RMS) $= \sqrt{\dfrac{\sum\limits_{t=1}^{n} e_t^2}{n}}$ (4-15)

2. Root Percent Mean Square (R%MS) $= \sqrt{\dfrac{\sum\limits_{t=1}^{n} (e_t^2/Y_t)}{n}}$ (4-16)

3. Mean Error (Bias): formula same as in equation (4-13)
4. Mean Percent Error (Percent Bias): formula same as in equation (4-14).

The root mean square error carries the same interpretation as the mean absolute deviation. It provides a measure of the average error measured in the same units as the actual observations. The root percent mean square is interpreted as the average error from the simulation measured in percentage terms and is similar to the MAPE. The final two statistics carry exactly the same interpretation as noted in the preceding sections of this discussion.

Table 4-4 presents the results of the six-period-ahead simulations from the four models and the respective simulation statistics. Applying these four ex post statistics to the alternative models under consideration here, the conclusion would be that model 2 provides the most accurate forecasts. An alternative approach to ex post forecast evaluation is to conduct a number of simulations in which we add one additional period to the data set with each simulation. Table 4-5 presents the results of this sequential set of simulations using model 3. These simulation statistics are then averaged for the set of sequential simulations. For example, the average RMS would be 11.06; the average R%MS equals 6.21 percent; the average BIAS equals -9.49; while the average percent BIAS is -5.37 percent. This process of conducting sequential simulations and computing average simulation statistics would then be repeated for all of the alternative models under consideration.

There are a number of alternative data-splitting strategies that differ

TABLE 4-4 Ex Post Simulation Results and Statistics

Date*	Actual	Simulation Forecast		Model 3	Model 4
		Model 1	Model 2		
1988:III	156.6	157.5	163.1	156.5	164.4
1988:IV	157.3	158.3	165.4	156.0	167.0
1989:I	160.8	159.1	167.7	155.5	169.6
1989:II	168.9	159.8	170.1	155.1	172.4
1989:III	178.6	160.6	172.4	154.6	175.2
1989:IV	188.3	161.4	174.7	154.2	178.2
		Simulation Statistics			
	RMS	11.13	6.07	15.53	6.54
	R%MS	6.25	3.71	8.75	4.10
	BIAS	− 7.50	1.95	− 11.63	4.18
	%BIAS	− 4.23	1.37	− 6.64	2.68

* Year and quarter

from the aforementioned approach. The appropriateness of a particular strategy is dependent on the number of available data points and the forecast horizon (how many periods into the future forecasts are to be prepared). One popular strategy is to use half of the sample data set to estimate the model and the other half to validate the model. Another strategy, called double cross-validation, splits the actual observations into two subsets. A model is estimated

TABLE 4-5 Sequential Simulations for Model 3

Dates Simulated*	1988:II	Model Estimated Through				
		1988:III	1988:IV	1989:I	1989:II	1989:III
1988:III	156.5					
1988:IV	156.0	156.2				
1989:I	155.5	155.8	157.5			
1989:II	155.1	155.5	157.7	162.7		
1989:III	154.6	155.1	157.9	164.8	174.1	
1989:IV	154.2	154.7	158.2	166.9	179.7	183.7
		Simulation Statistics				
RMS	15.53	16.64	16.02	11.39	2.21	4.60
R%MS	8.75	9.37	9.01	6.39	1.24	2.50
BIAS	− 11.63	− 13.55	− 14.13	− 10.86	− 2.14	− 4.60
%BIAS	− 6.64	− 7.73	− 8.03	− 6.13	− 1.20	− 2.50

* Year and quarter

from the first subset and tested on the other subset; this procedure is then repeated, with the second subset serving as the in-sample estimation set and the first subset serving as the test set.

THE RELATIONSHIP OF MODEL FIT TO FORECASTING

Forecasters learn through bitter experience that a forecasting model that seems well suited to historical data does not necessarily provide the best forecasts. Despite the fact that there is ample evidence to prove this claim, virtually all of the tools that we have presented for assessing the accuracy of various forecasting models are based on how well the models fit the pattern exhibited by the historical data. The primary reason for this approach to model evaluation is that information relative to the success of an actual forecast (a prediction beyond the time period for which we have actual values for Y) can only be obtained after the actual results are recorded. While it is true that the data-splitting process that was used in our discussion of model evaluation does provide a crude method for testing the model against values that were not included in the model, it is also true that we do not know how the model will perform in generating future forecasts. The general assumption is that the model that grades out the highest based on its accuracy in the historical simulation will also be the best forecasting model.

The accuracy statistics generated from the historical simulation should serve only as guidelines. Thus, for example, if the average percent error of the historical simulation is 2.5 percent, forecasts for future time periods will most certainly yield an average error of at least 2.5 percent—a shocking conclusion for first-time forecasters (or top management) who assume that historical reliability can be taken as a gauge of the accuracy of their future forecasts.

MODELS AND FORECASTING

Business and economic forecasts, if properly constructed and presented, are an integral part of decision making. Although the primary goal of forecasting is to assist management in understanding the implications of currently available courses of action (choices) on the future success of the organization, forecasting models such as those presented in Table 4-1 are abstractions from reality. A complete listing of all factors affecting the outcome of a firm's decisions would be overwhelming. Models focus on a few characteristics in a way that is simple to understand and manipulate yet realistic enough to permit satisfactory results whenever the model is used in decision making. The acid test of a model's utility is whether or not it provides reliable predictions. Since models must be continually revised, modeling implies a learning process in which the original model is formulated and the parameters (measurable relationships) are estimated. Once they are estimated, this model provides decision makers with the likely outcomes of alternative choices. The resulting decisions, in turn, lead to actual outcomes that are then compared with the forecast outcome. If the predicted result varies widely from the actual outcome, a critical appraisal must first be made to see if the underlying set of forecast assumptions has been seriously violated. If the assumptions are incorrect, the model should be resimulated to determine whether the ex post forecast is accurate given a proper set of assumptions. If the forecasts are still at variance with the actual results, the model must be either revised or replaced. Thus, forecasting is a continuous process of technique selection, model construction, and forecast evaluation.

SUMMARY

A key element in the forecasting process is the development and implementation of reliable tools for evaluating the reliability of both ex ante and ex post forecasts. The objectives in this chapter have been to set forth (1) the basic concepts of forecasting and (2) the various methods of forecast evaluation. Prior to becoming involved in the development of specific forecasting models, the analyst would do well to understand both the various forecasting strategies and the factors that relate to technique selection.

In the process of evaluating forecasting models, there are numerous graphical and statistical tools available to the practitioner. The utility of these tools lies in the comparison of alternative models and their implications regarding the accuracy of forecasts into the future.

QUESTIONS FOR DISCUSSION AND ANALYSIS

1. Suppose that the following four models have been given to you for your evaluation (sales are measured in thousands of units):

| Date | Actual Sales | Historical Simulations | | | |
		Model 1	Model 2	Model 3	Model 4
1987: Jan.	16,299				14,638
Feb.	16,669				15,632
Mar.	17,171	17,039		16,743	16,597
Apr.	17,801	17,607	17,607	17,433	17,533
May	18,507	18,302	18,367	18,249	18,441
June	19,245	19,059	19,175	19,091	19,319
July	19,965	19,834	19,967	19,914	20,169
Aug.	20,622	20,576	20,694	20,668	20,990
Sept.	21,208	21,240	21,311	21,311	21,783
Oct.	21,715	21,822	21,830	21,852	22,546
Nov.	22,176	22,317	22,262	22,295	23,281
Dec.	22,639	22,764	22,660	22,696	23,988

(Continued)

Historical Simulations

Date	Actual Sales	Model 1	Model 2	Model 3	Model 4
1988: Jan.	23,168	23,215	23,101	23,125	24,665
Feb.	23,784	23,740	23,664	23,666	25,313
Mar.	24,518	24,360	24,357	24,333	25,934
Apr.	25,378	25,105	25,193	25,152	26,525
May	26,328	25,983	26,175	26,119	27,088
June	27,334	26,955	27,233	27,173	27,622
July	28,324	27,983	28,312	28,262	28,127
Aug.	29,294	28,992	29,322	29,291	28,603
Sept.	30,160	29,978	30,274	30,268	29,051
Oct.	30,920	30,853	31,078	31,091	29,470
Nov.	31,536	31,616	31,733	31,773	29,860
Dec.	31,966	32,229	32,224	32,279	30,221
1989: Jan.	32,251	32,647	32,489	32,562	30,554
Feb.	32,342	32,916	32,609	32,695	30,858
Mar.	32,310	32,984	32,530	32,617	31,133
Apr.	32,129	32,926	32,339	32,430	31,380
May	31,871	32,715	32,022	32,101	31,598
June	31,582	32,427	31,652	31,724	31,787
July	31,350	32,109	31,309	31,357	31,947
Aug.	31,223	31,852	31,090	31,110	32,079
Sept.	31,224	31,704	31,043	31,027	32,182
Oct.	31,356	31,690	31,161	31,117	32,256
Nov.	31,575	31,812	31,422	31,362	32,301
Dec.	31,850	32,024	31,750	31,688	32,318

a. Plot the fitted versus actual values. Which of the four models most closely matches the pattern in actual data?

b. Plot a control chart diagram using 1.5 percent as the control limit. Which of the models performs best according to this graph?

c. Plot the error diagrams. Can you determine which of the four models is most accurate? What problems do you have with these diagrams?

d. Plot the turning-point diagrams. Which of the four models performs best when viewed relative to its accuracy in predicting turning points?

e. Determine how many missed and false signals each of the four models generates.

f. Derive the consistency of performance statistics for the four models. Which of the models performs best according to this criteria?

g. What is the range of error for each of the models? Which of the models performs best according to this criteria?

h. Compute the MSE, MAD, and MAPE statistics for each of the four models. Which model performs best according to these statistics?

i. Compute the bias and percent bias statistics for each of the four models. Which model performs best according to each of these measures? What information do we obtain from these two statistics that we do not get from the preceding statistical measures?

j. What are the limitations of the various statistical evaluation statistics? What are their advantages?

k. The simulations for each of the four models are as follows:

Date	Actual Sales	Model 1	Model 2	Model 3	Model 4
1990: Jan.	32,088	32,294	32,097	32,047	32,306
Feb.	32,250	32,739	32,358	32,258	32,265
Mar.	32,297	33,183	32,612	32,470	32,196
Apr.	32,222	33,627	32,870	32,681	32,098
May	32,062	34,072	33,125	32,893	31,971
June	31,845	34,516	33,382	33,104	31,815

Using the four simulation statistics presented in the text (RMS, R%MS, bias, percent bias), which of the four models performs best according to each of these criteria?

2. Suppose that we have conducted a series of sequential simulations based on model 2 in the text. The results of these sequential simulations are as follows:

Sequential Simulations from Model 2

Dates Simulated*	Actual Sales	Model Estimated Through					
		1988:II	1988:III	1988:IV	1989:I	1989:II	1989:III
1988: III	156.6	163.1					
IV	157.3	165.4	160.3				
1989: I	160.8	167.7	163.5	167.7			
II	168.9	170.1	166.6	167.9	168.1		
III	178.6	172.4	169.7	178.1	178.7	175.1	
IV	188.3	174.7	184.8	187.2	188.9	186.8	185.1

* Year and quarter

a. Compute the mean error (bias) and the mean percent error (percent bias) for each of these simulations.

b. Compute the average of each of the statistics derived in step a.

c. How does this model compare with the results presented for model 3 in the text?

3. Describe the key factors that might influence the selection of a specific forecasting technique in the women's clothing industry? Are these the same factors one would consider in the men's clothing industry? How would these two examples differ from the situation in the home microwave industry?

4. What potential problems occur when a forecast is used as a goal? Is the process of setting a growth target of 6 percent in company sales the same as taking a statistical forecast for 6 percent growth and converting it into a goal?

5. What is the most important factor when selecting a forecasting technique? Consider the three industries mentioned in question 1.

6. How has the introduction of high-powered microcomputers altered cost as a factor in the selection of forecasting techniques? In the need for a large corporate staff to carry out forecasting projects?

7. Consider the case of a corporation that runs a regional chain of department stores. How would the corporation's five-year plan differ from its five-year forecast?

8. What is the principal objective in making a business-as-usual forecast? A worst-case forecast? A best-case forecast?

9. Discuss the various types of forecasting strategies available to an analyst in the personal computer industry.

10. When conducting a turning-point analysis of a forecasting technique, how are false signals distinguished from missed signals?

11. "As long as the accuracy from forecasts can be increased by allocating more resources to the forecasting function, management should approve the allocation." Evaluate the validity of this argument.

12. In the case of the regional department store chain, what are the likely sources of uncertainty in its economic future? How could forecasts reduce the uncertainty? Increase the uncertainty?

13. Despite the criticism leveled at forecasters and forecast accuracy, there has been a tremendous growth in the demand for economic projections by businesses, government, and nonprofit institutions. How can these two facts be reconciled?

14. What is the difference between a deterministic and symptomatic strategy? Between a symptomatic and systematic strategy?

15. What is the central distinction between qualitative and quantitative forecasting? How does a forecaster develop qualitative forecasting techniques?

16. Distinguish between autoregressive and regression approaches to forecasting.

17. How is the pattern of the data related to the time frame when choosing among various forecasting techniques? How do these factors affect technique selection?

18. What information do forecasters obtain from fitted versus predicted diagrams? From error plots? From control charts? From turning-point or prediction-realization diagrams?

19. What are the advantages (limitations) of various graphical techniques when used for model evaluation?

20. What is the difference between evaluating a model's performance in historical simulations and its accuracy in forecasting into the future?

21. Suppose that you are given the following results with respect to the historical reliability of five alternative forecasting models:

Date*	Actual	Model 1	Model 2	Model 3	Model 4	Model 5
1989: 1	98,991	98,646	99,124	99,096	99,158	99,526
2	100,440	100,671	101,174	101,220	101,148	101,631
3	101,398	102,111	102,625	102,311	102,170	103,736
4	102,248	103,042	103,556	102,724	102,602	105,840
5	103,239	103,862	104,375	103,179	103,152	107,945
6	104,139	104,831	105,346	104,124	104,159	110,049

(Continued)

Date*	Actual	Model 1	Model 2	Model 3	Model 4	Model 5
7	104,803	105,707	106,222	105,107	105,085	112,154
8	105,392	106,341	106,852	105,644	105,585	114,259
9	106,270	106,899	107,405	106,037	106,019	116,363
10	107,713	107,758	108,264	106,931	107,004	118,468
11	109,719	109,199	109,717	108,732	108,874	120,572
12	112,016	111,221	111,761	111,302	111,444	122,677
1990: 1	114,454	113,540	114,108	114,095	114,168	124,781
2	117,000	116,004	116,601	116,786	116,822	126,886
3	119,760	118,577	119,206	119,465	119,492	128,991
4	122,709	121,368	122,033	122,360	122,413	131,095
5	125,727	124,351	125,056	125,516	125,563	133,200
6	128,629	127,404	128,149	128,693	128,710	135,305
7	131,361	130,336	131,119	131,618	131,589	137,409
8	133,946	133,092	133,909	134,220	134,178	139,513
9	136,548	135,697	136,545	136,641	136,605	141,618
10	139,239	138,318	139,198	139,137	139,142	143,723
11	142,135	141,030	141,942	141,863	141,886	145,827
12	144,868	143,950	144,899	144,877	144,928	147,932
1991: 1	147,247	146,702	147,684	147,723	147,682	150,037
2	149,625	149,092	150,100	149,892	149,803	152,142
3	152,497	151,481	152,514	152,004	152,004	154,246
4	156,356	154,374	155,441	154,999	155,122	156,351
5	161,073	158,271	159,393	159,475	159,721	158,455
6	166,220	163,042	164,235	165,147	165,361	160,560
7	171,432	168,249	169,522	171,045	171,152	162,664
8	176,574	173,520	174,874	176,595	176,611	164,769
9	181,501	178,718	180,151	181,769	181,751	166,873
10	186,022	183,695	185,202	186,589	186,536	168,978
11	190,092	188,256	189,830	190,847	190,746	171,083
12	194,520	192,358	193,988	194,500	194,388	173,187

* Year and month

a. Conduct a graphical analysis of the reliability of these five models. Specifically, plot an actual versus predicted graph, an error plot, control charts, and a prediction-realization diagram.

b. Based on your work in part a, which of the five models would you select as your final model(s)? Why?

c. Carry out a statistical analysis of the reliability of the five models. Specifically, use the consistency of performance (± 1 percent), range of error, false and missed signals, mean square error, mean absolute deviation, mean error, and mean percent error analysis.

d. Based on your work in part c, which of the five models would you select as your final model(s)? Why?

22. Suppose that you have made a sales forecast for the next six months as shown in the following table. Further, suppose that this six-month period has passed and you are asked to evaluate the accuracy of your forecast.

Date	Actual	Forecast
1991: 1	246,710	239,717
2	249,064	242,231
3	240,000	244,746
4	250,964	247,261
5	246,498	249,775
6	253,390	254,805

a. Compute the RMS, the R%MS, the mean error (bias), and mean percent error (percent bias) statistics for these forecasts.

b. Evaluate the reliability of this model based on your answers in part a.

23. Suppose that you are given the following results with respect to the historical projections of four alternative forecasting models:

Date*	Actual	Model 1	Model 2	Model 3	Model 4
1989: 1	19,865	18,646			
2	21,468	20,671			
3	23,086	23,111			21,170
4	24,738	24,042	24,556	24,724	24,602
5	26,507	26,862	26,375	26,179	26,152
6	28,521	28,831	28,346	28,124	28,159
7	30,750	30,707	30,222	30,107	30,085
8	33,036	32,341	32,852	32,644	33,585
9	35,424	34,899	35,405	35,037	35,019
10	37,928	37,758	37,264	37,931	38,004
11	40,685	39,199	40,717	40,732	40,874
12	43,604	43,221	43,761	43,302	43,444
1990: 1	46,551	45,540	46,108	46,095	46,168
2	49,432	49,004	49,601	49,786	49,822
3	52,279	51,577	52,206	52,465	52,492
4	55,231	54,368	55,033	55,360	55,413
5	58,315	57,351	58,056	58,516	58,563
6	61,345	60,404	61,149	61,693	61,710
7	64,101	63,336	64,119	64,618	64,589
8	66,340	66,092	67,909	66,220	67,178
9	68,411	68,697	68,545	68,641	68,605
10	70,361	70,318	70,198	70,137	70,142
11	71,994	72,030	72,942	72,863	72,886
12	73,214	74,950	73,899	73,785	73,928
1991: 1	74,317	75,702	74,684	74,723	74,682
2	75,695	76,092	75,100	75,892	75,803
3	77,720	77,481	76,514	76,004	76,004
4	80,352	79,374	79,441	79,999	79,122
5	82,686	83,271	82,393	82,475	82,721
6	83,884	84,042	85,235	85,147	85,361
7	84,431	86,249	85,522	85,045	86,152

(Continued)

Date*	Actual	Model 1	Model 2	Model 3	Model 4
8	85,287	86,520	85,874	85,595	87,611
9	87,390	87,718	85,151	89,769	87,751
10	90,623	89,695	88,202	93,589	88,536
11	94,310	88,256	93,830	97,847	83,746
12	98,148	92,358	97,988	98,500	93,388

* Year and month

a. Conduct a graphical analysis of the reliability of these four models. Specifically, plot an actual versus predicted graph, an error plot, control charts, and a prediction-realization diagram.

b. Based on your work in part a, which of the four models would you select as your final model(s)? Why?

c. Carry out a statistical analysis of the reliability of the four models. Specifically, use the consistency of performance (± 1 percent), range of error, false and missed signals, mean square error, mean absolute deviation, mean error, and mean percent error analysis.

d. Based on your work in part c, which of the four models would you select as your final model(s)? Why?

24. Suppose that you have made an inventory forecast for a six-month period as shown in the following table. Further, suppose that this six-month period has passed and you are asked to evaluate the accuracy of your forecast.

Date	Actual	Forecast
1991: 1	102,142	100,130
2	106,298	103,801
3	110,624	106,167
4	115,125	111,245
5	119,810	120,226
6	124,685	138,966

a. Compute the RMS, the R%MS, the mean error (bias), and mean percent error (percent bias) statistics for these forecasts.

b. Evaluate the reliability of this model based on your answers in part a.

25. Suppose that you are given the following results with respect to the historical projections of four forecasting models:

Date*	Actual	Model 1	Model 2	Model 3	Model 4
1988: 1	46,647				
2	50,570				
3	51,813	54,493	54,823		21,170
4	55,544	54,042	54,456	55,724	24,602
5	58,504	58,862	58,375	57,179	26,152
6	62,749	61,831	61,346	62,124	28,159
7	66,478	65,707	66,222	66,107	30,085

(Continued)

Date*	Actual	Model 1	Model 2	Model 3	Model 4
8	69,041	69,341	70,852	70,644	33,585
9	70,937	72,899	73,405	72,037	35,019
10	69,890	73,758	74,264	73,931	38,004
11	68,952	72,199	73,717	71,732	40,874
12	67,217	71,221	71,761	67,302	43,444
1989: 1	70,619	69,540	69,108	66,095	46,168
2	74,101	72,004	73,601	70,786	49,822
3	84,054	76,577	76,206	77,465	52,492
4	79,648	86,368	87,033	89,360	55,413
5	82,908	81,351	82,056	86,516	58,563
6	83,224	85,404	86,149	80,693	61,710
7	85,849	85,336	86,119	85,618	64,589
8	88,561	88,092	88,909	86,220	67,178
9	86,186	90,697	91,545	91,641	68,605
10	89,486	88,318	88,198	87,137	70,142
11	85,717	91,030	92,942	88,863	72,886
12	77,123	87,950	88,899	87,785	73,928
1990: 1	72,428	78,702	78,684	72,723	74,682
2	74,629	73,092	73,100	64,892	75,803
3	80,128	75,481	76,514	71,004	76,004
4	85,614	81,374	81,441	83,999	79,122
5	88,623	87,271	87,393	91,475	82,721
6	86,404	90,042	90,235	93,147	85,361
7	101,941	98,249	98,522	100,045	86,152
8	100,115	103,520	104,874	109,595	109,611
9	101,962	101,718	102,151	103,769	103,751
10	104,841	103,695	104,202	101,589	101,536
11	106,843	106,256	107,830	106,847	106,746
12	110,183	108,358	109,988	109,500	109,388
1991: 1	110,320	111,998	113,043	112,519	112,606
2	108,193	112,089	113,108	112,859	112,161
3	111,362	109,856	110,797	107,764	107,811
4	113,092	113,095	114,057	110,559	110,054
5	116,705	114,795	115,804	115,901	115,946
6	121,703	118,456	119,527	118,905	118,502
7	123,926	123,533	124,701	125,662	125,519
8	129,428	125,765	126,960	128,230	128,859
9	121,957	131,353	132,657	132,470	132,764
10	131,766	123,668	124,770	124,215	124,559
11	132,406	133,657	134,973	128,615	128,901
12	138,108	134,270	135,573	139,923	139,905

* Year and month

a. Conduct a graphical analysis of the reliability of these four models. Specifically, plot an actual versus predicted graph, an error plot, control charts, and a prediction-realization diagram.

b. Based on your work in part a, which of the four models would you select as your final model(s)? Why?

c. Carry out a statistical analysis of the reliability of the four models. Specifically, use the consistency of performance (± 1 percent), range of error, false and missed signals, mean square error, mean absolute deviation, mean error, and mean percent error analysis.

d. Based on your work in part c, which of the four models would you select as your final model(s)? Why?

REFERENCES FOR FURTHER STUDY

Butler, William F., Robert A. Kavesh, and Robert B. Platt, eds., *Methods and Techniques of Business Forecasting*. Englewood Cliffs, N.J.: Prentice Hall, 1976.

Chambers, J. C. et al., "How to Choose the Right Forecasting Techniques," *Harvard Business Review*, July–August 1971, pp. 45–74.

Eby, Frank and William O'Neill, *The Management of Sales Forecasting*. Lexington, Mass.: Lexington Books—Heath Company, 1977.

Hanke, John E. and Arthur G. Reitsch, *Business Forecasting*, 3rd ed. Boston: Allyn and Bacon, 1989.

Makridakis, S. and M. Hibon, "Accuracy of Forecasting: An Empirical Investigation," *Journal of the Royal Statistical Society*, series A, vol. 142, 1979, pp. 97–145.

Makridakis, Spyros, "Metaforecasting: Ways of Improving Forecasting, Accuracy and Usefulness," Working Paper from the European Institute of Business Administration, May 1987.

Makridakis, Spyros and Steven C. Wheelwright, *The Handbook of Forecasting: A Managers Guide*. New York: John Wiley & Sons, 1982.

McLaughlin, R. L., "A New Five-Phase Economic Forecasting System," *Business Economics*, September 1975, pp. 49–60.

McNees, Stephen K., "Forecasting Accuracy of Alternative Techniques: A Comparison of U.S. Macroeconomic Forecasts," *Journal of Business and Economic Statistics*, vol. 4, no. 1, January 1986, pp. 5–15.

Montgomery, D. C. "An Introduction to Short-Term Forecasting," *Journal of Industrial Engineering*, 19, 1968, pp. 500–503.

Robinson, Richard, "Forecasting and Small Business: A Study of the Strategic Planning Process," *Journal of Small Business Management*, vol. 17, July 1974, pp. 19–27.

Sartorius, Lester C. and N. Carroll Mohn, *Sales Forecasting Models: A Diagnostic Approach*. Research monograph no. 69. Georgia State University: Publishing Services Division, College of Business, 1976.

Studenmund, A. H. and Henry J. Cassidy, *Using Econometrics: A Practical Guide*. Boston: Little, Brown and Company, 1987.

Thompson, Arthur H. and A. J. Strickland, *Strategy Formulation and Implementation*. Dallas: Business Publications, Inc., 1980.

Wecker, William E., "Predicting the Turning Points of a Time Series," *Journal of Business*, vol. 52, no. 1, January 1979, pp. 57–85.

Wheelwright, Steven C. and Darral Clarke, "Corporate Forecasting: Promise and Reality," *Harvard Business Review*, November–December 1976, pp. 40–48.

Willis, Raymond E. *A Guide to Forecasting for Planners and Managers.* Englewood Cliffs, N.J.: Prentice Hall, 1987.

5

Simple Linear Regression

INTRODUCTION

In the discussion of trend estimation in the preceding chapters, we implicitly assigned a causal role to the passage of time—that is, we acted as if the passage of time "caused" the predicted growth or decline in the trend variable. While this approach assists forecasters in data analysis and satisfies the purely mechanical function of model building, forecast analysts often have access to economic data that can be used to develop a model built around a cause-and-effect relationship. For example, we know that camera sales are partially determined by household income levels, and that the demand for steel is influenced by automobile production. Thus, instead of relying on time as an explanatory variable, we can develop models that link changes in camera sales to fluctuations in household income, or shifts in automobile production to the demand for steel. Causal models allow managers to evaluate the impact of shifts in internal, company-level variables (such as changes in prices and advertising budgets) and the effect of external economic factors (disposable income, interest rates, etc.) on company sales.

Regression analysis is a statistical technique that is widely used by forecasters to quantify behavioral relationships that exist between two or more economic and business variables. In this chapter, we begin our study with the simplest case: the two-variable linear regression model. Even though this model is oversimplified, the results can easily be extended to more complex (and realistic) regression models.

REGRESSION ANALYSIS: THE LINEAR MODEL

There are two fundamental questions to be dealt with in using regression analysis to measure the relationship between two variables:

1. What is the appropriate mathematical model to use in a given situation?

Should we use a linear, parabolic, or logarithmic function, or some other type of mathematical model?

2. Once the functional form of the model has been determined, how do we estimate the best-fitting model for the two variables under consideration? In this chapter, we focus exclusively on the two-variable linear model.[1]

The starting point in regression analysis is an equation (model) that postulates a specific relationship between a dependent variable and one independent variable. For example, we might want to estimate home computer sales based on knowledge of income levels, or alternatively, predict steel production as it relates to automobile output. These relationships are quantified by means of an equation such as the following:[2]

$$\hat{Y} = \hat{\beta}_0 + \hat{\beta}_1 X. \tag{5-1}$$

This equation provides estimates of an unknown variable, $\hat{Y}$ (sometimes referred to as the dependent variable), when the value of another variable, X (the independent or causal variable, or the regressor), is known and the parameters, $\hat{\beta}_0$ and $\hat{\beta}_1$, have been estimated.

The following step-by-step description provides an overview of the next three chapters and will help you understand the process involved in estimating a regression equation:

1. Assume that a linear model is appropriate and estimate the best-fitting straight line (linear model).
2. Test the estimated linear model for goodness of fit.
3. Test whether the mathematical assumptions of the linear model are satisfied.
4. If the estimated line passes the goodness of fit tests and the mathematical assumptions are satisfied, use the model to generate forecasts.
5. Evaluate the estimated model in terms of its forecasting reliability. There may be situations in which the model performs admirably when viewed from a historical perspective yet fails miserably as a forecasting tool.

The model suggested by equation (5-1) assumes that a theoretical relationship between X and Y exists and that it can be represented by a particular mathematical linear function.[3] The unknown parameters are estimated with

---

[1] Once the two-variable linear model is mastered, these techniques can easily be extended to multiple variables and to other nonlinear formulations.

[2] In fact, the linear regression model is but a special case of the general linear model. For a detailed treatment, see F. A. Graybell, *Theory and Application of the Linear Model* (North Scituate, Mass.: Duxbury Press, 1976).

[3] This assumption is not as restrictive as it might appear. It will become evident that the majority of business and economic data approximate linearity either directly or by some form of transformation.

available sample data, and a fitted equation is obtained. Since we cannot be certain about the reliability of our model, predictions based on the regression equation must be gauged for accuracy and checks made regarding the validity of the underlying assumptions. Additionally, parameters or coefficients of the estimated line are evaluated by subjecting the estimated equation to statistical tests of significance.[4]

Implicit in equation (5-1) are two hypotheses, one statistical and one theoretical. The statistical hypothesis is that the relationship between X and Y is closely approximated by a linear equation that satisfies certain mathematical or statistical assumptions. The theoretical hypothesis is that changes in X (the independent variable) cause or lead to changes in Y (the dependent variable). Thus, before we become immersed in statistical estimation of regression equations, a brief overview of this theoretical hypothesis is in order.

THEORETICAL RELATIONSHIPS AND HYPOTHESES

Consider the following question: What causes quarter-to-quarter fluctuations in consumer expenditures on personal computers? To answer this question, one must identify those explanatory variables that are linked to consumer purchasing decisions. Questions about consumer expenditures on personal computers suggest, in turn, the theory of demand. Therefore, the theory of consumer demand is a logical place to turn for guidance in selecting variables. Similarly, if the process being studied involved forecasting corporate profitability, financial theory and topics such as the rate of return and the cost of capital would be considered.

This process of variables selection is generally referred to as model specification. At this point, it may be useful to introduce a general equation:

$$Y = f(X_1, X_2, X_3, X_4, \ldots X_k). \tag{5-2}$$

This equation suggests that Y, the variable of interest, depends on or is a function of k independent variables. The process of model specification begins by identifying the appropriate theory (demand, production, financial, trade) to serve as a sieve for selecting the explanatory factors (X's) and to winnow the "real-world factors" down to a select list of major variables.

Additionally, economic theory should help to indicate the directional change in Y resulting from changes in any of the independent variables. For example, if Y is the sale of personal computers and X is income, the theory of consumer choice predicts that an increase in income will lead to an increase in personal computer sales. These theoretical expectations are an integral part of regression modeling.

---

[4] The reason for including the error term (e_t) in equation (5-1) will become apparent in succeeding sections.

To illustrate more concretely some of these ideas, let us say that we are trying to develop a predictive model for the sales of a particular company's products. The theory of consumer choice suggests that some of the factors that are likely to affect sales (S) are the ratio of the company's price to the competitor's price (P/P_c), the company's advertising expenditures relative to its competitors' (A/A_c), and household income (I). This model can then be written as

$$\hat{S} = \hat{\beta}_0 - \hat{\beta}_1(P/P_c) + \hat{\beta}_2(A/A_c) + \hat{\beta}_3(I) \qquad (5\text{-}3)$$

with the expectation that $\hat{\beta}_1$ will be negative and $\hat{\beta}_2$ and $\hat{\beta}_3$ positive. Once the model has been specified, the analyst collects sample data and derives estimates for the regression parameters $(\hat{\beta}_1, \hat{\beta}_2, \hat{\beta}_3)$. This estimated model is then subjected to various statistical tests of reliability, and these tests lead, in turn, to new insights regarding the proper formulation of the model (for example, regional employment may be a better variable than income in equation 5-3). Thus, to be an effective applied researcher, the forecaster must have a rigorous understanding of statistical theory and the appropriate economic theory.

SELECTION OF EXPLANATORY OR PREDICTOR VARIABLES

CRITERIA

When evaluating possible explanatory or predictive variables (the X's) for inclusion in forecasting models, four questions should be asked. First, is there a sound theoretical basis for including the variable in the model? When a forecasting model does not have a sound theoretical basis, the resulting forecasts will be unreliable. (Unfortunately, the reverse is not always true. That is, a sound theoretical model does not necessarily generate reliable forecasts.)

Second, do we have access to an adequate data base for all of the variables of interest? There must be enough historical data on the selected variables to ensure that the true nature of the relationship with the dependent variable can be captured. Indeed, the amount of data required to estimate a given model is directly related to the total number of variables in the model. A rule of thumb is that there should be at least five observations for each independent variable (X) included in the model. Thus, if the final equation has three independent variables, there should be at least 15 historical observations on each variable. Further, the data that exist must be available in the appropriate time frame. Thus, if we are estimating a quarterly forecasting model and the only available time frame for a given variable is annual, this variable must either be modified or eliminated from consideration.

Third, are future projections available for the independent variables $(X$'s) selected for inclusion in the model? Look at equation (5-3) for company sales (S). We may be able to gain access to historical information for our competitors' advertising expenditures (A_c) and prices (P_c), but how will we get estimates for future movements in these two variables so we can predict company sales (S)? Accurate estimates of future values of the predictor variables must be readily attainable.

Fourth, is the historical relationship between the variables likely to continue into the future? The strength of regression analysis lies in the fact that knowledge of historical relationships between economic phenomena assists us in making accurate forecasts. This advantage only holds if the relationship suggested by the estimated equation remains relatively stable into the future. As an example of what occurs when relationships change over time, consider the case of the demand for steel, which, for a number of years, was closely associated with the production of automobiles. In recent years, however, plastic, aluminum, and other substitutes have been used to a greater degree in automobiles, and the relationship between the demand for steel and automobile production has changed drastically. To some extent, this draws us back to the importance of basing models on a sound theoretical foundation. If we were to prepare a theoretical model of the demand for steel, we would certainly incorporate substitutes for steel.

SCATTER DIAGRAMS

As a first step in variable selection, we can rely on a graphical device known as a scatter diagram. Scatter diagrams are constructed by plotting paired observations of the dependent variable and the independent variable. Figure 5-1

FIGURE 5-1   Scatter Diagram for Computer Sales and Real Income

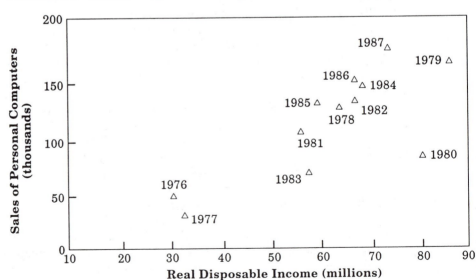

TABLE 5-1   **Sales of Personal Computers and Real Disposable Income, 1976–1987**

Year	Sales of Personal Computers (thousands) Y	Real Disposable Income (millions) X
1976	73.1	31.9
1977	50.2	29.8
1978	128.3	63.7
1979	170.4	84.6
1980	87.5	79.5
1981	108.6	55.4
1982	135.7	66.3
1983	69.8	57.2
1984	148.9	68.1
1985	132.1	59.0
1986	150.2	65.9
1987	180.3	72.8

contains the scatter diagram for sales of personal computers and income for the years 1976 to 1987, while the corresponding data are presented in Table 5-1.

By convention, the values of the independent variable (income, in this case) are plotted along the horizontal axis and the values of the dependent variable (sales of personal computers) along the vertical axis. For example, the observation for 1976 is plotted at the intersection of a line drawn vertically from an income level (X) of \$31.9 million and horizontally from a sales level (Y) of \$73.1 thousand. When the points for each of the remaining years are plotted in a similar fashion, the result is the scatter diagram depicted in Figure 5-1.

An examination of Figure 5-1 indicates that there is considerable variation in the level of personal computer sales for any given income level. Nonetheless, there does seem to be a positive relationship between personal computer sales and income levels. Specifically, as real disposable income increases, sales of personal computers also increase, but the relationship is not perfect. For example, disposable income levels in 1981 and 1985 are virtually identical, while personal computer sales are significantly different. As one would expect from the theory of consumer choice, there are factors other than income (prices of personal computers, advertising, prices of complements, etc.) that affect the sales of personal computers. While scatter diagrams are useful, they do not provide us with a quantitative measure of the relationship between personal computer sales and income levels.

CORRELATION AND COVARIANCE MEASURES

Correlation and covariance measures provide quantitative estimates of how closely two variables are linearly related. As seen in Figure 5-1, there is a tendency for sales of personal computers and income to move or vary together. Statistically, we can measure how the variation of X about its mean $(\overline{X})$ is linked to the variation of Y about its mean $(\overline{Y})$. The formula for covariance is given by (the summation sign, Σ, means that we sum the products for all n observations)

$$\text{COV}_{xy} = \left(\frac{1}{n-1}\right) \sum_{t=1}^{n} (X_t - \overline{X})(Y_t - \overline{Y}), \qquad (5\text{-}4)$$

which when applied to our personal computer sales and income data set (sample size $= n = 15$ pairs of observations) yields a value of 502.943. The fact that the covariance is positive confirms the theoretical expectation of a positive relationship between income and computer sales. If the relationship between the two variables had been negative, the covariance value would have been negative; if there were no relationship, it would have been close to zero. However, this measure of covariance is hard to interpret because it is influenced by the units in which X and Y are measured. That is, if we had measured personal computer sales in thousands of units rather than of dollars, the absolute value of the COV coefficient would have changed significantly (the sign would have remained positive, however).

To eliminate the measurement problem, analysts more commonly rely on correlation computations when studying the relationship between variables. The correlation coefficient (r) is a pure number (no units to worry about) and is given by this formula:

$$r = \text{COV}_{xy}/S_xS_y \qquad (5\text{-}5)$$

where S_x and S_y refer to the standard deviations of the respective variables. The correlation coefficient is bounded by

$$-1 \leq r \leq +1.$$

For the personal computer and household income example, the correlation coefficient is computed as 0.7275, and this value confirms that the two variables are positively correlated. In essence, the correlation coefficient measures how the two variables $(X$ and $Y)$ vary or move together. This interpretation is expanded later in the chapter in equations (5-48) and (5-49).

LINEAR REGRESSION MODEL

STATISTICAL FORMULATION

The linear regression model is a shorthand mathematical way of expressing the statistical relationship that we believe exists between the two variables. The principal elements of this statistical relationship are (1) the tendency of the dependent variable, Y, to vary in a systematic way with the independent variable, X; and (2) the dispersion or scatter of points about the line that represents the relationship between X and Y. The objective is to specify the model that produces the best straight line relating X and Y.

To illustrate, we continue our investigation of the relationship (based on 12 yearly observations) between personal computer sales and real disposable income detailed in Table 5-1 and Figure 5-1.[5] Many straight lines can be chosen to fit the plotted data points. For example, one could connect the points from the lowest Y value to the highest Y value (G_1 in Figure 5-2), or one could simply draw a line that appears to fit the full scatter of data points (G_2 in Figure 5-2).

In developing our regression model, our objective is to select (estimate)

FIGURE 5-2   Scatter Diagram and Alternative Regression Lines

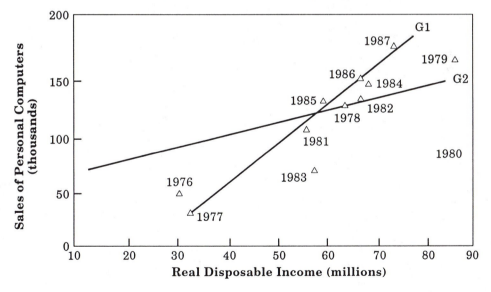

[5] To reduce sampling error, a sample larger than 12 ought to be obtained. The small number used here is only for ease in showing calculations. In fact, the example used throughout this section must be regarded as pedagogical.

the best line from among all possible lines. Let us define the best line as the line with the least total error. These errors are generally referred to as deviations or residuals about the regression line. There are many possible ways to minimize error, but the criterion most frequently relied on is the least-squares model, which minimizes the sum of the squared deviations (errors) about the regression line. Formally, the objective is to find the line, $\hat{Y}_t = \hat{\beta}_0 + \hat{\beta}_1 X_t$, in which the values $\hat{\beta}_0$ and $\hat{\beta}_1$ ensure that the squared deviations (errors) from the data points to the line are minimized. That is, we want to find values for $\hat{\beta}_0$ and $\hat{\beta}_1$ that minimize

$$\sum_{t=1}^{n} (Y_t - \hat{Y}_t)^2 = \sum (\text{errors})^2 = \sum e_t^2 \tag{5-6}$$

where $\hat{Y}_t = \hat{\beta}_0 + \hat{\beta}_1 X_t$ is the fitted (estimated) value of Y_t corresponding to a particular observation on X_t, n is the total number of observations, and $(Y_t - \hat{Y}_t)$ is the regression error. Figure 5-3 graphically illustrates this process.

We are interested in finding values for $\hat{\beta}_0$ and $\hat{\beta}_1$ that will minimize the sum of the squares of these vertical deviations (errors). As can be seen in Figure 5-3, the regression line does not completely describe the relationship between the two variables. Some points lie directly on the line while others do not. Once again, this reflects the fact that the stated model is a simplification of

FIGURE 5-3 Fitting Points with a Regression Line: Error Analysis

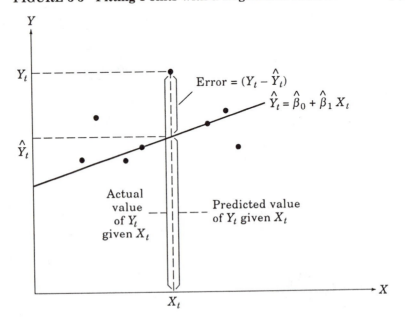

reality. These differences between the actual values of Y and the regression, or predicted, values of $\hat{Y}$ correspond to the residuals or error terms (e) that we are interested in minimizing. That is, $e_t = Y_t - \hat{Y}_t$.

Mathematically, it may be shown that the estimated values of $\hat{\beta}_0$ and $\hat{\beta}_1$ must simultaneously satisfy the following expressions referred to as the normal equations:[6]

$$\sum Y_t = n\hat{\beta}_0 + \hat{\beta}_1 \sum X_t \tag{5-7}$$

$$\sum X_t Y_t = \hat{\beta}_0 \sum X_t + \hat{\beta}_1 \sum X_t^2. \tag{5-8}$$

Solving equations (5-7) and (5-8), we get the following definitional formulas:[7]

$$\hat{\beta}_1 = \frac{n\sum X_t Y_t - \sum X_t \sum Y_t}{n\sum X^2 - (\sum X_t)^2} \tag{5-9}$$

$$\hat{\beta}_0 = \frac{\sum Y_t}{n} - \hat{\beta}_1 \frac{\sum X_t}{n} \tag{5-10}$$

$$\hat{\beta}_0 = \overline{Y} - \hat{\beta}_1 \overline{X}. \tag{5-11}$$

In equations (5-9), (5-10), and (5-11), the symbols are defined as follows:

n = number of sample observations
$\sum$ = summation of observations

---

[6] Formally, this process is as follows:

a. Substitute into equation (5-1) the definition of $\hat{Y}$, obtaining

$$\sum (Y_t - \hat{\beta}_0 - \hat{\beta}_1 X_t)^2.$$

b. To minimize this expression, we take the partial derivatives with respect to $\hat{\beta}_0$ and $\hat{\beta}_1$ and set them equal to zero:

$$\frac{\delta}{\delta \beta_0} \sum (Y_t - \beta_0 - \beta_1 X_t)^2 = -2\sum (Y_t - \beta_0 - \beta_1 X_t)$$

$$\frac{\delta}{\delta \beta_1} \sum (Y_t - \hat{\beta}_0 - \hat{\beta}_1 X_t)_2 = -2\sum X_t (Y_t - \hat{\beta}_0 - \hat{\beta}_1 X_t).$$

Equating these to zero yields

$$\sum (Y_t - \hat{\beta}_0 - \hat{\beta}_1 X_t) = 0$$
$$\sum X_t (Y_t - \hat{\beta}_0 - \hat{\beta}_1 X_t) = 0.$$

Rewriting these, we obtain equations (5-7) and (5-8).

[7] If you are forced to compute a significant number of regression equations, shorthand formulas are available. See R. J. Wonnacott and T. H. Wonnacott, *Econometrics* (New York: John Wiley & Sons, 1970), pp. 6–9.

$$X = \text{independent variable}$$
$$Y = \text{dependent variable}$$
$$\overline{Y} = \text{arithmetic mean of } Y$$
$$\overline{X} = \text{arithmetic mean of } X.$$

STATISTICAL ESTIMATION

Calculations for $\hat{\beta}_0$ and $\hat{\beta}_1$ are carried out in the first four columns of Table 5-2 (the remaining columns may be ignored for the present). The regression equation can now be stated as

$$\hat{Y}_t = 7.431 + 1.833X_t. \qquad \text{(5-12)}$$

This estimated line is graphed, along with the actual data points, in Figure 5-4.

Historical estimates of personal computer sales for any given income level are easily obtainable from equation (5-12). For example, if real disposable income equals $72.8 million (the actual value in 1987), the regression estimate

TABLE 5-2   Least-Squares Calculations: Sales of Personal Computers

	(1) Y [a]	(2) X [b]	(3) XY	(4) X^2	(5) $\hat{Y}$ [c]	(6) $(Y - \hat{Y})$	(7) $(Y - \hat{Y})^2$
1976	73.1	31.9	2,331.89	1,017.61	65.9098	7.1902	51.6983
1977	50.2	29.8	1,495.96	888.04	62.0615	−11.8601	140.6632
1978	128.3	63.7	8,172.71	4,057.69	124.2051	4.0948	16.7675
1979	170.4	84.6	14,415.84	7,157.16	162.5187	7.8812	62.1135
1980	87.5	79.5	6,956.25	6,320.25	153.1695	−65.6695	4312.4880
1981	108.6	55.4	6,016.44	3,069.16	108.9897	−.3897	0.1519
1982	135.7	66.3	8.996.91	4,395.69	128.9714	6.7285	45.2731
1983	69.8	57.2	3,992.56	3,271.84	112.2894	−42.4894	1805.3550
1984	148.9	68.1	10,140.09	4,637.61	132.2712	−16.6288	276.5167
1985	132.1	59.0	7,793.90	3,481.00	115.5892	16.5108	272.6062
1986	150.2	65.9	9,898.18	4,342.81	128.2381	21.9618	482.3207
1987	180.3	72.8	13,125.84	5,299.84	140.8871	39.4128	1553.3690

$$\Sigma\, Y = 1{,}435.1 \qquad \Sigma\, X = 734.2 \qquad \Sigma\, XY = 93{,}336.57 \qquad \Sigma\, X^2 = 47{,}938.70$$

$$\Sigma(Y - \hat{Y}) \approx 0 \qquad \Sigma(Y - \hat{Y})^2 = 9{,}019.324 \qquad \overline{Y} = 119.6 \qquad \overline{X} = 61.2$$

$$\hat{\beta}_0 = 7.431 \qquad \hat{\beta}_1 = 1.833$$

[a] Y = sales of personal computers (thousands of dollars).
[b] X = real disposable income (millions of dollars).
[c] $Y_t = 7.431 + 1.833X_t.$

FIGURE 5-4   Regression Line between Computer Sales and Real Income

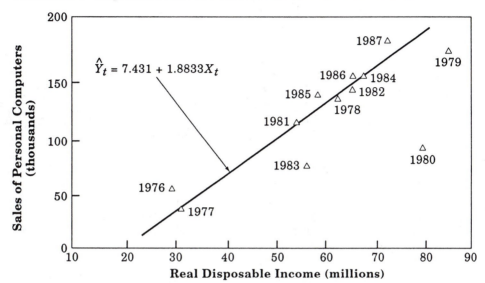

of personal computer sales would be

$$\hat{Y}_t = 7.431 + 1.833X_t$$

$$= 7.431 + 1.833(72.8) \tag{5-13}$$

$$\hat{Y}_t = 140.887.$$

That is, if we input the actual value of real disposable income ($72.8) in 1987, we would estimate personal computer sales at $140,887 (there is a slight difference due to rounding between the numbers calculated directly from equation 5-13 and those presented in Table 5-1), compared to the actual value of $180,300—an underestimate of $39,413 (or 21.9 percent).

What, precisely, do the regression coefficients tell us? The slope of the line, $\hat{\beta}_1$, is an estimate of the average change in Y resulting from a one-unit change in X. That is, for every one million dollar change in real disposable income, personal computer sales will, on the average, increase by $1,833. Note that the slope coefficient tells us only the average change in computer sales that accompanies a unit change in real disposable income.

It might also be argued that the slope coefficient provides a measure of the average change in Y (computer sales) *caused* by a unit change in the independent variable, X (real disposable income). This may or may not be an appropriate interpretation. The statistical process of regressing one variable on another variable cannot establish causality, it can only support it. To appreciate this critical point, suppose that we were to apply the least-squares methodology to the following equation:

$$\hat{X}_t = \alpha_0 + \alpha_1 Y_t \tag{5-14}$$

where X and Y are defined respectively as real disposable income and personal computer sales. Obviously, such a computational exercise would not suddenly reverse the causal order of X and Y in the real world. The correct causal relationship between two variables is determined outside of the statistical estimation process. That is, it is based on theoretical considerations and not on statistical estimation.

The interpretation of the intercept, $\hat{\beta}_0$, depends on whether observations near $X = 0$ are available. If so, $\hat{\beta}_0$ may be interpreted as the estimate of Y when X equals zero. However, if sufficient observations near $X = 0$ are not available (generally true in business and economic data, and clearly true in this case), then the intercept is simply the height of the least-squares regression line. The majority of computer programs simply refer to the intercept as the constant term.

In using the regression line to generate estimates, one must distinguish between interpolation and extrapolation. The former uses the regression equation to estimate Y based on an X value within the observed data-base range, whereas extrapolation produces an estimate of Y based on an X value falling outside the actual range of X values observed in the sample. The estimate of $140,887 thousand for personal computer sales was based on a real disposable income level of $72.8 million, an income level actually contained within the sample data base. If however, we were to estimate computer sales based on an income level of 0, we obtain a sales level of $7,431. The reliability of this estimate is questionable both statistically (we have no sample observations with which to compare this estimate) and theoretically (we would not expect people to spend money on personal computers when they have no income).

MATHEMATICAL MODEL

PROPERTIES OF THE LEAST-SQUARES MODEL

In this section, we focus on the statistical validity of applying the least-squares regression model to a particular data set. The principal statistical advantage of regression analysis (as compared to the other techniques presented in this book) is that it is based on a model that yields a number of statistical measures designed to check the validity of each application. We will next discuss, therefore, the underlying assumptions of the two-variable model, analyze the statistical properties of the least-squares estimators, and examine the usefulness of the estimated regression line as a predictive device.

FIGURE 5-5   Scatter Diagram for Computer Purchases and Income

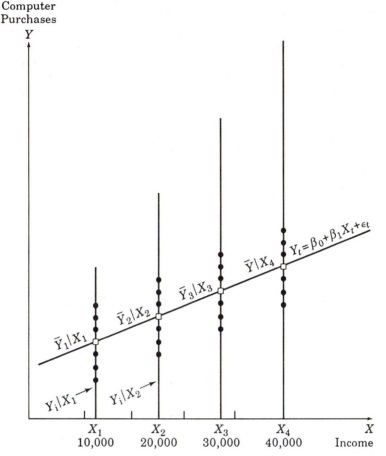

Note: Y_i/X_i denotes the alternative values Y can take for a given value of X.

To emphasize the probabilistic nature of the least-squares model, note that for a given observed value of X, we may observe many possible values of Y.[8] For example, consider the expenditures on personal computers by different families, each of whom earns \$10,000 per year (X_1). Even though income (X) is the same, we would not observe exactly the same expenditures by each family. Instead, there would be fluctuations in the Y values, with a clustering about the central or mean value of expenditures (shown by the box in Figure 5-5). Further, if the income level were \$20,000, \$30,000, etc., we would observe

[8] For a more thorough discussion, see Wonnacott and Wonnacott, *Econometrics*; and R. S. Pindyck and D. L. Rubinfeld, *Econometric Models and Economic Forecasts*, 3rd ed., (New York: McGraw-Hill, 1991).

a similar pattern with fluctuations around some central or mean value. Note that these mean values are correctly referred to as conditional means, since the mean or average value of Y is conditional on a given X value being recorded or observed. If we then connect these conditional mean values, we would obtain the least-squares regression line. These results are depicted in Figure 5-5.

In the absence of additional information, we will assume that for each X value, observations on Y will vary in a random fashion. Formally, this situation can be described by adding an error term and expressing the theoretical model as

$$Y_t = \beta_0 + \beta_1 X_t + \epsilon_t \tag{5-15}$$

where for each observation, Y_t is a random variable, X_t is fixed, and ϵ_t is a random error term. Equation (5-15) is the equation for the theoretical or unknown true regression relationship linking Y_t to X_t. When we gather data and estimate the coefficients, the "hat" symbol ($\hat{}$) is used to denote sample estimates, and the specific model that has been estimated can be written as

$$\hat{Y}_t = \hat{\beta}_0 + \hat{\beta}_1 X_t + e_t \tag{5-16}$$

Equation (5-15) is the formal model of the relationship that we believe exists. We begin by assuming that the least-squares method is an appropriate or valid model for the problem being analyzed, and then we statistically test this hypothesis based on the output of our regression statistics. That is, since we wish to make accurate inferences about the actual population values, the classical regression model (in equation 5-15) should satisfy the following assumptions:[9]

1. No specification error
   a. The relationship between the X_i's and Y is linear.
   b. No relevant independent variables have been excluded.
   c. No irrelevant independent variables have been included.
2. No measurement error
   a. The variables are measured accurately.
3. The following assumptions relate to the error term, ϵ_t:
   a. Zero mean: $E(\epsilon_t) = 0$. For each observation, the expected value of the error term is zero.
   b. Homoscedasticity: The variance of the error term is constant for all values of X_t. This variance is denoted as $E(\epsilon_t)^2 = \sigma^2$.
   c. No autocorrelation: That is, the error terms are uncorrelated with each other.

---

[9] In our discussion of the multiple regression model in chapter 6, we introduce two additional assumptions.

d. The independent variables are uncorrelated with the error term. Alternatively, the values of the independent variables are fixed.

e. Normality: The error term is normally distributed.

The statistical power of the least-squares regression model is built on this series of critical assumptions, all of which were implicitly assumed to hold in the personal computer regression line. Figure 5-6 illustrates the classical linear model. Specifically, Figure 5-6 implies that for every X, there exists a probability distribution of the Y's that satisfies the preceding assumptions.

Furthermore, the fact that the error term is a random variable implies that its values can be described by a probability distribution with a mean and a variance. Because the error terms are unobservable, the mean and variance of the distribution cannot be directly computed and must be estimated based on sample error patterns.

In particular, we assume that the random variables, Y_t, are statistically independent, with

$$\text{Mean} = \beta_0 + \beta_1 X_t \tag{5-17}$$

$$\text{Var} = \sigma_2. \tag{5-18}$$

FIGURE 5-6 Conditional Population of Y Assumed in Simpler Linear Regression

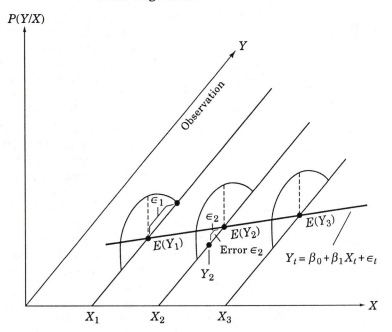

Additionally, it is occasionally useful to describe the model in terms of the error term. In this case, the model and its assumptions may be written as

$$Y_t = \beta_0 + \beta_1 X_t + \epsilon_t \tag{5-19}$$

where the ϵ_t are independent random variables with

$$\text{Mean} = E(\epsilon_t) = 0 \tag{5-20}$$
$$\text{Var} = V(\epsilon_t) = \sigma^2.$$

These alternative formulations highlight four significant facets of the classical linear model. First, the distributions of Y_t and ϵ_t are identical, except that their means differ. Second, while assumptions concerning the shapes of the Y_t and ϵ_t distributions are needed to conduct statistical tests, they are not required for purposes of estimating the model. Third, the variance, σ^2, is an unknown parameter and must be estimated as part of the regression model. Finally, before the models developed by the forecaster are actually used, the validity of the assumptions must be checked.

When all of these assumptions are satisfied, the least-squares estimators possess the desirable statistical characteristics of unbiasedness, consistency, efficiency, and robustness.[10] In statistical jargon, the least-squares estimators are said to be the "best linear unbiased estimates," or BLUE. As long as the normality assumption also holds, we can carry out tests of statistical significance.

While we will have occasion to investigate many of these assumptions in detail in later chapters, a brief overview here is warranted. While it may seem that the addition of the error term in the population regression line (ϵ_t) is both arbitrary and capricious, there are fundamental reasons for its inclusion. The error term, ϵ_t, may be regarded as the sum of specification and measurement errors.

Specification errors appear because all regression models are simplifications of reality. For example, we assumed that income was the sole determinant of personal computer sales. In fact, we have omitted such determinants as prices and advertising. The effect of all of these omitted variables is captured by the error term. In addition to omitting relevant variables, it is also possible that we might, erroneously, include variables in the model that are irrelevant. Finally, in applying the linear model, we are implicitly assuming that a straight line is the proper functional form of the model. In fact, it is highly unlikely that any economic or business relationship is perfectly linear.

Measurement error exists because economic and business data are difficult to measure with complete accuracy. Rounding error, recording error, and

---

[10] For a more detailed discussion of these characteristics, see N. R. Draper and H. Smith, *Applied Regression Analysis*, 2nd ed. (New York: John Wiley & Sons, 1981).

missing data points are all potential causes of measurement error. Simply stated, if the data are measured inaccurately, then our estimates will be inaccurate (or, euphemistically, "garbage in, garbage out").

The assumption of a zero mean for the error term is generally of little concern in empirical estimation. If this assumption is violated, the intercept is the only coefficient of the regression model that is affected. That is, even if this assumption does not hold, the least-squares estimate of the slope coefficient(s) remains unchanged.

The assumption that the error term is normally distributed is necessary only for the statistical tests of significance. Thus, even if this assumption does not hold, it has no effect on the estimates of the regression coefficients. Furthermore, even when applying the statistical tests of significance, the normality assumption is critical only with small samples. In large samples (more than 25 observations), we can rely on the central limit theorem to ensure that even if the error term is not normally distributed in the population, the sampling distribution of the individual regression coefficients will be normally distributed.

The remaining assumptions—homoscedasticity, no autocorrelation, and no correlation between the independent variables and the error term—are critical to practicing forecasters, but this discussion is deferred to later chapters.

STATISTICAL PROPERTIES

In the estimation of the regression equation for personal computer sales, a significant distinction was glossed over. This is the relationship between the true regression line denoted by equation (5-15):

$$Y_t = \beta_0 + \beta_1 X_t + \epsilon_t \tag{5-15}$$

and the estimated regression line denoted by equation (5-16):

$$\hat{Y}_t = \hat{\beta}_0 + \hat{\beta}_1 X_t + e_t \tag{5-16}$$

The true regression line is generally unknown to the forecaster, and we are forced to use equation (5-16), the least-squares line, as the best estimate of equation (5-15). Figure 5-7 highlights this distinction. In all likelihood, the estimated regression line will differ from the true regression line. This difference occurs because of the impossibility of reproducing economic phenomena perfectly, even in a random sample.

In Figure 5-7, β_0 and β_1 (without "hats") are the unknown regression parameters contained in the *true* or population regression line describing the relationship between Y and X. Since these two parameters are not known in advance (a priori) in a regression problem, they must be estimated from sample

FIGURE 5-7   **True and Estimated Regression Lines**

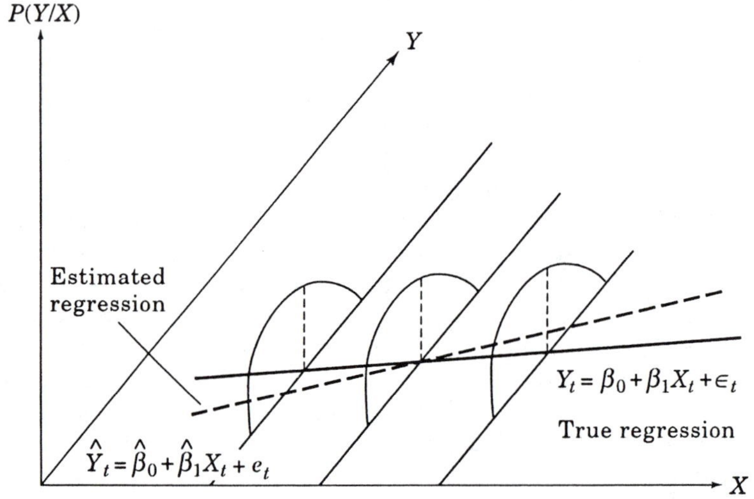

data. The estimated values are referred to as the regression coefficient estimates and are denoted by $\hat{\beta}_0$ and $\hat{\beta}_1$—our best statistical guess of the unknown parameters, β_0 and β_1. This is analogous to taking a random sample of a certain number of nineteen-year-olds, calculating their average weight $(\overline{X})$, and using this as an estimate of the average weight (μ) of all nineteen-year-olds in the United States.

Return to the estimated least-squares equation, equation (5-16). The most important theoretical justification for use of this least-squares criterion is the Gauss-Markhov theorem, which we state without formal proof:

> Within the class of linear unbiased estimates of β_0 and β_1, the least-squares estimators have minimum variance.

There are several noteworthy features of this theorem. First, the theorem applies only to linear estimators. Thus, it is possible that a nonlinear estimator may have a lower variance (have a better fit) than does the least-squares estimator. Second, the variance of the estimates derived from the least-squares estimators can be shown to be both unbiased and consistent.

STATISTICAL VALIDATION

HYPOTHESIS TESTING

Having obtained estimates of the regression coefficients, $\hat{\beta}_0$ and $\hat{\beta}_1$, the next step is to evaluate statistically the usefulness of the model. This involves the computation and interpretation of summary statistics. The meaning and use of these statistics are especially valuable in applied regression analysis. Textbook problems in which the model is correctly specified and the data are clean are rarely encountered in real-world forecasting. Thus, applied regression requires a great deal of judgment at various stages of research, using summary statistics and tests to feel one's way through the data. Since regression estimates are mathematically derived, it is possible to make statistical statements regarding the significance and accuracy of estimated regression equations. The use of these statistical properties, along with our knowledge of $\hat{\beta}_0$ and $\hat{\beta}_1$ and the normality assumption, will also allow us to make statements about the likelihood that future values will vary from the forecast (estimate), the confidence that we place in having estimated the best line, and finally, the accuracy of the coefficients. Since the estimated regression line is based on a sample, sampling error is present. The primary goal of all these statistical tests is to take this sampling error into consideration. Indeed, one of the key advantages of regression analysis is that statistical procedures can be used to evaluate the accuracy of estimated models.

Hypothesis testing returns us to the task of statistical estimation and forces us to ask what we can learn about the real world based on the data contained in the sample. How likely is it that the empirical results could have been obtained by chance? Can the theory be rejected using the results of the sample? If the theory is correct, what are the odds that this particular sample would have been observed? Thus, our estimate of the slope coefficient, $\hat{\beta}_1$, is only one of many possible estimates that could have been obtained from repeated samples. As a result, classical hypothesis testing involves a three-step procedure:

1. Statement of the null and alternative hypotheses to be tested concerning a specific parameter (such as β_1);
2. Selection of the appropriate statistical test and specification of the level of significance;
3. Testing of the significance of the statistic (say, $\hat{\beta}_1$) obtained from the regression analysis.

There is an important distinction to be made between theoretical significance and statistical significance. For example, economic theory suggests that computer purchases should be influenced by income levels; however, theory makes no statement as to how strong the statistical relationship should be for any given time frame. Thus, it is possible that income levels are statistically insignificant based on the specific sample under consideration. This is not meant to suggest that we should discard the theory. Rather, it should be taken to mean that we simply do not have a sufficient amount of data to measure or record a statistically measurable relationship.

The first step in hypothesis testing is the statement of the null hypothesis, H_0, and the alternative hypothesis, H_1. Because there are relatively few instances in forecasting where the intercept has an obvious theoretical interpretation, our attention will be concentrated on the slope coefficient.[11] In stating a hypothesis, the forecaster must state carefully what he or she believes is untrue and what is thought to be true. The null hypothesis is typically a statement of the value (or range of values) of the regression coefficient that could be expected to occur if the observed results were not significant. The most frequently tested null hypothesis is that the slope coefficient, β_1, is either greater or less than zero. That is,

$$H_0: \beta_1 \geq 0$$

or

(5-21)

$$H_0: \beta_1 \leq 0.$$

The justification for using a zero value as the benchmark is that the variable would not be included in an equation if its expected coefficient were zero. Furthermore, since we are generally interested in the sign of a coefficient rather than a specific value, the null hypothesis focuses on a range of values. The direction noted in the formulation of the null hypothesis is entirely a function of the theory being applied. For example, if theory suggests that a specific variable (personal income) should be positively related to another variable (personal computer sales), the coefficient should have a positive sign in the estimated regression equation. Therefore, the appropriate null hypothesis would be $H_0 \leq 0$. Conversely, if you expect the regression coefficient to have a negative coefficient, the null hypothesis would be $H_0 \geq 0$. Note that the null hypothesis under either case still represents what we hope to be incorrect. If H_0 is true, then our estimated regression line is of no use to us as a predictive device. For the personal computer example, the null hypothesis to be tested is

$$H_0: \beta_1 \leq 0.$$

(5-22)

Since only 12 periods of data were used in estimating the personal computer sales regression model in equation (5-12), it is possible that the estimated value of $\hat{\beta}_1$ (1.833) occurred by chance or was the result of sampling error. Stated differently, if the true value of β_1 is ≤ 0, what is the chance that we could have obtained the value of 1.833 for $\hat{\beta}_1$?

The alternative hypothesis is used to specify the value(s) that would occur if the null hypothesis were incorrect. The alternative hypothesis, H_1, can be written as

$$H_1: \beta_1 > 0.$$

(5-23)

---

[11] Suffice it to say that if the intercept carried some theoretical interpretation, it would be necessary to apply the same procedure to this coefficient.

We state the null and alternative hypotheses in this fashion so we can make a strong statement when we reject the null hypothesis. Specifically, only when we define the null hypothesis as signifying no relationship can we control the probability (often referred to as the alpha or Type I error) of rejecting the null hypothesis when it is, in fact, true. The converse does not hold. That is, we can never actually know the probability of accidentally accepting a false null hypothesis. The primary implication of this approach is that we can never "technically" say that we accept the null hypothesis. Alternatively, we must always say that we cannot reject the null hypothesis.

Equations (5-22) and (5-23) imply a one-tailed test, since a direction is specified. That is, since the alternative hypothesis has values on only one side of the null hypothesis, a one-tailed or one-sided test would be required. There will be situations wherein theory provides a consistent explanation for either a positive or negative sign associated with a given variable. For example, if we were interested in generating estimates of costs of production, a negative sign could signify that we are on the down-sloping portion of a short-run cost curve, while a positive sign could indicate that we have expanded output beyond the most efficient point, thereby leading to increased costs. In this situation, the regression coefficient associated with the cost variable could have either a positive or negative sign. Thus, the null hypothesis would be stated as

$$H_0: \beta_1 = 0 \tag{5-24}$$

and the alternative hypothesis would be

$$H_1: \beta \neq 0. \tag{5-25}$$

As we have seen, the typical approach in forecasting is to hypothesize an expected sign for each of the regression coefficients and then determine whether to reject the null hypothesis. However, since the regression coefficients are only estimates (based on one specific sample) of the true population parameters, we must accept that we will not always be right. In particular, there are two kinds of errors that we can make when testing a specific hypothesis:

Type I: We reject a true null hypothesis.
Type II: We accept (do not reject) a false null hypothesis.

The probability of committing a Type I error is equal to the level of statistical significance that we select in testing the null hypothesis. While there is an incentive to minimize the probability of committing a Type I error, as the level of statistical significance is increased, the probability of committing a Type II error increases. Attempting to strike an ideal balance between the two types of errors is difficult and requires judgment.

Having formulated the null and alternative hypotheses, the next step is to select a level of significance and to state the appropriate statistical test. The most common levels of significance (denoted by α, alpha) are 0.01, 0.05, and 0.10. For our example, we will arbitrarily select an α level of 0.05. In effect, we are stating that we are willing to incorrectly reject the null hypothesis 5 percent of the time—implying that we will be correct, in a statistical sense, 95 percent of the time.

The statistical test used in accepting or rejecting H_0 is the t test.[12] This is the relevant distribution because σ^2 is unknown.[13] t_e is calculated as

$$t_e = \frac{\hat{\beta}_1 - \beta_1}{S_{\hat{\beta}_1}}. \qquad (5\text{-}26)$$

t_e has $n - 2$ degrees of freedom (d.f.) and is the calculated t value based on the sample results. In effect, the calculated t value is a measure of the number of standard errors (standard deviations) the estimated value of the coefficient ($\hat{\beta}_1$) deviates from 0.

$$t_e = \frac{\hat{\beta}_1 - 0}{S_{\hat{\beta}_1}} \quad \text{or} \quad t_e = \frac{\hat{\beta}_1}{S_{\hat{\beta}_1}}$$

$$\beta_1 = 1.833 \qquad (5\text{-}27)$$

$$t_e = (1.833)/(0.547)$$

$$= 3.353$$

The standard error of the regression coefficient is given by

$$\hat{S}_{\beta_1} = \frac{S}{\sqrt{\sum (X_t - \overline{X})^2}} \qquad (5\text{-}28)$$

where S^2 equals

$$S^2 = \frac{\sum (Y_t - \hat{Y}_t)^2}{n - 2} \qquad (5\text{-}29)$$

[12] Technically speaking, we do not accept H_0; we simply cannot reject it.

[13] While it is true that the t distribution is the statistically correct distribution and statistic to be used, it can be shown that whenever the sample size is relatively large (greater than 30), the t and z distributions are nearly identical.

$$S^2 = (9019.324)/10 = 901.9324 \text{ (Table 5-2)}$$
$$S = 30.032$$

(5-30)

$$\sum (X_t - \overline{X})^2 \approx 3{,}017.88$$

$$S_{\hat{\beta}_1} = \frac{30.032}{\sqrt{3017.88}}$$
$$= 0.547.$$

(5-31)

The calculated value of t, t_e, is commonly referred to as the t statistic on computer printouts, while S is the standard error of the estimate. Further, the standard error of the estimate, 0.547, is similar to a standard deviation of the mean in that it measures the preciseness with which we have estimated a regression coefficient. As a general guideline, the smaller the standard error of the coefficient is relative to the estimated coefficient, the more reliable the estimate is. Alternatively, the standard error of the regression coefficient describes the distribution of sample coefficients around the actual population value of the regression parameter (β_1).

The final step involves the statement of a decision rule which specifies the appropriate interval over which we will accept or reject H_0. A critical value of t, denoted by t_{cr}, must be selected.

$$t_{cr} = 1.812$$

$$\alpha = 0.05 \quad \text{and} \quad \text{d.f.} = n - 2 = 10.$$

This critical value for t can be found in the appropriate column (or α value) and row (degrees of freedom) in Appendix A. Thus, the decision rule is as follows: If $t_e \leq 1.812$, accept H_0; if $t_e > 1.812$, reject the null hypothesis (accept the alternative hypothesis).

In effect, selection of the appropriate level of significance and the determination of the degrees of freedom allows us to divide the entire probability distribution into two segments, an area of acceptance and an area of rejection. Figure 5-8 illustrates the t distribution for our personal computer problem. Based on our decision rule, any value of t_e that falls within the right-hand extreme tail falls within the area of rejection, meaning that we would reject the null hypothesis.

With the decision rule specified, the next step is to compare t_e with t_{cr}.

$$t_e = 3.353$$

$$t_{cr} = 1.812$$

Since 3.353 is greater than 1.812, the decision is to reject H_0. Therefore, we

FIGURE 5-8 The *t* Test and Hypothesis Testing

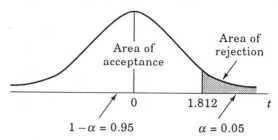

can conclude that the relationship between personal computer sales and per-household real disposable income is statistically significant.

Because we specified the level of significance at $\alpha = 0.05$, there is a 5 percent chance that we will err in rejecting the null hypothesis. That is, there is a 5 percent possibility that we will reject H_0 when it is true. We can say, however, that we will make the statistically correct decision 95 percent of the time. The arbitrary selection of the level of significance is subject to criticism, which can be avoided by using the Prob-Value approach.[14] The important issue is not whether statistical significance is achieved, but rather at what level it is achieved. The level at which we cross over from insignificance to significance is referred to as the critical confidence level. To determine this value, calculate the t_e value as before, locate this value in Appendix A, and find the appropriate α level. For our problem, a calculated t_e of 3.353 and 10 degrees of freedom implies a Prob-Value of less than 0.0025. In other words, if real disposable income is unrelated to personal computer sales, there are less than 25 chances out of 10,000 that we would observe a $\hat{\beta}_1$ value as large as 1.833.

Because the *t* test is so widely applied and is an integral part of most computer printouts, it is important that we understand what the *t* test does not do or show. First, recall that the purpose of the *t* test is to assist us in making statistical inferences about a population parameter based on the estimate that has been generated from our specific sample. Thus, we can say that the *t* test is a test for statistical significance and should not be used to test the theoretical validity of any estimated relationship. Numerous examples exist to demonstrate that nonsensical relationships are statistically significant. Consider the following regression model for the consumer price (P) index in the United Kingdom:

$$\hat{P} = 10.9 - 3.2C + 0.39C^2. \qquad (5\text{-}32)$$
$$t_e \qquad\qquad 13.9 \quad\ 19.5$$

[14] R. J. Wonnacott and T. H. Wonnacott, *Introductory Statistics* 2d ed. (New York: John Wiley & Sons, 1977), pp. 246–51. Copyright © 1977 John Wiley & Sons, Inc. Reprinted by permission.

Both of the regression coefficients can be shown to be statistically significant at an alpha level of 0.01. The problem occurs because the C variable is the cumulative rainfall in the United Kingdom. Despite the fact that C is statistically significant, there is no underlying theory to support this statistical relationship.[15]

A second limitation of the t test is that it does not assist us in determining which independent variable has the largest relative effect on the dependent variable. In various situations, forecasters are interested in ranking the importance of each of the independent variables in the model. The t test cannot be used to accomplish this task.

POINT AND INTERVAL ESTIMATES

By applying the method of least squares, we have estimated the slope coefficient from a sample of 12 observations and determined that $\hat{\beta}_1 = 1.833$. This is the best point estimate of the population parameter, β_1. Similarly, the best point estimate of $\hat{\beta}_0$ is $\beta_0 = 7.431$. The difficulty with these numbers is that we do not have a means of measuring the accuracy of the estimates. That is, we must now focus our attention on determining how precise our point estimates are relative to the actual population values. Confidence intervals, or interval estimates, provide us with a measure of the reliability of these estimates. They provide a range of values within which the true values of β_0 and β_1 are likely to fall. Thus, a confidence interval contains the area inside the critical region (the middle area of acceptance in Figure 5-8). Alternatively, a specific level of significance can be converted into a level or degree of confidence by subtracting the level of significance (α) from 100 percent. Thus, a 0.95 (95 percent) confidence interval is equivalent to a 0.05 level of significance.

As before, we will concentrate on the slope coefficient, $\hat{\beta}_1$. The confidence interval for β_1 is given by

$$\beta_1 = \hat{\beta}_1 \pm t_{cr} \, S_{\beta_1} \tag{5-33}$$

where t_{cr} denotes the critical value determined by the degree of significance or confidence we would be satisfied with. It is possible to calculate confidence intervals for any level of significance. As previously noted, confidence intervals provide us with a statement about the range within which the parameter, β_1, will fall. Equation (5-33) states that, if we repeat this experiment over and over, an interval of (t_{cr}) standard deviations on either side of the estimated slope value, $\hat{\beta}_1$, has a probability of 0.95 (assuming that 0.05 has been selected as our α level of significance) of containing the true slope parameter, β_1. For

[15] This example is taken from David F. Hendry, "Econometrics—Alchemy or Science?," *Economica*, November 1980, pp. 383–406.

our example, the 95 percent confidence interval for β_1 is computed as follows:

$$\beta_1 = \hat{\beta}_1 \pm t_{cr} S_{\beta_1}$$

$$= 1.833 \pm 1.812(0.547)$$

$$= 1.833 \pm 0.991 \qquad \textbf{(5-34)}$$

$$0.842 < \beta_1 < 2.824.$$

We can state with 95 percent confidence that the true value of β_1 falls within this range, a span wide enough to expose the lack of precision in the estimated point value and the model.

As an interesting corollary, this confidence interval can be used to test the null hypothesis, H_0. Once we have determined the confidence interval for β_1, we do not have to go through the lengthy process of hypothesis testing. The simplest procedure is to examine the confidence interval for β_1 and see if it contains the hypothesized value—that is, $\beta_1 \leq 0$. If it does, then H_0 cannot be rejected. Since equation (5-34) does not contain zero, we can reject the null hypothesis that there is no statistical relationship between disposable income and computer sales.

EXAMPLE 5-1   Use of confidence intervals to test H_0: $\beta_1 = 0$

To illustrate the use of confidence intervals in the testing of the null hypothesis, suppose that we have estimated the following model for automobile sales:

$$\hat{Y}_t = 5{,}807 + 3.24X_t. \qquad \textbf{(5-35)}$$

Further, suppose that $S_{\hat{\beta}_1} = 1.634$ and that $n = 16$. The 90 and 95 percent confidence intervals are calculated as follows:

90% Confidence Interval:

$$3.24 \pm (1.761)(1.634)$$

$$0.363 < \beta_1 < 6.117$$

95% Confidence Interval:

$$3.24 \pm (2.145)(1.634)$$

$$-0.265 < \beta_1 < 6.745.$$

The null hypothesis to be tested is H_0: $\beta_1 = 0$. This hypothesis can be tested by seeing if the confidence interval contains the assumed value of the population parameter, $\beta_1 = 0$. If so, then the null hypothesis is accepted; if not, it is rejected. An examination of the 90 percent confidence level indicates that it does not contain zero; therefore, we will reject the null hypothesis of no relationship. Conversely, the 95 percent confidence interval does contain the value zero, indicating that we would accept the null hypothesis of no relationship at a 95 percent level of significance. Further, it can be shown that the Prob Value for this example is approximately 0.07, indicating that the critical value of t where we cross from statistical significance to insignificance occurs when $\alpha = 0.07$ or a 93 percent confidence level.

This example, while simple, does serve to highlight the critical role played by selection of the level of significance, α. Specifically, the acceptance or rejection of the null hypothesis is crucially affected by which of the two values that we select. This is the reason that many practitioners prefer the Prob-Value approach.

STANDARD ERROR OF THE ESTIMATE

Because a regression estimate represents a type of average, we do not expect all the actual values to lie on this average line. This claim is analogous to the fact that the arithmetic mean, 10, of the numbers 4, 6, 14, and 16 is not one of the elements in the data set. Knowing this, we are interested in determining the average regression error.

The statistic that enables us to measure regression error is the standard error of the estimate:

$$\text{SEE} = S_{y \cdot x} = \sqrt{\frac{\sum (Y_t - \hat{Y}_t)^2}{n - 2}}. \tag{5-36}$$

As can be seen from this formulation, the SEE focuses on deviations about the regression line. Hence, it should be interpreted as the average error in guessing $\hat{Y}_t$. That is, the difference between the observed and the estimated (predicted) value of the dependent variable, $\hat{Y}_t - Y_t$, can be regarded as either the prediction error in time period t or as the standard deviation of all actual values from the predicted values. Returning to the personal computer example, the average error, SEE, is computed as follows:

$$\text{SEE} = \sqrt{\frac{9{,}019.324}{12 - 2}}$$

$$= \$30{,}032 \text{ dollars}. \tag{5-37}$$

Although the standard error of the estimate may be used to gauge the reliability of estimates, it has several deficiencies. First, it can be shown that the SEE depends on the unit of measurement of the dependent variable. This occurs because the SEE relies on the residual term, $\hat{Y}_t - Y_t$, to measure goodness of fit. This residual is not unit-free. If we divide all values of Y by 100, this yields a different result for SEE. Second, the standard error is a measure of a single-period error; it does not provide us with any measure of the error in future multiperiod forecasts. Third, the SEE is calculated based on known values of the independent variables (X_t). This certainly is not the situation that prevails in the future periods for which estimates are desired. Finally, without some frame of reference an exact interpretation of the SEE is difficult. As a result of this difficulty, practitioners frequently rely on the average percentage regression error (APE), which is computed as follows:

$$APE = \frac{SEE}{\overline{Y}_t} \cdot 100. \tag{5-38}$$

For the personal computer example, the APE is computed as

$$APE = \frac{30.032}{119.5917} \cdot 100$$
$$= 25.112\%. \tag{5-39}$$

On average, the regression estimates have been in error by 25.112 percent, which once again confirms the observation that, despite the fact that the estimated model is statistically significant, the model does not generate very precise estimates.

ANALYSIS OF VARIANCE

Analysis of variance, hereafter called AOV (and sometimes called ANOVA), focuses on the ability of a regression line to explain or account for the variation in Y. Return to our personal computer example and begin by asking the question, Why would different individuals spend different amounts on personal computers? Stated another way, what *explains* this variation in purchases of personal computers and how can this explanation assist in the forecasting process? The objective in model building is to identify those variables that assist in explaining the observed variation in the variable of interest (personal computer sales).

This can best be seen by concentrating our attention on Figure 5-9. Assume, again, that you are a business-conditions analyst interested in predicting personal computer sales. Further assume that you are doing this in the absence of any knowledge about household income levels. In this case, your best guess will be the average observed value of personal computer sales—that is, $\overline{Y}$. In Figure 5-9, this guess $(\overline{Y})$ involves a large estimating error. This error can be depicted as $(Y_t - \overline{Y})$, the deviation in Y_t from its mean. The regression line allows us to obtain another, perhaps better, estimate of Y. That

FIGURE 5-9 Explained and Unexplained Deviation: Simple Regression

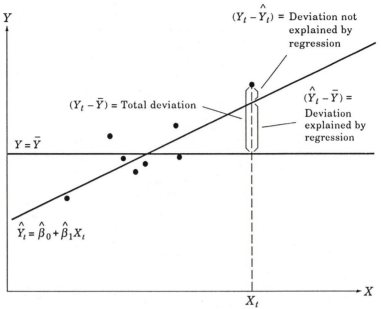

is, instead of estimating personal computer sales as $\overline{Y}$, we use $\hat{Y}$, which is derived from the regression line. Figure 5-9 presents this comparison.

A large part of the deviation, $(\hat{Y}_t - \overline{Y})$, is now explained by the regression. This leaves only a relatively small portion of the deviation unexplained, $(Y_t - \hat{Y}_t)$. Formally, the total deviation in Y can be regarded as the sum

$$(Y_t - \overline{Y}) = (\hat{Y}_t - \overline{Y}) + (Y_t - \hat{Y}_t)$$

$$\underset{\text{Deviation}}{\text{Total}} = \underset{\text{Deviation}}{\text{Explained}} + \underset{\text{Deviation}}{\text{Unexplained}} \qquad \textbf{(5-40)}$$

which holds for all t. It therefore follows that

$$\sum (Y_t - \overline{Y}) = \sum (\hat{Y}_t - \overline{Y}) + \sum (Y_t - \hat{Y}_t). \qquad \textbf{(5-41)}$$

Furthermore, it can be shown that this same equality holds when these deviations are squared. Thus,

$$\sum (Y_t - \overline{Y})^2 = \sum (\hat{Y}_t - \overline{Y})^2 + \sum (Y_t - \hat{Y}_t)^2$$

$$\underset{\text{Variation}}{\text{Total}} = \underset{\text{Variation}}{\text{Explained}} + \underset{\text{Variation}}{\text{Unexplained}} \qquad \textbf{(5-42)}$$

$$\text{TSS} = \text{RSS} + \text{ESS}$$

TABLE 5-3 Analysis of Variance Table for Linear Regression

Sources of Variation	Variation	Degrees of Freedom[b]	Variance[c]	F_e [d]
Explained by Regression[a]	$\sum (\hat{Y}_t - \overline{Y})^2$ or $\hat{\beta}_1^2 \sum (X_t - \overline{X})^2$	1	$\dfrac{\sum (\hat{Y}_t - \overline{Y})^2}{1}$	
Unexplained or Residual/ Error[a]	$\sum (Y_t - \hat{Y}_t)^2$	$n - 2$	$S^2 = \dfrac{\sum (Y_t - \hat{Y}_t)^2}{n - 2}$	
Total	$\sum (Y_t - \overline{Y})^2$	$n - 1$		$\dfrac{\hat{\beta}_1^2 \sum (X_t - \overline{X})^2}{S^2}$

[a] See equations (5-42) and (5-43).
[b] Based on a sample of size n. If used for a multiple regression equation with a sample of size N and K regression coefficients, the corresponding degrees of freedom would be $K, N - (K + 1)$, and $N - 1$. The K value does not include the constant.
[c] Variation divided by degrees of freedom.
[d] This is the observed or estimated F value. It is compared to the theoretical or critical F value to determine the significance of the regression equation. See equations (5-45) and 5-46).

where variation is defined as the sum of squared deviations and TSS refers to the total sum of squares, RSS to the regression sum of squares, and ESS to the error sum of squares. It is occasionally convenient to rewrite equation (5-42) as

$$\sum (Y_t - \overline{Y})^2 = \hat{\beta}_1^2 \sum (X_t - \overline{X})^2 + \sum (Y_t - \hat{Y}_t)^2$$

$$\begin{array}{ccc} \text{Total} \\ \text{Variation} \end{array} = \begin{array}{c} \text{Variation} \\ \text{Explained} \\ \text{by } X \end{array} + \begin{array}{c} \text{Unexplained} \\ \text{Variation.} \end{array} \qquad (5\text{-}43)$$

This formulation highlights the role of X in accounting for or explaining variations in Y.

The components noted in equations (5-42) and (5-43) are commonly presented in an AOV table similar to Table 5-3.

The goal in regression analysis is to derive a regression line that will assist us in predicting Y. If we can link the variation (change) in Y to variations (changes) in X, we can use our knowledge of changes in per-household real disposable income to predict changes in personal computer sales. The AOV table incorporates the F test of the regression equation's significance. The F test may be viewed as a test that $\beta_1 = 0$.[16] The issue under consideration is

[16] The observant reader will notice that this is identical to the situation of testing H_0: $\beta_1 = 0$ with the t test. However, this equality is not true in general (in multiple regression); therefore, both are presented here. Further, the F test has a special applicability in the case of stepwise regression. This is discussed in chapter 8.

whether or not the ratio of the explained variance to unexplained variance is sufficiently large to reject the hypothesis that Y is unrelated to X. Specifically, the test statistic and the hypothesis are

$$H_0: \beta_1 = 0$$

$$F_e = \frac{\text{Variance Explained by Regression } (X)}{\text{Unexplained Variance}}. \tag{5-44}$$

Formally,

$$F_e = \frac{\beta_1^2 \sum (X_t - \overline{X})^2}{S^2} \tag{5-45}$$

or

$$F_e = \frac{\sum (\hat{Y}_t - \overline{Y})^2}{\sum (Y_t - \hat{Y}_t)^2/(n - 2)}. \tag{5-46}$$

A 0.05 significance test involves finding the critical F value that leaves 5 percent of the distribution in the right-hand tail. Thus, the decision rule becomes: If the calculated value of F_e exceeds the critical value of F_{cr}, reject H_0. Table 5-4 illustrates the AOV table for the personal computer sales example.[17]

To test the null hypothesis, calculate F_e:

$$F_e = (10,142)/902 \tag{5-47}$$
$$F_e \approx 11.24.$$

Since F_e is greater than 4.96 (the critical value of F taken from Appendix B), we reject H_0. Therefore, knowledge of the level of real disposable income

TABLE 5-4   Analysis of Variance Table for Personal Computer Example

Source of Variation	Variation	d.f.	Variance
Explained by Regression	$\hat{\beta}_1 \sum (X_t - \overline{X})^2 \approx (1.833)^2(3017.88)$	1	10,142
Unexplained	$\sum (Y_t - \hat{Y}_t)^2 \approx 9,019$	10	902
Total	19,161	11	

[17] Some computer software packages will refer to variation as sum of squares and variance as mean square or mean square error.

does provide us with useful knowledge in predicting changes in personal computer sales.

COEFFICIENTS OF DETERMINATION AND CORRELATION

Practitioners are principally interested in the explanatory or predictive power of our estimated regression models. While it is true that we could compare the estimated regression model to a scatterplot of the actual observations, we obviously need a more formal measure of this goodness of fit. The most straightforward measure available to use is the coefficient of determination, r^2.[18]

There are a variety of formulas for calculating and interpreting the coefficient of determination, r^2. The most convenient method follows from the development of AOV. The coefficient of determination can be defined as

$$r^2 = \frac{\sum (\hat{Y}_t - \overline{Y})^2}{\sum (Y_t - \overline{Y})^2} \tag{5-48}$$

$$= \frac{\text{Explained Variation}}{\text{Total Variation}}.$$

This formulation permits a clear interpretation. The coefficient of determination is the proportion of the total variation in Y that is explained or accounted for by an estimated regression line. Alternatively, it provides a measure of the proportion or percentage of the changes in the dependent variable (Y) that can be explained by changes in the independent variable(s). Since the explained variation cannot exceed the total variation, the maximum value of r^2 is 1—that is, 100 percent of the variation in the dependent variable (Y) has been explained. The coefficient of correlation (r) is simply the square root of the coefficient of determination. That is,

$$r = \sqrt{r^2}. \tag{5-49}$$

Returning to the personal computer example in Table 5-2,

$$r^2 = \frac{\sum (\hat{Y}_t - \overline{Y})^2}{\sum (Y_t - \overline{Y})^2}$$

$$= (10{,}142)/(19{,}161) \tag{5-50}$$

$$r^2 = 0.5293$$

$$r = 0.7275.$$

[18] r^2 is used when a simple (one independent variable) linear regression model has been estimated, while R^2 is the more common notation when a multiple (more than one independent variable) regression model has been estimated.

Thus, we have explained only 52.93 percent of the observed changes (variation) in personal computer sales (Y) with observed changes (variations) in real disposable income (X). This provides further evidence that our simple model is an inadequate explanatory model.

There are several potential problems with both the coefficient of determination and the correlation coefficient. First, unwary readers or users will frequently confuse the interpretation of the correlation coefficient with the coefficient of determination. Thus, for example, if the correlation coefficient, r, is reported as 0.7275, it may be interpreted as implying that 72.75 percent of the variation in the dependent variable has been explained or accounted for. However, from the personal computer sales example, a correlation coefficient of .7275 implies that the independent variable(s) explains only 52.93 percent of the variations in Y. (It is true that as r approaches 1, r^2 also approaches 1.) Hence, if our interest is in measuring the strength of the relationship between Y and X, the coefficient of determination, r^2, is the preferred measure.

Second, although it is a common practice to associate high values of r and r^2 with a good fit and low values with a poor fit, this interpretation can be misleading in forecasting models if not supported by other evaluation statistics. For example, time series models generally have much higher r^2 values than do cross-sectional models. In the former case, the units of observation are typically aggregates, such as average prices, total disposable income, or total sales. When using these aggregates, a lot of variation is averaged out of the observations. Cross-sectional data are generally based on micro units when this variation has not been averaged out. Furthermore, there is no such thing as a good, best, optimal, or acceptable r^2 in applied areas such as forecasting.

Third, it can be shown that these measures are somewhat dependent on the number of independent variables in the regression model. In particular, as will be seen in our discussion of multiple regression models, both the coefficient of determination and the correlation coefficient will increase as the number of independent variables increases.

Finally, it is important to remember that neither the coefficient of determination nor the correlation coefficient imply anything about causation.

CONCLUDING COMMENTARY

Prior to the presentation of more realistic examples and the use of regression for forecasting, the reader is reminded that the example used throughout this section was selected for illustrative purposes. In the majority of cases, the forecaster will have access to computers. The formulas, calculations, and tests previously noted were presented and analyzed to develop a conceptual understanding.

Second, we have not verified the assumptions of the classical linear model.

This process of assumption verification is delayed until multiple regression models have been estimated and discussed in succeeding chapters.

Third, we have made an important distinction between theoretical significance and statistical significance. The former derives from theory; the latter from statistical tests applied to a specific set of sample data. If, for example, the null hypothesis, H_0, is not rejected, an obvious question arises: Is the theory inconsistent with the real world or, conversely, is the real world (as measured by our model) inconsistent with the theory? As we will see in succeeding sections of this chapter and in the next chapter, problems such as incorrect signs on individual independent variables or statistical insignificance for some models may be a result of either improper specification or violation of the assumptions of the classical linear model. For this reason, regression equations should not be used to "prove" cause and effect. These models can be used, however, to measure whether an association exists between two or more variables and the strength of the relationship.

Finally, and most significantly, we have not evaluated the usefulness of regression as a predictive device. The tests presented here are designed primarily to measure the statistical reliability of regression. Although there is a relationship between statistical reliability and forecast accuracy, they are not synonymous. To evaluate regression equations as forecasting techniques, we need to develop additional concepts and tools.

EXAMPLE 5-2   Air Miles Traveled

The head of a forecasting division received a request from a senior vice-president of purchasing to provide a quarterly estimate that can be used to plan crude-oil purchases to minimize costs. The firm is a major supplier of fuel to the airlines, and advance estimates of fuel demand are critical because of erratic fluctuations in both the price and the supply of crude oil. The goal is to develop a model that will provide a quarterly estimate of the demand for airline fuel.

The preparation of a forecast presupposes several items. The first item of concern is the selection of a variable that can be used to measure the demand for high-octane airplane fuel. After a review of past research, it was decided to use air miles flown as a proxy variable. The advantage of this variable is that there is a fairly stable relationship between miles flown and fuel consumption. Once estimated, the mileage can simply be used to determine the probable demand for fuel.

Since total miles flown is related to economic activity on a national level, real gross national product was selected as the independent or causal factor that best measures aggregate activity. The model becomes

$$\widehat{AM}_t = \hat{\beta}_0 + \hat{\beta}_1 RGNP_t + e_t \qquad (5\text{-}51)$$

where

$$\widehat{AM}_t \;=\; \text{quarterly air miles traveled in time period } t; \text{ seasonally adjusted; billions of miles}$$

$$RGNP_t \;=\; \text{real gross national product in quarter } t; \text{ seasonally adjusted; billions of dollars}$$

$$\hat{\beta}_0, \hat{\beta}_1 \;=\; \text{regression coefficients to be estimated.}$$

We would expect the slope coefficient, $\hat{\beta}_1$, to have a positive value, implying that as real gross national product increases, air miles traveled increases. Since we do not have any observations on $\widehat{AM}_t$ when $RGNP_t$ is equal to zero, we cannot assign any theoretical interpretation to the value or the sign of the intercept $(\hat{\beta}_0)$.

Time series data were collected on a quarterly basis for the period from the first quarter of 1970 (1970:I) to the first quarter of 1987 (1987:I). The actual data used in this example are documented in Appendix C, Table C-1. As an initial step, a scatter diagram was plotted, and the clustering in Figure 5-10 verified the belief that there was a positive relationship between air miles traveled and RGNP.

The results of fitting a linear regression model to the data (Table C-1) were as follows:

$$\widehat{AM}_t \;=\; -66.834 + 0.037 RGNP_t. \qquad\qquad \textbf{(5-52)}$$

Standard Error	0.000814
t_e	45.24
95% Confidence Interval for β_1	0.035–0.038
Range of Data	1970:I to 1987:I
Number of Observations	69
$r^2 = 0.9683$	$r = 0.984$
$F_{1,67} = 2,047$	SEE $= 2.60$
APE $= 5.76$	

This output is typical of the cryptic summarization of regression information provided by computer-generated statistical programs. A business-conditions analyst interested in forecasting applications must squeeze the maximum possible information from each of the regression statistics. Looking first at the regression coefficients, the intercept value, -66.834, provides no meaningful information; interpreted literally, it implies that if GNP equals zero (that is, if we have no economic activity), we will have a negative level of air travel. The slope coefficient implies that a \$1 billion increase in real GNP will lead to an increase of approximately 37 million air passenger miles traveled.

Immediately below the regression coefficient associated with RGNP are the statistics used to evaluate its reliability. The standard error of

FIGURE 5-10   Scatter Diagram for Air Miles Traveled and Real Gross National Product

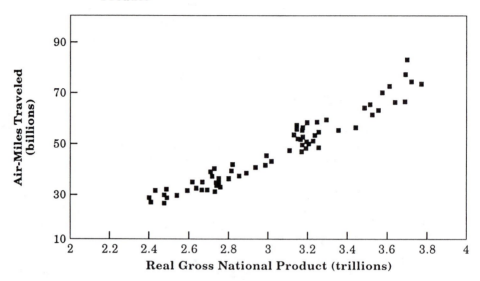

the coefficient is used in calculating the t statistic and in computing the confidence interval. To check the null hypothesis that the observed slope of 0.037 is significantly different from zero (that is, it did not occur by chance), we can use either of the following two procedures:

1. A comparison of the calculated t statistic, t_e, with the critical value of this statistic, t_{cr}, can be used to accept (or reject) H_0: $\beta_1 \leq 0$. In this case, t_e (45) exceeds t_{cr} (≈ 2.5) at an α level of 0.99. We can reject H_0.

2. The information needed to construct a 95 percent confidence interval is presented immediately below the t statistic. In this case, the actual confidence interval is

$$0.035 \leq \beta_1 \leq 0.038. \tag{5-53}$$

Since this interval does not contain zero, we can reject H_0. Given these test results, we can be confident that the observed slope coefficient, 0.037, is significantly different from zero. Thus, the equation can be used to estimate air miles traveled.

Continuing with the analysis, note that the regression equation explained approximately 97 percent of the variation in the dependent variable. Alternatively, we could have relied on the analysis-of-variance table, Table 5-5, to test the statistical reliability of the regression equation. This is accomplished by computing the F

TABLE 5-5   Analysis of Variance for Air Miles Traveled

Source of Variation	Variation	d.f.	Variance
Explained	13,824	1	13,824
Unexplained	452	67	6.75
Total	14,276	68	$F_e = 2047$

Source: Equation (5-52)

statistic as follows:

$$F_e = F_{1,67} = \frac{\text{Explained Variance}}{\text{Unexplained Variance}}$$
$$= 13,824/6.75 \text{ (Table 5-5)} \qquad \textbf{(5-54)}$$
$$= 2,047.$$

Since F_e exceeds the critical value of 4, we conclude that the regression equation is statistically significant. That is, the observed relationship will provide a better estimate of $\widehat{AM}_t$ than could be obtained by simply relying on the mean of air miles traveled.

As a final check on the average precision of the regression estimates, we can use the standard error of the estimate (SEE).

As noted earlier, the SEE is the average error $(AM_t - \widehat{AM}_t)$ one would have made by mechanically plugging the historical values of RGNP into the regression equation.

Since it is futile to interpret this average quarterly error without reference to the actual values of AM_t, the average percentage regression error is preferred:

$$\begin{array}{c}\text{Average Percentage}\\ \text{Regression Error}\end{array} = \text{APE} = \frac{\text{SEE}}{\text{AM}_t}$$
$$= 2.5987/45.10 \qquad \textbf{(5-55)}$$
$$\text{APE} = 5.76\%.$$

On average, regression estimates have been in error by 5.76 percent.

EXAMPLE 5-3   Consumption Function

Suppose that we are interested in estimating a simple form of the Keynesian consumption function. Specifically, we want to derive estimates of consumption spending as it relates to income. After some investigation of the various measures of income, we decide to use disposable personal

FIGURE 5-11   **Scatter Diagram: Consumption Expenditures versus Disposable Income**

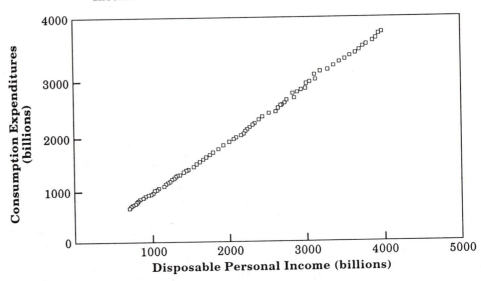

income as our predictor or explanatory variable. Traditional macroeconomic theory suggests that consumption should be positively related to income. Thus, the model that we are interested in is

$$\hat{C}_t = \hat{\beta}_0 + \hat{\beta}_1 YD_t \tag{5-56}$$

where

C_t = quarterly consumption expenditures, billions of dollars, SAAR

YD_t = quarterly disposable personal income, billions of dollars, SAAR.

The data base is a quarterly tabulation for the period from 1970:I to 1990: IV and is presented in Appendix C, Table C-2. The scatter diagram in Figure 5-11 along with the simple correlation coefficient of 0.999 provide initial verification that high values of income are indeed associated with high levels of consumption.

The results of fitting a regression line to the scatter diagram are shown in Table 5-6. By all statistical tests, the estimated relationship between consumption and disposable income is statistically significant. The coefficient itself indicates that if income changes by $1 billion dollars,

TABLE 5-6   Regression Equation for Consumption Function

$$\hat{C}_t = -53.979 + 0.94216YD_t \tag{5-57}$$

Standard error $\approx (0.00260)$

$t_e \approx 363$

$r^2 \approx 0.99$

$r \approx 0.99$

SEE ≈ 24.0

consumption expenditures will change by 0.94216 billion dollars ($942,160,000). The average percentage error is

$$\text{APE} = (\text{SEE}/\overline{YD}_t) = \frac{24.0}{2046.5} \approx 1.17. \tag{5-58}$$

EXAMPLE 5-4   Appliance Shipments

Suppose that you are the warehouse credit manager for a firm whose primary line of business is serving as a shipping facility for a group of household appliance manufacturers. To determine your transportation requirements, you decide to develop quantitative estimates of shipments. You have reason to believe that appliance shipments (APP_t) will be responsive to the production of these appliances ($PROD_t$). You would expect higher production levels to lead to an increase in appliance shipments. Since you are interested in making short-term predictions, you decide to examine a quarterly model. Data for this example is presented in Appendix C, Table C-3.

The results of estimating the quarterly model are presented in Table 5-7.

TABLE 5-7   Appliance Shipments Regression Model

Time Frame	Constant	Coefficient	Standard Error	t_e	95% Confidence Interval
1986:I–1990:III	−85,318	1027.604	51.39	20	919–1,136

Summary Statistics

$r^2 \approx 0.96$	$r \approx 0.98$	$F_e \approx 400$	SEE $\approx 1,047$

The model can be written as

$$\widehat{APP}_t = -85{,}318 + 1027.60439PROD_t \qquad (5\text{-}59)$$

Time Frame: 1986:I to 1990:III

with the 95 percent confidence interval for the production coefficient, PROD, given by

$$919 \leq \beta \leq 1{,}136. \qquad (5\text{-}60)$$

The model passes all statistical tests of significance, and the positive sign on the income variable matches theoretical expectations. Further, since the confidence interval does not contain zero, we would reject the null hypothesis of no significant statistical relationship. However, as we see in the next section, the pattern exhibited by the error terms suggests that there may be an underlying problem with using the model to generate forecasts of automobile sales.

FORECASTING WITH LINEAR REGRESSION MODELS

FORECASTING MODELS

Previous sections of this chapter focused on fitting a regression line and on how to evaluate the statistical reliability of these models. We now turn to the task of using regression models in forecasting. That is, our attention shifts from estimating and statistically evaluating regression coefficients to using a regression equation for forecasting and predicting. Interest shifts from the properties of regression coefficients to the properties of forecasts or predictions made with the regression equation.

The basic premise of regression models is that changes in the value of a particular variable (the dependent variable, Y) are closely associated with changes in some other independent variable(s). Therefore, if accurate information is available on the future value of the independent variables, it can be used to forecast the future value of the dependent variable. We return to this point later, but it is worth emphasizing here that the reliability of forecasts generated by regression models is crucially related to the accuracy of the predicted values of the independent variable(s).

TYPES OF FORECASTS

A forecast or prediction (the words are used interchangeably) is a numerical estimate concerning the probability of future events based on past and current information. The estimated regression equation contains all the past and current information at our disposal. By extending our models beyond the reference period, we can use this information to obtain quantitative guesses about future values of specific variables. Thus, the past and current information is summarized by the regression equation

$$\hat{Y}_t = \hat{\beta}_0 + \hat{\beta}_1 X_t \tag{5-61}$$

In the context of our definition, the numerical estimate has the following structure: If X were to take on the value X^*, the associated value of Y would be Y^*. In other words, forecasting or prediction is concerned with the value of Y, given that $X = X^*$.

Forecasts of future values of Y involve a two-step process. First, we must derive a point estimate of Y based on a specific value of X; second, we must derive a confidence interval around this point. Formally, the first step can be stated as (assuming that we are interested in a one-period-ahead forecast):

$$\hat{Y}_{t+1} = \hat{\beta}_0 + \hat{\beta}_1 X_{t+1}. \tag{5-62}$$

Once we have estimated $\hat{\beta}_0$ and $\hat{\beta}_1$ by the least-squares procedure from our sample data and have obtained an estimated value for X_{t+1}, we can obtain a forecast value for Y_{t+1}. In the personal computer sales example, suppose that the estimate for real disposable income in 1988 (X_{t+1}) is \$82.5 million. Based on this information, the best point estimate for personal computer sales can be obtained as follows:

$$\hat{Y}_{t+1} = \hat{Y}_{1988} = \hat{\beta}_0 + \hat{\beta}_1 X_{t+1}$$

$$= 7.431 + 1.833 X_{t+1} \tag{5-63}$$

$$= 7.431 + 1.833(82.5)$$

$$\hat{Y}_{1988} = \$158,654 \text{ thousand.}$$

It is important to recognize that although the estimated regression line yields a precise forecast value, this model should really be viewed as providing a range of values within which the true forecast value is likely to fall. For example, based on our estimated personal computer model, the "forecast" of personal computer sales for 1988 was \$158,654,000. It is highly unlikely that actual sales would match this figure. The difference between the "forecast" and actual sales highlights the fact that the estimated model enables us to construct an interval band around the actual values, with the same interpretation that we can be reasonably confident that actual sales will fall within this interval.

Construction of a confidence interval for this point estimate requires a measure of the forecasting error. It can be shown that the variance involved in this process is

$$V_f = \sigma^2 \left[\frac{1}{n} + \frac{(X_{t+1} - \overline{X})^2}{\sum (X_t - X)^2} + 1 \right]. \tag{5-64}$$

Since the variance for the population, σ^2, is generally unknown, it is estimated by s^2, the sample variance. Equation (5-64) is of immediate interest because it tells us that the forecast error is sensitive to (1) sample size, (2) variance of X, and (3) the distance between X_{t+1} and $\overline{X}$. This latter point deserves further clarification. The best forecasts for Y can be made for values of X close to $\overline{X}$. In fact, when $X_{t+1} = \overline{X}$, the middle term in equation (5-64) disappears, and the error is simply a function of sample size. Thus, the farther we extend X_{t+1} away from $\overline{X}$ (the farther into the future we go), the larger the error becomes and the less reliable the forecast is likely to be. The confidence interval for the point estimate, equation (5-63), can be shown to be equal to[19]

$$Y_{t+1} = \hat{Y}_{t+1} \pm t_\alpha s \sqrt{\frac{1}{n} \frac{(X_{t+1} - \overline{X})^2}{\sum (X_t - X)^2} + 1}. \tag{5-65}$$

When $X_{t+1} = X_{1988} = \$82.5$ and $\alpha = 0.10$, the calculations are

$$\hat{Y}_{1988} = 158,654 \pm 1.812(30.032) \sqrt{\frac{1}{12} + \frac{(82.5 - 61.2)^2}{3017.88} + 1} \tag{5-66}$$

$$= \$158,654,000 \pm \$60,442,000$$

$$\$98,212,000 \le Y_{t+1} \le \$219,096,000. \tag{5-67}$$

The forecaster can be 90 percent confident that the true value of Y_{t+1} falls somewhere in this confidence interval. Furthermore, we can obtain 90 percent confidence intervals for all other values of X. This permits the derivation of confidence or interval bands—a confidence interval for all values of X. Figure 5-12 illustrates the 90 percent confidence band for the personal computer sales example. The principal usefulness of this diagram is to highlight the fact that the greater the distance between X and $\overline{X}$, the larger our confidence interval becomes. Thus, once we attempt to extrapolate too far into the future, we are likely to encounter ever-larger forecast errors.

---

[19] Technically, this confidence interval is for small samples. The interval for large samples $(n > 30)$ is given by

$$Y_0 = \hat{Y}_0 \pm t_\alpha s.$$

For details, see, for example, H. Theil, *Principles of Econometrics* (New York: John Wiley & Sons, 1971), chapter 8.

FIGURE 5-12 **Ninety Percent Prediction Interval for Personal**
Computer Sales

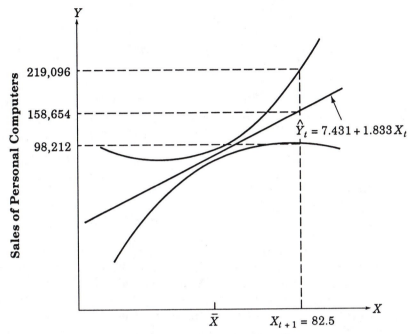

Real Disposable Income Per Household

It is useful to differentiate among (1) ex post and ex ante forecasts, and (2) conditional and unconditional forecasts. Both ex post and ex ante forecasts provide estimated values of the dependent variable beyond the time period for which the model has been fitted. However, in an ex post forecast, the forecast period is such that observations on both the dependent and independent variables are known with certainty. Ex post forecasts can be compared with existing data for Y, thereby providing a means of evaluating the forecasting reliability of the model. Indeed, as we see in the next section, one of the best techniques for evaluating forecasts from regression models is ex post forecasting. Whereas an ex post forecast is made with certain knowledge of both the independent and dependent variable, an ex ante forecast is made without any knowledge regarding the value of the actual dependent variable. The value of the independent variable may or may not be known with certainty. This distinction can be seen by examining Figure 5-13.

To better illustrate these concepts, suppose that we return to the personal computer sales example. In particular, suppose that we estimated the model for the years 1976 to 1986, excluding 1987 from the estimation procedure. The

FIGURE 5-13 Types of Forecasts

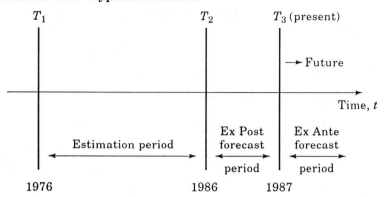

estimated model for this time frame is

$$\hat{Y}_t = 14.310 + 1.659X_t. \tag{5-68}$$

It is helpful to think of a time continuum consisting of three segments. The first represents the time period used for estimating the regression equation (the years 1976 to 1986, for example). The second segment refers to the period of time from the last year (period) of the estimation period to the present (1987, for example). The third period represents the future (all years following 1987). Referring to Figure 5-13, during the T_2 to T_3 time interval, actual values for the dependent and independent variables are known. This may not appear to be forecasting in the true sense, but, as we see in the next section, the making of ex post forecasts is an important evaluation tool. Ex ante forecasting involves making predictions about the period following T_3. This distinction can be further clarified by referring to our personal computer sales example. Equation (5-68) includes 1986 as the last data point in the estimated model. An ex post forecast can be prepared for 1987 because the actual values for real disposable income ($72.8 million) and personal computer sales ($180.3 thousand) are available. Thus, the ex post forecast value is

$$\hat{Y}_t = 14.310 + 1.659X_t \tag{5-69}$$

$$\hat{Y}_{1987} = 14.310 + 1.659X_{1987}$$

$$= 14.310 + 1.659(72.8) \tag{5-70}$$

$$= \$135,085 \text{ thousand.}$$

The critical feature in this computation is that the estimate of $135,085,000 can be compared with the actual value of $180,300,000. Furthermore, this ex post forecast is based on an actual value for real GNP. An ex ante forecast does not require any information regarding the value of the dependent variable. Continuing with the personal computer example, an ex ante forecast would be of the form

$$\hat{Y}_{1990} = 14.310 + 1.659X_{1990}. \tag{5-71}$$

The preceding discussion leads to a second important distinction. If, at the time the forecast is made, the values of the independent variable(s) are known with certainty, then an unconditional forecast can be made. If, on the other hand, the values of the independent variable(s) are not known with certainty, then a conditional forecast is made—a forecast conditional on the assumed values of the independent variables. Equation (5-70) is an unconditional forecast because the 1987 value of real disposable income is known with certainty. All ex post forecasts are unconditional, but ex ante forecasts may also be unconditional. For example, it is possible that we would know the exact value of real disposable income in 1988 but would not have the exact value for personal computer sales for the same period. Ex post forecasts require certain knowledge for both dependent and independent variables. Unconditional forecasts require that only independent variables be known with certainty. In a conditional forecast, values for one or more independent variables are not known with certainty. The implication is that with conditional forecasts, we must have a method of forecasting (estimating) values for the independent variables. Equation (5-71) exemplifies a conditional forecasting equation.

The practicing forecaster is apt to rely on all four of these classifications at various stages of research. For example, ex post forecasts are made with the intention of evaluating forecast reliability (see the next section). Alternatively, development of ex ante forecasts, which focus on estimating unknown values for the dependent variable, is the primary point of interest throughout this text. The previous discussion pointed out the distinction between conditional and unconditional forecasts; the former uses projections for the independent variables, whereas the latter incorporates known values. Even though in most cases future values of the independent variables are not known, many variables can be estimated with a high degree of accuracy. Because conditional forecasting requires a high level of mathematical sophistication, many business forecasters use estimates of the independent variables prepared by commercial forecast vendors.

FORECAST EVALUATION

Prior to preparing unconditional forecasts, we need to develop techniques for evaluating the forecasting reliability of regression estimates. This is quite a different problem from statistical evaluation. In all previous examples, we have highlighted the t, F, R^2, SEE, and confidence intervals. A single-equation regression model may have a high t and F, yet may fail as a forecasting device. This can occur because of inherent volatility in the forecast variable being analyzed. For example, if we estimate a monthly equation, the irregular component can dominate and produce low t and F statistics. However, if the errors in estimating tend to offset each other, it may be a satisfactory forecasting equation. Conversely, a high SEE or a high R^2 does not guarantee that the model will generate useful forecasts.

As has been pointed out several times, the best test of the reliability for any model is its ex ante forecasting performance. However, if this were the only test, forecasting as we know it would cease to exist. Some pretesting on actual data is essential to an evaluation of models. Included in this pretesting are computation and validation of the various statistical tools introduced in this chapter. The most common measure of goodness of fit is the correlation coefficient (R) or its counterpart, the coefficient of determination (R^2). This is unfortunate, because, to quote Michael Evans,

> In all of the thousands of equations which I have estimated for predictive purposes, probably less than five percent of those selected for forecasting were those with the highest R^2. The reason is simple. If one calculates several regression equations in order to determine the best one, it is likely that certain variables will appear to be significant when in fact they have only a spurious correlation. If one leaves these variables in the equation, he is likely to generate a very poor forecast.[20]

If this is true, how do we exclude those variables that do not belong? Once again, we quote Evans: "Part of the answer to this question goes back to my earlier remarks about the importance of choosing a reasonable theory as a guide toward estimating the best forecasting equation."[21]

The other part of the answer involves computation and interpretation of measures specifically devised to measure and test the forecasting reliability of models. Virtually all practitioners test their empirical work by estimating an equation, looking at the size of the error terms, and then reestimating the equation in an attempt to reduce the error terms. The specific criteria most commonly relied on are (1) the mean absolute deviation (MAD), (2) mean square error (MSE), (3) mean absolute percentage error (MAPE), (4) average percentage error (APE), (5) turning-point error graphs and computations, and (6) ex post forecast analysis. Additionally, there are four simulation-type statistics that can be computed: (1) root mean square (RMS), (2) root percent mean square (RPMS), (3) mean error (bias), and (4) mean percent error (percent bias). A detailed discussion of all of these evaluation statistics was presented in

---

[20] Michael K. Evans, "Econometric Models," in William F. Butler, Robert A. Kavesh, and Robert B. Platt, eds., *Methods and Techniques of Business Forecasting* (Englewood Cliffs, N.J.: Prentice Hall, 1974), pp. 172–73.

[21] Ibid., p. 173.

chapter 4; hence, our primary purpose here is to apply these tools to the personal computer example.

Returning to the personal computer sales example, suppose that we omit the last three years, 1985 to 1987, from our analysis and estimate the equation based on this shortened time frame (1976 to 1984). The resulting model is

$$\hat{Y}_t = 12.406 + 1.605X_t. \tag{5-72}$$

This model can thus be used to generate estimates for personal computer sales based on known values of per-household real disposable income for the three years that we have omitted. The results of this estimation and the comparison with the actual values are presented in Table 5-8. An examination of the error and percent error columns in Table 5-8 clearly indicates that the estimated model is generating forecasts that are, for all purposes, erroneous and unreliable. This observation is true despite the fact that the model as estimated passes all statistical tests of significance.

The information in Table 5-8 can also be used to compute the historical evaluation and simulation statistics. However, prior to presenting the simulation statistics, a word on terminology is in order. When a regression model is estimated, one of the evaluation tools that is relied on is a comparison of the actual and fitted values that are generated by the model. This comparison is generally referred to as a historical simulation. That is, we are using the estimated model to generate a series of fitted values that are then compared with the actual values of the dependent variable. The simulation that results from ex post forecasting is sometimes referred to as an ex post simulation. An ex post simulation provides us a measure of the dynamic behavior of the dependent variable, given changes in the independent variable(s).

Table 5-9 presents the various ex post simulation statistics (equation 5-72) and the historical evaluation statistics (equation 5-12) for the personal computer sales example. Based on the truncated model, the ex post simulation statistics suggest that the model as specified does not generate reliable forecasts. The average percentage error is 22.87 percent, implying that on the average, the ex post forecast values are 22.87 percent below actual sales levels. As is the case with all these types of statistics, they are most useful when

TABLE 5-8 Ex Post Versus Actual Personal Computer Sales: 1985–1987

Year	Ex Post Forecast	Actual Value	Error	Percent Error
1985	107.075	132.100	25.03	18.9
1986	118.146	150.200	32.05	21.3
1987	129.218	180.300	51.08	28.3

TABLE 5-9   **Calculation of Ex Post Simulation and Historical Evaluation Statistics***

Year	$\hat{Y}_t - Y_t$	$(\hat{Y}_t - Y_t)^2$	$[(\hat{Y}_t - Y_t)/(Y_t)]$	$[(\hat{Y}_t - Y_t)/(Y_t)]^2$
1985	25.03	626	18.94	359
1986	32.05	1,027	21.34	455
1987	51.08	2,609	28.33	803
	108.16	4,262	68.61	1,617

$$\text{RMS} = \sqrt{(4,262/3)}$$

$$= 37.69$$

$$\text{RPMS} = \sqrt{(1,617)/3}$$

$$= 23.22\%$$

$$\text{Bias} = 108.16/3$$

$$= 36.05$$

$$\text{Percent Bias} = 68.61/3$$

$$= 22.87\%$$

HISTORICAL EVALUATION STATISTICS

MAPE = 20.22   MSE = 751.6   MAD = 20.07   APE = 25.11

* The simulation statistics are based on equation (5-72), while the historical evaluation statistics are derived from equation (5-12).

comparing models and have the same characteristic that the smaller the values the more reliable the model. Additionally, the historical evaluation statistics serve to illustrate further the lack of forecasting reliability of the estimated regression model.

For the complete personal computer sales example, equation (5-12), the turning-point diagram is presented in Figure 5-14. Figure 5-15 illustrates a comparison of the actual versus fitted values, from equation (5-12), for the entire time period. These two figures can then be used to prepare the turning-point information presented in Table 5-10. The information in the TP (Actual) and TP (Fitted) columns refers to directional changes in the actual and historical columns. For example, between 1976 and 1977, actual personal computer sales declined and estimated personal computer sales also declined. Conversely, between 1978 and 1979 there was no directional change. That is, the change between these two years was positive, which was also the case between the preceding two years.

These directional changes are summarized in Table 5-11. Of the eight turning points in actual personal computer sales (1976–1977, 1977–1978, 1979–1980, 1980–1981, 1982–1983, 1983–1984, 1984–1985, 1985–1986), the

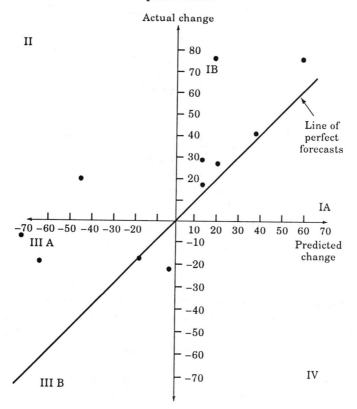

FIGURE 5-14   Turning-Point Analysis for Personal
Computer Sales

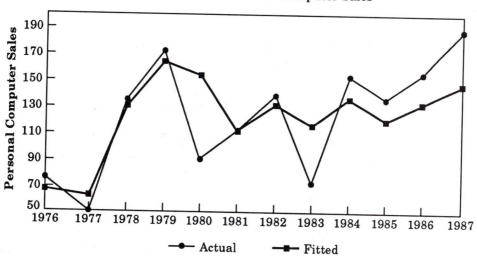

FIGURE 5-15   Actual versus Fitted Personal Computer Sales

TABLE 5-10   Fitted versus Actual Personal Computer Sales

Year	Actual (1)	Fitted (2)	TP (Actual) (3)	TP (Fitted) (4)
1976	73.1	65.9		
1977	50.2	62.1	−	−
1978	128.3	124.2	+	+
1979	170.4	162.5	N	N
1980	87.5	153.2	−	−
1981	108.6	109.0	+	−
1982	135.7	129.0	N	+
1983	69.8	112.3	−	−
1984	148.9	132.3	+	+
1985	132.1	115.6	−	−
1986	150.2	128.2	+	+
1987	180.3	140.9	N	N

estimated model picked up seven of the turning points in the actual data. The only actual turning point (directional change) that the estimated model missed (TN) occurred during the 1980–1981 time period, when actual computer sales increased and the prediction was for a continued decline in sales. Conversely, the only false signal occurred during the 1981–1982 time period, when actual personal computer sales continued to increase and the fitted values resulted in a directional change from a decline to an increase. In terms of the false signal ratio, we obtain

$$\overline{E}_{T1} = \frac{1}{1 + 7} = \frac{1}{8} \tag{5-73}$$

implying that the estimated model generated one false signal out of eight turning points. Similarly, the missed signal ratio is

$$\overline{E}_{T2} = \frac{1}{1 + 7} = \frac{1}{8}, \tag{5-74}$$

TABLE 5-11   Turning-Point Analysis

	Forecast	
Actual	No TP	TP
No TP	2 (NN)	1 (NT)
TP	1 (TN)	7 (TT)

which once again indicates that the estimated model misses one of the directional changes or turning points in actual personal computer sales.

In addition to computing the false and missed signal values, analysts rely heavily on graphs similar to Figure 5-15 in which the actual and fitted values of the dependent variable are compared visually. An examination of these two time plots confirms that the estimated model appears to be fairly useful in picking up the turning points in actual personal computer sales but does not appear to capture the volatility of actual sales.

The pragmatic empiricist uses all of these tests when developing his or her model. Due to space limitations, we do not attempt to present all tests with all models. Nevertheless, in real forecasting situations, you should, at various stages of your analysis, rely on these measures in conjunction with the standard statistical and theoretical considerations. Indeed, they are all integral parts of any successful forecasting effort.

EXAMPLE 5-5 Air Miles Traveled (Continued)

In example 5-2, the primary emphasis was on checking the statistical validity of the regression equation. We now turn to the task of appraising the forecasting reliability of the estimated equation. In the original equation, equation (5-52) (which is reproduced here for convenience),

$$\widehat{AM}_t = -66.834 + 0.037 RGNP_t \qquad (5\text{-}52)$$

the model was estimated for the time period 1970:I to 1987:I. This model was then used to develop ex post forecasts for the second through fourth quarters of 1987. The results of this ex post simulation are presented in Table 5-12.

An examination of the forecast errors and the ex post simulation statistics suggests that the estimated model is generating reliable forecasts. That is, the changes that are occurring in real GNP are capturing the changes that are occurring in air miles traveled.

Based on the relative reliability of this truncated model, the model

---

TABLE 5-12 Ex Post Forecast for Air Miles Traveled

Year and Quarter	Actual	Ex Post Forecast	Error	Percent Error
1987: II	75.82	72.96	2.86	3.77
1987: III	75.06	74.47	0.59	0.78
1987: IV	76.01	75.50	0.51	0.67

RMS = 1.71; RPMS = 2.26; Bias = 1.32; Percent Bias = 1.74

was reestimated using the full data range with the results as follows:

$$\widehat{AM}_t = -67.526 + 0.037RGNP_t \qquad \text{(5-75)}$$
$$t_e \qquad\qquad (50)$$

$$R^2 = 0.97 \qquad SEE = 2.56 \qquad APE = 5.53 \qquad MAD = 1.98$$
$$MAPE = 4.74 \qquad MSE = 6.39 \qquad\qquad\qquad F = 2509.$$

Thus, by all statistical criteria, equation (5-75) passes all tests.

Figures 5-16 and 5-17 provide an analysis of the reliability of the estimated model. An examination of both of these figures suggests that the model is reliably simulating the actual pattern of changes in air miles traveled. This information can be evaluated further by computing the missed and false signal ratios. The missed signal ratio is given by

$$\overline{E}_{T1} = \frac{9}{9 + 13} = \frac{9}{22} \qquad \text{(5-76)}$$

while the false signal ratio is

$$\overline{E}_{T2} = \frac{13}{13 + 13} = \frac{13}{26}. \qquad \text{(5-77)}$$

FIGURE 5-16 Efficiency of Regression Equation in Simulating Air Miles Traveled

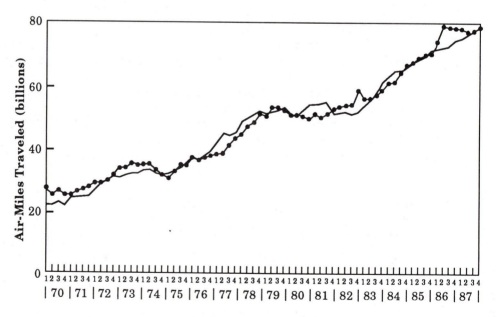

FIGURE 5-17 **Turning-Point Analysis of Air Miles Traveled Regression**

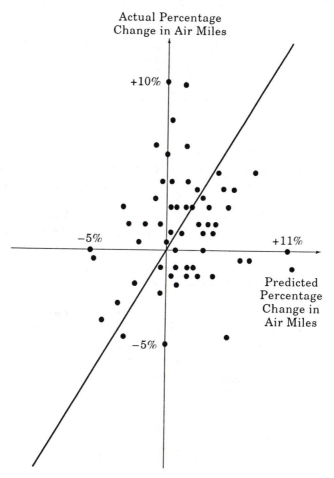

Thus, while the model does appear to capture the patterns in the actual data, the fact that it leads to nine missed changes in direction and generates 13 false signals is somewhat disturbing for a forecasting equation.

Two additional factors deserve mention at this stage of our analysis. First, to use the estimated model to generate forecasts, reliable forecasts for the independent variable, real GNP, must be available. Based on forecasts from a commercial vendor, the forecasts for the year 1988 for real GNP are as follows: 1988:I = $3,878, 1988:II = $3,893, 1988:III = $3,912,

TABLE 5-13 **Conditional Forecasts for Air Miles Traveled**

Date	Lower	Middle	Upper
1988:I	71.2	76.3	81.3
1988:II	71.8	76.8	81.9
1988:III	72.5	77.5	82.6
1988:IV	73.5	78.5	83.6

and 1988:IV = \$3,939. The conditional forecasts for air miles traveled as well as the forecast intervals are presented in Table 5-13.

A second factor relates to the observation that the forecasting equation for air miles traveled, equation (5-75), was estimated using seasonally adjusted quarterly data. This implies that any estimates obtained from the equation will also be seasonally adjusted. The relationship between seasonally adjusted and unadjusted data is given by

$$\text{Seasonally Adjusted Data} = \frac{\text{Unadjusted (Raw) Data}}{\text{Seasonal Factor}}. \quad \text{(5-78)}$$

For our example, the predicted value for the first quarter of 1988 is 76.3 billion miles. This value must be multiplied by the seasonal factor associated with the first quarter, 1.01, yielding the unadjusted value for air miles traveled of 77.06 billion miles. The remaining unadjusted values would be obtained via a similar procedure.

EXAMPLE 5-6   Appliance Shipments (Continued)

Prior to using estimated regression equations for forecasting purposes, we can frequently assess the probable usefulness by scanning a plot of the error terms. The advantage of this approach is that the majority of computer packages automatically provide this graph. For example, Figure 5-18 presents the plot of error terms for the quarterly appliance shipments model, equation (5-60).

A visual inspection of Figure 5-18 suggests that the error terms form a consistent pattern, and this violates the assumption of randomly distributed error terms. Specifically, the estimated model is generating errors that exhibit a distinct pattern of underestimates (depicted by a positive sign) followed by a series of overestimates (depicted by a negative sign) followed by a series of underestimates, etc. In chapter 6, we develop

FIGURE 5-18 **Error Pattern from Regression of Appliance Sales on Production**

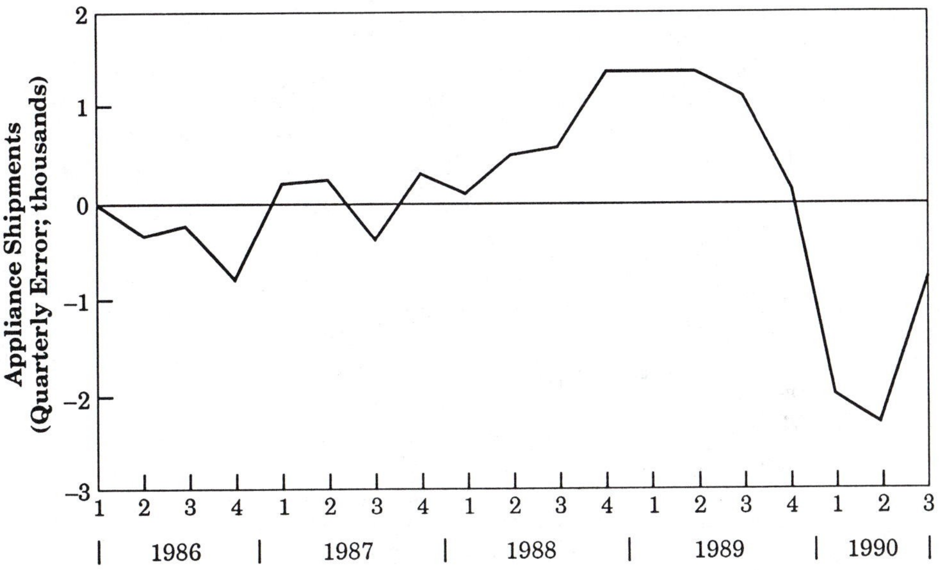

techniques for measuring and correcting nonrandom error patterns, and we turn to these more advanced techniques and models.

SUMMARY

Our purpose here has been to provide you with the introductory tools needed to use regression models in forecasting situations. In succeeding chapters, the widespread applicability of regression analysis is extended and more realistic examples are presented. These extensions are presented in a less formal and less mathematical style than has been used in this chapter. Nonetheless, virtually everything that we have presented in this chapter can be incorporated into the more sophisticated and realistic examples.

QUESTIONS FOR DISCUSSION AND ANALYSIS

1. In analyzing equation (5-1), we made the statement that there are two hypotheses. What are these two hypotheses and what is their importance?
2. Define what is meant by model specification and explain the role that theory plays in this process.
3. What advantage does the simple correlation coefficient have over the covariance?

4. What are the assumptions implicit in the ordinary least-squares model?

5. Why is an error term included in the population (true) regression model?

6. What is the difference between the error term in the population model and the error term in the sample model?

7. What is the relationship between the standard deviation, the standard error of the regression coefficient, and the standard error of the estimate (SEE)?

8. What advantage do interval estimates have over point estimates?

9. What criteria are involved in selecting independent variables in regression models?

10. Explain the process of using confidence intervals to conduct hypothesis tests.

11. How is the standard error of the estimate interpreted?

12. In conducting hypothesis tests, how are the calculated and estimated values of t used?

13. Explain the difference between an ex post and ex ante forecast; between a conditional and unconditional forecast.

14. Explain the process of conducting a turning-point analysis on an estimated regression equation.

15. Making use of the following regression results, answer these questions and fill in the blanks in the tables.

   a. The regression equation is $\hat{Y} =$ _____.

   b. Give a precise interpretation for the numerical values of $\hat{\beta}_0$ and $\hat{\beta}_1$ in the regression equation.

   c. How many observations are there in the sample?

   d. What is the standard error of the estimate (SEE)?

   e. What is the standard error of the intercept (constant)?

   f. What is the estimated value of the t statistic (t_e) for the slope (β_1) coefficient?

   g. We can be 95 percent confident that β_1 is between _____ and _____.

   h. What is the coefficient of determination?

   i. What is the coefficient of correlation?

   j. What is the estimated value of the F statistic, F_e?

	Coefficient	Standard Error	t statistic
Constant	48.489	_____	4.29
X	12.855	2.241	_____
SEE = _____			
R^2 = _____			

Analysis of Variance

Source of Variation	Variation	d.f.	Variance
Explained by Regression	1,581	1	_____
Unexplained	433	_____	48
Total	_____	10	_____

16. Suppose that you are a marketing analyst and are asked to develop a forecasting equation relating sales to income levels from the following data set.

Year	Sales (thousands)	Income (thousands)
1979	14	6
1980	17	8
1981	15	9
1982	18	10
1983	16	11
1984	22	12
1985	26	14
1986	25	16
1987	30	18
1988	34	20

a. Prepare a scatter diagram.
b. Estimate the covariance and correlation coefficients. Do they confirm your theoretical expectations?
c. Estimate the regression coefficient for this data set.
d. How is the income coefficient interpreted?
e. Conduct a 90 percent hypothesis test on the income coefficient.
f. How much of the variation in sales is explained by the income variable?
g. Plot a turning-point diagram.
h. How well does the estimated model pick up the turning points? Does it generate any false signals or does it miss any of the turning points?
i. What is the standard error of the income coefficient?
j. Does the intercept or constant term have any theoretical interpretation? If so, what does it mean? If not, why not?
k. What is the average percentage error, APE?

17. You are given the following data set and are asked to estimate a regression equation.

Y	X
20	2
25	3
34	5
30	4
60	10
41	5
42	7
45	9

a. Prepare a table similar to Table 5-2.
b. What is the regression equation?
c. What is the standard error of the slope coefficient?
d. What is the estimated value of t for the slope coefficient?
e. What is the standard error of the estimate?

18. As a marketing analyst, you are given the following data sets relating sales levels to advertising expenditures and are asked to develop a forecasting model. Both data sets are measured in thousands of dollars.

Year	Sales	Advertising	Year	Sales	Advertising
1971	710	2.35	1980	764	3.39
1972	713	2.58	1981	774	3.56
1973	720	2.56	1982	776	3.48
1974	722	2.65	1983	784	3.71
1975	738	2.76	1984	796	3.05
1976	740	2.99	1985	800	3.02
1977	747	3.06	1986	805	3.08
1978	755	3.09	1987	809	2.97
1979	760	3.54			

a. Estimate a trend equation for sales.
b. Estimate a regression equation relating sales levels to advertising expenditures.
c. How would the trend coefficient be interpreted?
d. What is the regression equation? The trend equation?
e. Based on an evaluation of the MAPE, MAD, APE, SEE, and a turning-point analysis, which of the two models would you use for forecasting purposes and why?
f. Reestimate the model leaving off the last three years' worth of data. What are the ex post forecasts for these three years? Compute and interpret the four ex post simulation statistics.
g. Based on the full model, what are the conditional forecasts for the years 1988 and 1989 if advertising expenditures are predicted to be 3.00 and 3.20, respectively?
h. Based on your answers in part g, develop a 95 percent confidence interval for your 1988 forecast.

19. As a pricing analyst, you are given the following data set relating units sold to changes in the relative price of the commodity.

Year	Units Sold (thousands)	Change in Relative Price (percent)
1979	65	2
1980	60	3
1981	62	2
1982	55	4
1983	50	5
1984	58	3
1985	64	2
1986	48	6
1987	53	4
1988	57	3

a. What are your theoretical expectations regarding the sign on the price coefficient?
b. Estimate a regression model where the change in the relative price is the independent variable.

   c. What is the meaning of the price coefficient?

   d. Compute a 95 percent confidence interval for the price coefficient.

   e. Based on your confidence interval, would you accept or reject the null hypothesis of no relationship between sales and the price variable?

20. How is a turning-point analysis used in developing and evaluating forecasting models? Specifically, what are the differences between a statistical evaluation of an estimated regression model and a forecasting evaluation of a model?

21. The finance officer in charge of short-term cash control has asked you to prepare an estimate of production costs. As a first step, you collect the following information on costs and size of production run. The costs are measured in per-unit average variable costs and the production-run numbers are measured in thousands of units.

Date*	Costs	Units Produced
1985: II	10.98	35.3
III	11.13	29.7
IV	12.51	30.8
1986: I	8.40	58.8
II	9.27	61.4
III	8.73	71.3
IV	6.36	74.4
1987: I	8.50	76.7
II	7.82	70.7
III	9.14	57.5
IV	8.24	46.4
1988: I	12.19	28.9
II	11.88	28.1
III	9.57	39.1
IV	10.94	46.8
1989: I	9.58	48.5
II	10.09	59.3
III	8.11	70.0
IV	6.83	70.0
1990: I	8.88	74.5
II	7.68	72.1
III	8.47	58.1
IV	8.86	44.6
1991: I	10.36	33.4
II	11.08	28.6

   * Year and quarter

   a. Estimate a cost function based on this data.

   b. Suppose that you are then told that the production run in the third quarter of 1991 will be between 35.6 and 42.6 thousand units. What is your estimate of costs? What would the 95 percent confidence interval for this estimate be?

22. Based on the following information, estimate a simple linear regression model that expresses the relationship between mail-order sales (measured in millions of dollars) and the per capita income in your sales area.

Year	Sales	Per Capita Income
1982	13.3	3,700
1983	14.5	4,000
1984	14.2	3,900
1985	13.5	3,600
1986	13.8	4,500
1987	14.2	4,600
1988	14.7	4,900
1989	13.6	3,700
1990	14.0	4,400
1991	13.4	3,800

a. Derive the simple linear regression model.
b. Interpret the coefficient on per capita income.
c. Conduct a graphical analysis of the reliability of the estimated model based on the tools provided in previous chapters. For example, plot the actual versus fitted values, the error terms, a control chart, and a turning-point diagram.
d. How does the model perform based on your analysis in part c?

REFERENCES FOR FURTHER STUDY

Chatterjee, Samprit and Bertram Price, *Regression Analysis by Example.* New York: John Wiley Interscience Series, 1977.

Chisholm, Roger K. and Gilbert R. Whitaker, Jr., *Forecasting Methods.* Homewood, Ill.: Richard D. Irwin, 1971.

Draper, Norman and Harry Smith, *Applied Regression Analysis*, 2nd ed. New York: John Wiley Interscience Series, 1981.

Granger, C. W. J., *Forecasting in Business and Economics.* New York: Academic Press, 1980.

Gujaranti, Damodar N., *Basic Econometrics*, 2nd ed. New York: McGraw-Hill, 1988.

Johnston, J., *Econometric Methods*, 3rd ed. New York: McGraw-Hill, 1984.

Klein, L. R., *An Essay on the Theory of Economic Prediction.* Chicago: Markham, 1971.

Kleinbaum, David G., Lawrence L. Kupper, and Keith E. Muller, *Applied Regression Analysis and Other Multivariable Methods*, 2nd ed. Boston: PWS-Kent Publishing Company, 1988.

Long, J. Scott, ed., *Common Problems/Proper Solutions.* Beverly Hills: Sage Publishers, 1988.

Montgomery, Douglas C. and Elizabeth A. Peck, *Introduction to Linear Regression Analysis.* New York: John Wiley Interscience Series, 1982.

Neter, John, William Wasserman, and Michael H. Kutner, *Applied Linear Statistical Models*, 2nd ed. Homewood, Ill.: Richard D. Irwin, 1985.

Ramanathan, Ramu, *Introductory Econometrics: With Applications.* San Diego: Harcourt Brace Jovanovich, 1989.

Studenmund, A. H. and Henry J. Cassidy, *Using Econometrics: A Practical Guide.* Boston: Little, Brown and Company, 1987.

Wonnacott, R. J. and T. H. Wonnacott, *Econometrics.* New York: John Wiley & Sons, 1970.

Wonnacott, T. H. and R. J. Wonnacott, *Regression.* New York: John Wiley and Sons, 1981.

6

Multiple Regression Models

INTRODUCTION

Regression equations that incorporate more than one independent variable are referred to as multiple regression equations, and they are the focus of this chapter. Few forecasters rely completely on simple regression models because the pattern exhibited by economic variables is a product of numerous factors. Since both the simple linear model and the multiple regression model are based on a specific set of statistical assumptions, this chapter also presents the procedures needed to test the regression results and to correct the model if the assumptions have been violated. Frequently, the most important outcome from multiple regression analysis is that it promotes a better understanding of a business environment. For example, a company that has developed a sales forecasting model incorporating external (macroeconomic) and internal factors (company-level pricing and marketing decisions) may find that it is better able to shape an alternative marketing strategy in response to a predicted recession.

While there are clear benefits associated with multiple regression analysis, there are also additional costs. First, when more than one independent variable is included in an estimated model, it may become more time consuming to select the best model. Second, it is more difficult to visualize (even in three dimensions) what the fitted model looks like. Third, interpreting the output from the model is a more complex task. Finally, as is always the case, increased complexity leads to increased monetary costs, and these costs must always be balanced against the expected gains in accuracy.

THE MULTIPLE REGRESSION MODEL

In any modeling effort, the forecaster has to make a choice: to construct a model as close as possible to the simple linear model, or to build a highly sophisticated and complex model in which an effort is made to include all independent variables influencing Y. Multiple regression analysis, merely an extension of simple regression, attempts to link changes in the dependent variable (Y) to changes in two or more independent variables (X_1, X_2, X_3, and so on).

In general, there are three reasons why multiple regression is preferable to simple regression:

1. To reduce unexplained error, thereby strengthening the statistical tests
2. To eliminate the bias that results when we ignore variables that have a significant impact on Y
3. To reduce forecasting error by more fully using all the information at our disposal.

However, the construction of a multiple regression model does involve added costs. First, the more sophisticated the model, the larger the amount of data the forecaster has to collect and analyze. Second, when the regression equation is used as a forecasting model, the analyst must have future values or estimates for the X_i's. With highly sophisticated models, in turn, there is a greater likelihood that errors will be made in estimating values for the X_i's. Thus, the trade-off is between greater accuracy and higher cost.

The general form for the multiple regression model may be set forth as

$$Y_t = \beta_0 + \beta_1 X_{1t} + \beta_2 X_{2t} + \cdots + \beta_k X_{kt} + \epsilon_t \tag{6-1}$$

where Y_t and ϵ_t are as before, and the X_{kt}'s denote the independent variables and k the number of regressors. For example, X_{2t} represents the recorded observation on variable X_2 in time period t. In comparison with the simple linear model, one assumption must be modified and two assumptions added. The modification is as follows: The dependent variable (Y) is a linear function of a number of independent variables rather than being linearly related to one independent variable. The two additional assumptions are

1. The X's must be independent of each other. That is, X_{1t} does not significantly influence X_{2t}, X_{3t}, etc., and X_{3t} is independent of X_{2t}, and so on. This is the non-multicollinearity assumption.
2. The number of observations, n, must exceed the number of regressors, k. That is, $n > k$.

In deriving the least-squares estimators, it is convenient to consider the special case of $k = 2$—that is, two independent variables.

$$\hat{Y}_t = \hat{\beta}_0 + \hat{\beta}_1 X_{1t} + \hat{\beta}_2 X_{2t} \tag{6-2}$$

Paralleling the development of estimators in the simple model, the general coefficients for the multiple regression model may be derived by solving a set of three normal equations in three unknowns:

$$\sum Y_t = \hat{n}\,\beta_0 + \hat{\beta}_1 \sum X_{1t} + \hat{\beta}_2 \sum X_{2t}$$

$$\sum X_{1t}Y_t = \hat{\beta}_0 \sum X_{1t} + \hat{\beta}_1 \sum X_{1t}^2 + \hat{\beta}_2 \sum X_{1t}X_{2t} \qquad \textbf{(6-3)}$$

$$\sum X_{2t}Y_t = \hat{\beta}_0 X_{2t} + \hat{\beta}_1 \sum X_{1t}X_{2t} + \hat{\beta}_2 \sum X_{2t}^2.$$

Solving these three equations simultaneously yields values for $\hat{\beta}_0$, $\hat{\beta}_1$, and $\hat{\beta}_2$. Finally, all the comments with respect to bias, consistency, and reliability noted in the case of simple linear regression hold here. That is, it can be shown that these estimators are also BLUE (best linear unbiased estimators). The procedures for hypothesis testing and interval estimation, as well as calculations of SEE, standard error of coefficients, t statistics, AOV, and correlation coefficients, are conceptually identical to those developed for simple linear regression.

The objectives and procedures in fitting a multiple regression equation are essentially the same as they were in the earlier simple linear regression case. Thus, the basic steps in estimating and evaluating a multiple regression model are (1) model specification and problem formulation, (2) selection of appropriate independent variables, (3) initial estimation of multiple regression model(s), (4) evaluation of statistical reliability of the estimated model, (5) reevaluation of alternative models, (6) validation of regression assumptions, (7) appraisal of the model's forecasting reliability, and (8) analysis of the model's contribution to managerial decision making. In other words, we will obtain estimates for the regression coefficients, $\hat{\beta}_0$, $\hat{\beta}_1$, and $\hat{\beta}_2$; test the statistical reliability of these coefficients; test the validity of all regressors (independent variables) taken together; use the regression equation to estimate Y given values for X_1 and X_2; measure the error involved in the estimations; and assess the model's efficiency as a forecasting device. Although the objectives and procedures remain similar, the calculations become more complex, and the summary statistical measures require a more detailed interpretation. From a practical standpoint, estimation of a multiple regression model requires access to computer programs; hence, our initial objective is to ensure that computer output can be understood and interpreted. We will not attempt to present the mathematics that undergird multiple regression techniques.

To develop an appreciation of the power of multiple regression analysis (as compared with simple regression analysis), suppose that we first estimate two simple linear regression models based on the data noted in Table 6-1. The first of the simple linear regression models (equation 6-4) focuses on the relationship between sales and real income (RINC) while the second model (equation 6-5) highlights the sales and advertising relationship (SOV):

$$\widehat{SALES}_t = 1.67784 + 0.01251RINC_t \tag{6-4}$$
$$r^2 = 0.83184; SEE = 0.51773$$

$$\widehat{SALES}_t = -2.48067 + 0.27708SOV_t \tag{6-5}$$
$$r^2 = 0.70034; SEE = 0.69112.$$

Table 6-2 presents the results of estimating a multiple regression model in which both real income and advertising are incorporated as explanatory variables.

Thus, the multiple regression model can be written as

$$\widehat{SALES}_t = -1.13991 + 0.00874927RINC_t + 0.14368SOV_t. \tag{6-6}$$

An examination of the information in Table 6-2 reveals that several additional

TABLE 6-1   Company Sales Analysis

Year	Sales (millions)	Share of Voice* (Percent)	Real Income (billions)
1969	2.68	19.9	113
1970	3.01	22.6	118
1971	3.61	26.0	121
1972	2.59	20.5	118
1973	4.41	21.5	271
1974	4.02	23.5	190
1975	3.58	21.5	175
1976	5.04	26.2	263
1977	5.81	28.5	334
1978	5.60	29.5	368
1979	5.05	24.5	305
1980	4.80	29.5	210
1981	6.02	26.1	387
1982	5.41	27.3	270
1983	4.14	22.3	218
1984	5.91	31.0	342
1985	4.91	28.0	173
1986	6.59	28.5	370
1987	3.61	23.1	170
1988	4.09	27.0	205
1989	6.81	32.0	331
1990	5.95	32.0	283

* "Share of Voice" refers to one firm's advertising expenditures as a percentage of total industry advertising.

TABLE 6-2   Least-Squares Estimates for Multiple Regression of Sales on Share of Voice and Real Income

	Constant	*Share of Voice*	*Real Income*
Coefficient	−1.13991	0.14368	0.00874927
Standard Error of Coefficient	0.4888	0.02296	0.00095115
t Statistic	−2.332	6.257	9.199
95% Confidence Interval		0.09561 to 0.19174	0.0067585 to 0.01074
Beta Coefficient		0.43395	0.63800
Part Coefficient of Determination		0.11321	0.24471
Partial Coefficient of Determination		0.67324	0.81662
Prob Value		0.00000	0.00000

Coefficient of Determination: R^2 = 0.94505
Correlation Coefficient: R = 0.97214
Adjusted Coefficient of Determination: ADJ R^2 = 0.93927
F Statistic = 163.39
Durbin-Watson Statistic = 2.157
Standard Error of the Estimate = .30364

statistics and measures are useful when dealing with multiple regression models.

The advantage of the multiple regression model (equation 6-6) over either of the single-variable regression models (equations 6-4 and 6-5) is perhaps best seen by comparing the coefficients of determination and standard errors of the estimates. In the case of the coefficient of determination (R^2), for the multiple regression equation we have accounted for 94.5 percent of the variation in sales.

The comparable figures for the simple income-sales model and advertising-sales model are 83.2 percent and 70.0 percent, respectively. Alternatively, the standard errors of the estimates are 0.30 for the multiple regression model and 0.52 and 0.69 for the income and advertising models, respectively. Clearly, the multiple regression model improves the explanatory power and, in all likelihood, the predictive power of the sales model.

INTERPRETATION OF THE MODEL

The first difference in interpretation between simple and multiple regression centers on the regression coefficients. In the former situation, $\hat{\beta}_1$ referred to the change in Y, the dependent variable, as a result of a one-unit change in the independent variable, X. In the two-variable model,

$$\hat{Y}_t = \hat{\beta}_0 + \hat{\beta}_1 X_{1t} + \hat{\beta}_2 X_{2t} \tag{6-7}$$

$\hat{\beta}_0$'s interpretation is unchanged, while $\hat{\beta}_1$ measures the average change in Y associated with a unit change in X_1 when all other independent variables remain constant. In the economist's vocabulary, this corresponds to the *ceteris paribus* assumption (Latin for "all other things being equal"). In calculus, these coefficients correspond to partial derivatives. A similar interpretation follows for all other coefficients in a multiple regression model.

We should also mention that this process of holding all other variables constant involves statistical control rather than experimental control. That is, since we are generally not able to actually hold the values of all other variables at some constant level, we must rely on the statistical control that multiple regression analysis provides.

The terms $\hat{\beta}_1$ and $\hat{\beta}_2$ are sometimes referred to as partial regression coefficients and can be shown to be systematically related to partial correlation coefficients. These interpretations follow from the assumption that the independent variables are unrelated. That is, if X_1 and X_2 vary systematically, the *ceteris paribus* assumption no longer holds. Thus, for the sales example, the coefficients have the following specific interpretation:

1. Sales will change by 8,749 units (0.00874927·1,000,000, since sales are measured in millions) for every 1 billion dollar change in income, under the assumption that share of voice remains constant.
2. Sales will change by 143,680 (0.14368·1,000,000) for every 1 percent change in share of voice, as long as real income does not change.

The analysis-of-variance table for a multiple regression equation is identical to that for a simple regression equation, except for the degrees of freedom column.[1] In the case of multiple regression, the null and alternative hypotheses being tested by the F test are[2]

$$H_0: \beta_1 = \beta_2 = 0 \tag{6-8}$$

and

$$H_0: \beta_1 \neq 0; \beta_2 \neq 0. \tag{6-9}$$

---

[1] The degrees of freedom in a multiple regression AOV table are k (as opposed to 1 in a simple regression model), $N - (k + 1)$ (as opposed to $n - 2$), and $n - 1$.

[2] In contrast, the null and alternative hypotheses being tested with a simple regression model are

$$H_0: \beta_1 = 0$$
and
$$H_1: \beta_1 \neq 0.$$

That is, the F test analyzes the joint effect of X_1 and X_2 (or, in general, all independent variables) on Y and measures the combined statistical significance of all regression coefficients, whereas the t test looks at the significance of the coefficients taken one at a time. The F test involves testing the significance of the coefficients simultaneously; that is,

$$F_{\text{cr}} = F_{\alpha,k,n-(k+1)}. \tag{6-10}$$

The prediction interval for a multiple regression equation is defined by

$$Y_{t+1} = \hat{Y}_{t+1} \pm t_{\text{cr}}s \sqrt{\frac{1}{n} + \frac{(X_{1t+1} - \overline{X}_1)^2}{\sum (X_{1t} - \overline{X}_1)^2} + \frac{(X_{2t+1} - \overline{X}_2)^2}{\sum (X_{2t} - \overline{X}_2)^2} + 1} \tag{6-11}$$

where $\hat{Y}_{t+1}$ is the point estimate. Conceptually, the confidence band for a multiple regression equation is identical to the simple regression band illustrated in Figure 5-12.

MULTIPLE AND SIMPLE CORRELATION

Significant areas of difference exist between simple and multiple regression, both in the interpretation of the coefficients of determination and correlation and in the various types of related coefficients that can be calculated. In the case of a multiple regression equation, it is common practice to refer to these terms as the multiple correlation coefficient and the multiple coefficient of determination, symbolized by R and R^2, respectively.[3] As would be expected, the coefficient of determination measures the variation in Y explained by the combined influence of all independent variables, X_1 and X_2 in the special case where the model includes two independent variables. That is,

$$R^2 = \frac{\sum (\hat{Y}_t - \overline{Y})^2}{\sum (Y_t - \overline{Y})^2} \tag{6-12}$$

where

$$\hat{Y}_t = \hat{\beta}_0 + \hat{\beta}_1 X_{1t} + \hat{\beta}_2 X_{2t} \quad \text{and} \quad R = \sqrt{R^2}. \tag{6-13}$$

At this juncture, a word of caution is in order concerning the multiple coefficient of determination and multiple correlation coefficient. Both of these measures are directly related to the number of independent variables (k) in-

---

[3] Recall that in chapter 5, we noted that the letters r and r^2 are sometimes reserved for simple regression models while R and R^2 are used with multiple regression analysis.

cluded in the regression equation. The addition of more independent variables can never lower R (or R^2) and will, for all practical purposes, increase the absolute size of both numbers. For this reason, it is necessary to correct both of these measures for the number of independent variables (regressors)—that is, correct for the degrees of freedom. These corrected coefficients are denoted by $\overline{R}^2$ (or ADJ R^2) and $\overline{R}$ (or ADJ R) and can be found by using equation (6-14)

$$\text{ADJ } R^2 = 1 - (1 - R^2) \left(\frac{n - 1}{n - k} \right) . \tag{6-14}$$

As n becomes larger, ADJ R^2 approaches R^2. An examination of the R^2 (0.94505) and the ADJ R^2 (0.93927) in Table 6-2 indicates that the latter measure is lower than the unadjusted measure by 0.00578. Intuitively, this suggests that 0.578 percent of the improvement in the coefficient of determination is simply a result of adding one more variable rather than as a result of adding a variable that contributes to our understanding of the observed changes in the dependent variable, Y. This adjustment for the number of independent variables included in the model is important because, while it is desirable to have as high an R^2 as possible, if this were the only goal we would simply add independent variables to the equation. Thus, after compensating for the number of regressors in the model, 93.927 percent of the observed changes in the dependent variable have been explained or accounted for by changes in both X_1 and X_2. We should also recall that because of its straightforward interpretation, the multiple coefficient of determination is preferred to the multiple correlation coefficient.

In addition to the multiple coefficient of determination, it is possible to calculate simple coefficients of determination and correlation, part coefficients [see equations (6-22) and (6-23)] of determination and correlation, and partial coefficients of determination and correlation [see equation (6-24)]. Simple coefficients of determination (and correlation) refer to the relationship between each independent variable and the dependent variable. A matrix of coefficients of determination documents the simple coefficients of determination among all combinations of the dependent variable and the independent variables. A simple coefficient of determination (r^2) can be calculated between each pair of variables of a given set of m variables, each with n observations, using the equation

$$r^2 = \frac{\sum\limits_{t=1}^{n} (X_{1t} - \overline{X})(Y_t - \overline{Y})}{\sqrt{\sum\limits_{t=1}^{n} (X_{1t} - \overline{X})^2 \sum (Y_t - \overline{Y})^2}} \tag{6-15}$$

where X_t and Y_t are variables in the model.

When applied to the sales, real income, and advertising model, the simple coefficients of determination are 0.70035 and 0.83184, respectively. The observant reader will note that these values can be derived from equation (6-15).[4] A word of warning: To the unwary user there is a tendency to believe that these simple coefficients are additive. That is, if we sum the simple coefficient of determination for the income variable and for the advertising variable, the result should be equal to the multiple coefficient of determination. In our example, a summation of the two simple coefficients of determination yields 1.53219, which would imply that we have been able to account for or explain 153 percent of the observed changes in Y. Obviously, we cannot explain more than 100 percent of anything, and this attests to the fact that simple coefficients of determination (or correlation) are not additive.

RANKING THE RELATIVE IMPORTANCE OF INDEPENDENT VARIABLES

When evaluating a multiple regression model, we frequently want to evaluate the relative importance of the independent variables in explaining the changes that have occurred in the dependent variable. An obvious (and incorrect) procedure would be to compare the regression coefficients and conclude that the largest regression coefficient is the most important, the second largest coefficient is the second most important, and so on. The problem with this procedure is that the independent variables may be measured in different units. In our example, we have measured real income in billions of dollars and share of voice in percentage terms. In other situations, we might have one variable measured in dollars, a second in tons, a third in percentage terms. Clearly, when the independent variables are measured in different units, a direct comparison of the regression coefficients is fraught with danger.

One potential solution to this unit problem is to standardize each of the variables, reestimate the regression model, and then evaluate and compare the coefficients. A variable is standardized by converting its values into standard deviation units from the mean. For example,

$$Y^* = \frac{Y - \overline{Y}}{s_y} \; ; X_1^* = \frac{X_1 - \overline{X}_1}{s_{x1}} \; ; X_2^* = \frac{X_2 - \overline{X}_2}{s_{x2}}. \qquad \textbf{(6-16)}$$

When formulated in this fashion, the model to be estimated would be written as

$$\hat{Y}_t^* = \hat{\beta}_1 X_{1t}^* + \hat{\beta}_2 X_{2t}^*. \qquad \textbf{(6-17)}$$

---

[4] From a practical perspective, these simple coefficients of determination or correlation coefficients are obtained from an examination of the correlation matrix. The correlation matrix is introduced in a later section of this chapter.

Note that when this standardized procedure is used, the intercept is forced to zero. An alternative procedure involves computing beta weights or beta coefficients. The beta coefficient corrects the unstandardized regression coefficients by the ratio of the standard deviation of the independent variable to the standard deviation of the dependent variable:

$$\beta_i^* = \beta_i(s_{xi}/s_y) \tag{6-18}$$

$$\text{Beta Coefficient for (RINC)} = (0.00874927)(89.847/1.232) \tag{6-19}$$
$$= 0.638$$

$$\text{Beta Coefficient for (SOV)} = (0.14368)(3.721/1.232) \tag{6-20}$$
$$= 0.43395.$$

The beta coefficients have a straightforward interpretation in that they indicate the average standard deviation change in Y associated with a standard deviation change in each independent variable, when all other independent variables are held constant. For example, the beta coefficient for real income, 0.638, implies that a one-standard-deviation change in this variable is associated with an average 0.638 standard deviation change in sales when share of voice is held constant. Conversely, a one-standard-deviation change in share of voice will elicit a 0.43395 standard deviation change in sales. Thus, we can conclude that the impact of real income, as measured in standard deviation units, is greater than the impact of share of voice, similarly measured. Alternatively, real income has 1.47 (0.638/0.43395) times the impact on sales as does share of voice.

There is, however, one significant limitation to these beta coefficients. The values of these coefficients are contingent on the other independent variables in the equation. That is, the beta coefficient for, say, real income, is influenced by the inclusion of the share of voice variable in the model. Alternatively, only in the extreme case of no statistically observed relationship between the independent variables would the beta coefficients provide a completely accurate representation of the relative importance of the independent variables.

Another procedure for assessing the relative importance of independent variables is to consider the increase in the multiple coefficient of determination, R^2, when a variable (say, share of voice) is entered into an equation that already contains another independent variable(s) (real income in our model). This increase can be expressed as[5]

$$R^2_{\text{change}} = R^2 - R_i^2 \tag{6-21}$$

---

[5] There are numerous formulas that would permit the computation of both the part and partial coefficients of determination. A consultation of any of the econometrics textbooks noted at the end of this chapter would provide this information.

where R_i^2 refers to the multiple coefficient of determination when all independent variables except the ith are in the equation. A large change in R^2 suggests that a variable provides unique information about the dependent variable that is not available from the other independent variables in the model. This measure is referred to as the part coefficient of determination. It is the relationship between X_i and Y when the linear effects of the other independent variables have been removed from X_i.

The part coefficient of determination for share of voice can be derived by comparing the information in equation (6-6) to the information provided in equation (6-4). An examination of equation (6-4) indicates that the coefficient of determination is 0.83184 for real income while for the combined model, equation (6-6), the multiple coefficient of determination equals 0.94505, which yields a part coefficient of determination (PART COD) of 0.11321:

$$\text{PART COD}_{\text{SOV}} = 0.94505 - 0.83184 = 0.11321. \qquad \text{(6-22)}$$

When applied to real income, the results are

$$\text{PART COD}_{\text{real income}} = 0.94505 - 0.70034 = 0.24471. \qquad \text{(6-23)}$$

Thus, when we add real income to an equation that already contains the share of voice variable, the percentage of the explained variation in sales, Y, increases by 24.471. Similarly, the percentage of the explained variation in sales as a result of adding share of voice is 11.321. Real income clearly would be ranked highest in terms of relative importance.

The part coefficient of determination does have one drawback. If most of the variation in Y has been explained by the variables already in the model, no part coefficient of determination can be large. For this reason it may, therefore, be difficult to compare part coefficients of determination.

This problem can be overcome by using the partial coefficient of determination:

$$Pr_i^2 = \frac{R^2 - R_i^2}{1 - R_i^2}. \qquad \text{(6-24)}$$

The partial coefficients of determination can be regarded as measuring the relationship between the dependent variable and one independent variable after netting out the linear effects of all other independent variables in the model. The partial coefficients of determination are 0.67324 and 0.81662 for share of voice and real income, respectively. As was the case with the part coefficient of determination and the beta coefficient, real income contributes more to explaining the observed changes in sales.

FORECASTING WITH MULTIPLE REGRESSION MODELS

FORECASTING EQUATIONS VERSUS EXPLANATORY EQUATIONS

In using a multiple regression equation for explanatory purposes, the independent variables are selected solely on a theoretical basis. The primary purpose of this type of analysis is to test the validity of the theory, and, therefore, past or historical changes are of primary consideration. Alternatively, analysis of future values for the dependent and independent variables is of little interest to the analyst.

By the very nature of a forecasting equation, the primary goal in developing it is to obtain reliable forecasts for future values of the dependent variable. Hence, the model's success in satisfying this goal depends on our ability to obtain future values for the independent variables. It is of little consolation to a forecaster to find that he or she has developed an equation that explains historical movements of the dependent variable accurately but is useless for forecasting because future values of the independent variables are impossible to obtain.

To elaborate on this distinction among regression models, suppose that a forecaster wishes to develop an equation to project sales of personal computers. Economic theory suggests that personal computer sales (PCS) are apt to depend on, among other things, the price of personal computers (PC), income (INC), the rate of technological change (TC), the existing stock of personal computers in use (SPC), the growth in computer literacy (CL), and the widespread availability of computer software (SOFT). Furthermore, this model might be subdivided into sales to households and sales to business users. Formally,

$$\widehat{PCS}_t = \hat{\beta}_0 - \hat{\beta}_1 PC_t + \hat{\beta}_2 INC_t + \hat{\beta}_3 TC_t$$
$$- \hat{\beta}_4 SPC_t + \hat{\beta}_5 CL_t + \hat{\beta}_6 SOFT_t. \quad \textbf{(6-25)}$$

Although this model makes perfect sense from the perspective of a theorist, it is highly unlikely that we will be able to obtain forecasts for variables such as the rate of technological change, the existing stock, the growth in computer literacy, and the availability of computer software. Instead of using equation (6-25), the forecaster might formulate the following model:

$$\widehat{PCS}_t = \hat{\beta}_0 - \hat{\beta}_1 PC_{t-1} + \hat{\beta}_2 EMESER_t + \hat{\beta}_3 PCS_{t-1} + \hat{\beta}_4 INV_t \quad \textbf{(6-26)}$$

where PC refers to the price of personal computers, EMESER to employment in services, and INV to inventory levels. The $t-1$ subscript indicates a lagged variable. The inclusion of personal computer sales lagged one time period is a surrogate for the stock of personal computers already owned by households.

The advantage of this latter formulation is obvious. Reliable estimates for the independent variables are readily available and reasonably accurate. The selection of independent (explanatory) variables in forecasting models is based on factors such as theoretical relationships, the strength of the relationship between the independent variable(s) and the dependent variable, and the availability of forecast values. Obtaining future values for the independent variables is one of the most perplexing problems facing the forecaster. The use of lagged values for the independent variables, as per equation (6-26), is one of the more popular approaches. Closely allied with simple lag relationships are more complex distributed lag models, which are discussed in succeeding chapters. The advantage of lagged relationships is not only that future values of the variables are available but also that there is some theoretical basis for their incorporation into regression models. For example, while economic theory indicates that prices should be inversely related to the unit sales of any good or service, theory does not imply that this relationship is perfectly synchronized in time. In fact, there is every reason to believe that consumer purchases will adjust to changes in prices, changes in income, and changes in advertising only after some lapse in time.

From the perspective of the industry or firm-level forecaster, the widespread availability of purchasable forecasts of economic variables from commercial forecast vendors is a cost-effective procedure for obtaining forecast values. That is, for many business forecasters, the selection of independent variables is a function of the work that has been done by these commercial forecast vendors to predict future movements for a vast array of "potential" independent variables. In fact, one of the most useful first steps in developing industry or firm-level forecasting models is to spend time examining the listing of several hundred variables that are forecast by the large commercial forecast vendors.

FORECASTING WITH MULTIPLE REGRESSION EQUATIONS

To illustrate the process of forecasting with a multiple regression model, suppose that we return to the sales model presented in Table 6-2 and in equation (6-6), which is reproduced here:

$$\widehat{SALES}_t = -1.13991 + 0.00874927 RINC_t + 0.14368 SOV_t. \qquad \textbf{(6-6)}$$

Table 6-3 and Figure 6-1 detail the reliability of the estimated model in the historical simulation. The various evaluation statistics as well as the fitted-versus-actual comparison in Figure 6-1 indicate that, with few exceptions, the model appears to simulate closely the historical changes in sales. Figure 6-2 further indicates that the error pattern is randomly dispersed around the line of perfect forecasts and, with the exception of 1978, the estimated model captures the turning points exhibited by actual sales.

TABLE 6-3   Actual versus Historical Sales

Date	Actual Sales (1)	Estimated Sales (2)	Error* (3)	Percent Error (4)
1969	2.68	2.71	0.03	1.04
1970	3.01	3.14	0.13	4.31
1971	3.61	3.65	0.04	1.23
1972	2.59	2.84	0.25	9.57
1973	4.41	4.32	-0.09	-2.04
1974	4.02	3.90	-0.12	-3.01
1975	3.58	3.48	-0.10	-2.78
1976	5.04	4.93	-0.11	-2.27
1977	5.81	5.88	0.07	1.16
1978	5.60	6.32	0.72	12.83
1979	5.05	5.05	0.00	0.00
1980	4.80	4.94	0.14	2.83
1981	6.02	6.00	-0.02	-0.40
1982	5.41	5.14	-0.27	-4.90
1983	4.14	3.97	-0.17	-4.07
1984	5.91	6.31	0.40	6.71
1985	4.91	4.40	-0.51	-10.45
1986	6.59	6.19	-0.40	-6.04
1987	3.61	3.67	0.06	1.56
1988	4.09	4.53	0.44	10.83
1989	6.81	6.35	-0.46	-6.70
1990	5.95	5.93	-0.02	-0.27

MAPE = 4.32%; APE = 6.45%;
MAD = 0.2061; MSE = 0.0796

* Recall that in chapter 3 we indicated that in making presentations to management, the signs on the error terms should be reversed for ease of interpretation.

To develop sales forecasts, future values for real income and share of voice are required. Suppose that we have obtained, from a commercial forecast vendor, a forecast value for real income in 1991 of $325 billion. Further, suppose that in consultations with the advertising department, we are able to determine that our share of voice for 1991 will be 34 percent. Based on this information, a forecast value for sales for 1991 can be prepared:

$$\widehat{SALES}_{1991} = -1.13991 + 0.00874927RINC_{1991} + 0.14368SOV_{1991}$$

$$= -1.13991 + 0.00874927(325) + 0.14368(34)$$

$$= -1.13991 + 2.84351 + 4.88512 \qquad \textbf{(6-27)}$$

$$= 6.58872$$

$$= 6,588,720$$

FIGURE 6-1 Performance of Regression Model in Simulating Historical Sales

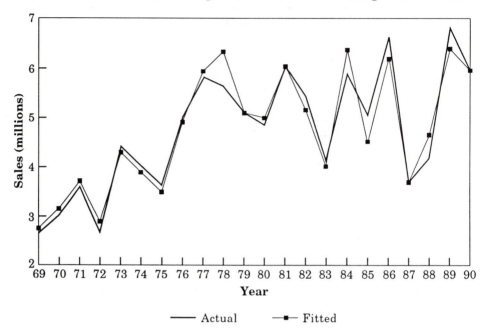

As a practical matter, when presenting these forecasts to management, analysts are well served to present this information as a range or interval, thereby highlighting that regression forecasts are probability-based estimates. By way of illustration, a 95 percent interval forecast would yield the following:[6]

$$Y_{1991} = \hat{Y}_{1991} \pm t_{cr}\,s$$

$$= 6{,}588{,}720 \pm 2.093(0.31196)$$

$$= 6{,}588{,}720 \pm 652{,}932 \qquad \textbf{(6-28)}$$

$$5{,}935{,}788 \le Y_{1991} \le 7{,}241{,}652$$

Thus, the forecaster can be 95 percent confident that the actual value of sales (assuming our forecasts for real income and share of voice are correct, and assuming that the relationships measured in regression model remain stable) will be between 5.9 million and 7.2 million units.

---

[6] The s term refers to the standard error component as noted in equation (6-11).

FIGURE 6-2   Turning-Point Reliability of Sales Model

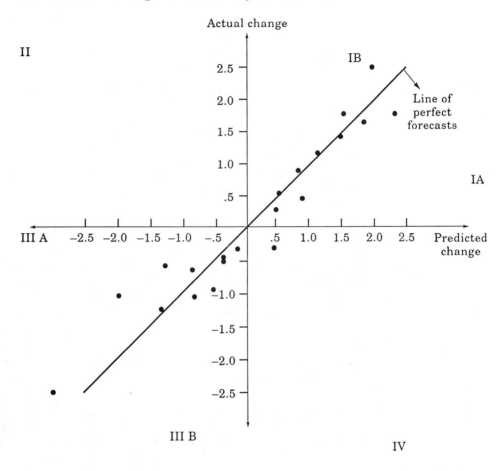

EXAMPLE 6-1   Automobile Sales Forecasts

Suppose that you are the credit manager for a firm whose primary line of business is the provision of short-term financing for inventories of retail automobile dealers. To determine the demand for cash to finance these inventories, you decide to develop quantitative estimates of automobile sales. Thus, the goal is to develop a forecasting model for automobile sales. In turn, this forecast will be used to determine cash needs for financing the inventories of retail automobile outlets. Suppose that the following model is formulated:

$$\widehat{USCAR}_t = f(YDP82_t, JCS_t, RUNC_t, RAUTO_t, REPCAR_t, RELP_t, TRP_t)$$

$$(6\text{-}29)$$

where:

$$
\begin{aligned}
\text{USCAR}_t &= \text{total retail sales, new passenger cars, millions of} \\
&\quad \text{units, SAAR} \\
\text{YDP82}_t &= \text{real disposable personal income, billions of 1982 dol-} \\
&\quad \text{lars, SAAR} \\
\text{JCS}_t &= \text{index of consumer sentiment, not seasonally ad-} \\
&\quad \text{justed, 1966:I} = 100.00 \text{ percent} \\
\text{RUNC}_t &= \text{unemployment rate, civilian, percent seasonally ad-} \\
&\quad \text{justed} \\
\text{RAUTO}_t &= \text{effective interest rate, new auto loans, percent, not} \\
&\quad \text{seasonally adjusted} \\
\text{REPCAR}_t &= \text{average auto finance period, months} \\
\text{RELP}_t &= \text{relative price of new-cars} \\
\text{TRP}_t &= \text{transfer payments to persons, billions of current dol-} \\
&\quad \text{lars, SAAR.}
\end{aligned}
$$

The data used in estimating equation (6-29) are detailed in Appendix D, Table D-1. Furthermore, an examination of the listing of forecast variables from a major commercial forecast vendor indicates that forecast values for all of these variables are available on a timely and consistent basis.

The theory of demand suggests that there should be a positive relationship between the level of personal income and automobile sales. Automobile sales should be inversely related to the unemployment rate (RUNC) since, as the rate of unemployment increases, purchases of automobiles should decline. Consumers' expectations regarding the state of the economy are likely to affect their willingness to commit themselves to large purchases such as automobiles. In general, the more optimistic people are with respect to future economic performance, the more willing they are to purchase automobiles. The index of consumer sentiment (JCS) tabulated by the University of Michigan is the most widely used measure of consumer expectations. The higher the index value, the larger the percent of consumers that expect economic growth to continue, hence the higher the sales of automobiles. Since the majority of automobile purchases are financed, the cost of this financing (RAUTO) and the length of the finance period (REPCAR) may be significant determinants of automobile sales. As the cost of financing increases, sales should decline while the length of the financing period should be positively related to auto sales. The relative price of automobiles (RELP) should be inversely related to automobile purchases. In an attempt to capture the complete impact of recessions, the transfer payments variable (TRP) is included in the model. An increase in transfer payments is likely to be indicative that the recession is adversely affecting income thereby adversely influencing the likely purchase of all consumer durables, including automobiles.

It should be emphasized that these a priori statements about the relationship between the dependent variable and each of the independent variables should be conducted prior to actually estimating the model. Table 6-4 summarizes the theoretical relationships for the specified automobile sales model.

Table 6-5 details the information pertinent to the estimated regression equation (6-30):

$$\widehat{USCAR}_t = 3.50139 + 0.006537YDP82_t + 0.061169JCS_t$$

$$- 0.09838RUNC_t - 0.114518RAUTO_t + 0.0945REPCAR_t \quad \textbf{(6-30)}$$

$$- 7.89014RELP_t - 0.02087TRP_t.$$

A comparison of the calculated t statistics (t_e, column 3, Table 6-5) with the critical values implies that, with the exception of the unemployment rate, all the coefficients taken individually are statistically significant at the 0.01 level (which means that the null hypothesis can be rejected). That is, there is less than one chance in 100 that these values would be observed if H_0 were true. Additionally, all the coefficients conform to a priori theoretical expectations. Interpreting these coefficients is a straightforward procedure. For example, automobile sales will increase by 6,537 units for each 1 billion dollar increase in real disposable income; will increase by 61,169 units for each 1 percent increase in the index of consumer sentiment; will decline by 98,380 units for each 1 percent increase in the unemployment rate; decline by 114,518 units for each 1 percent increase in the interest rate; increase by 94,450 units for each month increase in the finance period; decline by 7,890 units for each one hundredth of a point increase in the relative price of automobiles; and decline by 20,870 units for each 1 billion dollar increase in transfer payments. As usual, all of these interpretations are based on the assumption that all other variables in the model remain constant.

**TABLE 6-4   Theoretical Relationships for
Automobile Sales Model**

Variable	Expected Sign in Estimated Model
YDP82	+
JCS	+
RUNC	−
RAUTO	−
REPCAR	+
RELP	−
TRP	−

TABLE 6-5 Regression Results for Automobile Sales

Variable	Regression Coefficient (1)	Standard Error of Coefficient (2)	t Statistic (3)	95% Confidence Interval		Mean (6)	Standard Deviation (7)	Part Correlation Coefficient (8)	Partial Correlation Coefficient (9)	Beta Coefficient (10)	Prob Value (11)
				Lower Limit (4)	Upper Limit (5)						
Personal Income in Constant 82$ (YDP82)	0.006537	0.002065	3.166	0.002432	0.010642	2152.744	413.741	0.193771	0.323082	2.23816	0.0021
Index of Consumer Sentiment (JCS)	0.061169	0.009619	6.359	0.042047	0.08029	83.043	11.489	0.389222	0.565542	0.58154	0.0000
Unemployment Rate (RUNC)	-0.098377	0.104414	-0.942	-0.305945	0.10919	6.327	1.684	-0.057667	-0.101078	-0.137135	0.3487
Effective Interest Rate, New Autos (RAUTO)	-0.114518	0.068284	-1.677	-0.250263	0.21227	11.536	1.801	-0.102646	-0.177957	-0.170716	0.0972
Length of Financing Period (REPCAR)	0.094454	0.04611	2.048	-0.00279	0.186118	43.752	6.269	0.125375	0.215689	0.489979	0.0436
Relative Price (RELP)	-7.890143	3.149474	-2.505	-14.151091	-1.629195	1.105	0.138	-0.15333	-0.260797	-0.899253	0.0141
Transfer Payments (TRP)	-0.02087	0.00347	-6.014	-0.027769	-0.013971	299.324	189.718	-0.368063	-0.54408	-3.276493	0.0000
Constant	3.501392	7.211908									

Durbin-Watson	1.60735	Coefficient of Determination	0.67784	Missed Turning Points	60.8%
Mean of Auto Sales	9.875	Correlation Coefficient	0.82331	False Turning Points	51.2%
Standard Deviation	1.208	ADJ Coefficient of Determination	0.65161	APE	7.72%
Standard Error of Estimate	0.71325			F Statistic	25.85889
				Range of Data: 1967:I to 1990:II	

The confidence intervals for each of the individual coefficients (columns 4 and 5, Table 6-5) suggest that the null hypothesis would be accepted for the unemployment rate, the interest rate, and the length of the financing period. However, an examination of the Prob-Value column (column 11, Table 6-5) suggests that, with the exception of the unemployment rate, all of the variables contribute to an explanation of the observed changes in automobile sales and hence should be retained in the model. The insignificance of the unemployment rate is related to the fact that the transfer payments variable captures the same cyclical movements in the economy.

The beta coefficients (column 10, Table 6-5) yield a ranking of the relative importance of the independent variables that proceeds from the most important variable, transfer payments, to real personal income, to the relative price, to the index of consumer sentiment, to the length of the financing period, to the effective interest rate, to the least important variable, the unemployment rate variable. However, if the part and partial coefficients of determination (columns 8 and 9, Table 6-5) are examined, the most important variable (in terms of accounting for changes in automobile sales) is the index of consumer sentiment, while the second most important variable is transfer payments.[7]

The multiple coefficient of determination corrected for the number of independent variables indicates that 65.16 percent of the observed changes in automobile sales have been accounted for by the collective set of independent variables. The standard error of the estimate suggests that the average regression estimate is in error by 713,250 units, which when converted to percentage terms yields the average percentage error of 7.72 percent. An examination of the predicted versus actual automobile sales levels in Figure 6-3 indicates that the estimated model matches the historical pattern with reasonable precision.

Despite the fact that the model appears to perform satisfactorily from a statistical perspective, there are several problems that relate to its reliability in forecasting. First, the APE of 7.72 percent is relatively high. This is especially important when we recall that it is highly unlikely that future forecasts will be more accurate than the historical simulation. Second, equation (6-30) missed 60.8 percent of the turning points in actual automobile sales and predicted false turning points 51.2 percent of the time. The pattern of these turning points suggests that the model is not capturing lagged relationships that are present in the automobile market. This possibility is confirmed in Figure 6-4.

---

[7] The astute reader will note that several of the part and partial coefficients of determination have negative signs. An examination of the formulas that are involved in computing these measures suggests that only positive values can be generated. The signs on the part and partial coefficients of determination are taken from the regression coefficients after the absolute number has been determined.

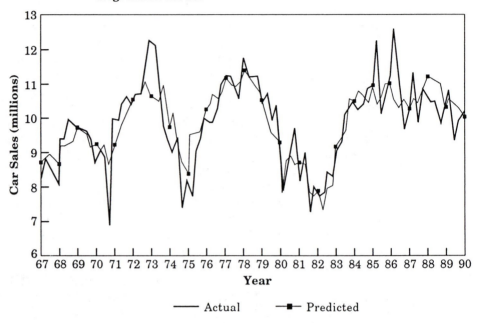

FIGURE 6-3 Estimated versus Actual Performance of Automobile Sales Regression Model

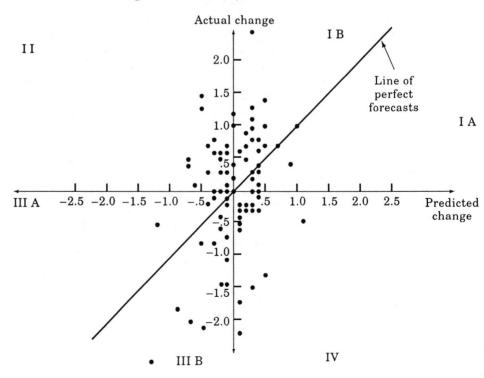

FIGURE 6-4 Turning-Point Reliability of Automobile Sales Model

TABLE 6-6   Forecast Values for Automobile Sales[8]

Date*	Automobile Sales Forecast	YDP82	JCS	RUNC	RAUTO	REPCAR	RELP	TRP
1990:III	10.255	3000.7	92.27	5.75	11.67	53.03	0.94	680.2
1990:IV	10.105	3011.1	92.25	5.72	11.64	53.03	0.94	690.9
1991:I	9.807	3029.1	91.52	5.68	11.62	53.03	0.94	709.0
1991:II	10.006	3052.1	90.90	5.65	11.61	53.03	0.93	708.8
1991:III	10.327	3074.0	90.89	5.57	11.60	53.03	0.93	700.7
1991:IV	10.064	3096.7	91.14	5.49	11.60	53.03	0.93	721.5
1992:I	10.069	3120.8	91.46	5.38	11.60	53.03	0.93	730.3
1992:II	9.945	3139.9	91.11	5.27	11.60	53.03	0.93	741.7
1992:III	10.026	3155.2	91.19	5.16	11.59	53.03	0.93	743.4
1992:IV	9.913	3170.2	91.63	5.04	11.59	53.03	0.93	755.4

* Year and quarter

Table 6-6 contains, in turn, information on the forecast values for each of the independent variables, as well as the forecast values for automobile sales based on these values.

An informal comparison of the automobile forecasts with current trends suggests that the model generates forecasts that are reasonably reliable (not a ringing endorsement, but the automobile model possesses obvious flaws).

EXAMPLE 6-2   Demand for Lumber

As a forecaster for a major lumber producer in the southeastern United States, you are assigned the task of developing a forecasting model for lumber sales used in the construction of housing units. As a first attempt in satisfying this requirement, the following model is specified:

$$DL_t = \beta_0 + \beta_1 HU_t + \beta_2 APT_t + \beta_3 RATE_t - \beta_4 P_t + \beta_5 INC_t \quad \text{(6-31)}$$

where

DL_t = lumber sales to housing industry, millions of tons, seasonally adjusted

HU_t = sales of new homes in southeastern United States, millions of units, seasonally adjusted

[8] At the time this model was estimated, the most current available data was through the second quarter of 1990. In fact, much of the 1990 data should be regarded as preliminary information.

$$\text{APT}_t = \text{multifamily units constructed, millions of units, season-}$$
ally adjusted

$$\text{RATE}_t = \text{rate of household formation, seasonally adjusted}$$

$$\text{P}_t = \text{price of ton of lumber, dollars}$$

$$\text{INC}_t = \text{personal income, southeastern United States, millions}$$
of dollars, seasonally adjusted.

The time frame of interest is 1977 to 1989 (quarterly data), and the data used in estimating this model is detailed in Appendix D, Table D-2.

After some initial testing, the final lumber sales model was estimated as

$$\hat{\text{DL}}_t = -916.419 + 226.316\text{HU}_t + 1.39741\text{APT}_t$$

t_e	3.59	1.76
PCD	0.22	0.063

$$+ \ 25.9193\text{RATE}_t - 0.14213\text{P}_t + 0.77785\text{INC}_t. \quad \textbf{(6-32)}$$

	1.39	−1.91	5.84
	0.04	−0.073	0.42

All individual coefficients are statistically significant at the 0.01 level or better. The partial coefficients of determination (PCD) indicate that income contributes most to explaining the observed changes in lumber sales, while the rate of household formation contributes the least.

Table 6-7 presents the summary statistics for the complete lumber model. The collective set of independent variables accounts for 89.6 percent of the observed changes in lumber sales, while the average percent error indicates that the regression estimates are in error by 15.92 percent. When compared with the critical value of the F statistic, the null hypothesis would be rejected.

Figure 6-5 illustrates the relationship between the actual lumber sales and the historically simulated or predicted values from the estimated model. While the estimated model appears to pass all statistical tests, there are two disturbing features of the model as presented. First, the APE of 15.92 percent is large. Second, the Durbin-Watson (DW) statistic (the DW statistic is discussed later in this chapter) of 0.49 is so low as to lead one to expect autocorrelation to be present; that is, the error terms (e_t) are positively related to each other. This relationship is confirmed by Figure 6-6, where a plot of the error terms is presented. The

TABLE 6-7 Summary Statistics for Lumber Sales Model

Time Frame: 1977:I to 1989:IV
ADJ R^2 = 0.896; SEE = 41.10; APE = 15.92%;
F_e = 88.49; DW = 0.49

FIGURE 6-5   Actual versus Predicted Performance of Lumber Sales Model

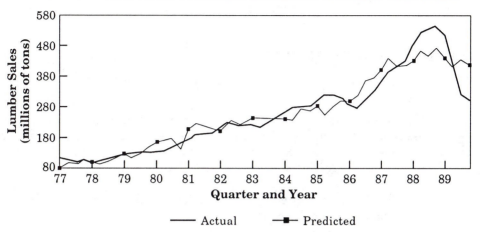

FIGURE 6-6   Error Pattern in Lumber Sales Model

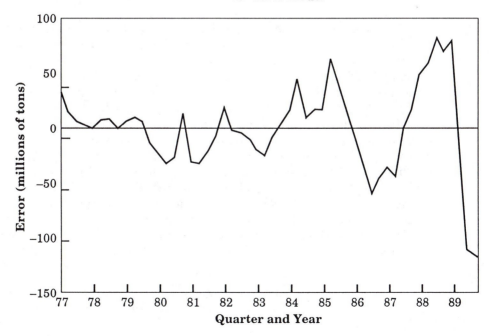

techniques for identification and correction of autocorrelation are discussed later in this chapter.

VALIDATION OF THE MODEL

INTRODUCTION

Up to this point, no attempt has been made to test the validity of the underlying assumptions of the regression model. The next step is to determine those situations in which the assumptions are violated and to investigate the proper techniques for correction. The assumptions of the linear model are as follows:

1. The relationship between the independent variables, X_i's, and the dependent variable, Y, is linear.
2. The X_i's are nonrandom variables whose values are fixed.
3. The error term has constant variance.
4. The random variables, Y_t, or the error terms, e_t, are statistically independent. That is, they are randomly distributed and exhibit no discernible pattern.
5. The error term has an expected value of zero.
6. The independent variables, X_i's, must be independent of each other.
7. The number of observations, n, must exceed the number of regressors, k.

Note that an assumption of normality is not included in the preceding list. Even without the normality assumption, it can be shown that the least-squares estimators are BLUE (best linear unbiased estimators). Although the assumption of normality is needed to perform the t and F tests, the central limit theorem provides the rationale of using statistical tests without a normality assumption whenever the sample size is large.[9]

The assumption that the error term has an expected value of zero is insignificant for purposes of forecasting. If the error has a nonzero expected value, the slope parameters remain unchanged, but the intercept ($\hat{\beta}_0$) reflects the difference between the actual expected value and the theoretical value of zero. Although this implies that the true intercept cannot be accurately estimated, the intercept generally has no theoretical interpretation; thus, the consequences of violating this assumption are minimal.

Thus far we have implicitly assumed that the independent variables are fixed and under the control of the forecaster. It must be obvious that this

[9] Ronald J. Wonnacott and Thomas H. Wonnacott, *Econometrics* (New York: John Wiley & Sons, 1970), pp. 15–34 and 38–40. Copyright © 1970 John Wiley & Sons, Inc. Reprinted by permission.

condition rarely holds in the problems being addressed by the business analyst. Fortunately, the majority of the results and their interpretations remain valid whether the X_i's are fixed or random, if the error terms are normally distributed and independent of the X_i's.[10]

The assumption that the number of observations must exceed the number of regressors follows from an examination of the normal equations. Specifically, in order to generate a set of independent normal equations, the number of unknowns must match the number of equations. This condition will be violated if there is an insufficient number of observations. For the practitioner, this assumption poses no real problem, because if it is violated estimates for the coefficients are mathematically unattainable.

The remaining four assumptions are important and are considered in some detail in the following sections of this chapter:

1. The assumption that the error term has a constant variance is referred to as the assumption of homoscedasticity. Alternatively, violation of the assumption is referred to as heteroscedasticity.

2. When the assumption that the error terms are statistically independent of each other is violated, the problem of autocorrelation is said to exist.

3. Multicollinearity refers to the violation of the assumption that the independent variables are unrelated to each other.

4. The linearity assumption essentially refers to the model specification assumption and, as we shall see, has both theoretical and mathematical aspects.

SPECIFICATION ERROR

Throughout our discussions of various regression models, we have implicitly assumed that the model to be estimated has been correctly specified. If indeed this assumption is true, model estimation, testing, and forecast generation become relatively straightforward procedures. However, as should be reasonably obvious, forecasters are never certain that a specific model has been correctly specified (that is, they have included the "correct" set of independent variables). Rather, it is much more likely that the practitioner has examined several alternative specifications and the final model is the one that "fits" the historical data the best. The typical approach is to formulate an initial model based on a combination of the underlying theory being applied, a forecaster's own knowledge of the underlying process being studied, and other similar studies. Even with all these tools, there is no unique way of quantifying the relationship between the dependent variable and the almost innumerable independent variables that could be selected for inclusion into the final model.

---

[10] Wonnacott and Wonnacott, *Econometrics*, pp. 38–40.

Our purpose here is to provide you with an overview of the costs involved in testing regression models for misspecification. There are four types of misspecification error that are of interest. The first occurs when relevant variables are omitted from the model; the second relates to the possibility that irrelevant variables are included in the model; the third happens when the functional form of the model is questionable; and the fourth relates to an analysis of the residuals or errors associated with any specific regression model.

LINEARITY ASSUMPTION

The assumption of linearity is not nearly as restrictive as it first appears. In fact, the techniques of regression analysis that we have described are applicable as long as the model under consideration is inherently (or intrinsically) linear. A model is said to be inherently linear if, via some appropriate transformation, the relationship can be estimated in a linear fashion. For example, a model of the form

$$\hat{Y}_t = \hat{\beta}_0 X_t^{\hat{\beta}_1} \tag{6-33}$$

is said to be inherently linear because it can be transformed via logarithms into the form

$$\log \hat{Y}_t = \log \hat{\beta}_0 + \hat{\beta}_1 \log X_t. \tag{6-34}$$

Thus, once the transformation to logarithms has been made, the techniques associated with linear regression analysis can be applied with the only qualification being that we now have a model that is linear in logarithms. This process of transformation to logarithms, along with several other possibilities, is presented in more detail in the next chapter.

Another aspect that relates to the linearity assumption is the possibility that a correctly specified model would include interactive variables in which the effects of the independent variables are multiplicative rather than additive. Thus, in our models we have implicitly assumed that Y is influenced, at least in part, by X_1 plus X_2 (not X_1 times X_2). While it is true that this additivity assumption dominates the use of regression analysis in forecasting applications, it nonetheless should be investigated for validity. To illustrate the interaction term, suppose that we are interested in deriving estimates for the level of consumption in any given time period. That is, we are interested in predicting consumption expenditures. Previously, we have hypothesized that the level of consumption was related to disposable income (example 5-3). Theory also suggests that asset holdings may affect consumption expenditures.[11]

---

[11] See, for example, L. R. Klein and J. N. Morgan, "Results of Alternative Statistical Treatment of Sample Survey Data," *Journal of American Statistical Association*, vol. 47, December 1951.

Specifically, it is argued that the marginal propensity to consume will depend not only on income but also on assets—a wealthier person is likely to have a different marginal propensity to consume out of income. With this formulation the consumption function would be

$$\hat{C}_t = \hat{\beta}_0 + \hat{\beta}_1 Y_t + \hat{\beta}_2 A Y_t \tag{6-35}$$

The AY term is the interaction term and reflects the belief that the income and asset effects on consumption are multiplicative.

There are essentially three procedures that can be applied to test the validity of the linearity assumption. The first approach would involve the estimation of various functional forms. For example, rather than assuming that the model should be estimated as

$$\hat{Y}_t = \hat{\beta}_0 + \hat{\beta}_1 X_{1t} + \hat{\beta}_2 X_{2t} \tag{6-36}$$

we could respecify as

$$\hat{Y}_t = \hat{\beta}_0 + \hat{\beta}_1 X_{1t}^2 + \beta_2 X_{2t}^2 \tag{6-37}$$

This second possibility is explored in the next chapter in the section on non-linear estimation.

A second approach for testing the linearity assumption (as well as other assumptions) focuses on an examination of the residual or error terms generated by a specific model. In particular, if the assumption of linearity is satisfied, there should be no relationship between the predicted values and the error terms.[12] If the plot of predicted and error terms resembles Figure 6-7(a) (which suggests that the residuals can be contained within a horizontal band), the assumption of linearity is satisfied. Conversely, if the error plot resembles that presented in Figure 6-7(b), it is indicative of a nonlinear relationship between the variables in the model.[13]

Figure 6-8 depicts the plot of error terms and predicted values (taken from columns 1 and 3 of Table 6-3) for the sales model in equation (6-6). A comparison of the pattern of error terms in Figure 6-8 and Figure 6-7(a) suggests that the linearity assumption has been satisfied for the sales model.

The third method of testing for linearity involves the use of a procedure called the Lagrange multiplier test. Lagrangian multiplier (LM) tests can be employed as either nonlinearity tests or as tests for the applicability of inter-

---

[12] The residuals or error terms should be plotted versus the predicted or fitted values and not the actual values, because the error term and the predicted value should be uncorrelated while the error term and the actual values are usually correlated.

[13] It should also be noted that this pattern may be indicative of a model that does not contain all relevant independent variables.

FIGURE 6-7 Error Plots

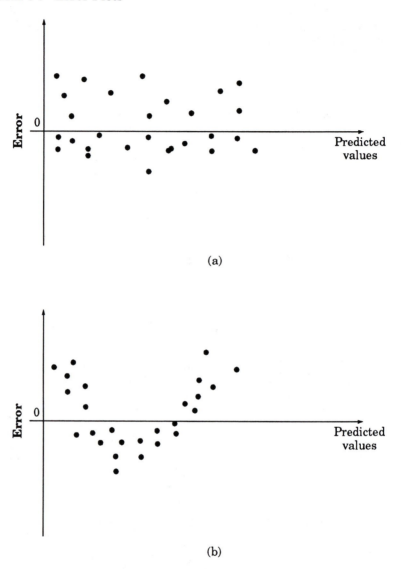

action terms. Consider the multiple regression model $Y = \beta_0 + \beta_1X + \beta_2Z + \epsilon$. Suppose that we are interested in testing for the possibility that the model should have included nonlinear terms such as X^2 and Z^2. This can be checked with the LM test as follows. Estimate the original model using ordinary least-squares procedures and calculate the residuals (actual minus predicted) as

$$e_t = Y_t - \beta_0 - \beta_1X - \beta_2Z. \tag{6-38}$$

FIGURE 6-8 Plot of Error Terms and Predicted Sales

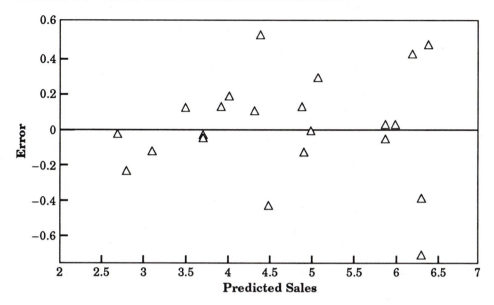

If the nonlinear terms, X^2 and Z^2, should have been included in the model, then their absence would be captured by e_t. More specifically, we can test for nonlinearity by running a second regression using the error term. The results of applying this procedure to the sales example in equation (6-6) are (as before, INC measures real income in billions and SOV measures share of voice, or company advertising as a percent of total industry advertising). The actual data for this example are provided in Appendix D, Table D-3:

$$e_t = -0.57686 + 0.005151033\text{RINC}_t + 0.005110986\text{SOV}_t$$
$$- 0.000172506\text{SOV}_t^2 - 0.0000103204\text{RINC}_t^2. \tag{6-39}$$

To see whether the nonlinear terms should have been included in the model, we can evaluate the t statistics for each of the terms in much the same fashion that has been previously discussed. In the case of equation (6-39), the t statistics were -0.031 and -0.998 for the squared share of voice and real income variables, respectively. Neither of these values indicates that the estimated coefficients on the nonlinear terms are significantly different from zero. Once again the linearity assumption appears to hold in the case of equation (6-6).[14]

---

[14] The LM method can be used to test for inclusion of all nonlinear terms simultaneously. A complete discussion of this procedure is presented in Ramu Ramanathan, *Introductory Econometrics: With Applications* (San Diego: Harcourt Brace Jovanovich, 1989), pp. 295–309.

EXAMPLE 6-3 Testing for Interaction

Suppose that you have been assigned the task of developing a forecasting model for the consumption of electrical power in a major Midwestern city. These forecasts are to be used to develop a long-term plan for construction of additional generating facilities. Because of the long-term nature of the request, you decide to focus on annual data and formulate the following model to be estimated:

$$\widehat{CONSEL}_t = \beta_0 + \beta_1 PRICE_t + \beta_2 NONAG_t + \beta_3 HCDD_t \quad (6\text{-}40)$$

where

$$
\begin{aligned}
\widehat{CONSEL}_t &= \text{consumption of electricity, millions of kilowatt hours} \\
PRICE_t &= \text{price of electricity relative to price of natural gas} \\
NONAG_t &= \text{nonagricultural employment, thousands} \\
HCDD_t &= \text{heating and cooling degree days.}
\end{aligned}
$$

Nonagricultural employment is included because it is the most comprehensive and readily available measure of the general economic health of a metropolitan area. We would expect there to be a positive relationship between the consumption of electricity and the level of employment. Consumption of electricity should also be related to the vagaries in the weather. Specifically, during the summer as the temperature increases, the consumption of electricity should increase. Conversely, during the winter months a decline in the temperature should be associated with increased electrical consumption. Utilities typically measure the variance in temperatures via variables referred to as heating and cooling degree days. These measures should be regarded as measuring the temperatures that actually existed versus some average measure of temperature. That is, as the number of heating and cooling degree days increases, either the summer has been warmer than normal or the winter has been colder than average. While these two values could be included as separate variables, the decision here was to aggregate them into one measure, HCDD, since the forecasts are to be used in a capital budgeting process. We would expect there to be a positive relationship between HCDD and the consumption of electricity.

There is one other possibility that warrants consideration. It is possible that the impact of temperature variations on the consumption of electricity might also depend on the price of electricity. That is, if electricity is relatively expensive, consumers might delay turning on the air conditioning or heat and/or switch it off sooner. This interactive effect can be tested by including a PRICEHCDD term in the model.

Data on the variables of interest were collected for the years 1978 through 1989 and are presented in Appendix D, Table D-4. The model as originally formulated is

$$\widehat{COMEL}_t = -14310.27924 + 150.22415NONAG_t$$
$$t_e \qquad\qquad\qquad\qquad 8.647$$

$$+ 1.79951HCDD_t - 212.62478PRICE_t. \quad \textbf{(6-41)}$$
$$1.370 \qquad\qquad -1.607$$

The signs on the independent variables satisfy theoretical expectations and all are significant enough to warrant inclusion into a forecasting model. The collective set of independent variables explains almost 89 percent of the observed variation in the consumption of electricity.

To test for the possibility of an interaction effect between price and heating and cooling degree days, a second model was estimated as

$$\widehat{COMEL}_t = 219159 + 149.91734NONAG_t + 43.16546HCDD_t$$
$$t_e \qquad\qquad\qquad 8.795 \qquad\qquad\qquad 1.10$$

$$- 3069.35348PRICE_t + 0.55035PRICEHCDD_t. \quad \textbf{(6-42)}$$
$$-1.23 \qquad\qquad\qquad 1.146$$

Of particular interest here is the PRICEHCDD interactive term. The t statistic is statistically significant at the 0.29 level of significance. Alternatively, we can be 71 percent confident that the interaction term has a significant impact on the observed changes in the consumption of electricity.

OMISSION OF AN IMPORTANT VARIABLE

A second type of specification error occurs if an important independent variable is excluded from the estimation process. Suppose that the true model is

$$Y_t = \beta_0 + \beta_1 X_{1t} + \beta_2 X_{2t} + \epsilon_t \qquad\qquad \textbf{(6-43)}$$

but we have estimated the model

$$Y_t = \beta_0 + \beta_1 X_{1t} + \epsilon_t. \qquad\qquad \textbf{(6-44)}$$

Implicitly we have assumed that the value of β_2 is zero when in fact it has a nonzero value. While there are some statistical issues associated with omitting important variables, the most significant practical implication is that the forecasting reliability of the model is likely to be unsatisfactory.

The simplest procedure for testing for omitted variables is to examine a plot of the error terms over time. If an important variable has been omitted, we should observe a nonrandom error pattern. Recall that the assumptions of the linear regression model imply that the error pattern should be randomly dispersed: that is, there should be no discernible pattern in the error terms.

A nonrandom error pattern is, therefore, a potential red flag. We defer our discussion of the diagnostic and correction procedures, since they are covered in detail later in this chapter in our discussion of autocorrelation.

INCLUSION OF AN IRRELEVANT VARIABLE

If we now suppose that the true model were represented by equation (6-44) and we have estimated the model as equation (6-43), we have erroneously included a variable that does not contribute to our understanding of the changes in the dependent variable. Fortunately, it can be shown that the forecasting consequences of including irrelevant variables are not nearly as serious as those that arise from omitting an important variable. Furthermore, testing for irrelevant variables is relatively easy. The simplest procedure is to examine the t statistics for statistical significance. If the variable is redundant in the sense that it does not contribute to explaining the changes in Y, the t statistic will be statistically insignificant. The possibility of redundant variables is discussed in some detail later in this chapter in our discussion of multicollinearity.

COSTS OF MODEL BUILDING

If, as is usually the case, the forecaster is not certain which explanatory variables ought to appear in a model, there are several trade-offs to be addressed. If a relevant variable is excluded, we run the risk of presenting unreliable forecasts to management. Conversely, if we simply add independent variables, we may run the risk of loss of efficiency. Specifically, unless the sample size is relatively large, we may exhaust the degrees of freedom available to us. Furthermore, simply adding independent variables to the model may not improve the forecasting reliability and in fact may reduce forecast accuracy. It should also be obvious that adding independent variables increases the costs associated with building and monitoring models.

The trade-off between increased forecast reliability and model-building costs may be approximated by the mean square error. That is, since the mean square error addresses both efficiency and bias issues, we might estimate several alternative models over a given time period and compare the mean square errors associated with each of these models. Finally, it should also be noted that, even if a variable has a statistically insignificant t statistic, it does not necessarily imply that it should be excluded from the model.

ANALYSIS OF RESIDUALS

In evaluating the various regression models that have been presented in this and the preceding chapter, we have relied on numerous summary statistics, such as the coefficient of determination, the standard error of the estimate, the mean square error, etc. Utilization of these summary statistics is valid only insofar as the assumptions concerning the residual or error terms are satisfied. A large value of R^2, a significant t, or a small mean average percent error does not guarantee that the estimated model "fits" the actual data well. To dramatize this point, Anscombe presented four data sets, each with a distinct pattern. If we were to estimate a regression model for each of these data sets, we would find virtually identical regression equations and virtually identical summary statistics.[15] The estimated regression lines versus the actual observations are reproduced in Figure 6-9.

By focusing exclusively on the summary statistics, the practicing forecaster would have been unable to detect the distinctly different patterns depicted in Figure 6-9. The simplest and most effective method for identifying problems with estimated models is to examine the residuals. The residual or error term associated with any time period has been previously defined as

$$e_t = Y_t - \hat{Y}_t. \tag{4-3}$$

Corresponding to e_t, the standardized residual, e_{ts}, can be defined as

$$e_{ts} = \frac{e_t}{s} \tag{6-45}$$

where s is the standard deviation of residuals as given by

$$s^2 = \frac{\sum (Y_t - \hat{Y}_t)^2}{n - 2}. \tag{6-46}$$

Alternatively, s refers to the standard error of the estimate. The standardized residuals sum to zero and have a variance of unity. Additionally, some computer programs present the analysis of error terms in the form of studentized residuals defined as

$$sr_t = \frac{e_t}{s\sqrt{1 - h_t}} = \frac{z_t}{\sqrt{1 - h_t}} \tag{6-47}$$

where h is commonly referred to as the leverage and is a measure of the importance of the tth observation in determining the model fit. Our purpose here is to illustrate the use of graphical residual analysis as a diagnostic tool. As such, we do not present all of the computations that are required to derive standardized or studentized residuals.

The practicing forecaster will generally find that significant violations

---

[15] F. J. Anscombe, "Graphs in Statistical Analysis," *American Statistician*, vol. 27, 1973, pp. 17–21.

FIGURE 6-9   **Fitting Regression Equations to Alternative Data Sets**

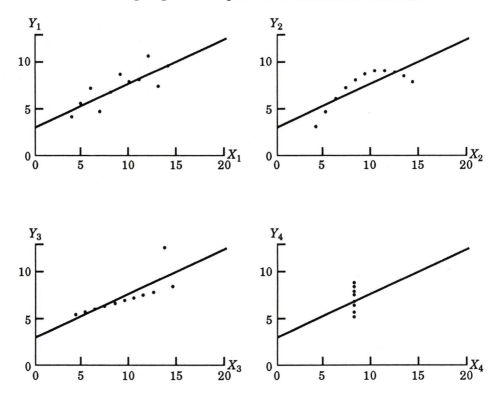

of the linearity assumption can be detected by examining various types of error plots.[16] Some of the more commonly used plots are as follows:

1. The predicted values, $\hat{Y}_t$, versus the error terms, e_t
2. The error terms versus time
3. Histograms of standardized residuals
4. Normal probability plots.

For purposes of presenting all of these residual plots, suppose that we concentrate on the lumber sales model that was presented in example 6-2 and in equation (6-32). The relationship between the predicted values and the residual term is presented in Figure 6-10. An examination of dispersion of points

---

[16] Statisticians would argue that an additional component of residual analysis would focus on the influence of potential outliers. It is our belief that much of what can be gleaned from the more sophisticated outlier procedures can be almost as readily derived from the various residual plots presented here.

FIGURE 6-10 Plot of Error Terms and Predicted Values for Lumber Sales Model

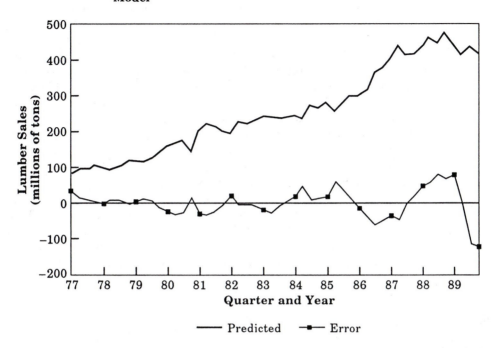

FIGURE 6-11 Standardized Error Plot for Lumber Sales Model

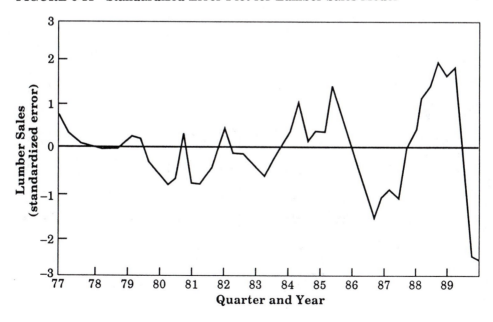

in Figure 6-10 appears to indicate that as the predicted demand for lumber, $\hat{D}L_t$, increases, the error associated with this value increases. This pattern is highlighted by the fanning out of the boundary lines in Figure 6-10.

Figure 6-11 (page 251) illustrates another of the residual plots that frequently proves to be useful to the forecaster. On this graph the standardized error terms are plotted versus time. The disturbing feature of this plot is that the error terms mirror what appears to be a cyclical pattern. That is, a series of overestimates are followed by a sequence of underestimates, which are followed by a series of overestimates, etc. This type of systematic pattern is clearly indicative of one or more violations of the underlying assumptions of the model, or an error in the specification of the model.

The assumption of normality can be studied by investigating a histogram of residuals (errors) and a normal probability plot. Figures 6-12 and 6-13 present these two plots for the lumber demand model, equation (6-32). The regression histogram, Figure 6-12, presents a comparison of the observed number of residuals (represented by a vertical line) and the number of residuals that would be expected in a normal distribution. It would be unreasonable for us

FIGURE 6-12   Histogram of Standardized Residuals for Lumber Sales

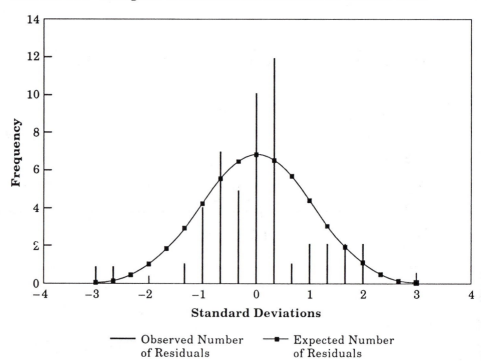

FIGURE 6-13   Normal Probability Plot for Lumber Sales

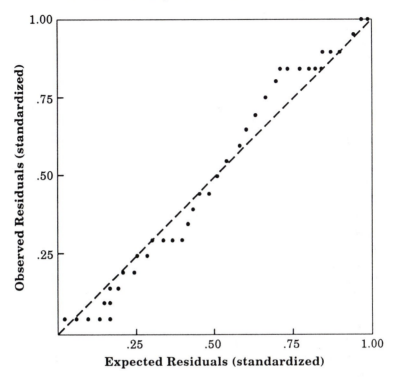

to expect the observed residuals to match exactly the normal distribution—some discrepancies are to be expected because of sampling variation. That is, even if the errors are normally distributed in the population, sample errors are only approximately normal. In Figure 6-12, the distribution does not appear to satisfy the assumption of normality since there is an exaggerated clustering of residuals toward the center and a straggling tail of positive values.

Figure 6-13 provides a second method of comparing the observed residuals (errors) to the expected pattern under the assumption of normality. If the two distributions (the expected distribution and the observed distribution) are identical, a straight line results. In Figure 6-13 we have graphed the two cumulative residual distributions. By observing how points scatter about the expected straight line, we can test the validity of the normality assumption. An analysis of this figure suggests that, initially, the observed residuals are below the straight line, with a smaller number of large negative residuals than expected. Once the greatest concentration of residuals is reached, the observed cumulative proportion exceeds the expected.

MULTICOLLINEARITY

Whenever more than one independent variable appears in a regression model, it is possible that the variables are related to or are dependent on each other. For example, when using time series data, all economic data move together as a result of underlying trends, business cycles, and other similar phenomena. The practical implications of such coincident movements is that time-measured data may exhibit some degree of incidental correlation. If independent variables are related to each other, multicollinearity among the variables is said to exist. In general, when two or more independent variables are related to each other, they are redundant—they contribute overlapping information. Although it is possible to obtain least-squares estimators (except in the case of perfect collinearity), the use, testing, and interpretation of the regression coefficients is troublesome when multicollinearity is present.

It can be proven that the presence of multicollinearity results in an overstatement of the standard errors (and, therefore, understatement of the t values) of the regression coefficients. Thus, even though the independent variables are related to Y, their statistical significance may be masked. Additionally, if the standard errors are overstated, the t test and confidence intervals are adversely affected, the process of partitioning the regression sum of squares is invalid, and the F test cannot be used in statistically checking the regression equation.

With respect to interpreting the regression coefficients, the effect of multicollinearity can be illustrated by examining a multiple regression equation of the form

$$\hat{Y}_t = \hat{\beta}_0 + \hat{\beta}_1 X_{1t} + \hat{\beta}_2 X_{2t} \tag{6-48}$$

In this equation, the coefficients, $\hat{\beta}_1$ and $\hat{\beta}_2$, were given specific meanings. For example, $\hat{\beta}_1$ measures the change in Y due to a change in X_1, other things (specifically X_2) remaining the same. However, if X_1 and X_2 are related to each other, this interpretation is no longer valid. That is, we cannot isolate the effect of X_1 on Y because X_1 also influences X_2, which in turn affects Y.

Methods of detecting and identifying the severity of multicollinearity follow from an understanding of the problem and its effects. There are three relatively simple schemes that are presented here.[17] Because multicollinearity is a problem with the data and not with the regression model itself, it becomes

---

[17] Statisticians have proposed a number of formal tests for multicollinearity. Among these would be a chi-square test, an F test, and a t test. The chi-square test is to identify whether multicollinearity is present, the F test to discover which variables are causing the multicollinearity, and the t test to discover the nature of the multicollinearity. Another formal testing procedure involves the computation of a condition number. The utility of these procedures is subject to some controversy and is beyond the scope of this text.

more appropriate to present these three schemes in connection with estimated models. The three schemes that signify the presence of multicollinearity are (1) a high R^2 with low values for the t statistics, (2) high values for simple correlation coefficients, and (3) regression coefficients that are sensitive to model specification.

EXAMPLE 6-4   Sales of Personal Computers Revisited

The first method involves examining the values of the regression coefficients to see if they are sensitive to changes in the specification of the model. For example, consider the model that was presented earlier:

$$\widehat{SALES}_t = -2.48067 + 0.277085SOV_t. \tag{6-5}$$

Now, if real income (RINC) and share of voice (SOV) are independent of each other, inclusion of RINC into equation (6-5) should not change the value of $\hat{\beta}_1$ (0.277085). Equation (6-6) provides this comparison:

$$\widehat{SALES}_t = 1.13991 + 0.14368SOV_t + 0.00874927RINC_t. \tag{6-6}$$

Clearly, the regression coefficient for share of voice was altered by the inclusion of real income in the model. Therefore, one could reasonably conclude that multicollinearity between share of voice and real income exists and is likely to affect adversely our ability to interpret the specific impact of the independent variables on changes in sales, the dependent variable.

Prior to presenting the other methods of detecting multicollinearity, we need to introduce the concept of a correlation matrix. A correlation matrix documents the simple correlation coefficients among all combinations of the dependent and independent variables. The format of the correlation matrix is given in Table 6-8. In this table, $r(Y_t Y_t)$ can be interpreted as the relationship between Y_t and Y_t (which, obviously, would be perfect or $r = 1$); $r(Y_t X_{1t})$ as measuring the relationship between Y_t and the first independent variable X_{1t}; $r(X_{1t} X_{2t})$ as measuring the relationship between X_{1t} and X_{2t}; and so on.

In Table 6-8, the cross diagonals measure the correlation between a variable and itself; hence the values here will always be equal to 1. Correlation coefficients are invariant with respect to the order of the variables; thus $r(X_1 Y)$, which measures the relationship between X_1 and Y, equals $r(Y X_1)$, which measures the relationship between Y and X_1. Because of this equality, it is commonplace for many computer programs to display only the bottom half (that portion below the cross diagonal) of a correlation matrix. The assumption that the independent variables are unrelated to each other implies that $r(X_1 X_2)$ and $r(X_2 X_1)$, boldfaced in the correlation matrix, are zero.

**TABLE 6-8   Simple Coefficient of Determination
Matrix for Three Variables**

Variable \\ Variable	Y	X_1	X_2
Y	1	$r(Y\ X_1)$	$r(Y\ X_2)$
X_1	$r(X_1\ Y)$	1	$r(X_1\ X_2)$
X_2	$r(X_2\ Y)$	$r(X_2\ X_1)$	1

EXAMPLE 6-5   Shipments of High-Value Packages

Suppose that our objective is to develop a forecasting model for a firm whose primary line of business is the shipment of high-value packages. The important theoretical aspect of this model is that the demand for package shipments is a derived demand in the sense that our shipments are entirely a function of the demand for our shippers' products. That is, package volumes will be dependent on economic activity in the industries that use our services. An examination of our historical data base indicates that shipments by nine industries account for over 80 percent of our package volumes. With this as background, the forecasting model is specified as follows:

$$PS_t = f(SER_t, PR_t, FIR_t, COMP_t, ELEC_t, INS_t, COMM_t, \quad \text{(6-49)}$$
$$DRUG_t, PRIN_t, AIR_t)$$

where

$$
\begin{aligned}
PS_t &= \text{package shipments, millions of packages} \\
SER_t &= \text{employment in service industries, millions} \\
PR_t &= \text{average price per package, dollars} \\
FIR_t &= \text{employment in finance, insurance, and real estate, millions} \\
COMP_t &= \text{industrial production in computer industry, } 1982 = 100 \\
ELEC_t &= \text{industrial production in electronics industry, } 1982 = 100 \\
INS_t &= \text{industrial production in instrument industry, } 1982 = 100 \\
COMM_t &= \text{industrial production in communication industry, } 1982 = 100 \\
DRUG_t &= \text{industrial production in drug industry, } 1982 = 100
\end{aligned}
$$

TABLE 6-9 Package Shipments Regression Model

$$PS_t = -1,993,736 - 1319.7AIR_t + 850.2ELEC_t + 1371.4INS_t$$
$$t_e \qquad\qquad\qquad -1.69 \qquad\qquad 1.17 \qquad\qquad 0.97$$

$$\qquad - 2869.5PR_t + 698.3COMM_t + 128.0DRUG_t + 151.6PRIN_t \quad \textbf{(6-50)}$$
$$\qquad -0.44 \qquad\quad 0.60 \qquad\qquad 0.11 \qquad\qquad 0.17$$

$$\qquad + 78,995SER_t - 929.3COMP_t + 90,603FIR_t$$
$$\qquad\quad 7.59 \qquad\qquad -1.02 \qquad\qquad 1.22$$

ADJ R^2 = 0.999;   SEE = 8,059.7; F = 1701;   DW = 2.21

PRIN$_t$ = industrial production in printing and publishing industry, 1982 = 100

AIR$_t$ = industrial production in aircraft parts industry, 1982 = 100

All variables were seasonally adjusted and are provided in Appendix D, Table D-6. The industrial production measures are the most common values that are used for charting economic growth in various sectors.[18]

All of the variables, except price, should be positively related to package shipments in the sense that the regression coefficients should have a positive sign in the estimated model. One of the more common indicators of the presence of multicollinearity is that the estimated regression coefficients have the "wrong" sign.[19] Another indication of multicollinearity occurs when the individual regression coefficients are statistically insignificant, while the multiple coefficient of determination suggests that the model in its entirety is acceptable.

The estimated package shipments model and its summary statistics are shown in Table 6-9. The disturbing aspects of equation (6-50) are that (1) the signs on two of the coefficients (AIR and COMP) do not satisfy theoretical expectations, and (2) that the INS, PR, COMM, DRUG, and PRIN variables are not statistically significant. When evaluated in its entirety, the collective set of independent variables accounts for 99.4 percent of the actual changes in package volume. This, when combined with the insignificant t statistics and the wrong signs, is indicative of a high degree of multicollinearity.

Table 6-10 presents the correlation matrix and confirms the multicollinearity between the independent variables. The correlation coef-

[18] For a complete explanation of these measures, consult any current issue of the *Federal Reserve Bulletin*.

[19] There are other potential explanations for regression coefficients having the "wrong" sign. For example, changes in economic behavior frequently exhibit lead-lag relationships, which unless correctly identified can lead to the same problem of "wrong" signs.

TABLE 6-10   Correlation Matrix for Package Shipments[20]

Variable \ Variable	PS	PR	FIR	SER	PRIN	DRUG	COMP	ELEC	COMM	INS	AIR
PS	1.00	0.93	0.96	0.99	0.97	0.97	0.99	0.50	0.95	0.98	0.96
PR	0.93	1.00	**0.98**	**0.91**	**0.92**	**0.93**	**0.90**	**0.36**	**0.91**	**0.87**	**0.96**
FIR	0.96	**0.98**	1.00	**0.95**	**0.95**	**0.97**	**0.94**	**0.35**	**0.96**	**0.90**	**0.99**
SER	0.99	**0.91**	**0.95**	1.00	**0.97**	**0.97**	**0.99**	**0.51**	**0.95**	**0.98**	**0.96**
PRIN	0.97	**0.92**	**0.95**	**0.97**	1.00	**0.95**	**0.97**	**0.51**	**0.91**	**0.96**	**0.95**
DRUG	0.97	**0.93**	**0.97**	**0.97**	**0.95**	1.00	**0.96**	**0.50**	**0.93**	**0.94**	**0.96**
COMP	0.99	**0.90**	**0.94**	**0.99**	**0.97**	**0.96**	1.00	**0.52**	**0.94**	**0.99**	**0.95**
ELEC	0.50	**0.36**	**0.35**	**0.51**	**0.51**	**0.54**	**0.52**	1.00	**0.29**	**0.56**	**0.40**
COMM	0.95	**0.91**	**0.96**	**0.95**	**0.91**	**0.93**	**0.94**	**0.29**	1.00	**0.89**	**0.95**
INS	0.98	**0.87**	**0.90**	**0.98**	**0.96**	**0.94**	**0.99**	**0.56**	**0.89**	1.00	**0.91**
AIR	0.96	**0.96**	**0.98**	**0.96**	**0.95**	**0.96**	**0.95**	**0.40**	**0.95**	**0.91**	1.00

ficients that are boldfaced in Table 6-10 provide a measure of the relationship between the independent variables. While there may be some theoretical explanation for the observed relationships between some of these measures (for example, between electronic components and communication equipment or between electronic components and computer components), it should also be obvious that some of the measured relationships (for example, between computer components and drugs) are simply a result of the consistent changes in time-related measures.

The assumption of no relationship between the independent variables assumes that the correlation coefficients should be zero. For all practical purposes, it is impossible to obtain a value of zero in real-world calculations. Therefore, a good rule of thumb is that the absolute value of the correlation between the independent variables should be less than 0.50. An examination of the correlation coefficients in Table 6-10 indicates that this rule of thumb is violated. This confirms the previous conclusions that the inconsistent signs and the insignificant t statistics are a result of the severe multicollinearity among the variables.

There is no single solution that will completely eliminate multicollinearity. Thus, it is true that in large-scale regression equations, some minimal levels of multicollinearity must be tolerated. In preceding paragraphs, this minimal level (rule-of-thumb value for the simple correlation coefficient) was postulated to be ± 0.5, but this is an arbitrary cut-off. Indeed, if the analyst is less interested in interpreting individual coefficients and more interested

[20] The negative signs on several of these simple correlation coefficients have been ignored for convenience.

in forecasting, multicollinearity may not be a serious problem. That is, in forecasting environments, multicollinearity may be ignored without any dire consequences because, as long as the multicollinearity can be expected to continue, short-run forecasts will be reasonably accurate. Further, even if there is a high degree of correlation among the independent variables, as long as the signs of the coefficients are theoretically logical, the forecaster need not be overly concerned with multicollinearity.

Whenever the problem of multicollinearity is severe enough to warrant elimination, many textbooks and forecasters suggest dropping one of the related variables from the equation. There are two drawbacks to this recommendation: first, which one should be dropped, and second, if there is a theoretical reason for including the variable, omitting it will inject bias into the results. Fortunately, there are several alternative methods of minimizing the effects of multicollinearity.

One acceptable alternative is to increase the sample size. This procedure is justified on the grounds that by increasing the sample size, the precision of estimators improves, thereby reducing the adverse effects of multicollinearity. However, an increase of sample size is easier said than done. In many cases the forecaster has already collected all of the data at his or her disposal. It is also possible that by expanding the sample size, other problems may adversely affect the forecasting reliability of any given model. For example, with time series data, an increase in the sample size may introduce the possibility of structural instability in the model (by extending the time horizon of the model into a period that was not stable).

Another common practice is to redefine the variables. The two most popular methods of accomplishing this are data aggregation and data transformation. These procedures are easier to illustrate than to explain. Suppose that the following forecasting model for retail sales (adjusted for inflation) has been estimated:

$$\widehat{FS}_t = -1110.98 - 8.20802POP_t + 1.77092YD82_t. \qquad \textbf{(6-51)}$$

FS_t refers to final sales adjusted for inflation and measured in billions of dollars; POP_t refers to total population in millions and $YD82_t$ to real disposable income in billions of dollars. The data for equation (6-51) are provided in Appendix D, Table D-7. While the multiple coefficient of determination of 0.993 suggests a useful model, the negative sign on the population variable contradicts both common sense and theoretical expectations. To check for the possibility of a relationship between population and real income, we estimate the correlation coefficient between these two variables. The correlation coefficient between population and disposable income is 0.989, which is clearly outside of our rule-of-thumb boundaries. While one of these variables could be eliminated, it is also true that by following this approach valuable information could be lost. We can transform final sales and income by simply dividing them by population.[21] These computations yield figures for per capita final sales $(PCFS_t)$ and per capita disposable income $(PCINC_t)$. The equation to be estimated now becomes

$$\widehat{PCFS}_t = \hat{\beta}_0 + \hat{\beta}_2 PCINC_t + e_t. \tag{6-52}$$

Implicitly, we have taken the effect of population on both these variables into account. Empirically, this yields

$$\widehat{PCFS}_t = -0.49587 + 1.485 PCINC_t. \tag{6-53}$$

The important facet of this process is that we have eliminated the existence of multicollinearity without ignoring information that is obviously relevant.

EXAMPLE 6-6   Package Shipments Revisited

As an example of aggregating independent variables to minimize the impact of multicollinearity, suppose that we return to the package shipments model presented in example 6-5. In aggregating these independent variables, the analyst needs to be cognizant of the classic problem of "adding apples and oranges." Thus, while it is mathematically possible for us to add employment in services with industrial production in the computer industry, there are some conceptual problems. In the package shipments example, numerous industrial production indices were used as independent variables. Because these variables are conceptually identical measures for different industries, a simple weighting of these indicators is reasonable and consistent.[22]

With this in mind, suppose that we derive a composite of the industrial production indices and then estimate the following model:

$$\widehat{PS}_t = -1,712,476 + 69,721 EME_t + 1,324.767 COMIND_t \tag{6-54}$$
$$t_e \qquad\qquad\qquad 11.852 \qquad\qquad\quad 0.999$$

where PS is defined as before, EME refers to a combination of the FIR and SER employment measures, and COMIND refers to the aggregated average of the industrial production indices. The encouraging aspect of this specification is that both independent variables have the appropriate signs. Although it has a relatively low t statistic, the COMIND variable is essential in capturing the turning points in the package shipments variable.

---

[21] Other types of transformations are illustrated in succeeding chapters.

[22] There are various weighting schemes that could be used in this aggregation process.

A final point for dealing with severe cases of multicollinearity: Econometricians have proposed several other complex procedures. Two of these techniques are ridge regression and principal components analysis. Neither of these procedures is discussed here, as they require an understanding of advanced mathematical statistics and access to sophisticated computer programs.[23]

HETEROSCEDASTICITY

The next critical assumption is constant variance of the error terms, often referred to as the homoscedasticity assumption. That is, if we do not have constant variance, we have heteroscedasticity. Variables which exhibit heteroscedasticity include interest rates, inflation rates, exchange rates, and stock prices. In the case of interest rates, the increased volatility stems from a change in Federal Reserve monetary policy targets, while in the case of exchange rates the change follows from the increased internationalization of the domestic economy. The introduction and control of program trading has dramatically altered the periodic changes in stock prices. These examples focus on exogenous sources of heteroscedasticity due to institutional change, but endogenous changes are also possible.

The effect of heteroscedasticity can best be seen by looking at the graphs in Figure 6-14. Figure 6-14(a) illustrates the case of constant variance. Note that the observations of Y given X fall within a constant band around the regression line. Thus, variance is not dependent on the X value specified. In Figures 6-14(b), (c), and (d), the variance fluctuates as the size of X changes. In (b), the variance increases as X increases; in (c), it decreases; and in (d), it varies over the entire range of X. To see the effect on future values of Y, assume that the pattern illustrated in (b) prevails, and observe that the difference between the observed and the estimated values increases over time. If the regression equation is used to forecast Y, the confidence intervals will be less and less likely to contain the true value of the dependent variable.

There are four statistical procedures that have been developed to test for the existence of heteroscedasticity: the Goldfeld-Quandt test, the Breusch-Pagan test, White's test, and Engle's ARCH test. In addition to these statistical procedures, the various error plots that were introduced earlier can be used as a quick visual check of the homoscedasticity assumption. For our purposes, we concentrate on the Goldfeld-Quandt test since it can be applied without introducing any new procedures.

---

[23] For an excellent discussion of these two techniques, consult Douglas C. Montgomery and Elizabeth A. Peck, *Introduction to Linear Regression Analysis* (New York: John Wiley & Sons, 1982), pp. 287–341.

FIGURE 6-14   Constant and Heteroscedastic Variance in the Residuals*

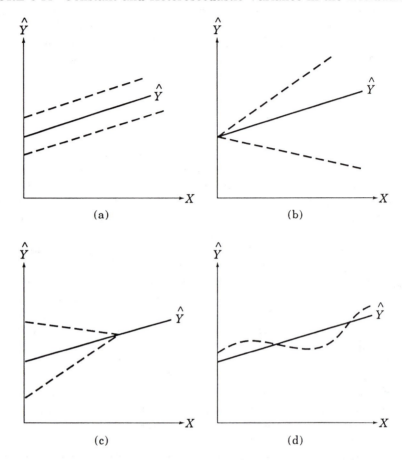

* Dashed lines indicate pattern of actual Y values about the estimated regression values ($\hat{Y}$).

The Goldfeld-Quandt test is based on the premise that if the error variances are equal across observations, then the variance of one part of the sample will be the same as the variance for another part of the sample. Bearing this in mind, we can test for the equality of error variances using the F test. The specific process becomes one of computing the ratio of two sample variances. The sample of observations is divided into three parts, and the middle observations are discarded. The model is then estimated for each of the other two sets of observations and the residual variances computed. Next, an F test is used to test for the equality of these variances.

EXAMPLE 6-7 Travel Expenditures: Testing for Heteroscedasticity[24]

Suppose that as a supplier to the tourism industry, we are interested in developing forecasts for travel expenditures. In conjunction with this endeavor, we have collected information on travel expenditures (TE) and income (INC) by state for all 50 states and the District of Columbia. The data used in this example are contained in Appendix D, Table D-8.

The results of an ordinary least-squares estimation were

$$\widehat{TE} = -0.26649 + 0.0675INC \tag{6-55}$$
$$t_e \qquad\qquad 19.288$$

The multiple coefficient of determination of 0.88362 indicates that the model fit is good, but not perfect. However, an examination of the error plot in Figure 6-15 reveals that the size of the residuals appears to increase as the income increases.[25]

One hypothesis (hunch) is that this increased variance can be related to the size of the population in the states. That is, states with larger populations are likely to have a greater variation in travel expenditures. To test for the possibility for a heteroscedastic distribution of the error terms, we first arrange the observations by population size. The next stage is to subdivide the observations into three equal segments; the first group contains the states ranging from Alaska to Utah, the second includes the states ranging from West Virginia to Louisiana, while the final segment begins with Tennessee and ends with California.[26]

According to the Goldfeld-Quandt testing procedure, we would first estimate separate models for the first and last groups of states. Once these two models are estimated, we would obtain the error sum of squares (ESS) from the analysis of variance table, sometimes referred to as the mean square. The ESS for the first grouping of states is 1.90037, while for the last group of states the ESS equals 7.48493. These two values are then combined to form the F statistic as follows:

$$F_e = \frac{ESS_2/(T_2 - k)}{ESS_1/(T_1 - k)} \tag{6-56}$$

[24] Condensed excerpts from *Introductory Econometrics: With Applications*, pp. 452–66, by Ramu Ramanathan, copyright © 1989 by Harcourt Brace Jovanovich, Inc., reprinted by permission of the publisher.

[25] In this error plot, we have retained the original error formulation since our purpose here is to conduct a statistical test rather than provide information to managerial decision makers.

[26] The exact subdivision into parts is obviously arbitrary. As a rule, the division should be made into thirds with as nearly an equal a number of observations in each part as possible. However, we need to ensure that the number of observations in each subset exceeds the number of coefficients to be estimated.

FIGURE 6-15   Heteroscedastic Error Plot from Travel Expenditures Model

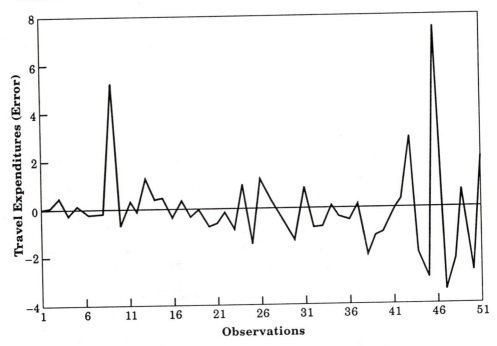

where the subscripts refer to the first (T_1) and the last (T_2) grouping of states, respectively, k to the number of coefficients (including the constant) to be estimated, and ESS to the error sum of squares from the respective model estimations. When applied to our sample the specific results are

$$F_e = \frac{7.48493/(17 - 2)}{1.90037/(17 - 2)} \quad \text{(6-57)}$$

$$= 3.94$$

which exceeds the critical value of F at a level exceeding 0.01. Thus, we can be 99 percent certain that the sample is characterized by a heteroscedastic variance pattern.

The correction for heteroscedasticity requires the use of weighted least squares, transformed variables, or respecification of the model. One frequently used procedure is the specification of two equations, with one being applied whenever condition A (small states, for example) prevails and the other applied when condition B (large states, for example) prevails. In fact, this procedure is closely related to the use of dummy variables, which is presented in chapter 7.

EXAMPLE 6-8   Travel Expenditures Revisited

In example 6-7 we concluded that the variance in travel expenditures increased as income increased. In particular, we found that states with larger populations had a much larger variance in travel expenditures. To offset this problem, suppose that we redefine the model as follows:

$$(TE/POP) = \beta_0(1/POP) + \beta_1(INC/POP) + e/POP. \qquad \textbf{(6-58)}$$

With this transformation, we are applying a form of weighted least squares. Note that with this transformation, travel expenditures and income are expressed on a per capita basis. As a general rule, whenever the size of the population is likely to affect the variance of a model, it is good practice to define the variables in per capita terms. Further, note that with this transformation, the model to be reestimated contains no constant term. As before, the data for this model are provided in Appendix D, Table D-8. The reestimated model is as follows:

$$(TE/POP) = 0.55396(1/POP) + 0.06439(INC/POP). \qquad \textbf{(6-59)}$$
$$t_e \qquad\qquad 2.464 \qquad\qquad\qquad 4.632$$

FIGURE 6-16   Elimination of Heteroscedasticy from Travel Expenditures Model

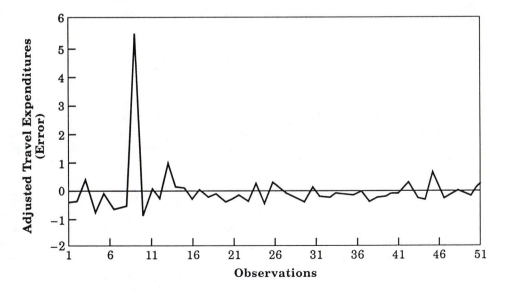

The transformed model accounts for 65 percent of the variation in the dependent variable, and an examination of Figure 6-16 (page 265) suggests that the problem of an increasing variance has been eliminated.

AUTOCORRELATION

From the perspective of a practicing forecaster, the most important assumption of the classical regression model is that the error terms, e_t, corresponding to different observations are unrelated to each other—that is, they are randomly distributed. This assumption implies that e_t is independent of e_{t-1}, e_{t-2}, as well as e_{t+1}, e_{t+2}, and so on. Alternatively, the random variable Y_t in period t is assumed to be unrelated to Y_t in any other period. These statements are identical in terms of their implications for forecasting models, and for time series data both assumptions are frequently violated. For example, suppose that consumption expenditures on durable goods is the dependent variable. Its value in 1990 is apt to be influenced by its value in 1989, which in turn is influenced by the 1988 value, and so on. Clearly, successive observations over time are related to each other. For such data, the error terms are said to exhibit autocorrelation or serial correlation. In fact, it is fair to say that autocorrelation is the most serious problem you are likely to incur in developing reliable forecasting models.

The major cause of autocorrelated error terms in forecasting models is misspecification of the model. In particular, whenever we have omitted one or more key explanatory variables, we are apt to observe a systematic pattern in the residual or error terms. For example, in formulating our model for travel expenditures (examples 6-6 and 6-7), we are dealing with a model of the form

$$\text{TE} = f(\text{INCOME, POPULATION}). \tag{6-60}$$

This specification ignores many variables, one of which is likely to be the price of gasoline, that have a significant bearing on travel expenditures. Another common cause of autocorrelation is that the data may have been collected or tabulated in such a way that measurement errors are systematically built into the model.

The most common type of autocorrelation is first-order autocorrelation, in which this time period's error is a function of (dependent on) the previous time period's error term. That is, e_t is correlated with e_{t+1}, e_{t-1}, and so on. It is, of course, possible that the autocorrelation that occurs in any given example is something other than first order. For example, second-order autocorrelation would imply that there is a two-period lag in the relationship between error terms, third-order autocorrelation a three-period lag, etc.

First-order autocorrelation can be expressed via the following equation:

$$\epsilon_t = \rho\epsilon_{t-1} + u_t \tag{6-61}$$

where

ϵ = the error term of the model under consideration

ρ = the parameter depicting the functional relationship between the error terms

u = the error term.

The new symbol, ρ (rho, pronounced "row"), is referred to as the first-order autocorrelation coefficient. The magnitude of ρ indicates the strength of the autocorrelation in an equation. If ρ is zero, there is no autocorrelation, while as the absolute value of ρ approaches 1 in absolute value, the stronger the relationship is between the current error and the error in the preceding time period. The sign of ρ indicates the nature of the autocorrelation in an equation. A positive value for ρ implies that the error term tends to have the same sign as the error term from the previous time period. Such a tendency implies that if ϵ_t takes on a large value in one time period, subsequent error terms would tend to retain a portion of this original large error and would have the same sign as the original error term. For example, if this situation occurs, the error term will tend to be positive (negative) for a number of observations (time periods), then negative (positive) for a number of periods, and then back to positive (negative). This fluctuating error pattern is called positive autocorrelation and can be depicted graphically by either of the patterns in Figure 6-17.

A negative value of ρ implies that the error pattern has a tendency to switch signs from negative to positive and back to negative in consecutive time-ordered observations. This alternating pattern is indicative of negative autocorrelation, a much less common occurrence in applied forecasting environments. Figure 6-18 illustrates the error pattern of a model with negative autocorrelation.

In forecasting, the consequences of autocorrelated error terms can be severe. If, for example, positive autocorrelation exists, the forecast error tends to increase (or decrease) in size over time. Given this occurrence, the forecasts themselves become less and less reliable over time. For example, if the forecast in time period $t + 1$ is in error by 10 percent, the error in $t + 2$ will be somewhat greater than 10 percent, with the effect being cumulative—10, 12, 15, 20 percent errors in $t + 1$, $t + 2$, $t + 3$, and $t + 4$, respectively.

Fortunately, in checking for the existence of autocorrelation, we have two readily accessible tools at our disposal. The first of these tools involves an

FIGURE 6-17 Error Patterns Associated with Positive Autocorrelation

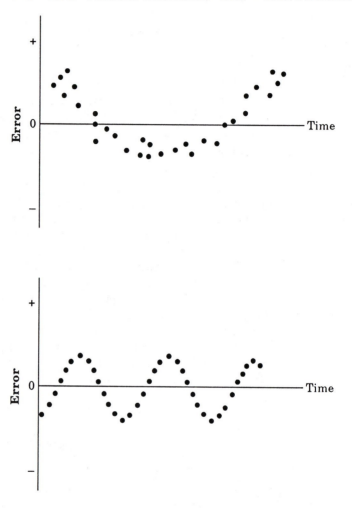

examination of either the signs of the error terms or a plot of the error terms. Once again returning to the example for final sales, equation (6-53), we can illustrate this technique. Table 6-11, column 3, documents the error terms obtained from the historical simulation for equation (6-53). In this case, the relevant information is derived by looking at the systematic sign pattern. The first three error terms have positive signs, the next four have negative signs, then one positive, then seven negative, then four positive, and finally two negative—in other words, a nonrandom error pattern. A similar conclusion could be reached via an examination of Figure 6-19.

A common procedure for testing for the presence of autocorrelation is

FIGURE 6-18 Error Patterns Associated with Negative Autocorrelation

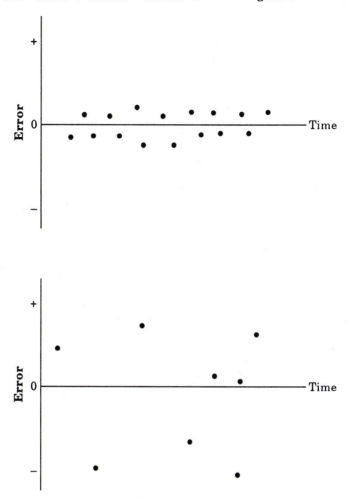

based on the Durbin-Watson (DW or d) statistic. This statistic is defined by[27]

$$DW = d = \frac{\sum\limits_{t=2}^{n} (e_t - e_{t-1})^2}{\sum\limits_{t=1}^{n} e_t^2} \qquad (6\text{-}62)$$

[27] The Durbin-Watson, d, statistic is not the appropriate measure when the estimated model includes lagged values for the independent variables. The Durbin h statistic, the appropriate measure with lagged independent variables, is introduced in the next chapter. If we were interested in testing for the existence of negative autocorrelation, the alternative hypothesis would be: H_1: $\rho < 0$, there is negative autocorrelation.

TABLE 6-11   Actual and Estimated Values for Final Per Capita Sales

Year	Actual Real Per Capita Final Sales (1)	Estimated Real Per Capita Final Sales (2)	$e_t =$ $PCFS_t -$ $\widehat{PCFS_t}$ (3)	e_t^2 (4)	$(e_t - e_{t-1})^2$ (5)	$e_t * e_{t-1}$ (6)	e_{t-1}^2 (7)
1970	11.8882	11.5835	0.3047	0.0928			
1971	12.0602	11.8621	0.1981	0.0392	0.0029	0.0604	0.092842
1972	12.5592	12.2200	0.3392	0.1151	0.0057	0.0672	0.039243
1973	12.9069	12.9303	-0.0234	0.0005	0.0131	-0.0079	0.115056
1974	12.6018	12.6730	-0.0712	0.0051	0.0000	0.0017	0.000547
1975	12.4499	12.7863	-0.3364	0.1132	0.0117	0.0240	0.005069
1976	12.9108	13.1301	-0.2193	0.0481	0.0042	0.0738	0.113164
1977	13.4588	13.4344	0.0244	0.0006	0.0023	-0.0054	0.048092
1978	13.9480	13.9611	-0.0131	0.0002	0.0000	-0.0003	0.000595
1979	14.0994	14.1012	-0.0018	0.0000	0.0000	0.0000	0.000171
1980	13.7738	13.9422	-0.1684	0.0284	0.0008	0.0003	0.000003
1981	13.7962	14.0114	-0.2152	0.0463	0.0003	0.0362	0.028358
1982	13.6050	13.9441	-0.3391	0.1150	0.0047	0.0730	0.046311
1983	14.0761	14.2508	-0.1747	0.0305	0.0071	0.0592	0.114988
1984	14.8639	14.9775	-0.1136	0.0129	0.0003	0.0198	0.030520
1985	15.5181	15.2819	0.2362	0.0558	0.0018	-0.0268	0.012904
1986	15.8977	15.6972	0.2005	0.0402	0.0002	0.0474	0.055790
1987	16.1727	15.7961	0.3766	0.1418	0.0103	0.0755	0.040200
1988	16.5251	16.3399	0.1852	0.0343	0.0116	0.0697	0.141827
1989	16.7724	16.8415	-0.0691	0.0048	0.0009	-0.0128	0.034299
1990	16.9661	17.0857	-0.1196	0.0143	0.0001	0.0083	0.004774
Total*				0.93906	0.078151	0.56321	0.924762

* The total for column (4) is used in the denominator of equation (6-62), while the total of column (5) is used for the numerator. Similarly, the totals for columns (6) and (7) are used for the numerator and denominator, respectively, of equation (6-71).

where

$$e_t = Y_t - \hat{Y}_t = \text{actual error in period } t$$
$$\hat{Y}_t = \text{estimate of forecasted value of the dependent variable}$$
$$Y_t = \text{actual or observed value of the dependent variable.}$$

The specific hypothesis test for autocorrelation is

$$H_0: \rho = 0, \text{ there is no autocorrelation}$$
$$H_1: \rho > 0, \text{ there is positive autocorrelation.}$$

FIGURE 6-19 Autocorrelated Error Terms from Final Sales Model

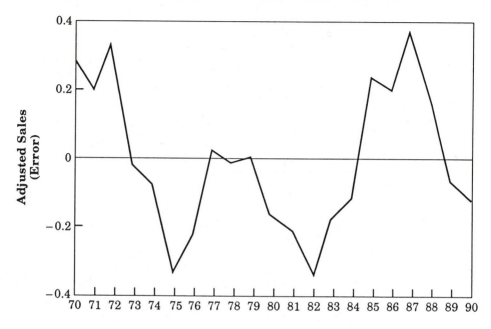

The actual value of the DW statistic is computed and compared against the upper and lower bounds (d_u and d_l, respectively) as presented in Appendix E. This value is compared to the critical values (d_u and d_l) using the following scheme shown in Table 6-12 ("Pos." and "Neg." indicate direction of the one-tail test).

The scheme shown in Table 6-12 can be simplified by noting that values of DW (d) close to zero and 4 indicate positive and negative autocorrelation, respectively. Conversely, values close to 2 indicate a random pattern. Appendix E contains the d_l and d_u values based on sample size (n) and number of regressors excluding the intercept (k) and level of significance ($\alpha = 0.025$).

For our example, $n = 21$, $k = 1$, there is a 2.5 percent level of significance, and the critical values are $d_l = 1.10$ and $d_u = 1.30$. Columns 4 and 5 of Table 6-11 furnish the calculations necessary for the Durbin-Watson statistic for our final sales example:

$$\text{DW} = (0.78151)/(0.939066) \qquad\qquad \textbf{(6-63)}$$
$$= 0.8322.$$

Since the calculated value of d, 0.8322, is less than the lower acceptance point, $d_l = 1.10$, we conclude that there is positive autocorrelation in the error terms.

TABLE 6-12   Testing Scheme for Autocorrelation

Value of the Calculated DW d	Conclusion
$d < d_l$	Positive autocorrelation (Pos. test)
$d > (4 - d_l)$	Negative autocorrelation (Neg. test)
$d_l < d < d_u$	Indeterminate (Pos. test)
$(4 - d_u) < d < (4 - d_l)$	Indeterminate (Neg. test)
$d_u < d$	No autocorrelation (Pos. test)
$d < (4 - d_u)$	No autocorrelation (Neg. test)

Two final comments are in order:

1. If we want to check for negative autocorrelation, the test statistic used is $4 - d_l$. The rest of the procedure is similar. That is, if $4 - d_l < d$, we conclude that negative autocorrelation exists; if $d < 4 - d_u$, accept H_0.
2. If the results are inconclusive, more observations are required.

Since autocorrelation is such a serious problem for the forecaster, techniques have been developed to overcome its existence. There are a great many schemes specifically designed to correct this situation. Among them we would find improved specification, use of generalized least squares, use of the Cochrane-Orcutt and Hildreth-Lu iterative procedures, differencing, and various autoregressive schemes. The first of these approaches, improved specification, has the most theoretical merit. However, it may not always be possible to improve the specification. For one thing, the missing variable, although known to us, may not be quantifiable. For example, while business investment in future periods is related to the optimism of investors, it is difficult to quantify this factor. Nevertheless, where possible, the model should be specified in accordance with theoretical insights. Blind application of any corrective technique to a theoretically unsound model will not solve the problem of autocorrelation.

Given the conclusion that the autocorrelation parameter is greater than zero for the model presented in equation (6-53), the first step is to derive an estimate for ρ. That is, in using the various corrective procedures, the original model must be transformed, based on our estimate for ρ, as follows:

$$Y_t^* = Y_t - \rho Y_{t-1} \tag{6-64}$$

$$X_{kt}^* = X_{kt} - \rho X_{kt-1}. \tag{6-65}$$

It can be shown that if we use these transformed variables, and if the appropriate substitutions are made, the new regression model will have independent error terms and retain the BLUE properties summarized in chapter 5:[28]

$$Y_t^* = \beta_0^* + \beta_1^* X_{1t}^* + \beta_{2t}^* X_{2t}^* + \beta_{3t}^* X_{3t}^* + \beta_4^* X_{4t}^* + \beta_5^* X_{5t}^* + \epsilon_t. \quad \textbf{(6-66)}$$

The relationship between the old and new parameters can be shown to be equal to

$$\beta_0 = \frac{\beta_0^*}{1 - \rho} \quad \textbf{(6-67)}$$

$$\beta_i = \beta_i^*. \quad \textbf{(6-68)}$$

Alternatively, these relationships can be illustrated by using the definitional statements in equations (6-64), (6-65), (6-67), and (6-68):

$$Y_t = \rho Y_{t-1} + \beta_0(1 - \rho) + \beta_1(X_{1t} - \rho X_{1t-1}) + \beta_2(X_{2t} - \rho X_{2t-1})$$
$$+ \beta_3(X_{3t} - \rho X_{3t-1}) + \beta_4(X_{4t} - \rho X_{4t-1}) + \beta_5(X_{5t} - \rho X_{5t-1}) + \epsilon_t. \quad \textbf{(6-69)}$$

Notice that if $\rho = 0$, we are back to the original model with no autocorrelation while if $\rho = 1$—that is, we have perfect positive autocorrelation—then we are taking first differences for all variables and dropping the constant term (since it equals zero).

Suppose, for example, a simple regression of Y on X is run:

$$\hat{Y}_t = \hat{\beta}_0 + \hat{\beta}_1 X_t + e_t. \quad \textbf{(6-70)}$$

Further, suppose that the Durbin-Watson statistic indicates that autocorrelation exists. The autocorrelation coefficient, ρ, is estimated by r_t, as follows:

$$r_t = \frac{\sum\limits_{t=2}^{n} e_t e_{t-1}}{\sum\limits_{t=2}^{n} e_{t-1}^2}. \quad \textbf{(6-71)}$$

The data are then transformed via equations (6-64) and (6-65), with the least-squares technique being applied to the transformed variables.

---

[28] To say that a model is BLUE (best linear unbiased estimator) does not guarantee that it will forecast well; it merely meets a series of statistical conditions that yield desirable properties for the estimators.

The regression equation to be estimated becomes

$$\hat{Y}_t^* = \hat{\beta}_0^* + \hat{\beta}_1^* X_t^*. \tag{6-72}$$

If $r_t = 1$, this equation is equivalent to first differencing. After the transformed regression model is estimated, the Durbin-Watson statistic is again checked. If autocorrelation still exists, the process can be repeated. This iterative procedure, known as the Cochrane-Orcutt process, produces unbiased standard errors and reliable statistical tests. Further, many computer software packages have this routine.

This iterative procedure can be illustrated for our final sales example in equation (6-53):

$$\widehat{PCFS}_t = -0.49487 + 1.485PCINC_t$$
$$t_e \qquad\qquad\qquad\qquad 31.97$$

$R^2 = 0.982$;	$F_{1,19} = 1,022$;
SEE = 0.2223;	DW = 0.83.

As noted, a comparison of the estimated DW statistic with the critical values indicates the presence of positive autocorrelation. To use the Cochrane-Orcutt iterative procedure, we must first estimate a value for ρ by applying equation (6-71):

$$r_t = 0.563213/0.924762 = 0.61. \tag{6-73}$$

Columns 2 and 4 of Table 6-13 present the figures based on transformations given by equations (6-64) and (6-65). The least-squares estimation based on these transformed values is

$$\widehat{PCFS}_t^* = -0.362 + 1.523PCINC_t^*. \tag{6-74}$$
$$t_e \qquad\qquad\qquad\quad 17.549$$

The Durbin-Watson statistic for this corrected equation is 1.87, which falls within the boundaries for accepting the null hypothesis. If the Durbin-Watson statistic for equation (6-74) had indicated the presence of autocorrelation, another iteration would have been run by performing a second transformation, rerunning the regression equation, and again testing the same null hypothesis for positive autocorrelation. To use equation (6-74) for forecasting, we must retransform the results back to their original form. For example, if PCINC in 1990 is equal to \$11.83942, then

$$PCINC_t^* = 11.83942 - 0.61(11.67498) \tag{6-75}$$
$$= 4.718$$

TABLE 6-13 Autocorrelated Transformations for Final Sales Model

Year, t	Real Per Capita Final Sales, PCFS (1)	PCFS* (2)	Real Per Capita Income, PCINC (3)	PCINC* (4)
1970	11.8882		8.134194	
1971	12.0602	4.808[a]	8.321858	3.360[b]
1972	12.5592	5.202	8.562887	3.487
1973	12.9069	5.246	9.041141	3.818
1974	12.6018	4.729	8.867890	3.353
1975	12.4499	4.763	8.944183	3.535
1976	12.9108	5.316	9.175742	3.720
1977	13.4588	5.583	9.380617	3.783
1978	13.9480	5.738	9.735294	4.013
1979	14.0994	5.591	9.829631	3.891
1980	13.7738	5.173	9.722590	3.727
1981	13.7962	5.394	9.769175	3.838
1982	13.6050	5.189	9.723831	3.765
1983	14.0761	5.777	9.930373	3.999
1984	14.8639	6.277	10.41978	4.362
1985	15.5181	6.451	10.62475	4.269
1986	15.8977	6.432	10.90439	4.423
1987	16.1727	6.475	10.97100	4.319
1988	16.5251	6.660	11.33718	4.645
1989	16.7724	6.692	11.67498	4.759
1990	16.9661	6.735	11.83942	4.718

a = $\text{PCFS*} = \text{PCFS}_t - r_t\text{PCFS}_{t-1}$
b = $\text{PCINC*} = \text{PCINC}_t - r_t\text{PCINC}_{t-1}$

and

$$\widehat{\text{PCFS}}_t^* = -0.362 + 1.523(4.718) \tag{6-76}$$
$$= 6.8235$$

This value for $\widehat{\text{PCFS}}_t^*$ would then have to be added to the prior value for per capita sales in 1989 to obtain our forecast value:

$$\widehat{\text{PCFS}}_{1990} = \widehat{\text{PCFS}}_{1990}^* + 0.61\text{PCFS}_{1989}$$
$$= 6.8235 + 0.61(16.7724) \tag{6-77}$$
$$= 17.0546$$

EXAMPLE 6-9   Interest Rate Forecasting; Correction for Autocorrelation

As the forecaster in charge of cash-flow forecasting, you are asked to construct an interest rate forecasting model. After much thought, you decide to estimate the following model:

$$\widehat{\text{INTRATE}}_t = \beta_0 + \beta_1\text{YDP}_t + \beta_2\text{PMONEY}_t + \beta_3\text{PPRICE}_t + e_t \quad \textbf{(6-78)}$$

where

$$
\begin{aligned}
\text{INTRATE}_t &= \text{the three-month Treasury bill rate, percent per year} \\
\text{YDP}_t &= \text{disposable personal income, billions of dollars, SAAR} \\
\text{PMONEY}_t &= \text{percent change in the money supply, M1 definition, billions of dollars, SA} \\
\text{PPRICE}_t &= \text{percent change in the consumer price index, index } 1982\text{--}1984 = 100
\end{aligned}
$$

The data used in this estimation are provided in Appendix D, Table D-9.

The interest rate should be positively related to the level of disposable income and the percentage change in the price level. The exact relationship between the percentage change in the money supply and the interest rate would depend to a large extent on the specific time-lag relationship that exists between changes in the money supply and the interest rate as well as a host of institutional factors.

When estimated over the time frame beginning in January 1970 and ending in November 1989, the results were

$$\widehat{\text{INTRATE}}_t = 3.94062 + 0.0011055\text{YDP}_t$$
$$- 54.4513\text{PMONEY}_t + 352.341\text{PPRICE}_t. \quad \textbf{(6-79)}$$

While the summary statistics seem to suggest a reliable model, the disturbing aspect of this formulation is the Durbin-Watson statistic of 0.30. An examination of the critical values from Appendix E clearly indicates that, as originally formulated, the model generates autocorrelated error terms.

The estimated ρ value from this model equals 0.969. After correcting for this autocorrelation, the reestimated model is

$$\widehat{\text{INTRATE}}_t^* = 6.90977 + 0.00040699\text{YDP}_t^*$$
$$- 35.02210\text{PMONEY}_t^* + 18.06260\text{PPRICE}_t^*. \quad \textbf{(6-80)}$$

The Durbin-Watson for this corrected model is 1.47 and falls within the range of acceptance.

A frequently used alternative to the Cochrane-Orcutt procedure is the Hildreth-Lu search procedure. The principal difference with this procedure is that a number of models are estimated and the error sum of squares is computed and compared for a sequential listing of ρ values, usually ranging from -1 to $+1$. The minimum error sum of squares ρ value is then used as the starting point in beginning an iterative procedure similar to that presented in our discussion of the Cochrane-Orcutt procedure. While there are some theoretical advantages to the Hildreth-Lu procedure, there are few significant differences when applied to forecasting situations.

SUMMARY

In this chapter the basic multiple regression model has been presented, and the procedures required to validate the assumptions underlying this model have been outlined. As was the case in chapter 5, our purpose has been to present these concepts in a relatively simple framework that facilitates understanding even as it abstracts from reality. Subsequent chapters build on this foundation by providing more advanced and specialized topics—stepwise regression, dummy variables, nonlinear estimation, distributed lag models, and multiple equation models. Additionally, the role of subjective interpretations and input in terms of minimizing forecast error is analyzed, and the potential sources of error in regression-based forecasting models is discussed.

QUESTIONS FOR DISCUSSION AND ANALYSIS

1. In example 6-2 a lumber sales model was estimated. Provide a precise interpretation of each of the coefficients in equation (6-32).
2. You are given the following forecast values for the independent variables in the lumber sales model, equation (6-32). Using these values, prepare quarterly forecasts for 1990.

Date*	HU	APT	RATE	P	INC
1990:I	1.312	275	6.063	2,305	1073.8
1990:II	1.269	240	6.950	2,275	1083.0
1990:III	1.279	249	7.226	2,699	1121.5
1990:IV	1.259	272	7.226	2,699	1128.6

* Year and quarter

3. Data on the consumption of electricity and natural gas, prices of both commodities, and heating and cooling degree days are likely to be readily available from your local utility. Collect this information on a quarterly basis and replicate the procedures noted in example 6-3. That is, formulate a model with and without an interaction term.

4. True of false? If false, why?
   a. Multicollinearity between independent variables is due to improper specification of the model.
   b. If there is an incorrect sign on the regression coefficient, it is due to multicollinearity.
   c. If all simple correlations between the independent variables are less than 0.5, then multicollinearity is not a significant problem.
   d. When judged from a forecasting perspective, the impact of multicollinearity on the individual regression coefficients is of paramount importance.

5. Suppose that you are attempting to estimate the following model for consumption spending. Specifically, you believe that consumption is a function of current income (Y_t), habit or past income levels (Y_{t-1}), and expectations or changes in income, ΔY_t. That is,

$$C_t = \beta_0 + \beta_1 Y_t + \beta_2 Y_{t-1} + \beta_3 \Delta Y_t + e_t.$$

What problems would you envision in estimating this model? *Hint:* What are the relationships among the independent variables?

6. In example 6-9, an interest rate model was presented.
   a. Is the Treasury bill rate independent of foreign rates?
   b. What variables might you include to link domestic rates to movements in international markets?

7. Explain the distinction between a multiple and simple correlation coefficient, and between a partial and part correlation coefficient.

8. Explain the difference between the correlation coefficient and the coefficient of determination. Which of these two measures is most widely cited by forecasters? Why?

9. Explain what a beta coefficient is and why it provides useful information to business forecasters.

10. What are the similarities and differences between a regression model formulated in a forecasting environment and one formulated for explanatory purposes? Should a forecaster ever make use of a purely explanatory model? Why or why not?

11. Can a model display statistical significance but be of little theoretical significance? Is theoretical significance important to the practitioner?

12. What is meant by specification error? What are its principal causes? How do we attempt to eliminate it?

13. What is meant by measurement error? What are its principal causes? How can we attempt to minimize its impact?

14. How can a forecaster test to determine whether the assumption of linearity is appropriate for a given model?

15. When is a forecaster theoretically justified in including interaction terms in forecasting models?

16. What is meant by multicollinearity? What are its consequences? How do we detect multicollinearity? How do we eliminate it? Under what conditions is multicollinearity unimportant?

17. Why is heteroscedasticity less prevalent in time series regression models than it is in cross-sectional models?

18. What is the difference between first-order and second-order autocorrelation? Between negative and positive autocorrelation?

19. Why is the problem of autocorrelation so critical? Is this a theoretical concern, or does it have practical meaning relative to forecast accuracy?

20. What is the most important explanation for the presence of autocorrelation? How should we attempt to eliminate autocorrelation in regression models?

21. Suppose that we have collected the following data on the sales of coal used in home heating, coal prices, and real household income.

Year	Sales	Price	Real Income
1969	10.98	35.3	20
1970	11.13	29.7	20
1971	12.51	30.8	23
1972	8.40	58.8	20
1973	9.27	61.4	21
1974	8.73	71.3	22
1975	6.36	74.4	16
1976	8.50	76.7	23
1977	7.82	70.7	21
1978	9.14	57.5	20
1979	8.24	46.4	20
1980	12.19	28.9	21
1981	11.88	28.1	21
1982	9.57	39.1	19
1983	10.94	46.8	23
1984	9.58	48.5	20
1985	10.09	59.3	22
1986	8.11	70.0	22
1987	6.83	70.0	17
1988	8.88	74.5	23
1989	7.68	72.1	20
1990	8.47	58.1	21
1991		44.6	20
1992		33.4	20
1993		28.6	22

In this table, sales are measured in thousands of tons, coal price is measured in dollars per ton, and real income is measured in thousands of dollars per household.

a. What are your theoretical expectations for the signs of the regression coefficients?

b. Estimate the multiple regression model (with sales per ton as the dependent variable) for the time period from 1969 to 1990.

c. Test the statistical significance of coal price and real income as explanatory variables in the regression model (make use of 95 percent confidence intervals for each of the regression coefficients).

d. What are the partial and part coefficients of determination for each of the variables?

e. Based on an examination of the beta coefficients, which of the two variables is the most important as an explanatory factor?

f. Interpret the multiple coefficient of determination.

g. Calculate the value of the Durbin-Watson statistic. What does it suggest about autocorrelation? Based on your analysis of the error plot, what conclusions can you draw about the variety of autocorrelation exhibited in this model?

h. What other variables might you consider for inclusion into this model? Why?

i. Based on your analysis of the histogram of standardized residuals and the normal probability plot, have we satisfied the assumption of linearity with this model?

j. Does multicollinearity appear to be a problem with this model?

k. Based on the estimated model and the additional data in the table, develop forecasts for 1991 through 1993.

22. Suppose that you have been hired as a consultant by a manufacturing firm and your task is to develop a forecasting model for the number of accidents that the firm can expect to have happen in any given plant. As a first step, you formulate a model where the number of workers is the independent variable and the number of accidents is the dependent variable. You then proceed to collect the following data set:

Number of employees (thousands)	Number of accidents
30	294
32	247
37	267
44	358
47	423
49	311
56	450
62	534
68	438
78	697
80	688
84	630
88	709
97	627
97	1,021
100	615
109	999
114	1,022
117	1,015
106	700
128	850
130	980
160	1,025
180	1,200
112	1,250
210	1,500
235	1,650

a. Estimate a regression model for this data set.

b. Based on an examination of the error plot, does the model violate the assumption of homoscedasticity? That is, does this plot indicate heteroscedasticity?

c. Divide the data set into three equal parts and conduct the Goldfeld-Quandt test for the existence of heteroscedasticity.

23. Suppose that you have collected information on the quarterly shipments of dishwashers, the price of dishwashers, and the quarterly production of dishwashers. This information is provided in the following table.

Date*	Shipments	Price	Production
1986:I	10,829	174.0	93.60
II	11,342	170.0	94.40
III	12,068	170.5	95.00
IV	13,119	167.3	96.60
1987:I	15,053	164.9	97.50
II	17,017	161.7	99.33
III	18,505	160.4	101.40
IV	19,476	156.4	101.70
1988:I	20,055	153.5	102.47
II	20,890	154.0	102.90
III	22,388	155.5	104.27
IV	23,623	153.6	104.70
1989:I	24,823	151.9	105.90
II	25,341	151.7	106.37
III	24,778	152.1	106.10
IV	24,773	153.3	107.07
1990:I	23,290	154.8	107.67
II	22,786	159.5	107.50
III	24,232	161.5	107.40

* Year and quarter.

Shipments are measured as the number of truckloadings, price is measured in dollars, and production refers to the industrial production index for dishwashers (base year $1982 = 100$).

a. Estimate a regression model with shipments as the dependent variable and price and production as independent variables.

b. Based on the estimated Durbin-Watson test, does the model suffer from autocorrelation?

c. Based on the procedure illustrated in this chapter, derive an estimate for ρ. Using this value for ρ, carry out the necessary transformations and reestimate the model. Did this help in eliminating the autocorrelation?

d. Using the procedure known as first differencing, carry out the appropriate transformations and reestimate the model. How does this model compare with the model derived in part c of this question?

e. Based on an analysis of the error plot from the first model that you estimated in part a, what variables can you identify that might capture the pattern exhibited by the error terms?

24. Suppose that you are interested in estimating a model for the sales of used automobiles and have collected the following data set:

Sales	Availability of Credit	Change in Population	Unemployment Rate
11.2	587	16.5	6.2
13.4	643	20.5	6.4
40.7	635	26.3	9.3
5.3	692	16.5	5.3
24.8	1,248	19.2	7.3
12.7	643	16.5	5.9
20.9	1,964	20.2	6.4
35.7	1,531	21.3	7.6
8.7	713	17.2	4.9
9.6	749	14.3	6.4
14.5	7,895	18.1	6.0
26.9	762	23.1	7.4
15.7	2,793	19.1	5.8
36.2	741	24.7	8.6
18.1	625	18.6	6.5
28.9	854	24.9	8.3
14.9	716	17.9	6.7
25.8	921	22.4	8.6
21.7	595	20.2	8.4
25.7	3,353	16.9	6.7

Sales are measured in thousands, availability of credit in millions of dollars, the change in population in thousands, and the unemployment rate in percent.

a. What are your a priori theoretical expectations for each of these variables?

b. Estimate a regression model for sales.

c. Do the signs in the estimated model satisfy your a priori expectations? If not, why not?

d. Interpret the results of your model. Include in this interpretation a complete discussion of the individual regression coefficients as well as all statistical tests carried out by the computer.

e. Have all of the assumptions of the linear model been satisfied? If not, which ones have been violated? Can you think of a way to correct these problems?

25. Suppose that you have been assigned the task of developing forecasts for your company's sales of videocassette tapes. As a first step, you collect quarterly data on SALES (company sales, measured in thousands), SOV (share of voice, measured as the ratio of company advertising to total industry advertising expenditures), PCI (per capita dollars of discretionary income available to the primary market), P (price in dollars per package), P_c (price of the major competitor's tape measured in dollars) and P_s (price of VCRs, a complementary good, measured in dollars).

Date*	SALES	SOV	PCI	P	P_c	P_s
1986:I	534	57.3	1059	4.65	5.38	84.1
II	535	65.1	1356	5.27	5.45	88.7
III	570	60.6	1273	4.94	5.21	92.0
IV	528	63.0	1151	4.89	5.03	87.9
1987:I	548	54.7	1135	5.31	5.19	91.5
II	555	55.7	1236	5.49	5.52	91.4
III	481	48.9	1231	5.62	4.52	82.4
IV	516	68.5	1564	5.66	4.43	91.3
1988:I	475	53.6	1182	5.92	4.64	85.4
II	486	68.5	1564	6.31	5.64	91.4
III	554	66.4	1588	5.06	4.81	86.7
IV	519	70.3	1335	5.19	4.84	81.2
1989:I	492	65.3	1395	6.25	5.19	89.2
II	517	58.6	1114	5.05	5.65	88.9
III	502	53.4	1143	5.21	5.70	88.9
IV	508	52.3	1320	5.05	6.12	91.9
1990:I	520	58.0	1249	5.46	6.08	95.4
II	506	44.8	1028	5.22	5.34	91.8
III	595	47.6	1057	4.29	5.32	92.9
IV	568	52.8	1057	4.24	5.66	90.9

* Year and quarter

Your assignment is to estimate a regression model for sales and prepare a detailed report to your vice-president on the results. This report should include among other things a discussion of why you selected these variables, your a priori theoretical expectations and why you hold these expectations, a complete statistical evaluation of the independent variables and the model in its entirety, an evaluation of the model's predictive power, and any other information of interest to your vice-president.

26. Following the procedures established in example 6-3 and making use of the following data, estimate a model for the residential consumption of natural gas. After you have estimated the original model, test for the possibility of interaction between the price variable and the heating and cooling degree-day variable.

Date	RSGAS	Price	Price of Electricity	Real Income	HCDD
1978	221,559	95.8	96.5	752	5529
1979	207,072	98.5	98.9	779	5055
1980	204,299	100.0	100.0	810	5368
1981	231,871	98.7	100.1	865	5176
1982	197,548	101.0	107.5	858	4483
1983	244,567	112.6	113.1	875	5066
1984	210,892	124.8	114.4	907	4825
1985	219,655	140.4	115.4	943	5637
1986	245,483	144.3	115.8	989	5751

Date	RSGAS	Price	Price of Electricity	Real Income	HCDD
1987	225,052	153.6	114.5	1016	5460
1988	205,216	166.1	120.1	1018	5926
1989	187,112	173.6	127.2	1043	5276
1990	197,300	197.2	132.0	1055	5532

The RSGAS variable is measured is millions of cubic feet, both price variables are measured with 1980 = 100, real income is in millions of dollars, and HCDD is the heating and cooling degree-day variable and is measured as described in example 6-3.

27. You have been charged with developing a forecasting model for the average number of beds in use on a daily basis. This information is required by management, which is considering building several new hospitals in medium-sized metropolitan areas. As a first step, you collect the following information from two areas similar to that of interest to management:

Average Daily Bed Usage (thousands)	Population (thousands)	Average Family Income (thousands)	Number of Physician Offices
11.2	587	16.5	62
13.4	643	20.5	64
40.7	635	26.3	93
5.3	692	16.5	53
24.8	1,248	19.2	73
12.7	643	16.5	59
20.9	1,964	20.2	64
35.7	1,531	21.3	76
8.7	713	17.2	49
9.6	749	14.3	64
14.5	895	18.1	60
26.9	762	23.1	74
15.7	793	19.1	58
36.2	741	24.7	86
18.1	625	18.6	65
28.9	854	24.9	83
14.9	716	17.9	67
25.8	921	22.4	86
21.7	595	20.2	84
25.7	553	16.9	67

a. Estimate a multiple regression model.
b. Provide management with an interpretation of each of the independent variables.
c. Are all of the variables statistically significant at the 95 percent level?
d. Do the signs on the independent variables match theoretical expectations? Explain.
e. Test for an interaction term between the number of physician offices and average

family income. Provide a theoretical explanation as to why there might be an interaction between these two variables.

f. What other variables might you be interested in with regards to the average number of beds in use in hospitals? Explain why these might be important and what relationship you would expect them to have with the dependent variable.

28. Management is interested in developing a forecasting model that will provide them with estimates of their market share in one of their major product lines. You are provided with the following information, where all variables are measured as changes in the respective variables.

Date*	Market Share	Income	Competitive Price	Advertising	Competitive Sales	Population	Price
1984:III	4.3	51	30	39	61	92	45
IV	6.3	64	51	54	63	73	47
1985:I	7.1	70	68	69	76	86	48
II	6.1	63	45	47	54	84	35
III	8.1	78	56	66	71	83	47
IV	4.3	55	49	44	54	49	34
1986:I	5.8	67	42	56	66	68	35
II	7.1	75	50	55	70	66	41
III	7.2	82	72	67	71	83	31
IV	6.7	61	45	47	62	80	41
1987:I	6.4	53	53	58	58	67	34
II	6.7	60	47	39	59	74	41
III	6.9	62	57	42	55	63	25
IV	6.8	83	83	45	59	77	35
1988:I	7.7	77	54	72	79	77	46
II	8.1	90	50	72	60	54	36
III	7.4	85	64	69	79	79	63
IV	6.5	60	65	75	55	80	60
1989:I	6.5	70	46	57	75	85	46
II	5.0	58	68	54	64	78	52
III	5.0	40	33	34	43	64	33
IV	6.4	61	52	62	66	80	41
1990:I	5.3	66	52	50	63	80	37
II	4.0	37	42	58	50	57	49
III	6.3	54	42	48	66	75	33
IV	6.6	77	66	63	88	76	72
1991:I	7.8	75	58	74	80	78	49
II	4.8	57	44	45	51	83	38
III	8.5	85	71	71	77	74	55
IV	8.2	82	39	59	64	78	39

* Year and quarter

The market share variable is measured as a percentage of total market, the income variable as the change in per capita income, competitive price in cents, advertising in dollars, competitive sales in thousands of dollars, population in number of people, and the change in price in cents.

a. What are your theoretical expectations with regards to each of these variables? Explain.

b. Estimate a multiple regression model using this data. Evaluate the statistical reliability of the estimated model. Are you satisfied with your final model? Why or why not?

29. Your manager has charged you with developing a model that focuses on the relationship between research and development expenditures and sales. You are provided with the following information:

Year	Sales	R&D Expenditures	Income
1977	45	17.2	9.7
1978	23	7.6	9.8
1979	48	19.6	9.2
1980	31	10.7	10.6
1981	42	16.8	10.0
1982	48	17.4	10.2
1983	55	21.5	10.4
1984	73	33.9	9.2
1985	44	18.1	9.5
1986	28	9.5	10.2
1987	45	18.3	9.2
1988	68	27.6	9.3
1989	28	8.5	10.5
1990	35	13.2	10.8
1991	33	12.0	9.6

Sales are measured in thousands of units, R&D expenditures are lagged one year and measured in thousands of dollars, and income refers to per capita income measured in thousands of dollars.

a. What theoretical justification would you provide for using a one-year lag on the R&D expenditures variable?

b. Estimate and evaluate a multiple regression model.

30. The operations manager has asked that you provide her with forecasts for fuel costs on a quarterly basis and has provided you with the following information:

Date*	Fuel Costs	Miles Flown	Price
1987:I	360	121	26.0
II	260	118	20.5
III	440	271	21.5
IV	400	190	23.5
1988:I	360	75	21.5
II	500	263	26.2
III	580	334	28.5
IV	560	368	29.5

Date*	Fuel Costs	Miles Flown	Price
1989:I	505	305	24.5
II	480	210	29.5
III	602	387	26.1
IV	540	270	27.3
1990:I	415	218	22.3
II	590	342	31.0
III	492	173	28.0
IV	660	370	28.5
1991:I		170	23.1
II		205	27.0
III		331	32.0
IV		283	32.0

* Year and quarter

Fuel costs are measured in thousands of dollars, miles flown in millions of miles, and price as the price per gallon.

a. Using the time frame beginning with the first quarter of 1987 and ending with the fourth quarter of 1990, estimate a multiple regression model.

b. Based on the model estimated in part a, generate forecasts for the next four quarters. What would your 95 percent forecast interval be for each of these quarters? What type of forecasts are these?

31. Suppose that you have estimated the following model:

$$\widehat{SHIP} = -28,722 + 779.89PROD - 1963PRICE.$$

Nineteen observations were used in estimating this model. All variables are statistically significant, and the model passes all significance tests. The Durbin-Watson statistic for this model is estimated to be 1.17. What does this suggest about the presence of autocorrelation in the model? Explain.

Now suppose that you reestimate the model as

$$\widehat{SHIP} = -3315 + 123.9PROD1 + 126.42PROD2 - 600PRICE.$$

Once again the model passes all statistical tests of significance. For this model, the Durbin-Watson statistic was estimated as 1.83. Is this model superior to the previous model? Why or why not? What does this suggest about the problem of autocorrelation and eliminating the problem?

REFERENCES FOR FURTHER STUDY

Aaker, D. A., ed., *Multivariate Analysis in Marketing.* Belmont, Calif.: Wadsworth, 1971.

Ascher, W., *Forecasting: An Appraisal for Policy Makers and Planners.* Baltimore: Johns Hopkins University Press, 1978.

Barten, A. P. and S. J. Turnovsky, "Some Aspects of Aggregation Problems for Composite Demand Functions," *International Economic Review*, vol. 7, 1966, pp. 231–59.

Belsley, D. A., E. Kuh, and R. E. Welsh, *Regression Diagnostics: Identifying Differential Data and Sources of Collinearity.* New York: John Wiley & Sons, 1980.

Brown, R. G., *Statistical Forecasting for Inventory Control.* New York: McGraw-Hill, 1959.

Chatterjee, Samprit and Bertram Price, *Regression Analysis by Example.* New York: John Wiley & Sons, 1977.

Draper, N. and H. Smith, *Applied Regression Analysis*, 2nd ed. New York: John Wiley & Sons, 1981.

Farrar, D. E. and R. R. Glauber, "Multicollinearity in Regression Analysis: The Problem Revisited," *Review of Economics and Statistics*, vol. 49, 1967, pp. 92–107.

Gaudry, M. and M. Dagenais, "Heteroscedasticity and the Use of Box-Cox Transformations," *Economic Letters*, vol. 2, 1979, pp. 225–29.

Goldfeld, S. M. and R. M. Quandt, "Some Tests for Homoscedasticity," *Journal of the American Statistical Society*, vol. 60, 1965, pp. 539–47.

Green, R. D., *Forecasting with Computer Models: Econometric, Populations and Energy Forecasting.* New York: Praeger, 1985.

McNown, R. F. and K. R. Hunter, "A Test for Autocorrelation in Models with Lagged Dependent Variables," *Review of Economics and Statistics*, vol. 62, 1980, pp. 313–17.

Montgomery, Douglas C. and Elizabeth A. Peck, *Introduction to Linear Regression Analysis.* New York: John Wiley & Sons, 1982.

Neter, John and William Wasserman, *Applied Linear Statistical Models.* Homewood, Ill.: Richard D. Irwin, 1974.

7

Advanced Topics in Regression Analysis

INTRODUCTION

Forecasting with regression models is not as straightforward as it may have appeared in the preceding two chapters, where estimates were derived under the assumptions that the model was clearly and correctly specified and that the variables were well defined and measured. In many of the models in chapter 6, only the final regression results were presented, since a complete cataloging of all the intermediate models would have been tedious. Nonetheless, there are innumerable tricks of the trade that the forecast analyst must master to move from the crude model to the final product. This chapter presents some of the more common techniques forecasters use to simplify the task of developing reliable forecasts. Although the techniques presented in this chapter may not appear to be as scientific as the methodology outlined in earlier chapters, these methods and tools can help in minimizing the cost of an investigation and in maximizing the utility of forecasting models. Additionally, they provide the tools that are necessary to carry out empirical research.

PROXY AND DUMMY VARIABLES

PROXY VARIABLES

Least-squares estimators are unbiased only when all relevant independent variables are specified and included in the regression. A forecaster often runs into a situation where one (or more) of the specified variables is not available as a data series. To avoid the bias that inevitably occurs when important variables are omitted, one can frequently find variables that are close substitutes (proxy variables). In essence, proxy variables stand in for theoretical measures that are not available in empirical form. For example, in forecasting consumer durables, consumer confidence is an important theoretical variable. We rely, however, on surveys of consumer buying intentions to serve as surrogates for consumer confidence.

In chapter 6 several proxy variables were used to develop the forecasting model for automobile sales given by equation (6-30):

$$\widehat{USCAR}_t = 3.50139 + 0.006537YDP82_t + 0.061169JCS_t$$
$$- 0.09838RUNC_t - 0.114518RAUTO_t + 0.0945REPCAR_t \quad \textbf{(6-30)}$$
$$- 7.89014RELP_t - 0.02087TRP_t.$$

Ideally, a forecaster would have an aggregate measure of individual income that netted out adjustments for taxes and transfer payments and that deducted expenditures for necessities such as food and shelter. Because automobiles are durable goods, a consumer can always postpone a new-car purchase by spending money to maintain his or her old car for one more year. No such deferral is possible for taxes, food, and shelter. Instead of the theoretically desirable income concept, equation (6-30) makes use of two variables—$YDP82_t$ (personal income in 1982 dollars) and TRP_t (transfer payments)—to substitute for theoretical income measure. These variables work well, but they are merely proxies for a theoretical concept that is otherwise impossible to obtain.

The third proxy variable used in developing the forecasting model for auto sales was consumer sentiment, JCS_t. Economic theory reinforces the notion that expectations influence consumer decision making; however, an exact formulation of this variable is dependent on the person making the decision to purchase a car. For example, some consumers may assign a high decision-making weight to the likelihood of future price changes, whereas others may feel that future income expectations are most relevant. In the present situation, the consumer-sentiment variable is the best available expression of a complex concept designed to quantify the net effect of a seemingly infinite range of human perceptions. It might also be argued that inclusion of the unemployment rate, $RUNC_t$, serves as a proxy for income expectations. Microeconomic theory points out the hazards of interpersonal comparisons, but, once again, the justification for the proxy variable is pragmatic—JCS_t is the best real-world quantitative measure of consumers' income expectations at the forecaster's disposal.

EXAMPLE 7-1 Forecasting Natural Gas Consumption

Management has placed you in charge of developing a forecasting model for the consumption of natural gas by business users. The results of this model are to be used in the creation of a long-term plan for the company's capital construction projects, and estimates of annual gas consumption will satisfy the charge from management. In an attempt to fulfill this charge, you specify the following model:

$$GAS_t = f(PRICE_t, ELECT_t, EMPLOY_t, HDD_t, CDD_t) \qquad (7\text{-}1)$$

where

$$
\begin{aligned}
GAS_t &= \text{consumption of natural gas, millions of cubic feet} \\
PRICE_t &= \text{price of cubic foot of natural gas, } 1981 = 100.0 \\
ELECT_t &= \text{price of electricity, a substitute power source for busi-} \\
&\quad \text{nesses, } 1981 = 100.0 \\
EMPLOY_t &= \text{total nonagricultural employment, thousands of em-} \\
&\quad \text{ployees} \\
HDD_t &= \text{heating degree days} \\
CDD_t &= \text{cooling degree days.}
\end{aligned}
$$

The two price measures should capture the substitution effects of the competing power sources. The PRICE variable should be inversely related to the consumption of natural gas, while the ELECT variable should be positively related. That is, as the price of natural gas increases, the business user will be more likely to shift to electricity as a power source. Similarly, EMPLOY captures the market changes that have occurred in the business sector and should be positively related to natural gas consumption.

While it is true that we might not be able to predict long-term weather patterns in the future, it is nonetheless true that weather patterns have influenced the consumption of natural gas in preceding years. While the ideal variable would measure the exact temperature over any given time frame, this variable is not available. However, all utilities compute variables that can be used as proxies for weather variations. The two variables of interest here are heating degree days (HDD) and cooling degree days (CDD). Both of these variables are calculated based on the natural gas that is used relative to a norm of 65 degrees fahrenheit. Specifically, when average daily temperatures exceed or fall below 65 degrees, this increases the number of heating and cooling degree days required to bring the inside temperature to 65 degrees. Thus, we would expect there to be a positive relationship between the consumption of natural gas and both heating and cooling degree days. The data used in this example can be found in Appendix F, Table F-1.

The results of estimating the gas consumption model for annual data running from 1979 to 1990 are as follows:

$$\widehat{\text{GAS}}_t = -371{,}551 - 2283.570\text{PRICE}_t + 2743.56\text{ELECT}_t$$

$$
\begin{array}{lcc}
t_e & -3.03 & 1.57 \\
\text{Prob Value} & 2.32 & 16.66
\end{array}
$$

$$+ 315.58\text{EMPLOY}_t + 39.623\text{CDD}_t + 64.827\text{HDD}_t.$$

$$
\begin{array}{ccc}
2.00 & 1.97 & 2.58 \\
9.23 & 9.58 & 4.14
\end{array}
$$

(7-2)

All variables, with the exception of the price of electricity variable (ELECT_t), are significant at the 90 percent or greater level of significance. The two proxy variables for average temperature, HDD_t and CDD_t, appear to provide reasonable measures for the influence of weather on the consumption of natural gas.

EXAMPLE 7-2   Permanent Income Hypothesis

In example 5-3 and equation (5-57), it was hypothesized that consumption was a function of disposable income. Implicit in this formulation is the theoretical belief that "current" income levels influence "current" consumption levels, an assumption that has proved to be only partially true when tested empirically. In an attempt to provide a better theoretical foundation for understanding variations in consumer spending, Milton Friedman put forth the permanent income hypothesis. His theory is based on the hypothesis that consumption behavior is a function of permanent income.[1] While Friedman develops the underlying basis of this theory, the key aspect from the perspective of a forecaster is to develop an operational measure of permanent income. Since there are no published data on permanent income, it is up to the imagination of the forecaster or researcher to construct a proxy variable for this theoretical concept called permanent income. The most common approach is to use a weighted average of the income that was earned in a given number of preceding years. That is, permanent income is taken to be approximated by

$$\text{YP}_t = f(Y_{t-1}, Y_{t-2}, \ldots Y_{t-n}) \tag{7-3}$$

where the number of terms in the model and the coefficients associated

[1] Milton Friedman, *A Theory of the Consumption Function* (Princeton, N.J.: Princeton University Press for the National Bureau of Economic Research, 1957). Published for NBER by Princeton University Press. Reprinted by permission of Princeton University Press.

with each preceding year's level of actual income are determined via empirical estimation.

EXAMPLE 7-3   Interest Rate Forecasting[2]

In an attempt to develop a forecasting model for interest rates, Leonard Lardaro, in a 1986 article in *Business Economics*, estimated the following model:

$$\widehat{INT}_t = 2.978 + 0.024VOLCKER_t + 0.106AVINE_t$$
$$t_e \qquad\qquad\qquad 1.09 \qquad\qquad\qquad 4.92$$

$$- 0.494VARINT_t - 0.179RESFHAT_t - 0.722VOLRSHAT_t$$
$$4.56 \qquad\qquad 2.49 \qquad\qquad 5.51$$

$$+ 0.149STKYLDHAT_t + 0.605INT_{t-1} \qquad\qquad\qquad (7\text{-}4)$$
$$2.62 \qquad\qquad 13.3$$

where

$$INT_t = \text{yield on Moody's Aaa seasoned corporate bonds}$$
$$VOLCKER_t = \text{a dummy variable that is included to test a specific hypothesis of interest to the author}$$
$$AVINF_t = \text{a proxy variable for inflationary expectations}$$
$$VARINT_t = \text{proxy for the volatility premium in interest rates}$$
$$RESFHAT_t = \text{predicted value of free reserves}$$
$$STKYLDHAT_t = \text{predicted value of stock yields}$$
$$VOLRSHAT_t = \text{an interaction term between VOLCKER and the level of free reserves.}$$

With the exception of VOLCKER, all the variables are statistically significant and display the signs expected by the author.

The theoretical premise for this model is that when an actual or potential bondholder evaluates the effective return on this bond, the uncertainties dictated by the time until maturity play a critical role. Investors will seek to protect the purchasing power of the capital tied up in a bond for the particular time in question by requiring a compensation for any inflationary losses that might occur. However, compensation for inflation is not the only protection required by these investors. Because resale of existing bonds determines effective yields on these assets, the

---

[2] Leonard Lardaro, "Interest Rate Volatility and the Level of Long-Term Interest Rates," *Business Economics*, January 1986, pp. 39–43. Copyright © 1986 National Association of Business Economists. Reprinted by permission.

value that will prevail, given the purchasing power in that time period, is also a relevant consideration. The inverse relationship between the price of bonds and the rate of interest dictates that if, for example, the resale price of a bond should fall below that anticipated by the bondholder, a capital loss will be incurred that lowers the actual effective yield below the level anticipated. The likelihood of this occurrence is directly related to the probability of fluctuations in bond prices. If this relationship is indeed true, the greater the volatility in bond prices, the higher the probability of incurring capital losses as a result of incorrect expectations.

The theoretical argument thus suggests that inflationary expectations and the impact of volatility will significantly influence interest rates. Having put forth this fancy argument, it now becomes important to recognize that data on these two variables are simply not available. In an attempt to overcome this data limitation, the author constructed proxy variables in the following fashion:

1. $AVINF_t$ is the proxy variable for inflationary expectations and is derived by taking a four-quarter geometric mean of annual inflation rates.
2. $VARINT_t$ is the proxy for the volatility premium in interest rates and is equal to an eight-quarter moving variance of 20-year government bonds.

An examination of examples 7-1, 7-2, and 7-3 suggests that the actual process of generating these proxy variables is based on an understanding of the underlying problem being studied. There are no set rules or procedures for developing these proxies, and the actual examples provided here are but illustrations of the trial-and-error process used by practitioners.

DUMMY VARIABLES

Up to this point in our application of regression analysis, all of the variables have been quantitative in nature; that is, they have numerically measurable values and have been continuous. The methods of regression analysis can be broadened by including qualitative factors. Thus, the behavior of economic variables may be a function of factors such as educational attainment, season, age, sex, and so on. Qualitative and discrete measurements can be incorporated into regression models through the use of dummy variables. We confine our attention to qualitative independent variables in this section. Qualitative dependent variables are presented in a later section of this chapter. There are many applications of the dummy variable approach, and four widely used applications are as follows:[3]

1. Dummy variables can be used to separate the population of interest into two or more categories. For example, in developing marketing plans, the process of market segmentation may dictate that we develop one model to forecast sales to females and a different model to forecast sales to males.
2. Dummy variables can be used to test for structural stability. In particular, dummy variables can be integrated into regression models for the purpose of testing for shifts (that is, significant changes in the numerical value of the coefficient) in the slope coefficients, the intercept, or a combination of these two components of the regression line.
3. Dummy variables provide an alternative for incorporating seasonal variations into time series regression models.
4. Finally, dummy variables can be used to eliminate the biasing effect of outliers (extreme values) on regression estimators.

EXAMPLE 7-4   Seasonal Factors and Dummy Variables

In previous chapters and examples, data have been seasonally adjusted via either the Census X-11 technique or a moving average approach. A disadvantage of both of these techniques is that they require a large number of data points. There are tremendous advantages to using the Census X-11 approach to seasonally adjusting data, but there are situations where the practitioner simply does not have enough data at his or her disposal to use this approach. Since seasonal patterns are qualitative in nature, seasonality may be included into regression models by using a set of dummy variables. Let Q_i be a dummy variable that takes the value 1 during the ith season and 0 otherwise. The formal regression equation incorporating $m + 1$ seasonal variables is

$$Y_t = \beta_0 + \beta_1 X_{1t} + \beta_2 X_{2t} + \beta_3 Q_1 + \beta_4 Q_2 + \dots \beta_m Q_m \quad \text{(7-5)}$$

where the $(m + 1)$th season is the excluded category. For example, if monthly data $(m + 1 = 12)$ were used, there would be 11 values for Q_i, with one month being excluded.[4]

Consider a company that sells communications systems and experiences strong seasonal sales patterns. The figures in column 1 of Table

---

[3] For a more complete discussion of the application of dummy variables in other situations, see David G. Kleinbaum, Lawrence L. Kupper, and Keith E. Muller, *Applied Regression Analysis and Other Multivariable Methods*, 2nd ed (Boston: PWS-Kent Publishing Company, 1988), pp. 260–313.

[4] For a technical explanation of why the number of dummy variables should be one less than the number of categories of interest, consult Ramu Ramanathan, *Introductory Econometrics: With Applications* (San Diego: Harcourt Brace Jovanovich, 1989), pp. 252–53.

TABLE 7-1 **Sales of Communications Systems: Seasonal Dummies**

Date*	Sales (thousands) (1)	Service Sector Employment (millions) (2)	Q_2 (3)	Q_3 (4)	Q_4 (5)
1987: I	$112,022	23.76	0	0	0
II	113,958	24.06	1	0	0
III	132,563	24.39	0	1	0
IV	144,832	24.70	0	0	1
1988: I	136,891	25.08	0	0	0
II	138,598	25.42	1	0	0
III	147,033	25.79	0	1	0
IV	158,970	26.11	0	0	1
1989: I	147,597	26.42	0	0	0
II	148,532	26.76	1	0	0
III	153,857	27.06	0	1	0
IV	163,697	27.30	0	0	1

* Year and quarter

7-1 depict the dramatic increases that occur in the third and fourth quarters and the decline that occurs in the first quarter of each year. If the forecaster is interested in using the relationship between growth in the service sector (the principal user of these communication systems) and growth in company sales, the extreme seasonality evidenced by column 1 can be statistically neutralized by adding dummy variables. Three dummy variables will suffice to measure quarterly seasonality, because Q_2, Q_3, and Q_4 measure the seasonality relative to a first-quarter base. The complete model to be estimated becomes

$$\hat{S}_t = \hat{\beta}_0 + \hat{\beta}_1 \text{EMPSER}_t + \hat{\beta}_2 Q_2 + \hat{\beta}_3 Q_3 + \hat{\beta}_4 Q_4. \quad (7\text{-}6)$$

The actual least-squares estimation is

$$\hat{S}_t = -129,470 + 10,429.439 \text{EMPSER}_t - 1880.94992 Q_2$$
$$t_e \qquad\qquad\qquad 3.08 \qquad\qquad\qquad -0.44$$
$$+ 5430.90389 Q_3 + 13,755.03338 Q_4. \quad (7\text{-}7)$$
$$1.24 \qquad\qquad\qquad 3.08$$

Quarterly, sales are predicted to increase by $10,429,439 (remember, the sales data is measured in thousands) per each increment of one million employees in the service sector; the remaining coefficients provide measures of the seasonality in each specific quarter. For example, the coefficient in front of Q_3 (5430.9) tells us that the seasonal surge in the third

FIGURE 7-1 Estimating Sales: Dummy Variable Techniques

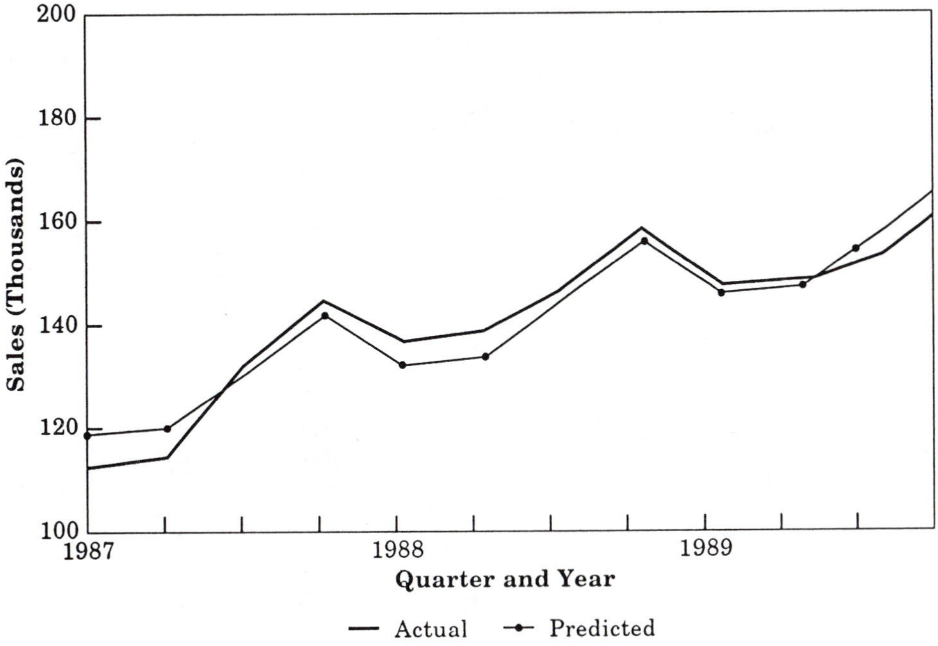

Quarter and Year

— Actual   —•— Predicted

quarter should (holding all other factors constant) pull sales upward by $5,430,904 relative to the first quarter of the year. Equation 7-7 is presented graphically in Figure 7-1, and the seasonal pattern is repeated each year; that is, the same upward or downward adjustments, $\hat{\beta}_2$, $\hat{\beta}_3$, and $\hat{\beta}_4$, occur in the fitted equation between the first and second, first and third, and first and fourth quarters, respectively. When first-quarter sales are estimated, the dummy variables drop out since they all have values of zero, and only the impact of changes in service sector employment remains.

The principal limitation of the dummy variable approach for seasonal fluctuations is the assumption of constancy from year to year. Thus, whenever a sufficient amount of data is available, the Census X-11 approach should be used in seasonally adjusting data because it automatically incorporates any shifts in seasonal patterns.

EXAMPLE 7-5 Dummy Variables and Outlier Adjustments

Another application of dummy variables, and one of primary significance in forecasting, involves incorporation of exogenous influences, such as prolonged strikes or severe weather, into regression models. As an illustration, consider the information in Table 7-2.

TABLE 7-2   High-Value Freight: Use of Dummy Variables

Date*	Shipments (millions) (1)	CED87 (billions) (2)	CEN87 (billions) (3)	CES87 (billions) (4)	Strike Adjustment (5)
1986: I	27,041	344.8	838.2	1,136.2	0
II	28,548	350.3	843.0	1,144.1	0
III	31,342	369.1	850.0	1,156.8	0
IV	34,052	356.4	858.3	1,172.2	0
1987: I	35,745	363.7	870.1	1,177.1	0
II	37,332	374.5	879.8	1,178.0	0
III	39,884	401.9	879.1	1,183.4	0
IV	43,012	397.5	883.5	1,196.8	0
1988: I	44,562	376.1	887.7	1,214.5	0
II	36,380	389.3	889.0	1,229.5	9,860
III	27,723	403.8	891.8	1,240.9	21,262
IV	64,549	389.4	892.9	1,250.0	(14,862)
1989: I	58,551	408.4	896.6	1,265.9	(5,239)
II	57,340	414.8	899.2	1,272.8	0
III	59,779	410.7	910.3	1,287.0	0
IV	61,960	420.5	912.0	1,295.2	0
1990: I	64,416	419.3	915.0	1,306.7	0
II	65,122	424.9	909.7	1,319.0	0
III	63,568	436.4	920.8	1,332.9	2,680

* Year and quarter

We have been assigned the task of developing a forecasting model for shipments of high-value freight packages via a commercial airline. An examination of the time plot of quarterly package shipments shown in Figure 7-2 suggests that the actual values in the second and third quarters of 1988 and the third quarter of 1990 are exceptionally low, while the fourth quarter of 1988 and the first quarter of 1989 appear to be unusually high. Further investigation reveals that the unusual declines during the middle quarters of 1988 and during the third quarter of 1990 all occurred in conjunction with prolonged strikes. Conversely, the larger than normal shipments levels during the fourth quarter of 1988 and the first quarter of 1989 correspond to the backlog in shipments that occurred after the strike period. If a forecaster chooses to ignore this information, he or she not only produces bad estimates in these periods but also introduces bias into the model.

The impact of this bias can be seen by examining the estimated model without any consideration of the impact of the strikes:

$$\widehat{SHIP}_t = -257{,}447 + 210.62151CES87_t$$

$t_e \qquad\qquad\qquad\qquad\qquad 2.20$

$$-100.103.03CED87_t + 94.99269CEN87_t \quad \textbf{(7-8)}$$

$\qquad\qquad\qquad\qquad -0.53 \qquad\qquad\qquad 0.362$

where

$\widehat{SHIP}_t$ = shipments of high-value freight, seasonally adjusted, in thousands

$CES87_t$ = consumption expenditures on services, SAAR, billions of 1987$

$CED87_t$ = consumption expenditures on durable goods, SAAR, billions of 1987$

$CEN87_t$ = consumption expenditures on nondurable goods, SAAR, billions of 1987$.

The bias that results from ignoring the impact of the outliers is best illustrated by the small t statistics for the CED87 and CEN87 variables, as well as the negative sign associated with the consumption of durables variables—in other words, the model does a poor job of explaining fluctuations in package shipments due to the strike-related volatility of the data.

FIGURE 7-2   Scatter Diagram of Freight Shipments

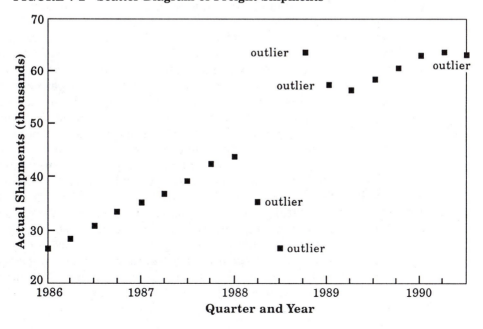

To construct the dummy variables presented in column 5 of Table 7-2, we fit a trend line to the data prior to the occurrence of the strike. This trend line was then used to generate estimated values for the next four quarters. Finally, these trend line estimates were compared to the actual values, and a dummy variable was constructed such that it equaled the difference between the actual and trend values. This same procedure was used in generating the dummy variable value for the third quarter of 1990.

The estimated model with the dummy variable included is

$$\widehat{SHIP}_t = -234,807 + 154.44366CES87_t + 54.93166CED87_t$$
$$t_e \qquad\qquad\qquad 10.73 \qquad\qquad\qquad 1.92 \qquad\qquad (7\text{-}9)$$
$$+ \; 79.58749CEN87_t - 1.01922STRIKE_t.$$
$$2.05 \qquad\qquad\qquad -25.86$$

The signs of each of the independent variables match our theoretical expectations, and each of the variables is significant at the 95 percent or greater level.

There are, however, two complicating factors associated with the use of dummy variables in the shipments example. First, the use of the trend line to derive the estimates upon which the dummy variables were based is arbitrary. That is, there may be other approaches that would yield a more accurate measure of the actual impact of the strikes. In addition, this general approach should only be used when there is overwhelming evidence of an exogenous shock. If used indiscriminately, the dummy variable seemingly becomes a way of forcing the model to have a high R^2.

The second complicating factor arises because decision makers may take anticipatory actions designed to mitigate the effect of unusual events such as strikes. For example, if decision makers anticipate a strike, a decision may be made to increase output prior to the strike to maintain sales at near-normal levels even though production has been curtailed. Alternatively, if economic agents do not anticipate these unusual events, adjustment decisions may be pushed into future time periods. For example, if consumers have not foreseen an automobile strike, their purchase plans may simply be delayed until after the strike is settled. Because events such as strikes not only influence sales during the strike but also alter sales in preceding and succeeding time periods, dummy values need to be created for periods surrounding the strike period. Dummy values will, ideally, provide a quantitative measure of the quarterly (or monthly) stimulus or drag generated by a strike. In this instance, the object is to evaluate past strikes to improve the historical fit and the specific estimates of the regression coefficients. Even though future strikes will differ qualitatively and quantitatively due to the unique characteristics of the economy, information about past strikes can provide a historical perspective concerning the likely spectrum of future outcomes.

Conceptually, the derivation of dummy values is based on ex post error analysis. For example, if the historical model starts to underestimate prior to a strike period, what part of this error is due to the strike? Similarly, what portion of the overestimate during the strike is strike related? There is no reason for the total strike effect to equal zero; that is, the positive and negative influences on the dependent variable need not cancel out. Theoretically, the adjustment process may span a long period before and after the strike, but it is necessary to truncate this process when estimating dummy values.

EXAMPLE 7-6 Housing Prices and Dummy Variables[5]

Suppose that we are interested in developing a model designed to predict the selling price of homes in a major metropolitan area in the Mid-South. As a first step, we postulate the following model:

$$P = f(\text{SQFT, BED, BATH, POOL}) \tag{7-10}$$

where

$$
\begin{aligned}
P &= \text{selling price in dollars} \\
\text{SQFT} &= \text{square footage of home} \\
\text{BED} &= \text{number of bedrooms} \\
\text{BATH} &= \text{number of bathrooms} \\
\text{POOL} &= \text{swimming pool.}
\end{aligned}
$$

Information on each of these variables is presented in Table 7-3.

The application of dummy variables can be seen by examining the specific values for the pool variable. This is a typical example of a categorical variable that can take on only a small number of discrete values. In this instance, the impact of a pool on housing prices can be captured with a variable that takes on a value of 0 if there is no pool and a value of 1 with a pool.

The least-squares regression model based on the data in Table 7-3 is

$$
\begin{array}{lll}
\hat{P} = & +87.03 + 0.07695\text{SQFT} - 27.10586\text{BED} \\
t_e & \qquad\qquad 3.41 \qquad\qquad\quad -2.12 \\
& + 27.46842\text{BATH} + 54.16610\text{POOL.} \\
& \qquad 1.19 \qquad\qquad\quad 2.88
\end{array} \tag{7-11}
$$

While it might seem normal to hypothesize that the number of bedrooms should be positively related to the selling price of a home, the importance of the all-other-things-being-equal assumption of these regression coef-

---

[5] Condensed excerpts from *Introductory Econometrics: With Applications*, pp. 161–78 and 247–49, by Ramu Ramanathan, copyright © 1989 by Harcourt Brace Jovanovich, Inc., reprinted by permission of the publisher.

TABLE 7-3 Housing Prices and Dummy Variables

Price (000) (dollars) (1)	Square Footage (000) (2)	Number of Bedrooms (3)	Number of Bathrooms (4)	Pool (5)
128.5	1,219	3	2.0	0
139.5	1,210	4	2.5	0
139.5	1,400	4	2.0	0
152.5	1,560	4	2.0	0
153.0	1,846	5	2.0	0
185.0	2,400	5	3.0	0
209.0	1,846	4	2.5	0
211.0	1,846	5	2.5	1
214.0	2,300	4	3.0	0
226.0	2,230	4	3.0	0
250.0	2,300	5	3.0	0
259.0	2,180	3	2.0	0
269.9	2,527	4	2.5	1
298.0	1,968	4	3.0	1

ficients comes to the front. In particular, the negative sign on the number of bedrooms variable suggests that, when the square footage of the home is held constant, an increase in the number of bedrooms reduces the square footage available for the other rooms. The implication of the negative sign is that for a given size home, consumers prefer fewer bedrooms. When used in this fashion, the dummy variable associated with the pool variable has a straightforward interpretation. The positive sign suggests that homes with pools have a higher selling price than would the same home without a pool. Furthermore, a home with a pool will, on the average, have a selling price that is approximately $54,000 higher than a home without a pool, as long as all of the other factors are identical.

EXAMPLE 7-7 Dummy Variables and Structural Stability

As a forecaster for a major firm in the packaging materials industry, you are required to develop quarterly forecasts for use in establishing long-term marketing strategies. An analysis of historical shipping records indicates that three industries account for over 80 percent of the firm's sales. These three industries are the service sector, the computer industry, and the job printing industry. The concentration in the package materials industry (i.e., small number of firms) is such that the price charged by each competitor is also felt to be important. With this information in hand, the conceptual model is formulated as

$$SALES_t = f(EMPSER_t, COMP_t, PRINT_t, PRICE_t). \quad \textbf{(7-12)}$$

Data for each of these variables are presented in Table 7-4.
The results of the least-squares estimation are

$$\widehat{SALES}_t = -261{,}248.97 + 13{,}279.366EMPSER_t + 614.17469COMP_t$$
$$t_e \qquad\qquad\qquad 2.94 \qquad\qquad\qquad 4.93$$
$$+\ 1263.71671PRINT_t - 1293.6905PRICE_t.$$
$$3.15 \qquad\qquad -2.32 \qquad\qquad \textbf{(7-13)}$$

The multiple coefficient of determination for this model indicates that over 99 percent of the observed variation in sales has been accounted for by this model. All variables are significant at the 98 percent or greater level. The Durbin-Watson statistic of 0.51 is disturbing in that it suggests that the error terms are autocorrelated. While it is true that we could correct this problem by simply applying the mechanical Cochrane-Orcutt or Hildreth-Lu approach, it is also possible that the autocorrelation could be a result of structural changes in the underlying model.

This possibility of structural change is especially relevant in light of the fact that in 1984 changes in federal government regulations allowed a major firm to enter the industry. Whenever time series data are used in conjunction with regression models, the structural stability of the model over time is an important consideration. Structural stability implies that the observed relationship between industrial production in the computer and job printing industries, employment in services, and the price level and packaging sales (millions of pounds) has remained relatively constant over the period for which the model was estimated (1980: I to 1990: IV). That is, the model builder implicitly assumes that, throughout the entire time period covered by the data set, a 1 unit change in the production index in the computer industry will lead to an increase of 614 million pounds of packaging material, that a 1 unit change in the production index in the job printing industry will lead to an increase of 1,264 million pounds, that a change of 1 million in service sector employment will lead to a change of 13,279 million pounds, and that a 1 dollar change in the price per hundred weight will lead to a decrease of 1,294 million pounds of packaging materials.

Two procedures that are commonly used to test the structural stability of an equation are the Chow test and dummy variables. In applying the Chow test, the following steps must be carried out: Divide the data base into two subperiods; estimate an equation for each subperiod; calculate the sum of squares from each regression; compute an actual F

TABLE 7-4   Sales of Packaging Materials and Structural Stability

Date*	Sales (millions of pounds) (1)	Employment in Services (millions) (2)	Industrial Production Index for Computers (1987 = 100.0) (3)	Industrial Production Index for Job Printing (1987 = 100.0) (4)	Price per Hundred Weight (dollars) (5)	Dummy Variable (6)
1980: I	50,907	17.63	155.03	122.30	127.47	0
II	52,521	17.78	154.10	120.13	127.60	0
III	57,219	17.96	160.93	124.13	129.23	0
IV	63,504	18.18	173.43	124.23	131.63	0
1981: I	69,605	18.39	178.37	123.77	132.40	0
II	72,796	18.53	183.00	124.63	134.87	0
III	79,556	18.69	187.93	126.03	136.63	0
IV	86,873	18.86	184.27	127.10	135.07	0
1982: I	93,688	18.96	187.50	126.93	133.53	0
II	95,219	18.99	183.90	126.30	132.73	0
III	97,879	19.06	181.97	125.50	132.23	0
IV	104,918	19.13	195.83	127.03	129.33	0
1983: I	114,168	19.26	197.60	130.47	129.73	0
II	120,893	19.55	209.37	134.37	131.83	0
III	129,884	19.86	216.27	141.97	136.60	0
IV	144,393	20.10	224.77	147.50	141.33	0
1984: I	154,893	20.36	241.03	155.20	149.50	1
II	162,977	20.67	252.40	157.23	153.10	1
III	173,503	20.92	262.33	159.70	154.57	1
IV	187,547	21.23	264.40	164.17	155.70	1
1985: I	208,171	21.56	268.73	158.80	155.77	1
II	209,246	21.84	275.23	163.87	157.33	1
III	209,336	22.12	269.07	164.23	157.30	1
IV	223,323	22.47	272.13	167.73	160.30	1
1986: I	227,772	22.69	274.83	171.73	162.13	1
II	233,809	22.92	263.63	177.17	163.10	1
III	233,954	23.16	266.20	178.70	163.33	1
IV	248,935	23.45	266.07	185.27	167.77	1
1987: I	255,338	23.77	271.77	189.03	168.03	1
II	262,958	24.08	280.60	197.37	170.73	1
III	268,018	24.39	284.97	199.30	171.70	1
IV	281,285	24.70	293.63	203.03	177.60	1
1988: I	292,720	25.08	305.33	207.33	178.93	1
II	299,139	25.42	314.97	212.67	182.20	1
III	310,719	25.78	318.97	217.47	185.80	1
IV	324,334	26.11	322.03	217.90	193.10	1
1989: I	332,870	26.42	338.67	219.60	194.30	1
II	331,328	26.76	351.50	221.66	195.76	1
III	332,345	27.06	351.43	223.43	196.46	1
IV	337,357	27.30	352.20	225.57	196.79	1
1990: I	342,511	27.53	353.23	227.38	196.24	1
II	354,720	27.76	356.79	229.60	196.93	1
III	358,778	28.00	364.00	231.83	198.64	1
IV	357,982	28.23	370.55	233.78	200.45	1

* Year and quarter

statistic and compare to a critical F value; and decide whether to accept or reject the assumption of structural stability.[6]

To illustrate this procedure, the model in equation (7-13) was reestimated over the period from the first quarter of 1980 to the fourth quarter of 1983.

$$\widehat{SALES}_t = -557{,}762 + 38{,}317.42749EMPSER_t - 74.39168COMP_t$$
$$t_e \qquad\qquad\qquad 10.53 \qquad\qquad\qquad -0.51$$
$$+ \ 822.70261PRINT_t - 1243.87614PRICE_t.$$
$$4.32 \qquad\qquad -5.33 \qquad\qquad\qquad \textbf{(7-14)}$$

One disturbing aspect of this truncated model is that the COMP variable has a sign that contradicts our theoretical expectations. However, an examination of the individual t statistics suggests that this variable is not statistically significant and should be deleted from the model.

The same model estimated from the first quarter of 1984 to the fourth quarter of 1990 is

$$\widehat{SALES}_t = -407{,}657 + 26{,}430.60081EMPSER_t - 290.76661COMP_t$$
$$t_e \qquad\qquad\qquad 5.99 \qquad\qquad\qquad -1.81$$
$$- \ 294.37281PRINT_t + 1011.97780PRICE_t.$$
$$-0.73 \qquad\qquad 1.44 \qquad\qquad\qquad \textbf{(7-15)}$$

On an intuitive level, the contradictory signs on all variables except the employment in services is most certainly indicative of some specification problems during this most recent time period.

To test the structural stability of the coefficients in these two equations (that is, to test whether or not the differences are the result of sampling error), the sum of squares of the residual (unexplained variation) was computed for equations (7-13), (7-14), and (7-15), with the results reproduced in Table 7-5.

The test statistic for structural stability is given by

$$F_{(k, n_1 + n_2 - 2k)} = \frac{(Q - Q_1)/k}{Q_1/(n_1 + n_2 - 2k)} \qquad \textbf{(7-16)}$$

where

$$n_1 = \text{number of observations in data set I, equation (7-14)}$$
$$n_2 = \text{number of observations in data set II, equation (7-15)}$$
$$k = \text{number of regressors, including constant}$$
$$Q = \text{error variation for equation (7-13)}$$
$$Q_1 = \text{combined error variation for equations (7-14) and (7-15).}$$

---

[6] Gregory C. Chow, "Tests of Equality between Sets of Coefficients in Two Linear Regressions," *Econometrica*, vol. 28, July, 1960, pp. 591–605.

TABLE 7-5   Sales of Packaging Material: Structural Stability

Data Set I: 1980, Quarter I—1983, Quarter IV; Equation (7-14)

Analysis of Variance	Sum of Squares	d.f.	Mean Square	F statistic
Explained by Regression	11,895,236,651	4	2,973,826,663	
Error Variation	56,085,786	11	5,098,708	583.25

Data Set II: 1984, Quarter I—1990, Quarter IV; Equation (7-15)

Analysis of Variance	Sum of Squares	d.f.	Mean Square	F statistic
Explained by Regression	108,580,729,039	4	27,145,182,260	
Error Variation	938,860,490	23	40,820,021	665.00

Data Set III: 1980, Quarter I—1990, Quarter IV; Equation (7-13)

Analysis of Variance	Sum of Squares	d.f.	Mean Square	F statistic
Explained by Regression	443,309,460,795	4	110,827,365,199	
Error Variation	3,659,151,567	39	98,824,399	1181.22

Table 7-6 contains all of the data necessary to compute the F statistic for structural stability. The error variation, Q, measures the variation not explained by the regression model in equation (7-13); thus $Q = 3,659,151,567$, as shown in Table 7-6. The combined sum of squares, Q_1, measures the total unexplained variation in equations (7-14) and (7-15); thus $Q_1 = 994,946,276$, as shown in Table 7-6. As illustrated in the formula for the actual F value in equation (7-16), the greater the difference between Q and Q_1, the greater the evidence against the null hypothesis of structural stability in the regression coefficients for the original model

TABLE 7-6   The Chow Test for Structural Stability: Package Materials

Residual or Error Variation	Sum of Squares	d.f.	Mean Square	F Statistic*
Regression error for complete equation (7-13)	Q = 3,659,151,567	39		
Combined error from equations (7-14) and (7-15)	Q_1 = 994,946,276	34	29,263,126	
			$\dfrac{532,841,058}{29,263,126}$ = 18.21	
Complete less combined error	$Q_2 = Q - Q_1$ = 2,664,205,291	5	532,841,058	

* The actual F statistic is based on equation (7-16). Statistics are taken from Table 7-5. The null hypothesis of structural stability is rejected since the critical F equals 3.61 when $\alpha = .01$.

in equation (7-13). A low F value implies that random forces have caused the observed differences in the regression coefficients for the equations analyzed in Tables 7-5 and 7-6. In the case of the package materials model, the actual F of 18.21 exceeds the critical value of 3.61 ($\alpha = .01$); hence the null hypothesis of structural stability is rejected. That is, we can conclude that the regression model and its coefficients in equation (7-13) are structurally unstable over the entire time frame.

The principal limitation of the Chow test in the package shipments model is that once we have concluded that the estimated relationship has changed over time, we are forced to go back to the beginning. That is, if the model is structurally unstable the specification has to be changed and reestimations attempted. The dummy variable approach simply involves creating a 0–1 dummy variable corresponding to different time periods. That is, the dummy variable shown in column 6 of Table 7-4 takes on a value of 0 prior to the entry of the new firm and a value of 1 after the entry. With the dummy variable included, the package materials model is

$$\widehat{SALES}_t = -328256 + 26{,}461.53645 EMPSER_t + 252.70945 COMP_t$$
$$\phantom{\widehat{SALES}_t = -328256 + }6.59 2.29$$
$$+\ 523.62069 PRINT_t - 1462.20029 PRICE_t + 30{,}438.315 DUM_t.$$
$$1.63 -3.56 5.84$$

$$(7\text{-}17)$$

The statistical significance of the dummy variable provides ample evidence that the observed changes in sales of packaging material have been due to the entry of the new competitor. Thus, the model was extremely sensitive to a structural change in the industry—namely, entry of a major new competitor. This example points out the necessity for forecasters to familiarize themselves with the industry before attempting to develop a model.

LINEAR TRANSFORMATIONS

Implicit in all of the regression models estimated in earlier examples has been the assumption of linearity, but this specification is not as restrictive as it might first appear. Indeed, the least-squares methodology can be applied to all systems that are intrinsically linear. A model is intrinsically linear if it can be expressed, by transformation of the variables, in a linear form. A transformation is simply a mathematical function or statistical process that changes the relative magnitudes of the numbers. This section presents the intrinsically linear models that the practicing forecaster encounters most frequently.

LOGARITHMIC TRANSFORMATIONS

A logarithmic transformation is useful when the underlying model is multiplicative:

$$Y = \beta_0 \beta_1^x \epsilon \tag{7-18}$$

where β_0 and β_1 are the parameters to be estimated, X and Y are the variables being studied, and ϵ is the error term. As it is formulated, this model is neither linear in the parameters (β_0 and β_1 are multiplied together) nor linear in X, since X appears as an exponent. However, equation (7-18) is said to be intrinsically linear because it can be expressed via a logarithmic transformation.

$$\log Y = \log \beta_0 + X \log \beta_1 + \log \epsilon. \tag{7-19}$$

The transformed error terms must satisfy all the conditions noted in conjunction with the error term in the standard model; for instance, error terms must be randomly distributed and independent of each other.

Additional models involving logarithmic transformations are

$$Y = \beta_0 + \beta_1 \log X + \epsilon \tag{7-20}$$

$$\log Y = \beta_0 + \beta_1 \log X + \log \epsilon. \tag{7-21}$$

Economists have used the formulation presented in equation (7-21) when interested in estimating various elasticity coefficients (which measure the percentage change in Y divided by the percentage change in X). Specifically, the coefficient β_1 represents the elasticity coefficient. For example, if X were price and Y were sales, the coefficient would be the price elasticity for sales; or, alternatively, if X were advertising expenditures and Y were sales, the coefficient would be interpreted as the advertising elasticity (that is, the percentage change in sales resulting from a 1 percent change in advertising).

EXAMPLE 7-8 Logarithmic Transformations and Growth

To illustrate the process of using a logarithmic transformation to capture nonlinear growth patterns, consider the shipment of low-value air freight (a model for high-value air freight was presented in example 7-5). Data for low-value shipments is presented in Appendix F, Table F-2. Using the data set, the linear estimation is

$$\widehat{\text{LVSHIP}}_t = -3{,}048{,}916 + 3695.315\text{CES87}_t$$
$$- 163.42082\text{CED87}_t - 755.48135\text{CEN87}_t. \tag{7-22}$$

While the same independent variables are used in equations (7-8) and (7-22), the results in equation (7-22) are not acceptable.

The negative signs on the consumption of durable (CED87) and non-durable (CEN87) goods contradict theoretical expectations. As an additional attempt to test this model, a logarithmic transformation is tested with the results as follows:

$$\widehat{\text{LOGLVSHIP}}_t = -16.62753 + 1.95134\text{LOGCES87}_t$$

$$t_e \qquad\qquad\qquad 4.07$$

$$+\ 4.22839\text{LOGCEN87}_t + 1.54328\text{LOGCED87}_t. \qquad \textbf{(7-23)}$$

$$3.25 \qquad\qquad\qquad 5.14$$

With this formulation, all signs match theoretical expectations and the *t* statistics are significant at the 99 percent level of significance. The Durbin-Watson statistic of 1.48 and the multiple coefficient of determination of .996 (when combined with the goodness of fit graph presented in Figure 7-3) indicate that this transformation provides us with a reliable model from a historical perspective. Notice that there may not be a theoretical basis for preferring the additive model in equation (7-22) vis-à-vis the multiplicative model in equation (7-23). Pragmatically, the logarithmic transformation works well, and this is the basis for its use.

Despite the fact that the logarithmic model portrayed in equation (7-23) passes all statistical tests, there remains one disturbing issue. An

FIGURE 7-3   Error Plot: Low-Value Freight Shipments

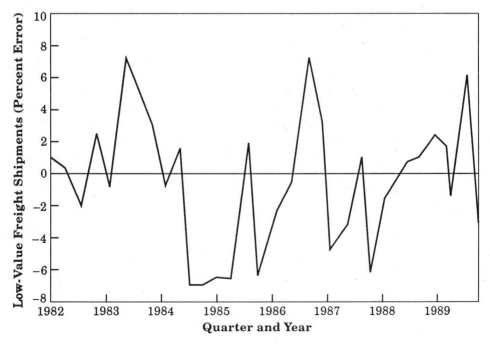

examination of the error pattern in Figure 7-3 suggests that while there is no consistent pattern, there are several quarters where the percentage error is exceptionally large, and this suggests the need for further analysis. This process of error identification and error analysis becomes an integral part of using forecasting models and is covered in greater detail in succeeding chapters.

EXAMPLE 7-9   Logarithmic Transformations and Elasticities

As a research analyst for the revenue department in Tennessee, you receive a request to prepare an estimate of the likely impact on tax revenue if the sales tax rate is increased. Specifically, the legislature is interested in using the tax elasticity concept to reach some policy decisions. Conceptually, the following model is formulated:

$$\text{REV}_t = f(\text{INC}_t, \text{RATE}_t) \qquad (7\text{-}24)$$

where

$$\text{REV}_t = \text{sales tax revenues in time } t$$
$$\text{INC}_t = \text{personal income in time } t$$
$$\text{RATE}_t = \text{sales tax rate in time } t.$$

Thus, sales tax revenues will increase if personal income (hence consumption spending) increases or if the tax rate is increased. The task is to advise the tax commission as to the responsiveness of sales tax revenues to changes in each of these two factors, or, more specifically, the tax elasticity of each variable.

As a preliminary step, data on sales tax revenue, personal income, and the sales tax rate have been collected and are presented in Appendix F, Table F-3. Preliminary examination of the data suggests the desirability of using the general model noted in equation (7-21). First, the data seem to follow an exponential growth pattern. Second, the tax commission is interested in determining the responsiveness of sales tax revenues (REV) to changes in either the tax rate (RATE) or economic growth as measured by income (INC). Thus, the model to be estimated by least squares is

$$\log \text{REV}_t = \log \hat{\beta}_0 + \hat{\beta}_1 \log \text{INC}_t + \hat{\beta}_2 \log \text{RATE}_t \qquad (7\text{-}25)$$

where

$$\text{REV}_t = \text{sales tax revenues in thousands of dollars}$$
$$\text{INC}_t = \text{personal income in billions of dollars}$$
$$\text{RATE}_t = \text{sales tax rate.}$$

Note that $\hat{\beta}_1$ and $\hat{\beta}_2$ measure the elasticity of sales tax revenue with respect to income and tax rates, respectively. That is, $\hat{\beta}_2$ measures the percentage change in REV from a 1 percent change in RATE, holding INC constant.

The results of applying this model to the data are

$$\log \widehat{\text{REV}}_t = 1.10353 + 0.98371 \log \text{INC}_t + 0.64346 \log \text{RATE}_t. \quad \textbf{(7-26)}$$
$$t_e \qquad\qquad\qquad 16.74 \qquad\qquad\qquad 4.29$$

$R^2 = 0.99$	$\text{SEE} = 0.02179$
$F_{2,27} = 5951$	$\text{DW} = 0.63.$

A brief response to the tax commission could be made as follows: (1) A 1 percent increase in the sales tax rate will lead to a 0.64346 percent increase in tax revenues; and (2) a 1 percent increase in personal income will increase revenues by 0.98371 percent. Clearly, the impact of economic growth and personal income is much more significant than are changes in the sales tax rate. The implication is that retail sales will be lost (perhaps to other nearby cities) when sales taxes are increased.

The model presented in equation (7-26) can be retransformed and written as

$$\widehat{\text{REV}}_t = (12.692) \cdot \text{INC}^{0.98371} \cdot \text{RATE}^{0.64346}. \quad \textbf{(7-27)}$$

The advantage of this formulation is that it highlights the multiplicative interrelationship between the independent variables.

RECIPROCAL TRANSFORMATIONS

A reciprocal transformation may be in order when a scatter diagram indicates the desirability of a curvilinear model similar to that shown in Figure 7-4. In this situation, the graph leads to a model of the form

$$Y = \beta_0 + (\beta_1/X). \quad \textbf{(7-28)}$$

By letting

$$X' = (1/X) \quad \textbf{(7-29)}$$

equation (7-28) becomes

$$Y = \beta_0 + \beta_1 X' \quad \textbf{(7-30)}$$

which conforms to the simple linear model. Here, the forecaster is simply using the reciprocal of the independent variable in fitting the equation. The same

FIGURE 7-4   Reciprocal Variable Transformations

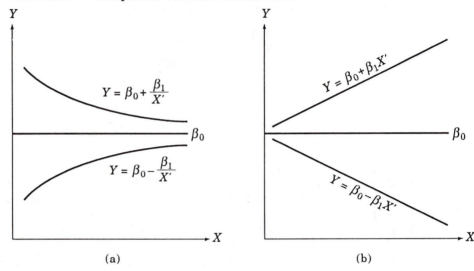

(a)   (b)

type of transformation can be made on the dependent variable, Y. Thus, the model

$$Y' = \beta_0 + \beta_1 X \qquad\qquad (7\text{-}31)$$

is still linear when Y' is equal to $(1/Y)$.

COMMENTS ON TRANSFORMATION ISSUES

In addition to the transformations suggested by the preceding sections, other transformations—the square root and the reciprocal—were presented in chapter 3. Whenever any of these transformations are used, the estimators, $\hat{\beta}_0$ and $\hat{\beta}_1$, obtained by least squares, are BLUE with respect to the transformed variable observations, not the original ones. Further, if a transformation is made, the forecaster must check the validity of the model's assumptions by applying the tests noted in chapter 6 to the transformed variables and error terms.

FINDING THE BEST SET OF INDEPENDENT VARIABLES

INTRODUCTION

In constructing a forecasting model via least squares, the forecaster is faced with two conflicting options:

1. Include as many X's as possible to make the equation representative of the process being studied and to make the equation useful for predictive purposes.

2. Include as few X's as possible to minimize the costs involved in obtaining information, estimating, and monitoring the model.

Thus, the practitioner wants a model that yields the "best" predictive value of Y (the dependent variable) given a collective "best" set of X_i's (independent variables). Further, the set of independent variables considered for inclusion in a regression model falls into one of three categories:

> Those that for purely theoretical reasons should be included
>
> Those that are likely to improve the overall fit of actual models. This would include such factors as proxy and dummy variables.
>
> Other variables that may have desirable intuitive appeal based on an understanding of the system or process being studied.

Theory can and should aid the analyst in selecting the independent variables (X's) to be used. Typically, the number of X's in purely theoretical models is rather large. Variables may be deleted prior to statistical analysis if they are not fundamental to the problem being studied, if they are subject to unacceptable measurement errors, if they are intercorrelated with other variables, or if they are not directly measurable. Unfortunately, even after this initial screening, the number of variables is likely to be quite large. The forecaster needs to pare his or her model, because a regression model with a large number of independent variables is expensive to maintain. Further, the presence of a large number of independent variables presents the forecaster with the complicated problem of obtaining future values for all these variables when the equation is to be used for prediction. Additionally, the inclusion of a large number of independent variables does not necessarily generate more reliable predictions than would a model with fewer variables. Finally, the presence of numerous interrelated variables adds little to the predictive capabilities of a model and tends to detract from its simulative power.

The problem, then, is to shorten the list of independent variables to obtain a set that is small enough to have manageable maintenance costs, yet large enough to represent accurately the real-world situation and to predict well. The purpose of this section is to develop the more common approaches used by practitioners to find the best set of independent variables.

ALL POSSIBLE REGRESSIONS

The all-possible-regressions procedure is just what its name implies. It literally entails an examination of all possible regression equations yielded by the list of potential independent variables and selection of the best equation(s). A major disadvantage of this procedure is the amount of computational time required. Since each X can either be or not be in the equation, and since this is true for every X_i, $i = 1, 2, \ldots, k$, there are altogether 2^k possible equations. For example, if there are 10 ($k = 10$) independent variables, then there are 1,024 possible (2^{10}) regression equations. Indeed, this approach is so costly that it has given way to other, more practical procedures.

STEPWISE REGRESSION

The stepwise regression technique does not require an examination of all possible regressions; rather, this search method computes a sequence of least-squares equations, and at each step of the sequence, independent variables are added or deleted according to a predetermined criterion.

First, the stepwise routine computes k simple regressions based on the k potential independent variables and calculates the F statistic to test whether or not the slope is significantly different from zero. Let this calculated F be symbolized by F_i, where i refers to the specific independent variable being used. Although there are criteria other than the F statistic upon which to judge regression equations, the majority of computer software packages rely on this statistic.

The F statistic is based on the following ratio:

$$F_i = \frac{\text{MSR}(X_i)}{\text{MSE}(X_i)} \tag{7-32}$$

where $\text{MSR}(X_i)$ measures the reduction in total variation of Y associated with the inclusion of X_i in the regression, and $\text{MSE}(X_i)$ represents the mean square error. The independent variable with the largest F_i value is the first variable added to the model *if* this value exceeds a predetermined minimum referred to as F_L. F_L is simply a critical or limiting F value based on a given level of significance (α). Before the stepwise regression process is begun, the forecaster selects an α value—say, $\alpha = .01$—and uses the F table (Appendix B) to determine F_L. If F_i is greater than F_L when $\alpha = .01$, then the analyst can be 99 percent confident that he or she has found a statistically significant relationship. If no F_i exceeds F_L, the regression process terminates and the forecaster must conclude that no regression equation provides better estimates than the mean value of the dependent variable.

For illustrative purposes, assume that X_5 is the independent variable entered at step 1. The stepwise regression routine now computes all two-variable regressions in which X_5 is combined with one of the remaining variables. Each F_i is obtained and compared with F_L, and the equation that explains the largest percentage of the variation in Y becomes the next building block, provided that $F_i > F_L$. If none of the combinations meets this condition, the program terminates and Y is assumed to be only a function of X_5.

Suppose X_2 is added at the second stage, so the model becomes

$$\hat{Y}_t = \hat{\beta}_0 + \hat{\beta}_5 X_5 + \hat{\beta}_2 X_2 + e_t. \tag{7-33}$$

Now the stepwise routine investigates whether any of the variables incorporated in the model prior to the inclusion of X_2 should be deleted. In our example, only one other independent variable was in the model, X_5, so only one conditional F_c statistic, $F(X_5/X_2)$, is obtained. At later stages there would be a number of these F_c statistics computed, one for each variable other than the last one added to the model. The variable for which the F_c value is the smallest is a candidate for deletion if the value falls below F_L; otherwise, all variables are retained.

Suppose that X_5 is retained and the model remains as noted in equation (7-33). The routine now examines which independent variable is the next candidate for inclusion with X_5 and X_2, specifies whether any of the variables already in the equation should be deleted, and continues on until no more independent variables can be added or deleted; at this point, the search process terminates. It must be noted that a true stepwise regression procedure allows an independent variable, brought into the model at an earlier stage, to be subsequently deleted if it is no longer statistically significant in conjunction with variables added at later stages.

FORWARD STEPWISE SELECTION

This process is a simplified version of the stepwise procedure discussed in the preceding paragraphs, the principal difference being that once a variable enters into the regression equation, it is never deleted because of the introduction of additional variables. Thus, the main drawback of this technique is that it makes no attempt to evaluate the effect that insertion of a new variable has on the variables selected at earlier stages.

BACKWARD STEPWISE ELIMINATION

Whereas the forward selection procedure begins with the smallest regression model, the backward elimination technique begins with a regression model based on all variables and subsequently reduces the number until a decision is reached on the *best* equation. This process is accomplished by comparing F_L and F_c according to the following rules:

1. If $F_c < F_L$, remove the variable that gave rise to F_c and recompute the regression equation with the remaining variables.
2. If $F_c > F_L$, adopt the regression as computed.

COMMENTS ON SEARCH PROCEDURES

None of the search procedures can be proved to yield the best set of independent variables. Indeed, there may be no unique best set. The entire variable-selection process is pragmatic and relies on judgment. The principal advantage of automatic search procedures is that the time and cost elements of the search are minimized, thereby allowing the forecaster to spend his or her time on judgmental questions. One of the mistakes commonly made by beginning forecasters is to ignore theory and blindly accept the results of the search routine.

Finally, it is essential to comprehend fully the specific features and/or options of the computer package being used. For example, various packages have the following options:

1. Regression lines can be forced through the origin.
2. Variables can be inserted into the models and tested in pairs or groupings as desired.
3. The partial correlation coefficient can be used to decide whether variables should be inserted or deleted.
4. F limits for adding or deleting can be varied.
5. Certain variables can be forced into the regression if the forecaster has an a priori belief that they should be included.

In addition, the forecaster may want to experiment with lower (or higher) F_L levels or may wish to compare the final equation obtained via one of the search procedures with an equation based on a priori expectations. The point of all of these comments is simple: Do not use search procedures as a substitute for intelligent reasoning.

EXAMPLE 7-10   Sales of Single-Family Homes, Stepwise Analysis

There are a number of variables that theoretically influence single-family home sales ($SALES_t$): additions to the available capital stock (ADD_t); index of consumer sentiment (JCS_t); number of households (HH_t); housing prices as measured by the consumer price index of housing ($PHOME_t$) and the median price of new single-family homes sold during the month ($MPNEW_t$), which is included to capture a measure of the change in the absolute selling price of homes; rental prices (REN_t); a measure of the affordability of housing (HAI_t); the interest rate on conventional mortgages (INT_t); vacancy rates of rental units ($RVAC_t$) and of housing units ($HVAC_t$); and real disposable income ($YDP82_t$). If this list comprised all relevant variables, then the theoretical model would be (omitting the subscripts for convenience):

SALES

$$= f(\text{ADD, JCS, HH, PHOME, MPNEW, REN, RVAC, HVAC, YDP82})$$

$$(7\text{-}34)$$

Figure 7-5 shows an abbreviated copy of the computer-generated output for the stepwise regression routine of the SPSS software package when applied to the housing sales example in equation (7-34). In this program, the F statistic is used to decide whether to insert or delete specific variables (that is, the step algorithm is based on F). The maximum number of steps is 18 to allow each variable noted in equation (7-34) to be entered and deleted from the model. In this example, the F_L limit for adding or deleting variables was set at 1.00. This corresponds to a significance level of approximately 0.25 for a single variable. The data used in this example are presented in Appendix F, Table F-4. Now the stepwise process can be traced:

1. While not presented here, the program computes the partial correlation coefficients and F_c values to enter for each variable, on the

FIGURE 7-5 **SPSS's Stepwise Regression Program Applied to Sales of Single-Family Houses (SALES)**

		VARIABLES IN EQUATION				*VARIABLES NOT IN EQUATION*			
Variable	*Coefficient*	*Standard Error of Coefficient*	*Beta Coefficient*	*Partial Correlation Coefficient*	*F-to-Remove*	*Variable*	*Beta In*	*Partial Correlation Coefficient*	*F-to-Enter*
				Variable Added on Step 1					
Constant	0.62568	0.34220				JCS	0.28372	0.36042	10.90
ADD	2.22816	0.32189	0.62692	0.62692	47.92	HH	0.55900	0.71414	75.98
						PHOME	0.53025	0.67105	59.80
$R^2 = 0.39302$		R^2 change = 0.39302		$F = 47.91577$		REN	0.51980	0.66390	57.54
ADJ $R^2 = 0.38482$		F change = 47.91577				HAI	−0.41631	−0.50226	24.63
SEE = 0.50838		Sig F change = 0.0000				INT	0.24628	0.27130	5.80
						RVAC	0.28602	0.36564	11.27
						YDP82	0.54941	0.70473	72.03
						MPNEW	0.54930	0.70498	72.13
						HVAC	0.45818	0.55981	33.318
				Variable Added on Step 2					
Constant	−2.64329	0.44588				JCS	0.04409	0.07179	0.37
ADD	2.42052	0.22793	0.68140	0.77913	112.77	PHOME	−3.53287	−0.60337	41.22
HH	0.03648	0.00418	0.55900	0.71414	75.98	REN	−1.07605	−0.33419	9.05
						HAI	−0.04465	−0.05775	0.24
$R^2 = 0.70258$		R^2 change = 0.69443		$F = 86.22197$		INT	−0.13049	−0.17471	2.27
ADJ $R^2 = 0.69443$		F change = 75.98				RVAC	−0.10666	−0.15163	1.69
SEE = 0.35830		Sig F change = 0.0000				YDP82	0.02368	0.00734	0.00
						MPNEW	0.06316	0.02099	0.03
						HVAC	−0.28398	−0.22863	3.971

(continued)

FIGURE 7-5 *(Continued)*

		VARIABLES IN EQUATION					VARIABLES NOT IN EQUATION		
Variable	Coefficient	Standard Error of Coefficient	Beta Coefficient	Partial Correlation Coefficient	F-to-Remove	Variable	Beta In	Partial Correlation Coefficient	F-to-Enter

Variable Added on Step 3

Constant	−14.63935	1.90250							
ADD	1.52306	0.23030	0.42853	0.61473	43.74	JCS	0.26601	0.48445	21.77
HH	0.26384	0.03557	4.04308	0.65812	55.01				
PHOME	−0.07809	0.01216	−3.53287	−0.60337	41.02				
						REN	0.27774	0.08324	0.50
$R^2 = 0.81086$		R^2 change = 0.10828	$F = 102.88902$			HAI	0.07464	0.11736	0.99
ADJ $R^2 = 0.80298$		F change = 41.21809				INT	−0.15418	−0.25850	5.08
SEE = 0.28771		Sig F change = 0.0000				RVAC	−0.06701	−0.11893	1.02
						YDP82	0.13115	0.05086	0.18
						MPNEW	0.04820	0.02008	0.03
						HVAC	−0.10272	−0.1004	0.723

Variable Added on Step 4

Constant	−18.89357	1.90795							
ADD	1.05621	0.22621	0.29718	0.48468	21.80				
HH	0.33001	0.03440	5.05705	0.75136	92.05				
PHOME	−0.10344	0.12010	−4.67947	−0.71469	74.13				
JCS	0.14510	0.00311	0.26601	0.48445	21.77	REN	−0.74533	−0.21934	3.54
						HAI	−0.15812	−0.23114	3.95
$R^2 = 0.85525$		R^2 change = 0.04439	$F = 104.87405$			INT	0.03846	0.05805	0.24
ADJ $R^2 = 0.84709$		F change = 21.77327				RVAC	−0.16003	−0.31058	7.47
SEE = 0.25346		Sig F change = 0.0000				YDP82	−0.60138	−0.23432	4.07
						MPNEW	−0.26047	−0.12007	1.02
						HVAC	−0.17350	−0.19204	2.68

Variable Added on Step 5

Constant	−19.13463	1.82863							
ADD	1.09431	0.21701	0.30709	0.51621	25.43				
HH	0.33973	0.03312	5.20600	0.77491	105.22				
PHOME	−0.10497	0.01151	−4.74879	−0.73675	83.11				
JCS	0.01698	0.00311	0.31139	0.54644	29.80	REN	0.79287	0.11742	0.97
RVAC	−0.11627	0.04253	−0.16003	−0.31058	7.47	HAI	0.12315	0.09082	0.57
						INT	−0.63466	−0.4789	20.42
$R^2 = 0.86921$		R^2 change = 0.01396	$F = 93.04255$						
ADJ $R^2 = 0.85987$		F change = 7.47278				YDP82	−0.18439	−0.05996	0.25
SEE = 0.24264		Sig F change = 0.0079				MPNEW	0.20097	0.07916	0.44
						HVAC	−0.12349	−0.14104	1.40

Variable Added on Step 6

Constant	−13.48494	2.04464							
ADD	0.70568	0.21038	0.19855	0.37444	11.25				
HH	0.31188	0.02994	4.77925	0.78181	108.48				
PHOME	−0.08051	0.01154	−3.64218	−0.64325	48.70				
JCS	0.00407	0.00397	0.07464	0.12259	1.05	REN	−4.92034	−0.49946	22.60
RVAC	−0.43203	0.07936	−0.59464	−0.54813	29.64	HAI	−1.28172	−0.60931	40.15
INT	−0.18024	0.03989	−0.63466	−0.47789	20.422				
$R^2 = 0.89908$		R^2 change = 0.02987	$F = 102.45215$						
ADJ $R^2 = 0.8903$		F change = 20.42221				YDP82	−1.24597	−0.39792	12.79
SEE = 0.21468		Sig F change = 0.0000				MPNEW	−1.17467	−0.38490	11.83
						HVAC	0.03654	0.04413	0.13

FIGURE 7-5   *(Continued)*

	VARIABLES IN EQUATION					VARIABLES NOT IN EQUATION			
Variable	*Coefficient*	*Standard Error of Coefficient*	*Beta Coefficient*	*Partial Correlation Coefficient*	*F-to-Remove*	*Variable*	*Beta In*	*Partial Correlation Coefficient*	*F-to-Enter*

Variable Added on Step 7

Variable	*Coefficient*	*Standard Error of Coefficient*	*Beta Coefficient*	*Partial Correlation Coefficient*	*F-to-Remove*	*Variable*	*Beta In*	*Partial Correlation Coefficient*	*F-to-Enter*
Constant	1.49502	2.87332							
ADD	0.62734	0.16849	0.17651	0.41151	13.862	REN	−1.35725	0.12297	1.029
HH	0.16922	0.3285	2.59318	0.52985	26.542				
PHOME	−0.04105	0.01112	−1.85716	−0.40857	13.625				
JCS	0.005024307	0.00317263	0.09212	0.1886	2.508				
RVAC	−0.33129	0.06535	−0.45598	−0.52369	25.696				
INT	−0.47408	0.5626	−1.66929	−0.71471	71.006				
HAI	−0.03392	0.0053566	−1.28172	−0.60931	40.152	YDP82	−0.61346	−0.22881	3.702
						MPNEW	−0.73535	−0.29311	6.297
						HVAC	−0.0713	−0.10623	0.765

$R^2 = 0.93655$ R^2 change $= 0.03747$ $F = 143.38023$
ADJ $R^2 = 0.93002$ F change $= 40.15161$
SEE $= 0.17147$ Sig F change $= 0.0000$

Variable Added on Step 8

Variable	*Coefficient*	*Standard Error of Coefficient*	*Beta Coefficient*	*Partial Correlation Coefficient*	*F-to-Remove*	*Variable*	*Beta In*	*Partial Correlation Coefficient*	*F-to-Enter*
Constant	−1.39047	2.99691							
ADD	0.58584	0.16313	0.16483	0.40178	12.897	REN	−0.11055	−0.00964	0.006
HH	0.22508	0.03868	3.4491	0.57938	33.856				
PHOME	−0.03836	0.1077	−1.73539	−0.39914	12.697				
JCS	0.0003121998	0.00358665	0.0057242	0.01063	0.008				
RVAC	−0.39841	0.06839	−0.54836	−0.57982	33.932				
INT	−0.518	0.05695	−1.82395	−0.74335	82.744	YDP82	−0.31397	−0.10838	0.782
HAI	−0.03039	0.00534589	−1.14491	−0.57037	32.306				
MPNEW	−0.0000169542	0.0000067562	−0.73535	−0.29311	6.297	HVAC	−0.14492	−0.21504	3.2

$R^2 = 0.94200$ R^2 change $= 0.00545$ $F = 136.01816$
ADJ $R^2 = 0.93507$ F change $= 6.29728$
SEE $= 0.16516$ Sig F change $= 0.0145$

Variable Removed on Step 9

Variable	*Coefficient*	*Standard Error of Coefficient*	*Beta Coefficient*	*Partial Correlation Coefficient*	*F-to-Remove*	*Variable*	*Beta In*	*Partial Correlation Coefficient*	*F-to-Enter*
Constant	−1.36945	2.96529							
ADD	0.58467	0.16138	0.1645	0.40224	13.126	JCS	0.005724	0.01063	0.008
HH	0.22542	0.03819	3.45441	0.58201	34.833	REN	−0.11942	−0.01045	0.007
PHOME	−0.03793	0.00949686	−1.71595	−0.43591	15.952				
RVAC	−0.40212	0.5312	−0.55346	−0.67625	57.303				
INT	−0.52028	0.05021	−1.83197	−0.78248	107.381				
HAI	−0.0303	0.00522289	−1.14491	−0.57543	33.662	YDP82	−0.29862	−0.10456	0.741
MPNEW	−0.000017262	0.0000057141	−0.74871	−0.34999	9.126				
						HVAC	−0.14041	−0.21083	3.117

$R^2 = 0.94199$ R^2 change $= 0.00000$ $F = 157.75052$
ADJ $R^2 = 0.93602$ F change $= 0.00758$
SEE $= 0.16395$ Sig F change $= 0.0821$

Variable Added on Step 10

Variable	*Coefficient*	*Standard Error of Coefficient*	*Beta Coefficient*	*Partial Correlation Coefficient*	*F-to-Remove*	*Variable*	*Beta In*	*Partial Correlation Coefficient*	*F-to-Enter*
Constant	−1.42784	2.92038			10.4				
ADD	0.52425	0.16257	0.1475	0.36656	37.797				
HH	0.23259	0.03783	3.56422	0.60056	12.463	JCS	0.02373	0.04457	0.131
PHOME	−0.03396	0.00961915	−1.53629	−0.39604	45.511	REN	−0.14735	−0.01319	0.011
RVAC	−0.38164	0.05509	−0.51151	−0.636	113.66	YDP82	−0.18135	−0.06354	0.268
INT	−0.53137	0.04984	−1.87103	−0.79318	36.502				
HAI	−0.03124	0.00517081	−1.18034	−0.59386	12.435				
MPNEW	−0.0000218967	0.0000062065	−0.94972	−0.39566	3.117				
HVAC	−0.33768	0.19127	−0.14041	−0.21083					

$R^2 = 0.94457$ R^2 change $= 0.00258$ $F = 142.71789$
ADJ $R^2 = 0.93795$ F change $= 3.11668$
SEE $= 0.16146$ Sig F change $= 0.0821$

assumption that none of the variables are in the equation. This step serves two purposes. First, it is possible that none of the simple regression coefficients would be significantly different from zero. If this were true, the best estimate of SALES would correspond to the constant term or the mean value of sales. Second, this step presents the ranking of each of the variables in terms of the variation in Y that is explained. The largest F-to-enter, 47.92, is associated with ADD.

2. Since the largest F-to-enter exceeds 2.00, ADD becomes the first variable in the regression equation.

3. The results of ADD's inclusion are shown in step 1 in Figure 7-5. The remaining statistics have the same interpretation as in previous examples.

4. Next, all regression equations containing ADD and another variable are estimated and the F_c statistics calculated. These values are listed under the "F-to-enter" heading. HH has the highest F_c and it exceeds F_L, so HH enters the model.

5. The results of including HH with ADD are summarized at the beginning of step 2. Next, the routine tests whether ADD should be dropped. This test is shown in the "F-to-remove" column. Since F_c(ADD/HH) exceeds F_L, ADD is retained in the equation.

6. Next, all regression equations containing ADD, HH, and one more variable are tabulated, and the F values are computed and shown in step 2. Since PHOME's F-to-enter value is the largest and exceeds F_L, PHOME enters the model.

7. The first portion of step 3 summarizes the results of the inclusion of PHOME. As before, the routine tests whether any of the previously entered variables (ADD and HH) have F-to-remove values less than 2. Neither of them does; hence, the equation has ADD, HH, and PHOME as independent variables. Additionally, the introduction of one more variable into the model is considered.

8. Step 4 summarizes the results of including JCS, the variable with the largest F-to-enter value, in step 3. The test for removal of any of the preceding variables is now conducted, and all of the variables remain in the model. Since RVAC has the largest F-to-enter value and exceeds F_L, RVAC becomes the next candidate for inclusion. The removal test is applied to all included variables.

9. Step 5 summarizes the results of including RVAC. The next variable to be included into the model is INT, with the results of inserting this variable into the model presented in step 6. The housing affordability index (HAI) and the median price measure (MPNEW) become the next two variables to enter the model. At each of these stages the previous variables are tested to ensure that they remain in the model.

10. When the MPNEW variable enters the model, the JCS variable falls below the critical value and hence is removed from the model. Once this deletion is completed, the process then continues to examine the remaining variables for inclusion into the model. In the next step, the HVAC variable enters the model and the routine next tests for further insertions or deletions. Since none of the remaining variables exceeds the critical F-to-enter value, the process terminates.

The least-squares regression model for sales of single-family units can now be stated as

$$\widehat{\text{SALES}}_t = -1.42784 + 0.52425\text{ADD}_t + 0.23259\text{HH}_t$$
$$t_e \qquad\qquad\qquad 3.22 \qquad\qquad 6.15$$

$$- 0.03396\text{PHOME}_t - 0.37164\text{RVAC}_t - 0.53137\text{INT}_t \qquad \textbf{(7-35)}$$
$$3.53 \qquad\qquad 6.75 \qquad\qquad 10.66$$

$$- 0.03124\text{HAI}_t - 0.0000218967\text{MPNEW}_t - 0.33768\text{HVAC}_t.$$
$$6.04 \qquad\qquad 3.53 \qquad\qquad 1.77$$

$F_{8,67} = 142$	DW $= 1.14$
SEE $= 0.16146$	False Signals $= 64\%$
ADJ $R^2 = 0.94$	Missed Signals $= 60\%$

Both the equation and the coefficients are significant at the 0.05 level.

FIGURE 7-6   Reliability of Stepwise Housing Model in Historical Simulation

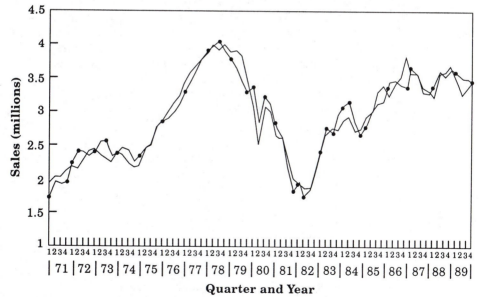

— Actual   —•— Predicted

FIGURE 7-7   Error Plot from Stepwise Housing Model

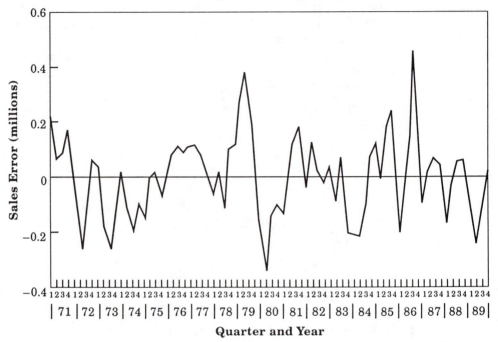

The coefficients are theoretically sound, since the signs match the a priori expectations. As a forecasting device, the equation tracks the historical data patterns reasonably well, as seen in Figures 7-6 (page 321) and 7-7. It is somewhat disturbing that the model generated false signals with respect to turning points 64 percent of the time and missed actual turning points or changes in direction 60 percent of the time; but this factor is mitigated somewhat by the fact that many of the turning-point errors occurred during periods of instability in the housing market. That is, one of the characteristics of the housing market is that during turbulent times, actual housing sales tend to exhibit almost a random pattern of changes alternating from increasing to decreasing to increasing, etc. However, the sensitivity of the model to turning-point errors suggests that forecasts must be monitored closely for their reliability.

LAGGED VARIABLES

INTRODUCTION

When all variables in a regression model are measured at time t (where t stands for a specific time period), the implicit assumption is that the effects of the independent variables on the dependent variable are completely felt during this time period. The validity of this assumption depends on the particular system being studied and modeled. There is, however, little reason to believe that all economic relationships are this perfectly synchronized in time. That is, in many markets a time lag is required before the participants can respond fully to changes in market forces. As a simple example of this delayed or lagged effect, consider the production and planting decision facing someone in the farming industry. In this environment, the price for a particular crop in a particular marketing year will be unknown at the time the planting decision must be made. In other words, production in time period t will not be determined by price in t because the price in t will be observable only after the crop has been harvested and taken to market. For this reason it seems much more reasonable to suggest that decision makers in this environment will make their planting decisions for this marketing year based on the observed price from the preceding marketing year. This pattern suggests that a more appropriate model in this situation would be

$$Q_t = \beta_0 + P_{t-1} + \epsilon_t \tag{7-36}$$

where P_{t-1} is a lagged variable.

Theoretical considerations may suggest either that the impact of a given economic factor may not manifest itself for several time periods or the impact may be distributed over several time periods. These delayed reactions or lags can range from extremely simple patterns such as that suggested by equation (7-36) to extremely complicated polynomial distributed lag patterns similar to

$$Y_t = \beta_0 + \beta_1 X_t + \beta_2 X_{t-1} + \beta_3 X_{t-2} + \ldots \beta_p X_{t-p} + \epsilon_t. \tag{7-37}$$

In these distributed lag models, the coefficient β_1 is the weight attached to X in the current time period and is frequently referred to as the impact multiplier, while the remaining coefficients are interim multipliers. Alternatively, the sum of all of the coefficients, β's, is the cumulative impact of X on Y, while β_1 is the short-term impact.

SIMPLE LAGGED RELATIONSHIPS

When an analyst sets out to construct a forecasting model, the choice of independent variables is influenced by theoretical considerations, statistical constraints, and data availability. Of particular interest here is the last constraint, data availability. For example, a sales forecasting equation might be formulated as

$$\hat{S}_t = \hat{\beta}_0 + \hat{\beta}_1 P_t + \hat{\beta}_2 Y_t + \hat{\beta}_3 \text{ADV}_t \tag{7-38}$$

where S_t is current dollar sales, P_t is price, Y_t is income, and ADV_t is advertising expenditures. Even if this equation is statistically significant and judged to be theoretically sound, estimates of future sales cannot be determined unless the variables, P_t, Y_t, and ADV_t, are determinable for the period in question. One common method of overcoming this difficulty is to use lagged values for the independent variables. Thus, equation (7-38) might be restated as

$$\hat{S}_t = \hat{\beta}_0 + \hat{\beta}_1 P_{t-1} + \hat{\beta}_2 Y_{t-1} + \hat{\beta}_3 \text{ADV}_{t-1}. \qquad \textbf{(7-39)}$$

With this formulation, estimates of sales in period t can be made based on prior-period values $(P_{t-1}, Y_{t-1},$ and $\text{ADV}_{t-1})$. Although the inclusion of lagged variables such as P_{t-1} presents no special problems in terms of satisfying the least-squares criteria, the issue of empirical identification of the length of these lags remains.

While there are numerous methods of identifying the nature of the lag pattern, the two most common are a graphical examination and estimating simple correlation coefficients. In applying these techniques, the time reference of the dependent variable is held constant and the independent variable is shifted forward n periods.

The simplest and generally the most reliable method is to graph the value of both variables over a number of time periods and then line up their peaks and troughs. Figure 7-8 presents a time plot of sales and income. A comparison

FIGURE 7-8 Relationship of Sales and Income Variables

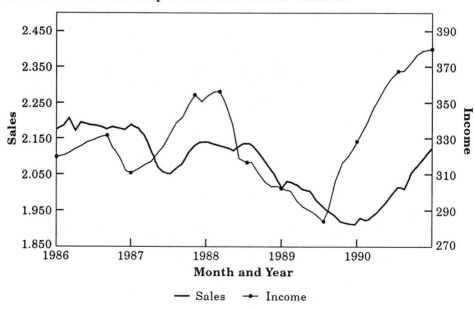

of the sales and income data in Figure 7-8 seems to indicate that turning points (changes of direction) in income occur approximately four months prior to sales turning points. Armed with this information, the regression model that would be estimated would be of the form

$$\hat{S}_t = \hat{\beta}_0 + \hat{\beta}_1 INC_{t-4}. \tag{7-40}$$

The second method would be to estimate a correlation matrix between the dependent variable and the independent variable(s) at different time lags. The time lag with the largest correlation coefficient would thus be used in the regression model.

EXAMPLE 7-11 Time Lags: Cash-Flow Forecasting

As an analyst with the accounts receivable department, you are charged with developing estimates of cash flows and of providing guidelines with respect to the percentage of credit sales that will remain unpaid (bad debts). An analysis of credit and discount policies indicates that payment within 10 days entitles the customer to a 2 percent discount while the full balance is due within 90 days.

Clearly, the cash flows or cash collections in any given month are a function of sales in the current and preceding time periods such that the following model seems appropriate:

$$\widehat{CF}_t = \hat{\beta}_0 + \hat{\beta}_1 S_t + \hat{\beta}_2 S_{t-1} + \hat{\beta}_3 S_{t-2} + \hat{\beta}_4 S_{t-3} \tag{7-41}$$

where CF refers to cash flows or collections in the current time period (t) and S to sales in the current and three preceding time periods. The length of the time lag is a function of credit and discount policies.

The least-squares model is derived from applying equation (7-41) to the data in Appendix F, Table F-5.

$$\widehat{CF}_t = 3480 + 0.62325 S_t + 0.19858 S_{t-1}$$
$$t_e \qquad\qquad 8.52 \qquad\qquad 2.58 \tag{7-42}$$
$$+ \ 0.05142 S_{t-2} + 0.0256 S_{t-3}$$
$$0.67 \qquad\qquad 0.35$$

ADJ R^2 = 0.87	SEE = 9427
$F_{4,64}$ = 119	DW = 2.16

An examination of the model statistics and Figure 7-9 indicates that the estimated model performs satisfactorily in the historical simulation. The coefficients associated with the sales figures imply that 62.3 percent of current-period sales generate cash, 19.9 percent of the preceding months sales generate cash in the current period, 5.1 percent of the sales two months ago generate cash, and 2.6 percent of sales three months ago

FIGURE 7-9   Development of a Cash-Flow Model with Lag Variables

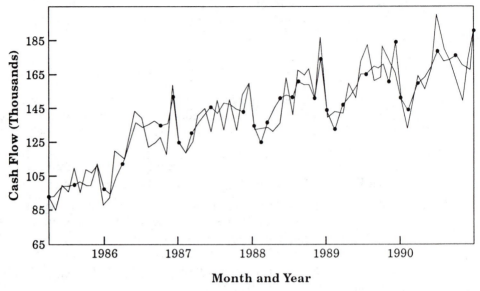

(a)
Historical Simulation of Cash Flow Model

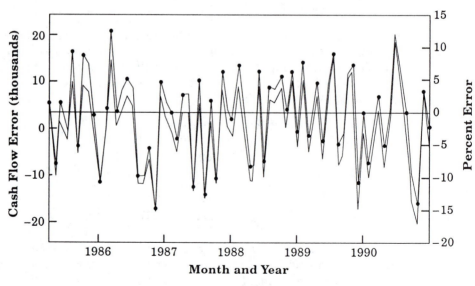

(b)
Error Plot from Cash Flow Projections

are received as cash in the current period. Furthermore, since these coefficients sum to 89.9, we would expect that an allowance for bad debts equal to approximately 10 percent of sales should be established.

DISTRIBUTED LAGS

A logical extension of simple lag models is the development of distributed lag models, which attempt to explain delayed responses when the effects of the independent variable(s) are spread out over a large number of periods. One way of estimating these lags is to include the value of the independent variable in each relevant period. For example, a new advertising campaign should generate a large sales increase the first month, with smaller and smaller increments in successive months. It is possible to express this theoretical model as

$$\hat{S}_t = \hat{\beta}_0 + \hat{\beta}_1 P_t + \hat{\beta}_2 Y_t + \hat{\beta}_3 \text{ADV}_t + \hat{\beta}_4 \text{ADV}_{t-1} + \hat{\beta}_5 \text{ADV}_{t-1} \qquad (7\text{-}43)$$
$$+ \hat{\beta}_6 \text{ADV}_{t-3} + \hat{\beta}_7 \text{ADV}_{t-4} + \ldots + \hat{\beta}_i \text{ADV}_{t-n}.$$

Direct estimation of equation (7-43) is likely to be difficult because of the high degree of multicollinearity between the advertising variables. That is, there is an insufficient amount of variation among the independent variables to permit statistically reliable estimation of the regression coefficients.

Since theoretical considerations suggest that current economic behavior is predicated on past values of certain variables, it is common practice for forecasters to include lags of different lengths for the same variable. The notion that the effect may be spread over several periods is the basis for the name *distributed lag*. In its most general form, the distributed lag model can be written as

$$Y_t = \beta_0 + \beta_1(w_0 X_t + w_1 X_{t-1} + w_2 X_{t-2} + \ldots) + \epsilon_t \qquad (7\text{-}44)$$

or

$$Y_t = \beta_0 + \beta_1 \sum_{i=1}^{n} w_i X_{1i} + \beta_2 \sum_{j=1}^{m} w_j X_{2j} + \epsilon_t. \qquad (7\text{-}45)$$

The only difference between these two equations is that in equation (7-45), Y_t is related to more than one independent variable. The distributed lag effect of the variable X on the variable Y is described by the specification of the weights, w's. Different sets of values for the weights imply different distributed lag schemes.[7]

---

[7] For a more complete understanding of the various schemes that fall within the category of distributed lag models, see either of the two following texts: J. Johnston, *Econometric Methods* (New York: McGraw-Hill, 1984), pp. 343–83; or Robert S. Pindyck and Daniel L. Rubinfeld, *Econometric Models and Economic Forecasts* 3rd ed., (New York: McGraw-Hill, 1991), pp. 204–215.

FIGURE 7-10   Geometric Lag Weights

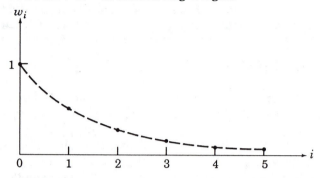

The general form of the geometric lag model is

$$Y_t = \beta_0 + \beta_1(X_t + wX_{t-1} + w^2X_{t-2} + w^3X_{t-3} + \ldots) + \epsilon_t \quad \textbf{(7-46)}$$

where $0 < w < 1$. In this lag scheme, the weights decline, so the effect of additional lagged variables is minimized. For example, the pattern where $w = \frac{1}{2}$ is graphically illustrated in Figure 7-10. Further, in this pattern, one half the effect of a change in X is registered in the first period. As formulated in equation (7-46), the model is difficult to estimate. This can be overcome by rewriting equation (7-46) as

$$Y_{t-1} = \beta_0 + \beta_1(X_{t-1} + wX_{t-2} + w^2X_{t-3} + \ldots) + \epsilon_t. \quad \textbf{(7-47)}$$

The next step is to calculate values for $Y_t - wY_{t-1}$:

$$Y_t - wY_{t-1} = \beta_0(1 - w) + \beta_1X_t + u_t \quad \textbf{(7-48)}$$

where $u_t = \epsilon_t - w\epsilon_{t-1}$. Rearranging, this becomes

$$Y_t = \beta_0(1 - w) + wY_{t-1} + \beta_1X_t + u_t \quad \textbf{(7-49)}$$

which can be more easily estimated with ordinary least squares (OLS).

To see how the analyst estimates a polynomial distributed lag model, consider the example of a second-degree polynomial (parabola) with a two-period lag. The general specification of this model is

$$Y_t = \beta_0 + w_0X_t + w_1X_{t-1} + w_2X_{t-2} + \epsilon_t. \quad \textbf{(7-50)}$$

The assumption of a second-degree polynomial for the weighting system implies that

$$w_i = c_0 + c_1i + c_2i^2 \quad i = 0, 1, 2. \quad \textbf{(7-51)}$$

Substituting this into equation (7-50) and rewriting yields

$$Y_t = \beta_0 + c_0 X_t + (c_0 + c_1 + c_2)X_{t-1} + (c_0 + 2c_1 + 4c_2)X_{t-2} + \epsilon_t \quad \textbf{(7-52)}$$

or

$$Y_t = \beta_0 + c_0(X_t + X_{t-1} + X_{t-2}) + c_1(X_{t-1} \quad \textbf{(7-53)}$$
$$+ 2X_{t-2}) + c_2(X_{t-1} + 4X_{t-2}) + \epsilon_t.$$

Equation (7-53) can be estimated using ordinary least-squares procedures. As long as the assumptions of the least-squares model are satisfied, the estimated c's are BLUE. Further, once the c's are estimated, the original lag weights, w's, can be determined by working backwards to equation (7-50). Two of the more common variations of equation (7-53) used in forecasting are the partial adjustment and the adaptive expectations models.

ADAPTIVE EXPECTATIONS MODEL

Reliance on lagged values, besides being helpful in forecasting, has some justification in theory. In time series models of economic behavior, a substantial period of time may elapse between the moment when a decision is made (price change) or an event occurs (income changes) and the period in which the total impact is measurable. People rarely change their behavior patterns immediately. Frequently, the response to a price change will be delayed as consumers assess the permanence of the change and their ability to respond to the change. In the case of a price decline, potential buyers may delay purchases in the belief that prices will decline even further. A similar time-lag pattern may exist between a change in income and a measurable change in consumer spending. Further, there are situations where contractual or informal commitments may extend beyond one time period. Indeed, this was the primary justification for the use of lagged sales values in the earlier cash-flow forecasting model.

The adaptive expectations model can be illustrated by

$$Y_t = \beta_0 + \beta_1 X_t^* + \epsilon_t \quad \textbf{(7-54)}$$

which suggests that Y_t depends on "expectations" concerning the causal variable, X_t. The "problem" with this model is that the expected value of the independent variable, X^*, is unobservable. If X^* were expected income, then it can be quantified by using income received in the previous period. The adaptive expectations model makes the following assumption:

$$X_t^* - X_{t-1}^* = \delta(X_t - X_{t-1}^*), \qquad 0 < \delta < 1 \quad \textbf{(7-55)}$$

which suggests that expectations are adjusted proportionally by the factor δ to the difference between expected values held in $t - 1$ and the actual value of X in t. That is, the adaptive expectations model assumes that expectations are revised each period in which an actual observation occurs by a proportion of the difference between the actual value of X_t and the previous expected value. In theory, this formulation suggests that decision makers or consumers learn by doing or observing actual values.

EXAMPLE 7-12   Adaptive Expectations and Forecasts of Consumption Expenditures

In attempting to develop forecasts for consumption expenditures, it is reasonable to approximate Friedman's permanent income hypothesis by specifying a model wherein consumption is a function of permanent income and the interest rate. Further, permanent income can be operationally measured as a function of income in the current time period as well as income in previous time periods. We would expect consumption to be positively related to permanent income and inversely related to the interest rate. To avoid the problems of autocorrelation and multicollinearity, a decision was made to use a polynomial distributed lag formulation of first differences. That is, the model as specified would be

$$\Delta C_t = \beta_0 + \beta_1 \Delta Y_t + \beta_2 \Delta Y_{t-1} + \ldots + \beta_k \Delta Y_{t-k} + \beta_4 r_t + \epsilon_t \quad \textbf{(7-56)}$$

where

$$
\begin{aligned}
C_t &= \text{quarterly personal consumption expenditures, billions of} \\
&\quad \text{dollars, seasonally adjusted} \\
\Delta C_t &= C_t - C_{t-1} \\
Y_t &= \text{quarterly disposable personal income, billions of dollars,} \\
&\quad \text{seasonally adjusted} \\
\Delta Y_t &= Y_t - Y_{t-1} \\
r_t &= \text{three-month average of three-month Treasury bills.}
\end{aligned}
$$

The data used in this example are contained in Appendix F, Table F-6.

There are three empirical issues that must be addressed in estimating equation (7-56). The first of these issues relates to the degree of the polynomial; the second to the number of lags to be included; and the third to the restrictions on the estimated coefficients associated with income levels. While previous research and theory offer some guidelines, to a large extent these issues will be resolved through a trial-and-error process of estimating various models. To illustrate this trial-and-error process, suppose for simplicity that we fit a third-degree polynomial with a five-period lag using varying end-point restrictions.[8]

Assuming no end-point restrictions, the first model estimated was

$$\Delta \hat{C}_t = 9.945 + 0.17498\Delta Y_t + 0.25031\Delta Y_{t-1} + 0.19380\Delta Y_{t-2}$$
$$t_e \qquad\qquad 2.48 \qquad\qquad 4.07 \qquad\qquad 4.06 \qquad (7\text{-}57)$$
$$+ 0.09513\Delta Y_{t-3} + 0.04401\Delta Y_{t-4} - 0.37317 r_t.$$
$$\qquad 1.50 \qquad\qquad 0.59 \qquad\qquad -0.60$$

ADJ R^2 = 0.48	DW = 1.91
1970: I to 1989:IV	F = 15.6
Mean Lag = 1.450	
Sum of Lag Coefficients = 0.76	

The interpretation of the coefficients of the lagged income variables would be as follows: An increase of $1 billion in the quarterly change in disposable personal income in the current time period leads to an increase in the change in consumption of $175 million in the first quarter, $250 million in the second quarter, $194 million in the fourth quarter, etc. The sum of the lag coefficients implies that changes in income in the preceding four periods leads to a total change in consumption of $760 million. The negative sign on the interest rate variable satisfies theoretical expectations, but it is not statistically significant.

The second model that was estimated is based on the zero-tail restriction. This restriction has the effect that the end weights become close to zero, as seen in equation (7-58):

$$\Delta \hat{C}_t = 9.99212 + 0.17646\Delta Y_t + 0.24069\Delta Y_{t-1} + 0.20110\Delta Y_{t-2}$$
$$t_e \qquad\qquad 2.51 \qquad\qquad 4.28 \qquad\qquad 4.60 \qquad (7\text{-}58)$$
$$+ 0.11176\Delta Y_{t-3} + 0.02671\Delta Y_{t-4} - 0.37391 r_t.$$
$$\qquad 2.36 \qquad\qquad 0.45 \qquad\qquad -0.61$$

The final model contained both a beginning and an end-point restriction and was estimated as

$$\Delta \hat{C}_t = 9.94917 + 0.18497\Delta Y_t + 0.23454\Delta Y_{t-1} + 0.19478\Delta Y_{t-2}$$
$$t_e \qquad\qquad 3.67 \qquad\qquad 5.37 \qquad\qquad 7.90 \qquad (7\text{-}59)$$
$$+ 0.11174\Delta Y_{t-3} + 0.03146\Delta Y_{t-4} - 0.37202 r_t.$$
$$\qquad 2.37 \qquad\qquad 0.60 \qquad\qquad -0.61$$

A comparison of equations (7-57), (7-58), and (7-59) indicates that the primary impact of the end-point restrictions is that the coefficients as-

---

[8] A five-period lag and a third-degree polynomial were selected by examining other models and through a trial-and-error process of estimating other forms.

sociated with income for longer time lags become smaller the longer the lag. The remaining coefficients, as well as the mean lag and sum of the lag coefficients, are virtually the same. Further, the lag pattern is identical for all three models.

EXAMPLE 7-13 Distributed Lags and the St. Louis Model[9]

The St. Louis equation provides an attempt to analyze and predict the impact of both monetary and fiscal policy on gross national product. Conceptually, the model can be stated as

$$\dot{Y}_t = \alpha_0 + \sum_{i=0}^{j} \beta_i \dot{M}_{t-i} + \sum_{i=0}^{k} \delta \dot{G}_{t-i} + \epsilon_t. \tag{7-60}$$

The dots over each variable signify that the measure that is used is a quarter-to-quarter annualized rate of change, and Y, M, and G represent nominal GNP, money (the M1 definition) and high-employment government expenditures, respectively.

Two models are presented in Table 7-7 for the study of the appropriate length of the lagged response. The impact of the different lag lengths manifests itself in the change in sign associated with the expenditures variable and the smaller SEE and the larger ADJ R^2 associated with the model containing a longer lag period. All of these statistics seem to suggest that the model with the longer lag structure is preferable to the alternative model.

The second consideration in evaluating the St. Louis model revolves around a determination of the appropriate polynomial degree. Three al-

---

TABLE 7-7 Alternative Lag Specifications of the St. Louis Model

	Specification 1	Specification 2
Terms in Model		
Money Supply	10	5
Expenditures	9	5
Sum of Coefficients		
Money Supply	1.163 (t_e = 4.50)	1.114 (t_e = 4.69)
Expenditures	−0.034 (t_e = 0.26)	0.082 (t_e = 0.82)
SEE	3.21	3.58
ADJ R^2	0.47	0.33
DW	2.17	2.01

---

[9] Dallas S. Batten and Daniel L. Thornton, "Polynomial Distributed Lags and the Estimation of the St. Louis Equation," *Federal Reserve Bank of St. Louis*, April 1983, pp. 13–25.

TABLE 7-8 Estimates of Various Specifications of St. Louis Model

	Model A	*Model B*	*Model C*
Sum of Coefficients			
Money Supply	1.143	1.081	1.086
Expenditures	−0.026	−0.008	0.110
SEE	3.24	3.42	3.65
ADJ R^2	0.46	0.39	0.31
DW	2.27	2.41	2.17

ternatives are presented in Table 7-8. In this table, model A has ninth-degree and seventh-degree polynomials on M and G, respectively; model B has sixth- and third-degree polynomials on M and G, respectively; and model C has four lags on both M and G and end-point constraints.

The results in Table 7-8 indicate that each of the two longer lag specifications performs better than the current specification (model C). In particular, while the long-run effects of monetary and fiscal policy are similar in all specifications, the short-run distributed lag response patterns are significantly different.

The final test involves an analysis of the impact of the end-point restrictions. The test of all four end-point constraints (head and tail on both M and G) is rejected for models A and B, but not for model C. The head constraint on M, however, is never rejected by the F test, and the tail constraint is rejected only for model B. These differences highlight that end-point restrictions should be analyzed for their validity.

PARTIAL ADJUSTMENT MODEL

Another common lag formulation arises in the context of habit or persistence in market behavior. For example, the number of automobiles that consumers buy in period t may in part be influenced by the number that they have purchased in $t - 1$. This type of behavior suggests the following formulation:

$$\hat{Y}_t = \beta_0 + \hat{\beta}_1 Y_{t-1}. \tag{7-61}$$

The rationale for this specification is that inertia (the high costs associated with making changes) or the lack of availability of resources can work to prevent a consumer or a producer from moving all the way from one "equilibrium" point to another distinct "equilibrium" point.

There are at least two problems with a partial adjustment model such as equation (7-61). First, the theoretical justification for such models is not rigorously stated. Second, the inclusion of the dependent variable as an independent variable poses serious problems when attempting to apply OLS techniques. Recall that one of the key assumptions behind the least-squares methodology is that there is no relationship between the independent variables and the error term. Clearly, this assumption is violated with this formulation since the "independent" variable is the dependent variable lagged one period. However, if the objective of the exercise is to maximize short-term forecasting accuracy, the enhanced predictive power of the model may outweigh its obvious statistical flaws.

EXAMPLE 7-14 Adjusting to Changing Fuel Prices

Suppose that the objective is to develop a forecasting model for the consumption of natural gas used for home heating as it relates to changing fuel prices. Since it is likely that consumers of natural gas cannot respond completely to any change in price in the immediate term, an appropriate model would be

$$\text{GAS}_t = \hat{\beta}_0 + \hat{\beta}_1 P_t + \hat{\beta}_2 \text{GAS}_{t-1} + e_t \tag{7-62}$$

where

$$\text{GAS}_t = \text{monthly consumption of natural gas, millions of cubic feet, seasonally adjusted}$$

$$P_t = \text{price per cubic foot of natural gas, } 1982 = 100.$$

The data for this example are provided in Appendix F, Table F-7. When equation (7-62) is fitted to the data from January 1975 to December 1989, the results are

$$\widehat{\text{GAS}_t} = 219.12988 - 0.47166 P_t + 0.82207 \text{GAS}_{t-1}. \tag{7-63}$$
$$t_e \qquad\qquad\qquad 2.87 \qquad\qquad 20.02$$

ADJ R^2 = 0.80	SEE = 42.990
$F_{2,177}$ = 350	APE = 4.2%

Figure 7-11 provides a comparison of the actual and predicted values.

In models where one of the independent variables is the dependent variable itself, the Durbin-Watson statistic is not an appropriate measure for autocorrelation. The Durbin h statistic is defined by

$$h = r\sqrt{\frac{n}{1 - n\,V(\hat{\beta}_i)}} \quad \text{for } n\,V(\hat{\beta}) < 1 \tag{7-64}$$

where $r \approx 1 - 0.5d$ and $V(\hat{\beta}_i)$ is the estimated variance of the regression coefficient associated with the lagged dependent variable, Y_{t-1}. If $h > 1.645$, we would reject the hypothesis that the residuals are not correlated. In this example, h equals 0.563, and we can accept the null hy-

FIGURE 7-11 Historical Reliability of Gas Consumption Model

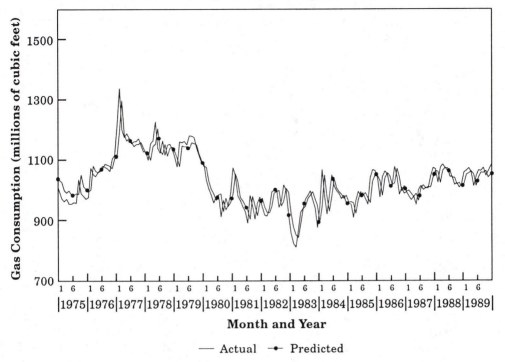

— Actual   -•- Predicted

pothesis that the residuals are not correlated (in other words, we conclude that the error terms are not autocorrelated).

QUESTIONS FOR DISCUSSION AND ANALYSIS

1. What is the difference between a proxy variable and a dummy variable?
2. Under what conditions would the use of a proxy variable be justified in a forecasting environment? Would these conditions change if your primary objective were the development of an explanatory model?
3. What theoretical justification can you make for including dummy variables in a regression model where outliers appear to be present?
4. What is the difference between the backward elimination and the forward inclusion method of stepwise regression analysis?
5. What explanations can you offer for using lagged variables in a regression model for forecasting? Would your explanations differ in an explanatory environment? Why or why not?

6. As a forecaster for a major metropolitan bank in a large southeastern city, one of your responsibilities is to provide management with forecasts of the number of new personal checking accounts on a quarterly basis. As a first step, you collect the information in the following table.

Date*	New Checking Accounts	Effective Monthly Service Charge	New Retail Outlets	Share of Voice	Interest Earned on Average Balance
1977:IV	80	5.8	3.8	7.2	1.42
1978:I	80	5.7	4.6	6.3	1.91
II	65	6.7	5.1	4.3	1.86
III	34	3.7	5.1	4.1	1.55
IV	58	8.7	4.5	2.3	2.52
1979:I	71	3.2	6.4	6.5	0.74
II	87	6.0	8.5	2.8	2.98
III	70	6.7	2.6	6.8	2.10
IV	72	5.2	5.4	5.6	2.71
1980:I	95	5.2	4.9	7.2	1.84
II	75	3.6	2.8	9.9	1.30
III	101	5.1	5.9	6.6	1.70
IV	101	6.5	7.3	4.1	2.01
1981:I	127	3.7	6.8	8.1	2.57
II	168	7.7	6.2	6.7	3.40
III	172	5.6	5.7	8.7	3.02
IV	109	5.2	5.2	7.6	2.85
1982:I	136	3.4	8.3	5.3	1.12
II	144	5.8	6.1	7.3	3.50
III	181	5.2	5.2	8.6	2.45
IV	178	5.8	7.6	5.9	2.58
1983:I	116	5.0	5.9	7.3	3.50
II	115	5.4	5.8	7.0	2.64
III	118	2.6	7.4	8.6	2.05
IV	120	4.3	0.8	11.9	2.85
1984:I	151	4.8	6.1	7.6	2.45
II	148	5.4	5.2	8.8	1.81
III	153	6.5	5.6	7.7	2.85
IV	191	3.4	7.7	9.3	1.48
1985:I	123	6.5	4.0	8.4	3.00
II	158	5.1	6.7	7.7	2.86
III	124	6.6	7.7	4.6	1.95
IV	125	6.1	8.5	4.0	1.21
1986:I	198	6.4	5.9	8.5	2.33
II	200	6.7	6.2	8.1	2.59
III	204	7.4	5.7	8.3	2.16
IV	202	6.0	6.7	9.3	2.50

Date*	New Checking Accounts	Effective Monthly Service Charge	New Retail Outlets	Share of Voice	Interest Earned on Average Balance
1987:I	203	3.7	7.6	9.4	2.40
II	215	7.3	6.8	7.4	3.56
III	217	7.4	7.4	6.8	2.40
IV	220	5.8	6.7	8.6	3.40
1988:I	276	6.3	5.9	10.0	2.95
II	295	5.8	7.2	9.3	3.30
III	184	5.3	5.1	9.9	2.60
IV	329	6.3	8.4	8.3	4.13
1989:I	330	5.8	8.3	8.8	3.95
II	311	4.5	7.3	10.6	3.05
III	398	4.8	8.6	10.1	4.10
IV	313	8.8	7.8	7.2	3.20
1990:I	310	3.9	8.2	10.3	4.55
II	483	8.8	8.6	8.8	6.40
III	509	7.8	6.5	11.5	4.30
IV	574	11.2	7.6	9.0	5.59
1991:1	830	5.8	9.6	11.4	3.95

* Year and quarter

The effective service charge is measured as dollars, SOV is measured as percentage of total industry advertising, and the effective interest rate on balances is measured as a percent.

Using the forward method stepwise procedure, develop your forecasting model.

7. Suppose that the primary consumer of your services is the legal industry, and your responsibility is to derive a forecasting model for sales to this industry. As a first attempt at developing this model, you collect the information presented in the following table.

Date*	Sales	Number of Legal Firms	Price
1986:I	24,624	1,396	17.40
II	26,724	1,400	17.00
III	29,223	1,403	17.05
IV	31,174	1,418	16.73
1987:I	33,020	1,439	16.49
II	34,633	1,448	16.17
III	35,709	1,460	16.04
IV	35,653	1,469	15.64
1988:I	36,303	1,484	15.35
II	37,832	1,494	15.40
III	38,502	1,508	15.55
IV	39,257	1,516	15.36

(*continued*)

Date*	Sales	Number of Legal Firms	Price
1989:I	39,206	1,521	15.19
II	38,372	1,527	15.17
III	38,436	1,539	15.21
IV	39,366	1,543	15.33
1990:I	38,663	1,553	15.48
II	36,934	1,560	15.95
III	36,692	1,573	16.15

* Year and quarter

a. Estimate a complete regression model for this data.
b. Despite the fact that the goodness-of-fit statistics suggest a reliable model, an examination of the error plot indicates that there may be problems with the model. Specifically, an examination of the actual data suggests that, beginning with the fourth quarter of 1988, sales have been relatively flat. Coincidentally, this corresponds to the quarter in which a new competitor entered the market.

   Test for the possibility that the stability of the model may have been altered as a result of the new entrant by using the dummy variable approach and the approach suggested by the Chow test in example 7-7.

8. Suppose that you are charged with developing a monthly forecasting model for tax collections. As a first step, you collect three years' worth of monthly data on tax collections as shown in the following table. An examination of the data indicates that there is a seasonal pattern in the data. Thus, prior to estimating a forecasting model, you decide to make an attempt at measuring the seasonality using the dummy variable approach.

Date	Tax Collections	Trend Factor
1988:Jan.	9,528	0
Feb.	17,979	1
Mar.	25,621	2
Apr.	18,415	3
May	9,743	4
June	7,887	5
July	6,629	6
Aug.	6,492	7
Sept.	7,308	8
Oct.	6,248	9
Nov.	5,544	10
Dec.	7,276	11
1989:Jan.	9,089	12
Feb.	20,133	13
Mar.	27,340	14
Apr.	16,831	15
May	9,901	16
June	8,742	17

Date	Tax Collections	Trend Factor
July	8,549	18
Aug.	7,738	19
Sept.	7,486	20
Oct.	6,820	21
Nov.	6,836	22
Dec.	7,155	23
1990:Jan.	11,806	24
Feb.	21,992	25
Mar.	27,307	26
Apr.	19,189	27
May	11,000	28
June	8,951	29
July	8,288	30
Aug.	8,135	31
Sept.	7,813	32
Oct.	7,137	33
Nov.	7,246	34
Dec.	7,507	35

Based on the data given, estimate a monthly model with the trend component and the relevant number of seasonal factors. How would you interpret each of the monthly seasonal factors?

9. In an attempt to provide management with a model that will measure the impact of pricing actions on shipments, you decide to develop a model relating shipments to price and production. The data for this example are as follows:

Date*	Shipments	Price	Production
1987:II	4,054	1.74	88.7
III	4,083	1.70	88.5
IV	4,376	1.71	88.2
1988:I	4,536	1.67	92.4
II	4,867	1.65	95.5
III	5,662	1.62	99.1
IV	6,549	1.60	101.5
1989:I	7,042	1.56	103.6
II	7,480	1.54	104.7
III	8,227	1.54	105.6
IV	8,858	1.56	109.7
1990:I	9,483	1.54	108.7
II	9,915	1.52	110.9
III	10,622	1.51	116.0
IV	12,115	1.45	116.2
1991:I	15,797	1.38	116.8

* Year and quarter

where price is measured in dollars and production is measured as thousands of units.

a. Estimate a regression model for shipments.
b. Estimate a logarithmic growth model for shipments.
c. Which of these two models appears to capture the pattern in the actual data?
d. What interpretation would give to the price variable in the logarithmic model?

10. Suppose you are charged with generating quarterly forecasts for the number of motel units that will be rented. You collect information on the number of tourists, the number of competitive units available, price, the average competitive price, and a top-of-mind awareness index. The top-of-mind awareness index provides information on the effectiveness of advertising programs, with the general belief that the higher this number, the more effective advertising programs are and the higher the rental rates. Information on these variables is provided in the following table.

Date*	Number of Units Rented	Number of Tourists (thousands)	Competitive Units Available	Price (dollars)	Competitive Price (dollars)	Top-of-Mind Awareness Index
1967:I	774	144.1	1,383	38.1	31.9	1.194
II	790	147.7	1,398	38.3	31.9	1.201
III	796	148.9	1,380	38.6	32.0	1.206
IV	832	150.6	1,425	38.8	32.3	1.201
1968:I	863	150.3	1,418	39.3	32.6	1.206
II	857	147.5	1,424	39.8	32.8	1.213
III	871	148.9	1,456	40.2	32.9	1.222
IV	861	145.8	1,515	40.4	33.2	1.217
1969:I	856	145.5	1,566	40.7	33.5	1.215
II	869	143.5	1,566	41.3	33.8	1.222
III	878	139.9	1,580	41.9	34.0	1.232
IV	880	135.1	1,562	42.4	34.4	1.233
1970:I	852	128.9	1,540	42.9	34.7	1.236
II	830	121.0	1,530	43.4	35.1	1.236
III	812	115.7	1,558	43.1	35.3	1.221
IV	780	112.0	1,488	43.4	35.7	1.216
1971:I	755	109.7	1,486	44.6	36.0	1.239
II	735	108.6	1,510	45.3	36.3	1.248
III	741	106.7	1,503	45.9	36.8	1.247
IV	753	104.3	1,541	46.2	37.0	1.249
1972:I	793	105.3	1,593	46.8	37.3	1.255
II	813	105.5	1,631	46.9	37.6	1.247
III	825	103.3	1,670	47.0	37.8	1.243
IV	845	103.1	1,805	46.7	38.2	1.223
1973:I	852	103.1	1,910	46.8	38.9	1.203
II	886	101.8	1,998	47.2	40.0	1.180
III	911	101.1	2,024	47.5	40.5	1.173
IV	915	101.6	2,051	47.8	41.8	1.144
1974:I	916	99.6	2,055	48.4	44.4	1.090
II	924	99.5	2,058	49.4	48.0	1.029
III	885	101.1	2,038	52.2	51.3	1.018
IV	944	101.6	1,957	54.7	53.2	1.028
1975:I	920	99.0	1,805	57.5	54.0	1.065
II	900	98.8	1,762	59.4	54.3	1.094
III	887	98.3	1,772	60.6	55.0	1.102
IV	873	98.0	1,798	61.5	56.3	1.092

Date*	Number of Units Rented	Number of Tourists (thousands)	Competitive Units Available	Price (dollars)	Competitive Price (dollars)	Top-of-Mind Awareness Index
1976:I	881	100.5	1,811	62.8	57.1	1.100
II	885	99.9	1,831	63.9	57.7	1.107
III	888	100.0	1,879	64.8	58.8	1.102
IV	928	100.1	1,927	66.0	60.0	1.100
1977:I	946	99.0	2,072	66.6	60.9	1.094
II	984	102.1	2,122	67.7	62.0	1.092
III	1,012	102.7	2,168	68.8	63.0	1.092
IV	1,058	96.3	2,266	70.1	64.0	1.095
1978:I	1,096	98.1	2,282	71.4	65.0	1.098
II	1,161	101.3	2,438	72.7	66.3	1.097
III	1,238	102.6	2,471	73.9	67.7	1.092
IV	1,285	102.9	2,521	75.0	69.3	1.082
1979:I	1,340	104.0	2,609	76.4	71.3	1.072
II	1,384	102.9	2,568	77.9	74.0	1.053
III	1,423	105.0	2,612	79.3	77.2	1.027
IV	1,466	110.3	2,562	80.7	80.6	1.001
1980:I	1,518	113.1	2,575	82.8	84.7	0.978
II	1,546	115.7	2,380	85.0	87.0	0.977
III	1,553	115.4	2,369	87.4	89.0	0.982
IV	1,569	117.4	2,396	88.8	91.1	0.975
1981:I	1,581	117.2	2,450	90.8	94.5	0.961
II	1,606	116.6	2,460	92.8	97.4	0.953
III	1,634	120.3	2,497	94.5	98.4	0.960
IV	1,653	125.2	2,448	96.5	99.2	0.973
1982:I	1,669	127.4	2,359	98.2	99.6	0.986
II	1,673	133.0	2,249	99.7	99.2	1.005
III	1,667	134.6	2,187	100.8	100.3	1.005
IV	1,667	136.9	2,141	101.5	100.8	1.007
1983:I	1,689	139.1	2,134	100.5	100.4	1.001
II	1,746	142.6	2,255	99.7	100.4	0.993
III	1,780	145.4	2,381	98.9	101.6	0.973
IV	1,837	145.4	2,588	99.1	101.9	0.973
1984:I	1,910	150.2	2,635	98.5	102.6	0.960
II	1,980	155.2	2,777	97.9	103.5	0.946
III	2,053	158.8	2,872	97.4	103.6	0.940
IV	2,121	161.4	2,973	97.0	103.4	0.938
1985:I	2,160	165.3	2,971	95.9	103.3	0.928
II	2,176	169.8	3,064	95.0	104.0	0.913
III	2,165	173.4	3,015	95.3	103.7	0.919
IV	2,156	176.9	3,111	95.0	103.9	0.914
1986:I	2,089	178.5	3,045	94.8	102.1	0.929
II	2,089	180.2	3,098	95.7	99.8	0.959
III	2,157	183.6	3,068	97.0	98.8	0.982
IV	2,189	185.8	3,123	96.8	99.0	0.978
1987:I	2,235	188.3	3,107	94.8	100.8	0.940
II	2,201	189.0	3,279	93.9	102.0	0.921
III	2,212	189.2	3,473	92.1	103.5	0.890
IV	2,189	189.3	3,470	92.1	104.0	0.886

(continued)

Date*	Number of Units Rented	Number of Tourists (thousands)	Competitive Units Available	Price (dollars)	Competitive Price (dollars)	Top-of-Mind Awareness Index
1988:I	2,224	190.5	3,618	92.7	104.6	0.886
II	2,214	186.0	3,753	92.5	106.1	0.872
III	2,202	184.8	3,780	92.9	107.0	0.868
IV	2,122	182.2	3,713	95.2	107.5	0.886
1989:I	2,113	179.3	3,799	94.4	110.1	0.857
II	2,104	180.6	3,932	94.1	112.3	0.838
III	2,103	182.3	3,976	93.9	111.9	0.839
IV	2,076	176.8	3,890	93.7	112.2	0.835
1990:I	2,088	178.6	3,951	94.6	114.2	0.828
II	2,103	179.8	3,984	95.1	114.0	0.834
III	2,126	180.3	4,011	95.4	114.1	0.836
IV	2,150	181.4	4,037	96.0	114.7	0.837

* Year and quarter

a. Estimate a regression model for the number of units rented.
b. Do the signs on all of the variables match theoretical expectations? Why or why not?
c. Estimate a model where the variables have been transformed to logs.
d. What happened to the signs on the variables?
e. What model would you select in making forecasts? Why?

11. Suppose that you estimate a regression model for the sales data presented in the following table. The sign on the price coefficient clearly contradicts theoretical expectations. Now carry out a reciprocal transformation on price and reestimate the model. What happened to the sign on the price variable?

Date*	Sales (thousands)	Price (dollars)	Reciprocal of Price
1984:IV	123	2.4	0.417
1985:I	500	2.7	0.370
II	558	3.1	0.323
III	653	2.9	0.345
IV	1,057	3.4	0.294
1986:I	1,137	3.6	0.278
II	1,144	4.0	0.250
III	1,194	4.1	0.244
IV	1,501	5.4	0.185
1987:I	1,562	4.6	0.217
II	1,582	5.0	0.200
III	1,737	5.8	0.172
IV	1,822	7.0	0.143
1988:I	1,822	6.0	0.167
II	1,866	6.2	0.161
III	1,930	6.4	0.156
IV	2,088	7.4	0.135

Date*	Sales (thousands)	Price (dollars)	Reciprocal of Price
1989:I	2,112	8.8	0.114
II	2,166	8.2	0.122
III	2,179	7.9	0.127
IV	2,236	10.0	0.100
1990:I	2,294	9.6	0.104
II	2,303	9.1	0.110
III	2,310	10.2	0.098
IV	2,386	9.7	0.103

* Year and quarter

12. Suppose that you are given the information provided in the following table and are charged with developing a forecasting model for sales. Based on this information, conduct a stepwise regression analysis to develop your final model.

Date*	Sales (thousands)	Households (thousands)	Number of Stores	Share of Voice (percent)	Price (dollars)	Competitive Price (dollars)	Income (billions of dollars)
1983:IV	272	783	34	40.55	16.66	13.20	542.5
1984:I	264	748	37	36.19	16.46	14.11	551.1
II	239	684	35	37.31	17.66	15.68	556.0
III	231	828	33	32.52	17.50	10.53	556.3
IV	252	860	36	33.71	16.40	11.00	570.0
1985:I	258	875	34	34.14	16.28	11.31	580.0
II	264	909	35	34.85	16.06	11.96	588.0
III	267	906	35	35.89	15.93	12.58	597.4
IV	229	756	36	33.53	16.60	10.66	619.3
1986:I	239	769	36	33.80	16.41	10.85	630.8
II	258	794	35	34.72	16.17	11.41	642.5
III	258	802	35	35.22	15.92	11.91	662.1
IV	267	820	34	36.50	16.04	12.85	683.2
1987:I	267	809	32	37.60	16.19	13.58	700.2
II	260	775	34	37.89	16.62	14.21	716.1
III	240	712	31	37.71	17.37	15.56	735.3
IV	227	695	36	37.00	18.12	15.83	748.1
1988:I	196	638	34	36.76	18.53	16.41	765.7
II	279	776	35	34.62	15.54	13.10	784.4
III	272	758	36	35.40	15.70	13.63	792.3
IV	267	753	36	35.96	16.45	14.51	791.7
1989:I	255	705	38	36.26	17.62	15.38	800.1
II	225	667	35	36.34	18.12	16.10	821.1
III	182	569	35	35.90	19.05	16.73	945.5
IV	227	653	36	31.84	16.51	10.58	871.0
1990:I	254	704	36	33.16	16.02	11.28	889.1
II	263	710	36	33.83	15.89	11.91	908.2
III	266	727	36	34.89	15.83	12.65	929.7
IV	264	697	37	36.27	16.71	14.06	949.8

* Year and quarter

13. Provide an intuitive explanation for the use of distributed lag models in a forecasting environment. Would this explanation suffice in an explanatory environment? Why or why not?

REFERENCES FOR FURTHER STUDY

Abraham, Bovas and Johannes Ledolter, *Statistical Methods for Forecasting.* New York: John Wiley & Sons, 1983.

Almon, Shirley, "The Distributed Lag Between Capital Appropriations and Expenditures," *Econometrica,* vol. 33, 1965, pp. 178–96.

Armstrong, J. S., "Forecasting with Econometric Methods: Folklore versus Fact," *Journal of Business,* vol. 51, 1978, pp. 549–64.

Dhrymes, P. J., *Distributed Lags: Problems of Estimation and Formulation.* San Francisco: Holden-Day, 1971.

Fair, R., "A Comparison of Alternative Estimators of Macroeconomic Models," *International Economic Review,* vol. 14, no. 2, June 1973, pp. 261–77.

Fair, R., "The Estimation of Simultaneous Equation Models with Lagged Endogenous Variables and First Order Serially Corrected Errors," *Econometrica,* May 1970.

Fisher, F. M., *The Identification Problem in Econometrics.* New York: McGraw-Hill, 1966.

Friedman, Milton, *A Theory of the Consumption Function.* Princeton, N.J.: Princeton University Press, 1957.

Glasser, M., "Linear Regression Analysis with Missing Observations among Independent Variables," *Journal of the American Statistical Association,* vol. 59, 1964, 834–44.

Hertz, D. B. and K. H. Schaffir, "A Forecasting Model for Management of Seasonal Style Goods Inventories," *Operations Research,* vol. 8, no. 2, 1960, pp. 45–52.

Intriligator, Michael D., *Econometric Models, Techniques, & Applications.* Englewood Cliffs, N.J.: Prentice Hall, 1978.

Johnston, J. *Econometric Methods.* New York: McGraw-Hill, 1984.

Kleinbaum, David G., Lawrence L. Kupper, and Keith E. Muller, *Applied Regression Analysis and Other Multivariable Methods.* Boston: PWS-Kent Publishing Company, 1988.

Koyck, L. M., *Distributed Lags and Investment Analysis.* Amsterdam: North-Holland, 1954.

Michael, G. C., "A Computer Simulation Model for Forecasting Catalog Sales," *Journal of Marketing Research,* May 1971, pp. 224–29.

Neter, John, William Wasserman, and Michael H. Kutner, *Applied Linear Statistical Models,* 2nd ed. Homewood, Ill.: Richard D. Irwin, 1985.

Ramanathan, Ramu, *Introductory Econometrics: With Applications.* San Diego: Harcourt Brace Jovanovich, 1989.

Schmidt, P. and R. N. Waud, "Almon Lag Technique and the Monetary versus Fiscal Policy Debate," *Journal of the American Statistical Association,* vol. 68, 1973, pp. 11–19.

Tabachnick, Barbara G. and Linda S. Fidell, *Using Multivariate Statistics,* 2nd ed. New York: Harper & Row, 1989.

Wallis, K. F., "Lagged Dependent Variables and Serially Corrected Errors: A Reappraisal of Three-Pass Least Squares," *Review of Economics and Statistics,* vol. 49, 1967, pp. 555–67.

Wonnacott, Ronald J. and Thomas H. Wonnacott, *Econometrics,* 2nd ed. New York: John Wiley & Sons, 1979.

8

Time Series Models

INTRODUCTION

Regression models make use of economic interrelationships between a specified set of independent variables, X_i's, and the dependent variable, Y, for the purpose of explaining fluctuations in the dependent variable. While a regression model designed to forecast sales of lettuce might incorporate such explanatory factors as the price of lettuce, the price of substitutes, and the level of consumer income, the model may still not work well because of the forecaster's inability to account for variables such as fluctuations in the weather, changes in tastes and preferences, and a host of other factors. Alternatively, the model may closely approximate the historical pattern exhibited by lettuce sales but fall short as a forecasting model because accurate future estimates of the independent variables are not available. Thus, there will be numerous situations in which regression or explanatory models do not generate reliable forecasts.

Such limitations for regression models lead us to consider the second general type of quantitative forecasting technique: time series or autoregressive models. The cardinal premise underlying all time series models is that the historical pattern of the dependent variable can be used as the basis for developing forecasts. In these models, historical data for the forecast variable are analyzed in an attempt to discern any underlying pattern(s). Once identified, this pattern is extrapolated into the future to generate the forecast values. While all time series models are based on this extrapolation of historical data patterns, they differ in the way in which they use or extrapolate the historical data. Moving average models assign equal weights to past periods, while exponential smoothing models assign heavier weights to more recent data points. No matter how mathematically simple or complex, all time series models rely on an analysis and extrapolation of historical data patterns.

Time series or autoregressive forecasting models will, as a result of their dependence on historical data patterns, be most useful when economic conditions can be expected to remain relatively stable. Alternatively, they will yield misleading results when conditions are in a state of flux. For example, a time series model can be used to estimate short-run company demand patterns as long as management expects to continue its present advertising and pricing policies. However, these models will be ineffectual in evaluating or predicting the probable change in sales resulting from either a new advertising campaign or a change in the structure of prices.

The reliance of time series models on analysis and extrapolation of historical patterns carries several important implications with respect to technique selection (see chapter 4):

1. Time series models are best applied when the time frame or horizon of interest is immediate or short term in nature. That is, forecasts from these techniques are most reliable when the forecast horizon is from one day to six months, a period in which historical data patterns dominate.

2. Time series models prove most satisfactory when the historical data contain either no systematic data pattern or when the changes are occurring very slowly or consistently.

3. Costs of estimating time series models can range from a few cents for models such as a naive model, to several hundred dollars for exponential smoothing models, to several thousand dollars for multivariate Box-Jenkins models.

4. Data requirements and ease of implementation are a function of the specific time series technique that is selected. The principal limitation of time series models is their reliance on the assumption that historical data patterns will continue into the future. Because management is frequently interested in turning points, forecasts generated by time series techniques must be augmented by intuitive judgments to determine cyclical highs and lows.

PATTERN IDENTIFICATION: DIFFERENCING

In time series analysis, specific models are applicable to particular trend patterns, and it is therefore necessary to review the technique of differencing (see chapter 3). To determine whether a linear trend, a nonlinear trend, or some other pattern exists in the data being studied, we look at the trend pattern in terms of its pattern of time-period-to-time-period changes. (For a complete review of the mathematics of differencing, consult the relevant section in chapter 3.) As a preliminary step in using time series techniques, the trend pattern should be identified:

1. If the original data are stationary, this is indicative of no trend pattern in the data.
2. If the first differences are stationary, the underlying trend pattern is linear.
3. If the second differences are stationary, the underlying trend pattern is best captured with a parabola or second-degree trend line.
4. If the first differences of the logarithms are stationary, this is indicative of a constant growth pattern.

SIMPLE TIME SERIES MODELS

INTRODUCTION

Elaborate statistical models are not always required for the development of accurate forecasts. Indeed, the principle of parsimony suggests that the simpler the model the better. The principal advantage of the simple time series models presented here is that they serve as a benchmark with which to gauge the applicability, reliability, and necessity of the more sophisticated models. That is, the utility of these techniques should not be overlooked because of their simplicity. Frequently, they provide more accurate forecasts than do the more complex techniques. Since these simple methods tend to be less costly and easier to implement and understand, it is possible that the higher cost and increased complexity of more sophisticated models may outweigh any gains in accuracy. The key to selection of the proper model is its ability to capture the pattern exhibited by the actual historical data, not its complexity. The principal limitation of these models is that they will not generally perform well if the time series is dominated by cyclical patterns or, in general, by turning points.

Suppose that we are interested in developing a monthly forecast for cash outflow in the form of wages. Column 1 of Table 8-1 provides historical detail relative to the total wages paid on a seasonally adjusted monthly basis for the time period ranging from January 1986 through March 1990. Further, for purposes of this discussion, suppose that we are at the end of March 1990 and are interested in developing a three-month forecast. In turn, this wage forecast will be used by others to plan cash-flow requirements. To illustrate several aspects of model selection with time series models, the first time series estimate will exclude the last three data points. That is, January through March 1990 will be excluded from initial model estimation, thereby permitting us to evaluate the model's reliability in generating ex post forecasts.

MEAN FORECAST

The general form for the mean forecasting technique is

$$\hat{Y}_{t+T} = \overline{Y}.$$

(8-1)

TABLE 8-1   Historical Simulations from Simple Time Series Models

Date	Total Wages Paid (dollars) (1)	Mean (2)	Naive (3)	Simple Average Change (4)	Simple Percentage Change (5)
1986: Jan.	134,394				
Feb.	140,376		134,394		
Mar.	145,561	137,385	140,376	146,358	146,625
Apr.	150,233	140,110	145,561	151,144	151,489
May	154,446	142,641	150,233	155,513	155,919
June	158,476	145,002	154,446	159,459	159,913
July	163,209	147,248	158,476	163,292	163,791
Aug.	169,708	149,528	163,209	168,012	168,583
Sept.	178,917	152,050	169,708	174,753	175,463
Oct.	189,900	155,036	178,917	184,482	185,439
Nov.	200,003	158,522	189,900	196,067	197,349
Dec.	207,361	162,293	200,003	206,564	208,127
1987: Jan.	212,602	166,049	207,361	213,994	215,712
Feb.	217,710	169,630	212,602	219,119	220,898
Mar.	223,878	173,064	217,710	224,119	225,955
Apr.	230,893	176,452	223,878	230,270	232,204
May	238,751	179,854	230,893	237,326	239,389
June	247,020	183,319	238,751	245,273	247,495
July	254,754	186,858	247,020	253,645	256,038
Aug.	261,207	190,431	254,754	261,441	263,981
Sept.	267,080	193,970	261,207	267,881	270,518
Oct.	272,360	197,451	267,080	273,714	276,425
Nov.	277,208	200,856	272,360	278,930	281,692
Dec.	281,762	204,176	277,208	283,700	286,499
1988: Jan.	286,187	207,409	281,762	288,169	290,996
Feb.	291,245	210,560	286,187	292,512	295,362
Mar.	298,425	213,663	291,245	297,519	300,415
Apr.	306,418	216,802	298,425	304,734	307,743
May	312,718	220,003	306,418	312,789	315,935
June	316,820	223,200	312,718	319,087	322,313
July	321,426	226,321	316,820	323,111	326,349
Aug.	326,749	229,389	321,426	327,660	330,927
Sept.	330,553	232,431	326,749	332,954	336,271
Oct.	332,051	235,405	330,553	336,683	340,005
Nov.	333,392	238,247	332,051	338,041	341,303
Dec.	337,518	240,966	333,392	339,245	342,448
1989: Jan.	344,985	243,648	337,518	343,322	346,544
Feb.	351,751	246,386	344,985	350,835	354,166
Mar.	354,678	249,159	351,751	357,626	361,046
Apr.	355,254	251,865	354,678	360,475	363,881
May	356,758	254,449	355,254	360,917	364,250
June	360,524	256,945	356,758	362,317	365,604
July	364,261	259,411	360,524	366,039	369,338
Aug.	365,832	261,849	364,261	369,734	373,045
Sept.	364,864	264,213	365,832	371,214	374,485
Oct.	364,531	266,449	364,864	370,102	373,276
Nov.	366,498	268,582	364,531	369,645	372,741
Dec.	369,386	270,665	366,498	371,544	374,616
1990: Jan.	371,555				
Feb.	373,004				
Mar.	373,875				

In this formulation, T equals the number of time periods into the future for which the forecast is desired and $\overline{Y}$ refers to the arithmetic mean of the actual historical time series. This methodology assumes that the forecast value of any variable is equal to the average value of the variable over the historical time period. Thus, at a given point, the forecast for every period will be the same and will be equal to the average of the historical data. Each time a new observation is recorded, the mean value should be recomputed and a new set of forecasts generated.

The mean forecast model will perform most satisfactorily when the historical time series contains no discernible pattern. That is, the historical data fluctuate around a constant or stationary value. To illustrate the use and updating of this method, suppose that we are at the end of period 2, February 1986, and are interested in generating a forecast for March 1986. An application of equation (8-1) to the first two time periods yields a mean value of 137,385 {(134,394 + 140,376)/2}. This average of the first two time periods thus becomes the forecast for the third time period. At the end of the third time period, this forecast is updated by recomputing a new mean value of 140,110 {(134,394 + 140,376 + 145,561)/3} and this becomes the forecast for April of 1986. This process is iteratively applied to the remainder of the actual data, with the results as presented in column 2 of Table 8-1.

The principal limitation of the average model is its assumption that the historical data contain no systematic pattern. This assumption severely limits the general applicability of the mean forecasting model. Nevertheless, there may be situations where this characteristic prevails. For example, in many businesses, one of the primary forecasting objectives is the prediction of required inventory levels. In these situations, the mean forecasting model can prove useful.

NAIVE MODEL

The naive forecasting technique is based on a model of the form

$$\hat{Y}_{t+T} = Y_t \qquad (8\text{-}2)$$

where T refers to the number of periods into the future for which a forecast is desired. With this particular model, all future forecasts are set equal to the actual observed value in the most recent time period. Thus, as was the case with the mean forecasting model, the naive model will prove most satisfactory when the actual historical data contain no systematic pattern, or a pattern that is changing very slowly.

Applying equation (8-2) to the wages data, the forecast value for February 1986 is equal to the observed value in January 1986, while the March forecast equals the actual value in February 1986, and so on. The remainder of the naive historically simulated values are presented in column 3 of Table 8-1.

When the data series in question is changing very slowly and with few turning points, this method can generate useful short-term forecasts.

AVERAGE CHANGE MODEL

The average change technique is based on the premise that the forecast value is equal to the actual value in the current time period plus the average of the absolute changes experienced up to that point in time (where *absolute* means that the changes are stated in numerical units consistent with the variable that we are interested in forecasting). That is,

$$\hat{Y}_{t+T} = Y_t + \text{Average of Changes.} \tag{8-3}$$

The average change model is similar to a trend model, with the exception that it is less influenced by all of the historical observations and it responds relatively quickly to changes in the actual time series. Further, this model is most useful when the historical data being analyzed are characterized by period-to-period changes that are approximately the same size. If these changes are randomly dispersed, the average change model will overreact to these random changes.

To apply the average change model to our wages example, suppose that we are at the end of period 3 (March 1986) and want to generate a forecast for period 4 (April 1986). The first step would be to compute the average of the previous changes as follows:

$$\text{Average of Changes} = \frac{(140{,}376 - 134{,}394) + (145{,}561 - 140{,}376)}{2}$$

$$= \frac{5{,}982 + 5{,}185}{2} \tag{8-4}$$

$$= 5{,}583.5.$$

This value is then added to the actual value in March 1986 to generate the forecast value for April of 151,144.5 (145,561 + 5,583.5). This process is then repeated at the end of April to generate a forecast of 155,513 {(15,839/3) + 150,233}. The remainder of the historically simulated values from the average change model are presented in column 4 of Table 8-1.

The principal limitations of this model are that it tends to lag behind turning points and that all periods are weighted equally in deriving the current forecast. Despite these limitations, the average change model can provide useful short- to intermediate-term forecasts when the actual time series is dominated by a consistent pattern of changes.

AVERAGE PERCENT CHANGE

The average percent method assumes that the forecast value of the dependent variable is equal to the actual level of that variable in the current time period plus the average of the percentage changes from one time period to the next. Thus, this model is similar to the average change model except that percentage changes are used instead of the absolute changes. The average percent change model can be formally stated as

$$\hat{Y}_{t+T} = Y_t + \text{Average of Percent Changes.} \qquad (8\text{-}5)$$

The most significant aspect of this model is that the forecasts are based on percentage changes in the historical data, and therefore this approach is most appropriate for time series that exhibit a constant percentage growth rate. For example, if a historical time series is growing at an accelerating percentage growth rate, the average percent method will tend to underestimate this growth. When applied to the wages data, the first step is to compute the absolute changes on a month-to-month basis. These absolute changes are then converted to percentage figures. Suppose that we are at the end of March 1986 and are interested in generating a forecast for April 1986:

$$
\begin{aligned}
\text{Average of} \atop \text{Percent Changes} &= \frac{\{(5{,}982/134{,}394) + (5{,}185/140{,}376)\}}{2} \\[2mm]
&\approx \frac{0.0445 + 0.0369}{2} \qquad (8\text{-}6) \\[2mm]
&\approx 0.0407 \text{ or } 4.07\%.
\end{aligned}
$$

This growth rate is then applied to the actual value in March 1986 in the following fashion:

$$
\begin{aligned}
\hat{Y}_{1986:\text{April}} &= Y_{1986:\text{March}} \cdot 1.0407 \\
&= (145{,}561) \cdot 1.0407 \qquad (8\text{-}7) \\
&\approx 151{,}489.
\end{aligned}
$$

The remainder of the historical simulations are generated in a similar fashion and are presented in column 5 of Table 8-1.

The principal feature of this model is that all forecasts are extrapolations of the growth rate that is present in the historical data. When this assumption is used to generate forecasts, there may be a tendency to overstate future growth. That is, this technique may be unsuitable for forecasting beyond one or two months since the compounding effect will, over time, produce very high forecasts. Additionally, this model assigns an equal weight to all historical time periods.

FIGURE 8-1 **Comparative Reliability of Simple Models in Historical Simulation of Wages**

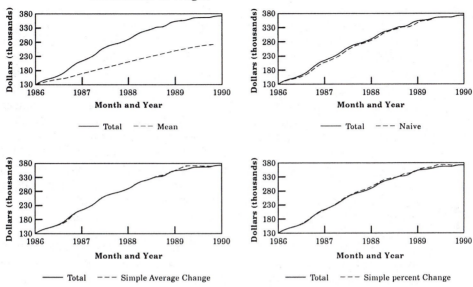

COMPARISON AND EVALUATION OF SIMPLE FORECASTING MODELS

Figure 8-1 and Table 8-2 provide the information that is required for an assessment of the simple forecasting models. The best model is the one that has the lowest MAPE and MAD and minimizes the bias inherent in the model.

TABLE 8-2 **Evaluation of Simple Forecasting Models**[1]

	Model			
Statistic	*Mean*	*Naive*	*Average Change*	*Average Percent Change*
MAPE*	24.32%	2.13%	0.76%	1.33%
MAD	72,085	5,055	2,123	3,915
Mean Error	−72,085	−5,000	988	3,407
Mean Percent Error	−24.32%	−2.13%	0.24%	1.05%

* See chapter 4 for definition of MAPE and MAD.

[1] Recall that in previous chapters we have suggested reversing the signs on the error terms when making managerial presentations. If this procedure is followed, care must be exercised in computing the evaluation statistics as some of them will be influenced by the sign on the error terms. For example, the sign on the mean error should be reversed.

Generally, one model performs better according to all the criteria. Should this not be the case, you must rely on your own judgment in selecting the most appropriate model.

A comparison of the evaluation statistics in Table 8-2 reveals that the average change model performs best in all categories. The MAPE and MAD are certainly within acceptable limits of forecasting error, while the mean error and mean percent error computations suggest that there is no consistent bias in the historically simulated values from the average change model. The mean forecasting model consistently lags behind the actual growth in checking accounts. This is a typical problem with this model when the actual time series exhibits some trend pattern. This same lag pattern occurs, albeit at a smaller level, with the naive model. The most reliable measure of this consistent underestimation is the mean percent error statistic; for the mean forecasting model it is −24.32 percent; for the naive model it is −2.12 percent. The negative sign indicates that these two models exhibit a consistent tendency to underestimate the change in the actual time series, while the numbers themselves indicate the magnitude of this tendency.

While the average percent change model appears to capture the pattern of changes in the actual data, it consistently overestimates the growth. An examination of Figure 8-1 indicates that the average change model captures the pattern exhibited by the actual historical data better than the remainder of the simple models.

Despite the fact that the average change model performs best in the historical simulation, it is possible that one of the other models would perform better as a forecast model. To test for this possibility, the last three actual data points, January through March 1990, were excluded from the original estimation. The results of this ex post simulation are presented in Table 8-3.

The mean and naive models consistently underestimate the growth that occurred during these three months, while the average change and average percent change models overestimate the growth. Further, in all cases the size of the error increases the further into the future we extrapolate the model. A comparison of the simulation statistics suggests that the naive model more closely captures the growth that occurred during this three-month period, with the average change model coming in second. Based on the performance in the historical simulation and the principle of parsimony, which suggests that we use the simplest model possible, we would use the naive model as our forecasting model. While we might not use either the naive or the average change model as the final forecasting model, they can be used as benchmarks against which other more sophisticated time series models can be evaluated. Prior to using any of these models to develop ex ante forecasts, we would have to reestimate the models, including all of the historical data points. This new model would then serve as the basis for generating forecasts and would be updated each time a new data point was recorded.

TABLE 8-3 Ex Post Simulations of Wages from Simple Time Series Models

Date	Actual (1)	Mean (2)	Percent Error (3)	Naive (4)	Percent Error (5)	Simple Average Change (6)	Percent Error (7)	Simple Percent Change (8)	Percent Error (9)
1990: Jan.	371,555	272,722	−26.6	369,386	−0.6	374,386	0.8	377,456	1.6
Feb.	373,004	272,722	−26.9	369,386	−1.0	379,386	1.7	385,702	3.4
Mar.	373,875	272,722	−27.1	369,386	−1.2	384,386	2.8	394,129	5.4

Evaluation Statistics

Root Mean Square		100,094		3,556		7,285		14,216	
Root Percent Mean Square		26.85		0.95		1.95		3.81	
Mean Error (Bias)		100,090		3,425		6,574		12,951	
Mean Percent Error (Percent Bias)		−26.85		−0.92		1.76		3.47	

EXAMPLE 8-1 Combining Forecasts

As noted earlier, the naive model consistently underestimates the actual growth in the wage payments while the average change model overestimates the changes. In an attempt to capture the actual pattern of changes in the cash flows associated with wages, one alternative is to combine the results of these two models. If forecasts are combined, one must first decide on the weights to be assigned to each of the individual forecasts. The simplest procedure is to assign an equal weight to each forecast, but a more appropriate method is to base the weighting scheme on the actual error patterns of the individual models.

In the historical simulation, the mean percent error for the naive model was −0.92 percent, while it was 1.76 percent for the average change model. In general, a weighting scheme should assign a higher weight to the model that generates the smallest error. To accomplish this objective, consider the steps presented in Table 8-4.[2] As shown in the first two columns of Table 8-4, if we ignore the sign associated with the mean percent error and add these two error averages together, then the naive model is responsible for 34 percent of the total error. If we take the reciprocal of the percentages in the second column, we derive the inverse percent shown in the third column of Table 8-4. In turn, when the entries in the third column are calculated as a percentage of the total, we get the weighting system shown in the last column.

Using this scheme, we would thus assign a weight of 0.66 to the naive forecast and a weight of 0.34 to the average change forecast. With this information in hand, the historically simulated forecasts would be derived as follows:

January 1990: $(374{,}386) \cdot 0.34 + (369{,}386) \cdot 0.66 = 371{,}086$

February 1990: $(379{,}386) \cdot 0.34 + (369{,}386) \cdot 0.66 = 372{,}786$

March 1990: $(384{,}386) \cdot 0.34 + (369{,}386) \cdot 0.66 = 374{,}486.$

When these estimates generated by the weighted model are compared to

TABLE 8-4 Weighting Scheme for Combining Forecasts

	Mean Error	Percent of Total Error	Inverse	Percent of Inverse Error
Naive	0.92%	0.34	2.94%	0.66
Average Change	1.76%	0.66	1.52%	0.34
Total	2.68%	1.00	4.46%	1.00

[2] In this simple exercise, the signs on the mean percent error statistic are ignored.

the actual values, the errors for January, February, and March are 0.13 percent, 0.06 percent, and −0.16 percent, respectively. The advantages of these combined forecasts are twofold. First, the size of the percent error in each of the three time periods is smaller than in either of the individual models. Second, the combined forecasts do not appear to consistently over- or underestimate the actual data pattern. While these results are impressive, there is no guarantee that such a weighting system will retain such accuracy when extrapolated into the future. Such models are fragile and must be closely monitored.

MOVING AVERAGE MODELS

INTRODUCTION

The moving average forecasting technique is one of the easiest time series models to use and understand. With this technique, the analyst assumes that the pattern exhibited by the historical observations can best be represented by an arithmetic mean of past observations. The "term" moving average follows from the fact that as each new observation or data point becomes available, a revised average is computed and used to generate a new set of forecasts.

Prior to preparing a forecast, the analyst must ensure that the number of historical observations exceeds the number of terms in the moving average. For example, if we are using a 12-term moving average (based on the last 12 monthly values for a time series), we must have 12 or more actual observations before we can generate a forecast for the thirteenth time period. In addition, the greater the number of observations that are included in the moving average, the more likely the average will mask subtle changes in the historical data. As a general rule, if the historical data contain a relatively large number of random changes, a large number of terms should be included in the moving average. Conversely, if the underlying pattern in the data is changing and you want to ensure that the model reacts to these fluctuations rapidly, a smaller number of terms should be used in computing the moving average. While including more terms in the final moving average model smooths out random fluctuations, it produces forecasts that lag behind actual patterns of growth or decline.

SIMPLE MOVING AVERAGES

The simple moving average model is set forth in equation (8-8):

$$M_t = \frac{Y_t + Y_{t-1} + Y_{t-2} + \cdots + Y_{t-n+1}}{n} \tag{8-8}$$

where

$$M_t = \text{moving average in time } t$$
$$Y_t = \text{actual value in period } t$$
$$n = \text{number of terms included in the moving average.}$$

For computational purposes, equation (8-8) can be restated as

$$M_t = M_{t-1} + \frac{Y_t - Y_{t-n}}{n}. \tag{8-9}$$

In both equations, the moving average for time period t is the arithmetic mean of the n most recent observations.

Several characteristics of this model are noteworthy. First, equal weights are assigned to each of the n most recent observations, with zero weight to all other previous observations. Second, as each new data point becomes available, it is included in the average and the data point for the nth period preceding the new data point is discarded. Thus, each *new* estimate of M_t is an updated version of the preceding estimate. Equation (8-9) highlights this characteristic. Third, the rate of response of the moving average to changes in the underlying data pattern depends on the number of periods included in the moving average. In general, the larger n is (that is, the more periods included), the less sensitive the moving average will be to changes in the pattern of the data. Conversely, a small value of n leads to a moving average that responds relatively rapidly to changes. Finally, to obtain forecasts for periods beyond the current period, t, equation (8-8) must be modified as follows:

$$\hat{Y}_{t+1} = M_t = \frac{Y_t + Y_{t-1} + Y_{t-2} + \cdots + Y_{t-n+1}}{n} \tag{8-10}$$

or

$$\hat{Y}_{t+3} = \frac{\hat{Y}_{t+2} + \hat{Y}_{t+1} + Y_t + Y_{t-1} + \cdots + Y_{t-n+3}}{n} \tag{8-11}$$

where the hats (^) refer to forecasted values.

Suppose that you are charged with developing forecasts for the number of production-line workers required in any given month and you decide to apply the simple moving average technique to the historical data provided in column 1 of Table 8-5. Since the production-line manager has to have a six-week lead time, the objective is to develop a model that will provide for short-term forecasts.

TABLE 8-5 Production-Line Requirements and Simple Moving Averages (Thousands of units)

Date	Period Number	Production Workers (1)	M_t (n = 2) (2)	Error (3)	M_t (n = 12) (4)	Error (5)
1986: Jan.	1	117.50				
Feb.	2	118.20				
Mar.	3	116.90	117.85	0.95		
Apr.	4	117.00	117.55	0.55		
May	5	117.10	116.95	−0.15		
June	6	116.00	117.05	1.05		
July	7	117.40	116.55	−0.85		
Aug.	8	117.20	116.70	−0.50		
Sept.	9	117.70	117.30	−0.40		
Oct.	10	116.90	117.45	0.55		
Nov.	11	117.40	117.30	−0.10		
Dec.	12	117.70	117.15	−0.55		
1987: Jan.	13	118.40	117.55	−0.85	117.25	−1.15
Feb.	14	117.30	118.05	0.75	117.33	0.03
Mar.	15	117.30	117.85	0.55	117.25	−0.05
Apr.	16	117.50	117.30	−0.20	117.28	−0.22
May	17	118.50	117.40	−1.10	117.33	−1.17
June	18	118.30	118.00	−0.30	117.44	−0.86
July	19	118.50	118.40	−0.10	117.63	−0.87
Aug.	20	118.60	118.40	−0.20	117.73	−0.88
Sept.	21	120.40	118.55	−1.85	117.84	−2.56
Oct.	22	121.30	119.50	−1.80	118.07	−3.23
Nov.	23	120.30	120.85	0.55	118.43	−1.87
Dec.	24	122.80	120.80	−2.00	118.68	−4.13
1988: Jan.	25	123.20	121.55	−1.65	119.10	−4.10
Feb.	26	122.40	123.00	0.60	119.50	−2.90
Mar.	27	122.70	122.80	0.10	119.93	−2.78
Apr.	28	123.00	122.55	−0.45	120.38	−2.63
May	29	123.30	122.85	−0.45	120.83	−2.47
June	30	123.40	123.15	−0.25	121.23	−2.17
July	31	123.60	123.35	−0.25	121.66	−1.94
Aug.	32	124.00	123.50	−0.50	122.08	−1.92
Sept.	33	124.20	123.80	−0.40	122.53	−1.67
Oct.	34	124.90	124.10	−0.80	122.85	−2.05
Nov.	35	125.00	124.55	−0.45	123.15	−1.85
Dec.	36	125.80	124.95	−0.85	123.54	−2.26
1989: Jan.	37	125.60	125.40	−0.20	123.79	−1.81
Feb.	38	127.10	125.70	−1.40	123.99	−3.11
Mar.	39	127.40	126.35	−1.05	124.38	−3.02
Apr.	40	128.40	127.25	−1.15	124.78	−3.63
May	41	128.60	127.90	−0.70	125.23	−3.38
June	42	129.20	128.50	−0.70	125.67	−3.53
July	43	129.10	128.90	−0.20	126.15	−2.95
Aug.	44	129.00	129.15	0.15	126.61	−2.39
Sept.	45	128.40	129.05	0.65	127.03	−1.38
Oct.	46	129.00	128.70	−0.30	127.38	−1.63
Nov.	47	130.00	128.70	−1.30	127.72	−2.28
Dec.	48	129.20	129.50	0.30	128.13	−1.07

(continued)

TABLE 8-5 (*Continued*)

Date	Period Number	Production Workers (1)	M_t ($n = 2$) (2)	Error (3)	M_t ($n = 12$) (4)	Error (5)
1990: Jan.	49	129.10	129.60	0.50	128.42	−0.68
Feb.	50	129.10	129.15	0.05	128.71	−0.39
Mar.	51	129.00	129.10	0.10	128.88	−0.13
Apr.	52	129.10	129.05	−0.05	129.01	−0.09
May	53	128.90	129.05	0.15	129.07	0.17
June	54	127.50	129.00	1.50	129.09	1.59
July	55	128.20	128.20	0.00	128.95	0.75
Aug.	56	127.20	127.85	0.65	128.88	1.67
Sept.	57	127.90	127.70	−0.20	128.73	0.82
Oct.	58	127.30	127.55	0.25	128.68	1.38
Nov.	59	126.50	127.60	1.10	128.54	2.04
Dec.	60	126.20	126.90	0.70	128.25	2.05
1991: Jan.	61	126.40	126.35	−0.05	128.00	1.60
Feb.	62	126.60	126.30	−0.30	127.78	1.18
Mar.	63	126.80	126.50	−0.30	127.57	0.77
Apr.	64	126.80	126.70	−0.10	127.38	0.58
May	65	126.90	126.80	−0.10	127.19	0.29
MAPE				0.4749		1.3879
MAD				0.5849		1.7371
Mean Error				−0.2119		−1.1739
Mean Percent Error				−0.1708		−0.9441

To illustrate the effect of lengthening or shortening the number of periods included in the moving average, columns 2 and 4 of Table 8-5 present the moving averages for $n = 2$ and $n = 12$, respectively. To apply equation (8-10) for $n = 2$ and 12, the relevant values are substituted as follows:

$$\hat{Y}_3 = M_2 = \frac{Y_2 + Y_1}{2}$$

$$= \frac{118.2 + 117.5}{2} \qquad (8\text{-}12)$$

$$= 117.85$$

$$\hat{Y}_{13} = M_{12} = \frac{Y_{12} + Y_{11} + Y_{10} + \cdots Y_3 + Y_2 + Y_1}{12}$$

$$= \frac{117.7 + 117.4 + 116.9 + \cdots + 116.9 + 118.2 + 117.5}{12}$$

$$= \frac{1{,}407}{12}$$

$$= 117.25. \qquad (8\text{-}13)$$

Note that the moving average for $n = 12$ fluctuates much less than does the series for $n = 2$. This smoothing out of the actual data patterns can best be seen by comparing the respective plots of the moving averages as presented in Figure 8-2.

As shown in Figure 8-2, the effect of including a large number of terms in the moving average is to delay the reaction of the model to changes in the historical data pattern. Determining which of the two values in n will likely provide better forecasts is a matter of comparing the mean absolute percentage error (MAPE), the mean absolute deviation (MAD), the mean, and mean percent error. Based on the data in Table 8-5, an n value of 2 performs better according to all four criteria. As a matter of course, the analyst should check other values of n prior to making a final decision.

Forecasting with moving average models is a straightforward application of equation (8-10). As an example, assume that $n = 2$, and that we want a forecast for period 67. Equation (8-10) is used as follows:

$$\hat{Y}_{67} = \frac{\hat{Y}_{66} + Y_{65}}{2}$$

$$= \frac{\hat{Y}_{66} + 126.9}{2}.$$

$$(8\text{-}14)$$

To complete this computation, an intermediate step is required, because an actual value for period 66 is unavailable. The best estimate for this period is

FIGURE 8-2 Relative Performance of Alternative Simple Moving Average Models

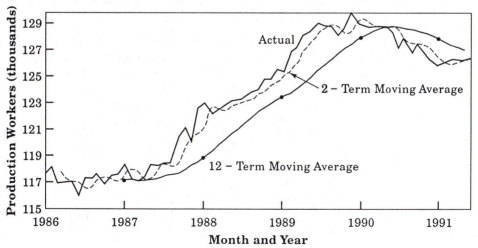

the moving average for period 65:

$$\hat{Y}_{66} = M_{65} = \frac{Y_{65} + Y_{64}}{2}$$

$$= \frac{126.9 + 126.8}{2} \tag{8-15}$$

$$= 126.85.$$

This value is then substituted into equation (8-14), yielding the following as the forecast value for period 67:

$$\hat{Y}_{67} = \frac{126.85 + 126.9}{2} \tag{8-16}$$

$$= 126.875.$$

There are two major limitations of the simple moving average model. First, it tends to either lag behind turning points in the actual data or it fails to capture them at all. This oversmoothing is especially noticeable whenever the number of terms included in the moving average is relatively large. Second, the simple moving average will not provide very reliable forecasts whenever there is a trend pattern in the data. In the production workers example, the negative figures shown for the mean error and mean percent error statistics are indicative of a consistent underestimation of the growth pattern in the actual data.

EXAMPLE 8-2   Simple Moving Averages: Rate of Change Forecasting

As a forecaster for a major airline, your assignment is to develop forecasts for the rate of change in the price of airline fuel. As a first step, you collect the information on actual prices paid as shown in Table 8-6.

Given that your assignment is the generation of rate of change forecasts, you compute percentage change figures as shown in column 2 of Table 8-6. An examination of these figures suggests that the percentage change figures fluctuate randomly within a narrow range of from -12.0311 percent to 13.9009 percent, thus suggesting that the simple moving average model would be appropriate.

Through a trial-and-error process it was determined that if the objective is to minimize the mean error, the appropriate number of terms in the moving average is 14. While it may seem unusual to include this many terms in a moving average, large values for n are indicative of a

TABLE 8-6   The Price of Fuel and Simple Moving Averages

Date	Actual Jet Fuel Prices (dollars per gallon) (1)	Actual Percent Change (2)	Simple Moving Average Estimate[a] (n = 14) (3)	Error[b] (4)	Predicted Change[c] (5)	Actual Change[d] (6)
1986: Jan.	0.864					
Feb.	0.872	0.9259				
Mar.	0.879	0.8028				
Apr.	0.860	−2.1615				
May	0.847	−1.5116				
June	0.858	1.2987				
July	0.872	1.6317				
Aug.	0.868	−0.4587				
Sept.	0.879	1.2673				
Oct.	0.873	−0.6826				
Nov.	0.928	6.3001				
Dec.	1.057	13.9009				
1987: Jan.	1.129	6.8117				
Feb.	1.100	−2.5686				
Mar.	1.043	−5.1818				
Apr.	1.031	−1.1505	1.455	2.61		
May	1.037	0.5820	1.307	0.73	−0.15	1.73
June	1.084	4.5323	1.291	−3.24	−0.02	3.95
July	1.082	−0.1845	1.769	1.95	0.48	−4.72
Aug.	1.056	−2.4030	1.864	4.27	0.09	−2.22
Sept.	1.041	−1.4205	1.600	3.02	−0.26	0.98
Oct.	1.037	−0.3842	1.382	1.77	−0.22	1.04
Nov.	1.047	0.9643	1.387	0.42	0.01	1.35
Dec.	1.049	0.1910	1.365	1.17	−0.02	−0.77
1988: Jan.	1.046	−0.2860	1.428	1.71	0.06	−0.48
Feb.	1.024	−2.1033	0.957	3.06	−0.47	−1.82
Mar.	1.030	0.5859	−0.186	−0.77	−1.14	2.69
Apr.	1.018	−1.1650	−0.631	0.53	−0.44	−1.75
May	0.911	−10.5108	−0.530	9.98	0.10	−9.35
June	0.993	9.0011	−0.911	−9.91	−0.38	19.51
July	1.019	2.6183	−0.186	−2.80	0.73	−6.38
Aug.	1.044	2.4534	−0.040	−2.49	0.15	−0.16
Sept.	1.161	11.2069	−0.189	−11.40	−0.15	8.75
Oct.	1.301	12.0586	0.625	−11.43	0.81	0.85
Nov.	1.363	4.7656	1.658	−3.11	1.03	−7.29
Dec.	1.512	10.9318	2.100	−8.83	0.44	6.17
1989: Jan.	1.527	0.9921	2.908	1.92	0.81	−9.94
Feb.	1.485	−2.7505	2.910	5.66	0.00	−3.74
Mar.	1.460	−1.6835	2.700	4.38	−0.21	1.07
Apr.	1.556	6.5753	2.600	−3.98	−0.10	8.26
May	1.544	−0.7712	3.220	3.99	0.62	−7.35
June	1.470	−4.7927	3.123	7.92	−0.10	−4.02
July	1.437	−2.2449	2.864	5.11	−0.26	2.55
Aug.	1.413	−1.6701	3.454	5.12	0.59	0.57
Sept.	1.243	−12.0311	2.692	14.72	−0.76	−10.36
Oct.	1.342	7.9646	1.646	−6.32	−1.05	20.00
Nov.	1.328	−1.0432	2.039	3.08	0.39	−9.01
Dec.	1.312	−1.2048	1.164	2.37	−0.88	−0.16
1990: Jan.	1.269	−3.2774	0.217	3.49	−0.95	−2.07
Feb.	1.279	0.7880	−0.358	−1.15	−0.57	4.07
Mar.	1.259	−1.5637	−1.082	0.48	−0.72	−2.35

[a] Estimated percent change.
[b] Column 3 minus Column 2.
[c] First difference of Column 3.
[d] First difference of Column 2.

widely fluctuating series. An analysis of the historical forecast errors in column 4 of Table 8-6 suggests that with a few exceptions the estimated model captures the essence of the pattern of changes. This is confirmed by the fact that the MAD is 4.303 and the mean error is 0.6679. Both of these values are well within acceptable limits for a forecasting model of a virtually random time series.

There is, however, one disturbing aspect of the estimated model. A comparison of the actual turning points (see columns 5 and 6) with the predicted turning points indicates that on seven occasions the model predicted a decline when the actual series increased and four times predicted an increase when the actual series declined. Alternatively, the model erred in predicting directional changes 31 percent of the time.

DOUBLE MOVING AVERAGES

If the data being analyzed have a linear or quadratic trend, then the simple moving average methodology may be inappropriate. Specifically, if a trend is present in the data, simple moving averages will lag behind the actual data. To correct for this bias, a double moving average, M_t^d, should be computed. To calculate M_t^d, one treats the simple moving average, M_t, as an individual data point and derives a second moving average based on the M_t observations:

$$M_t^d = \frac{M_t + M_{t-1} + M_{t-2} + \cdots + M_{t-n+1}}{n}. \tag{8-17}$$

Suppose that you are working as the manager of a distribution warehouse for a major appliance producer and that one of your responsibilities is to ensure that you have arranged for a sufficient number of trucks to deliver the needed appliances on a monthly basis. You have at your disposal the information on monthly shipments of these appliances measured in thousands of units recorded in column 1 of Table 8-7 (pages 366–67).

An examination of actual shipments data suggests that there is, at the very least, a linear trend pattern in the data, and you decide to use the double moving average technique. Through a trial-and-error process, you determine that the most appropriate number of terms to include in the moving average is two months.

Based on this information, the first M_t^d computation ($n = 2$) is

$$M_t^d = \frac{M_2 + M_1}{2} \tag{8-18}$$

where M_2 and M_1 are the simple moving averages for the respective time periods as shown in column 2 of Table 8-7. Applying equation (8-18) to the shipments data, the double moving average through March 1986 is

$$M^d_{\text{March}} = \frac{276.25 + 272.3}{2}$$

$$= 274.275.$$

(8-19)

The remainder of the double moving averages are computed in a similar fashion by dropping the oldest observation (simple moving average) and adding the most recent observation. They are presented in column 4 of Table 8-7.

The calculated difference between the double moving average (M^d) and the simple moving average (M) serves as the starting point for the double moving average forecast. To understand the logic of using the difference calculation, suppose that we first plot the values for the simple and double moving averages along with the actual data, as shown in Figure 8-3.

A comparison of these two moving average lines indicates that the simple moving average values lag behind the growth pattern in the actual data, while the double moving average values lag behind the simple moving average values. However, what is important for our purposes is the fact that the distance between the simple and the double moving average lines is approximately the same as the distance between the simple moving average line and the actual shipments line. Therefore, it follows that if the difference between the simple moving average value and the double moving average value is added back to

FIGURE 8-3 Moving Average Models and Trend Patterns

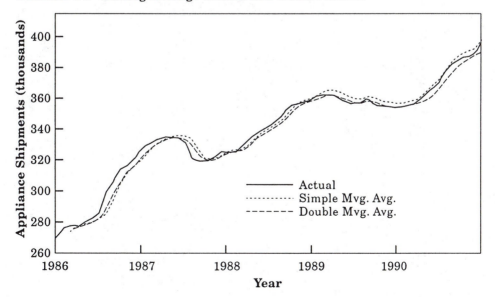

TABLE 8-7 Double Moving Average Forecast and Appliance Shipments

Date	Actual Appliance Shipments (thousands) (1)	Simple Moving Average (n = 2) (2)	Simple Moving Average Forecast (3)	Double Moving Average (n = 2) (4)	a_t (5)	b_t (6)	Double Moving Average Forecast (7)	Absolute Changes (8)	Moving Average Absolute Changes (9)	Moving Average Absolute Change Forecast (10)	Percent Changes (11)	Moving Average Percent Changes (12)	Moving Average Percent Change Forecast (13)
1986: Jan.	269.5												
Feb.	275.1	272.30						5.6			2.08		
Mar.	277.4	276.25	272.30	274.275	278.225	3.95		2.3			0.84		
Apr.	277.3	277.35	276.25	276.800	277.900	1.10	282.175	-0.1			-0.04		
May	279.2	278.25	277.35	277.800	278.700	0.90	279.000	1.9			0.69		
June	281.8	280.50	278.25	279.375	281.625	2.25	279.600	2.6			0.93		
July	285.4	283.60	280.50	282.050	285.150	3.10	283.875	3.6			1.28		
Aug.	299.1	292.25	283.60	287.925	296.575	8.65	288.250	13.7			4.80		
Sept.	306.9	303.00	292.25	297.625	308.375	10.75	305.225	7.8			2.61		
Oct.	313.4	310.15	303.00	306.575	313.725	7.15	319.125	6.5			2.12		
Nov.	316.4	314.90	310.15	312.525	317.275	4.75	320.875	3			0.96		
Dec.	320.4	318.40	314.90	316.650	320.150	3.50	322.025	4			1.26		
1987: Jan.	327.1	323.75	318.40	321.075	326.425	5.35	323.650	6.7			2.09		
Feb.	329.6	328.35	323.75	326.050	330.650	4.60	331.775	2.5			0.76		
Mar.	333.0	331.30	328.35	329.825	332.775	2.95	335.250	3.4			1.03		
Apr.	333.9	333.45	331.30	332.375	334.525	2.15	335.725	0.9			0.27		
May	334.4	334.15	333.45	333.800	334.500	0.70	336.675	0.5			0.15		
June	334.0	334.20	334.15	334.175	334.225	0.05	335.200	-0.4			-0.12		
July	331.2	332.60	334.20	333.400	331.800	-1.60	334.275	-2.8			-0.84		
Aug.	320.0	325.60	332.60	329.100	322.100	-7.00	330.200	-11.2			-3.38		
Sept.	318.9	319.45	325.60	322.525	316.375	-6.15	315.100	-1.1			-0.34		
Oct.	319.5	319.20	319.45	319.325	319.075	-0.25	310.225	0.6			0.19		
Nov.	321.4	320.45	319.20	319.825	321.075	1.25	318.825	1.9			0.59		
Dec.	325.6	323.50	320.45	321.975	325.025	3.05	322.325	4.2			1.31		
1988: Jan.	324.6	325.10	323.50	324.300	325.900	1.60	328.075	-1			-0.31		
Feb.	325.5	325.05	325.10	325.075	325.025	-0.05	327.500	0.9			0.28		
Mar.	330.0	327.75	325.05	326.400	329.100	2.70	324.975	4.5			1.38		
Apr.	334.7	332.35	327.75	330.050	334.650	4.60	331.800	4.7	2.41		1.42		
May	337.8	336.25	332.35	334.200	338.200	3.90	339.250	3.1	2.32	337.11	0.93	1.0082	337.43
June	340.1	338.95	336.25	337.600	340.300	2.70	342.100	2.3	2.32	340.12	0.68	1.0077	340.41
July	343.7	341.90	338.95	340.425	343.375	2.95	343.000	3.6	2.46	342.42	1.06	1.0077	342.71
Aug.	347.2	345.45	341.90	343.675	347.225	3.55	346.325	3.5	2.52	346.16	1.02	1.0081	346.47
Sept.	354.1	350.65	345.45	348.050	353.250	5.20	350.775	6.9	2.68	349.72	1.99	1.0086	350.05
Oct.	356.8	355.45	350.65	353.050	357.850	4.80	358.450	2.7	2.64	356.78	0.76	1.0084	357.14
Nov.	358.0	357.40	355.45	356.425	358.375	1.95	362.650	1.2	2.18	359.44	0.34	1.0067	359.80
Dec.	359.4	358.70	357.40	358.050	359.350	1.30	360.325	1.4	1.94	360.18	0.39	1.0059	360.41

TABLE 8-7 (Continued)

Date	Actual Appliance Shipments (thousands) (1)	Simple Moving Average (n = 2) (2)	Simple Moving Average Forecast (3)	Double Moving Average (n = 2) (4)	a_t (5)	b_t (6)	Double Moving Average Forecast (7)	Absolute Changes (8)	Moving Average Absolute Changes (9)	Moving Average Absolute Change Forecast (10)	Percent Changes (11)	Moving Average Percent Changes (12)	Moving Average Percent Change Forecast (13)
1989: Jan.	363.0	361.20	358.70	359.950	362.450	2.50	360.650	3.6	1.84	361.34	1.00	1.0055	361.53
Feb.	364.4	363.70	361.20	362.450	364.950	2.50	364.950	1.4	1.78	364.84	0.39	1.0053	365.00
Mar.	363.3	363.85	363.70	363.775	363.925	0.15	367.450	−1.1	1.59	366.18	−0.30	1.0047	366.33
Apr.	361.8	362.55	363.85	363.200	361.900	−1.30	364.075	−1.5	1.29	364.89	−0.41	1.0038	365.01
May	358.8	360.30	362.55	361.425	359.175	−2.25	360.600	−3	1.08	363.09	−0.83	1.0032	363.17
June	357.8	358.30	360.30	359.300	357.300	−2.00	356.925	−1	0.92	359.88	−0.28	1.0027	359.95
July	358.6	358.20	358.30	358.250	358.150	−0.10	355.300	0.8	0.91	358.72	0.22	1.0027	358.77
Aug.	361.0	359.80	358.20	359.000	360.600	1.60	358.050	2.4	0.99	359.51	0.67	1.0029	359.57
Sept.	356.7	358.85	359.80	359.325	358.375	−0.95	362.200	−4.3	0.84	361.99	−1.19	1.0025	362.04
Oct.	356.1	356.40	358.85	357.625	355.175	−2.45	357.425	−0.6	0.92	357.54	−0.17	1.0027	357.59
Nov.	356.1	356.10	356.40	356.250	355.950	−0.30	352.725	0	1.34	357.02	0.00	1.0040	357.08
Dec.	354.6	355.35	356.10	355.725	354.975	−0.75	355.650	−1.5	1.32	357.44	−0.42	1.0040	357.52
1990: Jan.	356.5	355.55	355.35	355.450	355.650	0.20	354.225	1.9	1.37	355.92	0.54	1.0041	356.01
Feb.	356.7	356.60	355.55	356.075	357.125	1.05	355.850	0.2	1.31	357.87	0.06	1.0039	357.96
Mar.	359.2	357.95	356.60	357.275	358.625	1.35	358.175	2.5	1.24	358.01	0.70	1.0037	358.09
Apr.	364.9	362.05	357.95	360.000	364.100	4.10	359.975	5.7	1.49	360.44	1.59	1.0044	360.52
May	368.4	366.65	362.05	364.350	368.950	4.60	368.200	3.5	1.59	366.39	0.96	1.0046	366.49
June	372.7	370.55	366.65	368.600	372.500	3.90	373.550	4.3	1.58	369.99	1.17	1.0045	370.10
July	381.0	376.85	370.55	373.700	380.000	6.30	376.400	8.3	1.71	374.28	2.23	1.0048	374.39
Aug.	385.2	383.10	376.85	379.975	386.225	6.25	386.300	4.2	1.76	382.71	1.10	1.0049	382.84
Sept.	388.6	386.90	383.10	385.000	388.800	3.80	392.475	3.4	1.80	386.96	0.88	1.0050	387.09
Oct.	389.7	389.15	386.90	388.025	390.275	2.25	392.600	1.1	1.70	390.40	0.28	1.0047	390.54
Nov.	391.7	390.70	389.15	389.925	391.475	1.55	392.525	2	1.65	391.40	0.51	1.0045	391.53
Dec.	400.8	396.25	390.70	393.475	399.025	5.55	393.025	9.1	1.73	393.35	2.32	1.0046	393.47

Note: a_t and b_t are defined in equations (8-20) and (8-21), respectively.

the simple moving average, a more reliable forecast is likely to emerge. The three equations used to incorporate this information into the forecast are

$$a_t = 2M_t - M_t^d \tag{8-20}$$

$$b_t = \frac{2}{n-1}(M_t - M_t^d) \tag{8-21}$$

$$\hat{Y}_{t+T} = \hat{M}_{t+T}^d = a_t + b_t T. \tag{8-22}$$

In using equation (8-22) to develop the one-period-ahead projections shown in column 7 of Table 8-7, T has a value of 1. Thus, the forecast for period 4 (April 1986) done at the end of period 3 (March 1986) would be determined as follows:

$$a_3 = 2M_3 - M_3^d$$

$$= (2 \cdot 276.25) - 274.275 \tag{8-23}$$

$$= 278.225$$

$$b_3 = \frac{2}{2-1}(276.25 - 274.275)$$

$$= 2 \cdot 1.975 \tag{8-24}$$

$$= 3.95$$

$$\hat{Y}_{3+1} = \hat{M}_{3+1} = a_3 + b_3(1)$$

$$= 278.225 + 3.95(1) \tag{8-25}$$

$$Y_4 = 282.175.$$

As each new observation becomes available, a_t and b_t are recalculated; these new coefficient values are substituted into equation (8-22), and a rolling one-period-ahead forecast is calculated. The results of this continual updating process are presented in columns 5, 6, and 7 of Table 8-7, respectively.

To develop forecasts for future time periods, we use the updated information from December 1990 as follows:

$$a_{\text{Dec}} = 2M_{\text{Dec}} - M_{\text{Dec}}^d$$

$$= 2(396.25) - 393.475 \tag{8-26}$$

$$= 399.025$$

$$b_{\text{Dec}} = \frac{2}{1}(396.25 - 393.475)$$

$$\tag{8-27}$$

$$= 5.55$$

$$\hat{Y}_{t+T} = \hat{Y}_{t+1} = \hat{Y}_{\text{Jan}} = 399.025 + 5.55(1) \tag{8-28}$$
$$= 404.575$$

$$\hat{Y}_{t+T} = \hat{Y}_{t+2} = \hat{Y}_{\text{Feb}} = 399.025 + 5.55(2)$$
$$= 410.125$$

$$\hat{Y}_{\text{Mar}} = 399.025 + 5.55(3)$$
$$= 415.675$$

$$\hat{Y}_{\text{Apr}} = 399.025 + 5.55(4) \tag{8-29}$$
$$= 421.225$$

$$\hat{Y}_{\text{May}} = 399.025 + 5.55(5)$$
$$= 426.775$$

$$\hat{Y}_{\text{Jun}} = 399.025 + 5.55(6)$$
$$= 432.325.$$

ABSOLUTE AND PERCENT CHANGE MOVING AVERAGE

Two variations of the simple moving average technique have proven useful in forecasting. The first of these, the absolute change moving average model, is a combination of the simple moving average technique and the absolute change model that was presented earlier in this chapter. Formally, a three-term absolute change moving average model can be stated as follows:

$$M_t = \frac{(Y_t - Y_{t-1}) + (Y_{t-1} - Y_{t-2}) + (Y_{t-2} - Y_{t-3})}{3}. \tag{8-30}$$

The forecast equation becomes:

$$\hat{Y}_{t+T} = Y_t + \text{Moving Average of Absolute Changes.} \tag{8-31}$$

The simple percent change moving average model is similar to the preceding model except that an average of percentage changes is used. The general form of the model for a two-term moving average model would be

$$M_t = \frac{\{(Y_t - Y_{t-1})/Y_{t-1}\} + \{(Y_{t-1} - Y_{t-2})/Y_{t-2}\}}{2}. \tag{8-32}$$

The forecast equation becomes

$$\hat{Y}_{t+T} = Y_t \cdot (1.0 + \text{Moving Average of Percent Changes}). \tag{8-33}$$

To illustrate the process of using these two models, consider the case of the shipments data presented in Table 8-7. In various tests it was found that the optimum number of terms in both of these moving averages was 27. Applying equation (8-30) to the shipments data, we obtain the information presented in column 9 of Table 8-7. Thus, through the end of April of 1988, the average of all preceding changes is 2.41 thousand units. This average is then added to the actual shipments value in April 1988 to obtain the forecast for May of 1988 as follows:

$$\hat{Y}_{\text{May}} = Y_{\text{Apr}} + \text{Average of Absolute Changes}$$

$$= 334.7 + 2.41 \tag{8-34}$$

$$= 337.11.$$

In generating forecasts for future time periods, equation (8-31) is used.

$$\hat{Y}_{t+T} = \hat{Y}_{t+1} = \hat{Y}_{\text{Jan}} = Y_{\text{Dec}} + \text{Average of Last 27 Changes}$$

$$= 400.8 + 1.73$$

$$= 402.53 \tag{8-35}$$

$$= \hat{Y}_{t+2} = \hat{Y}_{\text{Feb}} = 400.8 + 1.73(2)$$

$$= 404.26$$

Percent change moving average forecasts are derived in a similar fashion except that we apply equations (8-32) and (8-33). The average of the first 27 percent changes is 0.0082 percent, which when incorporated into equation (8-33) yields the forecast value for May 1988:

$$\hat{Y}_{t+T} = \hat{Y}_{t+1} = \hat{Y}_{\text{May}} = Y_{\text{April}} \cdot (1 + \text{Moving Average})$$

$$= 334.7 \cdot 1.0082 \tag{8-36}$$

$$= 337.43$$

with forecasts into the future being derived in a fashion similar to that illustrated with the absolute change moving average process in equation (8-35).

$$\hat{Y}_{t+T} = \hat{Y}_{t+1} = \hat{Y}_{\text{Jan}} = Y_{\text{Dec}} \cdot 1 + \text{Moving Average of Percent Changes}$$

$$= 400.8 \cdot 1.0046(1) \tag{8-37}$$

$$= 402.64$$

Columns 8 through 13 contain all of the information relative to the historical simulations for the absolute and percent change moving average models.

LIMITATIONS OF MOVING AVERAGES

There are four primary limitations associated with moving average techniques. First, moving average models often require lengthy time series. For example, in the case of the shipments model developed for Table 8-7, we had to use 27 observations. Second, when using moving average models we are implicitly assigning an equal weight to each of the last n observations. A strong argument can be made that the most recent observations contain the most pertinent information about future patterns of change and that they should, therefore, be assigned a larger weight than previous observations. Third, a determination of the optimal number of terms to include in the final moving average model can involve a great deal of trial-and-error testing. Finally, as with all of the techniques described in this chapter, moving average models are mechanistic in nature and tend to be unreliable when used in an environment that requires anything other than immediate- or short-term forecasts.

EXPONENTIAL SMOOTHING TECHNIQUES

INTRODUCTION

Exponential smoothing is perhaps the most widely used time series model. Despite the awesome name, it is an extremely simple technique to understand and apply: New forecasts are derived by adjusting the prior forecast to reflect its forecast error. In this way, the forecaster can continually revise the forecast based on previous experiences. In addition to this feature, exponential smoothing offers several advantages vis-à-vis moving average models. First, exponential smoothing models mesh very easily with computer systems. That is, exponential smoothing forecasting systems can be created with simple spreadsheet programs. Second, data-storage requirements are minimal when compared with other forecasting models—this is true despite the fact that exponential smoothing models use all previous historical observations. Finally, this type of model embodies the advantages of a weighted moving average since current observations are assigned larger weights. An exponential smoothing model reacts, however, more quickly to changes in data patterns (economic conditions) than do moving average models.

SINGLE EXPONENTIAL SMOOTHING

In single exponential smoothing models, the forecast for the next and all subsequent periods is determined by adjusting the current-period forecast by a portion of the difference between the forecast and the actual value. Intuitively, this is a very appealing characteristic for any forecasting system. If recent forecasts have proved accurate, it seems reasonable to base subsequent forecasts on these estimates. On the other hand, if recent predictions have been subject to large errors, new forecasts should take this into consideration.

The basic formula for computing the single exponential smoothing statistic is

$$S_t^1 = \alpha Y_t + (1 - \alpha)S_{t-1}^1 \tag{8-38}$$

where S_t^1 is the single exponential smoothing statistic; Y_t is the actual value in time period t; and α is the smoothing constant ($0 \leq \alpha \leq 1$) selected by the analyst. Equation (8-38) can be restated as

$$\text{New Estimate} = \alpha(\text{New Data}) + (1 - \alpha)(\text{Previous Estimate}). \tag{8-39}$$

Exponential smoothing has the advantage of requiring retention of only a limited amount of data. There is no need to store data for many periods, because the historical profile is recorded in concise form in one number—the current smoothed statistic. Equation (8-38) can be restated in terms of time period $t - 1$ as:

$$S_{t-1}^1 = \alpha Y_{t-1} + (1 - \alpha)S_{t-2}^1. \tag{8-40}$$

Substituting equation (8-40) into equation (8-38), we get

$$S_t^1 = \alpha Y_t + \alpha(1 - \alpha)Y_{t-1} + (1 - \alpha)^2 S_{t-2}^1 \tag{8-41}$$

but

$$S_{t-2}^1 = \alpha Y_{t-2} + (1 - \alpha)S_{t-3}^1. \tag{8-42}$$

Substituting again, we obtain

$$S_t^1 = \alpha Y_t + \alpha(1 - \alpha)Y_{t-1} + \alpha(1 - \alpha)^2 Y_{t-2} + (1 - \alpha)^3 S_{t-3}. \tag{8-43}$$

Substituting recursively for S_{t-3}^1, S_{t-4}^1, and so on, we obtain

$$S_t^1 = \alpha Y_t + \alpha(1 - \alpha)Y_{t-1} + \alpha(1 - \alpha)^2 Y_{t-2}$$
$$+ \cdots + \alpha(1 - \alpha)^{t-1} Y_1 + (1 - \alpha)^t S_0. \tag{8-44}$$

In other words, S_t is a weighted average of $Y_t, Y_{t-1}, Y_{t-2}, \ldots, Y_1$, and the initial estimate of S_0^1. The coefficients of the observations

$$\alpha, \alpha(1 - \alpha), \alpha(1 - \alpha)^2, \ldots, \alpha(1 - \alpha)^{t-1} \tag{8-45}$$

are the weights and measure the contribution each observation makes to the most recent estimate. Additionally, it can be seen that these coefficients decrease geometrically with the age of the observation. That is, the most recent observation, Y_t, makes the largest contribution to the current estimate, and past observations make successively smaller contributions to S_t^1. Thus, distant observations are dampened out with the passage of time. The rate at which this dampening occurs depends on the value of the smoothing constant, α. In particular, the larger α is, the more quickly the influence of distant observations is minimized. For example, when $\alpha = 0.8$, the weights are 0.8, 0.16, 0.032, and 0.0064 for Y_t, Y_{t-1}, Y_{t-2}, and Y_{t-3}, respectively, and periods past Y_{t-3} have almost no effect on the current estimate, S_t^1.

The preceding discussion also highlights the critical role of the smoothing constant in obtaining reliable forecasts. Indeed, from the analyst's viewpoint, the main input in any smoothing technique is the size of alpha. As noted in the preceding paragraph, the value of α determines the extent to which past observations influence forecasts. Since small values of the smoothing constant dampen previous observations slowly, a small α should be used with time series data that are relatively stable. Conversely, if we are dealing with a series that changes rapidly, a large smoothing constant is desirable because it assigns larger weights to more recent observations. Unfortunately, the rapid response rate of an exponential smoothing model with a large α value may place too much emphasis on irregular variations while ignoring the underlying data patterns. In practice, values of α from 0.1 to 0.6 usually work best. One way of selecting the smoothing constant is to simulate the historical data set using alternative values of α. That is, for each value of α, a set of forecasts is generated and compared with the actual observations. The value of α that yields the *best* forecasts thus becomes the appropriate smoothing constant to be used in future analysis. The determination of the best forecast model is made by examining the forecast errors obtained in the simulation. Typically, the set of forecasts that has the smallest sum of squared errors is judged to be the best. This corresponds to the mean square error criterion introduced earlier. Computer programs that have integrated exponential smoothing in their forecasting methods typically use this type of procedure.

The principal difficulty with the preceding technique is that it involves a time-consuming and costly trial-and-error process. An alternative approach to selecting the smoothing constant is to investigate a plot of the variable over time. It can be shown that the appropriate value of α is fundamentally related to the data pattern. In general, if the data plot reveals a time series with an insignificant irregular component (that is, little random variation), the smoothing constant should be relatively small. Alternatively, if there are large fluctuations in the actual data plot, a relatively large value for α should be used. If a smoothing value greater than $\alpha = 0.6$ seems to provide the best fit, the values of the error terms are likely to be autocorrelated. Although single exponential smoothing techniques are occasionally successful in such situa-

FIGURE 8-4 **Inventory Forecasting and Alternative Single Smoothing Statistics**

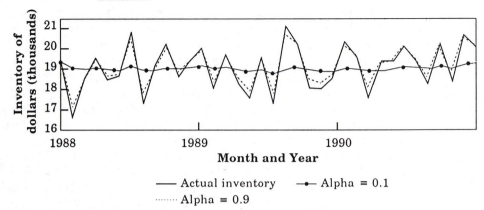

——— Actual inventory   •—— Alpha = 0.1
········ Alpha = 0.9

tions, other smoothing techniques, such as double exponential smoothing or the Winter's method, may be more appropriate.

Further, it can be shown that α is related (approximately) to the number of terms in a simple moving average by the relationship

$$\alpha = \frac{2}{n + 1}. \tag{8-46}$$

Equation (8-46) implies that when α is close to zero, an exponential smoothing model behaves like a mean forecast or a moving average model with a large n (that is, when $\alpha = 0.1$, the results are similar to a moving average model when $n = 19$). When α is close to 1, the exponential model responds quickly to changes in the data pattern and corresponds to a small value of n (that is, if $\alpha = 0.9$, $n = 1.2$).[3]

Using exponential smoothing, consider the monthly inventory data listed in Table 8-8 and graphed in Figure 8-4. To begin the smoothing process, the analyst must make an initial estimate of S_0^1 and select a value for α. The value for S_0^1 is needed to determine the smoothed statistic for S_1^1, as seen by

$$S_1^1 = \alpha Y_1 + (1 - \alpha)S_0^1. \tag{8-47}$$

The quickest way of determining a value for S_0^1 is to let it equal Y_1. (Alternative approaches for computing S_0^1 are noted in succeeding sections of this chapter.) To illustrate the effect of different smoothing constants, consider $\alpha = 0.1$ and $\alpha = 0.9$. Intuitively, it seems reasonable to base the smoothed statistic on

---

[3] For example, if we assume that $\alpha = 1.00$, equation (8-38) becomes $S_t^1 = 1.00$; thus, the forecast for period $t + 1$ is simply Y_t.

TABLE 8-8 Single Exponential Smoothing: Forecasting Inventory Levels

Date	Period	Inventory Level (1)	Single Smoothing Statistic S_1 Alpha = 0.1 (2)	Single Smoothing Statistic S_1 Alpha = 0.9 (3)	Forecast† (4)	Forecast Error (5)	Percent Error (6)
1988: Jan.	1	19,290	19,290*	19,290*			
Feb.	2	16,430	19,004	16,716			
Mar.	3	18,435	18,947	18,263	19,004	569	3.09
Apr.	4	19,565	19,009	19,435	18,947	(618)	−3.16
May	5	18,364	18,944	18,471	19,009	645	3.51
June	6	18,602	18,910	18,589	18,944	342	1.84
July	7	20,860	19,105	20,633	18,910	(1,950)	−9.35
Aug.	8	17,154	18,910	17,501	19,105	1,951	11.37
Sept.	9	19,041	18,923	18,887	18,910	(131)	−0.69
Oct.	10	20,252	19,056	20,116	18,923	(1,329)	−6.56
Nov.	11	18,562	19,007	18,717	19,056	494	2.66
Dec.	12	19,454	19,051	19,380	19,007	(447)	−2.30
1989: Jan.	13	20,042	19,150	19,976	19,051	(991)	−4.94
Feb.	14	17,926	19,028	18,131	19,150	1,224	6.83
Mar.	15	19,806	19,106	19,638	19,028	(778)	−3.93
Apr.	16	18,255	19,021	18,393	19,106	851	4.66
May	17	17,518	18,870	17,606	19,021	1,503	8.58
June	18	19,708	18,954	19,498	18,870	(838)	−4.25
July	19	17,254	18,784	17,478	18,954	1,700	9.85
Aug.	20	21,262	19,032	20,884	18,784	(2,478)	−11.65
Sept.	21	20,292	19,158	20,351	19,032	(1,260)	−6.21
Oct.	22	18,091	19,051	18,317	19,158	1,067	5.90
Nov.	23	18,037	18,950	18,065	19,051	1,014	5.62
Dec.	24	18,622	18,917	18,566	18,950	328	1.76
1990: Jan.	25	20,419	19,067	20,234	18,917	(1,502)	−7.36
Feb.	26	19,663	19,127	19,720	19,067	(596)	−3.03
Mar.	27	17,632	18,977	17,841	19,127	1,495	8.48
Apr.	28	19,357	19,015	19,205	18,977	(380)	−1.96
May	29	19,363	19,050	29,347	19,015	(348)	−1.80
June	30	20,307	19,176	20,211	19,050	(1,257)	−6.19
July	31	19,430	19,201	19,508	19,176	(254)	−1.31
Aug.	32	18,290	19,110	18,412	19,201	911	4.98
Sept.	33	20,435	19,243	20,233	19,110	(1,325)	−6.48
Oct.	34	18,454	19,164	18,632	19,243	789	4.28
Nov.	35	20,926	19,340	20,697	19,164	(1,762)	−8.42
Dec.	36	20,255	19,431	20,299	19,340	(915)	−4.52

* This value is based on an assumed value for S_0 = 19,290.
† Based on Alpha = 0.1.

recent observations rather than distant observations. This can be accomplished by starting with the initial estimate, S_0^1, and using equation (8-38) to revise recursively this smoothed statistic. Thus, at the end of the first period, the smoothed statistic is computed as follows:

$$S_1^1 = \alpha Y_1 + (1 - \alpha)S_0^1$$

$$= (.1)(19,290) + (1 - .1)(19,290) \tag{8-48}$$

$$= 19,290.$$

The smoothed statistic for period 2 may now be computed as

$$S_2^1 = \alpha Y_2 + (1 - \alpha)S_1^1$$

$$= (.1)(16,430) + (1 - .1)(19,290) \tag{8-49}$$

$$= 1,643 + 17,361$$

$$= 19,004$$

or, when $\alpha = .9$,

$$S_2^1 = (.9)(16,430) + (1 - .9)(19,290)$$

$$= 14,787 + 1,929 \tag{8-50}$$

$$= 16,716.$$

In a similar fashion, the single smoothed statistic is continually updated using the remainder of the actual observations in column 1 of Table 8-8. The results for $\alpha = 0.1$ and $\alpha = 0.9$ are summarized in columns 2 and 3 of Table 8-8 and are plotted in Figure 8-4.

Selection of the most appropriate smoothing constant can be made either by examining plots similar to that presented in Figure 8-4 or by using the various evaluation statistics presented in chapter 4. Table 8-9 presents a comparison of the evaluation statistics for various values for the smoothing constant.

A comparison of the evaluation statistics presented in Table 8-9 indicates that the model with an α value of 0.1 performs best according to the MAPE and the MAD statistics, while the model with an α value of 0.9 is best according to the bias and percent bias statistics. However, there are two factors that suggest that the model with an α value of 0.1 is superior. First, a value of 0.9 for α makes the model sensitive to random fluctuations in the data. Second, the improvement in the bias and percent bias statistics from the higher α value is minimal when compared to the loss of reliability suggested by MAD and MAPE. Therefore, the model with $\alpha = 0.1$ is used throughout the remainder of this discussion.

TABLE 8-9　Evaluation Statistics for Alternative Smoothing Constants

				Smoothing Constant Values (α)					
	.1	.2	.3	.4	.5	.6	.7	.8	.9
MAPE	5.22	5.33	5.48	5.75	6.04	6.35	6.70	7.15	7.60
MAD	1001	1024	1051	1101	1156	1212	1279	1364	1450
Bias	-126	-143	-141	-138	-133	-129	-125	-121	-117
Percent Bias	-0.31	-0.40	-0.38	-0.35	-0.32	-0.29	-0.26	-0.23	-0.21

The quantities in Table 8-8 may now be used to generate forecasts of monthly inventory levels. Thus, at the end of period 2, the forecast for period 3 is 19,004. However, when the actual data for period 3 become available, the forecast must be revised. For example, at the end of period 3, the actual inventory level is observed as 16,430. Now the forecast for period 3 is recomputed as 18,947:

$$S_3^1 = \alpha Y_3 + (1 - \alpha)S_2^1$$

$$= (.1)(18,435) + (.9)(19,004) \tag{8-51}$$

$$= 1,843.5 + 17,103.6$$

$$= 18,947.1.$$

The remainder of the one-period-ahead forecasts are prepared in a like manner and are presented in column 4 of Table 8-8.

At the end of period 36, December 1990, the forecast for period 37, January 1991, would be prepared as follows:

$$\hat{Y}_{37} = S_3^1 = \alpha Y_{36} + (1 - \alpha)S_{35}^1$$

$$= (.1)(20,255) + (.9)(19,340) \tag{8-52}$$

$$= 19,431.5.$$

Furthermore, this would be the forecast for all future periods as long as the forecast is made in period 36. Thus, the forecast for February of 1991 would be 19,431.5.

The preceding computations highlight two of the more significant limitations of single exponential smoothing models. First, the model must be updated each time a new data point becomes available. This updating is useful in regression analysis, but it is critical and required in the case of exponential smoothing models. Second, to be technically correct, this model will provide decision makers with forecasts for only one period into the future, and it will only be useful when immediate-term forecasts are required.

ADAPTIVE RESPONSE RATE EXPONENTIAL SMOOTHING

Adaptive response rate exponential smoothing is conceptually similar to single exponential smoothing.[4] The only difference (and it is an important one) is that with adaptive response rate exponential smoothing, the value of the smoothing constant varies. Specifically, the value of α changes (adapts) automatically whenever a change in the data pattern dictates that a change is desirable. The advantage is that the adaptive response rate exponential smoothing technique is capable of representing almost all data patterns.

The basic equation for adaptive response rate exponential smoothing is

$$\hat{Y}_{t+1} = \alpha_t Y_t + (1 - \alpha_t)Y_t. \tag{8-53}$$

For preparation of forecasts using this technique, several intermediate computations are required. Using β as the error-smoothing parameter, we get

$$\alpha = \left| \frac{E_t}{AE_t} \right| \tag{8-54}$$

$$E_t = \beta e_t + (1 - \beta)E_{t-1}; \, 0 < \beta < 1 \tag{8-55}$$

$$AE_t = \beta \, | \, e_t \, | + (1 - \beta)AE_{t-1} \tag{8-56}$$

$$e_t = Y_t - \hat{Y}_t \tag{8-57}$$

where E_t refers to the smoothed average error and AE_t to the smoothed absolute error. The following example illustrates the use of adaptive response rate exponential smoothing.

Juloy Incorporated, a small manufacturing firm, makes the Dalene doll. Management would like to develop a forecasting model that can be used to generate monthly sales forecasts for the doll. If a reliable forecasting model can be developed, Juloy can more efficiently plan its production schedule and determine its inventory requirements. Since the company's policy is to ensure that retail outlets can be immediately supplied out of existing stock of Dalene dolls, Juloy has to balance its inventory carefully against future demand. The marketing department has recorded monthly sales (in thousands of dollars) for the past two years. The sales history is recorded in column 1 of Table 8-10.

Using the data in Table 8-10 and assuming an initial value of $\alpha = .2$, the forecast for period 2 (made in period 1) is

---

[4] S. Makridakis and S. C. Wheelwright, *Forecasting: Methods and Applications* (New York: John Wiley & Sons, 1978), pp. 53–55. Copyright © 1978 John Wiley & Sons, Inc. Reprinted by permission.

TABLE 8-10   Forecasting Doll Sales Based on Adaptive Response Rate Exponential Smoothing[a]

Date	Period	Sales (thousands) (1)	Single Smoothing Statistic Y_t (2)	Single Smoothing Statistic e_t (3)	E_t (4)	AE_t (5)	α_t (6)
1989: Jan.	1	215			0.00	0.00	0.200
Feb.	2	216	215	1	0.20	0.20	0.200
Mar.	3	243	215	28	5.76	5.76	0.200
Apr.	4	204	221	-17	1.21	8.01	0.151
May	5	212	218	-6	-0.23	7.61	0.030
June	6	240	218	22	4.38	10.49	0.418
July	7	238	227	11	5.70	10.59	0.438
Aug.	8	218	233	-15	1.56	11.47	0.136
Sept.	9	221	231	-10	-0.75	11.18	0.067
Oct.	10	260	230	30	5.40	14.94	0.361
Nov.	11	268	241	27	9.72	17.35	0.560
Dec.	12	296	256	40	15.78	21.88	0.721
1990: Jan.	13	300	285	15	15.62	20.50	0.762
Feb.	14	280	296	-16	9.30	19.60	0.474
Mar.	15	329	289	40	9.44	23.68	0.399
Apr.	16	365	305	60	19.55	30.94	0.632
May	17	382	343	39	23.44	32.55	0.720
June	18	338	371	-33	12.15	32.64	0.372
July	19	332	359	-27	4.32	31.51	0.137
Aug.	20	328	355	-27	-1.94	30.61	0.064
Sept.	21	358	353	5	-0.55	25.49	0.022
Oct.	22	372	353	19	3.36	24.19	0.139
Nov.	23	384	356	28	8.29	24.95	0.332
Dec.	24	389	365	24	11.43	24.76	0.462

[a] For column (2), see equation (8-53); for column (3), see (8-57); for column (4), see (8-55); for column (5), see (8-56); and for column (6), see (8-54).

$$\hat{Y}_{t+1} = \alpha_t Y_t + (1 - \alpha_t) Y_t$$

$$\hat{Y}_2 = (.2)(215) + (.8)(215) \tag{8-58}$$

$$= 215.$$

This forecast value is recorded in column 2 of Table 8-10. The computations necessary to compute values for E_t, AE_t, and e_t are as follows (using $\beta = 0.2$):

1. $e_t = Y_t - \hat{Y}_t$

$$e_2 = Y_2 - \hat{Y}_2$$

$$= 216 - 215 = 1; \text{ see column 3}$$

$$2.\ E_t = .2e_t + .8E_{t-1}$$

$$E_2 = .2e_2 + .8E_1$$

$$= (.2)(1) + (.8)(0)$$

$$= .2;\ \text{see column 4}$$

$$3.\ AE_t = .2\,|\,e_t\,| + .8AE_{t-1}$$

$$= .2\,|\,e_2\,| + .8AE_1$$

$$= .2\,|\,1\,| + .8(0)$$

$$= .2;\ \text{see column 5.}$$

To allow the system to adjust to the initial value of α and the fact that we assumed $\hat{Y}_1 = Y_1 = 215$, let us assume that $\alpha = .2$ for periods 2 and 3. Thus, the forecast for period 3 is

$$\hat{Y}_{2+1} = \alpha_2 Y_2 + (1 - \alpha_2)Y_2$$

$$= (.2)(216) - (.8)(215) \tag{8-59}$$

$$\approx 215.$$

To revise α in period 4, the intermediate computations are

$$1.\ e_4 = Y_4 - \hat{Y}_4$$

$$= 204 - 221$$

$$= -17$$

$$2.\ E_4 = .2e_4 + .8E_3$$

$$= (.2)(-17) + (.8)(5.76)$$

$$= 1.21$$

$$3.\ AE_4 = .2\,|\,e_4\,| + .8AE_3$$

$$= (.2)(17) + (.8)(5.76)$$

$$= 8.01.$$

Steps 2 and 3 provide the final information needed to calculate α_4:

$$\alpha_4 = \left|\,\frac{E_4}{AE_4}\,\right|$$

$$= 1.21/8.01 \tag{8-60}$$

$$= 0.151;\ \text{see column 6 of Table 8-10.}$$

This revised α value is now used to prepare the forecast for May 1989 (period 5) as follows:

$$\hat{Y}_5 = \alpha_4 Y_4 + (1 - \alpha_4)\hat{Y}_4$$

$$= (.151)(204) + (.849)(221) \qquad \text{(8-61)}$$

$$= \$218.$$

Equations (8-54), (8-55), (8-56), and (8-57) must be re-solved for the values needed to compute α_5. Columns 2 through 6 of Table 8-10 contain the results of these computations for the entire historical data base. The information from period 24 (December 1990) can now be used to prepare a forecast for January 1991, as follows:

$$\hat{Y}_{25} = \alpha_{24} Y_{24} + (1 - \alpha_{24})\hat{Y}_{24}$$

$$= (.462)(389) + (.538)(365) \qquad \text{(8-62)}$$

$$= \$376.$$

While this adaptive technique has intuitive appeal, there are nonetheless two major limitations of adaptive response rate smoothing. First, the process of recomputing the necessary statistics each time a new observation becomes available is relatively cumbersome. Second, the forecasts from this technique lag turning points by one time period; that is, it does not anticipate turning points in the forecasted time series.

BROWN'S LINEAR EXPONENTIAL SMOOTHING

Whenever there is a growth pattern or trend in a time series, the single exponential smoothing model's statistics (and forecasts) will tend to lag behind the movements in the actual time series. This occurs because the single exponential smoothing model is based on the assumption of a random variation around a constant value. If there is a linear trend, either positive or negative, in the data, Brown's linear exponential smoothing technique is apt to generate superior forecasts.

The underlying rationale for this linear exponential smoothing technique is relatively simple. Since both the single- and double-smoothed values lag the actual data whenever a trend exists, the difference between these two values can be added to the single-smoothed value and adjusted for trend. The basic equations used in this process are

$$S_t^1 = \alpha Y_t + (1 - \alpha)S_{t-1}^1 \qquad \text{(8-63)}$$

$$S_t^2 = \alpha S_t^1 + (1 - \alpha)S_{t-1}^2 \qquad \text{(8-64)}$$

where S_t^1 refers to the single-smoothed statistic and S_t^2 to the double-smoothed statistic. To apply equations (8-63) and (8-64), the analyst must have values for these two smoothing statistics. However, when $t = 1$, these values are mathematically indeterminate and have to be specified at the outset of the smoothing process. This problem exists with all exponential smoothing models, but it can be overcome with relative ease. The most common methods of assigning these initial values are either by letting $S_1^1 = S_1^2 = Y_1$, or by computing some type of average of the first few observations. This problem of arbitrarily fixing the initial value is not critical, because it can be shown that this value is quickly discounted and the technique adjusts rapidly even if the initial estimate is grossly in error.

The figures shown in Table 8-11 (pages 384–85) are an example of applying Brown's technique for data with a significant trend component. These data represent appliance shipments, and management would like to use these forecasts to plan transportation requirements in the short term.

To begin the process, assume that $S_1^1 = S_1^2 = (Y_1 + Y_2)/2 = 272.3$ and that $\alpha = 0.68$. Columns 2 and 3 of Table 8-11 provide the single- and double-smoothed statistics that result from applying equations (8-63) and (8-64) to the shipments data in column 1. For example, the computations for period 2 are

$$S_t^1 = \alpha Y_t + (1 - \alpha)S_{t-1}^1 \tag{8-63}$$

$$S_2^1 = \alpha Y_2 + (1 - \alpha)S_1^1$$

$$= (.68)(275.1) + (.32)(272.3)$$

$$= 274.2 \tag{8-64}$$

and

$$S_t^2 = \alpha S_t + (1 - \alpha)S_{t-1}^2 \tag{8-65}$$

$$S_2^2 = \alpha S_2 + (1 - \alpha)S_1^2$$

$$= (.68)(274.2) + (.32)(272.3)$$

$$= 273.592. \tag{8-66}$$

The remaining figures in columns 2 and 3 are computed in an analogous manner. Additionally, the single- and double-smoothed statistics are plotted in Figure 8-5. Both the single- and double-smoothed statistics underestimate the trend pattern in Figure 8-5, and it is this defect that necessitates the use of Brown's linear exponential technique.

Several additional formulas must be introduced to clarify the linkages

FIGURE 8-5   Alternative Smoothed Statistics for Appliance Shipments

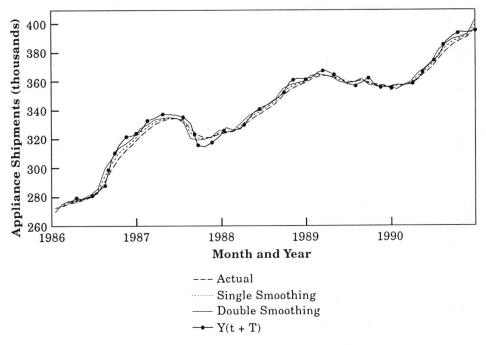

--- Actual
.... Single Smoothing
——— Double Smoothing
—•— Y(t + T)

between single and double exponential smoothing and Brown's technique:

$$\hat{Y}_{t+T} = a_t + b_t T \tag{8-67}$$

where T is the number of time periods from the present period, t, to the future period for which a forecast is desired, and a_t and b_t are defined as

$$a_t = 2S_t^1 - S_t^2 \tag{8-68}$$

$$b_t = \left(\frac{\alpha}{1 - \alpha}\right)(S_t^1 - S_t^2). \tag{8-69}$$

As an example, suppose that we are currently in period 2 and want to develop a forecast for period 3. Based on the data in Table 8-11, the necessary calculations for equation (8-67) are

$$a_2 = 2S_2^1 - S_2^2$$

$$= 2(274.2) - 273.59 \tag{8-70}$$

$$= 274.81$$

TABLE 8-11 Application of Brown's Linear Exponential Smoothing to Appliance Shipments

Date	Period	Actual Appliance Shipments (thousands) (1)	Single Smoothing Statistic S_1 (2)	Double Smoothing Statistic S_2 (3)	a_t (4)	b_t (5)	Y_{t+T} (6)	Forecast Error (7)	Percent Error (8)
1986: Jan.	1	269.5	272.30[c]	272.30[c]					
Feb.	2	275.1	274.20	273.59	274.81[d]	1.29[d]			
Mar.	3	277.4	276.38	275.49	277.27	1.89	276.11[e]	-1.29[f]	-0.47
Apr.	4	277.3	277.00	276.52	277.49	1.03	279.16	1.86	0.67
May	5	279.2	278.50	277.86	279.13	1.35	278.52	-0.68	-0.24
June	6	281.8	280.74	279.82	281.66	1.96	280.48	-1.32	-0.47
July	7	285.4	283.91	282.60	285.22	2.78	283.62	-1.78	-0.62
Aug.	8	299.1	294.24	290.52	297.96	7.91	288.00	-11.10	-3.71
Sept.	9	306.9	302.85	298.90	306.80	8.39	305.88	-1.02	-0.33
Oct.	10	313.4	310.02	306.46	313.58	7.56	315.18	1.78	0.57
Nov.	11	316.4	314.36	311.83	316.89	5.37	321.15	4.75	1.50
Dec.	12	320.4	318.47	316.34	320.59	4.51	322.25	1.85	0.58
1987: Jan.	13	327.1	324.34	321.78	326.90	5.44	325.10	-2.00	-0.61
Feb.	14	329.6	327.92	325.95	329.88	4.17	332.33	2.73	0.83
Mar.	15	333.0	331.37	329.64	333.11	3.69	334.05	1.05	0.32
Apr.	16	333.9	333.09	331.99	334.20	2.35	336.79	2.89	0.87
May	17	334.4	333.98	333.34	334.62	1.36	336.54	2.14	0.64
June	18	334.0	333.99	333.79	334.20	0.44	335.98	1.98	0.59
July	19	331.2	332.09	332.64	331.55	-1.15	334.65	3.45	1.04
Aug.	20	320.0	323.87	326.67	321.07	-5.96	330.40	10.40	3.25
Sept.	21	318.9	320.49	322.47	318.51	-4.21	315.10	-3.80	-1.19
Oct.	22	319.5	319.82	320.67	318.97	-1.80	314.31	-5.19	-1.63
Nov.	23	321.4	320.89	320.82	320.97	0.15	317.16	-4.24	-1.32
Dec.	24	325.6	324.09	323.05	325.14	2.23	321.12	-4.48	-1.38
1988: Jan.	25	324.6	324.44	323.99	324.88	0.95	327.37	2.77	0.85
Feb.	26	325.5	325.16	324.79	325.53	0.79	325.83	0.33	0.10
Mar.	27	330.0	328.45	327.28	329.62	2.49	326.33	-3.67	-1.11
Apr.	28	334.7	332.70	330.97	334.44	3.69	332.12	-2.58	-0.77
May	29	337.8	336.17	334.50	337.83	3.54	338.12	0.32	0.10
June	30	340.1	338.84	337.45	340.23	2.95	341.37	1.27	0.37
July	31	343.7	342.15	340.64	343.65	3.19	343.18	-0.52	-0.15
Aug.	32	347.2	345.58	344.00	347.16	3.36	346.84	-0.36	-0.10
Sept.	33	354.1	351.37	349.02	353.73	5.01	350.52	-3.58	-1.01
Oct.	34	356.8	355.06	353.13	357.00	4.11	358.75	1.95	0.55
Nov.	35	358.0	357.06	355.80	358.32	2.67	361.11	3.11	0.87
Dec.	36	359.4	358.65	357.74	359.56	1.94	360.99	1.59	0.44

TABLE 8-11 (Continued)

Date	Period	Actual Appliance Shipments (thousands) (1)	Single Smoothing Statistic S_1 (2)	Double Smoothing Statistic S_2 (3)	a_t (4)	b_t (5)	Y_{t+T} (6)	Forecast Error (7)	Percent Error (8)
1989: Jan.	37	363.0	361.61	360.37	362.85[d]	2.63[d]	361.50[e]	−1.50[f]	−0.41
Feb.	38	364.4	363.51	362.50	364.51	2.13	365.48	1.08	0.30
Mar.	39	363.3	363.37	363.09	363.64	0.59	366.64	3.34	0.92
Apr.	40	361.8	362.30	362.55	362.05	−0.54	364.23	2.43	0.67
May	41	358.8	359.92	360.76	359.08	−1.79	361.51	2.71	0.76
June	42	357.8	358.48	359.21	357.75	−1.55	357.29	−0.51	−0.14
July	43	358.6	358.56	358.77	358.35	−0.44	356.19	−2.41	−0.67
Aug.	44	361.0	360.22	359.76	360.68	0.99	357.91	−3.09	−0.86
Sept.	45	356.7	357.83	358.44	357.21	−1.31	361.67	4.97	1.39
Oct.	46	356.1	356.65	357.23	356.08	−1.22	355.90	−0.20	−0.06
Nov.	47	356.1	356.28	356.58	355.97	−0.65	354.86	−1.24	−0.35
Dec.	48	354.6	355.14	355.60	354.67	−0.98	355.33	0.73	0.21
1990: Jan.	49	356.6	356.06	355.91	356.21	0.32	353.69	−2.91	−0.82
Feb.	50	356.7	356.50	356.31	356.68	0.40	356.53	−0.17	−0.05
Mar.	51	359.2	358.33	357.69	358.98	1.38	357.08	−2.12	−0.59
Apr.	52	364.9	362.80	361.16	364.44	3.48	360.36	−4.54	−1.24
May	53	368.4	366.61	364.87	368.35	3.70	367.91	−0.49	−0.13
June	54	372.7	370.75	368.87	372.63	4.00	372.05	−0.65	−0.17
July	55	381.0	377.72	374.89	380.55	6.02	376.64	−4.36	−1.15
Aug.	56	385.2	382.81	380.27	385.34	5.39	386.57	1.37	0.36
Sept.	57	388.6	386.75	384.67	388.82	4.40	390.73	2.13	0.55
Oct.	58	389.7	388.75	387.45	390.06	2.77	393.22	3.52	0.90
Nov.	59	391.7	390.76	389.70	391.82	2.25	392.84	1.14	0.29
Dec.	60	400.8	397.59	395.06	400.11	5.36	394.07	−6.73	−1.68
MAD								2.55	
MSE								11.04	
MAPE								0.76	
Mean Error (Bias)								−0.15	
Mean Percent Error (Percent Bias)								−0.05	

c This value has been computed as (269.5 + 275.1)/2 = 272.3, which is the average of sales in periods 1 and 2. Also, we assume that alpha = .68. S_1 and S_2 are defined in equations (8-63) and (8-64), respectively.

d The coefficients a_t and b_t are defined in equations (8-68) and (8-69), respectively.

e See equation (8-67).

f Column 1 less column 6.

$$b_2 = \left(\frac{\alpha}{1 - \alpha}\right)(S_2^1 - S_2^2)$$

$$= \left(\frac{.68}{.32}\right)(274.2 - 273.59) \tag{8-71}$$

$$\approx 1.29$$

$$\hat{Y}_{t+T} = a_t + b_t T$$

$$\hat{Y}_{2+1} = a_2 + b_2(1) \tag{8-72}$$

$$= 274.81 + 1.29(1)$$

$$\approx 276.1$$

Thus, the forecast for period 3 made in period 2 is 276.1, as compared to the actual shipments level of 277.4, an error of -1.3, or -0.47 percent. One-period-ahead forecasts for periods 3 through 60 are listed in column 6 of Table 8-11. The errors associated with these forecasts are presented in columns 7 and 8, and the evaluation statistics are shown at the bottom of Table 8-11. The reliability of the forecasts can be seen by examining Figure 8-5.

Forecasting for time periods that extend beyond the data base involves the same procedure. From the values of S_{60}^1 and S_{60}^2, the analyst can calculate the values of a_{60} and b_{60}:

$$a_{60} = 2(397.59) - 395.06 \tag{8-73}$$

$$\approx 400.11$$

$$b_{60} = (2.125)(397.59 - 395.06) \tag{8-74}$$

$$\approx 5.36.$$

Thus, the forecasts for periods 61 to 65 *made in period 60* are

$$\hat{Y}_{61} = a_{60} + b_{60}(1) = 400.11 + 5.36(1) \approx 405.47$$

$$\hat{Y}_{62} = a_{60} + b_{60}(2) = 400.11 + 5.36(2) \approx 410.84$$

$$\hat{Y}_{63} = a_{60} + b_{60}(3) = 400.11 + 5.36(3) \approx 416.20$$

$$\hat{Y}_{64} = a_{60} + b_{60}(4) = 400.11 + 5.36(4) \approx 421.56$$

$$\hat{Y}_{65} = a_{60} + b_{60}(5) = 400.11 + 5.36(5) \approx 426.93.$$

HOLT'S TWO-PARAMETER LINEAR EXPONENTIAL SMOOTHING

An alternative methodology of dealing with a time series with a linear trend component is Holt's two-parameter model. Conceptually, the two techniques are similar, except that with Holt's method the trend present in the time series is dealt with by a smoothing constant that is different from the smoothing constant applied to the actual observations. Using Holt's technique, the analyst gains some flexibility, but the gain in flexibility requires that two smoothing parameters (as compared to one in Brown's model) be specified. Since two parameters must be quantified, the trial-and-error process of finding the best combination of parameters may be costly and time-consuming.

The basic equations in Holt's two-parameter exponential smoothing are

$$S_t^h = \alpha Y_t + (1 - \alpha)(S_{t-1}^h + c_{t-1}) \tag{8-75}$$

$$c_t = \beta(S_t^h - S_{t-1}^h) + (1 - \beta)c_{t-1}. \tag{8-76}$$

The terms in these equations parallel those given earlier for Brown's exponential smoothing models. Equation (8-75) yields a smoothed statistic that adjusts for trend to eliminate the lag that occurs when a single-smoothed statistic is computed; this is similar to the double-smoothing process of Brown's model. Equation (8-76) revises the trend estimate from the previous period and is similar to that of single exponential smoothing models. The forecasting equation for Holt's model is

$$\hat{Y}_{t+T} = S_t^h + c_t T. \tag{8-77}$$

A direct comparison with Brown's technique can be made by referring to the appliance shipments data and computations in Table 8-11. The actual data are reproduced in column 1 of Table 8-12.

As is the case with all exponential smoothing models, an initial value for the smoothed statistic, S_t^h, in period 1, is required. Assume that $S_1^h = 269.5 = Y_1$. With Holt's model, an initial value for c_1 is also required, and we will assume that

$$c_1 = \frac{Y_2 - Y_1}{2} + \frac{Y_4 - Y_3}{2}. \tag{8-78}$$

Finally, let the smoothing constants, α and β, equal 0.9 and 0.4, respectively. Generally, low values for α and β should be used when there are frequent random fluctuations in the data, whereas high values should be assigned when there is some pattern (that is, linear trend) in the data. High values of α and β also imply that recent observations of the forecast variable are weighted more heavily than are distant observations. Conceptually, the forecasting process can be illustrated by looking at the ex post forecast for period 3 made in period 2:

$$\hat{Y}_{t+T} = S_t^h + c_t T$$

$$\hat{Y}_{2+1} = S_2^h + c_2(1)$$

$$Y_3^h = S_2 + c_2$$

where

$$S_2^h = \alpha Y_2 + (1 - \alpha)(S_1^h + c_1)$$

$$= (.9)(275.1) + (.1)(269.5 + 2.75) \tag{8-79}$$

$$\approx 274.82$$

and

$$c_2 = \beta(S_2^h - S_1^h) + (1 - \beta)c_1$$

$$= (.4)(274.82 - 269.5) + (.6)(2.75) \tag{8-80}$$

$$\approx 3.78.$$

TABLE 8-12 Forecasting Appliance Shipments with Holt's Two-Parameter Exponential Smoothing Model

Date	Period	Actual Appliance Shipments (thousands) (1)	S_t^h (2)	c_t (3)	$\hat{Y}_{t+T}$ (4)	Forecast Error (5)	Percent Error (6)
1986: Jan.	1	269.5	269.50[d]	2.75[e]			
Feb.	2	275.1	274.82	3.78			
Mar.	3	277.4	277.52	3.35	278.59[f]	1.19	0.43
Apr.	4	277.3	277.66	2.06	280.87	3.57	1.29
May	5	279.2	279.25	1.88	279.72	0.52	0.19
June	6	281.8	281.73	2.12	281.13	−0.67	−0.24
July	7	285.4	285.25	2.68	283.85	−1.55	−0.54
Aug.	8	299.1	297.98	6.70	287.92	−11.18	−3.74
Sept.	9	306.9	306.68	7.50	304.68	−2.22	−0.72
Oct.	10	313.4	313.48	7.22	314.18	0.78	0.25
Nov.	11	316.4	316.83	5.67	320.70	4.30	1.36
Dec.	12	320.4	320.61	4.92	322.50	2.10	0.66
1987: Jan.	13	327.1	326.94	5.48	325.53	−1.57	−0.48
Feb.	14	329.6	329.88	4.47	332.42	2.82	0.86
Mar.	15	333.0	333.13	3.98	334.35	1.35	0.40
Apr.	16	333.9	334.22	2.82	337.11	3.21	0.96
May	17	334.4	334.66	1.87	337.04	2.64	0.79
June	18	334.0	334.25	0.96	336.54	2.54	0.76
July	19	331.2	331.60	−0.49	335.21	4.01	1.21
Aug.	20	320.0	321.11	−4.49	331.12	11.12	3.47
Sept.	21	318.9	318.67	−3.67	316.62	−2.28	−0.71
Oct.	22	319.5	319.05	−2.05	315.00	−4.50	−1.41
Nov.	23	321.4	320.96	−0.47	317.00	−4.40	−1.37
Dec.	24	325.6	325.09	1.37	320.49	−5.11	−1.57

TABLE 8-12   *(Continued)*

Date	Period	Actual Appliance Shipments (thousands) (1)	S_t^h (2)	c_t (3)	$\hat{Y}_{t+T}$ (4)	Forecast Error (5)	Percent Error (6)
1988: Jan.	25	324.6	324.79^d	0.70^e	326.46^f	1.86	0.57
Feb.	26	325.5	325.50	0.71	325.49	−0.01	0.00
Mar.	27	330.0	329.62	2.07	326.21	−3.79	−1.15
Apr.	28	334.7	334.40	3.15	331.69	−3.01	−0.90
May	29	337.8	337.78	3.24	337.55	−0.25	−0.07
June	30	340.1	340.19	2.91	341.02	0.92	0.27
July	31	343.7	343.64	3.13	343.10	−0.60	−0.17
Aug.	32	347.2	347.16	3.28	346.77	−0.43	−0.12
Sept.	33	354.1	353.73	4.60	350.44	−3.66	−1.03
Oct.	34	356.8	356.95	4.05	358.33	1.53	0.43
Nov.	35	358.0	358.30	2.97	361.00	3.00	0.84
Dec.	36	359.4	359.59	2.30	361.27	1.87	0.52
1989: Jan.	37	363.0	362.89	2.70	361.88	−1.12	−0.31
Feb.	38	364.4	364.52	2.27	365.59	1.19	0.33
Mar.	39	363.3	363.65	1.01	366.79	3.49	0.96
Apr.	40	361.8	362.09	−0.02	364.66	2.86	0.79
May	41	358.8	359.13	−1.19	362.07	3.27	0.91
June	42	357.8	357.81	−1.24	357.93	0.13	0.04
July	43	358.6	358.40	−0.51	356.57	−2.03	−0.57
Aug.	44	361.0	360.69	0.61	357.89	−3.11	−0.86
Sept.	45	356.7	357.16	−1.05	361.30	4.60	1.29
Oct.	46	356.1	356.10	−1.05	356.11	0.01	0.00
Nov.	47	356.1	356.00	−0.67	355.05	−1.05	−0.29
Dec.	48	354.6	354.67	−0.93	355.32	0.72	0.20
1990: Jan.	49	356.6	356.22	0.06	353.74	−2.86	−0.80
Feb.	50	356.7	356.66	0.21	356.28	−0.42	−0.12
Mar.	51	359.2	358.97	1.05	356.87	−2.33	−0.65
Apr.	52	364.9	364.41	2.81	360.02	−4.88	−1.34
May	53	368.4	368.28	3.23	367.22	−1.18	−0.32
June	54	372.7	372.58	3.66	371.51	−1.19	−0.32
July	55	381.0	380.52	5.37	376.24	−4.76	−1.25
Aug.	56	385.2	385.27	5.12	385.90	0.70	0.18
Sept.	57	388.6	388.78	4.48	390.39	1.79	0.46
Oct.	58	389.7	390.06	3.20	393.26	3.56	0.91
Nov.	59	391.7	391.86	2.64	393.25	1.55	0.40
Dec.	60	400.8	400.17	4.91	394.49	−6.31	−1.57
MAD						2.5	
MSE						11.07	
MAPE						0.74	
Mean Error (Bias)						−0.07	
Mean Percent Error (Percent Bias)						−0.02	

^{d} Equation (8-75); initial value of $S_1^h = y_1$
^{e} Equation (8-76); initial value of $c_1 = 2.75$; see equation (8-78).
^{f} Equation (8-77)

Therefore,

$$\hat{Y}_3 = 274.82 + 3.78 \tag{8-81}$$
$$= 278.6.$$

The remaining smoothed statistics (S_t^h), trend revisions (c_t), and forecasts $(\hat{Y}_{t+T})$ are listed in columns 2 through 4 in Table 8-12. The sales forecast for period 61, January 1991, is made as follows:

$$\hat{Y}_{60+1} = S_{60}^h + c_{60}(1)$$
$$= 400.17 + 4.91(1) \tag{8-82}$$
$$\approx 405.08.$$

Further, the forecast for April 1991 (period 64) made in December 1990 (period 60) is

$$\hat{Y}_{60+4} = S_{60}^h + c_{60}(4)$$
$$= 400.17 + 4.91(4) \tag{8-83}$$
$$\approx 419.8.$$

Alternatively, we would forecast that we will make an average of 419,800 shipments during April of 1991.

The performance of Holt's two-parameter exponential smoothing model in simulating the historical sales observations can be seen in Table 8-12. The evaluation statistics are also presented at the bottom of Table 8-12. Although the technique missed the turning points (as do most exponential smoothing models), it did capture the basic changes in the data pattern. A comparison of the evaluation statistics of the two models indicates that while Holt's performs marginally better according to the two bias statistics (mean error and mean percent error), the gain in accuracy is not likely to justify the increased complexity.

TRIPLE EXPONENTIAL SMOOTHING

Just as single exponential smoothing techniques fail when a linear trend is present in the data, Brown's and Holt's techniques fail whenever the data exhibit a nonlinear trend pattern. Consider a situation in which the average level of the time series changes over time in a quadratic or curvilinear fashion. An appropriate model for such a time series is

$$Y_t = \beta_0 + \beta_1 t + \beta_2 t^2. \tag{8-84}$$

Such a model implies that the time series being studied is either increasing at an increasing/decreasing rate or decreasing at an increasing/decreasing rate.

Triple exponential smoothing, sometimes called quadratic smoothing, involves the use of three smoothed statistics:

$$S_t^1 = \alpha Y_t + (1 - \alpha)S_{t-1}^1 \tag{8-85}$$

$$S_t^2 = \alpha S_t^1 + (1 - \alpha)S_{t-1}^2 \tag{8-86}$$

$$S_t^3 = \alpha S_t^2 + (1 - \alpha)S_{t-1}^3 \tag{8-87}$$

where S_t^1 and S_t^2 are the single- and double-smoothed statistics used in Brown's linear exponential smoothing, and S_t^3 is the triple-smoothed statistic that is derived by smoothing the output of the double-smoothing equation (8-86).

Forecasts based on triple exponential smoothing require the estimation of three additional coefficients:

$$a_t = 3S_t^1 - 3S_t^2 + S_t^3 \tag{8-88}$$

$$b_t = \frac{\alpha}{2(1 - \alpha)^2}\{(6 - 5\alpha)S_t^1 - (10 - 8\alpha)S_t^2 + (4 - 3\alpha)S_t^3\} \tag{8-89}$$

$$c_t = [\{\alpha/1 - \alpha\}]^2(S_t^1 - 2S_t^2 + S_t^3). \tag{8-90}$$

In turn, a_t, b_t, and c_t are used as follows:

$$\hat{Y}_{t+T} = a_t + b_t T + (1/2)c_t T^2. \tag{8-91}$$

The terms in equation (8-91) are defined as they were in previous models.

Consider the case of a company which has been very successful in expanding sales of computer paper. The historical data for paper sales (measured in standard size boxes) is set forth in column 1 of Table 8-13. To begin the triple-smoothing process, initial values for the smoothed statistics (S_t^1, S_t^2, and S_t^3) and α must be specified by the analyst. Based on an $\alpha = 0.65$ and the initialization of the smoothing constants (S's), the smoothed statistics for computer paper sales are computed in columns 2, 3, and 4 of Table 8-13. Once these values have been determined, the forecasting procedure is similar to that presented in connection with linear exponential smoothing. In each time period, the relevant smoothed statistics are entered into equation (8-91) to produce the needed forecast. For example, in preparing a forecast for period 49, January 1991, the initial step is to compute a_{48}, b_{48}, and c_{48} based on values for S_{48}^1, S_{48}^2, and S_{48}^3. Assuming that $\alpha = 0.65$, these statistics can be

TABLE 8-13 Application of Triple Exponential Smoothing to Sales of Computer Paper

Date	Period	Sales: Boxes of Computer Paper (1)	Single Smoothed Statistic S_t^1 (2)	Double Smoothed Statistic S_t^2 (3)	Triple Smoothed Statistic S_t^3 (4)	a_t (5)	b_t (6)	c_t (7)	$\hat{Y}_{t+T}$ (8)	Forecast Error (9)	Percent Error (10)
1987: Jan.	1	36,118	36,465[d]	36,465[d]	36,465[d]	36,797[e]	297[e]	95[e]			
Feb.	2	36,812	36,691	36,612	36,560	39,602	2,591	801			
Mar.	3	39,712	38,654	37,939	37,457	40,671	1,674	250	37,142[f]	(2,570)	-6.47
Apr.	4	40,585	39,909	39,220	38,603	41,734	1,266	38	42,594	2,009	4.95
May	5	41,701	41,074	40,425	39,787	44,938	3,020	589	42,470	769	1.84
June	6	45,024	43,641	42,516	41,561	47,932	3,323	497	43,019	(2,005)	-4.45
July	7	47,918	46,421	45,054	43,832	51,207	3,555	412	48,252	334	0.70
Aug.	8	51,194	49,524	47,959	46,515	58,578	7,194	1,448	51,504	310	0.61
Sept.	9	58,740	55,514	52,870	50,646	62,482	5,054	296	54,968	(3,772)	-6.42
Oct.	10	62,302	59,926	57,457	55,073	65,679	3,558	(279)	66,496	4,194	6.73
Nov.	11	65,589	63,607	61,454	59,221	73,868	7,544	1,090	67,683	2,094	3.19
Dec.	12	74,082	70,416	67,279	64,459	79,594	6,521	412	69,097	(4,985)	-6.73
1988: Jan.	13	79,488	76,313	73,151	70,109	84,242	5,075	(185)	81,957	2,469	3.11
Feb.	14	84,149	81,406	78,517	75,574	90,025	5,606	45	86,321	2,172	2.58
Mar.	15	90,061	87,032	84,052	81,084	93,815	4,008	(482)	89,225	(836)	-0.93
Apr.	16	93,733	91,388	88,820	86,113	100,916	6,505	474	95,654	1,921	2.05
May	17	101,065	97,678	94,578	91,615	101,844	1,783	(1,194)	97,582	(3,483)	-3.45
June	18	101,584	100,217	98,243	95,923	103,106	656	(1,172)	107,658	6,074	5.98
July	19	103,109	102,097	100,748	99,059	105,967	1,979	(371)	103,030	(79)	-0.08
Aug.	20	106,092	104,694	103,313	101,824	116,552	9,467	2,151	103,176	(2,916)	-2.75
Sept.	21	116,946	112,658	109,387	106,740	118,310	3,766	(369)	107,760	(9,186)	-7.85
Oct.	22	117,917	116,076	113,735	111,287	120,087	1,783	(887)	127,094	9,177	7.78
Nov.	23	120,006	118,631	116,917	114,946	127,759	6,557	930	121,892	1,886	1.57
Dec.	24	128,043	124,749	122,008	119,536				121,427	(6,616)	-5.17

TABLE 8-13 (*Continued*)

Date	Period	Sales: Boxes of Computer Paper (1)	Single Smoothed Statistic S_t^1 (2)	Double Smoothed Statistic S_t^2 (3)	Triple Smoothed Statistic S_t^3 (4)	a_t (5)	b_t (6)	c_t (7)	$\hat{Y}_{t+T}$ (8)	Forecast Error (9)	Percent Error (10)
1989: Jan.	25	133,426	130,389[d]	127,455[d]	124,684[d]	133,484[e]	6,327[e]	558[e]	134,781[f]	1,355	1.02
Feb.	26	139,263	136,157	133,112	130,162	139,298	6,177	331	140,090	827	0.59
Mar.	27	150,944	145,769	141,339	137,427	150,717	11,045	1,787	145,641	(5,303)	−3.51
Apr.	28	154,896	151,701	148,074	144,348	155,229	6,194	(344)	162,655	7,759	5.01
May	29	157,940	155,756	153,068	150,016	158,082	3,018	(1,253)	161,250	3,310	2.10
June	30	165,316	161,970	158,854	155,761	165,108	5,908	77	160,473	(4,843)	−2.93
July	31	158,744	159,873	159,517	158,202	159,272	(4,547)	(3,304)	171,055	12,311	7.76
Aug.	32	165,818	163,737	162,260	160,840	165,272	3,053	196	153,072	(12,746)	−7.69
Sept.	33	177,429	172,637	169,005	166,147	177,043	10,955	2,670	168,423	(9,006)	−5.08
Oct.	34	189,993	183,918	178,699	174,306	189,965	14,190	2,851	189,333	(660)	−0.35
Nov.	35	199,822	194,256	188,811	183,734	200,069	12,115	1,270	205,580	5,758	2.88
Dec.	36	207,598	202,928	197,987	192,999	207,822	8,918	(164)	212,819	5,221	2.51
1990: Jan.	37	212,868	209,389	205,398	201,058	213,030	5,512	(1,205)	216,658	3,790	1.78
Feb.	38	216,910	214,278	211,170	207,631	216,954	3,426	(1,487)	217,940	1,030	0.47
Mar.	39	229,937	224,456	219,806	215,545	229,495	10,751	1,341	219,636	(10,301)	−4.48
Apr.	40	238,233	233,411	228,649	224,063	238,348	9,796	604	240,917	2,684	1.13
May	41	240,337	237,913	234,671	230,958	240,685	3,462	(1,623)	248,446	8,109	3.37
June	42	236,214	236,809	236,060	234,274	236,519	(4,253)	(3,579)	243,336	7,122	3.01
July	43	249,072	244,780	241,728	239,119	248,273	8,078	1,528	230,477	(18,595)	−7.47
Aug.	44	253,583	250,502	247,431	244,522	253,735	6,583	558	257,116	3,533	1.39
Sept.	45	264,253	259,440	255,237	251,487	264,096	10,269	1,562	260,596	(3,657)	−1.38
Oct.	46	267,338	264,574	261,306	257,869	267,673	5,151	(582)	275,147	7,809	2.92
Nov.	47	267,597	266,539	264,707	262,314	267,809	346	(1,938)	272,533	4,936	1.84
Dec.	48	289,066	281,182	275,416	270,830	288,128	17,128	4,071	267,186	(21,880)	−7.57
MAD										5,052	
MAPE											3.56
MSE										46,246,439	
Mean Error (Bias)										−314.66	
Mean Percent Error (Percent Bias)											−0.13

[d] The value of 36,465 is the average of actual sales in periods 1 and 2; that is, 36,465 = (36,118 + 36,812)/2.
[e] The coefficients a_t, b_t, and c_t, are defined in equations (8-88), (8-89), and (8-90), respectively.
[f] The forecast values are derived from equation (8-91).

393

calculated as

$$S_{48}^1 = (.65)(289{,}066) + (.35)(266{,}539) \tag{8-92}$$
$$\approx 281{,}182$$

$$S_{48}^2 = (.65)(281{,}182) + (.35)(264{,}707) \tag{8-93}$$
$$\approx 275{,}416$$

$$S_{48}^3 = (.65)(275{,}416) + (.35)(262{,}314) \tag{8-94}$$
$$\approx 270{,}830.$$

Substituting into the equations for a_{48}, b_{48}, and c_{48}, we get

$$a_{48} = 3(281{,}182) - 3(275{,}416) + 270{,}830 \tag{8-95}$$
$$\approx 288{,}128$$

$$b_{48} = 2.65\{[6 - 5(.65)]281{,}182 - [10 - 8(.65)]275{,}416$$
$$+ [4 - 3(.65)]270{,}830\} \tag{8-96}$$
$$\approx 17{,}128$$

$$c_{48} = \frac{0.65^2}{(1 - .65)^2} [281{,}182 - 2(275{,}416) + 270{,}830) \tag{8-97}$$
$$\approx 4{,}071.$$

Thus, the forecast for period 49 is

$$\hat{Y}_{48+1} = a_{48} + b_{48}T + (1/2)c_{48}T^2$$
$$= 288{,}128 + 17{,}128(1) + (1/2)(4{,}071)(1^2) \tag{8-98}$$
$$\approx 307{,}292.$$

Similarly, the forecast for period 54, June 1991, would be

$$\hat{Y}_{48+6} = a_{48} + b_{48}(6) + (1/2)c_{48}(6)^2$$
$$\approx 288{,}128 + 17{,}128(6) + (1/2)(4{,}071)(36) \tag{8-99}$$
$$\approx 464{,}180.$$

WINTERS' SEASONAL EXPONENTIAL SMOOTHING

Exponential smoothing techniques can be generalized so both trend and seasonal patterns are incorporated in time series forecasts. Winters' seasonal ex-

FIGURE 8-6   Monthly Shipments of Steel: Actual versus Trend Values

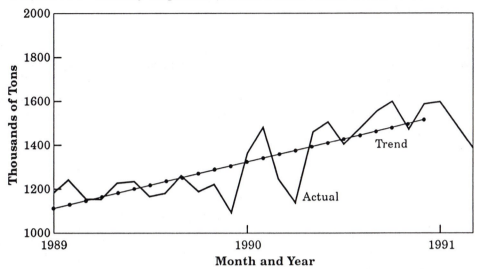

ponential smoothing technique applies the smoothing process three times:[5]

1. To estimate the average value of the time series
2. To estimate the trend component
3. To estimate the seasonal index.

Each of the three stages has its own smoothing constant, which can be adjusted as the situation warrants, and these individual modifications can be made to any one of the constants without having to alter the others.

The flexibility and power of Winters' seasonal exponential smoothing is best illustrated through an actual application to a time series that has a trend and a seasonal component. Sample data for steel shipments are listed in Table 8-14 and illustrated in Figure 8-6.

Several preliminary steps must be completed before applying Winters' model. These steps are designed to provide the initial estimates of trend and seasonality. The trend estimates can be generated via a simple linear trend regression model of the form

$$\hat{Y}_t = a + bX_t \qquad \text{(8-100)}$$

where X_t is the trend variable measuring time, and it is incremented by one

[5] P. R. Winters, "Forecasting Sales by Exponentially Weighted Moving Averages," *Management Science*, vol. 6, no. 3, 1960. Copyright © 1960 The Institute of Management Sciences. Reprinted by permission.

unit for each month beyond the beginning point. For the steel shipment data in column 1 of Table 8-14, the estimated trend line is[6]

$$\hat{Y}_t = 1{,}091 + 18.479X_t$$

$$X_t = 0 \text{ in December of 1988.}$$

(8-101)

This equation can be used to prepare trend estimates for any month simply by substituting the specific X_t value.[7] For example, the trend estimate for December 1990 (period 24) is

$$\hat{Y}_t = 1{,}091 + 18.479X_t$$

$$= 1{,}091 + 18.479(24)$$

$$= 1{,}534 \text{ Thousand Tons.}$$

(8-102)

Trend values for the historical period (January 1989 to December 1990) are derived in an identical fashion and are noted in column 2 of Table 8-14. Figure 8-6 provides a visual comparison of the actual and the trend magnitudes. The trend figures serve as the initial trend values in Winters' exponential technique, and they are also used in deriving the seasonal factors.

Seasonal factors are determined by dividing the actual values by the trend estimates and averaging these preliminary estimates. The first step in this process is to divide the actual values (Y_t) in column 1 of Table 8-14 by the trend estimates ($\hat{Y}_t$) in column 2. Thus, January 1989 steel shipments were 6 percent greater (1,178 versus 1,109) than the trend level. The ratios listed in column 3 must be averaged by month to determine the initial seasonal estimates used in Winters' exponential method. For example, the initial seasonal value for January is 1.045—(1.06 + 1.03)/2—and for February it is 1.105—(1.10 + 1.11)/2. Therefore, at time $t = 24$ (December 1990), the initial estimates of the multiplicative seasonal factors are as follows: January, 1.045; February, 1.105; March, 0.965; April, 0.91; May, 1.045; June, 1.05; July, 0.97; August, 0.99; September, 1.035; October, 1.01; November, 0.985; December, 0.905. These values are listed in column 4 of Table 8-14.

Once these initial estimates of trend and seasonality are made, Winters' model incorporates them into an exponential smoothing process, thereby permitting estimates of the intercept, the slope, and the seasonal factors to be updated continuously. The following four equations are used to derive the revisions prior to actually making a forecast:

---

[6] The derivation of least-squares estimators was illustrated in chapter 3.

[7] The data for 1991 were excluded from the trend line computations for reasons that will become apparent later in this section.

TABLE 8-14 **Forecasts of Monthly Steel Shipments Based on Winters' Seasonal Exponential Smoothing**

Date	Period	Steel Shipments (thousands of tons) Y_t (1)	Trend $\hat{Y}_t$ (2)	Ratio of Actual to Trend $Y_T/\hat{Y}_T$ (3)	Initial Estimates of Seasonal Factors (4)
1989: Jan.	1	1,178	1,109[a]	1.06	
Feb.	2	1,239	1,127	1.10	
Mar.	3	1,158	1,145	1.01	
Apr.	4	1,150	1,164	0.99	
May	5	1,231	1,182	1.04	
June	6	1,236	1,201	1.03	
July	7	1,173	1,219	0.96	
Aug.	8	1,188	1,238	0.96	
Sept.	9	1,266	1,256	1.01	
Oct.	10	1,195	1,275	0.94	
Nov.	11	1,224	1,293	0.95	
Dec.	12	1,101	1,312	0.84	
1990: Jan.	13	1,369	1,330	1.03	1.045[b]
Feb.	14	1,494	1,349	1.11	1.105
Mar.	15	1,252	1,367	0.92	0.965
Apr.	16	1,150	1,386	0.83	0.910
May	17	1,469	1,404	1.05	1.045
June	18	1,521	1,423	1.07	1.050
July	19	1,413	1,441	0.98	0.970
Aug.	20	1,488	1,460	1.02	0.990
Sept.	21	1,573	1,478	1.06	1.035
Oct.	22	1,615	1,497	1.08	1.010
Nov.	23	1,492	1,515	1.02	0.985
Dec.	24	1,605	1,534	0.97	0.905
1991: Jan.	25	1,611			
Feb.	26	1,512			
Mar.	27	1,402			
Apr.	28				

[a] These estimates are based on equation (8-101).
[b] This technique ignores the cyclicality present in column 1.

1. The current estimate of the intercept of the trend line at time t is

$$a_t = \alpha\, \frac{Y_t}{\text{SF}_{t-N}} + (1 - \alpha)(a_{t-1} + b_{t-1}) \qquad \textbf{(8-103)}$$

2. The current estimate of the slope of the trend line at time t is

$$b_t = \beta(a_t - a_{t-1}) + (1 - \beta)b_{t-1} \qquad \textbf{(8-104)}$$

3. Seasonal factors are revised according to

$$\text{SF}_t = \sigma \frac{Y_t}{a_t} + (1 - \sigma)\text{SF}_{t-N} \tag{8-105}$$

4. The forecast (made in period t) for a point T periods in the future is

$$\hat{Y}_{t+T} = (a_t + b_t T)\text{SF}^*_{t+T}. \tag{8-106}$$

The terms in equations (8-103), (8-104), (8-105), and (8-106) are defined as

$$
\begin{aligned}
Y_t &= \text{actual data value for period } t \\
a_t &= \text{estimated intercept of the trend line at time } t \\
b_t &= \text{estimated slope of the trend line at time } t \\
N &= \text{number of periods in the seasonal pattern (12 in the case of} \\
&\quad \text{monthly data, 4 with quarterly data, etc.)} \\
\text{SF}_t &= \text{estimated seasonal factor for period } t \\
\alpha, \beta, \sigma &= \text{exponential smoothing constants, where } 0 < \alpha, \beta, \sigma < 1 \\
\text{SF}^*_{t+T} &= \text{the best estimate of the seasonal factor in period } t + T \\
\hat{Y}_{t+T} &= \text{estimated value } T \text{ periods in the future.}
\end{aligned}
$$

The applicability of these equations can best be illustrated through the development of a one-period-ahead steel shipments forecast. Suppose that we are now at the end of December 1990 (period 24) and a forecast for January 1991 (period 25) is desired. Our best initial estimate of the intercept value of the trend value in period 24 is 1,534, as shown in equation (8-101). The best estimate for the slope of the trend line in period 24 is 18.479. The best estimate of the seasonal factor for January 1991 is the previous estimate of January's seasonality; that is, $\text{SF}^*_{24+1} = 1.045$. Our January estimate of steel shipments can then be computed as follows for January 1991:

$$
\begin{aligned}
\hat{Y}_{24+1} = \hat{Y}_{25} &= [a_{24} + b_{24}(1)] \cdot \text{SF}^*_{25} \\
&= (1,534 + 18.479) \cdot 1.045 \tag{8-107} \\
&\approx 1,622.
\end{aligned}
$$

At the end of period 25, actual steel shipments are recorded as 1,611 thousand tons for January 1991. Once this latest observation is recorded, we can develop revisions for the seasonal factors, intercept, and slope values, based on this latest information. To solve equations (8-103), (8-104), and (8-105), we must specify values for the smoothing constants α, β, and σ. For illustrative purposes, assume that $\alpha = \beta = \sigma = 0.4$.[8] The revisions are made as follows:

---

[8] The forecaster should experiment with alternative values of α, β, and σ.

1. $a_{25} = \alpha \dfrac{Y_{25}}{\text{SF}_{25-12}} + (1 - \alpha)(a_{24} + b_{24})$

   $= .4(1611/1.045) + (.6)(1{,}534 + 18.479) = 1{,}548$

2. $b_{25} = \beta(a_{25} - a_{24}) + (1 - \beta)b_{24}$

   $= (.4)(1{,}548 - 1{,}534) + (.6)(18.479)$

   $= 16.82$

3. $\text{SF}_{25} = \sigma(Y_{25}/a_{25}) + (1 - \sigma)\text{SF}_{25-12}$

   $= (.4)(1{,}611/1{,}548) + (.6)(1.045)$

   $= 1.043.$

Note that the value used for a_{24} is 1,534, the predicted trend value from equation (8-102). This is the intercept of the trend equation when the origin is moved to period 24. SF_{25} becomes the new estimated seasonal factor for January, and SF_{13} is eliminated from future computations. This revised information can then be used to develop forecasts for future periods. For example, February's forecast (made in January) would be

$$\hat{Y}_{t+T} = (a_t + b_t T)\text{SF}^*_{t+T}$$

$$\hat{Y}_{25+1} = (a_{25} + b_{25}T)\text{SF}^*_{t+T} \qquad \text{(8-108)}$$

$$\hat{Y}_{26} = [1{,}548 + 16.82(1)]1.105$$

$$= 1{,}729 \text{ Thousand Tons.}$$

This is as opposed to the actual value of 1,512 produced by the peak in the economy. Alternatively, the forecast for August 1991 (period 32) made in January 1991 is

$$\hat{Y}_{t+T} = (a_t + b_t T)\text{SF}^*_{t+T}$$

$$\hat{Y}_{25+7} = [(a_{25} + b_{25}(7)]\text{SF}^*_{25+7} \qquad \text{(8-109)}$$

$$\hat{Y}_{32} = [1{,}548 + 16.82(7)]0.99$$

$$= 1{,}649 \text{ Thousand Tons.}$$

By repeating this procedure of revising a_t, b_t, and SF^*_t each time an actual observation becomes available, we adapt the forecast values to changes in the activity being monitored. To see this, assume that period 26's observation of 1,512 thousand tons is recorded and a revised forecast for August 1991 is desired:

1. $a_{26} = \alpha(Y_{26}/SF_{26-12}) + (1 - \alpha)(a_{25} + b_{25})$

   $= (.4)(1,512/1.105) + (.6)(1,548 + 16.82)$

   $= 1,486$

2. $b_{26} = \beta(a_{26} - a_{25}) + (1 - \beta)b_{25}$

   $= (.4)(1,486 - 1,548) + (.6)(16.82)$

   $= -14.61$

3. $SF_{26} = \sigma(Y_{26}/a_{26}) + (1 - \sigma)SF_{26-12}$

   $= (.4)(1,512/1,486) + (.6)(1.105)$

   $= 1.070.$

Therefore, the August 1991 forecast is revised downward from 1,649 to

$$\hat{Y}_{26+6} = (a_{26} + b_{26}T)SF^*_{26+6}$$

$$\hat{Y}_{32} = [1,486 - 14.6(6)]0.99 \qquad \text{(8-110)}$$

$$= 1,384 \text{ Thousand Tons.}$$

There are two principal limitations associated with Winter's exponential smoothing. First, the existence of the cyclical component in economic time series data is difficult to build into Winter's model. Second, the selection of the smoothing constants (α, β, σ) is made through a trial-and-error process, which can become extremely time-consuming with three constants to select. In the illustration developed in this section, $\alpha = \beta = \sigma = 0.4$. Generally, higher values are assigned to the smoothing constants to place more emphasis on current observations, but the selection of parameter values remains highly judgmental. Finally, the revision of the seasonal factors tends to be unduly influenced by random variations in the data.

EXAMPLE 8-3 Turning-Point Reliability of Exponential Smoothing Model

One of the more important challenges facing the forecaster is to provide management with advance warning of turning points in economic and business activity. The ability of a forecaster to predict either the end of a recession or the onset of a contraction can be critical to the profitability of a firm. To illustrate one of the primary limitations of exponential smoothing, suppose that you are a forecaster for a large retailer of small to medium-size trucks and your assignment is the development of monthly sales forecasts. As a first step, you collect the monthly sales data presented in column 1 of Table 8-15.

A preliminary analysis of the data in column 1 indicates that a linear trend pattern dominates the data, so you decide to test the applicability of Brown's linear exponential model. The results of the historical simulation of the sales data using this technique are presented in column 3 of Table 8-15. The evaluation statistics of the estimated model are presented in Table 8-16.

TABLE 8-15 Turning-Point Reliability of Exponential Smoothing Model

Date	Period	Sales of Trucks (thousands) (1)	Actual Turning Point (2)	Brown's Linear Forecast (3)	Predicted Turning Point (4)
1987: Jan.	1	128.0			
Feb.	2	130.9	2.90		
Mar.	3	130.1	−0.80	131.31	
Apr.	4	130.8	0.70	130.36	−0.95
May	5	132.7	1.90	131.02	0.67
June	6	138.7	6.00	133.45	2.43
July	7	139.2	0.50	141.14	7.69
Aug.	8	140.6	1.40	141.78	0.64
Sept.	9	142.2	1.60	142.60	0.82
Oct.	10	137.7	−4.50	143.93	1.34
Nov.	11	134.5	−3.20	137.64	−6.30
Dec.	12	132.3	−2.20	132.75	−4.89
1988: Jan.	13	127.1	−5.20	130.02	−2.73
Feb.	14	131.9	4.80	123.94	−6.08
Mar.	15	132.9	1.00	130.59	6.65
Apr.	16	129.2	−3.70	133.27	2.68
May	17	129.4	0.20	128.73	−4.54
June	18	136.9	7.50	128.59	−0.14
July	19	134.8	−2.10	138.50	9.91
Aug.	20	136.3	1.50	136.44	−2.06
Sept.	21	138.8	2.50	137.42	0.98
Oct.	22	131.5	−7.30	140.29	2.87
Nov.	23	129.2	−2.30	130.71	−9.58
Dec.	24	125.9	−3.30	126.85	−3.86
1989: Jan.	25	126.0	0.10	123.09	−3.76
Feb.	26	126.5	0.50	123.88	0.79
Mar.	27	127.2	0.70	125.49	1.61
Apr.	28	127.5	0.30	127.01	1.52
May	29	129.4	1.90	127.67	0.66
June	30	135.4	6.00	130.12	2.45
July	31	136.2	0.80	137.82	7.70
Aug.	32	140.6	4.40	138.85	1.03
Sept.	33	148.1	7.50	143.53	4.68
Oct.	34	142.5	−5.60	152.54	9.01
Nov.	35	139.7	−2.80	144.72	−7.82
Dec.	36	139.6	−0.10	139.21	−5.51

(continued)

TABLE 8-15 *(Continued)*

Date	Period	Sales of Trucks (thousands) (1)	Actual Turning Point (2)	Brown's Linear Forecast (3)	Predicted Turning Point (4)
1990: Jan.	37	142.7	3.10	138.57	−0.64
Feb.	38	145.7	3.00	142.88	4.31
Mar.	39	149.1	3.40	147.20	4.33
Apr.	40	148.2	−0.90	151.50	4.30
May	41	150.5	2.30	149.92	−1.58
June	42	157.2	6.70	151.96	2.03
July	43	157.7	0.50	160.20	8.24
Aug.	44	160.7	3.00	160.68	0.48
Sept.	45	164.8	4.10	163.36	2.68
Oct.	46	156.8	−8.00	167.87	4.51
Nov.	47	153.0	−3.80	156.95	−10.91
Dec.	48	152.1	−0.90	150.61	−6.34
1991: Jan.	49	150.7	−1.40	149.62	−1.00
Feb.	50	151.4	0.70	148.71	−0.90
Mar.	51	153.9	2.50	150.31	1.59
Apr.	52	151.7	−2.20	154.16	3.85
May	53	156.0	4.30	151.74	−2.42
June	54	161.8	5.80	156.91	5.17
July	55	162.0	0.20	164.63	7.72
Aug.	56	164.3	2.30	164.73	0.10
Sept.	57	165.8	1.50	166.57	1.84
Oct.	58	166.6	0.80	167.80	1.23
Nov.	59	167.6	1.00	168.16	0.37
Dec.	60	171.5	3.90	168.85	0.69

From an examination of the evaluation statistics presented in Table 8-16 and the performance of the historical simulation shown in Figure 8-7, it seems that the model will fulfill your objective. However, there remains one other aspect of the model that requires investigation. The capability of the model in capturing turning points will assist management in both minimizing the costs of excess inventory levels and in ensuring that the probability of lost sales is minimized. The turning-point performance of Brown's linear exponential model can be evaluated with the aid of Figure 8-8.

TABLE 8-16 **Evaluation Statistics for Truck Sales Model**

MAPE	2.04%
MAD	2.90
MSE	14.6457
Mean Error (Bias)	−0.07
Mean Percent Error (Percent Bias)	−0.0461%

FIGURE 8-7 Historical Reliability of Truck Sales Model

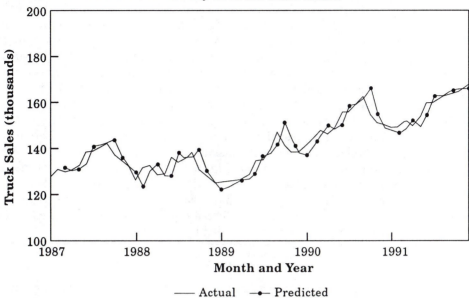

— Actual   —•— Predicted

FIGURE 8-8 Turning-Point Efficiency of Truck Sales Model

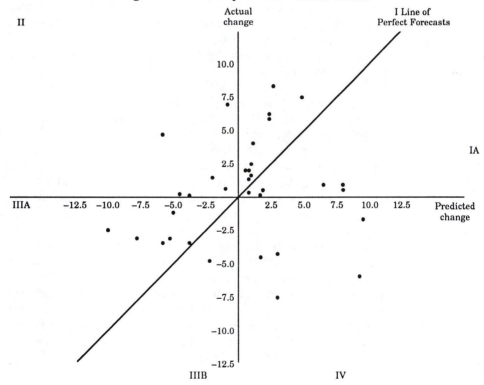

Of particular interest in this example are the points located in quadrants II and IV, since these represent periods in which turning-point errors occurred. There are 18 months in which turning-point errors occurred. That is, in 32 percent (18 of 57 observations) of the months, the time series model produced a forecast that involved a turning-point error.

The purpose of Figure 8-8 is to emphasize the weakness of time series models at upper and lower turning points. If the variable to be estimated is extremely sensitive to cyclical patterns in the economy, which is clearly true for truck sales, then exclusive reliance on a time series model is unwise. It may still be worthwhile, however, to use a time series model as both a cross-check against an established regression model and to generate immediate- to short-term forecasts. When the two models (time series and regression) give radically different signals, it is in the forecaster's best interest to diagnose the source of the discrepancy so that the decision maker is not forced to make a decision in the face of clearly contradictory signals provided by the forecaster.

EXAMPLE 8-4   Time Series Models: A Comparative Test

Suppose that, as a forecaster for a state department of revenue, you are responsible for developing monthly forecasts for the largest source of tax revenue, the gross receipts tax. It is highly unlikely that you will be able to obtain monthly measures of economic activity in the state on a timely basis, so you decide to rely on time series techniques rather than on estimating a regression equation.

The actual data to be used in developing the forecasts are presented in Table 8-17 and in Figure 8-9 (page 407). An examination of the time plot in Figure 8-9 indicates that the series for gross tax revenues exhibits an upward growth pattern. However, these changes appear to be occurring relatively slowly, and it is possible that a simple nonlinear model might perform adequately as a forecasting system. Thus, as a first step in the modeling process, you decide to evaluate statistics from each of the time series models. These statistics are documented in Table 8-18 (page 407).

A comparison of these statistics suggests that, as a first step in model(s) selection, the naive, simple average change, simple percent change, simple moving average, and single exponential smoothing models can be eliminated from further consideration. Furthermore, while it appears that Brown's linear exponential smoothing and triple exponential smoothing perform best in the historical simulation (the evaluation statistics are derived from this simulation), it does not necessarily follow that they provide the best forecasts.

TABLE 8-17   Time Series Forecasts for Gross Receipts Tax Revenues

Date	Actual	Double Moving Average Forecast[a]	Error	Absolute Change Moving Average Forecast[b]	Error	Percent Change Moving Average Change Forecast[c]	Error	Brown's Linear Exponential Smoothing Forecast[d]	Error	Triple Exponential Smoothing Forecast[e]	Error
	(1)	(2)	(3)	(4)	(5)	(6)	(7)	(8)	(9)	(10)	(11)
1984: Jan.	8,004										
Feb.	8,122										
Mar.	8,237							8,180	(57)	8,193	(44)
Apr.	8,352	8,354	2					8,351	(1)	8,385	33
May	8,463	8,467	4					8,467	4	8,502	39
June	8,612	8,577	(35)					8,574	(38)	8,594	(18)
July	8,763	8,732	(31)					8,760	(3)	8,776	13
Aug.	8,922	8,912	(10)					8,914	(8)	8,931	9
Sept.	9,057	9,075	18					9,081	24	9,093	36
Oct.	9,163	9,210	47					9,192	29	9,196	33
Nov.	9,241	9,291	50					9,270	29	9,259	18
Dec.	9,278	9,340	62					9,320	42	9,299	21
1985: Jan.	9,282	9,346	64					9,316	34	9,288	6
Feb.	9,295	9,311	16					9,287	(8)	9,253	(42)
Mar.	9,326	9,301	(25)					9,308	(18)	9,282	(44)
Apr.	9,406	9,344	(62)					9,357	(49)	9,349	(57)
May	9,564	9,449	(115)					9,485	(79)	9,498	(66)
June	9,809	9,664	(145)					9,720	(89)	9,758	(51)
July	10,129	9,989	(140)					10,052	(77)	10,113	(16)
Aug.	10,511	10,393	(118)					10,447	(64)	10,521	10
Sept.	10,949	10,846	(103)					10,892	(57)	10,965	16
Oct.	11,402	11,345	(57)					11,386	(16)	11,454	52
Nov.	11,838	11,844	6					11,855	17	11,909	71
Dec.	12,196	12,287	91					12,274	78	12,303	107
1986: Jan.	11,619	12,612	993					12,556	937	12,548	929
Feb.	11,515	11,743	228					11,061	(454)	10,838	(677)
Mar.	11,406	11,056	(350)					11,402	(4)	11,134	(272)
Apr.	11,284	11,301	17					11,297	13	11,238	(46)
May	11,154	11,172	18					11,162	8	11,158	4
June	11,023	11,030	7					11,024	1	11,024	1
July	10,934	10,893	(41)					10,892	(42)	10,890	(44)
Aug.	10,891	10,814	(77)					10,844	(47)	10,852	(39)
Sept.	10,923	10,814	(109)					10,847	(76)	10,871	(52)
Oct.	10,997	10,899	(98)					10,953	(44)	10,996	(1)
Nov.	11,122	11,040	(82)					11,070	(52)	11,123	1
Dec.	11,296	11,209	(87)					11,246	(50)	11,298	2
1987: Jan.	11,497	11,433	(64)					11,469	(28)	11,520	23
Feb.	11,709	11,678	(31)					11,697	(12)	11,743	34
Mar.	11,918	11,913	(5)					11,921	3	11,955	37
Apr.	12,100	12,129	29					12,127	27	12,147	47
May	12,236	12,302	66					12,283	47	12,285	49
June	12,324	12,407	83					12,373	49	12,357	33
July	12,366	12,448	82					12,413	47	12,381	15
Aug.	12,364	12,442	78					12,409	45	12,368	4
Sept.	12,328	12,395	67					12,363	35	12,318	(10)
Oct.	12,272	12,318	46					12,293	21	12,250	(22)
Nov.	12,219	12,231	12					12,216	(3)	12,180	(39)
Dec.	12,179	12,164	(15)					12,166	(13)	12,142	(37)

(continued)

TABLE 8-17   Time Series Forecasts for Gross Receipts Tax Revenues (*Continued*)

Date	Actual	Double Moving Average Forecast[a]	Error	Absolute Change Moving Average Forecast[b]	Error	Percent Change Moving Average Change Forecast[c]	Error	Brown's Linear Exponential Smoothing Forecast[d]	Error	Triple Exponential Smoothing Forecast[e]	Error
	(1)	*(2)*	*(3)*	*(4)*	*(5)*	*(6)*	*(7)*	*(8)*	*(9)*	*(10)*	*(11)*
1988: Jan.	12,138	12,129	(9)	12,268	130	12,290	152	12,139	1	12,130	(8)
Feb.	12,116	12,098	(18)	12,223	107	12,244	128	12,097	(19)	12,097	(19)
Mar.	12,086	12,080	(6)	12,199	113	12,218	132	12,094	8	12,099	13
Apr.	12,065	12,062	(3)	12,165	100	12,183	118	12,056	(9)	12,062	(3)
May	12,058	12,037	(21)	12,142	84	12,158	100	12,044	(14)	12,048	(10)
June	12,075	12,040	(35)	12,131	56	12,146	71	12,051	(24)	12,057	(18)
July	12,110	12,074	(36)	12,145	35	12,159	49	12,092	(18)	12,104	(6)
Aug.	12,142	12,132	(10)	12,178	36	12,190	48	12,145	3	12,162	20
Sept.	12,188	12,176	(12)	12,208	20	12,220	32	12,174	(14)	12,188	0
Oct.	12,240	12,224	(16)	12,252	12	12,264	24	12,234	(6)	12,244	4
Nov.	12,303	12,288	(15)	12,304	1	12,315	12	12,292	(11)	12,301	(2)
Dec.	12,369	12,358	(11)	12,367	(2)	12,379	10	12,366	(3)	12,375	6
1989: Jan.	12,434	12,433	(1)	12,435	1	12,446	12	12,435	1	12,443	9
Feb.	12,517	12,500	(17)	12,501	(16)	12,513	(4)	12,499	(18)	12,504	(13)
Mar.	12,609	12,586	(23)	12,585	(24)	12,597	(12)	12,600	(9)	12,606	(3)
Apr.	12,703	12,694	(9)	12,677	(26)	12,690	(13)	12,701	(2)	12,710	7
May	12,800	12,796	(4)	12,770	(30)	12,782	(18)	12,797	(3)	12,805	5
June	12,883	12,895	12	12,864	(19)	12,874	(9)	12,897	14	12,903	20
July	12,958	12,976	18	12,942	(16)	12,951	(7)	12,966	8	12,967	9
Aug.	13,024	13,039	15	13,010	(14)	13,017	(7)	13,033	9	13,028	4
Sept.	13,089	13,097	8	13,068	(21)	13,073	(16)	13,090	1	13,083	(6)
Oct.	13,146	13,155	9	13,125	(21)	13,128	(18)	13,154	8	13,147	1
Nov.	13,186	13,209	23	13,174	(12)	13,176	(10)	13,203	17	13,197	11
Dec.	13,187	13,239	52	13,207	20	13,209	22	13,226	39	13,218	31
1990: Jan.	13,163	13,217	54	13,220	57	13,223	60	13,189	26	13,172	9
Feb.	13,111	13,158	47	13,198	87	13,201	90	13,140	29	13,114	3
Mar.	13,049	13,080	31	13,147	98	13,150	101	13,060	11	13,032	(17)
Apr.	12,996	12,994	(2)	13,087	91	13,090	94	12,987	(9)	12,963	(33)
May	12,972	12,936	(36)	13,035	63	13,039	67	12,943	(29)	12,929	(43)
June	12,977	12,926	(51)	13,013	36	13,017	40	12,947	(30)	12,949	(28)
July	13,020	12,960	(60)	13,020	0	13,025	5	12,981	(39)	12,997	(23)
Aug.	13,094	13,034	(60)	13,065	(29)	13,070	(24)	13,062	(32)	13,088	(6)
Sept.	13,209	13,145	(64)	13,140	(69)	13,145	(64)	13,167	(42)	13,198	(11)
Oct.	13,338	13,293	(45)	13,256	(82)	13,261	(77)	13,323	(15)	13,357	19
Nov.	13,491	13,456	(35)	13,385	(106)	13,390	(101)	13,467	(24)	13,499	8
Dec.	13,662	13,626	(36)	13,538	(124)	13,542	(120)	13,644	(18)	13,670	8
1991: Jan.	13,854	13,820	(34)	13,708	(146)	13,712	(142)	13,833	(21)	13,856	2
Feb.	14,048	14,030	(18)	13,900	(148)	13,904	(144)	14,046	(2)	14,067	19
Mar.	14,217	14,240	23	14,093	(124)	14,097	(120)	14,242	25	14,259	42
Apr.	14,358	14,405	47	14,262	(96)	14,266	(92)	14,386	28	14,391	33
May	14,471	14,520	49	14,403	(68)	14,407	(64)	14,500	29	14,489	18
June	14,568	14,605	37	14,517	(51)	14,521	(47)	14,585	17	14,564	(4)
July	14,567	14,677	110	14,615	48	14,619	52	14,665	98	14,643	76
Aug.	14,717	14,640	(77)	14,614	(103)	14,618	(99)	14,568	(149)	14,530	(187)
Sept.	14,777	14,754	(23)	14,768	(9)	14,773	(4)	14,864	87	14,850	73
Oct.	14,812	14,904	92	14,830	18	14,836	24	14,839	27	14,849	37
Nov.	14,847	14,866	19	14,867	20	14,873	26	14,847	0	14,832	(15)
Dec.	14,864	14,882	18	14,904	40	14,910	46	14,882	18	14,863	(1)

[a] There are two terms in the final double moving average model.
[b] There are 47 terms in the absolute change moving average.
[c] There are 47 terms in the percent change moving average.
[d] The smoothing constant used in Brown's linear exponential smoothing model is 0.99.
[e] The smoothing constant used in the triple exponential smoothing model is 0.73.

FIGURE 8-9 **Growth in Gross Receipts Tax Revenues**

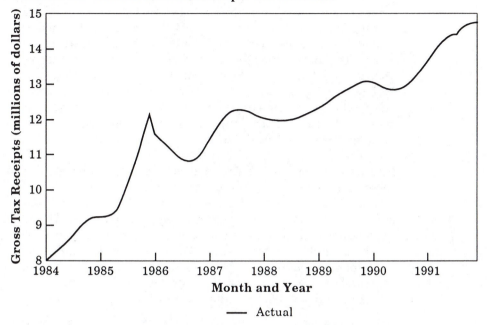

— Actual

TABLE 8-18 **Evaluation Statistics for Gross Receipts Tax Models**

	Evaluation Statistic				
	MAPE	*MAD*	*MSE*	*Mean Error*	*Mean Percent Error*
Naive	0.97	111	23,570	−72	−0.64
Average Change	0.80	94	19,297	22	0.19
Average Percent Change	0.85	99	21,110	42	0.35
Simple Moving Average	1.41	162	46,852	−108	−0.95
Double Moving Average	0.50	57	15,307	2	0.00
Absolute Change Moving Average	0.42	55	4,843	−2	0.00
Percent Change Moving Average	0.43	57	5,252	6	0.07
Single Exponential Smoothing	1.01	116	25,533	−76	−0.67
Brown's Linear Exponential Smoothing	0.37	42	12,941	−0	−0.01
Triple Exponential Smoothing	0.38	44	16,158	1	0.00

Having narrowed the potential list to five models, there are several other tests that can be carried out. The first of these tests focuses on the turning-point performance of each of the models in the historical simulation. The double moving average model leads to turning-point errors 11.5 percent of the time; the absolute change moving average model erred 18.8 percent of the time; the percent change moving average model erred 16.7 percent of the time; Brown's linear exponential smoothing model erred 9.6 percent of the time; and the triple exponential smoothing model erred 13.8 percent of the time. Thus, based solely on turning-point performance, Brown's linear exponential model would be selected.

The second of these additional tests involves a six-month, ex post forecast from each of the five models. Table 8-19 presents the details of these ex post forecasts for each of the models along with the summary statistics from these forecasts. In the ex post forecast, the absolute and percent change moving average models perform the best. The double moving average and Brown's linear exponential smoothing models both tend to consistently overestimate actual changes in gross receipts taxes, while the triple exponential smoothing model leads to underestimates (indeed, it predicts a downturn in receipts beginning in November).

In summary, here are the test results:

1. According to the evaluation statistics in Table 8-18, Brown's linear exponential smoothing performs best.

2. Brown's linear exponential smoothing also performs best in the turning-point test.

TABLE 8-19   Ex Post Forecast of Gross Receipts Taxes

				Model		
1991	*Actual*	*Double Moving Average*	*Absolute Change Moving Average*	*Percent Change Moving Average*	*Brown's Linear Exponential Smoothing*	*Triple Exponential Smoothing*
July	14,567	14,677	14,615	14,619	14,665	14,643
August	14,717	14,782	14,663	14,671	14,763	14,696
September	14,777	14,887	14,712	14,726	14,860	14,728
October	14,812	14,992	14,764	14,784	14,957	14,739
November	14,847	15,097	14,818	14,884	15,055	14,728
December	14,864	15,202	14,875	14,907	15,152	14,696
RMS		199	46	41	166	97
R%MS		1.34%	0.31%	0.28%	1.12%	0.65%
Bias		176	− 23	− 6	145	− 59
Percent Bias		1.19%	− 0.15%	− 0.04%	0.98%	− 0.40%

3. The absolute change moving average model does best in the ex post forecast.

As a result of these tests, you decide to use both the absolute change moving average model and Brown's linear exponential smoothing model. It is not uncommon for practicing forecasters to use more than one time series model to generate forecasts, especially when they are just beginning the forecasting process.

EXAMPLE 8-5 Confidence Intervals for Exponential Smoothing Models

Throughout this chapter, we have explicitly chosen to present only the basic equations needed to develop point forecasts. In doing this, we have ignored the general statistical theory underlying these models, which can be used to derive confidence intervals or ranges that are centered on a point forecast—$Y_{t+T}(t)$—made at time t for T periods into the future.[9]

$$Y_{t+T}(t) = \hat{Y}_{t+T}(t) \pm e^{\alpha}_{t+T}(t). \tag{8-111}$$

The superscript α refers to the degree of confidence specified by the analyst, and (t) denotes that the confidence interval was α computed in time period t. In turn, $e_{t+T}(t)$ generates the interval about the point forecast:

$$e^{\alpha}_{t+T}(t) = zk_T \Delta(t). \tag{8-112}$$

The symbol z is the number of standard deviations under the normal curve associated with the level of confidence and

$$k_T = 1.25 \tag{8-113}$$

for single exponential smoothing forecasts. For Brown's linear exponential model, k_T is no longer a constant and is defined as

$$k_T = 1.25 \left[\frac{1 + \dfrac{\alpha}{(1+v)^3}[(1 + 4v + 5v^2) + 2\alpha(1 + 3v)T + 2\alpha^2 T^2]}{1 + \dfrac{\alpha}{(1+v)^3}[(1 + 4v + 5v^2) + 2\alpha(1 + 3v) + 2\alpha^2]} \right]^{1/2} \tag{8-114}$$

Further, $\Delta(t)$ is computed by

$$\Delta(t) = \frac{\displaystyle\sum_{t=1}^{n} |e_t|}{d}. \tag{8-115}$$

---

[9] B. L. Bowerman and R. T. O'Connell, *Time Series Forecasting* (Boston, Mass.: Duxbury Press, 1987), pp. 272–292.

In equation (8-114), α refers to the smoothing constant and v equals $1 - \alpha$; the term d in equation (8-115) stands for number of terms in the numerator. In equation (8-112), α stands for level of significance.

To apply these formulas, suppose that we consider the example in Table 8-20, in which Brown's linear exponential smoothing model was applied to monthly sales data.

In this example, the smoothing constant, α, was equal to 0.4. Further, let us assume we are interested in computing a 95 percent confidence interval for a one-period-ahead forecast made in period 20. As a first step, $\Delta(t)$ and the forecast errors must be computed. Table 8-20 contains the information needed to solve equation (8-115) in time period 20:[10]

$$\Delta(20) = \frac{\sum\limits_{t=3}^{20} |e_t|}{18}$$

$$= (5{,}888/18)(\text{see column 7 of Table 8-20}) \qquad \textbf{(8-116)}$$

$$= 327.$$

The next step in the process is to solve equation (8-112):

$$e_{20+1}^{.05}(20) = 1.96(k_T)\Delta t \qquad \textbf{(8-117)}$$

If the forecast is made in period 20 for period 21, $k_T = 1.25$.[11] The coefficient value of 1.96 in equation (8-117) comes from a normal probability table, since 95 percent of the area under the normal curve falls within 1.96 standard deviations of the mean. Therefore,

$$e_{21}^{.05}(20) = (1.96)(1.25)(327)$$
$$e_{21}^{.05}(20) \approx 801. \qquad \textbf{(8-118)}$$

Thus, given the approach outlined in Table 8-20 and the forecast error in equation (8-118), the 95 percent confidence interval for a one-period-ahead forecast made in period 20 is[12]

$$\hat{Y}_{t+T}(t) - e_{t+T}^{\delta}(t) \leq Y_{t+T}(t) \leq \hat{Y}_{t+T}(t) + e_{t+T}^{\delta}(t)$$

$$13{,}084 - 801 \leq Y_{21}(20) \leq 13{,}084 + 801 \qquad \textbf{(8-119)}$$

$$12{,}283 \leq Y_{21} \leq 13{,}885.$$

Confidence intervals for more than one period ahead can be determined by resolving equation (8-114) for the required value for k_T. For example, if the forecast is made for period 22, then $k_T = 1.53$ and the forecast

---

[10] Because we did not make forecasts for periods 1 and 2, $t = 18$.
[11] Equation (8-114) can be shown to be equal to 1.25 when $T = 1$.
[12] See equation (8-111).

TABLE 8-20   Application of Brown's Linear Exponential Smoothing to Department Store Sales

Date	Period	Sales (1)	S_t^1 (2)	S_t^2 (3)	a_t (4)	b_t (5)	Y_{t+T} (6)	Error (7)
1990: Jan.	1	9,074	9,601	9,601				
Feb.	2	10,128	9,812	9,685	9,939	85		
Mar.	3	10,155	9,949	9,791	10,107	105	10,024	131
Apr.	4	9,746	9,868	9,821	9,915	31	10,212	−466
May	5	9,397	9,679	9,765	9,593	−57	9,946	−549
June	6	9,012	9,412	9,624	9,200	−141	9,536	−524
July	7	9,084	9,281	9,487	9,075	−137	9,059	25
Aug.	8	9,447	9,347	9,431	9,263	−56	8,938	509
Sept.	9	10,062	9,633	9,512	9,754	81	9,207	855
Oct.	10	10,420	9,948	9,686	10,210	175	9,835	585
Nov.	11	10,754	10,270	9,920	10,620	233	10,384	370
Dec.	12	10,826	10,493	10,149	10,837	229	10,854	−28
1991: Jan.	13	11,421	10,864	10,435	11,293	286	11,065	356
Feb.	14	11,442	11,095	10,699	11,491	264	11,579	−137
Mar.	15	11,665	11,323	10,949	11,697	249	11,756	−91
Apr.	16	11,559	11,417	11,136	11,698	187	11,947	−388
May	17	12,046	11,619	11,349	11,989	213	11,886	160
June	18	12,024	11,811	11,534	12,088	185	12,202	−178
July	19	12,350	12,026	11,731	12,321	197	12,273	77
Aug.	20	12,978	12,407	12,001	12,813	271	12,519	459

interval is

$$\hat{Y}_{t+T}(t) - e_{t+T}^{\delta}(t) \leq Y_{t+T}(t) \leq \hat{Y}_{t+T}(t) + e_{t+T}^{\delta}(t)$$

$$13{,}355 - 981 \leq Y_{22}(20) \leq 13{,}355 + 981 \qquad \textbf{(8-120)}$$

$$12{,}374 \leq Y_{22} \leq 14{,}336.$$

EVALUATION OF SMOOTHING TECHNIQUES

The major advantages of the smoothing methods introduced here are their relative simplicity and low cost. This latter point cannot be overstated. For example, if a business has 5,000 items in inventory and wants forecasts of each, the fact that exponential smoothing requires only the latest smoothed statistics can lead to substantial cost savings when compared to other forecasting procedures. Although greater accuracy may be attainable with either regression models or the more advanced time series models introduced in chapter 9, the additional cost may outweigh the gain in accuracy.

The appropriate smoothing technique is dependent on the data pattern exhibited by the data. If the data fluctuate around a relatively constant value, single exponential smoothing is preferable. Whenever a trend is present in the data, the analyst must determine whether the trend is linear or nonlinear. In addition to the smoothing techniques presented here, others are available that are applicable to different types of data patterns.

Despite the attractiveness of exponential smoothing, it has several limitations. First and foremost is the fact that the forecasts generated via exponential smoothing techniques are sensitive to the specification of the smoothing constant. The decision as to the *correct* constant(s) is pragmatic, in that it is based on a trial-and-error process. Second, exponential smoothing techniques either miss or lag behind the turning points in actual time series data. Third, exponential models are most useful when the objective is the generation of immediate- to short-term forecasts. Fourth, forecasts can involve a large error because of large random fluctuations in the more recent periods. This follows from the fact that with exponential smoothing the more recent time periods carry a heavier weight. Finally, because these techniques are based on the assumption of constancy, they cannot be used to evaluate the effect of a managerial decision such as a price change or a modification in marketing strategies.

SUMMARY

The time series forecasting methods presented in this chapter provide the forecaster with a relatively simple set of techniques that frequently prove to be useful in immediate- to short-term forecasting situations. The advantage of simple models is their relative simplicity. The moving average models prove to be more useful when there is a pattern in the data. Exponential smoothing models, because of their simplicity and their flexibility in capturing various historical patterns, have generally been found to be the most popular time series technique among forecasters.

Time series techniques have clear limitations, since they are based on a basic extrapolation of historical patterns. Further, these techniques do not provide management with clear insights when it comes to evaluating policies, such as changes in pricing or advertising. Despite these limitations, time series models are used widely, and an understanding of them is crucial for the practicing forecaster.

QUESTIONS FOR DISCUSSION AND ANALYSIS

1. What type of time series data for businesses might lend themselves to the models presented in this chapter?

2. What are the basic differences between the time series models presented in this chapter and regression models presented in preceding chapters?

3. How is the process of differencing used in identifying the appropriate time series model?

4. What are the principal limitations of the simple time series models? What are their advantages?

5. What is meant by the principle of parsimony, and how does it apply in selecting among the myriad of time series techniques?

6. Explain the role and importance of the number of terms in a moving average.

7. Explain the role and importance of the smoothing constant in exponential smoothing models.

8. What are the principal limitations of moving average models? What are their advantages?

9. What is the difference between the smoothing constant and the smoothing statistic?

10. What advantages do exponential smoothing models have relative to moving average models?

11. Why does it appear that all of the time series models presented in this chapter fail to capture turning points?

12. What are the principal limitations of exponential smoothing models? What are their advantages?

13. Suppose that you are given the information on average package weight presented in the following table. Test all of the simple models presented in this chapter. Based on the statistical evaluation tools presented in this text, which model would you select? Conduct an ex post forecast analysis by excluding the last several points of actual data. Which model performs best in this ex post forecast simulation?

Date	Average Weight per Package (pounds)	Date	Average Weight per Package (pounds)
1988: Jan.	9.48	May	10.30
Feb.	9.42	June	10.67
Mar.	9.68	July	11.06
Apr.	9.72	Aug.	11.42
May	9.77	Sept.	11.22
June	10.14	Oct.	11.26
July	10.30	Nov.	11.29
Aug.	10.15	Dec.	11.33
Sept.	10.31	1990: Jan.	11.40
Oct.	10.51	Feb.	11.52
Nov.	10.40	Mar.	11.65
Dec.	10.76	Apr.	11.75
1989: Jan.	10.65	May	11.84
Feb.	10.05	June	11.90
Mar.	10.12	July	12.03
Apr.	10.50	Aug.	12.11

14. Using the data presented in question 13, test the moving average models. Which model would you select based on the evaluation techniques? Conduct an ex post forecast anal-

ysis. Which model performs best in the ex post simulation? Which model would you select as your final model? Why?

15. The personnel manager has charged you with the responsibility for developing a forecasting model for wage rates, and she has provided you with the data in the following table. Using the moving average and exponential smoothing models presented in the text, conduct a complete comparative analysis of these models. Which model(s) would you select as your final model(s)?

Date	Hourly Wage Rates (dollars per hour)	Date	Hourly Wage Rates (dollars per hour)
1985: Jan.	6.82	1988: Jan.	10.47
Feb.	6.94	Feb.	10.04
Mar.	6.84	Mar.	9.783
Apr.	6.51	Apr.	9.593
May	7.39	May	9.27
June	7.60	June	8.838
July	7.76	July	8.477
Aug.	7.93	Aug.	9.23
Sept.	8.20	Sept.	9.137
Oct.	8.47	Oct.	9.24
Nov.	8.55	Nov.	9.053
Dec.	9.13	Dec.	8.4
1986: Jan.	9.31	1989: Jan.	8.06
Feb.	9.24	Feb.	8.447
Mar.	9.27	Mar.	8.513
Apr.	9.17	Apr.	8.12
May	8.36	May	8.91
June	8.40	June	9.543
July	8.50	July	10.22
Aug.	7.92	Aug.	10.76
Sept.	6.54	Sept.	11.24
Oct.	7.30	Oct.	11.18
Nov.	8.08	Nov.	11.25
Dec.	8.29	Dec.	11.25
1987: Jan.	8.63	1990: Jan.	11.15
Feb.	8.78	Feb.	11.83
Mar.	8.89	Mar.	11.33
Apr.	9.12	Apr.	11.32
May	9.61	May	11.39
June	9.88	June	11.43
July	10.23	July	11.65
Aug.	10.29	Aug.	11.79
Sept.	9.967	Sept.	11.99
Oct.	10.473	Oct.	11.81
Nov.	10.547	Nov.	12.07
Dec.	10.533	Dec.	12.12

16. Suppose that you are assigned the task of developing a daily forecast of the number of calls coming into a call center. This information is vital in terms of hiring part-time personnel to operate the telephone switchboard. You are provided with the daily information in the following table and decide to test the various exponential smoothing models. Which model would you select as your final model? Why?

Day Number	Telephone Calls Into Call Center	Day Number	Telephone Calls Into Call Center
1	892.0	39	1,469.7
2	893.9	40	1,489.8
3	888.8	41	1,397.2
4	926.8	42	1,468.5
5	976.9	43	1,459.0
6	969.1	44	1,302.8
7	932.9	45	1,353.0
8	860.6	46	1,356.2
9	833.5	47	1,381.0
10	851.8	48	1,480.4
11	872.6	49	1,509.1
12	981.6	50	1,530.9
13	1,015.5	51	1,650.0
14	1,037.4	52	1,638.4
15	907.4	53	1,614.1
16	1,012.8	54	1,611.8
17	1,015.5	55	1,686.3
18	974.6	56	1,592.2
19	939.7	57	1,626.5
20	901.2	58	1,622.0
21	908.4	59	1,463.2
22	944.7	60	1,824.2
23	1,006.2	61	1,899.5
24	1,042.0	62	1,972.2
25	1,075.4	63	2,134.8
26	1,082.6	64	2,074.7
27	1,142.1	65	2,157.3
28	1,144.2	66	2,200.5
29	1,165.5	67	2,450.6
30	1,155.9	68	2,623.6
31	1,204.6	69	2,521.0
32	1,202.4	70	2,513.5
33	1,235.0	71	2,484.3
34	1,297.8	72	2,294.9
35	1,199.5	73	2,389.7
36	1,419.1	74	2,536.0
37	1,393.4	75	2,298.2
38	1,407.0		

17. As an analyst for a department of revenue in a southeastern state, you are required to develop short-term forecasts of the major revenue sources. You are provided with the following historical information and are required to select the most applicable time series model(s) for this data.

Forecasting State Revenue
(monthly tax revenue in thousands of dollars)

Date*	Gasoline Taxes	Tobacco Taxes	Sales Taxes	Gross Receipts Taxes	Alcohol Taxes	Beer Taxes
1984: 1	6,595	1,544	10,923	320	338	219
2	6,401	1,400	7,395	270	449	191
3	5,169	1,512	7,491	281	310	188
4	5,686	1,509	8,508	292	415	296
5	6,747	1,690	8,685	685	416	241
6	6,350	1,667	9,298	386	637	288
7	6,409	1,633	8,977	2,378	547	312
8	6,245	1,762	9,138	286	426	283
9	7,108	1,596	9,241	268	569	285
10	6,248	1,629	9,700	299	686	254
11	6,508	1,580	9,325	271	808	262
12	5,700	1,520	9,658	272	455	228
1985: 1	7,386	1,675	11,332	283	457	228
2	6,516	1,416	7,942	269	462	193
3	5,030	1,609	8,107	280	455	196
4	6,544	1,577	9,363	279	528	287
5	6,307	1,815	9,572	535	490	276
6	6,497	1,667	10,251	420	413	316
7	7,629	1,823	10,219	2,365	443	346
8	6,877	1,798	9,873	300	471	324
9	7,469	1,557	9,986	275	523	348
10	6,322	1,768	10,152	298	725	262
11	7,305	1,755	10,473	274	831	285
12	6,203	1,554	10,467	270	395	238
1986: 1	6,734	1,754	11,943	286	501	230
2	6,191	1,473	8,507	272	439	217
3	5,465	1,506	8,347	280	440	190
4	6,892	1,852	9,885	280	517	275
5	6,731	1,610	10,315	599	440	327
6	8,082	2,736	11,101	430	1,071	330
7	6,689	2,519	12,075	3,122	562	321
8	7,142	2,382	11,914	348	626	356
9	6,737	2,345	12,164	299	834	324
10	6,512	2,384	11,779	340	828	271
11	7,319	2,280	12,741	309	881	336
12	7,528	2,253	12,368	287	481	257
1987: 1	7,042	2,055	14,220	316	635	220
2	6,953	1,750	11,223	318	696	251

Forecasting State Revenue
(monthly tax revenue in thousands of dollars) *(Continued)*

Date*	Gasoline Taxes	Tobacco Taxes	Sales Taxes	Gross Receipts Taxes	Alcohol Taxes	Beer Taxes
3	6,257	2,160	11,073	309	537	258
4	7,061	2,335	12,123	337	674	300
5	7,354	2,279	12,336	738	566	340
6	7,182	2,471	13,293	654	614	346
7	8,232	2,614	13,110	3,038	660	375
8	7,479	2,367	13,106	738	754	396
9	7,428	2,486	12,957	343	863	344
10	7,054	2,330	13,179	224	860	313
11	7,764	2,321	13,987	349	863	296
12	7,564	2,433	12,792	332	662	305
1988: 1	7,478	2,274	16,024	349	662	291
2	6,933	2,012	11,955	351	670	290
3	5,435	2,366	11,970	355	841	225
4	7,343	2,531	13,077	362	543	358
5	7,542	2,292	13,899	760	604	357
6	7,797	2,585	14,515	715	650	361
7	8,227	2,497	14,263	1,781	724	409
8	8,270	2,547	14,545	2,110	686	392
9	8,051	2,522	14,538	385	964	376
10	8,194	2,325	14,195	405	888	346
11	7,660	2,417	15,548	408	1,021	300
12	8,098	2,444	14,794	376	735	325
1989: 1	7,775	2,354	18,307	416	662	316
2	6,957	2,210	12,589	388	774	303
3	7,458	2,492	13,089	392	748	265
4	7,679	2,329	15,141	412	685	383
5	8,064	2,549	15,426	1,161	827	376
6	7,938	2,585	15,301	975	959	381
7	8,566	2,446	15,902	1,618	662	438
8	8,903	2,812	16,021	2,687	621	443
9	8,334	2,520	16,128	473	1,188	420
10	9,047	2,483	15,777	514	932	377
11	8,337	2,447	15,552	482	832	320
12	7,760	2,376	15,635	452	771	364
1990: 1	9,016	2,432	18,759	498	803	341
2	8,253	2,284	14,164	500	725	313
3	6,914	2,458	13,383	477	778	325
4	8,142	2,557	15,547	502	723	424
5	9,191	2,585	15,478	1,242	847	455
6	9,138	3,167	16,117	1,094	1,177	459
7	8,539	2,798	16,903	2,157	2,689	407
8	8,840	2,984	16,454	2,864	1,380	418

(continued)

Forecasting State Revenue
(monthly tax revenue in thousands of dollars) *(Continued)*

Date*	Gasoline Taxes	Tobacco Taxes	Sales Taxes	Gross Receipts Taxes	Alcohol Taxes	Beer Taxes
9	9,092	2,644	16,619	620	1,607	432
10	9,305	2,813	17,108	787	1,503	366
11	8,632	2,719	16,699	671	1,583	349
12	8,929	2,623	16,856	597	1,166	382
1991: 1	8,924	2,944	20,143	754	1,409	376
2	8,042	2,573	15,050	670	1,149	385
3	7,364	2,508	15,585	591	1,748	324
4	8,228	2,958	17,142	704	644	425
5	8,868	2,971	17,482	1,010	1,380	378
6	9,327	2,730	18,352	1,291	1,371	481
7	9,004	3,194	18,889	2,415	799	487
8	9,777	3,015	18,407	1,231	1,062	532
9	10,150	2,850	19,435	682	1,247	534
10	9,543	2,908	18,097	947	1,743	428
11	8,748	2,711	18,970	745	1,686	422
12	9,335	2,993	18,984	638	1,558	389

* Year and month

18. In chapter 3, question 25, you were provided with information on housing starts, total retail sales, and total employment. Estimate a model using Winter's exponential smoothing model. Compare the results of this model with the best exponential smoothing model based on the seasonally adjusted data for these time series.

19. In chapter 3, question 27, you were provided with data on the sale of hard disks. Which of the exponential smoothing and moving average models provides the most reliable forecasts for this time series?

REFERENCES FOR FURTHER STUDY

Berry, William L. and Friedheld W. Bliemel, "Selecting Exponential Smoothing Constants: An Application of Pattern Search," *International Journal of Production Research*, vol. 12, no. 4, 1974, pp. 483–99.

Bowers, David A., *An Introduction to Business Cycles and Forecasting*. Reading, Mass.: Addison-Wesley Publishing Company, 1985.

Brillinger, D. R., *Time Series—Data Analysis and Theory*, expanded ed. San Francisco: Holden-Day, 1981.

Brodie, Roderick J. and Cornelis A. DeKluyver, "A Comparison of the Short Term Forecasting Accuracy of Econometric and Naive Extrapolation Models of Market Share," *International Journal of Forecasting*, vol. 3, 1987, pp. 423–37.

Brown, R. G., *Smoothing, Forecasting, and Prediction of Discrete Time Series*. Englewood Cliffs, N.J.: Prentice Hall, 1962.

Brown, R. G., *Statistical Forecasting for Inventory Control.* New York: McGraw-Hill, 1959.

Bunn, D. W., "A Comparison of Several Adaptive Forecasting Procedures," *OMEGA: The International Journal of Management Science,* vol. 8, no. 4, 1980, pp. 485–91.

Chambers, J. C., S. K. Mullick, and D. D. Smith, "How to Choose the Right Forecasting Technique," *Harvard Business Review,* vol. 49, 1971, pp. 45–74.

Chatfield, C., *The Analysis of Time Series: An Introduction,* 2nd ed. New York: Chapman and Hall, 1980.

Chatfield, C., "The Holt-Winters Forecasting Procedure," *Applied Statistics,* vol. 27, 1978, pp. 264–79.

Chatfield, C., "What is the Best Method of Forecasting," *Journal of Applied Statistics,* vol. 15, no. 1, 198, pp. 19–38.

Chow, W. M., "Adaptive Control of the Exponential Smoothing Constant," *Journal of Industrial Engineering,* vol. 16, no. 5, 1965, pp. 315–17.

Cleveland, W. S. and G. C. Taio, "Decomposition of Seasonal Time Series: A Model for the Census X-11 Program," *Journal of the American Statistical Association,* vol. 75, 1976, pp. 581–87.

Crane, D. G. and J. R. Crotty, "A Two-State Forecasting Model: Exponential Smoothing and Multiple Regression," *Management Science,* vol. 13, no. 8, 1967, pp. 501–7.

Gardner, E. S. and D. G. Dannenbring, "Forecasting with Exponential Smoothing: Some Guidelines for Model Selection," *Decision Sciences,* vol. 11, 1980, pp. 370–83.

Granger, C. W. J. and P. Newbold, *Forecasting Economic Time Series,* 2nd ed. Boston: Academic Press, 1989.

Makridakis, Spyros and Steven C. Wheelwright, *Interactive Forecasting.* San Francisco: Holden-Day, 1977.

Makridakis, Spyros, Steven C. Wheelwright, and Victor E. McGee, *Forecasting: Methods and Applications,* 2nd ed. New York: John Wiley & Sons, 1983.

Schnaars, Steven P., "A Comparison of Extrapolation Models on Yearly Sales Forecasts," *Journal of Forecasting,* vol. 3, 1984, pp. 27–36.

Trigg, D. W. and D. H. Leach, "Exponential Smoothing with an Adaptive Response Rate," *Operational Research Quarterly,* vol. 18, 1967, pp. 53–59.

Whybark, D. C., "A Comparison of Adaptive Forecasting Techniques," *Logistics and Transportation Review,* vol. 6, 1960, pp. 324–42.

Winters, P. R., "Forecasting Sales by Exponentially Weighted Moving Averages," *Management Science,* April 1960, pp. 324–42.

9

Advanced Time Series Models

INTRODUCTION

While the simple time series models discussed in the preceding chapter prove to be successful in many circumstances, they have some serious drawbacks. First, the limited number of models available to the practitioner may not capture the patterns exhibited by many time series. Second, since we use a combination of visual and statistical evaluation, identifying the "best" model from the alternatives can be an extremely cumbersome trial-and-error process. Finally, with many of these models there are few guidelines for judging whether or not the model that we have selected as the final model will provide accurate forecasts. Alternatively, there are few statistical guidelines for assessing the uncertainty associated with many of these models.

These limitations have led to the widespread application of the Box-Jenkins (B/J) methodology to business and economic forecasting situations. Specifically, the B/J methodology

- Encompasses a wide variety of models that capture a myriad of data patterns
- Provides for a systematic approach to identifying the "best" model for a given set of data
- Provides for the development of statistical tests for verifying the validity of the model that has been selected
- Allows statistical measurement of the reliability of forecasts generated from any specific model.

In regression models the objective is to establish (quantitatively) the ways in which one or more independent variables explain or capture the pattern of changes in the dependent variable. This knowledge of the relationship between the independent variable(s) and the dependent variable is useful, but it may not be sufficient to develop a forecasting model.[1] Much of the information obtained from regression analysis may already be present in the pattern exhibited by the dependent variable in its period-to-period (week-to-week, month-to-month, or quarter-to-quarter) movements. That is, if a predictable pattern exists in the time series between its value this period and its values in past periods, we may be able to use this pattern to generate future values of the time series based on current information about the series.[2] Rather than examine the relationship between a dependent variable (say, lettuce sales) and other independent variables (price, income, etc.), the Box-Jenkins methodology is used to develop a forecasting model for lettuce sales that is based solely on statistical linkages between current and past values of observed lettuce sales.

THE BOX-JENKINS APPROACH

OVERVIEW

The Box-Jenkins methodology analyzed here is frequently referred to as univariate Box-Jenkins because the forecast for, say, electricity demand is completely based on an analysis of the pattern of changes in past electricity demand.[3] Univariate Box-Jenkins modeling follows the three-phase process outlined in Figure 9-1:

Model identification: A particular category of Box-Jenkins model is identified by using various statistics computed from an analysis of the historical data.

Model estimation and verification: Once identified, the "best model" is estimated such that the fitted values come as close as possible to capturing the pattern exhibited by the actual data.

Forecasting: The final model is used to forecast the time series and to develop confidence intervals that measure the uncertainty associated with the forecast.

---

[1] In estimating such a model the issue of simultaneity would have to be addressed. Our purpose here is to state as simply as possible the possibility that there are likely to be situations where regression models fail as forecasting devices.

[2] The pattern that we observe in the dependent variable may indeed be a result of the pattern of changes in the independent variables selected for inclusion in the regression model.

[3] The concepts used in univariate Box-Jenkins have been extended to incorporate the basic cause-and-effect implications of regression analysis. This approach is referred to as either multivariate Box-Jenkins or transfer functions.

FIGURE 9-1   The Box-Jenkins Model-Building Process

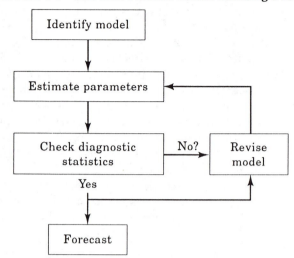

As suggested by Figure 9-1, this process of determining the final or "best" model is generally an iterative procedure in which the analyst goes back and forth between the first two phases, each time revising the model until one estimated model is superior to all the competing models. While not suggested by the figure, the forecasts produced by the model are monitored and, if a revision is necessary, the process begins anew.

ASSUMPTIONS OF BOX-JENKINS METHODOLOGY

To apply the basics of the Box-Jenkins methodology, we must first assume that the data series of interest is stationary. Intuitively, a series is said to be stationary when it fluctuates randomly around some fixed value, generally the mean value of the series. While it may seem that this assumption limits the applicability of the methodology, we will see that by using various transformations, we can, once we have analyzed the period-to-period changes in a series, transform many nonstationary time series into stationary series. For convenience, we will assume that the mean or average value of the variable under study fluctuates randomly around a fixed value of zero. The assumption allows us to illustrate the basic features of the Box-Jenkins methodology as simply as possible.

First-time users of Box-Jenkins modeling procedures are frequently intimidated by the mathematics accompanying the majority of theoretical and applied references. The basics of Box-Jenkins procedures can, however, be grasped without introducing sophisticated mathematics. While it is true that a nonmathematical approach may be labeled as a "black box" technique in which the forecaster does not understand what is going on inside the model, there is little to be gained in the initial stages of Box-Jenkins analysis by concentrating solely on the mathematics.

In addition to the mathematics, the calculations involved in deriving the parameters are time-consuming and laborious, and it is essential to have access to both a computer and a Box-Jenkins program. For this reason, we have focused on interpreting the computerized output rather than on the specific formulas that are used in producing the results.

CLASSIFICATIONS OF BOX-JENKINS MODELS

To set the stage, suppose that we consider a time-measured or temporal set of observations on a variable, y, taken at regular time intervals, t, over n periods:

$$y_t = \{y_1, y_2, y_3, \ldots, y_n\}. \tag{9-1}$$

The objective is to establish whether the pattern of these observations is due to some systematic relationship over time, and, if so, to determine the process that generates this pattern. In the generalized model, each observation on y is composed of two parts: an explainable or predictable component (p_t) and a random error component (ϵ_t):

$$y_t = p_t + \epsilon_t. \tag{9-2}$$

For historical values of the series, p_t represents the explainable component, but for forecasts of y_t this component would be called the forecast or predicted value. The difference between the actual and fitted values of y_t is designated as ϵ_t and is referred to as the residual. As was the case with regression analysis, the expected value of the residuals is zero, and they are assumed to be uncorrelated with one another:

$$E(\epsilon_t) = 0, \text{ and } E(\epsilon_t\epsilon_{t-1}) = 0. \tag{9-3}$$

FIGURE 9-2 Example of a Stationary Time Series

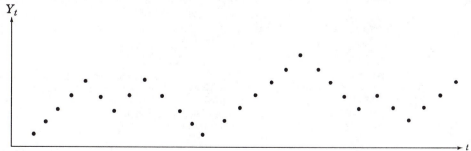

As noted earlier, we begin the discussion of Box-Jenkins by assuming that the time series of interest is stationary and fluctuates around the mean value, as shown in Figure 9-2 (page 423). While the majority of business and economic time series exhibit seasonal variations and long-term trend patterns and do not satisfy this assumption of stationarity, in subsequent sections we introduce tools and techniques to account for time series that exhibit nonstationarity and seasonality.

Within the framework of the Box-Jenkins methodology, there are three basic models:[4]

- Autoregressive (AR) models
- Moving average (MA) models
- Mixed autoregressive and moving average (ARMA) models.

When a model is autoregressive (AR), the current value of the variable is a function of its previous values plus an error term:[5]

$$y_t = \delta + \phi_1 y_{t-1} + \phi_2 y_{t-2} + \ldots + \phi_p y_{t-p} + \epsilon_t. \tag{9-4}$$

The ϕ's are parameters to be estimated and δ is a constant term that is related to the trend in the series. The model is called autoregressive because y_t is actually being regressed on itself. The order of this model, p, refers to the number of lagged terms.

To understand better how the autoregressive parameters work and how they are interpreted, suppose we look at a model with only one AR parameter and a mean or constant value of zero. This type of model would be written as

$$y_t = \phi_1 y_{t-1} + \epsilon_t. \tag{9-5}$$

In equation (9-5), the model has an order of 1, ϕ_1 refers to the AR parameter, $\phi_1 y_{t-1}$ represents the fitted value, and ϵ_t is the random error term measured in time period t. While the symbols in equation (9-5) appear cumbersome, their interpretation is relatively simple:

> The observed value of y in period t (y_t) is directly proportional (ϕ) to the previous value of y (y_{t-1}). Alternatively, our best estimate of the current value of y is the previous value plus a random error component.

---

[4] When we introduce the possibility of nonstationary time series, there are actually three more possibilities: ARI, MRI, and ARIMA. The only difference is that the letter I refers to integrated and suggests that the model uses data that have been differenced to achieve stationarity.

[5] Throughout this discussion, the use of plus and minus signs is for convenience only and is not meant to suggest any directional relationship.

As suggested by equation (9-4), it is likely that the fitted value (or forecast), y_t, will be related to more than one previous value. For example, a second-order autoregressive model would contain two AR parameters and would be written as

$$y_t = \phi_1 y_{t-1} + \phi_2 y_{t-2} + \epsilon_t. \tag{9-6}$$

As you would expect, this simply suggests that the current value of y, y_t, is a function (ϕ_1 and ϕ_2) of the immediately preceding two values of y (y_{t-1}, y_{t-2}) plus a random error component. In the terminology of Box-Jenkins, the highest order p is referred to as the order of the model. Furthermore, there is nothing to suggest that we cannot exclude some of the lower-order terms (earlier time periods) in arriving at the final model. For example, the final model might be estimated as

$$y_t = \phi_3 y_{t-3} + \phi_5 y_{t-5} + \epsilon_t. \tag{9-7}$$

The second general type of model within the B/J framework is a moving average (MA) model. A moving average model links the current value of the time series to random errors that have occurred in previous time periods rather than to the actual series values themselves. Thus, we can write a moving average model as

$$y_t = \delta - \Theta_1 \epsilon_{t-1} - \Theta_2 \epsilon_{t-2} - \ldots - \Theta_q \epsilon_{t-q} + \epsilon_t \tag{9-8}$$

where δ is the mean about which the series fluctuates, the Θ's are moving average parameters to be estimated, and the ϵ_{t-q}'s are the error terms. That is, with moving average models, the value of the series in time period t, y_t, is simply a function of the mean value, δ, and some combination of error terms from preceding time periods. The highest order of the model is called q and refers to the number of lagged time periods in the model.

Once again, referring to the simplest type of MA model, consider a moving average model with one term:

$$y_t = -\Theta_1 \epsilon_{t-1} + \epsilon_t. \tag{9-9}$$

Equation (9-9) implies that the observed value of the series, y_t, is directly proportional (measured by Θ_1) to the error in the previous time period. Like AR models, MA models can be extended to include a number of terms and need not include all intermediate terms. Note that a moving average model assumes that the current value of the series is a direct and predictable result of past random errors.

The final Box-Jenkins model (mixed autoregressive and moving average, or ARMA) contains both AR and MA parameters:

$$y_t = \delta + \phi_1 y_{t-1} + \phi_2 y_{t-2} + \ldots + \phi_p y_{t-p}$$
$$- \Theta_1 \epsilon_{t-1} - \Theta_2 \epsilon_{t-2} - \Theta_q \epsilon_{t-q} + \epsilon_t. \quad \textbf{(9-10)}$$

The order of the model is expressed in terms of both p and q, usually written as ARMA (p, q).[6] Inclusion of the mean value, δ, in equation (9-10) may seem to violate the previously noted assumption of a mean of zero. We have included the mean or constant value to generalize the model and in recognition of later models that will not be as restrictive of the value of δ. The assumption of a zero mean is simply a special case where δ equals zero.

MODEL IDENTIFICATION

NONSTATIONARY TIME SERIES

One of the critical assumptions of the Box-Jenkins methodology is the assumption of stationarity. However, even a cursory examination of the data in the examples used in this text for estimating regression equations and other time series models indicates the presence of, at the very least, a trend pattern.[7]

If, as is generally the case, actual time series are nonstationary, how can we expect to apply the Box-Jenkins methodology with any regularity? The answer is simple—a nonstationary time series can be converted to a stationary time series through the process of differencing. Intuitively, differencing involves a transformation in which the underlying pattern in the data is eliminated to make it easier to analyze the fluctuations around this pattern.[8]

To illustrate the utility of differencing and its relationship to the Box-Jenkins methodology, suppose that we are charged with developing a monthly forecasting model for the number of daily calls coming into a national call center for a major pest control firm. These daily forecasts will provide information to both the personnel department and the supervisors of the call center relative to the number of telephone lines that need to be accessed and the

---

[6] As a matter of course, once differencing is added to the model-building process, the notation that is used would be of the form ARIMA(p, d, q), where p is the order of the autoregressive term, d is the level of differencing, and q is the order of the moving average term.

[7] Nonstationarity can also occur when there are significant random changes in the level about which the series fluctuates or when there are changes both in levels and slopes. Further, the assumption of a stationary time series can be violated when seasonality is present in the activity being analyzed. We deal with seasonal patterns in a succeeding section of this chapter.

[8] If you need to review the process of computing first, second, and other degrees of differencing, consult the appropriate material in chapter 3.

number of people required to handle the calls. As a first step, suppose that we collect the information provided in column 1 of Table 9-1. An examination of a graphical presentation of the actual data, provided in Figure 9-3, clearly indicates the presence of a trend pattern. That is, the data do not randomly fluctuate around some fixed level. Since we have violated the assumption of stationarity, the next stage in our call station analysis would be to take first

TABLE 9-1 Average Daily Calls

Date	Actual Calls (1)	First Differences (2)	Seasonal Factors (3)	Seasonally Adjusted (4)	First Differences (5)
1984: Jan.	278,279		0.996	279,417	
Feb.	289,006	10,727	1.006	287,358	7,941
Mar.	300,653	11,647	1.023	293,865	6,507
Apr.	305,850	5,197	1.009	303,104	9,239
May	326,146	20,296	1.014	321,515	18,411
June	329,822	3,676	0.998	330,537	9,023
July	333,538	3,716	0.954	349,789	19,252
Aug.	348,448	14,910	0.967	360,321	10,533
Sept.	373,555	25,107	0.995	375,507	15,185
Oct.	379,254	5,699	0.998	380,149	4,642
Nov.	389,013	9,759	0.994	391,335	11,187
Dec.	407,143	18,130	1.045	389,682	(1,653)
1985: Jan.	406,079	(1,064)	0.997	407,252	17,570
Feb.	461,544	55,465	1.006	458,839	51,587
Mar.	451,477	(10,067)	1.024	440,956	(17,883)
Apr.	456,281	4,804	1.009	452,266	11,309
May	462,823	6,542	1.014	456,603	4,338
June	473,817	10,994	0.998	474,981	18,378
July	457,145	(16,672)	0.955	478,927	3,946
Aug.	471,203	14,058	0.968	486,973	8,045
Sept.	495,855	24,652	0.995	498,193	11,221
Oct.	523,105	27,250	0.998	524,355	26,162
Nov.	534,268	11,163	0.992	538,601	14,246
Dec.	572,682	38,414	1.046	547,718	9,117
1986: Jan.	554,642	(18,040)	0.999	555,315	7,597
Feb.	567,401	12,759	1.005	564,878	9,564
Mar.	591,544	24,143	1.025	577,223	12,344
Apr.	602,374	10,830	1.009	596,926	19,703
May	610,073	7,699	1.012	603,027	6,102
June	614,378	4,305	0.997	616,225	13,198
July	594,274	(20,104)	0.956	621,848	5,623
Aug.	617,231	22,957	0.969	637,160	15,312
Sept.	648,229	30,998	0.996	650,644	13,484
Oct.	656,833	8,604	0.997	658,604	7,960
Nov.	675,289	18,456	0.990	681,993	23,389
Dec.	717,011	41,722	1.048	684,128	2,135

(continued)

TABLE 9-1   Average Daily Calls (*Continued*)

Date	Actual Calls (1)	First Differences (2)	Seasonal Factors (3)	Seasonally Adjusted (4)	First Differences (5)
1987: Jan.	684,375	(32,636)	1.001	683,936	(192)
Feb.	708,906	24,531	1.003	706,680	22,744
Mar.	746,823	37,917	1.025	728,592	21,912
Apr.	741,087	(5,736)	1.008	735,154	6,562
May	771,569	30,482	1.009	764,873	29,719
June	765,463	(6,106)	0.995	769,012	4,140
July	731,728	(33,735)	0.957	764,542	(4,470)
Aug.	788,401	56,673	0.970	813,099	48,557
Sept.	811,947	23,546	0.998	813,739	640
Oct.	827,879	15,932	0.994	833,271	19,533
Nov.	813,937	(13,942)	0.988	823,855	(9,416)
Dec.	868,177	54,240	1.050	826,917	3,062
1988: Jan.	873,874	5,697	1.004	870,705	43,789
Feb.	881,943	8,069	1.004	878,875	8,170
Mar.	908,390	26,447	1.027	884,585	5,710
Apr.	905,156	(3,234)	1.007	889,101	14,516
May	904,164	(992)	1.007	897,594	(1,507)
June	919,407	15,243	0.994	925,103	27,510
July	911,445	(7,962)	0.959	950,674	25,570
Aug.	921,502	10,057	0.972	948,151	(2,523)
Sept.	969,245	47,743	1.001	968,789	20,639
Oct.	974,763	5,518	0.992	982,962	14,172
Nov.	972,789	(1,974)	0.985	987,906	4,944
Dec.	1,066,072	93,283	1.050	1,014,926	27,020
1989: Jan.	1,034,829	(31,243)	1.006	1,029,180	14,254
Feb.	1,024,556	(10,273)	1.004	1,020,247	(8,933)
Mar.	1,047,206	22,650	1.027	1,019,262	(985)
Apr.	1,091,893	44,687	1.005	1,086,830	67,568
May	1,090,336	(1,557)	1.006	1,084,017	(2,813)
June	1,078,425	(11,911)	0.992	1,086,971	2,955
July	1,056,840	(21,585)	0.961	1,100,351	13,380
Aug.	1,080,062	23,222	0.973	1,110,158	9,806
Sept.	1,136,408	56,346	1.003	1,133,188	23,030
Oct.	1,121,390	(15,018)	0.989	1,134,101	913
Nov.	1,141,206	19,816	0.983	1,161,204	27,102
Dec.	1,274,444	133,238	1.051	1,212,731	51,527
1990: Jan.	1,190,034	(84,410)	1.007	1,181,343	(31,388)
Feb.	1,212,303	22,269	1.005	1,206,507	25,164
Mar.	1,226,607	14,304	1.028	1,193,359	(13,148)
Apr.	1,177,155	(49,452)	1.004	1,172,406	(20,953)
May	1,184,930	7,775	1.005	1,179,629	7,224
June	1,182,393	(2,537)	0.991	1,192,780	13,150
July	1,161,215	(21,178)	0.961	1,207,890	15,111
Aug.	1,228,840	67,625	0.972	1,263,747	55,857
Sept.	1,233,870	5,030	1.003	1,229,853	(33,895)
Oct.	1,203,553	(30,317)	0.987	1,219,087	(10,765)

FIGURE 9-3 Average Daily Calls

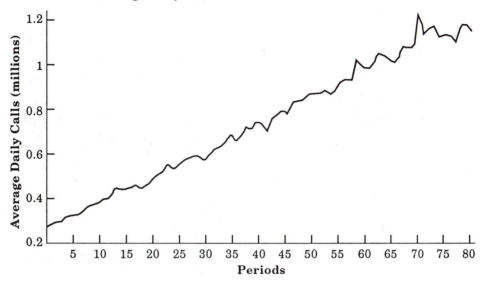

differences. Figure 9-4 provides a visual perspective of the fluctuations of the first differenced series.[9]

A study of the scatter of points in Figure 9-4 about the horizontal line suggests that we have eliminated the trend pattern that characterizes the original data. That is, by computing first differences, we have been able to convert a nonstationary time series into one that satisfies the condition of stationarity. There are situations in which the actual data is dominated by a nonlinear trend pattern. In the case of a parabolic trend, we would need to compute second differences, and in the case of a growth curve, we would need to transform the original time series into logarithms and then take first differences. The point to keep in mind is that by applying the appropriate level of differencing to a nonstationary time series, we can convert or transform it to a stationary time series.

AUTOCORRELATION (AC) AND PARTIAL AUTOCORRELATION (PAC) COEFFICIENTS

To identify the model that best describes the time series under consideration, two sets of statistics or tools are used: autocorrelations (ACs) and partial auto-

---

[9] The observant reader will note that the width of the variation about the mean line seems to be increasing over time. Thus, to be technically correct we would say that the first differences are stationary in terms of the mean, but not in terms of the variance. Specifically, the variance is increasing over time. However, this is a different issue and will be dealt with in succeeding sections of this chapter.

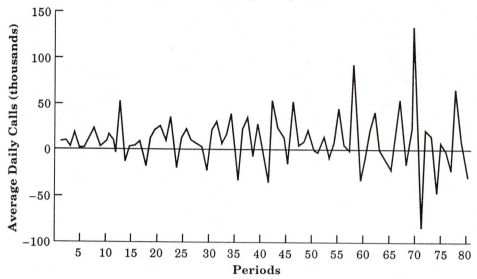

FIGURE 9-4   First Differences of Average Daily Calls

correlations (PACs). The ACs and PACs measure how much interdependency there is among the observations and take values that range between -1 and $+1$, depending on the pattern of the relationship. If, for example, values of the time series that are above the average value are immediately followed by values that are below the mean, then both the AC and the PAC will be negative. Alternatively, if above-average values tend to be followed by above-average values and below-average values followed by below-average values, the AC and PAC will be positive. The AC and PAC are typically calculated for various lags (depending on the type of data and its periodicity—daily, weekly, monthly, etc.).

Autocorrelation coefficients provide us with a numerical measure of the relationship of specific values of a time series to other values in the time series. That is, they measure the relationship of a variable to itself over time. ACs are normally computed for different time lags; thus an AC for a one-period lag measures the relationship of y_t and y_{t-1}, for a two-period lag between y_t and y_{t-2}, etc. Specifically, the autocorrelation coefficient for a lag of k periods is given by

$$R_k = \frac{\text{cov}(y_t, y_{t-k})}{[\text{var}(y_t)\,\text{var}(y_{t-k})]^{1/2}} = \frac{\text{cov}(y_t, y_{t-k})}{\text{var}(y_t)}. \qquad \textbf{(9-11)}$$

The simplified formulation of equation (9-11) follows from the assumption of stationarity in the series. That is, if y_t is stationary, then the mean and variance will not change over time, hence $\text{var}(y_t) = \text{var}(y_{t-1})$ for all lags. While we do not attempt to illustrate the specific mathematics of computing an autocorrelation coefficient, equation (9-11) does focus attention on the fact that we are analyzing the relationship of the variable with itself over time.

Partial autocorrelations, PACs, are closely related to ACs. They also take on values between -1 and $+1$. The specific computational procedures for PACs are complicated, but these formulas do not need to be understood for us to use PACs in the model identification phase. Their utility lies in the fact that PACs produce patterns that are complementary to those of the ACs.

Autocorrelations and partial autocorrelations are generally displayed either as a table of values or as a plot of the coefficients in a correlogram. Table 9-2 depicts a tabular display of the ACs and PACs for both versions of the average call data presented in Table 9-1.

TABLE 9-2 **Autocorrelation and Partial Autocorrelation Coefficients for Call Center Data**

Time Lags	Original Series		First Differences	
	AC (1)	PAC (2)	AC (3)	PAC (4)
1	0.964	0.964	-0.343	-0.343
2	0.929	-0.007	-0.213	-0.374
3	0.896	0.006	0.326	0.128
4	0.863	-0.019	-0.200	-0.114
5	0.830	-0.008	-0.110	-0.135
6	0.797	-0.022	0.194	-0.018
7	0.761	-0.056	-0.276	-0.281
8	0.725	-0.033	0.093	-0.052
9	0.688	-0.020	0.185	0.039
10	0.650	-0.044	-0.209	-0.035
11	0.609	-0.082	-0.065	-0.230
12	0.575	0.096	0.429	0.291
13	0.538	-0.085	-0.247	0.058
14	0.504	0.040	-0.056	0.030
15	0.472	0.003	0.166	-0.034
16	0.439	-0.030	-0.040	0.213
17	0.405	-0.045	-0.138	-0.075
18	0.370	-0.029	0.078	-0.086
19	0.333	-0.074	-0.123	-0.318
20	0.299	0.025	0.022	-0.075
21	0.266	-0.011	0.113	-0.043
22	0.232	-0.050	-0.106	-0.040
23	0.198	-0.025	-0.057	-0.042
24	0.170	0.065	0.271	-0.042

FIGURE 9-5   Preliminary Analysis of Call Center Data

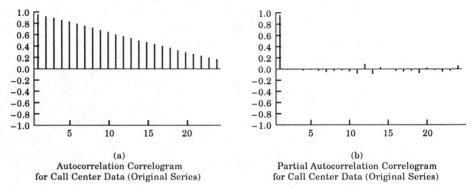

<table>
<tr><td>(a)
Autocorrelation Correlogram
for Call Center Data (Original Series)</td><td>(b)
Partial Autocorrelation Correlogram
for Call Center Data (Original Series)</td></tr>
</table>

While some information can be gleaned from an examination of a tabular presentation of the ACs and PACs, a much more useful and common approach is to transfer this data to a correlogram, as in Figures 9-5 and 9-6. In the correlograms, the lags are placed on the horizontal axis and the coefficients on the vertical axis. The magnitude of each of the coefficients is represented by a bar or spike. As we will see in later sections of this chapter, the pattern of the ACs and the PACs depicted in correlograms is an invaluable tool in identifying the type of model that will most closely capture the variation in the time series of interest. The complementarity of the AC and PAC correlograms stems from the fact that while moving average (MA) models can frequently be identified solely from the ACs, the same cannot be said for the cases of autoregressive (AR) and autoregressive-moving-average (ARMA) models. For example, it is quite easy to confuse the AC correlogram of an AR process with that of an ARMA process—that is, the correlogram for an ARMA(1,1) process will closely resemble that of an AR(1) process. Furthermore, it is difficult to distinguish the order of an AR model from an examination of the

FIGURE 9-6   Secondary Analysis of Call Center Data

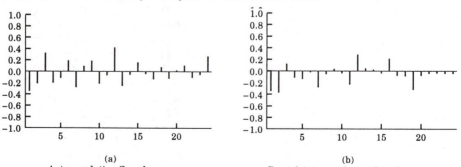

<table>
<tr><td>(a)
Autocorrelation Correlogram
for Call Center Data (First Differences)</td><td>(b)
Partial Autocorrelation Correlogram
for Call Center Data (First Differences)</td></tr>
</table>

correlogram. For these reasons, analysts generally study the pattern of spikes in both the autocorrelation and partial autocorrelation correlograms.

AUTOCORRELATION AND PARTIAL AUTOCORRELATION ANALYSIS FOR THEORETICAL MODELS

In this section we use the AC and PAC correlograms to recognize certain patterns that characterize moving average (MA), autoregressive (AR), and mixed ARMA models when the assumption of stationarity has been satisfied. While it might appear fruitless to focus on theoretical models, it facilitates recognition of similar patterns in actual time series. That is, by comparing actual AC and PAC patterns to the theoretical patterns presented here, we will be able to identify the specific type of B/J model to use based on the following general guidelines:

- If the autocorrelation coefficients decay and the partial autocorrelation coefficients have spikes, the process can best be captured by an AR model where the order equals the number of significant spikes.
- If the partial autocorrelation coefficients decay and the autocorrelation coefficients have spikes, the process can best be captured by an MA model where the order equals the number of significant spikes.
- If both the autocorrelation and partial autocorrelation correlograms are characterized by irregular patterns, the process can best be captured by an ARMA model where the order equals the number of significant spikes.

AC patterns for moving average models are among the easiest to recognize. Starting with a moving average model with one parameter of order 1, MA(1), it can be shown that the autocorrelation coefficients for this model will be

$$R_k = 1 \qquad \text{for } k = 0$$

$$= \frac{-\Theta_1}{1 + \Theta_1^2} \qquad \text{for } k = 1 \qquad \textbf{(9-12)}$$

$$= 0 \qquad \text{for } k \geq 2.$$

Correlograms for an MA(1) model are plotted in Figure 9-7.[10] Both of the correlograms contain a single large "spike" corresponding to the moving average parameter (0.80), with the direction of the spike determined by the sign

---

[10] We should note that all autocorrelation and partial autocorrelation correlograms are generated by specific equations. However, as a rule in forecasting we are much more interested in the pattern exhibited by the correlograms rather than the specific equation which generates the pattern.

FIGURE 9-7   Correlograms for MA(1) Model

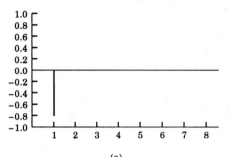

(a)
Autocorrelation Correlogram
for MA(1) Models

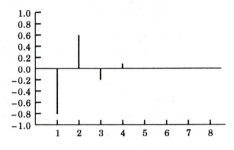

(b)
Partial Autocorrelation Correlogram
for MA(1) Models

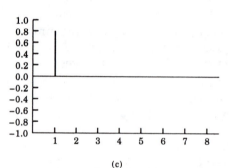

(c)
Autocorrelation Correlogram
for MA(1) Models

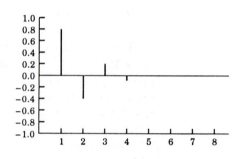

(d)
Partial Autocorrelation Correlogram
for MA(1) Models

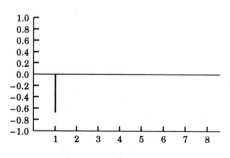

(e)
Autocorrelation Correlogram
for MA(1) Models

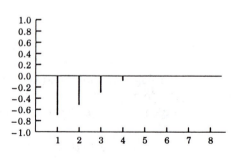

(f)
Partial Autocorrelation Correlogram
for MA(1) Models

FIGURE 9-7 (*Continued*)

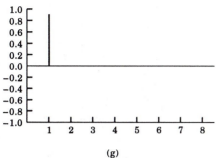

(g)
Autocorrelation Correlogram
for MA(1) Models

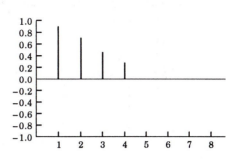

(h)
Partial Autocorrelation Correlogram
for MA(1) Models

on the parameter. Additionally, the PAC correlograms are characterized by spikes that gradually decay as the number of time lags increases or may be characterized by alternating spikes.[11] Finally, in the case of a first order MA model, the estimated value for the parameter, Θ must lie between -1 and $+1$.

Consider a moving average model with two parameters, MA(2), of the form

$$y_t = \delta - \Theta_1 \epsilon_{t-1} - \Theta_2 \epsilon_{t-2} + \epsilon_t. \tag{9-13}$$

For this model, it can be shown that the autocorrelation coefficients are given by

$$R_k = \frac{-\Theta_1 + \Theta_1 \Theta_2}{1 + \Theta_1^2 + \Theta_2^2} \quad k = 1$$

$$= \frac{-\Theta_2}{1 + \Theta_1^2 + \Theta_2^2} \quad k = 2 \tag{9-14}$$

$$= 0 \quad k > 2.$$

The estimated parameters in a second order MA model must satisfy the following condition

$$\Theta_2 - \Theta_1 < 1$$

$$\Theta_2 + \Theta_1 < 1$$

$$1 < \Theta_2 < 1$$

Figure 9-8 depicts correlograms for all possible MA(2) models.

---

[11] As a point of information, the mean of the stationary time series is sometimes included as part of the model. The value of this coefficient has no bearing on the computation or the interpretation of the correlograms.

FIGURE 9-8   Correlograms for MA(2) Models

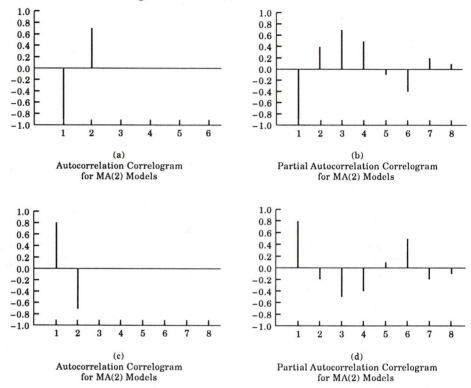

(a)
Autocorrelation Correlogram
for MA(2) Models

(b)
Partial Autocorrelation Correlogram
for MA(2) Models

(c)
Autocorrelation Correlogram
for MA(2) Models

(d)
Partial Autocorrelation Correlogram
for MA(2) Models

In general, the autocorrelations for an MA(q) process are given by

$$R_k = \frac{-\Theta_k + \Theta_1\Theta_{k+1} + \Theta_2\Theta_{k+2} + \ldots + \Theta_{p-k}\Theta_p}{1 + \Theta_1^2 + \Theta_2^2 + \ldots + \Theta_p^2} \qquad k = 1, 2, \ldots, q$$

$$= 0 \quad \text{for } k > q \tag{9-15}$$

with the correlogram depicting spikes at each of the applicable time lags.

The ACs and the correlograms, while somewhat more complicated, can nonetheless be used in identifying autoregressive (AR) models. To illustrate, suppose that we begin with the case of an autoregressive model of order 1, AR(1). It can be shown that the autocorrelation for an AR(1) model will be

$$R_k = \phi_1^k. \tag{9-16}$$

Whenever the time series is stationary, the sum of the AR coefficients (i.e., $\phi_1 + \phi_2 + \ldots + \phi_q$) will be less than one. In the case of the AR(1) model, this implies that ϕ_1 will be less than one so the ACs will be decreasing in absolute value as the lag period increases. That is, $\phi_1 > \phi_1^2 > \ldots > \phi_1^k$, which

FIGURE 9-8 (*Continued*)

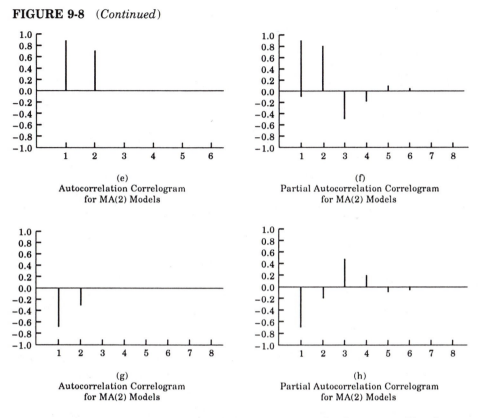

(e)
Autocorrelation Correlogram
for MA(2) Models

(f)
Partial Autocorrelation Correlogram
for MA(2) Models

(g)
Autocorrelation Correlogram
for MA(2) Models

(h)
Partial Autocorrelation Correlogram
for MA(2) Models

simply says that the relationship weakens as we go back in time. Further, as a practical matter, the autocorrelations should decline fairly rapidly, generally within six lags. Finally, we must impose the condition that the estimated parameter, ϕ, must lie between -1 and $+1$. Figure 9-9 shows the correlograms for an AR(1) model when the estimated parameter, ϕ, is positive.

FIGURE 9-9 **Correlograms for AR(1) Model**

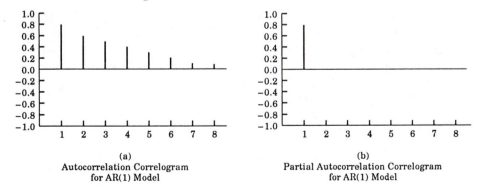

(a)
Autocorrelation Correlogram
for AR(1) Model

(b)
Partial Autocorrelation Correlogram
for AR(1) Model

FIGURE 9-10 Correlograms for AR(1) Model with a Negative Autoregressive Parameter

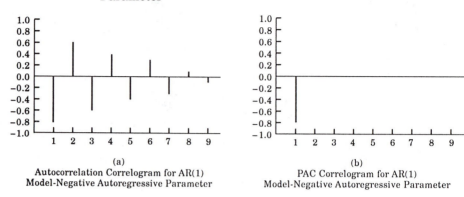

(a)
Autocorrelation Correlogram for AR(1)
Model-Negative Autoregressive Parameter

(b)
PAC Correlogram for AR(1)
Model-Negative Autoregressive Parameter

While it is relatively easy to identify an AR(1) model when the spikes occur as in Figure 9-9, it becomes somewhat more difficult when the autoregressive parameter, ϕ, is negative. When the AR parameter for an AR(1) model is negative, the correlograms will conform to the patterns suggested by Figure 9-10.

The correlogram for an AR(2) model will have a similar pattern, with a twist. The ACs will also fluctuate in a cyclical or sinusoidal manner. The autocorrelations for an AR(2) model can be shown to be

$$R_1 = \frac{\phi_1}{1 - \phi_2} \tag{9-17}$$

$$R_2 = \frac{\phi_2 + \phi_1^2}{1 - \phi_2} \tag{9-18}$$

$$R_k = \phi_1 R_{k-1} + \phi_2 R_{k-2}. \tag{9-19}$$

These equations are called the Yule-Walker equations. Notice that if we know that the time series can be modeled with an AR(2) process, then we can use the autocorrelations calculated from the data to estimate the parameters, by solving equations (9-17) and (9-18) for ϕ_1 and ϕ_2. There are other methods for estimating the parameters, but we do not deal with estimation methods for time series models as they are outside the scope of this book. Further, when dealing with an AR(2) model, the estimated parameters, ϕs, must satisfy the conditions that

$$\begin{array}{cc} \begin{array}{c} -1 < \phi_1 < 1 \\ -1 < \phi_2 < 1 \end{array} & \text{and} & \begin{array}{c} -1 < \phi_1 + \phi_2 < 1 \\ -1 < \phi_2 - \phi_1 < 1 \end{array} \end{array}$$

The basic AC and PAC patterns associated with an AR(2) model are presented in Figure 9-11. An examination of the various patterns presented in Figure 9-11 highlights the basic aspect of AR(2) models. The autocorrelation coefficients trail off to zero, while the partial autocorrelation coefficients tend to decay toward zero after only the second time lag. The signs of the parameters

FIGURE 9-11   Correlograms for AR(2) Models

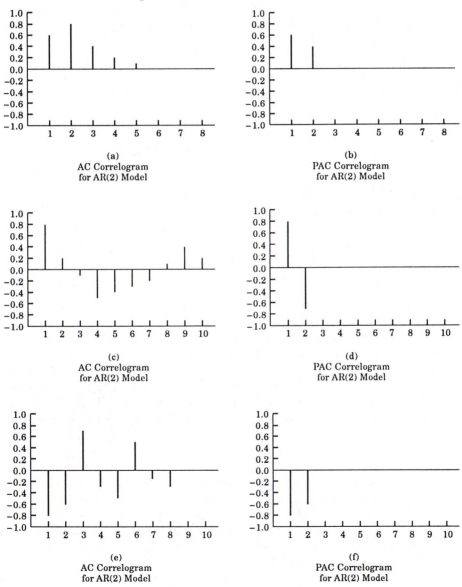

(a)
AC Correlogram
for AR(2) Model

(b)
PAC Correlogram
for AR(2) Model

(c)
AC Correlogram
for AR(2) Model

(d)
PAC Correlogram
for AR(2) Model

(e)
AC Correlogram
for AR(2) Model

(f)
PAC Correlogram
for AR(2) Model

FIGURE 9-11 *(Continued)*

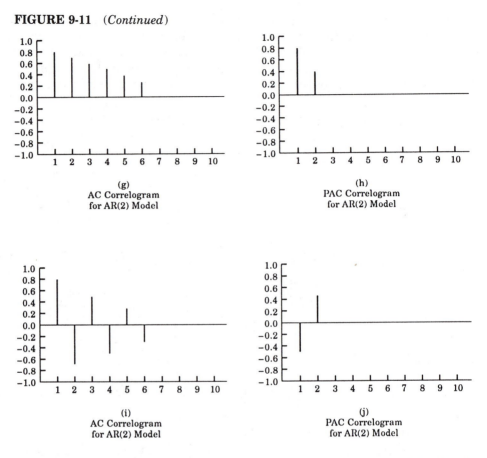

(g)
AC Correlogram
for AR(2) Model

(h)
PAC Correlogram
for AR(2) Model

(i)
AC Correlogram
for AR(2) Model

(j)
PAC Correlogram
for AR(2) Model

will determine whether or not the ACs decay or are characterized by the decaying and fluctuating pattern.

The final basic model within the B/J framework is a mixture of the previous two models in that it contains both an autoregressive (AR) and a moving average (MA) parameter, hence the abbreviation ARMA. The simplest autoregressive moving average process is one of the order (1,1), that is,

$$y_t = \delta + \phi_1 y_{t-1} - \Theta_1 \epsilon_{t-1} + \epsilon_t. \tag{9-20}$$

The process of deriving the computational formulas for the autocorrelation coefficients for various time lags is relatively complicated and hence need not be reproduced here. The correlograms in Figure 9-12 present the basic patterns exhibited by a mixed ARMA(1,1) model. An examination of all of the potential patterns inherent in an ARMA(1,1) model reveals the difficulties associated with identifying these models.

FIGURE 9-12   Correlograms for Mixed ARMA(1,1) Models

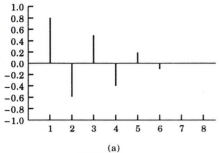

(a)
AC Correlogram
for ARMA(1, 1) Model

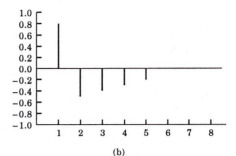

(b)
PAC Correlogram
for ARMA(1, 1) Model

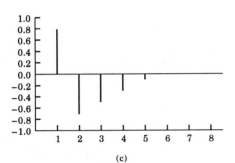

(c)
AC Correlogram
for ARMA(1, 1) Model

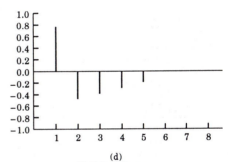

(d)
PAC Correlogram
for ARMA(1, 1) Model

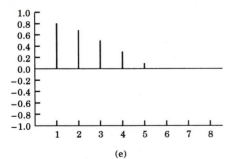

(e)
AC Correlogram
for ARMA(1, 1) Model

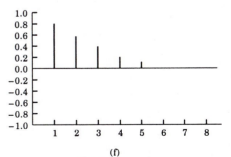

(f)
PAC Correlogram
for ARMA(1, 1) Model

FIGURE 9-12 *(Continued)*

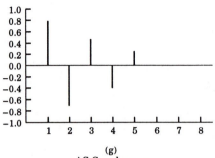

(g)
AC Correlogram
for ARMA(1, 1) Model

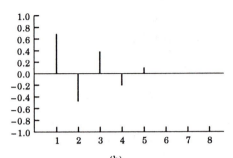

(h)
PAC Correlogram
for ARMA(1, 1) Model

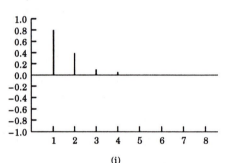

(i)
AC Correlogram
for ARMA(1, 1) Model

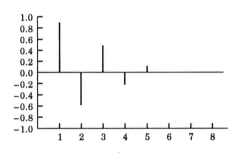

(j)
PAC Correlogram
for ARMA(1, 1) Model

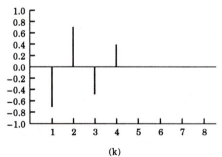

(k)
AC Correlogram
for ARMA(1, 1) Model

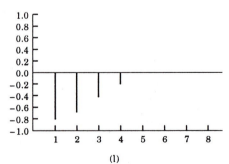

(l)
PAC Correlogram
for ARMA(1, 1) Model

INTERPRETING CORRELOGRAMS ESTIMATED FROM ACTUAL DATA

Until now, the discussion has focused on the situation in which the actual form of the process or model is known. In practice, the usual problem is to estimate the ACs and PACs for a given time series to identify the process or model that best describes the actual data.

Generally, the estimated ACs and PACs will not precisely match the theoretical patterns set forth in the preceding discussion. In particular, any given set of data may lead to nonzero autocorrelations when the actual autocorrelations are equal to zero. Thus, it is necessary to develop a procedure to evaluate the statistical significance of the observed autocorrelation. That is, some of the observed ACs and PACs may not be truly characteristic of the process under consideration. If this is indeed the case, the question is which of the nonzero ACs and PACs should be ignored and which should be considered significant. Confidence limits can frequently be used as guidelines in deciding which nonzero ACs and PACs to rely on in identifying the appropriate model. In using confidence limits, there is always the possibility that an autocorrelation or partial autocorrelation may appear significant when in fact it is not, or vice versa.[12]

Computer programs that feature Box-Jenkins estimation procedures will plot the ACs and PACs, along with the confidence limits. An example of a typical statistical estimation program's AC and PAC correlograms is given in Figure 9-13. The confidence limits in Figure 9-14(a) are denoted by dashed

FIGURE 9-13 Correlograms and Associated Confidence Limits

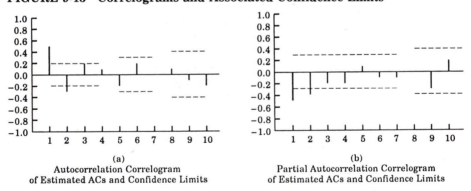

(a)
Autocorrelation Correlogram
of Estimated ACs and Confidence Limits

(b)
Partial Autocorrelation Correlogram
of Estimated ACs and Confidence Limits

[12] For example, an AR series can have an exponentially decreasing set of autocorrelation coefficients. However, usually only the first two or three will fall outside of the confidence limits. In the absence of a PAC correlogram, we might incorrectly conclude that the model is representative of an MA process.

lines. Further, the limits used in the AC plots are a result of the rule of thumb that $r_k = 0$ for $k > q$ if

$$|t_k| = \left| \frac{r_k}{s_k} \right| \leq 2. \tag{9-21}$$

The formula for s_k is given by

$$s_k = \frac{1}{(n+1)^{\frac{1}{2}}}\left(1 + 2\sum_{i=1}^{k-1} r_i^2\right)^{\frac{1}{2}}. \tag{9-22}$$

Note that t_k is a "t-like" statistic, it is asymptotically normal, and the use of t_k parallels the application of the t statistic in regression analysis.[13] The confidence limits for each AC are determined by equation (9-21) and are equal to $[+2s_k, -2s_k]$. Equation (9-22) tells us that s_k increases as k increases, hence the confidence limits will widen as we consider longer lag periods.

The use of ACs and PACs is somewhat overwhelming at first. With a little practice using the rules of thumb that describe the confidence limits, practitioners gradually become more proficient in "reading" the correlograms generated from actual data. In fact, before proceeding to deal with nonstationary data patterns in the subsequent sections of this chapter, we suggest that you attempt to apply the theoretical AC and PAC patterns to the data series in questions 1 and 2 at the end of the chapter.

EXAMPLE 9-1   Inventory Forecasting

As the forecasting expert in the production management division of a major corporation, one of your responsibilities is to develop inventory forecasts for the company's major product line. As a first step, you collect data on weekly inventory levels presented in Table 9-3. A visual inspection of the data in Table 9-3 clearly indicates that there is a trend pattern in the data. After conducting a differencing analysis it was determined that first differences were sufficient to eliminate this pattern.

Once the first differences were computed, the next stage was to identify the appropriate model from an analysis of the AC and PAC correlograms shown in Figure 9-14.

An examination of the autocorrelation correlogram shows that the only significant coefficient, -0.484, is associated with a one-period lag. The partial autocorrelation correlogram has significant spikes for both a

---

[13] *Asymptotically normal* means that as the size of the sample increases, the computed t statistic's distribution approximates a normal distribution. As indicated in previous chapters, this means you can use the normal distribution table to conduct tests of statistical significance if you have a large enough sample.

TABLE 9-3   Weekly Inventory Levels

Week	Inventory Level	Week	Inventory Level
1	682	42	1,142
2	657	43	931
3	720	44	1,001
4	768	45	1,070
5	685	46	1,044
6	682	47	1,078
7	817	48	1,138
8	903	49	1,153
9	774	50	1,151
10	774	51	1,197
11	711	52	1,143
12	721	53	1,232
13	596	54	1,339
14	746	55	1,359
15	716	56	1,264
16	639	57	1,347
17	824	58	1,314
18	831	59	1,405
19	840	60	1,292
20	820	61	1,514
21	799	62	1,594
22	890	63	1,399
23	854	64	1,660
24	902	65	1,719
25	963	66	1,790
26	825	67	1,706
27	821	68	1,695
28	911	69	1,822
29	1,090	70	1,742
30	1,053	71	1,818
31	1,093	72	1,976
32	972	73	1,931
33	1,070	74	1,946
34	919	75	1,878
35	930	76	2,093
36	774	77	2,030
37	989	78	2,108
38	794	79	2,090
39	981	80	2,229
40	884	81	2,057
41	930		

FIGURE 9-14 Correlograms for Weekly Inventory Levels

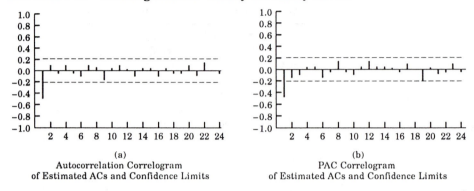

(a)
Autocorrelation Correlogram
of Estimated ACs and Confidence Limits

(b)
PAC Correlogram
of Estimated ACs and Confidence Limits

one- and two-period time lag. Both of these patterns are consistent with a moving average (MA) model with one parameter. Thus, the next stage would be to estimate an MA(1) model.

EXAMPLE 9-2 Predicting Average Package Weight

Suppose that we are charged with developing a forecasting model for the average daily weight of packages. This forecast is used to determine how many trucks are required to deliver the packages to the final customers. As a first step you collect the information presented in Table 9-4.

Stationarity was achieved by removing the trend pattern through a first differencing process. Figure 9-15 depicts the AC and PAC correlograms for the stationary time series. The decaying pattern of the AC coefficients for the first 4 time lags, when combined with the significant spike for the time lag shown in the PAC correlogram, indicates that an autoregressive (AR) model with one term is certainly worth further con-

FIGURE 9-15 Correlograms for Average Daily Package Weight

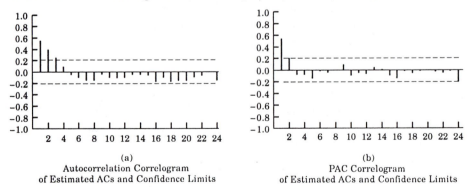

(a)
Autocorrelation Correlogram
of Estimated ACs and Confidence Limits

(b)
PAC Correlogram
of Estimated ACs and Confidence Limits

TABLE 9-4   **Average Daily Package Weight**

Package Weight	Package Weight	Package Weight
14.56	9.49	8.54
15.33	9.64	7.79
15.66	8.49	6.55
17.81	6.03	5.93
20.31	5.66	5.39
21.69	6.46	5.16
22.17	6.95	6.21
24.24	7.45	5.55
22.76	7.52	5.80
21.61	9.44	5.17
18.74	10.44	6.08
15.99	12.60	5.87
14.28	12.65	6.11
12.98	14.60	6.16
12.18	15.05	7.01
12.08	14.69	8.56
10.50	14.11	8.96
9.46	13.98	10.78
8.46	11.69	11.59
6.41	10.94	11.87
3.96	11.04	12.93
3.71	9.54	
4.20	8.75	
3.33	8.20	
3.98	8.05	
4.18	7.45	
5.17	6.95	
6.02	7.34	
6.87	7.27	
7.74	8.17	

sideration. Additionally. since the partial autocorrelation coefficient associated with a two-period lag is relatively large, it could indicate that an ARIMA(1,1,1) model may be worthy of evaluation.

EXAMPLE 9-3   Model Identification for Call Center Data

Return to Figures 9-6(a) and 9-6(b), which provide the AC and PAC correlograms for the first differences of the call center data. While not a perfect match, an examination of these two correlograms seems to suggest that the most appropriate model for the call center data is an autoregressive model with two parameters, AR(2). That is, the large spikes shown in the AC correlogram for a one- and a three-period time lag (with a smaller spike for a two-period lag), when combined with the two significant spikes for a one- and two-period time lag in the PAC correlogram, most closely parallel the theoretical pattern we would observe for an AR(2) model or process. While this conclusion is subject to revision after further testing, the AR(2) model would serve as our initial starting point.

EXAMPLE 9-4   Automobile Sales Revisited

Recall that in example 6-1 (using Appendix D, Table D-1) we developed a regression model for automobile sales. As a comparative study, suppose that we investigate the possibility of developing a Box-Jenkins model. Figure 9-16 illustrates the growth exhibited by automobile sales over the time frame of interest. In an attempt to eliminate the trend pattern inherent in the original data, the first differences are computed and plotted in Figure 9-17. Based on an initial inspection (see Appendix G, Table G-1), it appears that the trend pattern has been eliminated.

　　The next stage is to examine the AC and PAC correlograms for the first differenced data presented in Figure 9-18. A comparison of the calculated ACs and PACs with the theoretical patterns indicates that a combined AR and MA model would be most appropriate. The choice of a

FIGURE 9-16   Growth in Automobile Sales

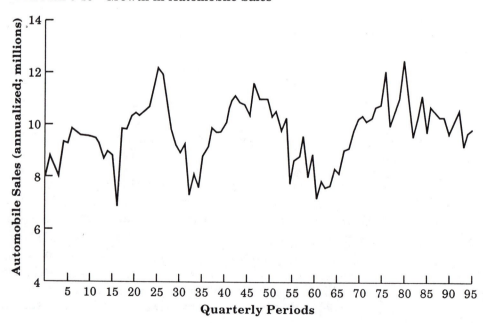

FIGURE 9-17   First Differences of Automobile Sales

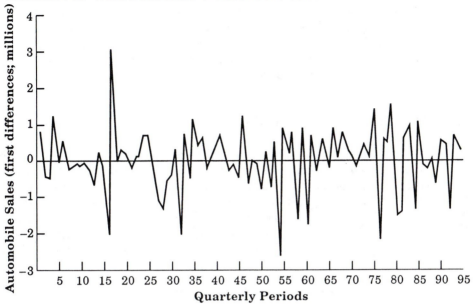

FIGURE 9-18   Correlograms for Auto Sales

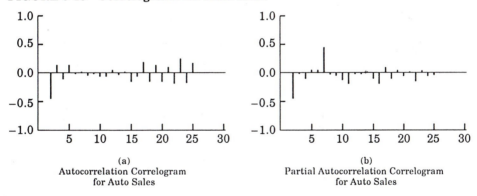

(a)
Autocorrelation Correlogram
for Auto Sales

(b)
Partial Autocorrelation Correlogram
for Auto Sales

specific ARIMA model is debatable. That is, an ARIMA(1,1,2), or an ARIMA(1,2,2), or an ARIMA(1,1,10) model are all candidates.

It has been pointed out that whenever a stationary time series contains a mean value that is significantly different from zero, this value must be included in the final model. This usually does not present any problem, since the majority of computer programs will include this parameter and will refer to it as the constant. However, many Box-Jenkins programs do not automatically include this parameter when using a differencing procedure to remove a trend pattern. Therefore, when you use a differencing process to obtain a stationary series, and if the mean value of the differenced time series does not equal zero, you must take care to include this parameter, generally called the trend parameter, in your final model.

SEASONALITY IN TIME SERIES

Seasonality consistently occurs in time-measured data, and, as was the case with a trend pattern, the existence of a seasonal pattern in the data violates the assumption of stationarity. Fortunately, AC and PAC correlograms can be used to identify seasonal patterns. Figure 9-19 depicts the most common AC and PAC patterns associated with the existence of pure seasonality. Panels (a), (b), and (f) present seasonal patterns of the moving average variety, while (c), (d), and (e) provide those of autoregressive seasonal patterns. Panels (a),

FIGURE 9-19   Correlograms for Seasonal Patterns

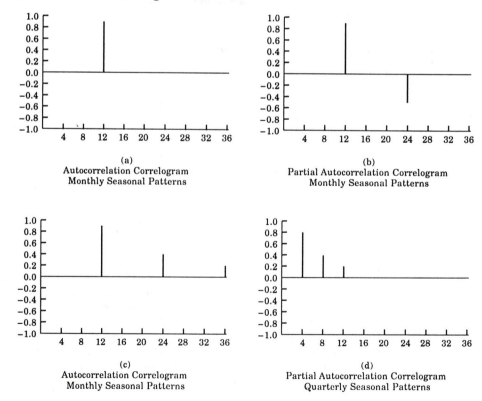

(a)
Autocorrelation Correlogram
Monthly Seasonal Patterns

(b)
Partial Autocorrelation Correlogram
Monthly Seasonal Patterns

(c)
Autocorrelation Correlogram
Monthly Seasonal Patterns

(d)
Partial Autocorrelation Correlogram
Quarterly Seasonal Patterns

FIGURE 9-19 *(Continued)*

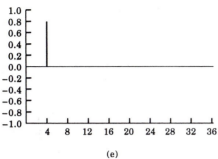

(e)
Autocorrelation Correlogram
Quarterly Seasonal Patterns

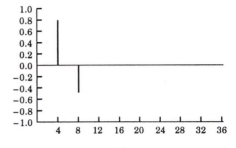

(f)
Partial Autocorrelation Correlogram
Quarterly Seasonal Patterns

(b), and (c) in Figure 9-20 are characteristic of monthly data, with (d), (e), and (f) symptomatic of quarterly data. In the case of weekly or daily data, the seasonal spikes would be entirely dependent on the process being studied. For example, if we were analyzing daily retail sales data, we would likely find significantly nonzero spikes for Saturday and Sunday.

EXAMPLE 9-5   Call Center Activity Revisited

As a practical matter, it is extremely difficult to identify seasonal patterns whenever the data contain a trend pattern. To illustrate, suppose that we once again refer to the AC and PAC correlograms for our call center data as presented in Figures 9-5(a) and (b). If there are seasonal patterns in the call center data, they are clearly overwhelmed by the dominant trend pattern. This is shown by the nonzero spikes for almost all time lags in the AC correlogram in Figure 9-5(a). Thus, to test for the existence of a seasonal pattern, we would be better served to study the AC and PAC correlograms for the differenced series as presented in Figures 9-6(a) and (b). In both of these cases, the existence of a monthly seasonal pattern is captured by the relatively large spikes for time lags of 12 months and 24 months. The call center data not only contain a trend pattern but also a seasonal pattern that must be eliminated prior to the model estimation phase.

EXAMPLE 9-6   Predicting Daily Riders

Suppose that you are employed by a local transit authority and are charged with developing a forecasting model for the number of daily riders. As a first step, you collect the information presented in Appendix G, Table G-2. An examination of a graphical display of the actual data seems

FIGURE 9-20   Correlograms for Daily Riders

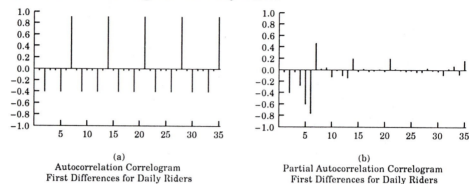

(a)
Autocorrelation Correlogram
First Differences for Daily Riders

(b)
Partial Autocorrelation Correlogram
First Differences for Daily Riders

to indicate that there is a trend pattern in the growth of riders. To investigate the possibility that there is also a seasonal pattern, you first eliminate the trend pattern through the use of first differences.

Having eliminated the trend pattern by first differencing, you then proceed to derive the AC and PAC correlogram for this time series, with the results as presented in Figure 9-20. An examination of the AC correlogram suggests that there is a large number of nonzero spikes that seem to occur at regular intervals. However, there is some variance in the time lags at which these spikes occur. As a result of this variance, you decide to examine the PAC correlogram where the seasonal pattern is much easier to recognize. Specifically, an examination of the spikes that occur at time lags of 7, 14, 21, 28, and 35 days would suggest that there is a recurring seasonal pattern within each week. In particular, the pattern of the spikes in both the AC and PAC correlograms seems to indicate an autoregressive seasonal pattern.

If seasonal patterns violate the assumption of stationarity, the next step is to eliminate this pattern prior to model estimation. There are two generally acceptable procedures for accomplishing this objective. The first procedure would be to use the Census X11 procedure discussed in chapter 3 to seasonally adjust the data. Once this seasonal adjustment has been completed, the seasonally adjusted data would be entered into the Box-Jenkins program. While this approach has some advantages, a problem occurs whenever we are working with hourly, daily, or weekly data. That is, the majority of the existing Census X11 programs cannot accommodate a time series measured in time increments of less than one month.

The second procedure is generally available within the majority of Box-Jenkins computer programs and closely parallels the elimination of trend patterns. Recall that to eliminate trend patterns in a nonstationary time series, we simply applied the process of differencing. The same approach can be used in eliminating seasonal patterns. That is, by computing seasonal differences to the trend-adjusted data, we can eliminate the seasonal pattern. As was the case with the elimination of a trend pattern, we may have to apply this process more than once in order to eliminate seasonality.

EXAMPLE 9-7 Daily Ridership Revisited

To illustrate the process of seasonal differencing, suppose that we reconsider the case of daily ridership first introduced in example 9-6. In our analysis of the AC and PAC correlograms in Figure 9-20, we concluded that the detrended data still contained a seasonal pattern, as suggested by the spikes at time lags that were multiples of 7.

In an attempt to eliminate this seasonal pattern, we decide to compute a seasonal first differences. To illustrate the process of computing seasonal first differences, consider the first seven observations of the daily ridership data shown in Table 9-5. After the difference between the first and second periods (1,940, as shown in column 2) has been calculated, the process is repeated for the eight and ninth periods (4,672). The first seasonal difference is shown in column 3 as 2,732 (4,672 − 1,940). This process was completed for the entire data set in Appendix G, Table G-2.

TABLE 9-5   Computing Seasonal First Differences

Actual Riders (1)	*First Difference* (2)	*Seasonal Difference* (3)
108,014		
109,954	1,940	
103,058	− 6,896	
18,231	− 84,827	
2,396	− 15,835	
107,332	104,936	
107,482	150	
109,388	1,906	
114,060	4,672	{4,672 − 1,940 = 2,732}
106,900	− 7,160	{−7,160 − (−6,896) = −264}
19,587	− 87,313	{−87,313 − (−84,827) = −2,486}
2,824	− 16,763	{−16,763 − (−15,835) = −928}
112,029	109,205	{109,205 − 104,936 = 4,269}
116,931	4,902	{4,902 − 150 = 4,752}
110,636	− 6,295	{−6,295 − 1,906 = 8,201}

FIGURE 9-21   Correlograms for Daily Riders After Seasonal Differencing

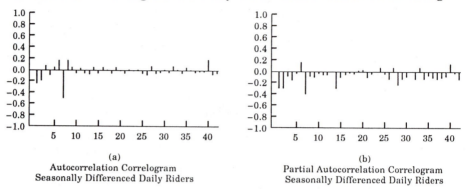

(a)
Autocorrelation Correlogram
Seasonally Differenced Daily Riders

(b)
Partial Autocorrelation Correlogram
Seasonally Differenced Daily Riders

Once the seasonal differences have been calculated, ACs and PACs are computed for this new time series, with the results as depicted in Figure 9-21. As suggested by the correlograms in Figure 9-21, seasonal differencing appears to have eliminated the majority of the seasonal patterns in the data. There are, however, some significantly nonzero spikes in both of the correlograms for a time lag of seven, and this indicates the need to include a seasonal moving average or autoregressive parameter in the final model.

As highlighted in Table 9-5, whenever differencing is used to create a stationary time series, data points are lost in the process. In the case of daily ridership, the first week of the data is lost. In the case of a monthly or quarterly time series, an entire year of data is lost. There are many cases when we simply cannot afford to lose this much data. Thus, as a general practice, seasonally adjust the data via the Census X11 procedure prior to beginning the identification phase of the Box-Jenkins methodology.

EXAMPLE 9-8   Call Center Identification Revisited

In example 9-5, the presence of significant spikes for time lags of 12 and 24 months in the AC and PAC correlograms indicated the likelihood of a seasonal pattern. While we could use the process of seasonal differencing to eliminate the pattern, an alternative approach would be to remove this pattern via the Census X11 approach. Columns 3 and 4 in Table 9-1 provide the seasonally adjusted call center data. Finally, adjusting the trend pattern in the data, the seasonally adjusted first differences are presented in column 5. Figure 9-22 provides the AC and PAC correlograms for the data in column 5 of Table 9-1. An examination of the correlograms does indeed suggest that we have eliminated both the trend

FIGURE 9-22   Correlograms for Seasonally Adjusted Call Center Data

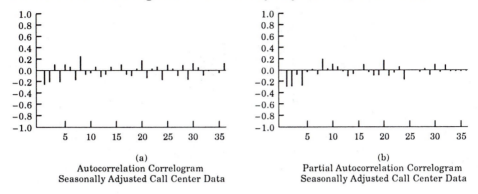

(a)
Autocorrelation Correlogram
Seasonally Adjusted Call Center Data

(b)
Partial Autocorrelation Correlogram
Seasonally Adjusted Call Center Data

and seasonal patterns in the original data. Further, these correlograms confirm that the best model will be an autoregressive model with either one or two terms.

APPROPRIATE LEVEL OF DIFFERENCING

Since the majority of the time series that are encountered in business settings will not be stationary, some level of differencing is required, but how much? To a large extent, the appropriate level of differencing can be determined via an analysis of the autocorrelation correlogram for the unadjusted or differenced data series. For example, consider the AC correlogram for the unadjusted call center data which is reproduced in Figure 9-23.

FIGURE 9-23   Autocorrelation Correlogram for Unadjusted Call Center Data

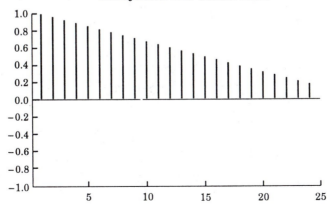

FIGURE 9-24   Correlograms for Sales Data

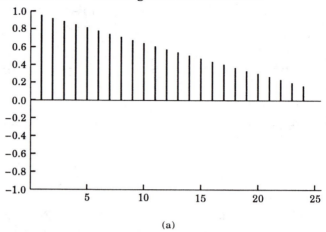

(a)

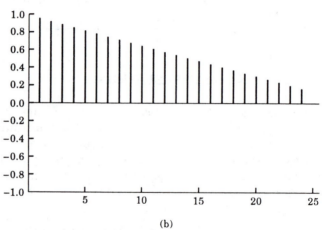

(b)

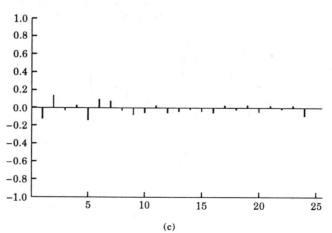

(c)

In this diagram, the AC coefficients are significant for a prolonged lag period, then decrease slowly, and finally appear to decline at a relatively constant rate. In fact, a straight line would connect the top of the spikes in Figure 9-23. When this AC pattern occurs with the unadjusted data, it is indicative of a trend pattern. To identify a specific trend pattern, compute successive differences and analyze the respective AC correlograms. There will be cases in which first differencing will not remove the trend pattern. Consider, for example, the monthly sales data presented in Appendix G, Table G-3. Figure 9-24, panels (a), (b), and (c), depicts the AC correlograms for the original series, the first differences, and the second differences.

The correlogram for the original data, Figure 9-24(a), clarifies the existence of a trend pattern and indicates the need for differencing. Figure 9-24(b) contains the correlogram for the first differenced data that displays an AC pattern virtually identical to the AC pattern for the unadjusted data, again suggesting the need for further differencing. Taking second differences and computing the ACs and PACs, we obtain the correlogram presented in Figure 9-24(c). An examination of Figure 9-24(c) confirms that the sales data contain a second-degree or parabolic trend pattern that requires the use of second differences to achieve stationarity.

To a large extent, determination of the appropriate level of differencing is subjective. Specifically, when you examine the AC and PAC correlograms and you are able to identify a pattern that matches either an autoregressive or moving average model, you are finished with the differencing procedure. In general, however, try to rely on as few differences as possible since each differencing procedure adds another layer of computations, complicates the estimation procedure, and causes a loss of data.

MODEL ESTIMATION AND VALIDATION[14]

ESTIMATION

The second stage in the Box-Jenkins model-building process is model estimation. That is, once we have analyzed the AC and PAC correlograms and tentatively identified the model, the next step is to derive estimates of the model's parameters that satisfy two overriding objectives:

- The fitted values should be as close as possible to the actual values.
- The models should require the fewest possible parameters consistent with a "good" fit.

---

[14] Different computer programs use different mathematical approaches in solving for the final estimates of Box-Jenkins models. This can lead to small differences in parameter estimations. Throughout this text, we are relying on the SPSSPC, Trends, version 4.0 computer program.

The process used to guarantee that the fitted values are as close as possible to the actual values is similar to that presented in the discussion of regression analysis. That is, within the B/J methodology, specific parameter values are estimated subject to the condition that the sum of the squared residuals is minimized (the least-squares criterion). While it is true that the mathematics associated with B/J is more complicated, the end result is identical in that the estimated parameters are sometimes called least-squares parameters.

The desire to use as few parameters as is necessary is based on the same arguments set forth earlier for regression models. That is, while the objective of achieving a close fit causes us to include all relevant variables, the desire to minimize parameters focuses on the need to exclude irrelevant variables. The inclusion of too many parameters in an estimated model complicates the estimation and forecasting process and may lead to unreliable forecasts (since we have included a variable that does not belong in the final model).

To illustrate the estimation and validation process, return to the call center example covered at various stages in this chapter. Analysis of the AC and PAC correlograms led us to conclude that the most appropriate model was an autoregressive model with two parameters (the term δ, the mean about which the series fluctuates, has been added to the original equation):

$$y_t = \delta + \phi_1 y_{t-1} + \phi_2 y_{t-2} + \epsilon_t. \tag{9-6}$$

If this model is applied to the first differences (denoted by lower-case ys) of the call center data, the specific model that results is

$$\hat{y}_t = 11{,}864 - 0.40308 y_{t-1} - 0.34057 y_{t-2}. \tag{9-23}$$

Prior to generating fitted or forecast values, there is one adjustment and one retransformation that must be performed on equation (9-23). The process mean of 11,864 must be modified to account for the two autoregressive parameters. This adjustment can be illustrated as follows:

$$\text{Final Mean} = 11{,}864 - 0.40308\,(-11{,}864) - 0.34057(-11{,}864)$$

$$= 11{,}864 - (-4{,}782) - (-4{,}041)$$

$$= 20{,}687. \tag{9-24}$$

Thus, the final model would be written as

$$\hat{y}_t = 20{,}687 - 0.40308 y_{t-1} - 0.34057 y_{t-2}. \tag{9-25}$$

As written in equation (9-25), fitted or forecast values are in terms of first differences—that is, $y_t = (Y_t - Y_{t-1})$. To convert this model back into its original nondifferenced form, substitute as follows (upper-case Ys denote nondifferenced form):

$$(Y_t - \hat{Y}_{t-1}) = 20{,}687 - 0.40308(Y_{t-1} - Y_{t-2}) - 0.34057(Y_{t-2} - Y_{t-3})$$

$$\hat{Y}_t = 20{,}687 + 0.59692Y_{t-1} + 0.06251Y_{t-2} + 0.34057Y_{t-3}. \quad \textbf{(9-26)}$$

Equation (9-26) can, in turn, be used to generate a fitted (historical) value for, say, October 1990:

$$\hat{Y}_{\text{Oct}} = 20{,}687 + 0.59692Y_{\text{Sep}} + 0.06251Y_{\text{Aug}} + 0.34057Y_{\text{July}}$$

$$= 20{,}687 + 0.59692(1{,}229{,}853) + 0.06251(1{,}263{,}747)$$

$$+ 0.34057(1{,}207{,}890)$$

$$= 1{,}245{,}178. \quad \textbf{(9-27)}$$

The remainder of the fitted values (as well as forecasts) in Table 9-6 would be obtained in an identical fashion.[15] Fortunately, you do not have to go through these time-consuming computations, as the majority of computer programs present the fitted values and the forecasts in terms of the original data.

EXAMPLE 9-9   Automobile Sales: Box-Jenkins Model

In Example 9-4, we pointed out that a combination ARIMA model appeared to be the most appropriate for the automobile sales data. As a first attempt, suppose that we estimate a model with one autoregressive parameter, AR(1), and two moving average parameters, MA(2). That is, the model to be tested is ARIMA(1,1,2) where AR refers to autoregressive; I to a differenced model; and MA to moving average. The first 1 signifies one AR parameter; the second 1 signifies that we have computed one difference; and the 2 refers to the number of moving average parameters.

When the model is estimated for the auto sales data, the results are as follows:

$$\hat{y}_t = 0.0209 - 0.996y_{t-1} - 0.6534e_{t-1} + 0.3139e_{t-2}. \quad \textbf{(9-28)}$$

The reliability of this model in simulating historical automobile sales is presented in Table 9-7 (pages 462–63).

---

[15] Recall that prior to estimating the model, we used the Census X11 methodology to seasonally adjust the data. For this reason, the forecast that is presented in equation (9-27) is in seasonally adjusted terms. To translate this back to nonseasonally adjusted data, we would simply multiply the seasonally adjusted forecast by the seasonal factor for November.

TABLE 9-6   Comparative Analysis of Fitted and Actual First Differences for Call Center Data

Date	Seasonally Adjusted (1)	Fitted Values* (2)	Residuals (3)	Percent Error (4)	Forecast Confidence Intervals Lower (5)	Upper (6)
1984: Jan.	279,417					
Feb.	287,358	291,281	(3,923)	−1.37	256,317	326,245
Mar.	293,865	300,402	(6,537)	−2.22	267,008	333,795
Apr.	303,104	309,224	(6,120)	−2.02	277,727	340,721
May	321,515	317,850	3,665	1.14	286,354	349,347
June	330,537	331,634	(1,097)	−0.33	300,137	363,130
July	349,789	341,317	8,472	2.42	309,820	372,813
Aug.	360,321	359,643	678	0.19	328,146	391,139
Sept.	375,507	370,206	5,301	1.41	338,709	401,703
Oct.	380,149	386,485	(6,336)	−1.67	354,989	417,982
Nov.	391,335	393,792	(2,457)	−0.63	362,296	425,289
Dec.	389,682	405,932	(16,250)	−4.17	374,435	437,428
1985: Jan.	407,252	407,225	27	0.01	375,728	438,722
Feb.	458,839	421,419	37,420	8.16	389,922	452,916
Mar.	440,956	452,748	(11,792)	−2.67	421,251	484,245
Apr.	452,266	451,282	984	0.22	419,785	482,779
May	456,603	474,484	(17,881)	−3.92	442,987	505,980
June	474,981	471,690	3,291	0.69	440,193	503,186
July	478,927	486,783	(7,856)	−1.64	455,286	518,279
Aug.	486,973	491,764	(4,791)	−0.98	460,267	523,261
Sept.	498,193	503,072	(4,879)	−0.98	471,576	534,569
Oct.	524,355	511,617	12,738	2.43	480,120	543,114
Nov.	538,601	530,675	7,926	1.47	499,178	562,172
Dec.	547,718	544,635	3,083	0.56	513,139	576,132
1986: Jan.	555,315	559,878	(4,563)	−0.82	528,381	591,375
Feb.	564,878	569,834	(4,956)	−0.88	538,337	601,331
Mar.	577,223	579,123	(1,901)	−0.33	547,626	610,619
Apr.	596,926	589,676	7,250	1.21	558,180	621,173
May	603,027	605,466	(2,439)	−0.40	573,969	636,963
June	616,225	614,544	1,681	0.27	583,047	646,041
July	621,848	629,514	(7,666)	−1.23	598,017	661,010
Aug.	637,160	635,773	1,387	0.22	604,276	667,270
Sept.	650,644	649,759	885	0.14	618,262	681,256
Oct.	658,604	660,680	(2,076)	−0.32	629,184	692,177
Nov.	681,993	671,490	10,503	1.54	639,993	702,987
Dec.	684,128	690,541	(6,413)	−0.94	659,044	722,038
1987: Jan.	683,936	695,988	(12,052)	−1.76	664,492	727,485
Feb.	706,680	703,973	2,707	0.38	672,476	735,469
Mar.	728,592	718,264	10,328	1.42	686,767	749,761
Apr.	735,154	732,700	2,454	0.33	701,204	764,197
May	764,873	745,733	19,140	2.50	714,236	777,229
June	769,012	771,345	(2,333)	−0.30	739,849	802,842
July	764,542	777,909	(13,367)	−1.75	746,412	809,406

TABLE 9-6 *(Continued)*

Date	Seasonally Adjusted (1)	Fitted Values* (2)	Residuals (3)	Percent Error (4)	Forecast Confidence Intervals	
					Lower (5)	Upper (6)
Aug.	813,099	785,621	27,478	3.38	754,124	817,117
Sept.	813,739	815,735	(1,996)	−0.25	784,239	847,232
Oct.	833,271	817,631	15,640	1.88	786,134	849,127
Nov.	823,855	845,867	(22,012)	−2.67	814,370	877,363
Dec.	826,917	841,685	(14,768)	−1.79	810,188	873,181
1988: Jan.	870,705	849,576	21,129	2.43	818,079	881,073
Feb.	878,875	872,699	6,176	0.70	841,202	904,195
Mar.	884,585	881,356	3,229	0.37	849,859	912,852
Apr.	899,101	900,188	(1,087)	−0.12	868,691	931,684
May	897,594	911,992	(14,398)	−1.60	880,495	943,489
June	925,103	913,944	11,159	1.21	882,447	945,441
July	950,674	935,215	15,459	1.63	903,718	966,711
Aug.	948,151	951,685	(3,534)	−0.37	920,188	983,181
Sept.	968,789	961,146	7,643	0.79	929,649	992,642
Oct.	982,962	982,016	946	0.10	950,519	1,013,513
Nov.	987,906	990,907	(3,001)	−0.30	959,410	1,022,403
Dec.	1,014,926	1,001,773	13,153	1.30	970,276	1,033,270
1989: Jan.	1,029,180	1,023,037	6,143	0.60	991,541	1,054,534
Feb.	1,020,247	1,034,919	(14,672)	−1.44	1,003,422	1,066,415
Mar.	1,019,262	1,039,680	(20,418)	−2.00	1,008,183	1,071,176
Apr.	1,086,830	1,043,388	43,442	4.00	1,011,891	1,074,884
May	1,084,017	1,080,616	3,401	0.31	1,049,120	1,112,113
June	1,086,971	1,082,826	4,145	0.38	1,051,329	1,114,322
July	1,100,351	1,107,425	(7,074)	−0.64	1,075,928	1,138,922
Aug.	1,110,158	1,114,638	(4,480)	−0.40	1,083,142	1,146,135
Sept.	1,133,188	1,122,335	10,853	0.96	1,090,838	1,153,831
Oct.	1,134,101	1,141,252	(7,151)	−0.63	1,109,755	1,172,748
Nov.	1,161,204	1,146,576	14,628	1.26	1,115,000	1,178,073
Dec.	1,212,731	1,170,655	42,076	3.47	1,139,158	1,202,151
1990: Jan.	1,181,343	1,203,417	(22,074)	−1.87	1,171,921	1,234,914
Feb.	1,206,507	1,197,133	9,374	0.78	1,165,636	1,228,630
Mar.	1,193,359	1,227,740	(34,381)	−2.88	1,196,243	1,259,236
Apr.	1,172,406	1,210,775	(38,369)	−3.27	1,179,278	1,242,272
May	1,179,629	1,206,016	(26,387)	−2.24	1,174,519	1,237,512
June	1,192,780	1,204,540	(11,761)	−0.99	1,173,043	1,236,037
July	1,207,890	1,205,705	2,185	0.18	1,174,209	1,237,202
Aug.	1,263,747	1,218,007	45,740	3.62	1,186,511	1,249,504
Sept.	1,229,853	1,256,773	(26,920)	−2.19	1,225,276	1,288,269
Oct.	1,219,087	1,245,178	(26,091)	−2.14	1,213,682	1,276,675

* See equations (9-25) and (9-26).

TABLE 9-7   Historical Reliability of Automobile Sales

Date[a]	Actual Auto Sales (1)	Fitted Auto Sales[b] (2)	Residual (3)	Percent Residual (4)
1967: I	7.99			
II	8.88	8.01	0.87	9.83
III	8.49	8.60	−0.12	−1.36
IV	8.06	8.62	−0.56	−6.99
1968: I	9.42	8.21	1.21	12.85
II	9.40	9.03	0.37	3.95
III	9.98	9.32	0.66	6.61
IV	9.82	9.75	0.07	0.67
1969: I	9.70	9.86	−0.16	−1.68
II	9.63	9.74	−0.11	−1.15
III	9.62	9.72	−0.11	−1.09
IV	9.39	9.64	−0.25	−2.71
1970: I	8.75	9.53	−0.78	−8.91
II	9.08	9.01	0.07	0.74
III	8.92	9.08	−0.16	−1.78
IV	6.86	8.99	−2.13	−31.03
1971: I	9.97	7.64	2.33	23.40
II	9.94	9.08	0.86	8.68
III	10.36	9.83	0.53	5.12
IV	10.63	10.05	0.58	5.49
1972: I	10.47	10.61	−0.14	−1.33
II	10.65	10.40	0.25	2.36
III	10.81	10.72	0.09	0.80
IV	11.56	10.67	0.89	7.73
1973: I	12.30	11.40	0.90	7.35
II	12.13	11.91	0.22	1.78
III	11.13	12.20	−1.07	−9.58
IV	9.84	11.41	−1.57	−15.99
1974: I	9.30	10.49	−1.19	−12.80
II	8.99	9.60	−0.61	−6.81
III	9.41	9.32	0.09	0.98
IV	7.40	9.29	−1.89	−25.61
1975: I	8.23	8.19	0.04	0.45
II	7.69	8.06	−0.38	−4.88
III	8.93	8.01	0.92	10.33
IV	9.31	8.45	0.86	9.22
1976: I	10.02	9.24	0.78	7.82
II	9.85	9.59	0.26	2.62
III	9.88	9.99	−0.11	−1.11
IV	10.23	9.74	0.48	4.74
1977: I	10.97	10.27	0.70	6.35
II	11.27	10.57	0.70	6.20
III	11.00	11.25	−0.25	−2.27
IV	10.95	10.93	0.02	0.16
1978: I	10.49	11.13	−0.64	−6.09
II	11.80	10.56	1.24	10.51
III	11.17	11.55	−0.38	−3.38
IV	11.19	11.20	−0.01	−0.07

TABLE 9-7 *(Continued)*

Date[a]	Actual Auto Sales (1)	Fitted Auto Sales[b] (2)	Residual (3)	Percent Residual (4)
1979: I	11.20	11.33	−0.13	−1.15
II	10.43	11.16	−0.73	−6.96
III	10.71	10.81	−0.10	−0.92
IV	9.89	10.64	−0.75	−7.59
1980: I	10.44	10.29	0.15	1.46
II	7.80	10.27	−2.47	−31.63
III	8.77	8.82	−0.05	−0.58
IV	8.92	8.60	0.31	3.53
1981: I	9.76	9.03	0.73	7.47
II	8.08	9.34	−1.26	−15.61
III	9.04	8.74	0.29	3.27
IV	7.27	8.71	−1.45	−19.89
1982: I	8.00	8.03	−0.03	−0.36
II	7.68	7.75	−0.07	−0.87
III	7.79	8.01	−0.22	−2.84
IV	8.45	7.60	0.85	10.02
1983: I	8.24	8.45	−0.21	−2.50
II	9.19	8.08	1.11	12.12
III	9.24	9.08	0.16	1.69
IV	10.04	8.98	1.06	10.57
1984: I	10.41	9.92	0.49	4.73
II	10.50	10.07	0.43	4.10
III	10.26	10.58	−0.32	−3.08
IV	10.38	10.20	0.18	1.77
1985: I	10.84	10.53	0.31	2.90
II	10.88	10.57	0.31	2.84
III	12.31	10.98	1.33	10.83
IV	10.11	11.70	−1.59	−15.69
1986: I	10.76	10.89	−0.13	−1.26
II	11.20	10.57	0.63	5.66
III	12.69	11.25	1.44	11.31
IV	11.16	11.99	−0.84	−7.49
1987: I	9.67	11.72	−2.06	−21.26
II	10.28	10.11	0.17	1.69
III	11.31	10.48	0.83	7.31
IV	9.86	10.82	−0.96	−9.77
1988: I	10.91	10.45	0.46	4.19
II	10.70	10.51	0.19	1.79
III	10.46	10.93	−0.47	−4.47
IV	10.49	10.37	0.12	1.10
1989: I	9.82	10.73	−0.91	−9.27
II	10.33	9.90	0.43	4.18
III	10.78	10.44	0.34	3.18
IV	9.30	10.46	−1.16	−12.47
1990: I	9.90	9.95	−0.05	−0.51
II	10.15	9.68	0.47	4.63

[a] Year and quarter   [b] See equation (9-28).

VALIDATION OF THE UNDERLYING BOX-JENKINS MODEL

As with regression models, B/J models are based on sample statistics that must be tested to assure their validity as estimates of the true population parameter values. The process of validation has three components:

- Statistical validation, or residual diagnostics
- Parameter validation
- Model validation.

Many of the statistics (MAD, the MAPE, and the MSE) used to evaluate the reliability of Box-Jenkins models were presented in earlier chapters. In this chapter, we present only those statistical evaluation tools that are unique to Box-Jenkins models.

STATISTICAL VALIDATION: RESIDUAL DIAGNOSTICS

Within the Box-Jenkins framework, a key assumption is made that the residual or error terms are not correlated with each other—that is, there is no systematic pattern in the residuals. When a systematic pattern is present, we have omitted an important parameter. While there are numerous residual diagnostic statistics, the ones unique to Box-Jenkins models and those covered here are as follows:

- The residual mean and mean percent error that measure the existence of any bias in the residuals
- Autocorrelations of the residuals that test the validity of the random error assumption
- Q statistics for the residual autocorrelations that test whether the autocorrelations of the entire residual series differ significantly from zero.

The first of the residual diagnostic statistics, the residual mean, should ideally be relatively close to zero. Alternatively, a significantly nonzero mean for the residuals would suggest that the fitted values are consistently higher or lower than the actual values. Furthermore, if the residual mean is not close to zero, the remaining diagnostic statistics are of questionable value. For the call center data, the residual mean is computed as -53.65 and, given that the call data in Table 9-1 are measured in hundreds of thousands of calls per month, this mean value can be said to closely approximate zero.

The mean percent error is similar to the residual mean except that the result is stated in percentage error terms. As was the case with the residual mean, the mean percent error should be relatively close to zero. Furthermore,

FIGURE 9-25   Residual Autocorrelation Correlogram
                for Call Center Data

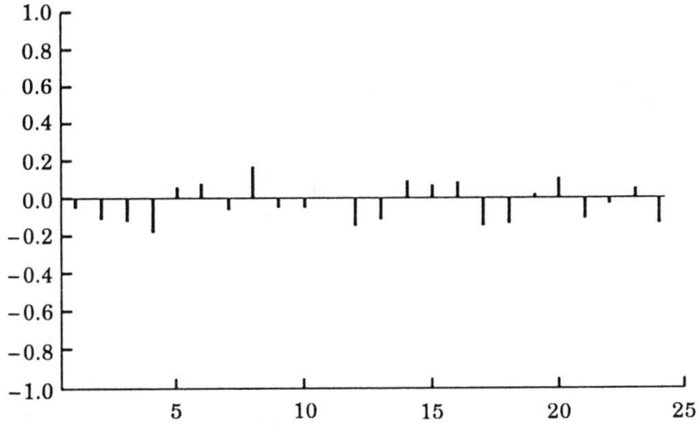

the size and sign of the mean percent error provides a measure of the tendency of a given model to generate either under- or over-estimates. For the call center data, the mean percent error equals -0.04 percent. When combined with the relatively small residual mean, this tends to confirm that the model, as estimated, is capturing the basic pattern in the call center data.

One of the basic attributes of a valid model is that the residual terms should be randomly distributed (i.e., uncorrelated with each other). To test for the existence of any relationship of the residual terms over time, we can compute an autocorrelation coefficient for the residuals in the same fashion as we did in the identification phase. For the call center data, the residual AC correlogram for the call center data is depicted in Figure 9-25. None of the autocorrelation spikes appear to be significantly different from zero, suggesting that error terms are randomly distributed.

EXAMPLE 9-10   Use of Residual Autocorrelation Correlogram as a Test for Model Validity

While there was no discernible pattern in the call center AC correlogram, this type of analysis can be extremely useful in evaluating the final model and in providing practitioners with some guidance as to how the model might be improved. To illustrate these possibilities, consider the AC correlogram presented in Figure 9-26. The relatively large nonzero spike that occurs at the two-period lag suggests the need to include a moving average parameter of order 2 in the final model.

FIGURE 9-26   Residual Autocorrelation Correlogram
for an Incorrectly Specified Model

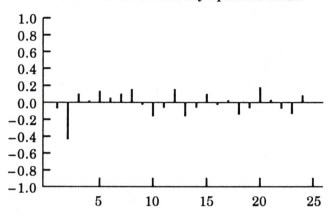

ARIMA models can also be tested for adequacy by conducting a chi-square test, more commonly known as the Box-Pierce Q statistic, on the autocorrelations of the residuals. The test statistic is

$$Q = (N - d) \sum_{i=1}^{k} r_k^2 \qquad (9\text{-}29)$$

which is approximately distributed as a chi-square distribution with $k - p - q$ degrees of freedom. In equation (9-29),

N = length of the time series
k = first k autocorrelations being tested
p = number of autoregressive terms
q = number of moving average terms
r_k = sample autocorrelations of the kth residual term
d = degree of differencing applied to original data.

If the calculated value of Q is less than the critical value, the model should be considered acceptable. The calculated value of Q for 24 time lags for the call center model was determined to be

$$Q_{\text{calc}} = (81)(.2473) = 20.03. \qquad (9\text{-}30)$$

The critical value of Q obtained from Appendix H is 32.7 (this assumes 22 degrees of freedom in the call center model). Since the calculated Q value is less than the critical value of Q, the model, as estimated, would be deemed to be statistically acceptable.

TABLE 9-8 **Parameter Statistics for Call Center Model**

Parameter	t statistic	Confidence Intervals	Prob Value
AR(1) = −0.40308	−3.64	−0.1817 to −0.6245	0.0005
AR(2) = −0.34057	−2.93	−0.1082 to −0.5729	0.0044

PARAMETER VALIDATION

In addition to the various residual diagnostics and goodness-of-fit tests, three parameter diagnostics have proven to be useful in evaluating the individual parameters in the model: (1) the correlations between parameters; (2) parameter t statistics; and (3) parameter confidence intervals. The principal advantage of these parameters is that they provide information on whether or not you have statistically insignificant parameters in the estimated model.

The correlation between parameters is computed and interpreted in the same fashion as are all other correlation coefficients. When used with Box-Jenkins models, it provides information on the redundancy of any of the estimated parameters.[16] In particular, if two (or more) of the parameters are highly correlated, we can, in all likelihood, eliminate one of the parameters without affecting the model's reliability. In the case of the call center data, the only parameter correlation coefficient that need concern us is that between the two autoregressive parameters, which is estimated at 0.353. Invoking the same rule of thumb that we introduced in evaluating the interrelationship between regression coefficients, as long as the correlation coefficient is less than 0.5, it should be regarded as spurious or insignificant. Since the estimated correlation is less than this rule-of-thumb value, we would retain both of the autoregressive parameters.

The parameter t statistics, confidence intervals, and prob values used in Box-Jenkins models carry the same interpretive value as was the case with estimated regression models. Table 9-8 provides information on the estimated t statistics, the confidence intervals, and the prob values for the two autoregressive parameters in our call center model.

When the computed t statistic exceeds the calculated t value, the estimated parameter is deemed to be statistically significant. For the two autoregressive parameters in the call center model, the calculated t statistics are −3.64 and 2.93, both of which exceed their respective critical values (indicating that both parameters should be retained in the model). The width of the confidence intervals provides us with a measure of the precision of each

---

[16] Recall that in our chapter 6 discussion of regression models we referred to the problem of multicollinearity wherein the independent variables were related to each other. The correlation between ARIMA parameters closely parallels this problem.

of the specific parameter estimates. Even more important, as was the case in regression analysis, the null hypothesis of no statistical relationship can be tested by simply examining the interval for the hypothesized value of zero. Since neither of the 95 percent confidence intervals presented in Table 9-8 contains zero, we would reject the null hypothesis of no statistical significance. That is, we would argue to retain both parameters in the model. The prob values provide us with a measure of the level at which the parameter becomes statistically significant. For example, the AR(2) parameter would be statistically significant at the 99.56 percent level.

MODEL VALIDATION

Model validation focuses on the reliability of the forecasts generated by the model. Virtually all of the statistics and tests that we have discussed in conjunction with previous models can be applied to Box-Jenkins models. That is, the numerous goodness-of-fit statistics (the MAD, the MAPE, the MSE, and the coefficient of determination, sometimes called the index of determination in Box-Jenkins computer programs) can be used in evaluating Box-Jenkins models. Since these statistics have been covered in some detail in our discussions of other models, they are not presented here.

One of the principal advantages of Box-Jenkins models, vis-à-vis other time series models, is that systematic approaches for the measurement of uncertainty have been developed based on the use of forecast confidence intervals. The forecast confidence intervals used in ARIMA programs generally rely on the residual standard error (RSE):

$$\text{Residual Standard Error (RSE)} = \sqrt{(1/N)(\text{Sum of } E^2)} \qquad \textbf{(9-30)}$$

where E refers to the residuals and N to the number of residual terms. For the call center data, the RSE can be computed as 15,428. The 95 percent confidence intervals for the historically fitted call center values are presented in columns 5 and 6 of Table 9-6. To illustrate, consider the case of the October 1990 fitted value of 1,245,178. This value corresponds to the best point estimate or best forecast for calls in October. Further, we can be 95 percent certain that the actual number of calls during October will be between 1,213,682 and 1,276,675. As a rule, the smaller this interval, the more reliable the point estimate.

The second procedure used as a gauge of the reliability of forecasts is the evaluation of ex post or after-the-fact forecasts. As previously noted, this procedure involves leaving out a certain number of actual data points from the estimation phase and then generating forecasts that can be compared with the actual values. Suppose, for example, that we decide to estimate an AR(2) model for the call center data, but omit the 10 months of 1990. The ex post forecasts from this "shortened" model are presented in Table 9-9.

An examination of the error and percentage error columns in Table 9-9

TABLE 9-9 Ex Post Forecasts for Call Center

Date	Actual	Ex Post Forecast	Error	Percent Error
January	1,181,343	1,198,061	−16,718	−1.42
February	1,206,507	1,199,071	7,435	0.62
March	1,193,359	1,233,729	−40,370	−3.38
April	1,172,406	1,213,968	−41,563	−3.55
May	1,179,629	1,215,428	−35,799	−3.03
June	1,192,780	1,211,428	−18,627	−1.56
July	1,207,890	1,207,974	−84	−0.01
August	1,263,747	1,219,217	44,529	3.52
September	1,229,853	1,252,495	−22,643	−1.84
October	1,219,087	1,246,848	−27,761	−2.28

Mean Error (Bias = −15,160

Mean Percent Error (Percent Bias) = −1.29%

indicates a tendency to overestimate relative to the actual number of calls coming into the call center. This consistency is measured by the mean error of −15,160 and the mean percent error of −1.29 percent. On average, the model overestimates by 15,160 (1.29 percent) calls. Additional analysis on the reliability of the model in capturing turning points reveals that the ex post simulation lagged two months behind the April 1990 decline and one month behind the September dip.

FORECASTING WITH BOX-JENKINS MODELS: CALL CENTER DATA

Suppose that we are at the end of October and are interested in generating a forecast for November 1990. The November forecast (and all subsequent forecasts) would be computed by making the appropriate substitutions into the estimated call center model (see equation 9-26) as follows:

$$\hat{Y}_{Nov} = 20{,}687 + 0.59692Y_{Oct} + 0.6251Y_{Sep} + 0.34057Y_{Aug}$$

$$= 20{,}687 + 727{,}697 + 76{,}878 + 430{,}394$$

$$= 1{,}255{,}656. \tag{9-31}$$

This point estimate would, in turn, be used to generate interval forecasts.

As additional data observations are recorded, the practitioner has two options. The first is to keep the existing model, substitute the new observations into the model as in equation (9-31), and generate revised forecasts based on this newly acquired information. This process of adding new data and using the original model to compute the revised forecasts should be continued as long as the results fall within acceptable limits. The second option involves reestimating the complete model and issuing a new set of forecasts. In the majority of situations, it is not necessary to reidentify the model when additional data points become available, since it is unlikely that the underlying structural relationships will change drastically from period to period.

As long as the model is generating acceptable forecasts, there is no need for reestimation, but because of the characteristics of most business and economic activities and because of the tendency of ARIMA models to lag behind turning points, the forecaster should establish some guidelines regarding the time frame for reestimation. That is, even if the model is generating reliable forecasts, a new model should be estimated after a specified period of time. The advantage of reestimation is that we are using the most current information as the basis for projecting into the future.

SUMMARY

Box-Jenkins or ARIMA models can be constructed to fit a wide variety of patterns, and this can be done with a minimum of effort as long as computer programs are available. While the process of model identification is cumbersome at first, it becomes relatively straightforward with sufficient practice. However, univariate ARIMA models suffer from the same limitations as do all other time series models. Specifically, they generally fail to capture turning points on time, and they provide management with little information on the potential impact of policies, such as pricing actions or advertising programs. To some extent, these limitations can be overcome with multivariate Box-Jenkins or transfer functions. The interested reader should consult some of the sources listed at the end of this chapter before attempting to apply multivariate ARIMA or transfer function models.

QUESTIONS FOR DISCUSSION AND ANALYSIS

1. Identify the model that corresponds to the theoretical AC and PAC patterns in the following correlograms.

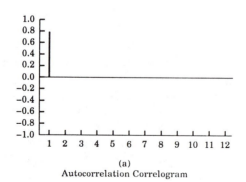

(a)
Autocorrelation Correlogram

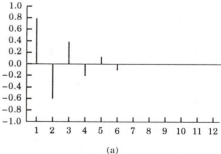

(a)
Partial Autocorrelation Correlogram

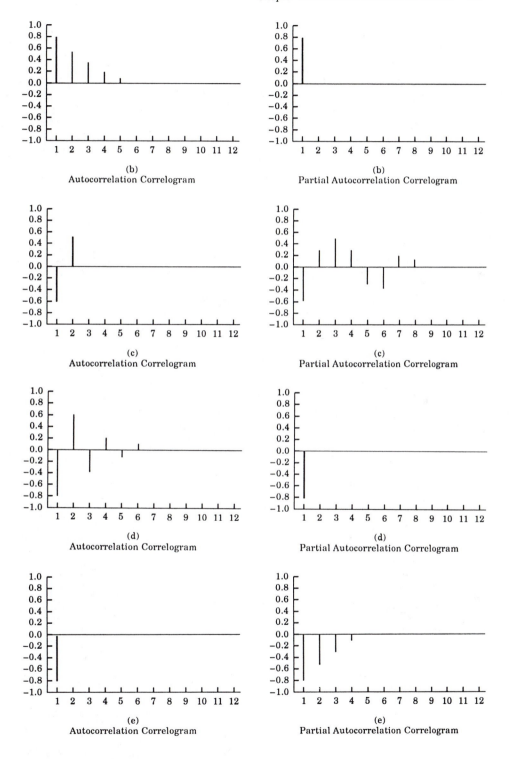

(b)
Autocorrelation Correlogram

(b)
Partial Autocorrelation Correlogram

(c)
Autocorrelation Correlogram

(c)
Partial Autocorrelation Correlogram

(d)
Autocorrelation Correlogram

(d)
Partial Autocorrelation Correlogram

(e)
Autocorrelation Correlogram

(e)
Partial Autocorrelation Correlogram

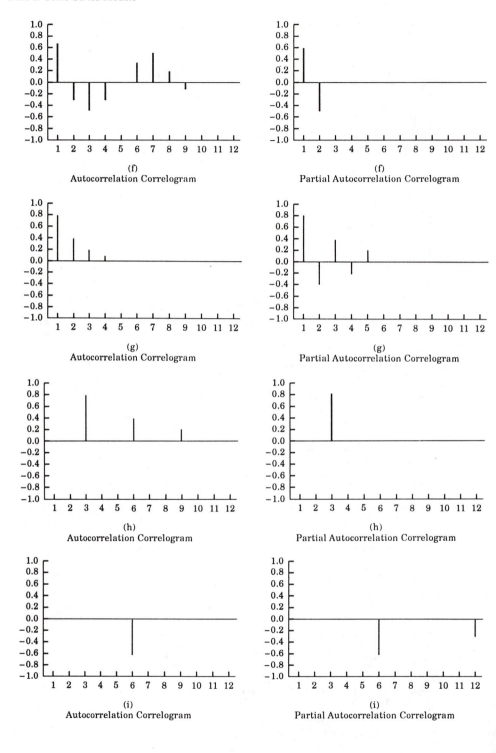

(f)
Autocorrelation Correlogram

(f)
Partial Autocorrelation Correlogram

(g)
Autocorrelation Correlogram

(g)
Partial Autocorrelation Correlogram

(h)
Autocorrelation Correlogram

(h)
Partial Autocorrelation Correlogram

(i)
Autocorrelation Correlogram

(i)
Partial Autocorrelation Correlogram

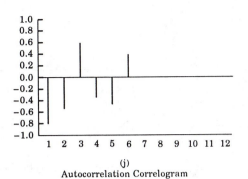

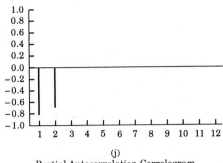

(j)
Autocorrelation Correlogram

(j)
Partial Autocorrelation Correlogram

2. Identify the model that corresponds to the actual AC and PAC patterns in the following correlograms.

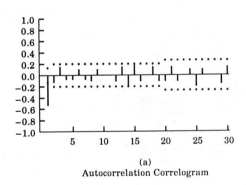

(a)
Autocorrelation Correlogram

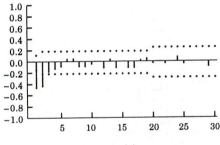

(a)
Partial Autocorrelation Correlogram

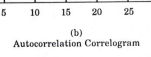

(b)
Autocorrelation Correlogram

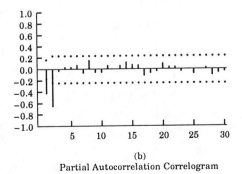

(b)
Partial Autocorrelation Correlogram

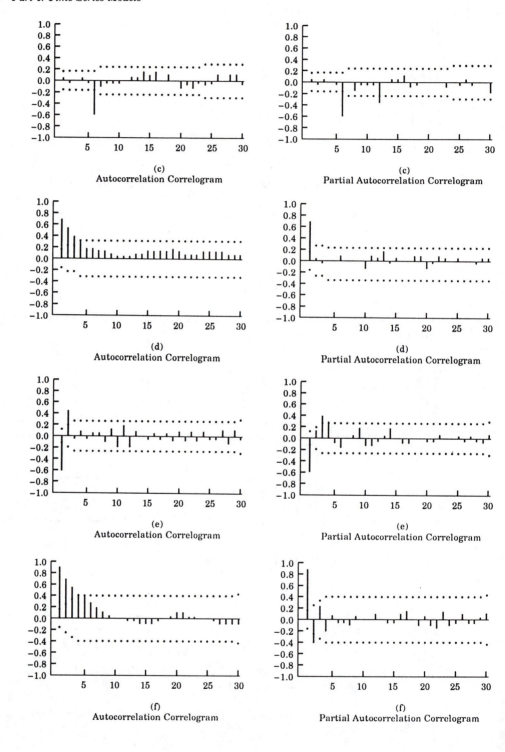

(c)
Autocorrelation Correlogram

(c)
Partial Autocorrelation Correlogram

(d)
Autocorrelation Correlogram

(d)
Partial Autocorrelation Correlogram

(e)
Autocorrelation Correlogram

(e)
Partial Autocorrelation Correlogram

(f)
Autocorrelation Correlogram

(f)
Partial Autocorrelation Correlogram

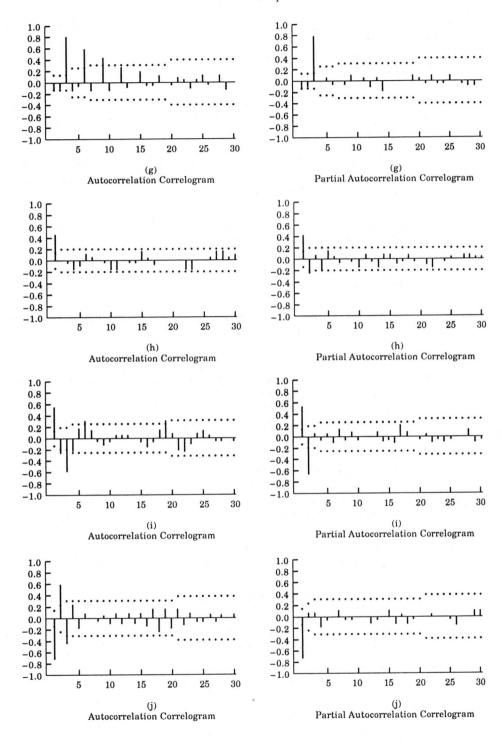

(g)
Autocorrelation Correlogram

(g)
Partial Autocorrelation Correlogram

(h)
Autocorrelation Correlogram

(h)
Partial Autocorrelation Correlogram

(i)
Autocorrelation Correlogram

(i)
Partial Autocorrelation Correlogram

(j)
Autocorrelation Correlogram

(j)
Partial Autocorrelation Correlogram

3. In the discussion on seasonal differencing for the daily riders example, we suggested that a second round of differencing might be required to eliminate all of the seasonality. Compute the second differences and examine the AC and PAC correlograms. Did this eliminate the seasonality from the data?

4. After you have successfully eliminated the seasonal pattern in the daily riders example, identify the type of model that appears to capture the process. That is, what type of model(s) would you estimate?

5. Compare the historical simulations from the Box-Jenkins automobile sales model and the regression sales model. Which of the two models would you select? What are the potential problems with both of these models?

6. Suppose that you decide to investigate another possible ARIMA model for the auto sales data. Specifically, try a model with two autoregressive parameters (AR 1 and 2) and two moving average parameters (MA10 and MA15). Compare the results of this model with the model presented in example 9-7. Which of the two models would you select as your final model?

7. Illustrate specifically how equation (9-28) would be used to generate the fitted value for the second quarter of 1990.

8. Conduct a residual analysis similar to that illustrated for the call center model for the auto sales model estimated in example 9-7. What do these results suggest about the reliability of the estimated model? Why?

9. For the sales data presented in Appendix G, Table G-3,
   a. Identify the appropriate model(s).
   b. Estimate the model(s).
   c. Conduct the residual diagnostics tests.
   d. Conduct the parameter evaluation tests.
   e. Reestimate the model, leaving off the last six data points, and conduct an ex post forecast test for reliability.

10. Explain, to someone conversant with forecasting but not with ARIMA models, the difference between autoregressive and moving average parameters.

11. What is meant by the order of an ARIMA model?

12. What is the difference between stationary and nonstationary data? How does this relate to the use and estimation of ARIMA models?

13. You have collected the following information on the three-month Treasury bill rate. Identify, estimate, and validate a model for the Treasury bill rate. Leave off the last nine months, re-estimate the model, and carry out an ex-post simulation.

Date	Three-Month Treasury Bill Rate	Date	Three-Month Treasury Bill Rate	Date	Three-Month Treasury Bill Rate	Date	Three-Month Treasury Bill Rate
1980: Jan.	12.00	1983: Jan.	7.86	1986: Jan.	7.07	1989: Jan.	8.27
Feb.	12.86	Feb.	8.11	Feb.	7.06	Feb.	8.53
Mar.	15.20	Mar.	8.35	Mar.	6.56	Mar.	8.82
Apr.	13.20	Apr.	8.21	Apr.	6.06	Apr.	8.65
May	8.58	May	8.19	May	6.15	May	8.43
June	7.07	June	8.79	June	6.21	June	8.15
July	8.06	July	9.08	July	5.83	July	7.88
Aug.	9.13	Aug.	9.34	Aug.	5.53	Aug.	7.90
Sept.	10.27	Sept.	9.00	Sept.	5.21	Sept.	7.75
Oct.	11.62	Oct.	8.64	Oct.	5.18	Oct.	7.64
Nov.	13.73	Nov.	8.76	Nov.	5.35	Nov.	7.69
Dec.	15.49	Dec.	9.00	Dec.	5.53	Dec.	7.63
1981: Jan.	15.02	1984: Jan.	8.90	1987: Jan.	5.43	1990: Jan.	7.64
Feb.	14.79	Feb.	9.09	Feb.	5.59	Feb.	7.74
Mar.	13.36	Mar.	9.52	Mar.	5.59	Mar.	7.90
Apr.	13.69	Apr.	9.69	Apr.	5.64	Apr.	7.77
May	16.30	May	9.83	May	5.66	May	7.74
June	14.73	June	9.87	June	5.67	June	7.73
July	14.95	July	10.12	July	5.69	July	7.62
Aug.	15.51	Aug.	10.47	Aug.	6.04	Aug.	7.45
Sept.	14.70	Sept.	10.37	Sept.	6.40	Sept.	7.36
Oct.	13.54	Oct.	9.74	Oct.	6.13		
Nov.	10.86	Nov.	8.61	Nov.	5.69		
Dec.	10.85	Dec.	8.06	Dec.	5.77		
1982: Jan.	12.28	1985: Jan.	7.76	1988: Jan.	5.81		
Feb.	13.48	Feb.	8.27	Feb.	5.66		
Mar.	12.68	Mar.	8.52	Mar.	5.70		
Apr.	12.70	Apr.	7.95	Apr.	5.91		
May	12.09	May	7.48	May	6.26		
June	12.47	June	6.95	June	6.46		
July	11.35	July	7.08	July	6.73		
Aug.	8.68	Aug.	7.14	Aug.	7.06		
Sept.	7.92	Sept.	7.10	Sept.	7.24		
Oct.	7.71	Oct.	7.16	Oct.	7.35		
Nov.	8.07	Nov.	7.24	Nov.	7.76		
Dec.	7.94	Dec.	7.10	Dec.	8.07		

14. You are interested in developing monthly forecasts for the price of jet fuel. As a first step, you collect the following information. Based on this information, identify, estimate, and validate a model for the price of jet fuel. Leave off the last nine months, reestimate the model, and carry out an ex-post simulation.

Date	Producer Price Index, Jet Fuel	Date	Producer Price Index, Jet Fuel	Date	Producer Price Index, Jet Fuel	Date	Producer Price Index, Jet Fuel
1980: Jan.	74.20	1983: Jan.	98.10	1986: Jan.	82.30	1989: Jan.	57.00
Feb.	78.40	Feb.	97.30	Feb.	80.10	Feb.	57.40
Mar.	84.30	Mar.	95.90	Mar.	75.20	Mar.	58.10
Apr.	87.10	Apr.	93.30	Apr.	63.10	Apr.	60.50
May	88.10	May	91.50	May	54.70	May	60.40
June	89.10	June	90.20	June	52.00	June	56.40
July	90.70	July	88.80	July	46.70	July	55.70
Aug.	91.90	Aug.	88.40	Aug.	41.90	Aug.	55.80
Sept.	91.90	Sept.	88.20	Sept.	43.20	Sept.	59.60
Oct.	91.00	Oct.	88.90	Oct.	44.00	Oct.	63.10
Nov.	90.90	Nov.	88.70	Nov.	43.50	Nov.	66.30
Dec.	92.20	Dec.	88.40	Dec.	43.90	Dec.	66.30
1981: Jan.	93.70	1984: Jan.	87.80	1987: Jan.	46.30	1990: Jan.	79.80
Feb.	97.30	Feb.	88.20	Feb.	51.10	Feb.	72.10
Mar.	103.80	Mar.	89.00	Mar.	50.30	Mar.	64.00
Apr.	108.40	Apr.	88.10	Apr.	52.00	Apr.	62.90
May	108.90	May	87.80	May	52.40	May	60.30
June	108.40	June	87.50	June	54.30	June	56.50
July	107.40	July	87.30	July	56.50	July	55.40
Aug.	105.80	Aug.	86.60	Aug.	59.00	Aug.	65.10
Sept.	105.30	Sept.	85.80	Sept.	59.10	Sept.	88.70
Oct.	105.30	Oct.	85.60	Oct.	60.90		
Nov.	105.10	Nov.	85.50	Nov.	61.50		
Dec.	104.30	Dec.	84.80	Dec.	59.90		
1982: Jan.	104.90	1985: Jan.	84.30	1988: Jan.	52.70		
Feb.	104.00	Feb.	84.00	Feb.	57.10		
Mar.	103.60	Mar.	83.10	Mar.	56.00		
Apr.	102.40	Apr.	82.60	Apr.	53.70		
May	99.20	May	82.20	May	55.00		
June	98.00	June	80.60	June	54.20		
July	98.10	July	79.00	July	51.90		
Aug.	97.90	Aug.	79.60	Aug.	50.10		
Sept.	97.80	Sept.	80.20	Sept.	49.10		
Oct.	97.40	Oct.	81.10	Oct.	47.20		
Nov.	98.20	Nov.	81.70	Nov.	48.00		
Dec.	98.70	Dec.	82.40	Dec.	51.40		

15. You are charged with developing a monthly forecasting model for the following sales figures. Identify and estimate the most appropriate model. Conduct an ex post forecast analysis by reestimating the model and omitting the 1990 values.

Date	Sales (thousands)	Date	Sales (thousands)	Date	Sales (thousands)	Date	Sales (thousands)
1980: Jan.	551	1983: Jan.	616	1986: Jan.	751	1989: Jan.	975
Feb.	569	Feb.	638	Feb.	747	Feb.	987
Mar.	562	Mar.	639	Mar.	745	Mar.	1,009
Apr.	554	Apr.	639	Apr.	763	Apr.	1,014
May	569	May	656	May	765	May	1,036
June	610	June	722	June	853	June	1,140
July	668	July	788	July	918	July	1,161
Aug.	708	Aug.	849	Aug.	961	Aug.	1,240
Sept.	713	Sept.	856	Sept.	945	Sept.	1,226
Oct.	644	Oct.	787	Oct.	921	Oct.	1,135
Nov.	590	Nov.	724	Nov.	861	Nov.	1,106
Dec.	570	Dec.	702	Dec.	863	Dec.	1,025
1981: Jan.	550	1984: Jan.	677	1987: Jan.	833	1990: Jan.	1,000
Feb.	571	Feb.	689	Feb.	858	Feb.	1,030
Mar.	554	Mar.	694	Mar.	874	Mar.	1,030
Apr.	558	Apr.	684	Apr.	904	Apr.	1,055
May	576	May	725	May	949	May	1,075
June	645	June	795	June	1,072	June	1,175
July	699	July	865	July	1,151	July	1,235
Aug.	723	Aug.	898	Aug.	1,182	Aug.	1,275
Sept.	709	Sept.	875	Sept.	1,152	Sept.	1,254
Oct.	660	Oct.	826	Oct.	1,079		
Nov.	612	Nov.	770	Nov.	991		
Dec.	607	Dec.	731	Dec.	954		
1982: Jan.	592	1985: Jan.	706	1988: Jan.	928		
Feb.	620	Feb.	734	Feb.	950		
Mar.	618	Mar.	731	Mar.	944		
Apr.	625	Apr.	753	Apr.	967		
May	647	May	790	May	976		
June	697	June	846	June	1,052		
July	752	July	866	July	1,139		
Aug.	788	Aug.	946	Aug.	1,224		
Sept.	784	Sept.	926	Sept.	1,177		
Oct.	711	Oct.	848	Oct.	1,100		
Nov.	662	Nov.	798	Nov.	1,029		
Dec.	616	Dec.	775	Dec.	993		

16. The following ARIMA model has been estimated from historical data:

$$\hat{Y}_t = 18 + .38e_{t-1} - .6e_{t-2}.$$

The last four actual values are 16.25, 18.3, 16.7, and 15.9. Further, assume that $e_{t-1} = .5$ and $e_{t-2} = .18$. Compute the forecast for the next two time periods. Assume that the adjustment to the mean has been completed and that all retransformations have been made.

17. Consider the following ARIMA model:

$$Y_t = 1{,}083 + .48Y_{t-1}.$$

Assume that the adjustment to the mean has been completed and that all retransformations have been made. Suppose that in the most recent time period, $t = 100$, the actual value is 2,166. Given this information,

a. Determine the forecasts for time periods 101 through 105.

b. The observed value for time period 101 equals 1,949.4. Revise the forecasts for periods 102 through 105.

c. The estimate of the residual standard error equals 26. Compute a 95 percent confidence interval for the forecast for period 102.

18. For the housing start data presented in chapter 3, question 31, assuming first that you have not seasonally adjusted the data,

a. Identify the appropriate model(s).

b. Estimate the model(s).

c. Conduct the residual diagnostics tests.

d. Conduct the parameter evaluation tests.

e. Reestimate the model, leaving off the last six data points, and conduct an ex post forecast test for reliability.

Now assume that you have seasonally adjusted the data, and repeat steps a through e. Which of the two models would you rely on? Why?

19. For the sales of fax machine data presented in chapter 3, question 33,

a. Identify the appropriate model(s).

b. Estimate the model(s).

c. Conduct the residual diagnostics tests.

d. Conduct the parameter evaluation tests.

e. Reestimate the model, leaving off the last six data points, and conduct an ex post forecast test for reliability.

20. For the construction employment data presented in chapter 3, question 35, assuming that you have not seasonally adjusted the data,

a. Identify the appropriate model(s).

b. Estimate the model(s).

c. Conduct the residual diagnostics tests.

d. Conduct the parameter evaluation tests.

e. Reestimate the model, leaving off the last six data points, and conduct an ex post forecast test for reliability.

Now assume that you have seasonally adjusted the data, and repeat steps a through e. Which of the two processes generates the more reliable ex post forecasts? Why do you think this is the case? Would a regression model be more appropriate for this type of a time series? Why or why not?

21. For the electricity consumption data presented in chapter 3, question 39, assuming that you have not seasonally adjusted the data,

a. Identify the appropriate model(s).

b. Estimate the model(s).

c. Conduct the residual diagnostics tests.

d. Conduct the parameter evaluation tests.

e. Reestimate the model, leaving off the last six data points, and conduct an ex post forecast test for reliability.

Now assume that you have seasonally adjusted the data, and repeat steps a through e. Which of the two processes generates the more reliable ex post forecasts? Why do you think this is the case? Would a regression model be more appropriate for this type of data? Why or why not?

22. In example 9-1, our analysis of the AC and PAC correlograms indicated that an MA(1) model appeared to be the most appropriate model. Estimate and evaluate an MA(1) model. Does this model pass all of the applicable tests? Now reestimate the MA(1) model leaving off the last six data points. Based on this new model, generate forecasts for the six data points that were omitted. How well does the model perform in this ex post forecast? Would you be comfortable using the full model in developing forecasts? Why or why not?

23. In example 9-2, our analysis of the AC and PAC correlograms indicated that an AR(1) model appeared to be the most appropriate model. Estimate and evaluate an AR(1) model. Does this model pass all of the applicable tests? Using this full model, generate 6 forecasts. Would you be comfortable using the full model in developing forecasts? Why or why not? Estimate an ARIMA(1,1,1) model. How does this ARIMA(1,1,1) model compare with the AR(1) model? Which of the two models would you select as your final model? Why?

REFERENCES FOR FURTHER STUDY

Aigner, D. J., "A Compendium on Estimation of the Autoregressive Moving Average Model from Time-Series Data," *International Economic Review*, vol. 12, 1971, pp. 348–71.

Anderson, O. D., *Time-Series Analysis and Forecasting: The Box Jenkins Approach.* London: Butterworths, 1975.

Anderson, T. W., *The Statistical Analysis of Time-Series.* New York: John Wiley & Sons, 1971.

Brillinger, D. R., *Time Series: Data Analysis and Theory.* New York: Holt, Rinehart and Winston, 1975.

Chatfield, C., *The Analysis of Time-Series: Theory and Practice.* London: Chapman & Hall, 1975.

Gottman, John M., *Time-Series Analysis.* New York: Cambridge University Press, 1981.

Granger, C. W. J. and Paul Newbold, *Forecasting Economic Time Series.* San Diego: Academic Press, Inc., 1986.

Harvey, A. C., *Time Series Models.* New York: John Wiley & Sons, 1981.

Hoff, John, *A Practical Guide to Box-Jenkins Forecasting.* Belmont, Calif.: Lifetime Learning Publications, 1983.

Libert, G., "The M-Competition with a Fully Automated Box-Jenkins Procedure," *Journal of Forecasting*, vol. 3, 1984, pp. 325–28.

Makridakis, Spyros and Steven Wheelwright, *The Handbook of Forecasting: A Manager's Guide*, 2nd ed. New York: John Wiley & Sons, 1987.

Montgomery, D. C. and L. A. Johnson, *Forecasting and Time-Series Analysis*. New York: McGraw-Hill, 1976.

Nazem, Sufi M., *Applied Time Series Analysis for Business and Economic Forecasting*. New York: Marcel Dekker, Inc., 1988.

O'Donovan, T. M., *Short Term Forecasting: An Introduction to the Box-Jenkins Approach*. New York: John Wiley & Sons, 1983.

Ostrom, C. W., Jr., *Time-Series Analysis: Regression Techniques*. Beverly Hills, Calif.: Sage Publishing, 1978.

Pindyck, Robert and Daniel Rubinfeld, *Econometric Models & Economic Forecasts*, 3rd ed. New York: McGraw-Hill, 1991.

10

Monitoring and Revising Forecasts

INTRODUCTION

Practicing forecasters recognize that their job is not completed when the technique has been selected and the forecast generated. In fact, the forecasting process has just begun. A tracking (monitoring) system must be put in place to continuously check actual results against forecasted magnitudes, to analyze forecast error patterns, and to reevaluate the underlying forecasting methodology when the error analysis suggests that the forecasting model is flawed. This chapter covers four primary topics:

1. Forecast guidelines
2. Identification of forecast error
3. Graphical and statistical techniques needed to track forecast results
4. Rules for auditing forecasts and comparing methodologies.

FORECAST GUIDELINES AND CONTROLS

The process of monitoring and auditing the output from a forecasting model assumes the existence of predetermined objectives and standards against which the results can be compared. Before we can develop tracking tools and monitoring procedures, however, key decision makers in the firm must provide guidance concerning the desired level of forecasting accuracy. These guideposts may be highly quantitative (a ± 5 percent error rate) or they may be a general statement concerning the relative merits of underestimating or overestimating the forecasting target. In other cases, the objective might be to reduce forecast error over time by a prespecified percentage relative to results of a previous year.

As a forecaster, you can assist management in designing the standards against which your forecasts and your performance are to be measured. First, prior to developing a forecasting model or generating a forecast, the forecaster should identify the recipients of the forecast and the intended uses to which it will be put. Acceptable error rates will be higher for long-range planning than for, say, short-term personnel requirements. Similarly, sensitivity to forecast error is likely to be higher for a project designed to reduce a company's monthly parts inventories.

Acceptable error rates are also a function of the product or service environment in which the company operates. The acceptable error range for a new product will be much larger than if a forecast is made for an established product. Alternatively, forecasts made in sectors that are subject to rapid technological change (such as the personal computer market) are different than forecasts in markets where product changes are occurring slowly over time (such as home roofing materials).

The establishment of future guidelines for accuracy must reflect the unique historical data patterns on which the model was built, as well as the actual historical errors generated by the model. For example, forecasts for steel demand (which has exhibited a volatile pattern over numerous cyclical turning points) cannot be held to the same standard of accuracy as projections for per capita meat consumption (which is dominated by trend patterns and cultural norms concerning food consumption). When a time series is very cyclical, the major focus may be with the prediction of turning points rather than the simpler task of predicting trend patterns or rates of growth. A reinforcing factor here is the accuracy of the model when subjected to historical simulation. That is, if a specific forecasting model had an average error of 4 percent in a historical simulation, it is not likely that we are going to be able to generate future forecasts with a smaller average percentage error.

SOURCES OF FORECAST ERROR

Forecasters spend much of their time answering questions such as these:

Why are actual sales 15 percent lower than forecasted sales?

Why did actual shipments decline when an increase was projected?

Why did the model fail to capture a significant change in trend growth patterns?

While it may seem that there is an infinite number of possible explanations for a given error, three general categories encompass most of the likely possibilities:

1. Changing external conditions
2. Modification of internal decisions and policies
3. Defects in the underlying forecasting methodology.

EXTERNAL FACTORS

When trying to discover reasons for an erroneous forecast, first look outside the firm or organization for possible sources of forecast error. Changes in institutional factors are often the culprit—for example, modifications in tax laws will most certainly influence certain types of expenditures and investments. If the federal government were to eliminate the tax deduction on primary family residences, the construction, sale, and financing of single-family homes would change dramatically, setting off a ripple effect through countless firms and industries tied to home construction. Further, changes in monetary and fiscal policies affect virtually all business organizations. Additionally, the increasingly global nature of world markets has had both beneficial effects (for example, increased sales for the cigarette industry) and adverse effects (for example, decreased sales for the auto industry) on U.S. firms. Finally, the forecaster must monitor the impact of special events—unusual weather patterns, strikes, fashions or fads, and technological changes—that may have an unexpected influence on many sectors of the economy. Once recognized, these structural changes can be built into the modeling process by using dummy variables in regression models, by creating a consistent set of data over time, or by adjusting the historical data to reflect the changing institutional environment.

"Changing external conditions" include the impact of recessions or expansions on the industry or firm, as well as changes in the competitive nature of the industry. While it is true that at least once a decade the business cycle is declared to be nonexistent, market-oriented business activity continues to be influenced by cyclical fluctuations (not necessarily, recessions) in the economy. Although business cycles are repetitive, their duration and severity vary considerably from cycle to cycle, making it extremely difficult to predict their impact in any specific situation. A forecaster must make certain that he or she does not confuse temporary cyclical changes (for example, a sudden surge in demand due to a rebound in the economy) with permanent changes in structural relationships (for example, a long-term modification of consumer tastes and preferences).

As an industry becomes more competitive—domestically or globally—forecasting becomes more difficult. An increase in competitive pressures will make previously stable relationships less reliable, since competitors (who will also be making forecasts) will formulate new strategies to take advantage of optimistic forecasts (or offset pessimistic forecasts). Forecasters must simultaneously monitor the reactions of domestic and international competitors to a company's policies. For example, while domestic producers in the automotive, steel, and textile industries have endorsed import quotas on foreign goods, foreign producers have circumvented the quotas by a series of competitive moves—setting up production facilities in the United States or relocating production to third-world countries not subject to quotas.

INTERNAL DECISIONS AND POLICIES

While well-established internal policies dealing with advertising programs or pricing strategies must be incorporated into the forecast, it is also possible that, subsequent to the issuance of the forecast, the marketing department may unveil a new advertising campaign, the finance department may implement new collection procedures, or top management may force cost-cutting policies throughout the organization. Each of these internal changes can significantly alter the current forecast and necessitate the revision of previously issued forecasts. Seemingly minor changes in internal policies (undertaken for a wide variety of reasons) may have a major impact on the company's forecast, and it is up to the individuals in charge of making the forecast to maintain close communications with forecast users in other departments. By failing to keep up with policies in other departments, forecasters may put themselves in adversarial positions with others in decision-making positions. For example, the marketing department's optimistic forecast for national sales may (unbeknownst to the forecaster) be based on highly successful testing in a regional market. The more frequently the forecaster makes mistakes due to a lack of information about internal changes, the less faith management will begin to have in the forecast, the forecasting process, and the forecaster.

FORECAST METHODOLOGY

In the case of both external factors and internal policies, the principal role of the forecaster is to monitor the impact of these factors on the forecast. While the forecaster has little, if any, control over either internal or external forces, he or she must be able to segregate forecast errors associated with defects in the forecasting model or methodology from errors resulting from internal or external forces.

The underlying model or methodology may be sound, but if the data used in generating the forecast are faulty, the forecast will likely be flawed, too. The forecaster must ask numerous questions:

Were the data revised prior to their use in the forecasting model?
Were any procedural errors made when the data were collected?

If the data were subjected to arithmetic manipulations or transformations, were the wrong transformations selected?

Data must be continuously monitored to catch any definitional changes. For example, a historical model developed to predict tire sales would be hopelessly flawed if data were not adjusted to reflect the introduction of radial tires. Another potential data problem area lies in the level of aggregation. The higher the level of data aggregation, the more accurate will be the forecast. Thus, a forecast for total tire sales will probably be more accurate than separate sales forecasts for individual product lines. Forecasters must constantly deal with the trade-offs between increased accuracy (a single forecast for total car sales) and increased cost (multiple models for separate tire categories). Finally, since the majority of forecasting models are based on seasonally adjusted data (a specific example of data transformation), it is possible that we have made errors in estimating and eliminating seasonality. While these types of mistakes and data problems are frequently difficult to uncover, the reward for their detection can be a substantial increase in forecast accuracy.

Virtually all of the forecasting methods discussed here assume that historical patterns will continue into the future. If they do not, the underlying model or methodology may be called into question. In the case of time series models, internal decisions such as pricing changes, advertising programs, and other types of policies can dramatically alter the pattern of change in the forecast variable. With regression models, new explanatory variables may emerge over time, old variables may no longer be valid, the existing regression coefficients may change, or policy changes may completely invalidate historical relationships.

EXAMPLE 10-1 Predicted Values for Independent Variables

With causal regression models, the precision of the forecast is largely dependent on the accuracy of the predicted values for the independent variables. When regression models are used to forecast, therefore, errors associated with the model (misspecification, etc.) must be separated from errors resulting from inaccurate forecasts for the independent variables. The process of decomposing the regression error is depicted in Figure 10-1. The personal computer sales model from chapter 5 (equation 5-12), in which computer sales (Y_t) are estimated as a function of personal income (X_t), can be used to illustrate the process of error decomposition:

$$\hat{Y}_t = 7.431 + 1.833X_t. \tag{5-12}$$

The model was based on data through 1987. If we assume that the original forecast for personal income (X) for 1988 was \$82.5 billion, the ex ante

FIGURE 10-1   Decomposition of Forecasting Errors

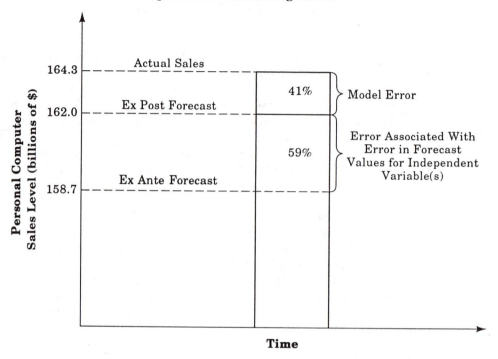

forecast—original forecast—for computer sales would be $158.7 billion:

$$\hat{Y}_t = 7.431 + 1.833 \,(82.5) \tag{10-1}$$
$$\approx \$158.7 \text{ billion.}$$

Now suppose that the actual value for personal income in 1988 turns out to be $84.3 billion. Armed with this new and revised information, the ex post forecast is

$$\hat{Y}_t = 7.431 + 1.833 \,(84.3) \tag{10-2}$$
$$\approx \$162.0 \text{ billion.}$$

Actual sales for 1988 are recorded as $164.3 billion. The forecast error can now be decomposed as

Total Error = Model Error

+ Error Due to Independent Variable

Total Error = ($164.3 − $158.7) = $5.6 billion

Error Associated with
Forecast of Independent = ($162.0 − $158.7) = $3.3 billion
Variable

Model Error = ($5.6 − $3.3) = $2.3 billion.

Thus, approximately 59 percent ($3.3/$5.6) of the observed error occurred as a result of using an incorrect value for the independent variable, with the remaining 41 percent of the error being attributable to the model. These results are summarized in Figure 10-1.

The importance of understanding and measuring these two separate sources of error in regression models cannot be overstated. If we were to focus simply on the total error of $5.6 billion (which is 3.4 percent of the observed sales level of $164.3 billion), we might conclude that the model required reestimation or significant revisions. But in this situation, the forecast can be improved significantly if the projections for the independent variable (personal income) can be more reliably determined.

EXAMPLE 10-2   Forecast Error and Pricing Actions

Suppose that as a forecaster for an amusement park you are charged with making forecasts of monthly attendance figures. As a first step, you collect and seasonally adjust the historical data presented in Appendix I, Table I-1. Based on the seasonally adjusted data, you decide to use Brown's linear exponential smoothing model to derive the forecasts presented in Table 10-1. When the April 1991 attendance figure of 217,654 is compared to the forecast of 223,829, it appears that the model is significantly overestimating. However, the percentage error rate of 3.5 percent is within acceptable standards for a monthly forecasting model. While it might seem that this is a relatively large error, an error of this magnitude is likely to be acceptable when you are analyzing an industry that is sensitive to weather patterns. While you should continue to monitor the performance of the model, you would probably not reestimate and revise the forecasts.

The disturbing aspect of the forecasts in Table 10-1 is that as actual attendance figures are recorded for May, June, and July, the model continues to overestimate, and the error rate increases over time. Clearly, it would be inexcusable to wait until July or August to reevaluate the

TABLE 10-1   Monthly Attendance Forecasts

Date	Forecast (SA)[a]	Seasonal Factor	Forecast (NSA)[b]	Actual	Error
1991:April	225,225	0.9938	223,829	217,654	+6,175
May	226,337	1.0039	227,220	207,350	+19,870
June	227,450	0.9857	224,198	187,413	+36,785
July	228,563	0.9215	210,621	170,519	+40,102
August	229,675	0.9588	220,212	204,300	+15,912

[a] SA = seasonally adjusted
[b] NSA = nonseasonally adjusted

forecasts. After the May results, you would begin to wonder why there was a sudden decline in growth relative to historical patterns. In this particular situation, it was found that the marketing department had implemented a significant increase in attendance fees beginning in April. As is normally the case, consumer reactions to price changes take time, and the full impact of the price increase was not felt until June. At this point, the model would be reestimated and a new set of forecasts would be issued based on the new set of prices for tickets to the park.

Finally, in considering forecasting methodology, it must be recognized that all practicing forecasters make subjective modifications to the results generated by their forecasting models. These subjective changes are commonly called add factors and usually reflect the forecaster's judgment or knowledge of some factor that cannot be built into the modeling process. The automobile industry provides us with a good example of what can occur when these add factors are incorporated into the final forecast. Prior to the OPEC oil embargo of 1974–1975, the majority of automobile sales forecasting models concentrated on such factors as price, advertising, income, and other traditional demand-side factors. The supply-side shock that occurred in 1974–1975 had such an influence on the automobile industry (among others) that some of these more traditional factors have been replaced by judgments regarding the potential for another disruption. The invasion of Kuwait by Iraq in August 1990 and the resulting disruption of oil shipments from the Middle East was clearly unexpected and once more forced forecasters to monitor forecasts and make substantial use of add factors.

TRACKING TECHNIQUES

Tracking techniques compare actual results with forecasted values over consecutive time periods. Tracking not only assists us in measuring where we are today relative to where we thought we would be, but it is also an integral part of the process of forecast revision. There is no "best" way to track forecast reliability, and a variety of techniques are used in differing situations. The specific tool(s) that the forecaster chooses to use in a particular case depends on historical data patterns, the nature of the industry, how often revisions are expected, and how rapidly a firm can adjust its plans as a result of forecast errors or revisions.

GRAPHICAL DEVICES

The first of the graphical tools used in tracking forecast reliability is the ladder chart.[1] Figure 10-2 depicts a common format for ladder charts based on the data for microwave sales presented in Table 10-2 (page 492). There are four

FIGURE 10-2   Ladder Chart for Microwave Sales

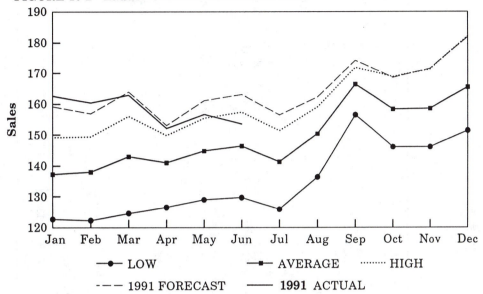

elements of information shown for each month (for a three-year period) on the four time plots contained in the ladder chart in Figure 10-2:

> Average sales level (AVERAGE) for each month (based on the last three observations for that month)
>
> Highest sales level (HIGH)
>
> Lowest sales level (LOW)
>
> 1991 forecast (FORECAST).

In addition, the actual observed values are shown for the first six months of 1991.

When the line for AVERAGE sales is compared with the line for 1991 FORECAST sales, it indicates whether the forecasted series adequately captures seasonal patterns in the data. In the case of microwave sales in Figure 10-2, the pattern of seasonal movements in the forecasted series is reflective

---

[1] The specific format of the ladder chart depends to a large extent on the specific environment under consideration. For example, a two- or five-year average may be more appropriate than a three-year average. Alternatively, in some cases it is useful to plot the actual data for the most recent year(s) along with other types of information.

TABLE 10-2 Tracking Microwave Sales with a Ladder Chart

	Jan.	Feb.	Mar.	Apr.	May	June	July	Aug.	Sept.	Oct.	Nov.	Dec.
SEASONAL FACTORS												
1988	0.974	0.967	0.980	0.992	0.997	0.958	0.925	0.970	1.057	1.025	1.046	1.084
1989	0.981	0.977	0.996	0.990	0.996	0.967	0.930	0.970	1.043	1.019	1.032	1.071
1990	0.990	0.987	1.014	0.987	0.996	0.973	0.935	0.968	1.030	1.014	1.023	1.062
FORECAST OF SEASONAL FACTORS												
1991	0.997	0.998	1.025	0.987	0.996	0.973	0.936	0.969	1.017	1.012	1.018	1.065
ACTUAL MICROWAVE SALES Thousands (Seasonally Adjusted)												
1988	126.0	126.5	127.2	127.5	129.4	135.4	136.2	140.6	148.1	142.5	139.7	139.6
1989	142.7	145.7	149.1	148.2	150.5	157.2	157.7	160.7	164.8	156.8	153.0	152.1
1990	150.7	151.4	153.9	151.7	156.0	161.8	162.0	164.3	165.8	166.6	167.6	171.5
FORECAST OF SALES (SEASONALLY ADJUSTED)												
1991	159.6	157.2	160.0	155.0	161.7	167.7	167.0	167.5	171.3	166.7	168.6	170.6
ACTUAL MICROWAVE SALES Thousands (Not Seasonally Adjusted)												
1988	122.7	122.3	124.6	126.5	129.0	129.7	125.9	136.4	156.5	146.1	146.1	151.4
1989	139.9	142.3	148.5	146.7	149.9	151.9	146.6	155.9	171.9	159.7	157.9	162.9
1990	149.2	149.4	156.0	149.8	155.4	157.4	151.4	159.0	170.8	168.9	171.4	182.1
1991	162.6	160.4	162.9	152.1	156.7	153.5						
FORECAST OF SALES (NOT SEASONALLY ADJUSTED)												
1991	159.1	156.9	163.9	153.0	161.1	163.1	156.4	162.2	174.2	168.6	171.6	181.8
Three-Year Average (1988 to 1990)												
Three-Year Average	137.3	138.0	143.0	141.0	144.8	146.4	141.3	150.4	166.4	158.3	158.5	165.5
Low	122.7	122.3	124.6	126.5	129	129.7	125.9	136.4	156.5	146.1	146.1	151.4
High	149.2	149.4	156	149.8	155.4	157.4	151.4	159	171.9	168.9	171.4	182.1

of the general seasonal swings. The reasonableness of the 1991 FORECAST level can be measured against the HIGH and LOW lines. Finally, a comparison of the 1991 actual values with the 1991 FORECAST series and with the HIGH series provides an indication of the accuracy of the forecast. In terms of forecast reliability, the difference between the FORECAST series and the six actual observations for 1991 values does not appear to be great for the first five months, but there is a significant error for June 1991. In addition, for April, May, and June of 1991, the forecast values exceed actual microwave sales and, more importantly, the size of the error becomes larger in each successive month. This could be a reflection of an inherent defect in the model, or it could indicate that the lagged effect of the recession (which started in July 1990) was finally starting to take hold in the microwave industry.

Another frequently used graphical tracking device is the modified turning-point error diagram (turning-point diagrams were discussed earlier), which allows the user to illustrate the accuracy of the forecasting model in capturing turning points and which provides a comparison of predicted changes versus actual changes. In the modified version of the turning-point diagram, the perfect forecasts line is rotated (see Figure 10-3) from its traditional 45-degree angle position so it becomes congruent with the horizontal axis.

FIGURE 10-3 Modified Turning-Point Error Diagram

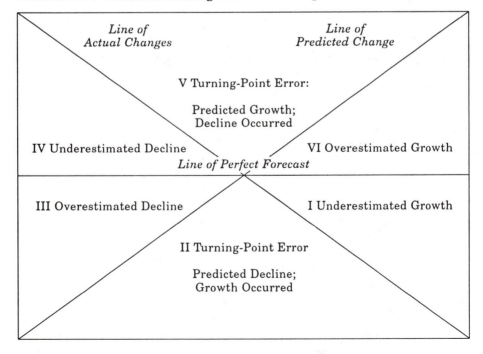

Of the six subdivided quadrants in Figure 10-3, turning-point errors occur in quadrant II (the model predicts a decline when an increase actually occurs) and in quadrant V (the model predicts growth when a decline actually occurs). The remaining quadrants involve forecasts that carried the correct sign (that is, predict the directional change correctly) but failed to accurately capture the magnitude of the change. Points that fall in quadrants III and VI reflect overestimates, while points in quadrants I and IV involve underestimates. Figure 10-4 depicts the potential error patterns of interest. Error patterns generated by models that consistently overestimate or underestimate are presented in panels (a) and (b) of Figure 10-4, respectively. Panel (c) illustrates the case of a random error pattern, while panel (d) displays the pattern created by a model that produces a large number of turning-point errors.

Figure 10-5 details a modified turning-point diagram for the automobile sales model previously estimated in equation (6-30), with the raw data contained in Table 10-3. For purposes of this and subsequent exercises in this chapter, assume that the model was estimated based on data available through the end of the second quarter of 1989 (1989:II). An examination of the turning-

FIGURE 10-4   Modified Turning-Point Diagrams

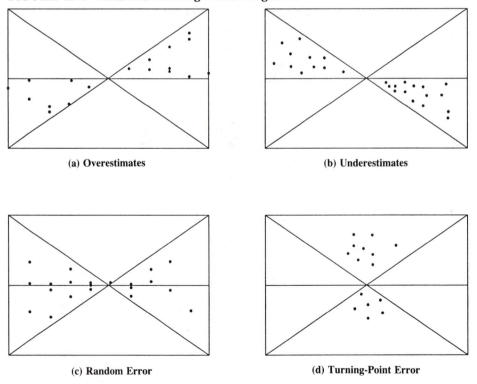

(a) Overestimates   (b) Underestimates

(c) Random Error   (d) Turning-Point Error

FIGURE 10-5   Turning-Point Evaluation of Auto Sales

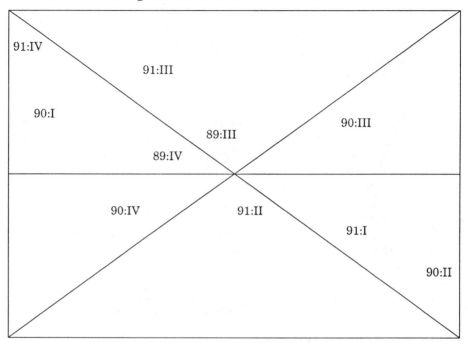

TABLE 10-3   Turning-Point Evaluation of Automobile Forecasts[2]

Year and Quarter	Predicted	Percent Change	Actual	Percent Change
1989: II			10.15	
III	10.29	1.38	9.96	−1.87
IV	10.14	−1.46	9.80	−1.61
1990: I	9.88	−2.56	9.15	−6.63
II	10.02	1.42	9.91	8.31
III	10.37	3.49	10.08	1.72
IV	10.09	−2.70	10.00	−0.80
1991: I	10.11	0.20	10.49	4.90
II	10.01	−1.00	10.60	1.05
III	10.10	0.90	10.26	−3.21
IV	9.97	−1.29	9.42	−8.19

[2] Prior to actually deriving the modified turning-point diagram, the forecaster should adjust the model forecasts to compensate for errors associated with errors in the independent variables.

point plot for the percentage change columns indicates that while the model appears to capture the magnitude of the changes, there were turning-point errors in 1989:III, 1991:II, and 1991:III. This might indicate that the model requires respecification or that it should be reestimated each quarter as new data become available.

A third graphical tracking device involves a plot of actual versus forecasted magnitudes, and this approach is illustrated in Figure 10-6 for actual and predicted automobile sales (as set forth in Table 10-3). The automobile sales model overestimated sales during the first six quarters, underestimated in the next three quarters, and then overestimated during the final quarter for which an actual and a predicted value are available. This alternating pattern of overestimates and underestimates, when combined with the questionable turning-point performance documented in Figure 10-5, suggests, again, that the model is not very reliable.

A fourth method of measuring the reliability of a forecasting model is to plot, on the same graph, sequential forecasts made by a model at different points in time (for example, sequential monthly forecasts for 1993 automobile sales could have been made in December 1991, March 1992, and June 1992). If the sequential forecasts made by a model at different points in time exhibit a wide spread or variation, it may indicate a structural problem with the model. The most useful models generate forecasts that are tightly bounded or clustered

FIGURE 10-6   Actual versus Forecast: Auto Sales

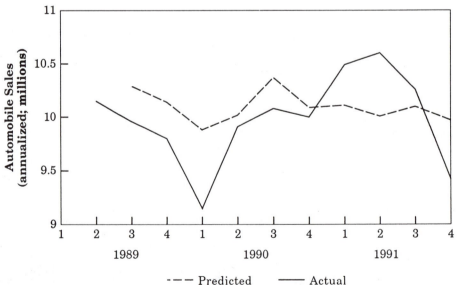

TABLE 10-4   Forecast Spread: Sales of Hard Cards

		Month in Which Forecast Made			
		March 1989	*June 1989*	*September 1989*	*December 1989*
1990:	January	458,536	454,342	444,910	441,933
	February	465,330	462,204	452,117	456,412
	March	477,917	475,100	463,188	462,575
	April	472,193	469,918	461,248	459,864
	May	484,601	482,624	471,647	470,232
	June	480,712	476,221	466,634	465,234
	July	464,867	460,542	451,543	450,188
	August	482,055	477,863	469,790	468,381
	September	504,378	500,094	491,933	491,617
	October	503,402	499,148	493,980	493,422
	November	497,351	492,851	488,790	488,240
	December	509,463	505,017	517,961	517,406
1991:	January	509,749	505,282	505,147	504,597
	February	515,464	511,242	512,030	511,488
	March	528,660	524,415	522,242	521,689
	April	519,707	515,724	523,244	522,662
	May	532,706	528,579	538,247	537,671

together. To illustrate, suppose that we have monitored the forecasts for sales of "hard cards" (boards that are inserted in microcomputers to enhance their memory capacity) from a specific model and have recorded the results in Table 10-4.

The graphical plot of the sequential forecast revisions in Table 10-4 is presented in Figure 10-7, and it suggests two conclusions:

1. There is a general downward trend in the sequential forecasts as they are revised over time.
2. The forecast model used to generate these sequential forecasts is behaving consistently in that there are no significant pattern variations (radical changes in the forecasted movement from month to month).

While it might seem that consistent downward revisions in sequential forecasts over time are indicative of a problem with the model, it is likely that increasingly negative external economic conditions (which would depress the values of the independent variables used in the forecasting model) are the cause. With regard to the pattern variations, the key to successful graphical tracking techniques is that sequential forecasts not produce wild fluctuations in predicted month-to-month (or quarter-to-quarter) movements.

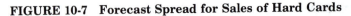

FIGURE 10-7   **Forecast Spread for Sales of Hard Cards**

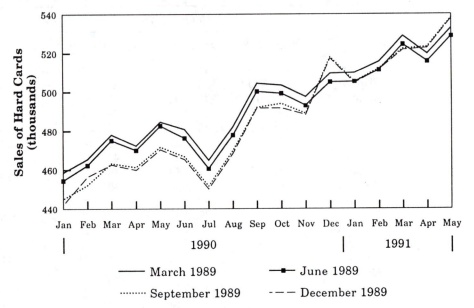

The final graphical device illustrated in this chapter involves the use of control and confidence limits.[3] With this technique, a succession of overestimates or underestimates can serve as an early warning signal of problems with a particular forecast model. Table 10-5 illustrates the use of the confidence limit graphical technique, with the information in the table derived from a 12-month forecast for hard card sales that was made at the end of March 1989. The forecasts for this 12-month period are presented in column 3, while the upper and lower confidence limits are provided in columns 2 and 4, respectively.

The forecast value for May 1989 is 425,005, while the lower confidence bound is 422,880 and the upper confidence bound is 427,130. The next stage is to compute the difference between the forecast value and the upper and lower confidence limits as follows:

$$\text{Lower Limit} = \text{Lower Confidence Bound} - \text{Forecast}$$ (10-3)
$$-2,125 = 422,880 - 425,005$$

$$\text{Upper Limit} = \text{Upper Confidence Bound} - \text{Forecast}$$ (10-4)
$$+2,125 = 427,130 - 425,005.$$

[3] The process of computing confidence intervals or limits for each of the forecasting techniques was presented in conjunction with the techniques themselves and hence is not presented here.

TABLE 10-5 Confidence Intervals for Hard Card Sales

Date	Actual Sales (1)	Lower Bound (2)	Forecast Sales (3)	Upper Bound (4)	Lower Limit (5)	Forecast Error (6)	Upper Limit (7)	Cumulative Forecast Error (8)	Cumulative Lower Limit (9)	Cumulative Upper Limit (10)
1989: May	418,332	422,880	425,005	427,130	(2,125)	6,673	2,125	6,673	(2,125)	2,125
June	418,881	426,528	430,836	435,144	(4,308)	11,955	4,308	18,628	(6,433)	6,433
July	409,747	416,041	422,377	428,713	(6,336)	12,630	6,336	31,258	(12,769)	12,769
August	421,486	429,740	438,510	447,280	(8,770)	17,024	8,770	48,282	(21,539)	21,539
September	447,706	435,902	447,079	458,256	(11,177)	(627)	11,177	47,655	(32,716)	32,716
October	438,626	434,770	448,216	461,662	(13,446)	9,590	13,446	57,245	(46,163)	46,163
November	435,114	428,506	444,048	459,590	(15,542)	8,934	15,542	66,179	(61,704)	61,704
December	463,376	439,509	457,822	476,135	(18,313)	(5,554)	18,313	60,625	(80,017)	80,017
1990: January	441,933	437,902	458,536	479,170	(20,634)	16,603	20,634	77,228	(100,651)	100,651
February	456,412	442,064	465,330	488,597	(23,267)	8,918	23,267	86,146	(123,918)	123,918
March	462,575	451,632	477,917	504,202	(26,285)	15,342	26,285	101,488	(150,203)	150,203

Finally, the forecast error itself needs to be derived:

$$\text{Forecast Error} = \text{Forecast Value} - \text{Actual Value} \tag{10-5}$$
$$6{,}673 = 425{,}005 - 418{,}332.$$

Similar computations are carried out for each monthly observation, with the resulting lower limit, upper limit, and forecast error plotted in Figure 10-8. An examination of Figure 10-8 suggests that for the first four months the model generates forecasts that exceed the upper limit, with the remainder of the forecasts relatively close to the zero error line. While the error pattern is generally within the upper and lower limits, only two errors are negative. This nonrandom error pattern (if it continues) would normally lead a forecaster to apply more sophisticated statistical tests (such as the Durbin-Watson test discussed in chapter 6).

An alternative method of analyzing the errors generated by a forecasting model is to make use of a cumulative error and cumulative confidence limit plot as shown in Figure 10-9 (based on the forecasts set forth in Table 10-5). Rather than plot the forecast error, upper limit, and lower limit, three new series were developed by keeping a running tally or total (see columns (8), (9), and (10) in Table 10-5). Thus, the observation for the cumulative error in August 1989 is the sum of the errors for May, June, July, and August. A cursory

FIGURE 10-8   Confidence Limits and Forecast Error

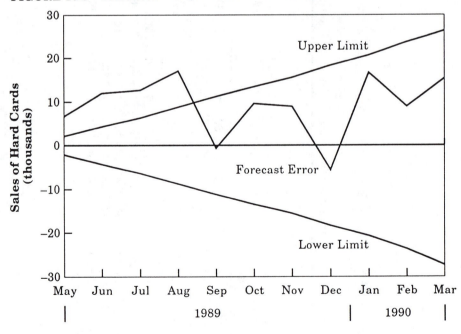

FIGURE 10-9 Confidence Limits and Cumulative Forecast Error

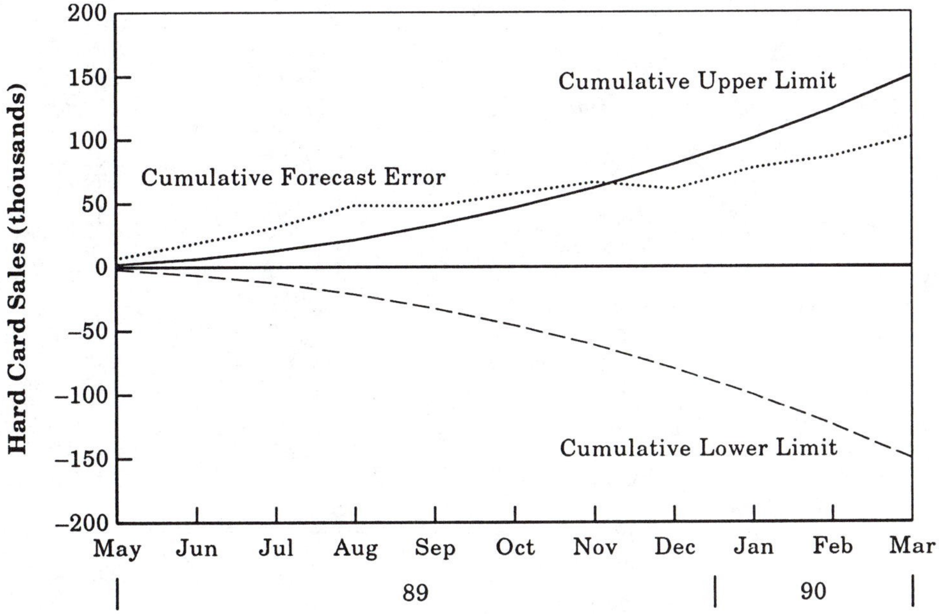

analysis of the error pattern in Figure 10-9 reveals that the cumulative error has stayed above the zero forecast line. The results presented in Figures 10-8 and 10-9 lead one to speculate that the model is overestimating either because of a change in market conditions or because the model, itself, is incorrectly specified. Furthermore, a forecast analyst would not necessarily have waited until the end of March 1990 to recommend a revision in the forecast. In all likelihood, the analyst would have recognized the nonrandom error pattern and called for a revision in July or August 1989.

An additional rule of thumb is to monitor the number of forecast errors falling outside the confidence limits. For example, with a 95 percent confidence interval, we would expect to observe only 5 percent of the monthly projections to fall outside of the confidence interval. Alternatively, with an 80 percent confidence interval, we would expect approximately two monthly forecasts per year to fall outside of the confidence interval. In the case of the hard card forecasts presented in Table 10-5, four of the monthly forecasts exceeded the upper limit, suggesting that the estimated model is unacceptable as a monthly forecasting system.

QUANTITATIVE TRACKING TOOLS

As with the graphical tracking tools, there are a number of quantitative or statistical tracking techniques. The first of these quantitative tracking tools

TABLE 10-6   Analysis of Sales

Date	Seasonally Adjusted Monthly Rate	Seasonally Adjusted Annual Rate
1990: January	14.125	169.5
February	14.333	172.0
March	14.500	174.0
Year-to-date SAAR		171.8
April	14.642	175.7
May	14.767	177.2
June	14.858	178.3
Year-to-date SAAR		174.5
July	14.858	178.3
August	15.017	180.2
September	15.075	180.9
Year-to-date SAAR		176.2
1990 Forecast =		184.9

is an extension of the seasonal adjustment process used for time series data. To illustrate, suppose that we have collected the information presented in Table 10-6. The seasonally adjusted annual rate (SAAR) converts monthly (or quarterly) observations into annualized or full-year rates. Specifically, to derive a SAAR from monthly data, we take the seasonally adjusted value and multiply by 12, while for quarterly data we would multiply by 4. The annualized rate provides a measure of what we would expect to observe for the year if a single monthly (quarterly) observation continued at the same level or rate for the full 12 months. To minimize the possibility that erratic behavior in any given month will be given undue influence, it is preferable to average two or more monthly SAARs. The basic premise of the SAAR as a tracking device is that annual forecasts are typically more accurate than are either monthly or quarterly forecasts because seasonal influence are not present, cyclical forecasts are dampened, and trend forces tend to dominate. An examination of the year-to-date SAARs indicates that the model is continually underestimating relative to the 1990 forecast of 184.9. Therefore, unless the forecaster has a good explanation for the continued shortfall, he or she would be wise to revise the forecast as soon as this trend becomes clear (certainly after the second quarter). That is, there is no reason to wait until the end of the third quarter to revise the forecast. Whenever a model is generating forecasts that are consistently low or high relative to the actual values, the sooner we can identify this problem and make revisions, the more useful the forecasting process is to management.

To quantify the revision that we might want to make in the case of the sales example presented in Table 10-6, we can go one step further and compute a target SAAR for the fourth quarter of 1990:

$$
\begin{array}{l}\text{Target SAAR} \\ \text{for Remaining} \\ \text{Months}\end{array} = \begin{array}{l}\text{Year-} \\ \text{to-Date} \\ \text{SAAR}\end{array} + \dfrac{12}{\begin{array}{c}\text{Number of Remaining} \\ \text{Months}\end{array}} \cdot \left[\begin{array}{l}\text{Forecast} \\ \text{Value}\end{array} - \begin{array}{l}\text{Year-} \\ \text{to-Date} \\ \text{SAAR}\end{array}\right]
$$

To illustrate, suppose that we are at the end of the third quarter and are interested in computing the target SAAR for the final three months of the year (that is, the level of sales which would have to be achieved in order to reach the annual forecast of 184.9):

$$
\text{Target SAAR} = 176.2 + (12/3) \cdot (184.9 - 176.2)
$$

$$
= 211.0. \tag{10-6}
$$

Unless sales in the fourth quarter increase to 211.0, a 14.1 percent increase, the company will not reach its 1990 forecast.

Another monitoring device commonly relied on is Trigg's tracking signal.[4] This method not only provides us with a measure of forecast reliability, but it also can be used to indicate the presence of a nonrandom error pattern. The tracking signal is defined by three equations:

$$
E_t = \alpha e_t + (1 - \alpha)E_{t-1} \tag{10-7}
$$

$$
M_t = \alpha |e_t| + (1 - \alpha)M_{t-1} \tag{10-8}
$$

$$
T_t = (E_t/M_t) \tag{10-9}
$$

where

α = an exponential smoothing constant
e = the forecasting error in the most recent time period
E = the smoothed or average error
M = the mean absolute deviation
T = Trigg's tracking signal.

The larger the value of the tracking signal, the more indicative it is of a needed forecast revision (given the condition that $0 \le T_t \le 1$). As a rule, the exponential smoothing constant, α, is usually constrained to be between 0.10

---

[4] D. W. Trigg, "Monitoring a Forecasting System," *Operational Research Quarterly*, vol. 15, 1964, pp. 272–74.

and 0.20. When using the tracking signal, the forecast user and preparer should jointly agree on the value of T_t that will trigger a revision. Trigg demonstrated that when T_t exceeds 0.5 (for $\alpha = 0.10$) or 0.74 (for $\alpha = 0.20$), the error pattern is nonrandom. Thus, if it was decided that management would be satisfied with an error rate of ± 1 percent (99 percent confidence level), and the smoothing constant were 0.10, a forecast would need revision whenever the tracking signal exceeded ± 0.50. The sign attached to the tracking signal provides information as to the direction of the revision. Whenever the forecast error is defined as the actual value minus the forecast value, negative values for the tracking signal indicate an upward revision, while positive values suggest the need for a downward revision. Alternatively, if the forecast error is defined as the forecast value minus the actual value, a positive value for the tracking signal would suggest a downward revision, while negative values would indicate an upward revision.

In chapter 8, we developed a model (using Brown's linear exponential smoothing) for estimating the average daily telephone calls coming into a call center. Table 10-7 provides us with the information needed to compute Trigg's tracking signal for the telephone call model. In this example, the smoothing constant for the tracking signal was assumed to be 0.10, E_{t-1} was assumed to be 0, while the smoothed absolute error, M_{t-1}, was set equal to the mean absolute deviation of 2.55 generated by the historical simulation. An examination of the tracking signals indicates that in July, the computed tracking signal exceeds the critical value of 0.50, and this implies that the forecast values are no longer capturing the pattern exhibited by the actual data. Specifically, the pattern of underestimation that began in April reached significant levels in July. Thus, based on Trigg's tracking signal, any forecasts beyond July 1991 should be revised upward. Finally, once it has been determined that a forecast revision is to be made, the tracking signal itself should be reset to a value of 0—otherwise it will continue to indicate the need for revisions.

TABLE 10-7 Trigg's Tracking Performance of Telephone Call Model

Date	Actual	Forecast	Error (e_t)	Smoothed Error (E_t)	Smoothed Absolute Error (M_t)	Tracking Signal (T_t)
1991: January	407.5	405.5	2.0	0.200	2.32	0.09
February	409.6	410.8	−1.2	0.060	2.21	0.03
March	415.8	416.2	−0.4	0.058	2.03	0.03
April	422.7	421.6	1.1	0.162	1.94	0.08
May	428.1	426.9	1.2	0.266	1.87	0.14
June	437.6	432.3	5.3	0.769	2.21	0.35
July	442.2	434.6	7.6	1.450	2.75	0.53

TABLE 10-8   Autocorrelation Tracking Signal of Telephone Call Model

Date	Actual	Forecast	e_t	Cov_t	MSE_t	AT_t
1991: January	407.5	405.5	2.0	13.46	55.23	0.24
February	409.6	410.8	−1.2	9.71	53.71	0.18
March	415.8	416.2	−0.4	9.22	49.78	0.19
April	422.7	421.6	1.1	7.86	44.96	0.17
May	428.1	426.9	1.2	8.39	41.67	0.20
June	437.6	432.3	5.3	13.91	38.94	0.36
July	442.2	434.6	7.6	52.80	63.14	0.84

The autocorrelation tracking signal is conceptually similar to Trigg's signal, and it is based on the following three equations:[5]

$$\text{Cov}_t = e_t e_{t-1} + (1 - \alpha)\text{Cov}_{t-1} \qquad \textbf{(10-10)}$$

$$\text{MSE}_t = e_{t-1}^2 + (1 - \alpha)\text{MSE}_{t-1} \qquad \textbf{(10-11)}$$

$$\text{AT}_t = \frac{\text{Cov}_t}{\text{MSE}_t} \qquad \textbf{(10-12)}$$

where

$$\alpha = \text{smoothing constant for the error term}$$
$$\text{Cov} = \text{covariance}$$
$$\text{MSE} = \text{mean square error}$$
$$\text{AT} = \text{autocorrelation tracking signal.}$$

For the majority of forecasting applications, a value for $\alpha = 0.10$ is suggested. While it is true that a higher value for α makes the tracking signal more responsive to actual changes in the data pattern, it also leads to a larger number of false signals. The more false signals generated, the more frequent, hence less useful, are the forecast revisions.

Making use of the telephone call model, suppose that we assume an α value of 0.10 and that the covariance in December 1990 equals zero. From the historical simulation, we obtain the initial value for the MSE in December 1990 of 11.04 and an error term of 6.73. The results of applying equations (10-10) through (10-12) to the telephone call model are detailed in the last three columns of Table 10-8.

[5] E. S. Gardner, "Automatic Monitoring of Forecast Errors," *Journal of Forecasting*, vol. 2, no. 1, 1983, pp. 1–22. Copyright © 1983 by John Wiley and Sons Limited. Reprinted by permission.

TABLE 10-9 Autocorrelation
Tracking Signals
for $\alpha = 0.10$

Cumulative Probability That Errors Are Not Random	AT_t
0.80	0.17
0.90	0.27
0.95	0.35
0.99	0.48

The autocorrelation tracking signal can be evaluated based on the cumulative probabilities illustrated in Table 10-9. Comparing the critical values in Table 10-9 with the tracking signals in Table 10-8 indicates that, beginning in June, the model requires revision at the 95 percent confidence level. As before, whenever a revision is needed, the values for the appropriate statistics should be reset to zero before the new tracking process is reinitiated. The principal limitation of this statistic is that it is not technically correct to use it for any model in which the forecasting errors are not independent, such as in exponential smoothing or moving average models.

THE FORECASTING AUDIT AND CONTROL CYCLE

While the exact stages of the forecast audit and control cycle depend on the industry or firm under study, it should include the stages shown in Figure 10-10. Begin in the upper, left-hand corner of this diagram with the box labeled "new information." There are countless ways in which new information is generated, but the most typical include changes in exogenous (external) forces, such as the competitive environment or the state of the business cycle, and internal policies, such as pricing actions or advertising programs. When this new information is combined with the monitoring and tracking procedures, it forms the basis for the feedback to the forecaster. Armed with this information, the forecaster would evaluate this new information in light of forecasted versus actual results for past and current periods, the model's forecast (without judgmental modifications) for the next period, and the methodology underlying the model (for example, a simple model that replies on extrapolation of historical trends would be unable to incorporate exogenous shocks). The new information may indicate that the methodology currently in use is satisfactory but that the forecast needs to be revised, or that the entire forecasting process needs to be reevaluated.

The use of a control cycle and a formal audit procedure involves not only the evaluation of forecasts but also prompt remedial actions when clear prob-

FIGURE 10-10 Forecast Control Cycle

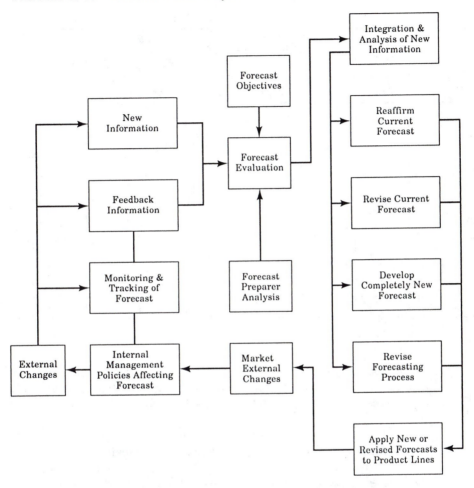

lems arise. Thus, the control flow suggested by Figure 10-10 must be internalized into a standard operating procedure that occurs continuously in both the short run and the long run—not just when special problems arise. While there are a number of formats by which the control cycle and audit may be formalized, Figures 10-11 and 10-12 illustrate two formats that have proven useful. Although these figures are stated in terms of units and dollars, other measurement units may be more appropriate depending on the model being studied. Figures 10-11 and 10-12 illustrate a monthly forecast, but the same format can be used for other time dimensions.

A third format that is useful both as an auditing procedure and as a means of monitoring forecast revisions is illustrated in Figure 10-13 (page 510). Once

FIGURE 10-11   Forecast Audit and Control Format

Time Period (Week, Month, Quarter) Ending _____

Forecast Variable	Current Time Period			Year to Date			Previous Year to Date	Percentage Change Versus Previous Year
	Actual Value	Forecast Value	Percent Achieved	Actual Value	Forecast Value	Percent Achieved		
Totals								

again, the format illustrated in Figure 10-13 can be adapted to other time frames and measurement units. The following four-step auditing procedure is one means of achieving an integrated system for producing and revising forecasts:

1. Evaluate the forecasting methodology independently of the forecast. Which methods were considered? Why were some methods originally rejected while others were accepted? What were the underlying assumptions for these models, and have they been violated?

2. Evaluate the data used in the forecast. Have the data remained consistent in terms of measurement? Have there been any significant changes in the seasonality exhibited by the data?

3. Have we incorporated useful guidelines for the uncertainty associated with making forecasts? Have the forecasts exceeded the upper or lower limits? Have we provided management with useful contingency forecasts? Is the level of uncertainty associated with a specific set of forecasts acceptable to management? Can managerial judgment be incorporated into the forecast, thereby reducing this uncertainty?

4. Have we incorporated an estimate of the costs associated with the forecasting effort?

FIGURE 10-12 Forecast Audit Format: Monthly Forecasts with Quarterly Revisions

Time Period		Jan.	Feb.	Mar.	Apr.	May	June	July	Aug.	Sept.	Oct.	Nov.	Dec.
Previous year actuals	Units												
	Dollars												
Original forecast January 1	Units												
	Dollars												
March 31 revised forecast	Units												
	Dollars												
June 30 revised forecast	Units												
	Dollars												
September 3 revised forecast	Units												
	Dollars												
Actuals	Units												
	Dollars												
		Jan.	Feb.	Mar.	Apr.	May	June	July	Aug.	Sept.	Oct.	Nov.	Dec.
Actuals	Units												
	Dollars												
January	Units												
	Dollars												
February	Units												
	Dollars												
March	Units												
	Dollars												
April	Units												
	Dollars												
May	Units												
	Dollars												
June	Units												
	Dollars												
July	Units												
	Dollars												
August	Units												
	Dollars												
September	Units												
	Dollars												
October	Units												
	Dollars												
November	Units												
	Dollars												
December	Units												
	Dollars												

FIGURE 10-13 Summarizing Forecast Revisions

Month	Actual Sales	Most Recent	Forecast Time Frame			
			Three Months Ago	Six Months Ago	Nine Months Ago	Twelve Months Ago
January						
February						
March						
• • •						
• • •						
• • •						
December						

REVISION OF FORECASTS

Throughout this chapter, we have repeatedly made reference to the task of forecast revision, and this may be incorrectly interpreted as a call for continuous revisions. In fact, the most common mistake made by forecasters is revising forecasts based on "new and improved" information. Two examples will serve to illustrate the potential problems inherent in forecast revision. In the case of long-run forecasts, as new information becomes available there is a tendency to mistake cyclical fluctuations for changes in trend. Caton offers an example of this phenomenon that focuses on the evolution of Data Resources Incorporated's (DRI's) long-term forecast over the period 1978–1983. We have reproduced a portion of his work in Table 10-10.[6] The most significant aspect of this example is that the forecast issued in December 1983 is virtually identical with the forecast that was made in December 1978. That is, after five successive revisions, DRI ended up where it started.

The second example comes from the authors' work in issuing short-term (monthly) forecasts for company sales. Each of the forecast revisions detailed in Table 10-11 was made to improve the model's accuracy based on the most current data. An analysis of the model's accuracy for the months for which actual observations were available indicates that the most accurate forecast is the one that was made with the "oldest" information. As a result of incorporating new information into our forecasts, the revisions became progressively worse relative to the final outcome. As management begins to notice this, and they will, their faith in forecasters diminishes rapidly. Before making forecast revisions, therefore, it is important to ask, What do we know now that

[6] Christopher Caton, "Forecast Revision—Coping with a Changing Future," *The Journal of Business Forecasting*, Fall 1988, pp. 15–35.

TABLE 10-10 Changes in Long-Term Macroeconomic Outlook

	Average Annual Increase, 1982–1985					
Forecast Reported In:	*December 1978*	*December 1979*	*September 1980*	*September 1981*	*December 1982*	*December 1983*
Real GNP	3.2	2.8	2.7	2.8	3.0	3.1
Industrial Production	4.2	3.6	3.6	3.5	3.9	4.2
Manufacturing Employment	0.8	0.4	0.4	0.4	0.8	1.1
Inflation	5.6	7.0	7.4	7.0	6.1	5.6
Output per Hour	2.1	2.1	1.6	1.7	1.7	1.9
Potential GNP	2.9	2.6	2.3	2.6	2.5	2.7

Source: Christopher Caton, "Forecast Revision—Coping with a Changing Future," *The Journal of Business Forecasting,* Fall 1988, pp. 15–35.

we did not know before? Alternatively, can we justify changing our existing forecast based on this new information? In the case of long-term forecasts, are we certain that the resulting revisions are not just normal cyclical fluctuations around a stable trend line? Is it possible that a cluster of irregular external factors are causing the observed variation? Have there been documentable structural changes simultaneously observed by other forecasters? These and other similar questions help us to avoid revising trend-oriented forecasts for the wrong reasons.

When dealing with short-term forecast revisions, there are even greater hazards due to ways in which short-term changes appear and disappear. By basing forecasts on the latest observations, the forecaster takes the chance of

TABLE 10-11 Revisions in 1990–1991 Sales Forecasts (thousands)

Forecast Reported In:	*June 1989*	*September 1989*	*December 1989*	*March 1990*	*Actual Sales*
1990: June	1,210.8	1,189.8	1,219.1	1,227.3	1,205.4
July	1,168.9	1,156.6	1,193.6	1,201.8	1,161.2
August	1,203.2	1,188.8	1,223.4	1,231.6	1,198.5
September	1,261.5	1,237.0	1,267.7	1,274.7	
October	1,256.9	1,242.4	1,265.9	1,272.1	
November	1,256.6	1,239.0	1,268.4	1,274.5	
December	1,368.5	1,335.5	1,387.1	1,393.3	
1991: January	1,288.0	1,272.1	1,309.6	1,315.6	
February	1,301.2	1,277.1	1,326.1	1,332.2	
March	1,347.8	1,317.9	1,360.7	1,366.7	
April	1,326.1	1,308.9	1,358.6	1,364.5	
May	1,341.1	1,326.0	1,377.2	1,383.2	

making the entire forecast unreliable and, ultimately, unusable. In many applications, the economic data series are subject to frequent (monthly, in terms of important series such as GNP) revisions. By blindly incorporating each new revision into the model, the forecast may yield greater volatility than can be reasonably explained to management. It is entirely possible that there are measurement or recording errors associated with short-term data observations. For example, there are numerous examples of economic data series that are recorded as below normal one month and above normal the next month. It is entirely possible that some of the sales or volume shift that was recorded in the second month should have been recorded in the first month. Fluctuations in reported government statistics are often thought to be due to incorrect estimates of seasonal patterns in the original data, which then produces distortions in the statistics reported for the latest month or quarter.

SUMMARY

As a forecaster, your responsibility does not end when the forecast is issued. A continuing reevaluation and monitoring of the forecast is required, and this forces the forecaster to be aware of changes in both external conditions and internal policies. Furthermore, you must always be in contact with forecast users for new information that you can use in improving the forecasting process. While the planning procedures developed in this chapter may not hold for all firms and industries, they do highlight the importance of planning geared to maximize a company's strengths in each cyclical phase. In this manner, forecasting becomes a valuable input into the planning process.

QUESTIONS FOR DISCUSSION AND ANALYSIS

1. Twice a week on Wednesday evening and Saturday evening, residents of the state of Virginia scurry to the television to see if they hold the winning ticket in the state's lottery. Lottery tickets are sold at thousands of outlets (typically, gas stations and other small retail stores) throughout the state. The purchaser of a lottery ticket picks six numbers between 1 and 45 and hopes to win (the chances of picking all six numbers are exceedingly small) a multimillion-dollar jackpot. Assume that you forecast lottery revenue (from the sale of lottery tickets) for the state of Virginia.
   a. What changes in external conditions might cause severe fluctuations in state lottery revenue? What types of internal decisions and policies would alter state lottery revenue?
   b. Suppose you decide, after witnessing declining ticket sales and lottery revenue for the first six months of the fiscal year, that you will calculate the target SAAR for the remaining months. First, set up a numerical example and explain how such a calculation would be prepared. Second, write a paragraph explaining the meaning of target SAAR for your boss, who is not trained in statistical and quantitative techniques.

   c. Making use of Figure 10-10, design an audit and control cycle for forecasts of state lottery revenue. Describe how the system might work.

2. Apply Trigg's tracking signal to the telephone call model in chapter 8, and replicate the results in Table 10-7.

3. Apply the autocorrelation tracking signal to the telephone call model, and replicate the results in Table 10-8.

4. Suppose that the vice-president of finance asks you for assistance in developing acceptable forecast error rates for the production department. What factors would you consider in responding to his request? Why? Would it make a difference if the request had originated in the sales department? Why or why not?

5. Suppose that you are given the following regression model on the relationship between the shipments of appliances and the production of these appliances:

$$\text{APP}_t = -85{,}320 + 1027.60439\text{PROD}_t.$$

Further suppose that you are asked to make a one-period-ahead forecast for appliance shipments (APP) based on a predicted value for production (PROD) of 108.623. What is your forecast? Now suppose that actual production in this time period turns out to be 109.5 and actual appliance shipments are recorded as 27,510. Based on this information, conduct an error decomposition analysis similar to that presented in Figure 10-1.

6. In chapter 6, a regression model was estimated for the relationship between sales and two explanatory variables, real personal income (RPINC) and share of voice (SOV). The specific model estimated is replicated here:

$$S = -1.13991 + 0.00874927\text{RPINC} + 0.14368\text{SOV}.$$

Now suppose that you are provided with a one-period-ahead estimate for RPINC of 296 and of 36 for SOV. What would your estimate of sales (S) be? Now suppose that actual sales are recorded as 6.47 and that real personal income is revised upward to 302, while the SOV estimate is revised downward to 33. Based on this information, conduct an error decomposition analysis similar to that presented in Figure 10-1.

7. In chapter 8, question 13, you were provided with information on average package weights. Estimate the most appropriate moving average and exponential models, omitting the last eight points. Based on these models and the resulting eight forecasts,
   a. Develop a ladder chart.
   b. Develop a modified turning-point diagram.
   c. Develop a control chart along with the appropriate confidence limits.
   d. Conduct a cumulative confidence limit analysis.
   e. Apply Trigg's tracking signal to these results.
   f. Apply the autocorrelation analysis to these results.
Which of these tracking tools is the most useful for these models? Why? What do they suggest about the reliability of the estimated models?

8. In chapter 8, question 15, you were provided with information on wage rates. Estimate the most appropriate moving average and exponential models, omitting the last 12 points. Based on these models and the resulting 12 forecasts,
   a. Develop a ladder chart.
   b. Develop a modified turning-point diagram.
   c. Develop a control chart along with the appropriate confidence limits.

    d. Conduct a cumulative confidence limit analysis.

    e. Apply Trigg's tracking signal to these results.

    f. Apply the autocorrelation analysis to these results.

    Which of these tracking tools is the most useful for these models? Why? What do they suggest about the reliability of the estimated models?

  9. In chapter 8, question 16, you were provided with information on the number of calls coming into a call center. Estimate the most appropriate moving average and exponential model, omitting the last six points. Based on these models and the resulting six forecasts,

    a. Develop a ladder chart.

    b. Develop a modified turning-point diagram.

    c. Develop a control chart along with the appropriate confidence limits.

    d. Conduct a cumulative confidence limit analysis.

    e. Apply Trigg's tracking signal to these results.

    f. Apply the autocorrelation analysis to these results.

    Which of these tracking tools is the most useful for these models? Why? What do they suggest about the reliability of the estimated models?

 10. Your manager has asked you to prepare a two-page report discussing the need (or lack thereof) for forecast revisions in a monthly forecasting model. What are the primary issues that you would include in this report? What dangers would you warn her of? How would you determine that revisions were needed and when there were dangers to revising existing forecasts?

 11. Explain how the concept of a SAAR can be used as a monitoring device. Do you foresee any problems associated with using this technique?

REFERENCES FOR FURTHER STUDY

Batty, M., "Monitoring an Exponential Smoothing Forecasting System," *Operational Research Quarterly*, vol. 20, 1969, pp. 319–25.

Brown, Robert G., "Detection of Turning Points in a Time Series," *Decision Sciences*, vol. 2, 1971, pp. 383–403.

Carbone, Robert and R. L. Longini, "A Feedback Model for Automated Real Estate Assessment," *Management Science*, vol. 24, 1977, pp. 241–48.

Dumaine, Brian, "How to Manage in a Recession," *Fortune*, November 5, 1990, pp. 58–72.

Ewan, W. D. and K. W. Kemp, "When and How to Use Cu-Sum Charts," *Technometrics*, vol. 5, 1963, pp. 1–22.

Gardner, Everette B., "Automatic Monitoring of Forecast Errors," *Journal of Forecasting*, vol. 2, no. 1, 1983, pp. 1–21.

Golder, E. R. and J. G. Settle, "Monitoring Schemes in Short-Term Forecasting," *Operational Research Quarterly*, vol. 27, 1976, pp. 489–501.

Harrison, P. J. and O. L. Davies, "Monitoring Schemes in Short-Term Forecasting," *Operational Research Quarterly*, vol. 12, 1963, pp. 325–33.

Makridakis, Spyros and Steven C. Wheelwright, *Forecasting Methods for Management*, 5th ed. (New York: John Wiley & Sons, 1989), pp. 385–91.

Makridakis, S. and S. C. Wheelwright, *The Handbook of Forecasting: A Manager's Guide.* New York: John Wiley & Sons, 1982.

Trigg, D. W., "Monitoring a Forecasting System," *Operational Research Quarterly*, vol. 15, 1964, pp. 271–74.

Van Dobben De Bruyn, C. S., *Cumulative Sum Tests: Theory and Practice.* London: Griffin, 1968.

Woodward, R. H. and P. L. Goldsmith, *Cumulative Sum Techniques.* London: Oliver and Boyd, 1964.

11

Communicating the Forecast to Management

INTRODUCTION

The focus in the first 10 chapters has been on the technical and judgmental facets of preparing a forecast, with less attention to the equally important responsibility of presenting the forecast to management in a form that will communicate most effectively to key decision makers who are not well versed in the arcane language of forecasters. This chapter first analyzes the complicated task of communicating the forecast to management and then focuses on the wide range of nonforecasting tasks that occupy forecasters.

HELPING MANAGEMENT TO UNDERSTAND
THE FORECASTING PROCESS

While novice forecasters may believe that their work is completed once the model has been estimated and the forecasts are generated, the job has, in fact, just begun. Forecasts must be easily understandable to the other members of the organization who will make critical decisions based, in part, on the picture painted by the economic projections. One should not expect that the president of the company will necessarily understand terms such as *SAAR* and *real GDP*. In other words, it is up to the forecaster to assure that the quality and understandability of the written reports to management match the care with which the statistical models were prepared. The purpose of this section is to examine how a company's forecast needs can be evaluated and how the work of the forecaster can be communicated most effectively.

People who engage in forecasting often assume that supply will create its own demand. That is, forecast preparers are apt to believe that once the forecast has been prepared, the users will automatically accept and use it in their decision making. Unfortunately, this is not true, and many otherwise good forecasts languish in bookcases due to the inability of users to fathom what is being said.

Forecasters most often serve as advisors (staff support) to management, and therefore to maximize their effectiveness they must first earn management's trust and respect by preparing reports that speak directly to the forecast user's needs. Before presenting a forecast to management, it is logical (but not always obvious) that the business analyst should find out what management expects from him or her. This can be accomplished by adopting the following strategy:

1. Involve management in the forecasting process at the appropriate times.
2. Understand management's objectives.

One of the major shortcomings of forecasting operations is a lack of managerial involvement and participation. Periodic meetings between the users and the preparer are critical to the success of any forecasting system. In the initial stages of developing a forecasting program, the forecaster should use meetings as a vehicle to determine who the major forecast users are in the organization, how the forecasts are to be used in the decision-making process (budgeting, capital allocations, hiring decisions, plant construction), and what the potential consequences of forecast error are to management.

From the forecaster's perspective, these meetings also serve to educate consumers (users) about the nature of forecasting:

The forecaster's goals

Problems inherent to the forecasting process

The alternative approaches to forecasting and the wide variety of models

The meaning and source of forecast error

The limits of forecasting: what forecasters cannot do.

While it may seem strange to discuss what forecasters cannot do, management must understand these limits if the forecaster is to build credibility within an organization. Managers must understand that a forecast is not a substitute for their own judgment. Rather, it is simply a tool to be used to improve their decisions.

A forecast preparer must go to great lengths to identify what each manager's job requires and what his or her goals are. Individuals with distinct functional responsibilities have different forecast needs that determine, to a large extent, their perspectives on the role of the forecaster and their toleration of forecast error. Production managers, for example, are likely to favor a forecast that errs on the high side since, in many situations, production planning is easier with steady production runs. A production forecast that turns out to be too low may force them to expedite orders or to operate production facilities overtime, which may strain capacity and lessen efficiency. Marketing and sales managers may prefer forecasts that are too low since, in many organizations, these forecasts are used to establish sales quotas and are critical in determining the salaries of people in these areas. Purchasing managers may prefer optimistic forecasts, because shortages in resources used in the production process can be disastrous. Finally, senior management is generally interested in minimizing the aggregate forecast error, with no apparent bias in favor of forecasts that are too high or too low. We are not suggesting that you should prepare a separate forecast for each of these functional areas. A very effective strategy for satisfying all of these needs is to develop interval forecasts so that production and purchasing managers can use the upper limit in their planning, marketing and sales can use the lower limits in establishing quotas, and senior management can focus on the most likely scenario. Again, this is not a contrived range but one that reflects the realities of the forecasting environment.

There are also a number of specific issues that can be addressed in meetings with functional managers:

- Forecast preparers must communicate in terms familiar to the user rather than relying on the technical vocabulary of the preparer. Managers focus on people and events, and they prefer to have the forecast translated relative to their own needs. For example, rather than saying "the computer industry is projected to decline by 5 percent," managers find it more useful when we say, "if there is a 5 percent decline in the computer industry, company sales will decline by 4 percent." Alternatively, while it is commonplace for forecasting models to use measures such as share of voice in their models, the advertising manager is much more interested in advertising dollars. The key is to translate your forecasts into terms and concepts that are most useful to the forecast user.

- Managers tend to be more aware of internal policies and potential changes in these policies than do forecasters. For this reason, the forecaster should spend some time in the departmental meetings where these possibilities are discussed and planned. It is difficult enough to develop reliable forecasts with all of the relevant information. When this information is not available to the forecaster, the process of forecasting becomes impossible.

- Forecasts must be distinguished from expectations or plans. This is especially critical when evaluating the impact of a new-product introduction or a change in marketing strategies. For example, it is not at all uncommon for advertising managers to believe that the latest advertising program will boost sales by an excessively large amount (after all, that is their job). As a forecaster, you must be objective in your evaluation of the most likely impact of these programs.

- Since managers are not technicians, they are generally not familiar with the various models available to the forecaster. This lack of familiarity limits their ability to provide the forecaster with adequate information. As preparers, it is our responsibility to work with users in defining information and data requirements.
- As forecasters, we must convey the uncertainty that is implicit in all forecasts. Managers are not only interested in what might happen, but they are also interested in why the projected change might not materialize. As always, this discussion should be conducted in terms familiar to the user. Thus, instead of saying that there is a 7 percent chance that our forecast will be in error, we might say that if interest rates change by a larger amount than assumed in our forecast, volumes will be 4 percent below the estimate contained in the control forecast.

An effective two-way flow of information between users and preparers helps users to understand what the forecaster can and cannot do for them, and it heightens the forecaster's appreciation of the difficulties management faces when using the forecast in real-world situations. The final result of this ebb and flow of information is that the forecaster develops the needed credibility within the organization.

CONFLICTS BETWEEN USERS AND PREPARERS

The basis for conflict between forecast users and preparers exists because of their relative placement within the organization. Managers are, in the main, in line positions that require them to make decisions involving the commitment of financial resources, materials, and personnel based on their analysis of the company's future. They are rewarded when they make the correct decision and are subject to criticism when they are wrong. Conversely, forecasters are, most commonly, advisors and do not make the final decision on whether management should pursue a specific organizational objective or policy.

Managers are generally hesitant to make their decisions based on a forecast that they do not understand or do not agree with. For this reason, it is imperative that the forecaster spend time with each user explaining the forecast methodology (not in terms of technical factors, but conceptually), outlining the underlying assumptions, and trying to clarify when there are disagreements concerning assumptions. It is not uncommon for the user to have access to information that invalidates the original assumptions. In many cases, this lack of agreement on assumptions can be tied to the fact that forecasters tend to view the world from the perspective of a technician, while users have a managerial viewpoint.

QUANTIFYING MANAGERIAL NEEDS

The preceding sections of this chapter have highlighted the importance of ongoing communication between forecast users and preparers as well as the importance of understanding the needs of management. In this section, we focus on two specific examples of responsiveness to forecast requests from functional area managers.

SUPPORT-STAFF PROJECTIONS FOR PERSONNEL

It would seem to be a straightforward task to estimate the needed secretarial staff and the number of computer support personnel required for data entry. A small company can operate effectively with a rule of thumb such as one secretary per office manager, but a major corporation employing hundreds of secretaries is forced to engage in detailed planning. A request to a forecaster in a large corporation from the personnel department might be initiated in the following fashion:

Dear Ms. Forecaster:

As you know, both the annual budget and the five-year company plan will be finalized this coming October. We have been asked to provide a monthly projection of labor-hours and average wage rates for the secretarial staff and the data entry personnel over the next ten years. We have attached monthly data for labor requirements and wage rates for the last five years. Would you please provide us with the requested forecast magnitudes no later than the end of next week so that we can complete our report?

I. M. Labor,
Vice-President of Personnel

Although this letter may appear farfetched, it is not uncommon for a forecast to be passed along from manager to manager until it finally reaches someone who can generate the needed set of numbers. The attachment of historical data by the forecast user is a rare practice; users typically are not oriented to time series data collection.

After the arrival of such a request, there are two separate paths the forecaster may follow. First, a simple trend line or moving average might be applied to the data and extrapolated over the five-year time horizon. This procedure would require no more than a couple of hours, and the numbers could be returned to personnel far in advance of the two-week deadline. Alternatively, the forecaster might initiate a round of meetings with personnel officials to better understand their needs and to determine whether a more elaborate study is warranted. The scope of such a study is, however, constrained by both users' and preparers' perceptions of the importance of the forecast to management and by the resources available to the forecast unit. An admittedly worthwhile study may be supplanted by a two-hour trend analysis if budgeted funds are inadequate to support the cost of developing a more sophisticated regression model.

Assume that resources are available and that the forecaster has sent the following response:

Dear Mr. Labor:

In response to your recent letter requesting a forecast of labor-hours and wage rates for secretarial staff and data entry personnel, we have carried out a preliminary analysis that suggests that these two labor categories made up 28 percent of our operating costs during the current fiscal year, as compared to 21 percent only five years ago. Present indications are that this upward trend will continue, and a meeting is needed to clarify the specific factors causing the rise in this labor-expense category. As a way of focusing the discussion, here are some initial questions and comments:

1. Are there historical data available on the departmental breakdown of hours worked by the secretarial staff?
2. Have any major labor-saving equipment purchases been made for either the secretarial or data entry staff? For example, has word-processing equipment been installed in place of traditional, single-typewriter installations? Are any such purchases contemplated in the five-year plan?
3. What is the company's position concerning the use of part-time workers and overtime as a means of meeting peak-period demand?
4. Is data entry work mainly related to information to be found on standard invoices? If so, is it possible to substitute optical machine readers for data entry operators?
5. Is the company willing to implement labor-saving programs that will reduce the labor force or keep its size constant?
6. By industry norms, is the company currently over- or understaffed with secretaries and data entry workers relative to the volume of production and total employment?
7. Are wage rates currently tied to a cost-of-living escalator? If not, are workers likely to secure such a benefit in the next five years?
8. Have any studies been done on worker productivity? For example, are there historical data on the number of invoices entered per hour?
9. Does the company purposely maintain excess secretarial and data entry capacity to meet recurring intramonth peaks, such as record keeping during the first 10 days of the month? If so, is it possible to smooth out these peaks and reduce this excess?
10. Other than the stated need to meet budgetary and planning requirements, would a monthly update of this forecast be of use in internal personnel-planning activities?

Sincerely,
Ms. Forecaster

Although the list appears to be voluminous, it is a necessary first step in attempting to project hours worked and wage rates paid. The preparer needs to develop a clear perception of how the forecasted figures mesh with the decisions and constraints faced by management. For example, several of the questions listed by the forecaster dealt with potential discretionary actions by management to substitute machinery for labor. In some companies, such a strategy would be viewed as progressive, but in others, the desire not to agitate union leaders might preclude introduction of any labor-saving technology. Alternatively, a company might be reluctant to change past procedures unless the potential increase in costs from following traditional techniques begins to erode profitability. In effect, issues such as the substitution of capital for labor form the basic parameters of the forecaster's analysis. If radical innovations are precluded because of managerial constraints, then the forecaster need not worry so seriously about structural changes altering the firm's demand function for secretarial or data entry personnel.

A user's response to this list of questions will reveal whether he or she has any serious appreciation of how a personnel forecast could be used by the personnel department. At one extreme, the user may disclaim any responsibility for the request, arguing instead that the projections are just meaningless numbers that he or she has requested to include as part of personnel's contribution to the company budget and five-year plan. In this case, the user becomes merely an intermediary, with no commitment to the forecast and probably little interest in exploring related issues such as worker productivity and capital-labor substitution. Alternatively, the user may have a clear perception of why the forecast is needed, how the personnel projections fit into the budget and five-year plan, and the degree to which management is willing to introduce labor-saving technology.

When the forecast user is knowledgeable and cooperative, a quick and productive interchange will expose the time series data available for analysis and the forecast package needed to meet management's requirements for decision making. In the case of a forecast user who is merely serving as an intermediary or conduit for information, the forecaster can either revert to the initial strategy of producing a simple trend projection for personnel or seek out the ultimate user of the forecast (perhaps the vice-president of finance) and solicit the same detailed information about the need for a personnel projection.

Ultimately, the forecast preparer must be willing to keep probing until the exact nature of a user's request can be pieced together. It may, in fact, turn out to be a rather whimsical, spur-of-the-moment request intended to fill a page in the five-year plan and serve no other apparent purpose. In this case, the forecast merits no more than an afternoon's work. Suppose, however, that there is a critical need for the personnel estimate. It is then up to the forecaster to help the vice-president of personnel translate the request into a usable forecast. For example, a linear-trend extrapolation of the past five years' growth in monthly labor-hours for secretarial and data entry support might illuminate a possible path for the company's labor needs over the next five years. Such a trend outlook would ignore, however, the company's own forecast of monthly sales volume. Thus, the second stage of the forecast analysis would call for two or more multiple-regression demand models linking the dependent variables (demand for secretarial and data entry services) to independent variables such as unit sales volume, hours of production labor, or thousands of sales invoices processed. For example, a forecast for secretarial services could be generated by inserting predictions of future company sales into a simple regression equation that measured the historical fit between unit sales and hours of secretarial labor.

Although the regression approach uses more information than the trend forecast, the regression model still assumes an absence of structural change over the forecast period. Just as the amount of labor needed to produce an automobile changes over time, so the amount of secretarial or data entry labor per unit of output may be altered by technological changes. If these alterations are continuous and steady over time, they may be adequately incorporated in a trend model or multiple-regression equation. In many cases, however, the demand for labor is altered in a lumpy fashion by factors such as major capital purchases. Management's goal is to maximize profits (given certain societal and company-level constraints), and it must therefore be concerned with productivity improvements. Based on trend extrapolations and multiple-regression estimates, management may become convinced that it faces labor-cost increases that will outpace revenue growth and damage profitability. As an aid to decision making, management may ask for a study incorporating a major labor-saving expenditure for word-processing equipment and computers in the second year of the five-year plan. A forecast can provide insights into a broad spectrum of decision alternatives, but these options may be inadequately explored if management is not prodded and compelled to articulate clearly both the underlying reasons for a personnel forecast and how it plans to use the projection.

Table 11-1 suggests one way in which the original, terse request for a trend extrapolation may actually be fulfilled. Forecasters must spend time thinking about the ways in which information can be most usefully presented to users, and this necessitates the laborious process of questioning and prodding the user to find out what he or she really needs. The hypothetical forecast in Table 11-1 contains the annualized percentage rate of change for the company's unit sales, dollar sales, secretarial hours, data entry hours, and wage rates, as well as a summary ratio for secretarial and data entry salaries as a percentage of operating costs. The high and low projections for unit sales and dollar sales correspond to alternative assumptions for variables such as cyclical growth in the economy and market share. Similarly, the high and low projections for labor requirements are partially linked to variability in sales growth. Since decision makers are apt to be more familiar with sales forecasts

TABLE 11-1   **Format for a Hypothetical Five-Year Support-Staff Forecast (Annual Percentage Change)**

	Forecast Category	Year 1	Year 2	Year 3	Year 4	Year 5
Unit Sales:	High	7	6	6	5	5
	Low	3	3	4	4	4
Dollar Sales:	High	15	14	14	9	9
	Low	11	11	11	7	7
Personnel trend (hours worked)[a]						
Secretarial		8.5	8.5	8.5	8.5	8.5
Data Entry		9	9	9	9	9
Regression estimate (hours worked)[b]						
Secretarial:	High	12	11	11	10	10
	Low	8	8	9	9	9
Data Entry:	High	13	12	12	11	11
	Low	9	9	10	10	10
New Technology (hours worked)[c]						
Secretarial:	High	12	8	7	2	0
	Low	8	5	5	2	2
Data Entry:	High	13	9	9	5	2
	Low	9	6	7	7	6
Wage rates ($/hour)[d]						
Secretarial:	High	8	8	8	6	6
	Low	6	6	6	4	4
Data Entry:	High	7	7	7	5	5
	Low	5	5	5	3	3
Secretarial and data entry expenses as a percentage of sales revenue[e]						
Trend		28	29	30	31	32
Regression:	High	29	31	33	34	35
New technology:	High	28	28	25	22	20
Regression:	Low	28	30	32	33	34
New technology:	Low	28	28	26	24	22

[a] Based on trend extrapolation of last five years.
[b] Uses statistical demand models for both labor categories.
[c] Assumes capital expenditures for word-processing equipment and computers beginning in second year.
[d] Based on forecast of consumer price index.
[e] Total dollar expenditures for secretarial and data entry labor as a percent of total sales revenue.

than with labor-demand projections, the first two sets of estimates for unit and dollar sales provide an understandable reference base. For example, trend growth rates of 8.5 and 9.0 percent for secretarial and data entry labor, respectively, may appear to be contradictory to management since they exceed even the high growth rate for unit sales. This dichotomy would have to be documented by another table detailing past growth trends for personnel and unit sales, as well as by analysis explaining the specific historical factors that have caused secretarial and data entry labor-hours to outpace unit sales. The regression model yields growth factors for secretarial and data entry labor that are even higher than the trend estimates. Again, supplementary tables would outline the regression model and describe why the high-growth scenario caused demand for secretarial and data entry labor to climb at such a fast rate. For example, the predicted growth in unit sales might be concentrated in high-service commodities that require more voluminous customer contact (including written correspondence) and record keeping (warranty and complaint records stored on computer).

The third set of personnel projections, shown in Table 11-1, labeled "New Technology," assumes that major capital expenditures for word-processing equipment and computers are begun in the second year of the five-year plan. In this instance, supplementary tables would describe how the regression estimates have been modified to reflect the substitution of capital equipment for labor. At the bottom of Table 11-1, ratios summarize the percentage of annual revenue that would be absorbed by secretarial and data entry salary expenses. Since the company hires this labor in a large and competitive labor market, the competitive setting of market wage rates would not be affected by company hiring practices. Even under the new-technology scenario, the secretarial to data entry expense ratio does not start to fall until the third year. This decline results not from a smaller secretarial and data entry work force (hourly growth factors are not negative) but from revenue outpacing salary expenses for secretarial and data entry personnel.

Table 11-1, together with the support tables and text, is the forecaster's response to the cryptic request originally sent by the personnel department. The utility of such a presentation to decision makers is dependent on whether management is able to interpret the information and draw policy conclusions that lead to specific decisions pertaining to secretarial and data entry labor.

FORMULATING THE BUDGET: THE ROLE OF THE FORECASTER

Of all the uses and applications of forecasts, none is more directly tied to the company's daily functioning and its financial-control systems than the company budget. A mystique often surrounds the budgetary process and keeps a host of issues intertwined in a seemingly insoluble maze. Consider these questions:

1. How does a forecast become part of a budget?
2. What is a company budget? a fixed budget? a variable budget?
3. What is the level of regional disaggregation in the budget? the level of product disaggregation?
4. How does the budget reconcile the field sales (bottom-up) forecast with the statistical (top-down) forecast?

5. How are budgeted dollar magnitudes decomposed into volume and price subcomponents?
6. How are actual company results analyzed and compared to the budget? What is budgetary variance analysis, and how is this process related to ex post forecast evaluation?
7. When is the old budget discarded in favor of a new set of numbers?
8. How do the forecast and budget fit into the management information system?
9. How can time series concepts such as seasonality be adapted to fit into the budgetary framework?
10. How can contingency forecasts and probabilistic assessments be incorporated within the budget?

TABLE 11-2   Lamp Sales by Product Category and Region (Millions of Lamps)

Region and Lamp Category	Last Year Sales	Last Year Market Share	Two Years Ago Sales	Two Years Ago Market Share	Three Years Ago Sales	Three Years Ago Market Share
Region 1	$18.0	16.0%	$18.9	17.0%	$21.0	18.5%
Lamp style						
A	6.5		7.0		9.0	
B	4.5		4.8		4.5	
C	3.6		3.9		4.1	
D	3.4		3.2		3.1	
Region 2	$25.0	19.0%	$23.0	18.5%	$20.0	17.0%
Lamp style						
A	8.0		7.5		7.0	
B	6.2		5.7		5.2	
C	3.8		3.3		2.8	
D	7.0		6.5		5.0	
Region 3	$26.8	23.0%	$23.9	21.0%	$21.2	20.0%
Lamp style						
A	4.7		4.0		3.3	
B	8.1		7.4		6.7	
C	9.1		8.4		7.7	
D	4.9		4.1		4.5	
Region 4	$22.2	19.0%	$23.6	21.0%	$22.9	22.0%
Lamp style						
A	7.0		7.8		7.2	
B	6.5		7.1		7.1	
C	5.4		5.4		5.2	
D	3.3		3.3		3.4	
Total	$92.0	19.6%	$89.4	19.5%	$85.1	19.5%

These general issues can best be discussed by reference to the lamp manufacturer whose sales history and budget for the past three years are summarized in Tables 11-2 and 11-3, respectively. As shown in Table 11-2, four basic lamp styles are sold in the four major regional markets; the individual lamp designations correspond to price categories from high to low. The first row of Table 11-3 reproduces the total sales figures from Table 11-2 and shows the linkages from dollar sales to gross profit, operating profit, profit before taxes, and profit after taxes. The regional sales totals in Table 11-2 are accompanied by market penetration or share figures, which illustrate an overall deterioration in the market share of regions 1 and 4 and an improvement in that of regions 2 and 3. As seen in Table 11-3, net profit after taxes has not been growing; it has actually been falling as a percent of sales. In addition, the company's return on average investment has been declining over the same three-year period.

In anticipation of the October budget meeting, the vice-president of finance, who is in charge of the budget, has sent around the schematic in Figure

TABLE 11-3   Income Statement of Lamp Manufacturer for Three Previous Years (Millions of Dollars)

	Last Year	*Two Years Ago*	*Three Years Ago*
Net sales*	$92.0	$89.4	$85.1
Cost of sales	69.4	66.6	62.1
Gross profit	22.6	22.8	23.0
Percent of sales	24.6%	25.5%	27.0%
Selling expenses	10.4	9.9	9.0
General and administrative	5.8	5.6	6.5
Operating profit	6.4	7.3	7.5
Percent of sales	6.9%	8.2%	8.8%
Other income	0.2	0.1	0.1
Other expense	0.1	0.1	0.1
Net profit before income taxes	6.5	7.3	7.5
Provision for taxes	3.3	3.7	3.8
Net profit	$ 3.2	$ 3.6	$ 3.7
Percent of sales	3.5%	4.0%	4.4%
Return on investment	11.3%	12.3%	12.8%

* As explained in the text, company revenue, or net sales, will serve as the main forecast variable in this example.

FIGURE 11-1 Budgetary Schema: Integration of Top-Down and Bottom-Up
Forecasts of Sales Revenue

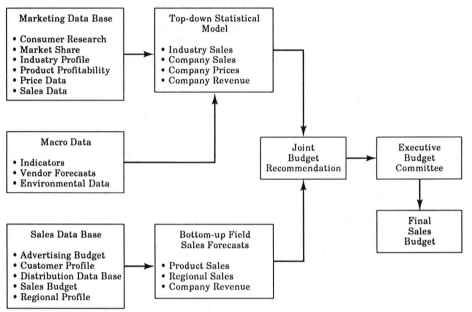

11-1 to illustrate the planning inputs needed from all departments and the logical flow of information during the preparation of the budget. Figure 11-1 helps to clarify the question concerning the logical relationship of the forecast to the budget. Literally all functional divisions in the lamp manufacturing company are represented in Figure 11-1, but the sales forecast marks the logical starting point for the planning information that flows throughout the company. The budget is a planning system designed to control and monitor all the functional activities within the company. In regard to the income statement in Table 11-3, forecasting activity will be defined as involving only the projection of total sales; the remainder of the activities related to the entries in the table have to do with cost and financial analysis and are viewed as outside the purview of forecasting. Although the forecaster is frequently called on to offer assumptions for inflation that can be used to estimate future materials costs and to provide interest rate projections needed in computing the cost of borrowed funds, the bulk of the forecaster's budgetary activity involves estimating unit and dollar sales for the company, using the time series techniques outlined in this text. It is revenue projections, not cost or net-income estimates, that are the focus of this discussion of budgeting.[1]

---

[1] For additional discussion of the role of forecaster, see: David I. Fisher, *The Corporate Economist*, Report No. 655 (New York: The Conference Board, 1975), pp. 6–12.

The budgetary schematic in Figure 11-1 is general enough to apply to almost any manufacturing organization, and it permits an overview that helps to integrate the examples for the lamp manufacturer provided in the following list. The first stage, as shown in Figure 11-1, involves the integration of statistical or top-down projections emanating from the marketing department, with field sales or bottom-up estimates provided by the sales department. The statistical, or top-down, approach involves the following general steps:

1. Develop the outlook for GDP and other key macroeconomic indicators, such as disposable income, that are closely related to lamp sales.
2. Prepare an industry-level forecast for lamp sales in physical units and dollars, and decompose these figures into the four main product subcategories.
3. Regionalize the national sales figures to match the four major markets served by the company.
4. Making use of external information concerning the competitive environment and internal market research related to consumer preferences and company capacity, develop market-share projections for the company.
5. Produce a forecast of total company sales in dollars and physical units for the coming budgetary year, and disaggregate by region and by product line (to match the historical detail in Table 11-2).

The procedures followed in linking aggregate economic measures to company lamp sales will be an amalgam of the many techniques outlined in the previous chapters of this text. Some statistical forecasters may jump from GDP to total lamp sales in one equation and may never make an explicit market-share assumption. Other business analysts might spend thousands of dollars to develop a disaggregated statistical model of industry lamp sales and then use nonstatistical or judgmental assessments of the company's market share for each major industry product line. There are literally hundreds of ways the top-down forecaster could arrive at a set of projections for lamp sales by region and product line that matched the format of Table 11-2; however, they would all share a common analytical view in which company sales were linked to an explicit set of numerical assumptions for aggregate economic performance.

There is equal, or perhaps even greater, diversity in the approaches followed by sales departments to generate the field sales projections for next year's budget. The underlying procedure of bottom-up forecasting is one of pyramiding sales estimates from individual salespeople to reach a grand total. For example, in the case of the lamp manufacturer, each of the four regions might be staffed by 10 salespeople. The head of company sales would request each of the 40 salespeople to project lamp sales by price category for the coming year, and then these projections would be totaled by region and by product category to match the categories in Table 11-2. On the other hand, each of the

40 salespeople would have privileged access to information about sales characteristics in his or her region that would permit incorporation of factors not available to top-down forecasters in the company's headquarters. For instance, the opening or closing of a major furniture store in a salesperson's territory might swamp cyclical forces that normally dominate lamp sales.

On the other hand, it is unlikely that the entire sales staff is operating with the same set of macroeconomic assumptions for the economy. Many salespeople will make no explicit assumptions at all about next year's real GDP growth, and even if the head of the sales department provides them with a baseline projection for the economy, it is unlikely that the sales force will be capable of interpreting and applying the information uniformly.[2] Field sales forecasts are nevertheless important, because they are compiled from internal or ground-level information about prospects in each of the company's subregions. The statistical projections are necessary because they build on the broader economic and sociopolitical environment surrounding the company.

Table 11-4 outlines a first-stage comparison between field sales and statistical projections of lamp sales for the coming year. These are, of course, hypothetical numbers, but they point out a number of questions that typically arise when the two groups get together to synthesize their projections:

1. Are the field sales estimates used to set quotas for the salespeople? If so, will they be biased on the low side?
2. If quotas or targets are independent of the budget, will the field sales estimates be merely wild guesses devoid of any serious thought?
3. Are salespeople in each region using the same set of assumptions for the prices of next year's lamps? Do they mesh with the top-down assumptions?
4. Are sales estimates affected by differentials in lamp profitability? That is, have salespeople inflated estimates for high-priced lamps because they yield higher commissions?
5. How can statistical projections incorporate unique regional influences, such as sales promotions by competitors?
6. Is it legitimate to assume that the company's promotional and advertising expenses will continue to absorb the same percentage of the sales dollar?

As shown in the first two columns of Table 11-4, the field sales and statistical forecasts differ substantially. For some users of the budget, the key characteristic is the level of total dollar sales; for others, it may be the composition of the physical units sold. For example, the marketing department, based on historical and industry norms, may always allocate 2.5 percent of total budgeted sales revenue for advertising and product promotion. The actual

---

[2] This is not meant to disparage the talent of sales personnel, who are, in fact, quite knowledgeable about the customer-to-company environment.

TABLE 11-4 **Comparative Estimates of Budgeted Lamp Revenue**
(Millions of Dollars)

Region and Lamp Category	Field Sales Forecast (1)	Statistical Projection (2)	Recommended Budget (3)	Optimistic Outlook (4)	Pessimistic Outlook (5)	Final Budget (6)
Region 1	$23.0	$19.0	$20.2	$23.0	$19.0	$21.0
Lamp style						
A	$8.0	$6.5	$6.7	$8.0	$6.5	$6.9
B	$6.0	$4.7	$5.2	$6.0	$4.7	$5.4
C	$5.0	$4.3	$4.3	$5.0	$4.3	$4.5
D	$4.0	$3.5	$4.0	$4.0	$3.5	$4.2
Region 2	$27.0	$24.0	$25.2	$27.0	$24.0	$26.0
Lamp style						
A	$8.0	$6.7	$6.8	$8.0	$6.7	$7.0
B	$6.8	$5.7	$6.8	$6.8	$5.7	$7.0
C	$4.2	$3.6	$3.6	$4.2	$3.6	$3.8
D	$8.0	$8.0	$8.0	$8.0	$8.0	$8.2
Region 3	$30.8	$26.8	$26.9	$30.8	$26.8	$27.7
Lamp style						
A	$4.7	$3.7	$3.7	$4.7	$3.7	$3.9
B	$9.1	$9.1	$9.1	$9.1	$9.1	$9.3
C	$10.5	$9.1	$9.1	$10.5	$9.1	$9.3
D	$6.5	$4.9	$5.0	$6.5	$4.9	$5.2
Region 4	$27.2	$24.0	$24.5	$27.7	$23.5	$25.3
Lamp style						
A	$8.0	$7.0	$7.0	$8.0	$7.0	$7.2
B	$7.5	$8.0	$7.5	$8.0	$7.5	$7.7
C	$6.4	$5.7	$6.0	$6.4	$5.7	$6.2
D	$5.3	$3.3	$4.0	$5.3	$3.3	$4.2
Total	$108.0	$93.8	$96.8	$108.5	$93.5	$100.0

distribution of advertising dollars for particular lamp product lines may be viewed as more important than the dollar value of budgeted total revenue. The purchasing department, however, needs to order materials and supplies for four physically distinct lamp styles, and it must also plan for the distribution of the finished products to four regional warehouses, depending on the regional sales volume incorporated in the budget.

The third column of Table 11-4 presents a recommended budget for the coming year, which the head forecaster prepared. Again, the numbers are hypothetical, but the steps used to arrive at the numbers are suggestive of the compromises that often occur. The process of arriving at a synthesis of sales and statistical forecasts involves a step-by-step discussion for each of the 16 lamp/region combinations (four regions multiplied by four products). For example, the sales forecast of $4 million of style D lamp sales in region 1 is higher than the statistical projection of $3.5 million. In turn, both those projections exceed the corresponding historical figures for past sales shown in Table 11-2. Whereas the statistical projection for style D lamp sales in region 1 envisions a continuation of the historical trend (see Table 11-2), the sales forecast of a substantial jump in sales of low-priced lamps was based on the assumed opening of a major new company employing low-wage laborers in region 1. Although there is substantial variance in the two forecasts, only a follow-up phone call is necessary to check the legitimacy of the salesperson's assumption. In this case, it was decided to accept the higher sales number. However, in region 3, just the opposite occurred for forecasted sales of high-priced, style A lamps. In this case, the sales numbers called for no growth, but the statistical projections yielded a substantial drop resulting from a predicted regional decline in disposable income. Of course, a phone call cannot be made to confirm a future decline in future income, but the underlying reasons can be articulated and discussed.

The act of merging the forecasts in the first two columns of Table 11-4 into the proposed budget in the third column involves compromise, analysis, and persuasion. In some unreconcilable cases, the proposed number may merely split the difference between the original bottom-up and top-down numbers. In addition to the proposed budget in column 3, optimistic and pessimistic projections were generated in columns 4 and 5 by summing the highest and lowest regional sales figures, respectively. The data in the first five columns of Table 11-4, together with an analysis of the key underlying controversies, would be forwarded to the vice-president of finance.

Budgets are not decided unilaterally, and the importance of the annual budget necessitates a meeting of the vice-president of finance with his or her counterparts throughout the company. Since all activity levels within the company will be geared to the budgeted figures for the coming year, all functional areas of the company must be able to respond to the proposed budgeted numbers in terms of the implications for the financial and physical operations of the company. For example, the forecasted jump in style D lamp sales in region 2 may cause warehouse demand to exceed local warehouse capacity, and the drop in style A lamp sales in region 3 may introduce inventory problems at the main factory. The company forecaster is likely to be called on to repeat many of the explanations presented earlier to the sales staff, as well as to discuss contingencies in the general economic outlook. The forecaster's persuasiveness will be one of the key factors shaping the final budget, shown in column 6 of Table 11-4, but the ultimate decision rests in the hands of the vice-president of finance. The final budget in column 6 is closest to the recommended budget presented in column 3. The statistical forecaster may feel that the budget in column 6 is too high, but the vice-president of finance is the person faced with the ultimate responsibility of achieving the targeted magnitudes for net income implied by the budget. The difference between the forecaster's original recommendation in column 2 and the final budget in column 6 may reflect a difference in optimism between a conservative forecaster and an optimistic finance officer, or it may be due to substantive issues, such as the predicted success of a planned advertising campaign or the effect of lamp imports on domestic sales. The process of formulating the revenue portion of the budget requires diplomacy and salesmanship; the task of explaining the variance between actual and budgeted figures is objective, analytical, and full of potential pitfalls.

In many companies, the top-down, or statistical, forecaster is also given the job of monitoring the monthly sales figures, writing explanations to reconcile the difference between actual and budgeted figures, and preparing analytical updates to management that can be used to determine when significant budget revisions are required. Part of the advantage of having an ongoing forecasting staff prepare preliminary budget figures is that the volume, price, and dollar magnitudes will be internally consistent. That is, when the forecasted dollar figures are deflated by prices, they should yield the original volume numbers projected by the forecast models. That is only true, however, of the preliminary forecast in column 2 of Table 11-4, which is directly under the control of the forecaster. The final budget in column 6 becomes a hybrid prediction that incorporates suggestions from many groups. The final budget of $100 million in column 6 may, for example, be a revised version of an earlier budget that was sent to the president and rejected because budgeted revenue and net income were inadequate to support capital expenditures to which the president was already emotionally committed. The vice-president of finance may simply have been forced to inflate all recommended budgeted revenue categories in column 3 to reach total revenue of $100 million. Thus, on top of compromises between alternative forecast figures, there are frequently unilateral additions to or subtractions from the consensus forecast that may partially or completely distort volume-price-revenue relationships. Ultimately, actual sales results must be explained and the budget critically appraised. The task of the forecaster becomes one of candidly analyzing the changing forces in the economy and bringing them to bear on management's monthly budget decisions.

Suppose that total revenue was below budgeted revenue by $2.1 million in January and February, and that corporate headquarters is seriously questioning the company's ability to achieve either the targeted revenue for the remainder of the year or the full-year projections. In effect, the forecaster's original set of statistical projections serves as a measuring stick for a host of interrelated questions:

1. How accurately did the original statistical projections for volume and the assumptions for lamp prices measure up against actual volume and prices?

2. Did the national and industrial assumptions vary significantly from actual economic conditions?

3. Using the original forecast models and the actual values for the independent variables in January and February, would the ex post forecasts have differed significantly from the forecaster's initial assessment in column 2 of Table 11-4?

4. In those cases where there was a significant difference between the forecaster's projections and the final budget, what part of the error (final budget less actual sales) was due to the forecaster's error (forecast less actual sales), and what part was due to managerial fiat (final budget less forecast)?

5. What unanticipated internal company-level events occurred? Will they lead to secondary repercussions during the remainder of the year?

6. What level of sales would be needed in each of the remaining months to achieve the final budget? the original forecast?

These and other questions must be answered before the forecaster responds to management's request for an explanation of actual results during January and February. Unless the forecaster saves information such as Table 11-4 for future comparisons, he or she may be falsely labeled the originator of the final budget. It is hard enough to explain one's own errors, but it is folly to assume the responsibility for budgetary adjustments made by others.

Question 4 in the preceding list can be used to set up a simple error-analysis model:

(Final Budget − Actual Sales)

$$= \text{(Forecast − Actual Sales)} + \text{(Final Budget − Forecast)} \quad \textbf{(11-1)}$$

or

$$\text{Actual Error} = \text{Forecast Error} + \text{Managerial Error.} \quad \textbf{(11-2)}$$

This error model decomposes the difference between actual and budgeted results into one portion that is the forecaster's direct responsibility, and the residual, which represents a discretionary adjustment made by management. As a starting point, the forecaster may use such an error model to gain some perspective on the primary sources of error.

Questions 2 and 5 in the preceding list focus on the external and internal framework of assumptions that can be used to highlight both forecast error and managerial error. That is, was the gap between the forecaster's recommended budget and the budget adopted by management due to differences in opinion about the economy and industry, or was it due to differing assessments of internal company programs? For example, at a prior budgetary meeting, management might have disavowed the forecaster's prediction of a severe decline in aggregate economic activity in January and February. Alternatively, management might have been more confident than the forecaster that a new advertising campaign would boost lamp sales and offset cyclical forces. Ideally, both the forecaster and management would have explicitly articulated their assumptions. Realistically, only the forecaster will have listed his or her assumptions explicitly, and the forecaster will have only general impressions of management's assumptions based on terse comments made at budgetary meetings.

Although the process of assessing management's reasons for altering the budget is highly subjective, feedback to management is necessary if past mistakes are to be avoided in the future. As necessary to the forecaster as the evaluation of errors in managerial judgment related to the budget is the attempt to quantify the impact of the forecaster's own erroneous assumptions. With a statistical forecasting model, it is a simple matter to incorporate actual values of the independent variables during January and February to produce an ex post forecast of lamp sales for these two months. The difference between the ex post forecast and the forecaster's original recommended budget becomes a precise measure of the forecast error arising from incorrect external assumptions about the economy. If the ex post forecast still differs significantly from the actual level of lamp sales in January and February, then the problem may lie within the structure of the forecasting model rather than with the assumed values of the independent variables. The analysis of the variance between actual and budgeted sales combines, therefore, traditional statistical error evaluation with a more subjective interpretation of the effect of managerial actions on budgetary levels.

A sample response to management's request for an explanation is as follows:

Lamp sales in both January and February were below budgeted levels, owing to the unexpected severity of the economic downturn in regions 2 and 3, the intense competition from off-brand lamps in region 1, the minimal success of the new advertising program in region 4, and the generally overly optimistic assessment of our field sales force. Although the forecast department had foreseen a softening in lamp demand in regions 2 and 3 because of a predicted economic slowdown, the decline in regional employment has been unprecedented based on past economic downturns. Two of the major employers in regions 2 and 3, plywood and automobile manufacturers, respectively, are extremely sensitive to interest rate movements, and the record interest rates recently experienced have devastated plywood and automobile sales. The subsequent decline in employment has undermined lamp sales in regions 2 and 3 by 3,000 units. The bad experience in region 1 can be ascribed to the appearance of off-brand lamps, which have made serious inroads into our market share of low-priced lamps and reduced region 1 lamp sales by 1,500 units. The new advertising campaign in region 4 has not been successful in taking away lamp sales from the established competition in this region. Based on marketing data collected from our retail distributors, the advertising campaign produced new sales of only 1,000 units. Finally, field sales estimates have been overly optimistic for practically all lamp categories in January and February. Although the following are only approximations of the relative contribution to budgetary error, it appears that incorrect cyclical assumptions by the forecast department were responsible for 20 percent of the budgetary error, off-brand lamp sales 10 percent, and independent adjustments by management 35 percent. Of these factors, none are viewed as temporary phenomena that will affect sales only in January and February. A revised forecast is attached.

An ex post budgetary analysis such as the foregoing one is an attempt to weave statistical and company-level institutional factors into a coherent fabric that is readily understood by decision makers faced with the task of reevaluating the budget. The next step is to move from an evaluation of past results to a reappraisal of the budget during the remaining portion of the budgetary year.

The springboard for budgetary changes is the error analysis carried out for lamp sales in January and February. Major changes in the budget are unsettling to all segments of a corporation, since an extensive web of plans has been built around the existing budget. Many of the participants in the budgetary reassessment have a vested interest in keeping the budget at its present size, since a host of maintenance, personnel, and production programs will be curtailed if the budget is significantly reduced. The forecaster is faced with the task of moving from a description of what has happened to cause sales to fall below the budget in January and February to the preparation of a new recommended budget. According to the foregoing analysis, roughly 20 percent of the budgetary error in January was due to the forecaster's model, with the remainder largely due to discretionary additions by management.

An attempt to reach the existing budget by offsetting the decline in the first two months with higher sales in the last 10 months might be the first method suggested by those unfamiliar with seasonally adjusted annualized rates (SAAR), but this analytical tool can help to cast aside what might otherwise appear to be a reasonable forecast revision. Although budget numbers have traditionally been presented to management on the basis of expected actual monthly magnitudes, it is important for management to be conversant with SAAR presentations, since forecasts are often prepared on a seasonally adjusted annual basis and then converted to a monthly rate and deseasonalized. Suppose, for example, that a company had budgeted sales of $200 million for the year and actual sales of $50 million for the first quarter. It does not necessarily follow that the company is achieving a level of sales consistent with the budget. If the first-quarter seasonal index for sales is 80, then sales are running at an SAAR of $250 million. If, however, the seasonal index for the first quarter is 110, then the SAAR is $181.8 million. In both cases, the results could be consistent with the quarterly budget, but budgetary data need to be annualized and seasonally adjusted before conclusions are reached about the achievability of the budget.

In Table 11-5, the monthly lamp sales figures have been seasonally adjusted and annualized. The actual sales results can be analyzed in several ways. First, as shown in column 3, if full-year sales maintain the SAAR of the first two months, then total lamp sales will be $91.9 million, or $8.1 million less than the original budget in column 1. Since total sales were below the budget by $2.1 million in January and February, this projection of continuity in the SAAR implies an actual worsening in terms of absolute deviation from the budget. Second, the sales data can be analyzed by asking what SAAR for sales would have to be maintained from March through December to hit the targeted budget of $100 million. As shown in column 4, lamp sales must attain an SAAR of $105 during the last 10 months to reach the original budget forecast of $100 million. When compared to the year-to-date's SAAR of $91.9 million, the annualized sales rate would have to increase roughly 12 percent.

At this point, the logical question is whether there is any reason to expect a budgetary turnaround. The analysis in the previous section suggested that much of management's past overoptimism was due to inflated field sales projections, misplaced confidence in the new advertising program, and lack of awareness concerning new regional competitors. The forecaster's original recommended budget in Table 11-4 called for sales of $93.8 million, with the new recommendation slightly lower at $91.0 million. In effect, the forecaster is saying that business conditions will degenerate, since the SAAR during the first two months was $91.9 million. In column 2, the actual sales results in the first two months are substituted for the original budgeted figures. The presentation of seasonally adjusted annualized data can help to move man-

TABLE 11-5   Budgetary Revenue Analysis (Millions of Dollars)

Lamp Style	Original Budget[a] (1)	Original Budget Less Year to Date[b] (2)	Year to Date[c] (SAAR) (3)	Needed Budget[d] (SAAR) (4)	Recommended Budget (5)
A	$25.0	$24.5	$23.0	$26.0	$22.7
B	$29.4	$28.9	$26.8	$30.5	$26.6
C	$23.8	$23.1	$21.6	$25.1	$21.5
D	$21.8	$21.4	$20.5	$23.4	$20.2
Total	$100.0	$97.9	$91.9	$105.0	$91.0

[a] Column 6 in Table 11-4.

[b] January and February lamp sales were $2.1 million below the budget. These numbers are substituted into the budget, with all other monthly figures kept at their budgeted levels.

[c] Rate for the first two months of the year.

[d] Sales rate needed for the last 10 months of the budget to achieve original budget target of $100 million.

agement away from a budget that it might otherwise cling to until too late in the year. That is, since actual sales were below the budget by $2.1 million in January and February (see column 2), it may not seem too unrealistic to simply add $210,000 to each of the original revenue projections for the remaining 10 months and stick with the original budget total of $100 million. When actual sales data are converted to a seasonally adjusted annualized rate (column 3), compared to the SAAR of sales needed to keep the budget and contrasted with current business conditions, the likelihood of being able to make up for past budgetary shortfalls can be appraised more objectively.

The budget is fixed only insofar as tradition and institutional rigidity keep it so, and the use of analytical tools such as SAARs, contingency forecasts, and subjective probability distributions provide additional information on which management can base budgetary decisions. The use of seasonally adjusted annualized data in the preceding example helped to clarify the actual results for lamp sales in January and February and to place the existing budget in sharper contrast. Before an existing budget is abandoned, however, management may request a contingency forecast that gives low, medium, and high sales prospects for lamp sales in the remainder of the year and attaches a subjective probability to each occurrence. Table 11-6 contains such a forecast assessment, and each sales scenario can be compared to the existing budget.

Only under the high-growth, or optimistic, scenario shown in Table 11-6 does sales revenue reach $100 million, and this outcome is given a subjective probability of only 10 percent. The control, or medium-growth, outlook calls for a 60 percent chance that revenue will reach $91 million, and the low-growth scenario attaches a 30 percent probability that sales will hit $88 million. This set of contingency projections would be accompanied by text material outlining the presumed economic environment and detailing the requisite assumptions. No comparable set of projections is likely to be available from the field sales force, since the rapid turnaround time required for a monthly budgetary review

TABLE 11-6   A Contingency Forecast for Lamp Sales (Millions of Dollars)

Lamp Style	Original Budget (1)	Pessimistic or Low Sales* (2)	Control or Medium Sales* (3)	Optimistic or High Sales* (4)
A	$25.0	$22.0	$22.7	$25.3
B	29.4	26.1	26.6	30.0
C	23.8	20.8	21.5	23.9
D	21.8	19.1	20.2	21.8
Total	$100.0	$88.0	$91.0	$101.0

* Low, control, and optimistic are assigned subjective probabilities of 30 percent, 60 percent, and 10 percent, respectively.

is more amenable to computerized modeling than is the time-consuming process of multiple contacts with the field sales force. Given the analysis of sales in January and February, the SAAR data, and the contingency projections in Table 11-6, management might still elect to stay with the existing budget for another month, but it is unlikely that it would do so without a sense of foreboding. The credibility of the forecaster affects management's willingness to abandon the old budget in favor of a new version that means lower profitability and greater stockholder discontent.

GETTING MANAGEMENT TO USE THE FORECAST

Much of an individual forecaster's success is dependent on management's understanding of forecasting as an ongoing process (rather than a once-a-month activity) and management's willingness to integrate forecasts into the decision-making process. In turn, there are several guidelines that enhance the likelihood of management's use of forecast output:

1. The forecaster should strive to have the forecast available prior to the time that management has to make critical decisions. For example, if purchasing has to place its orders in the early spring, the forecast must be available by early in the fourth quarter. Alternatively, advertising decisions frequently have a lead time of up to a year. Finally, personnel requirements may depend on conditions specified by labor contracts.

2. The forecast should be delivered to management in a useful format. Some functional managers (purchasing, operations, and personnel, for example) prefer the forecast in terms of units while others (sales, finance, and top management) prefer dollar forecasts. An additional aspect of the format is the time frame—some managers prefer monthly forecasts while others are content with quarterly or annual forecasts.

3. The usefulness of the forecast will be maximized if contingency forecasts are included. While managers frequently focus on the most likely outcome, the inclusion of contingency projections enhances the utility of the forecast by providing a quantitative picture of the likely outcomes and by encouraging managers to think in terms of forecast ranges.

4. Technical jargon should be kept to a minimum. As a rule, management is most comfortable with forecasts that are presented to them in terms that match the daily vocabulary of the business environment. For example, rather than using phrases such as "autoregressive models," or "correlation coefficients," you will be better served to refer to "historical patterns" and "percentage of change explained," respectively.

5. Make certain that you are comfortable with and understand the forecast techniques that you are using. If you do not thoroughly understand the

techniques you are using, you will not be able to answer questions effectively—that is, you will tend to fall back on technical jargon rather than translating the explanation into understandable prose. Inability to explain what you are doing to top management means that you will lessen your credibility (regardless of how accurate your forecasts turn out to be).

6. Strive to make the forecasts available to all potential users. As the person in charge of forecasting, it is your responsibility to determine who is likely to benefit from having access to the forecasts.

7. Always incorporate a discussion of historical forecast accuracy with your forecast analysis. If you have been accurate in the past, this heightens the credibility of your current forecast. If you have not been accurate, it is better to candidly assess past problems and place the current forecast in that context.

EVOLUTION OF THE FORECASTING PROCESS: SHARING THE RESPONSIBILITY

THE FORECASTER'S RESPONSIBILITIES

Aside from the obvious responsibilities of developing forecasts and providing these to management in a timely fashion, the evolving nature of corporate forecasting suggests several new directions for research effort:[3]

- Macroeconomic or aggregate forecasting must increasingly focus on change and risk. The first step in forecasting is the collection and analysis of large volumes of data. The constantly changing nature of the external environment, however, requires that we shift the focus from quantitative absolutes—"When will the recession end or begin?" or "What will volumes be next year?"—to qualitative or contingency-based assessments— "What could go wrong?" or "Will average growth be greater or less than historical patterns suggest?"

- The role of industry- and firm-level forecasting must be upgraded from a secondary to a primary position. Historically, forecasters have been able to predict changes in their specific sectors by relying on an analysis of aggregate trends. Over the course of the past 20 years, however, there has been a tremendous divergence in the growth paths followed by various sectors of the aggregate economy. For example, the service sector appears to be relatively recession proof (although the recession of 1990–1991 showed the service sector to have problems, too), especially when con-

---

[3] Lawrence Chimerine, "The Changing Role of Economists in Planning," *The Journal of Business Forecasting*, Spring 1988, pp. 2–7.

trasted with the durable goods industries. However, even within the durable goods industries we find that some industries (for example, the computer industry) are expanding at the same time that others (for example, the automobile industry) are declining (to be fair, these shifts also represent a long-run, or noncyclical, decline in the size of GM, Ford, and Chrysler relative to the world industry). Forecasters, must, if they are to continue to play a useful role in advising top management, spend much more time on the dynamics of growth and decline at the industry and firm level.

- Research on the impact of the environment must be expanded. Managers need to know more about how the changing environment will affect their business. Much could be gained, for example, by incorporating the implications of market research into the modeling process. Changes in consumption patterns, product substitutions, and alterations in distribution channels are but a few of the areas where market research studies can enhance the effectiveness of the forecaster.

- Furthermore, every effort should be made to communicate frequently with managers, using the vocabulary of the workplace. While this point has been made earlier, the necessity of frequent conversations with top management and with managers in functional areas cannot be overstated. Management must be advised when economic trends do or do not correspond to expectations. Similarly, managers must be notified of the reasons for a major revision in the sales forecast, as well as the risks associated with specific changes in the external environment.

- The increasingly competitive nature of the economy dictates that forecasters delve into the area of cost forecasting (this is different than cost accounting, but hopefully forecasters will try to incorporate internal information available from the accounting department). Cost forecasting is especially appropriate when considering the possibility of substituting capital for labor, raw-materials substitutions, and alternative sources for the resources used in the specific production process.

- The marketplace for many goods and services has been internationalized over the past 15 years, and forecasters must be familiar with global trends in macroeconomic activity as well as the shifts in microeconomic patterns that may cause, for example, a docile competitor in Germany to seek out new markets in the United States.

SHAPING THE FORECAST ENVIRONMENT: MANAGEMENT'S RESPONSIBILITIES

As a starting point, senior management should formally establish, in writing, a plan that outlines the purposes of the forecasting department. Since the forecaster generally serves in an advisory capacity, this statement of purposes should be concise and objective. Rather than stating that "the objective shall be to provide forecasts," the purpose statement should be explicit—"the forecasting department will provide monthly and annual forecasts of sales revenue and unit sales."

The second aspect of the managerial plan should be an explicit statement of the areas of responsibility. This should include statements regarding the level of detail, the time frame, the forecast format, methods of evaluation and monitoring, and other similar factors:

> The monthly and annual forecasts will be prepared for the 13 major product lines in 10 regions within the United States and six regions in foreign markets. The forecast will incorporate the plans of both the marketing and sales divisions. Each month, actual sales and volume results will be contrasted with budgeted estimates, with the variances highlighted and explained.

The third and final aspect of the managerial plan should be a statement of the measures that will be used to evaluate the forecasting department's performance. Some of these measures will be quantitative in nature while others will be subjective. For example, we might include a statement that revenue forecasts should fall within ±5 percent of actual revenues (an unforeseeable exogenous shock would not be counted against the forecaster). By establishing a measure of accuracy such as ±5 percent, top management provides important information to the forecaster about the consequences of forecast error to the company. Such a measure should not be arbitrarily pulled from the air, and it should be a topic for discussion and reflection between top management and the corporate forecaster.

The three areas most closely tied to forecasting are budgeting, planning, and scheduling, and the procedures put in place for these areas must be applied consistently to forecasting. A well-structured forecasting environment provides management with several advantages:

- It provides management with a consistent environment within which to evaluate the impact of both external and internal events. Since the forecasting, budgeting, planning, and scheduling projections were prepared under the same set of "old" assumptions, they will be revised under the same set of "new" assumptions.
- It permits management to react more quickly to changing economic, political, and environmental circumstances.
- It enables management to incorporate their perceptions of uncertainty into the decision-making process, thereby minimizing the impact of "surprises."

THE POLITICS OF FORECASTING

Diagnosing the needs of forecast users is an important task, but the forecaster must never forget that business forecasts are inherently political. Having devoted considerable time and effort to the technical task of preparing a forecast and to the equally arduous job of translating the projections into a report, the business forecaster may make the mistake of naively offering a forecast and waiting for universal acclaim. Since control of the forecast implies, to a large extent, control over major expenditure and resource allocation decisions within the company, a politically naive forecaster may become a pawn in a struggle for power within the company. Unfortunately, many forecasters, while superbly trained and skilled in the techniques of statistical model building, are unprepared for the hostile political environment in which they operate. Forecasters, who may have purposely chosen to work in a quantitative area as a way of escaping political in-fighting, suddenly find themselves in the midst of a power struggle among vice-presidents who wish to control the forecast.

Political and human-relations skills are likely to be much more important than technical expertise when it comes to determining the success or failure of a company's forecasting department. In many cases, a forecast is perceived as a threat to the job security of those individuals whose department is placed in the spotlight by what the forecaster views as an objective projection. A forecast can be a threat regardless of its accuracy; the following case serves to highlight the nature of this conflict.

Several years ago, a large and profitable financial consulting company undertook the task of upgrading its marketing and forecasting functions. The marketing organization had been reorganized, and market development managers were made responsible for creating business opportunities within major sectors such as the banking, automotive, lumber, and chemical industries. Since the company was mainly serving the western and midwestern sections of the United States, it was the forecaster's responsibility to develop statistical models that would link national activity to these two regions. It immediately became apparent that a market development manager would be able to get more resources if he or she could demonstrate high profit potential in his or her industrial sector. For example, the manager of market development for lumber products touted his area, arguing that the pent-up demand for housing and, therefore, lumber products meant increased demand for consulting services. The forecaster, however, correctly projected that the bulk of the increase in lumber activity would be confined to the southeastern and southwestern portions of the country, regions not served by the consulting company. Unfortunately, the forecaster did not anticipate the devastating impact his projection would have on the lumber manager's credibility, and he unveiled his findings after the vice-president of marketing had publicly proclaimed a glowing outlook for consulting services in the lumber industry. Rather than discuss his preliminary findings with the market manager of lumber products and the vice-president of marketing to discover in advance any potential areas of controversy, the forecaster inadvertently placed himself in an adversarial position and caused a permanent rift between the marketing and forecasting departments.

The inherently political dimension of forecasting can logically be traced to the independent nature of the functional areas that comprise the modern corporation. A seemingly minor forecast change in the company's annual budget can lead to major revisions in production plans, estimated cash-flow patterns, and projected inventory requirements. Thus, in a sense, the powerful political tremors generated by a forecast are merely a reflection of the important role economic forecasts play in the overall planning process of a business. Forecasts are an integral part of the overall information system that continuously feeds new data into the company's strategic planning process.

Here are some basic guidelines to assist you in dealing with the political nature of the forecasting process:

- Know the people who use the forecast.
- Know the users' concerns.
- Work to resolve problems before they become insurmountable.
- Make certain that forecast users are not misapplying or misinterpreting your estimates and your reports.
- Defend your forecasts against purely political arguments designed to postpone bad news or artificially create good news.

COMMUNICATION, ORGANIZATION, AND POLITICS: SUMMARY AND OVERVIEW

The task of conveying economic forecast information to management cannot be separated from the job of analyzing management's forecast needs. It is not the responsibility of management to present the forecaster with a predetermined format into which the economic projections are merely entered and passed back to management. The quality and quantity of prepared forecast information depends on the technical skills of the forecaster and the resources at his or her disposal, but management must be able to articulate the general steps followed in making key business decisions. If no coherent or logical process is followed in deciding whether to build a new regional plant or expand an existing factory, a forecaster will be hard pressed to provide information that enhances the decision-making process. If, however, an established decision-making framework for capital expenditures is in existence, the forecaster can analyze the needed information flows and determine where forecast information can best be used.

Literally all companies have formalized budgeting systems, so it would seem that budgeting is one activity for which the forecaster would always be able to make productive use of his or her skills. Even here, however, the forecaster remains at the mercy of company traditions, as well as management's technical and economic literacy. If decision makers do not wish to deal with contingency forecasts, subjective probabilities, and seasonally adjusted data, the breadth of the forecaster's potential contribution will be reduced correspondingly.

Even if the forecaster has a clear mandate and a willing executive audience, the ability to communicate effectively with top management may be muted if the forecaster is misplaced in the organization. Often the forecaster is the bearer of bad, or at least unpopular, news, and the farther that position is removed from key decision makers, the less likely the forecaster is to be able to present forecast data in the most appropriate format. A manager of forecasting who successively reports to a director, a manager, an assistant vice-president, and a vice-president may find that the budgetary report has been reformulated and watered down by the time it reaches the vice-president. In the end, therefore, effective forecasting is as much bound up with institutional considerations and communication with management as it is with quantitative forecasting techniques.

As a forecaster, you must be aware that your work will be used by people who have different goals and responsibilities than you do. These people deal with issues such as product design, inventory levels, customer complaints, product liability, competition, television coverage, lawsuits, and a host of other matters. You need to be cognizant of their positions and the goals that they are striving to achieve. Much of what they do falls under the title "crisis management," and you will go a long ways toward building trust if you help them in these situations. In fact, the value of the forecaster is often tied to nonforecasting activities in support of top management's quest to find answers to the interrelated questions regarding the outlook for the firm. It is to these nonforecasting activities that we now turn.

THE BUSINESS ECONOMIST AT WORK: NONFORECASTING ACTIVITIES

Table 11-7 is a duplicate of Table 1-1 in Chapter 1, and, as a starting point and ending point, it helps to illuminate the problem of evaluating management's forecast needs. As pointed out in a study of corporate economists completed in the early 1970s by the Conference Board, forecasters are also called on to provide the following:

Economic advice for management

Assignments in public relations

TABLE 11-7 Forecast Users Within the Corporate Structure and Their Forecast Needs*

Business Areas

Personnel	Finance	Marketing	Production	Law	Purchasing	Top Management
General economic conditions	General economic conditions	General economic conditions	General economic conditions	General economic conditions	General economic conditions	General economic conditions
Labor demand	Total dollar sales	Total dollar sales	Labor demand	Environmental constraints	Labor demand	Total sales and cost
Wage rates	Production costs	Unit sales by product and region	Unit sales by product and region	Social trends	Product demand by region and customer	Environmental constraints
Economic trends and turning points	Economic trends and turning points	Economic trends and turning points	Plant production	Economic trends	Raw-materials demand	Social trends
Personnel projections	Product inventory	Product prices	Product inventory	New-product technology	Product backlog	Economic trends and turning points
Fringe benefits	Cash flow	Consumer preferences	Equipment expenditure		Economic trends and turning points	Capital expenditures
	Interest rates	New-product technology	Plant expansion		Interest rates	New-product technology
	Capital expenditures	Product inventory	Environmental constraints		Product prices	
			New-product technology		Capital expenditures	
					Environmental constraints	

* These are merely generalizations about the most obvious forecast needs of each functional area. Although the law department is not ordinarily seen as a user of personnel projections, such information could become very useful if a new pension law was being analyzed.

Counsel on management-science techniques

Analysis of industry competition

Acquisition studies

Responses to government agency requests

Service on executive committees[4]

Although a forecaster needs to have the overall forecast profile of Table 11-7 firmly in mind, the reality is that the forecasting activities listed in this table provide a starting point for a wide variety of nonforecasting projects which make use of the forecaster's training in economics, business, and statistics.

NEW DIRECTIONS FOR THE BUSINESS FORECASTER

Unfortunately, economic forecasting and economic forecasters fell on relatively hard times during the second half of the 1980s. Many companies either eliminated their forecasting departments or radically reduced the size of the forecasting staff in response to the phenomenon of disinflation (a generally falling price level). The problems associated with collapsing prices were particularly acute in the oil sector, in the real estate industry, and in the financial sector. These trends were compounded by the forces of deregulation which led banks, savings and loans, and other financial-service businesses to retrench.

When businesses face declining prices and falling asset values, they must economize and attempt to cut their overhead costs. Unfortunately for forecasters, the demand for their services is income elastic, and a sharp drop in prices, sales, and profits in many businesses meant these companies were forced to eliminate a wide range of staff services. When political uncertainty (for example, in the Middle East) begins to overwhelm predictable economic trends and cycles, the demand for traditional business forecasts and related services begins to fade. Just as all other goods and services in the economy, forecasters found that the demand for their services was, in fact, cyclical.

Marina v.N. Whitman, Vice President and Group Executive for the Public Affairs Staff of General Motors Corporation, has recently noted that forecasters make their greatest contributions to management when they quantify the trade-offs facing management, when they focus on most-likely outcomes (rather than budgeted targets), and when they utilize contingency analysis to highlight alternative strategic options.[5]

---

[4] David I. Fisher, *The Corporate Economist*, Report No. 655 (New York: The Conference Board, 1975), p. 13.

[5] Marina v.N. Whitman, "New Directions for the Business Economist," *Business Economics*, January 1987, pp. 51–55.

As suggested above, individuals trained as forecasters spend much of their time performing other, complementary, analytical services:

- Analyzing regional, industry, and global growth prospects
- Projecting inflation rates and interest rates
- Preparing short-run and long-run corporate plans
- Evaluating industry and company pricing policies
- Preparing position papers on major policy issues
- Working with legal departments on antitrust issues
- Carrying out productivity studies
- Forecasting the impact of exchange rate movements
- Linking forecasts to investment plans
- Evaluating the impact of government policies
- Developing detailed cost projections.

While the range of topics is great, there is a common thread—namely, the application of economic and business theory and statistical techniques to problems brimming with uncertainty. As suggested in the preceding list, it is the forecaster's ability to provide a service of high value in times of uncertainty which will be the key to the future success of this profession.

QUESTIONS FOR DISCUSSION AND ANALYSIS

1. In problem 1 at the end of chapter 10, a forecaster was charged with the responsibility of projecting revenue from state lottery ticket sales in Virginia.
   a. How might the simple error model in equation (11-2) be used by the forecaster? What "managerial" actions might state employees take that would produce "managerial" error?
   b. Could the contingency approach set forth in Table 11-6 be used to facilitate projections for lottery revenue? What contingencies does Virginia face?
2. It is frequently argued that the process of communicating the forecast to management is as important as the actual development of forecasts. Why do you think this is true? Specifically, once the forecast has been prepared, has the forecaster fulfilled his or her responsibility? Why or why not?
3. Explain the relationship between budgeting, planning, and forecasting.
4. What is meant by a contingency forecast, and how are they useful to management?
5. Is it important to distinguish between macroeconomic and microeconomic issues in dealing with management? Why or why not?
6. What are the responsibilities of management in the forecasting process? of the forecaster?
7. Why do you think there are conflicts between forecast users and forecast preparers?
8. What is meant by the phrase, *the politics of forecasting*?

REFERENCES FOR FURTHER STUDY

Adams, F. Gerald, *The Business Forecasting Revolution.* New York: Oxford University Press, 1986.

Armstrong, J. Scott, *Long-Range Forecasting, From Crystal Ball to Computer.* New York: Columbia University Press, 1978.

Ascher, William, *Forecasting: An Appraisal for Policy Makers and Planners.* Baltimore: The Johns Hopkins University Press, 1979.

Bell, Daniel, "Twelve Modes of Prediction," in *Penguin Survey of the Social Sciences,* J. Gould, ed. Baltimore: Penguin Books, 1966.

Dalrymple, D. J., "Sales Forecasting Practices: Results from a United States Survey," *International Journal of Forecasting,* vol. 3, 1987, pp. 379–92.

Lendblom, Charles, "The Science of Muddling Through," *Public Administration Review,* vol. 19, Spring 1959, pp. 79–88.

Makridakis, S., "The Art and Science of Forecasting: An Assessment and Future Directions," *International Journal of Forecasting,* vol. 2, 1986, pp. 15–39.

Makridakis, S. and S. C. Wheelwright, eds., *The Handbook of Forecasting: A Manager's Guide,* 2nd ed. New York: John Wiley & Sons, 1987.

Milne, Thomas E., *Business Forecasting: A Managerial Approach.* New York: Longman Group, 1975.

Naylor, Thomas, *Corporate Planning Models.* Reading, Mass.: Addison-Wesley, 1978.

Naylor, Thomas and Horst Schouland, "A Survey of Users of Corporate Planning Models," *Management Science,* vol. 22, no. 9, May 1976, pp. 927–37.

Strauch, Ralph E., "'Squishy' Problems and Quantitative Methods," *Policy Sciences,* vol. 6, no. 2, June 1975, pp. 175–84.

Wolf, Charles, Jr., "Scoring the Economic Forecasters," *The Public Interest,* vol. 88, Summer 1987, pp. 48–55.

Appendices

Appendix A

Student t Distribution

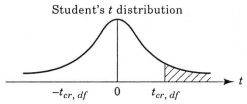

Student's t distribution

TABLE A-1   Student's t Distribution

Degrees of Freedom	Probability of a Value Greater in Value than the Table Entry					
	0.005	0.01	0.025	0.05	0.1	0.15
1	63.657	31.821	12.706	6.314	3.078	1.963
2	9.925	6.965	4.303	2.920	1.886	1.386
3	5.841	4.541	3.182	2.353	1.638	1.250
4	4.604	3.747	2.776	2.132	1.533	1.190
5	4.032	3.365	2.571	2.015	1.476	1.156
6	3.707	3.143	2.447	1.943	1.440	1.134
7	3.499	2.998	2.365	1.895	1.415	1.119
8	3.355	2.896	2.306	1.860	1.397	1.108
9	3.250	2.821	2.262	1.833	1.383	1.100
10	3.169	2.764	2.228	1.812	1.372	1.093
11	3.106	2.718	2.201	1.796	1.363	1.088
12	3.055	2.681	2.179	1.782	1.356	1.083
13	3.012	2.650	2.160	1.771	1.350	1.079
14	2.977	2.624	2.145	1.761	1.345	1.076
15	2.947	2.602	2.131	1.753	1.341	1.074
16	2.921	2.583	2.120	1.746	1.337	1.071
17	2.898	2.567	2.110	1.740	1.333	1.069
18	2.878	2.552	2.101	1.734	1.330	1.067
19	2.861	2.539	2.093	1.729	1.328	1.066
20	2.845	2.528	2.086	1.725	1.325	1.064
21	2.831	2.518	2.080	1.721	1.323	1.063
22	2.819	2.508	2.074	1.717	1.321	1.061
23	2.807	2.500	2.069	1.714	1.319	1.060
24	2.797	2.492	2.064	1.711	1.318	1.059
25	2.787	2.485	2.060	1.708	1.316	1.058
26	2.779	2.479	2.056	1.706	1.315	1.058
27	2.771	2.473	2.052	1.703	1.314	1.057
28	2.763	2.467	2.048	1.701	1.313	1.056
29	2.756	2.462	2.045	1.699	1.311	1.055
30	2.750	2.457	2.042	1.697	1.310	1.055
∞	2.576	2.326	1.960	1.645	1.282	1.036

Source: Reprinted from Table IV in Sir Ronald A. Fisher, *Statistical Methods for Research Workers,* 13th ed. (Edinburgh: Oliver & Boyd Ltd. 1963), with the permission of the publisher and the late Sir Ronald Fisher's literary executor.

Appendix B _____

Critical Values for the *F* Distribution

TABLE B-1 5% (Roman type) and 1% (boldface type) points for the distribution of F

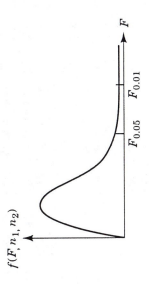

$f(F, n_1, n_2)$

$F_{0.05}$ $F_{0.01}$

F

n_1 Degrees of Freedom in the Numerator

n_2	1	2	3	4	5	6	7	8	9	10	11	12	14	16	20	24	30	40	50	75	100	200	500	∞	n_2
1	161	200	216	225	230	234	237	239	241	242	243	244	245	246	248	249	250	251	252	253	253	254	254	254	1
	4,052	**4,999**	**5,403**	**5,625**	**5,764**	**5,859**	**5,928**	**5,981**	**6,022**	**6,056**	**6,082**	**6,106**	**6,142**	**6,169**	**6,208**	**6,234**	**6,258**	**6,286**	**6,302**	**6,323**	**6,334**	**6,352**	**6,361**	**6,366**	
2	18.51	19.00	19.16	19.25	19.30	19.33	19.36	19.37	19.38	19.39	19.40	19.41	19.42	19.43	19.44	19.45	19.46	19.47	19.47	19.48	19.49	19.49	19.50	19.50	2
	98.49	**99.00**	**99.17**	**99.25**	**99.30**	**99.33**	**99.34**	**99.36**	**99.38**	**99.40**	**99.41**	**99.42**	**99.43**	**99.44**	**99.45**	**99.46**	**99.47**	**99.48**	**99.48**	**99.49**	**99.49**	**99.49**	**99.50**	**99.50**	
3	10.13	9.55	9.28	9.12	9.01	8.94	8.88	8.84	8.81	8.78	8.76	8.74	8.71	8.69	8.66	8.64	8.62	8.60	8.58	8.57	8.56	8.54	8.54	8.53	3
	34.12	**30.82**	**29.46**	**28.71**	**28.24**	**27.91**	**27.67**	**27.49**	**27.34**	**27.23**	**27.13**	**27.05**	**26.92**	**26.83**	**26.69**	**26.60**	**26.50**	**26.41**	**26.35**	**26.27**	**26.23**	**26.18**	**26.14**	**26.12**	
4	7.71	6.94	6.59	6.39	6.26	6.16	6.09	6.04	6.00	5.96	5.93	5.91	5.87	5.84	5.80	5.77	5.74	5.71	5.70	5.68	5.66	5.65	5.64	5.63	4
	21.20	**18.00**	**16.69**	**15.98**	**15.52**	**15.21**	**14.98**	**14.80**	**14.66**	**14.54**	**14.45**	**14.37**	**14.24**	**14.15**	**14.02**	**13.93**	**13.83**	**13.74**	**13.69**	**13.61**	**13.57**	**13.52**	**13.48**	**13.46**	
5	6.61	5.79	5.41	5.19	5.05	4.95	4.88	4.82	4.78	4.74	4.70	4.68	4.64	4.60	4.56	4.53	4.50	4.46	4.44	4.42	4.40	4.38	4.37	4.36	5
	16.26	**13.27**	**12.06**	**11.39**	**10.97**	**10.67**	**10.45**	**10.27**	**10.15**	**10.05**	**9.96**	**9.89**	**9.77**	**9.68**	**9.55**	**9.47**	**9.38**	**9.29**	**9.24**	**9.17**	**9.13**	**9.07**	**9.04**	**9.02**	
6	5.99	5.14	4.76	4.53	4.39	4.28	4.21	4.15	4.10	4.06	4.03	4.00	3.96	3.92	3.87	3.84	3.81	3.77	3.75	3.72	3.71	3.69	3.68	3.67	6
	13.74	**10.92**	**9.78**	**9.15**	**8.75**	**8.47**	**8.26**	**8.10**	**7.98**	**7.87**	**7.79**	**7.72**	**7.60**	**7.52**	**7.39**	**7.31**	**7.23**	**7.14**	**7.09**	**7.02**	**6.99**	**6.94**	**6.90**	**6.88**	
7	5.59	4.74	4.35	4.12	3.97	3.87	3.79	3.73	3.68	3.63	3.60	3.57	3.52	3.49	3.44	3.41	3.38	3.34	3.32	3.29	3.28	3.25	3.24	3.23	7
	12.25	**9.55**	**8.45**	**7.85**	**7.46**	**7.19**	**7.00**	**6.84**	**6.71**	**6.62**	**6.54**	**6.47**	**6.35**	**6.27**	**6.15**	**6.07**	**5.98**	**5.90**	**5.85**	**5.78**	**5.75**	**5.70**	**5.67**	**5.65**	
8	5.32	4.46	4.07	3.84	3.69	3.58	3.50	3.44	3.39	3.34	3.31	3.28	3.23	3.20	3.15	3.12	3.08	3.05	3.03	3.00	2.98	2.96	2.94	2.93	8
	11.26	**8.65**	**7.59**	**7.01**	**6.63**	**6.37**	**6.19**	**6.03**	**5.91**	**5.82**	**5.74**	**5.67**	**5.56**	**5.48**	**5.36**	**5.28**	**5.20**	**5.11**	**5.06**	**5.00**	**4.96**	**4.91**	**4.88**	**4.86**	

n_2 degrees of freedom in the denominator.

TABLE B-1 (Continued)

n₁ Degrees of Freedom in the Numerator

n_2	1	2	3	4	5	6	7	8	9	10	11	12	14	16	20	24	30	40	50	75	100	200	500	∞	n_2
9	5.12	4.26	3.86	3.63	3.48	3.37	3.29	3.23	3.18	3.13	3.10	3.07	3.02	2.98	2.93	2.90	2.86	2.82	2.80	2.77	2.76	2.73	2.72	2.71	9
	10.56	8.02	6.99	6.42	6.06	5.80	5.62	5.47	5.35	5.26	5.18	5.11	5.00	4.92	4.80	4.73	4.64	4.56	4.51	4.45	4.41	4.36	4.33	4.31	
10	4.96	4.10	3.71	3.48	3.33	3.22	3.14	3.07	3.02	2.97	2.94	2.91	2.86	2.82	2.77	2.74	2.70	2.67	2.64	2.61	2.59	2.56	2.55	2.54	10
	10.04	7.56	6.55	5.99	5.64	5.39	5.21	5.06	4.95	4.85	4.78	4.71	4.60	4.52	4.41	4.33	4.25	4.17	4.12	4.05	4.01	3.96	3.93	3.91	
11	4.84	3.98	3.59	3.36	3.20	3.09	3.01	2.95	2.90	2.86	2.82	2.79	2.74	2.70	2.65	2.61	2.57	2.53	2.50	2.47	2.45	2.42	2.41	2.40	11
	9.65	7.20	6.22	5.67	5.32	5.07	4.88	4.74	4.63	4.54	4.46	4.40	4.29	4.21	4.10	4.02	3.94	3.86	3.80	3.74	3.70	3.66	3.62	3.60	
12	4.75	3.88	3.49	3.26	3.11	3.00	2.92	2.85	2.80	2.76	2.72	2.69	2.64	2.60	2.54	2.50	2.46	2.42	2.40	2.36	2.35	2.32	2.31	2.30	12
	9.33	6.93	5.95	5.41	5.06	4.82	4.65	4.50	4.39	4.30	4.22	4.16	4.05	3.98	3.86	3.78	3.70	3.61	3.56	3.49	3.46	3.41	3.38	3.36	
13	4.67	3.80	3.41	3.18	3.02	2.92	2.84	2.77	2.72	2.67	2.63	2.60	2.55	2.51	2.46	2.42	2.38	2.34	2.32	2.28	2.26	2.24	2.22	2.21	13
	9.07	6.70	5.74	5.20	4.86	4.62	4.44	4.30	4.19	4.10	4.02	3.96	3.85	3.78	3.67	3.59	3.51	3.42	3.37	3.30	3.27	3.21	3.18	3.16	
14	4.60	3.74	3.34	3.11	2.96	2.85	2.77	2.70	2.65	2.60	2.56	2.53	2.48	2.44	2.39	2.35	2.31	2.27	2.24	2.21	2.19	2.16	2.14	2.13	14
	8.86	6.51	5.56	5.03	4.69	4.46	4.28	4.14	4.03	3.94	3.86	3.80	3.70	3.62	3.51	3.43	3.34	3.26	3.21	3.14	3.11	3.06	3.02	3.00	
15	4.54	3.68	3.29	3.06	2.90	2.79	2.70	2.64	2.59	2.55	2.51	2.48	2.43	2.39	2.33	2.29	2.25	2.21	2.18	2.15	2.12	2.10	2.08	2.07	15
	8.68	6.36	5.42	4.89	4.56	4.32	4.14	4.00	3.89	3.80	3.73	3.67	3.56	3.48	3.36	3.29	3.20	3.12	3.07	3.00	2.97	2.92	2.89	2.87	
16	4.49	3.63	3.24	3.01	2.85	2.74	2.66	2.59	2.54	2.49	2.45	2.42	2.37	2.33	2.28	2.24	2.20	2.16	2.13	2.09	2.07	2.04	2.02	2.01	16
	8.53	6.23	5.29	4.77	4.44	4.20	4.03	3.89	3.78	3.69	3.61	3.55	3.45	3.37	3.25	3.18	3.10	3.01	2.96	2.89	2.86	2.80	2.77	2.75	
17	4.45	3.59	3.20	2.96	2.81	2.70	2.62	2.55	2.50	2.45	2.41	2.38	2.33	2.29	2.23	2.19	2.15	2.11	2.08	2.04	2.02	1.99	1.97	1.96	17
	8.40	6.11	5.18	4.67	4.34	4.10	3.93	3.79	3.68	3.59	3.52	3.45	3.35	3.27	3.16	3.08	3.00	2.92	2.86	2.79	2.76	2.70	2.67	2.65	
18	4.41	3.55	3.16	2.93	2.77	2.66	2.58	2.51	2.46	2.41	2.37	2.34	2.29	2.25	2.19	2.15	2.11	2.07	2.04	2.00	1.98	1.95	1.93	1.92	18
	8.28	6.01	5.09	4.58	4.25	4.01	3.85	3.71	3.60	3.51	3.44	3.37	3.27	3.19	3.07	3.00	2.91	2.83	2.78	2.71	2.68	2.62	2.59	2.57	
19	4.38	3.52	3.13	2.90	2.74	2.63	2.55	2.48	2.43	2.38	2.34	2.31	2.26	2.21	2.15	2.11	2.07	2.02	2.00	1.96	1.94	1.91	1.90	1.88	19
	8.18	5.93	5.01	4.50	4.17	3.94	3.77	3.63	3.52	3.43	3.36	3.30	3.19	3.12	3.00	2.92	2.84	2.76	2.70	2.63	2.60	2.54	2.51	2.49	
20	4.35	3.49	3.10	2.87	2.71	2.60	2.52	2.45	2.40	2.35	2.31	2.28	2.23	2.18	2.12	2.08	2.04	1.99	1.96	1.92	1.90	1.87	1.85	1.84	20
	8.10	5.85	4.94	4.43	4.10	3.87	3.71	3.56	3.45	3.37	3.30	3.23	3.13	3.05	2.94	2.86	2.77	2.69	2.63	2.56	2.53	2.47	2.44	2.42	
21	4.32	3.47	3.07	2.84	2.68	2.57	2.49	2.42	2.37	2.32	2.28	2.25	2.20	2.15	2.09	2.05	2.00	1.96	1.93	1.89	1.87	1.84	1.82	1.81	21
	8.02	5.78	4.87	4.37	4.04	3.81	3.65	3.51	3.40	3.31	3.24	3.17	3.07	2.99	2.88	2.80	2.72	2.63	2.58	2.51	2.47	2.42	2.38	2.36	
22	4.30	3.44	3.05	2.82	2.66	2.55	2.47	2.40	2.35	2.30	2.26	2.23	2.18	2.13	2.07	2.03	1.98	1.93	1.91	1.87	1.84	1.81	1.80	1.78	22
	7.94	5.72	4.82	4.31	3.99	3.76	3.59	3.45	3.35	3.26	3.18	3.12	3.02	2.94	2.83	2.75	2.67	2.58	2.53	2.46	2.42	2.37	2.33	2.31	
23	4.28	3.42	3.03	2.80	2.64	2.53	2.45	2.38	2.32	2.28	2.24	2.20	2.14	2.10	2.04	2.00	1.96	1.91	1.88	1.84	1.82	1.79	1.77	1.76	23
	7.88	5.66	4.76	4.26	3.94	3.71	3.54	3.41	3.30	3.21	3.14	3.07	2.97	2.89	2.78	2.70	2.62	2.53	2.48	2.41	2.37	2.32	2.28	2.26	

n_2 degrees of freedom in the denominator.

TABLE B-1 (Continued)

n₁ Degrees of Freedom in the Numerator

n₂	1	2	3	4	5	6	7	8	9	10	11	12	14	16	20	24	30	40	50	75	100	200	500	∞	n₂
24	4.26	3.40	3.01	2.78	2.62	2.51	2.43	2.36	2.30	2.26	2.22	2.18	2.13	2.09	2.02	1.98	1.94	1.89	1.86	1.82	1.80	1.76	1.74	1.73	24
	7.82	**5.61**	**4.72**	**4.22**	**3.90**	**3.67**	**3.50**	**3.36**	**3.25**	**3.17**	**3.09**	**3.03**	**2.93**	**2.85**	**2.74**	**2.66**	**2.58**	**2.49**	**2.44**	**2.36**	**2.33**	**2.27**	**2.23**	**2.21**	
25	4.24	3.38	2.99	2.76	2.60	2.49	2.41	2.34	2.28	2.24	2.20	2.16	2.11	2.06	2.00	1.96	1.92	1.87	1.84	1.80	1.77	1.74	1.72	1.71	25
	7.77	**5.57**	**4.68**	**4.18**	**3.86**	**3.63**	**3.46**	**3.32**	**3.21**	**3.13**	**3.05**	**2.99**	**2.89**	**2.81**	**2.70**	**2.62**	**2.54**	**2.45**	**2.40**	**2.32**	**2.29**	**2.23**	**2.19**	**2.17**	
26	4.22	3.37	2.98	2.74	2.59	2.47	2.39	2.32	2.27	2.22	2.18	2.15	2.10	2.05	1.99	1.95	1.90	1.85	1.82	1.78	1.76	1.72	1.70	1.69	26
	7.72	**5.53**	**4.64**	**4.14**	**3.82**	**3.59**	**3.42**	**3.29**	**3.17**	**3.09**	**3.02**	**2.96**	**2.86**	**2.77**	**2.66**	**2.58**	**2.50**	**2.41**	**2.36**	**2.28**	**2.25**	**2.19**	**2.15**	**2.13**	
27	4.21	3.35	2.96	2.73	2.57	2.46	2.37	2.30	2.25	2.20	2.16	2.13	2.08	2.03	1.97	1.93	1.88	1.84	1.80	1.76	1.74	1.71	1.68	1.67	27
	7.68	**5.49**	**4.60**	**4.11**	**3.79**	**3.56**	**3.39**	**3.26**	**3.14**	**3.06**	**2.98**	**2.93**	**2.83**	**2.74**	**2.63**	**2.55**	**2.47**	**2.38**	**2.33**	**2.25**	**2.21**	**2.16**	**2.12**	**2.10**	
28	4.20	3.34	2.95	2.71	2.56	2.44	2.36	2.29	2.24	2.19	2.15	2.12	2.06	2.02	1.96	1.91	1.87	1.81	1.78	1.75	1.72	1.69	1.67	1.65	28
	7.64	**5.45**	**4.57**	**4.07**	**3.76**	**3.53**	**3.36**	**3.23**	**3.11**	**3.03**	**2.95**	**2.90**	**2.80**	**2.71**	**2.60**	**2.52**	**2.44**	**2.35**	**2.30**	**2.22**	**2.18**	**2.13**	**2.09**	**2.06**	
29	4.18	3.33	2.93	2.70	2.54	2.43	2.35	2.28	2.22	2.18	2.14	2.10	2.05	2.00	1.94	1.90	1.85	1.80	1.77	1.73	1.71	1.68	1.65	1.64	29
	7.60	**5.42**	**4.54**	**4.04**	**3.73**	**3.50**	**3.33**	**3.20**	**3.08**	**3.00**	**2.92**	**2.87**	**2.77**	**2.68**	**2.57**	**2.49**	**2.41**	**2.32**	**2.27**	**2.19**	**2.15**	**2.10**	**2.06**	**2.03**	
30	4.17	3.32	2.92	2.69	2.53	2.42	2.34	2.27	2.21	2.16	2.12	2.09	2.04	1.99	1.93	1.89	1.84	1.79	1.76	1.72	1.69	1.66	1.64	1.62	30
	7.56	**5.39**	**4.51**	**4.02**	**3.70**	**3.47**	**3.30**	**3.17**	**3.06**	**2.98**	**2.90**	**2.84**	**2.74**	**2.66**	**2.55**	**2.47**	**2.38**	**2.29**	**2.24**	**2.16**	**2.13**	**2.07**	**2.03**	**2.01**	
32	4.15	3.30	2.90	2.67	2.51	2.40	2.32	2.25	2.19	2.14	2.10	2.07	2.02	1.97	1.91	1.86	1.82	1.76	1.74	1.69	1.67	1.64	1.61	1.59	32
	7.50	**5.34**	**4.46**	**3.97**	**3.66**	**3.42**	**3.25**	**3.12**	**3.01**	**2.94**	**2.86**	**2.80**	**2.70**	**2.62**	**2.51**	**2.42**	**2.34**	**2.25**	**2.20**	**2.12**	**2.08**	**2.02**	**1.98**	**1.96**	
34	4.13	3.28	2.88	2.65	2.49	2.38	2.30	2.23	2.17	2.12	2.08	2.05	2.00	1.95	1.89	1.84	1.80	1.74	1.71	1.67	1.64	1.61	1.59	1.57	34
	7.44	**5.29**	**4.42**	**3.93**	**3.61**	**3.38**	**3.21**	**3.03**	**2.97**	**2.89**	**2.82**	**2.76**	**2.66**	**2.58**	**2.47**	**2.38**	**2.30**	**2.21**	**2.15**	**2.08**	**2.04**	**1.98**	**1.94**	**1.91**	
36	4.11	3.26	2.86	2.63	2.48	2.36	2.28	2.21	2.15	2.10	2.06	2.03	1.98	1.93	1.87	1.82	1.78	1.72	1.69	1.65	1.62	1.59	1.56	1.55	36
	7.39	**5.25**	**4.38**	**3.89**	**3.58**	**3.35**	**3.18**	**3.04**	**2.94**	**2.86**	**2.78**	**2.72**	**2.62**	**2.54**	**2.43**	**2.35**	**2.26**	**2.17**	**2.12**	**2.04**	**2.00**	**1.94**	**1.90**	**1.87**	
38	4.10	3.25	2.85	2.62	2.46	2.35	2.26	2.19	2.14	2.09	2.05	2.02	1.96	1.92	1.85	1.80	1.76	1.71	1.67	1.63	1.60	1.57	1.54	1.53	38
	7.35	**5.21**	**4.34**	**3.86**	**3.54**	**3.32**	**3.15**	**3.02**	**2.91**	**2.82**	**2.75**	**2.69**	**2.59**	**2.51**	**2.40**	**2.32**	**2.22**	**2.14**	**2.08**	**2.00**	**1.97**	**1.90**	**1.86**	**1.84**	
40	4.08	3.23	2.84	2.61	2.45	2.34	2.25	2.18	2.12	2.07	2.04	2.00	1.95	1.90	1.84	1.79	1.74	1.69	1.66	1.61	1.59	1.55	1.53	1.51	40
	7.31	**5.18**	**4.31**	**3.83**	**3.51**	**3.29**	**3.12**	**2.99**	**2.88**	**2.80**	**2.73**	**2.66**	**2.56**	**2.49**	**2.37**	**2.29**	**2.20**	**2.11**	**2.05**	**1.97**	**1.94**	**1.88**	**1.84**	**1.81**	
42	4.07	3.22	2.83	2.59	2.44	2.32	2.24	2.17	2.11	2.06	2.02	1.99	1.94	1.89	1.82	1.78	1.73	1.68	1.64	1.60	1.57	1.54	1.51	1.49	42
	7.27	**5.15**	**4.29**	**3.80**	**3.49**	**3.26**	**3.10**	**2.96**	**2.86**	**2.77**	**2.70**	**2.64**	**2.54**	**2.46**	**2.35**	**2.26**	**2.17**	**2.08**	**2.02**	**1.94**	**1.91**	**1.85**	**1.80**	**1.78**	
44	4.06	3.21	2.82	2.58	2.43	2.31	2.23	2.16	2.10	2.05	2.01	1.98	1.92	1.88	1.81	1.76	1.72	1.66	1.63	1.58	1.56	1.52	1.50	1.48	44
	7.24	**5.12**	**4.26**	**3.78**	**3.46**	**3.24**	**3.07**	**2.94**	**2.84**	**2.75**	**2.68**	**2.62**	**2.52**	**2.44**	**2.32**	**2.24**	**2.15**	**2.06**	**2.00**	**1.92**	**1.88**	**1.82**	**1.78**	**1.75**	
46	4.05	3.20	2.81	2.57	2.42	2.30	2.22	2.14	2.09	2.04	2.00	1.97	1.91	1.87	1.80	1.75	1.71	1.65	1.62	1.57	1.54	1.51	1.48	1.46	46
	7.21	**5.10**	**4.24**	**3.76**	**3.44**	**3.22**	**3.05**	**2.92**	**2.82**	**2.73**	**2.66**	**2.60**	**2.50**	**2.42**	**2.30**	**2.22**	**2.13**	**2.04**	**1.98**	**1.90**	**1.86**	**1.80**	**1.76**	**1.72**	

n₂ degrees of freedom in the denominator.

TABLE B-1 (Continued)

n_2	1	2	3	4	5	6	7	8	9	10	11	12	14	16	20	24	30	40	50	75	100	200	500	∞	n_2
											n_1 *Degrees of Freedom in the Numerator*															
48	4.04	3.19	2.80	2.56	2.41	2.30	2.21	2.14	2.08	2.03	1.99	1.96	1.90	1.86	1.79	1.74	1.70	1.64	1.61	1.56	1.53	1.50	1.47	1.45	48
	7.19	**5.08**	**4.22**	**3.74**	**3.42**	**3.20**	**3.04**	**2.90**	**2.80**	**2.71**	**2.64**	**2.58**	**2.48**	**2.40**	**2.28**	**2.20**	**2.11**	**2.02**	**1.96**	**1.88**	**1.84**	**1.78**	**1.73**	**1.70**	
50	4.03	3.18	2.79	2.56	2.40	2.29	2.20	2.13	2.07	2.02	1.98	1.95	1.90	1.85	1.78	1.74	1.69	1.63	1.60	1.55	1.52	1.48	1.46	1.44	50
	7.17	**5.06**	**4.20**	**3.72**	**3.41**	**3.18**	**3.02**	**2.88**	**2.78**	**2.70**	**2.62**	**2.56**	**2.46**	**2.39**	**2.26**	**2.18**	**2.10**	**2.00**	**1.94**	**1.86**	**1.82**	**1.76**	**1.71**	**1.68**	
55	4.02	3.17	2.78	2.54	2.38	2.27	2.18	2.11	2.05	2.00	1.97	1.93	1.88	1.83	1.76	1.72	1.67	1.61	1.58	1.52	1.50	1.46	1.43	1.41	55
	7.12	**5.01**	**4.16**	**3.68**	**3.37**	**3.15**	**2.98**	**2.85**	**2.75**	**2.66**	**2.59**	**2.53**	**2.43**	**2.35**	**2.23**	**2.15**	**2.06**	**1.96**	**1.90**	**1.82**	**1.78**	**1.71**	**1.66**	**1.64**	
60	4.00	3.15	2.76	2.52	2.37	2.25	2.17	2.10	2.04	1.99	1.95	1.92	1.86	1.81	1.75	1.70	1.65	1.59	1.56	1.50	1.48	1.44	1.41	1.39	60
	7.08	**4.98**	**4.13**	**3.65**	**3.34**	**3.12**	**2.95**	**2.82**	**2.72**	**2.63**	**2.56**	**2.50**	**2.40**	**2.32**	**2.20**	**2.12**	**2.03**	**1.93**	**1.87**	**1.79**	**1.74**	**1.68**	**1.63**	**1.60**	
65	3.99	3.14	2.75	2.51	2.36	2.24	2.15	2.08	2.02	1.98	1.94	1.90	1.85	1.80	1.73	1.68	1.63	1.57	1.54	1.49	1.46	1.42	1.39	1.37	65
	7.04	**4.95**	**4.10**	**3.62**	**3.31**	**3.09**	**2.93**	**2.79**	**2.70**	**2.61**	**2.54**	**2.47**	**2.37**	**2.30**	**2.18**	**2.09**	**2.00**	**1.90**	**1.84**	**1.76**	**1.71**	**1.64**	**1.60**	**1.56**	
70	3.98	3.13	2.74	2.50	2.35	2.23	2.14	2.07	2.01	1.97	1.93	1.89	1.84	1.79	1.72	1.67	1.62	1.56	1.53	1.47	1.45	1.40	1.37	1.35	70
	7.01	**4.92**	**4.08**	**3.60**	**3.29**	**3.07**	**2.91**	**2.77**	**2.67**	**2.59**	**2.51**	**2.45**	**2.35**	**2.28**	**2.15**	**2.07**	**1.98**	**1.88**	**1.82**	**1.74**	**1.69**	**1.62**	**1.56**	**1.53**	
80	3.96	3.11	2.72	2.48	2.33	2.21	2.12	2.05	1.99	1.95	1.91	1.88	1.82	1.77	1.70	1.65	1.60	1.54	1.51	1.45	1.42	1.38	1.35	1.32	80
	6.96	**4.88**	**4.04**	**3.56**	**3.25**	**3.04**	**2.87**	**2.74**	**2.64**	**2.55**	**2.48**	**2.41**	**2.32**	**2.24**	**2.11**	**2.03**	**1.94**	**1.84**	**1.78**	**1.70**	**1.65**	**1.57**	**1.52**	**1.49**	
100	3.94	3.09	2.70	2.46	2.30	2.19	2.10	2.03	1.97	1.92	1.88	1.85	1.79	1.75	1.68	1.63	1.57	1.51	1.48	1.42	1.39	1.34	1.30	1.28	100
	6.90	**4.82**	**3.98**	**3.51**	**3.20**	**2.99**	**2.82**	**2.69**	**2.59**	**2.51**	**2.43**	**2.36**	**2.26**	**2.19**	**2.06**	**1.98**	**1.89**	**1.79**	**1.73**	**1.64**	**1.59**	**1.51**	**1.46**	**1.43**	
125	3.92	3.07	2.68	2.44	2.29	2.17	2.08	2.01	1.95	1.90	1.86	1.83	1.77	1.72	1.65	1.60	1.55	1.49	1.45	1.39	1.36	1.31	1.27	1.25	125
	6.84	**4.78**	**3.94**	**3.47**	**3.17**	**2.95**	**2.79**	**2.65**	**2.56**	**2.47**	**2.40**	**2.33**	**2.23**	**2.15**	**2.03**	**1.94**	**1.85**	**1.75**	**1.68**	**1.59**	**1.54**	**1.46**	**1.40**	**1.37**	
150	3.91	3.06	2.67	2.43	2.27	2.16	2.07	2.00	1.94	1.89	1.85	1.82	1.76	1.71	1.64	1.59	1.54	1.47	1.44	1.37	1.34	1.29	1.25	1.22	150
	6.81	**4.75**	**3.91**	**3.44**	**3.14**	**2.92**	**2.76**	**2.62**	**2.53**	**2.44**	**2.37**	**2.30**	**2.20**	**2.12**	**2.00**	**1.91**	**1.83**	**1.72**	**1.66**	**1.56**	**1.51**	**1.43**	**1.37**	**1.33**	
200	3.89	3.04	2.65	2.41	2.26	2.14	2.05	1.98	1.92	1.87	1.83	1.80	1.74	1.69	1.62	1.57	1.52	1.45	1.42	1.35	1.32	1.26	1.22	1.19	200
	6.76	**4.71**	**3.88**	**3.41**	**3.11**	**2.90**	**2.73**	**2.60**	**2.50**	**2.41**	**2.34**	**2.28**	**2.17**	**2.09**	**1.97**	**1.88**	**1.79**	**1.69**	**1.62**	**1.53**	**1.48**	**1.39**	**1.33**	**1.28**	
400	3.86	3.02	2.62	2.39	2.23	2.12	2.03	1.96	1.90	1.85	1.81	1.78	1.72	1.67	1.60	1.54	1.49	1.42	1.38	1.32	1.28	1.22	1.16	1.13	400
	6.70	**4.66**	**3.83**	**3.36**	**3.06**	**2.85**	**2.69**	**2.55**	**2.46**	**2.37**	**2.29**	**2.23**	**2.12**	**2.04**	**1.92**	**1.84**	**1.74**	**1.64**	**1.57**	**1.47**	**1.42**	**1.32**	**1.24**	**1.19**	
1,000	3.85	3.00	2.61	2.38	2.22	2.10	2.02	1.95	1.89	1.84	1.80	1.76	1.70	1.65	1.58	1.53	1.47	1.41	1.36	1.30	1.26	1.19	1.13	1.08	1,000
	6.66	**4.62**	**3.80**	**3.34**	**3.04**	**2.82**	**2.66**	**2.53**	**2.43**	**2.34**	**2.26**	**2.20**	**2.09**	**2.01**	**1.89**	**1.81**	**1.71**	**1.61**	**1.54**	**1.44**	**1.38**	**1.28**	**1.19**	**1.11**	
∞	3.84	2.99	2.60	2.37	2.21	2.09	2.01	1.94	1.88	1.83	1.79	1.75	1.69	1.64	1.57	1.52	1.46	1.40	1.35	1.28	1.24	1.17	1.11	1.00	∞
	6.64	**4.60**	**3.78**	**3.32**	**3.02**	**2.80**	**2.64**	**2.51**	**2.41**	**2.32**	**2.24**	**2.18**	**2.07**	**1.99**	**1.87**	**1.79**	**1.69**	**1.59**	**1.52**	**1.41**	**1.36**	**1.25**	**1.15**	**1.00**	

n_2 degrees of freedom in the denominator.

Source: George W. Snedecor and William G. Cochran, *Statistical Methods*, 6th ed. (Ames, Iowa: The Iowa State University Press, 1967). Copyright © 1967 by the Iowa State University Press; reprinted by permission.

Appendix C

Sample Data for Examples in Chapter 5

TABLE C-1 Air Miles Traveled: Sample Data

Date	Air Miles Traveled, AM (Billions of miles)	Real Gross National Product, RGNP (Billions of dollars)	Date	Air Miles Traveled, AM (Billions of miles)	Real Gross National Product, RGNP (Billions of dollars)
1970: I	24.49	2,408.6	1980: I	49.02	3,233.4
II	26.14	2,406.5	II	50.73	3,157.0
III	29.21	2,435.8	III	53.73	3,159.1
IV	24.31	2,413.8	IV	46.38	3,199.2
1971: I	23.81	2,478.6	1981: I	46.32	3,261.1
II	26.87	2,478.4	II	51.65	3,250.2
III	29.40	2,491.1	III	52.73	3,264.6
IV	26.33	2,491.0	IV	47.45	3,219.0
1972: I	27.10	2,545.6	1982: I	49.01	3,170.4
II	29.42	2,595.1	II	53.99	3,179.9
III	32.43	2,622.1	III	55.63	3,154.5
IV	29.17	2,671.3	IV	50.04	3,159.3
1973: I	28.86	2,734.0	1983: I	54.77	3,186.6
II	32.10	2,741.0	II	56.89	3,258.3
III	38.42	2,738.3	III	57.82	3,306.4
IV	30.48	2,762.8	IV	53.26	3,365.1
1974: I	30.87	2,747.4	1984: I	54.69	3,451.7
II	33.75	2,755.2	II	62.19	3,498.0
III	35.11	2,719.3	III	63.59	3,520.6
IV	30.00	2,695.4	IV	59.46	3,535.2
1975: I	29.95	2,642.7	1985: I	61.59	3,568.7
II	32.63	2,669.6	II	68.75	3,587.1
III	36.78	2,714.9	III	71.33	3,623.0
IV	32.34	2,752.7	IV	64.88	3,650.9
1976: I	33.63	2,804.4	1986: I	64.81	3,698.8
II	36.97	2,816.9	II	75.52	3,704.7
III	39.71	2,828.6	III	81.93	3,718.0
IV	34.96	2,856.8	IV	72.89	3,731.5
1977: I	35.78	2,896.0	1987: I	71.87	3,772.2
II	38.59	2,942.7	II		3,795.3
III	42.96	3,001.8	III		3,835.9
IV	39.27	2,994.1	IV		3,864.1
1978: I	40.77	3,020.5	1988: I		3,878.2
II	45.31	3,115.9	II		3,892.9
III	51.45	3,142.6	III		3,912.1
IV	45.13	3,181.6	IV		3,939.2
1979: I	48.13	3,181.7			
II	50.35	3,178.7			
III	56.73	3,207.4			
IV	48.83	3,201.3			

See example 5-2 and equation (5-52).

All data have been seasonally adjusted.

TABLE C-2 Consumption Function: Sample Data

Date	Consumption Expenditures, C (Billions of dollars)	Disposable Personal Income, YD (Billions of dollars)	Date	Consumption Expenditures, C (Billions of dollars)	Disposable Personal Income, YD (Billions of dollars)
1970: I	625.1	691.1	1981: I	1862.9	2065.6
II	635.1	711.1	II	1896.4	2095.8
III	646.8	726.5	III	1940.9	2162
IV	653	733.7	IV	1960.2	2187
1971: I	671.7	754.5	1982: I	1996.3	2207.2
II	685.2	774.1	II	2023.8	2241.8
III	696.8	784.2	III	2065.6	2278.6
IV	712.4	794.4	IV	2117	2318.1
1972: I	729.3	807.2	1983: I	2146.6	2345.7
II	747	821.2	II	2213	2395.4
III	764.8	845.3	III	2262.8	2443.2
IV	789.2	884.6	IV	2315.8	2527.9
1973: I	813.2	911	1984: I	2361.1	2611.8
II	827.9	936.1	II	2417	2642.8
III	846.2	959.9	III	2450.3	2691.1
IV	861.6	992.1	IV	2493.4	2728.6
1974: I	880	1006.5	1985: I	2554.9	2764.6
II	907.8	1022.1	II	2599.3	2850.7
III	935.3	1052.8	III	2661.4	2840
IV	943	1072	IV	2700.4	2899.5
1975: I	967.4	1080.4	1986: I	2734.3	2959.2
II	996.6	1148.3	II	2761	3006.5
III	1029.6	1155.7	III	2826	3024.3
IV	1057.5	1186.7	IV	2868.5	3063.4
1976: I	1091.8	1218	1987: I	2919.5	3139.8
II	1111.2	1236.8	II	2987.2	3125.7
III	1139.8	1263.2	III	3051.6	3211.1
IV	1174.6	1292.5	IV	3079.1	3302.3
1977: I	1211.8	1317.9	1988: I	3147.7	3378.6
II	1239.2	1359	II	3204.3	3439.4
III	1270.2	1404	III	3268.2	3520.1
IV	1307.6	1436.4	IV	3332.6	3578.9
1978: I	1332.6	1474.9	1989: I	3371.7	3661.7
II	1391.1	1534.3	II	3425.9	3697.3
III	1424.6	1573.6	III	3484.3	3743.4
IV	1465.7	1622.1	IV	3518.5	3799.6
1979: I	1501.8	1666.6	1990: I	3588.1	3887.7
II	1537.6	1701.5	II	3622.7	3925.7
III	1590	1752.9	III	3693.4	3969.1
IV	1637.5	1796.3	IV	3724.9	4001.9
1980: I	1682.2	1857.6			
II	1688.9	1869.8			
III	1749.3	1934.1			
IV	1810	2010.3			

See example 5-3 and equation (5-57).

TABLE C-3 Appliance Shipments: Sample Data

Date	Appliance Shipments, APP	Appliance Production (1982 = 100), PROD
1986: I	10,829	93.600
II	11,342	94.400
III	12,068	95.000
IV	13,119	96.600
1987: I	15,053	97.500
II	17,017	99.333
III	18,505	101.400
IV	19,476	101.700
1988: I	20,055	102.467
II	20,890	102.900
III	22,388	104.267
IV	23,623	104.700
1989: I	24,823	105.900
II	25,341	106.367
III	24,778	106.100
IV	24,773	107.067
1990: I	23,290	107.667
II	22,786	107.500
III	24,232	107.396

See example 5-4 and equation (5-59).

Appendix D

Sample Data Sets for Chapter 6

TABLE D-1   Automobile Sales: Sample Data

Date	USCAR	RELP	TRP	JCS	REPCAR	RUNC	RAUTO	YDP82
1967: I	7.993	1.40	53.50	92.20	37.30	3.83	9.40	1,474.0
II	8.883	1.41	54.70	94.90	37.30	3.83	9.44	1,487.9
III	8.485	1.41	56.20	96.50	37.30	3.80	9.48	1,500.1
IV	8.057	1.42	57.50	92.90	37.30	3.90	9.53	1,510.7
1968: I	9.420	1.39	59.90	95.00	38.00	3.73	9.59	1,530.5
II	9.401	1.38	63.70	92.40	38.00	3.57	9.67	1,554.7
III	9.980	1.37	65.40	92.90	38.00	3.53	9.76	1,555.1
IV	9.816	1.37	67.00	92.10	38.00	3.40	9.81	1,565.1
1969: I	9.697	1.35	69.10	95.10	38.70	3.40	9.94	1,566.4
II	9.629	1.33	70.60	91.60	38.70	3.43	10.13	1,584.7
III	9.615	1.32	72.10	86.40	38.70	3.57	10.39	1,617.5
IV	9.386	1.32	74.00	79.70	38.70	3.57	10.62	1,630.6
1970: I	8.750	1.30	76.50	78.10	39.40	4.17	10.80	1,638.0
II	9.077	1.28	86.80	75.40	39.40	4.77	10.90	1,666.2
III	8.921	1.29	87.90	77.10	39.40	5.17	10.96	1,686.2
IV	6.861	1.32	92.30	75.40	39.40	5.83	10.92	1,682.1
1971: I	9.974	1.33	94.50	78.20	40.20	5.93	10.70	1,708.1
II	9.943	1.31	102.60	81.60	40.20	5.90	10.44	1,731.9
III	10.360	1.26	103.40	82.40	40.20	6.03	10.25	1,734.2
IV	10.634	1.22	105.40	82.20	40.20	5.93	10.04	1,739.6
1972: I	10.471	1.23	108.90	87.50	40.90	5.77	10.19	1,750.9
II	10.651	1.22	109.70	89.30	40.90	5.70	9.98	1,767.6
III	10.806	1.22	111.90	94.00	35.10	5.57	10.00	1,801.5
IV	11.564	1.17	122.60	90.80	34.90	5.37	10.01	1,869.4
1973: I	12.304	1.16	125.30	80.80	35.00	4.93	10.03	1,893.2
II	12.126	1.15	127.90	76.00	35.30	4.93	10.06	1,907.6
III	11.133	1.13	130.80	71.80	35.37	4.80	10.30	1,922.2
IV	9.837	1.10	134.60	75.70	35.10	4.77	10.50	1,942.1
1974: I	9.300	1.09	140.90	60.90	35.30	5.13	10.53	1,907.2
II	8.988	1.10	149.20	72.00	35.67	5.20	10.65	1,888.3
III	9.412	1.11	157.40	64.50	35.93	5.63	11.14	1,898.6
IV	7.396	1.11	165.10	58.40	36.20	6.60	11.57	1,892.4
1975: I	8.227	1.09	177.70	58.00	37.17	8.27	11.53	1,873.1
II	7.685	1.10	194.20	72.90	37.73	8.87	11.36	1,965.7
III	8.933	1.08	198.30	75.80	37.77	8.47	11.31	1,935.0
IV	9.308	1.08	202.20	75.40	37.73	8.30	11.24	1,953.1
1976: I	10.024	1.09	206.80	84.50	38.20	7.73	11.17	1,983.1
II	9.848	1.09	206.20	82.20	38.80	7.57	11.04	1,992.8
III	9.880	1.09	213.50	88.80	39.10	7.73	11.07	2,005.9
IV	10.225	1.09	216.50	86.00	39.20	7.77	11.03	2,022.2

Date	USCAR	RELP	TRP	JCS	REPCAR	RUNC	RAUTO	YDP82
1977: I	10.966	1.08	220.40	87.50	39.87	7.50	11.03	2,026.9
II	11.269	1.07	222.60	89.10	40.53	7.13	10.82	2,049.6
III	11.000	1.07	228.70	87.60	41.03	6.90	10.85	2,086.9
IV	10.948	1.08	232.60	83.10	41.27	6.67	10.87	2,102.8
1978: I	10.491	1.08	236.80	82.27	42.07	6.33	10.83	2,128.2
II	11.800	1.07	238.90	81.50	42.77	6.00	10.84	2,162.7
III	11.172	1.07	248.10	80.40	43.30	6.03	11.09	2,176.4
IV	11.192	1.06	252.40	73.47	43.40	5.90	11.29	2,202.0
1979: I	11.201	1.07	258.20	71.47	43.90	5.87	11.60	2,216.6
II	10.434	1.07	264.10	66.63	44.20	5.70	11.73	2,206.6
III	10.711	1.07	280.90	63.87	44.60	5.87	11.88	2,213.7
IV	9.889	1.06	289.10	62.13	44.30	5.97	12.85	2,213.7
1980: I	10.442	1.06	300.90	63.47	44.50	6.30	13.28	2,225.6
II	7.802	1.06	308.50	54.37	44.40	7.33	15.24	2,185.7
III	8.769	1.06	341.60	67.77	45.00	7.67	13.91	2,207.2
IV	8.915	1.04	347.70	72.07	44.80	7.40	14.29	2,238.8
1981: I	9.759	1.02	354.50	68.27	45.00	7.43	15.49	2,242.9
II	8.079	1.04	358.90	73.93	45.20	7.40	16.04	2,235.0
III	9.035	1.03	377.20	74.80	45.50	7.40	15.54	2,262.9
IV	7.265	1.02	381.80	65.70	45.30	8.23	16.55	2,253.7
1982: I	8.001	1.01	388.10	66.50	45.60	8.83	17.05	2,245.7
II	7.683	0.99	400.40	66.23	45.90	9.43	14.78	2,260.9
III	7.789	0.98	418.30	66.70	46.07	9.90	17.08	2,263.4
IV	8.446	0.98	435.40	72.47	46.23	10.67	12.82	2,276.1
1983: I	8.244	0.99	438.20	75.27	45.93	10.37	12.05	2,288.4
II	9.194	0.99	445.30	91.53	45.60	10.13	11.94	2,311.1
III	9.236	0.98	441.40	91.57	45.93	9.37	12.77	2,335.4
IV	10.041	0.99	445.50	91.53	46.27	8.53	13.46	2,392.7
1984: I	10.412	0.98	450.60	99.50	46.47	7.87	13.32	2,446.9
II	10.500	0.98	454.50	96.57	47.67	7.43	13.53	2,456.6
III	10.264	0.98	458.50	98.87	49.10	7.43	14.08	2,479.2
IV	10.384	0.98	463.00	94.97	49.97	7.30	13.91	2,496.3
1985: I	10.844	0.98	482.30	94.47	51.43	7.27	13.37	2,509.4
II	10.879	0.98	486.40	94.30	51.23	7.27	11.87	2,563.5
III	12.314	0.98	493.20	92.83	51.33	7.20	12.46	2,535.4
IV	10.113	0.98	497.50	91.07	51.87	7.07	11.71	2,562.8
1986: I	10.755	0.99	510.30	95.53	51.17	7.00	9.70	2,609.2
II	11.204	1.00	517.70	96.77	49.83	7.20	9.49	2,648.6
III	12.685	1.00	526.70	94.83	47.97	6.97	9.29	2,637.3
IV	11.155	1.01	531.20	92.03	50.67	6.87	10.58	2,646.2
1987: I	9.665	1.00	539.00	90.47	53.70	6.57	10.35	2,672.3
II	10.284	1.00	547.60	91.80	53.80	6.30	10.24	2,632.5
III	11.307	1.00	550.80	93.90	52.07	6.00	9.63	2,675.6
IV	9.857	1.00	555.50	86.40	54.57	5.90	10.86	2,726.2
1988: I	10.907	1.00	575.80	92.33	55.80	5.70	10.72	2,757.2
II	10.702	0.99	581.80	93.57	56.23	5.50	10.55	2,773.3
III	10.462	0.99	587.40	96.03	56.40	5.47	10.93	2,806.4
IV	10.485	0.98	593.80	93.00	56.27	5.33	11.22	2,835.9
1989: I	9.820	0.98	616.40	95.87	55.77	5.17	11.76	2,881.7
II	10.332	0.97	626.80	90.93	53.03	5.27	11.80	2,887.6
III	10.783	0.96	636.40	92.47	53.03	5.23	12.10	2,920.6
IV	9.300	0.95	648.27	93.11	53.03	5.42	11.98	2,924.5
1990: I	9.900	0.95	667.79	93.52	53.03	5.61	11.82	2,955.5
II	10.150	0.94	667.92	92.28	53.03	5.75	11.72	2,970.2

See example 6-1, Table 6-5, and equation (6-30).

TABLE D-2 Demand for Lumber: Sample Data

Date	Lumber Sales (millions of tons) (SA) DL	New Home Sales (millions of units) (SA) HU	Multi-Family Units Constructed (millions of units) (SA) APT	Rate of Household Formation (SA) RATE	Price per Ton (dollars) P	Personal Income (millions of dollars) (SA) INC
1977: I	114.0	0.914	132	7.633	1,157	737.4
II	109.1	0.918	138	7.867	1,258	752.5
III	101.8	0.899	138	7.733	1,241	760.1
IV	108.9	0.902	216	5.400	1,486	756.2
1978: I	100.9	0.893	154	8.436	1,538	771.1
II	105.0	0.864	166	8.249	1,649	779.9
III	110.6	0.872	160	8.706	1,654	780.7
IV	117.0	0.879	134	9.211	1,423	785.2
1979: I	126.8	0.860	150	8.959	1,513	792.0
II	126.5	0.847	143	9.130	1,521	798.7
III	132.5	0.858	149	9.139	1,613	812.4
IV	132.8	0.872	159	9.728	1,836	838.1
1980: I	137.8	0.868	153	10.420	1,883	855.2
II	137.2	0.879	153	10.269	1,857	862.3
III	149.3	0.873	143	9.539	1,594	867.9
IV	160.5	0.928	147	8.126	1,712	873.3
1981: I	174.1	1.057	164	7.771	1,529	860.2
II	192.8	1.129	138	7.747	1,241	859.7
III	194.1	1.100	158	7.929	1,483	859.4
IV	196.6	1.043	189	6.010	1,395	850.8
1982: I	217.0	1.031	208	6.515	1,711	854.1
II	229.4	1.037	204	6.115	1,570	891.4
III	222.3	1.084	184	7.292	1,640	878.2
IV	224.3	1.082	153	7.881	1,427	885.1
1983: I	224.3	1.056	136	8.663	1,362	899.5
II	217.5	1.041	139	8.481	1,367	904.1
III	232.3	1.037	157	8.330	1,550	908.8
IV	245.5	1.047	169	8.459	1,730	914.6
1984: I	262.7	1.049	168	9.120	1,846	919.5
II	283.3	1.046	201	8.999	2,270	933.9
III	285.7	1.024	210	8.866	2,134	952.2
IV	285.6	1.030	187	8.899	2,049	965.9
1985: I	301.4	1.018	195	8.516	1,975	973.4
II	323.1	0.911	173	9.760	2,040	982.8
III	322.3	0.993	183	9.129	2,043	994.2
IV	314.7	1.019	174	9.250	1,942	1,004.8
1986: I	292.3	1.044	197	8.998	2,204	1,011.1
II	283.2	1.161	236	7.967	2,467	1,011.7
III	305.3	1.301	210	8.466	2,245	1,019.8
IV	332.9	1.363	243	7.489	2,399	1,020.1
1987: I	368.3	1.512	255	7.782	2,660	1,025.8
II	399.1	1.527	274	5.667	2,135	1,012.0
III	419.6	1.485	267	6.416	2,342	1,019.2
IV	435.3	1.460	275	6.460	2,454	1,029.6
1988: I	484.3	1.556	262	7.203	2,555	1,040.7
II	526.4	1.544	286	5.771	2,310	1,045.6
III	534.6	1.470	248	6.797	2,239	1,068.1
IV	548.5	1.437	303	5.063	2,202	1,064.3
1989: I	525.0	1.413	272	5.821	2,180	1,055.1
II	413.5	1.243	263	5.661	2,021	1,060.2
III	328.0	1.342	285	5.572	2,217	1,059.3
IV	308.7	1.328	292	5.978	2,468	1,066.1

See example 6-2 and equation (6-32).

TABLE D-3   Lagrangian Multiplier Test for Linearity

Date	Error E	RINC	SOV	RINC Squared	SOV Squared	Interaction Term RINC * IN
69	−0.0280	113	19.9	12,769	396.01	2,248.7
70	−0.1296	118	22.6	13,924	510.76	2,666.8
71	−0.0444	121	26.0	14,641	676.00	3,146.0
72	−0.2479	118	20.5	13,924	420.25	2,419.0
73	0.0898	271	21.5	73,441	462.25	5,826.5
74	0.1211	190	23.5	36,100	552.25	4,465.0
75	0.0997	175	21.5	30,625	462.25	3,762.5
76	0.1145	263	26.2	69,169	686.44	6,890.6
77	−0.0672	334	28.5	111,556	812.25	9,519.0
78	−0.7183	368	29.5	135,424	870.25	10,856.0
79	0.0012	305	24.5	93,025	600.25	7,472.5
80	−0.1360	210	29.5	44,100	870.25	6,195.0
81	0.0239	387	26.1	149,769	681.21	10,100.7
82	0.2652	270	27.3	72,900	745.29	7,371.0
83	0.1685	218	22.3	47,524	497.29	4,861.4
84	−0.3964	342	31.0	116,964	961.00	10,602.0
85	0.5133	173	28.0	29,929	784.00	4,844.0
86	0.3978	370	28.5	136,900	812.25	10,545.0
87	−0.0564	170	23.1	28,900	533.61	3,927.0
88	−0.4430	205	27.0	42,025	729.00	5,535.0
89	0.4562	331	32.0	109,561	1,024.00	10,592.0
90	0.0161	283	32.0	80,089	1,024.00	9,056.0

See equation (6-39).

TABLE D-4 Forecasting Electrical Consumption: Sample Data

Date	Consumption of Electricity (millions of KWH) COMEL	Nonagricultural Employment (thousands) NONAG	Relative Price of Electricity (percent) PRICE	Heating and Cooling Degree Days HCDD	Interaction Term PRICE · HCDD
1978	19,628	278.6	79.4	5,529	439,003
1979	21,663	286.3	78.4	5,055	396,312
1980	24,464	315.6	83.4	5,368	447,691
1981	26,556	335.4	87.6	5,176	453,418
1982	26,239	341.6	83.8	4,483	375,675
1983	27,927	328.3	72.9	5,066	369,311
1984	29,710	335.9	79.5	4,825	383,588
1985	34,055	349.1	82.0	5,637	462,234
1986	33,928	364.8	84.4	5,751	485,384
1987	31,870	373.5	85.6	5,460	467,376
1988	33,566	371.1	79.1	5,926	468,747
1989	34,352	370.7	78.5	5,276	414,166

See example 6-3 and equations (6-41) and (6-42).

TABLE D-5 Testing the Reliability of Quantitative Statistics: Sample Data

Observation Number	Y_1	X_1	Y_2	X_2	Y_3	X_3	Y_4	X_4
1	8.04	10	9.14	10	7.46	10	6.58	8
2	6.95	8	8.14	8	6.77	8	5.76	8
3	7.58	13	8.74	13	12.74	13	7.71	8
4	8.81	9	8.77	9	7.11	9	8.84	8
5	8.33	11	9.26	11	7.81	11	8.47	8
6	9.96	14	8.10	14	8.84	14	7.04	8
7	7.24	6	6.13	6	6.08	6	5.25	8
8	4.26	4	3.10	4	5.39	4	12.50	19
9	10.84	12	9.13	12	8.15	12	5.56	8
10	4.82	7	7.26	7	6.42	7	7.91	8
11	5.68	5	4.74	5	5.73	5	6.89	8

See Figure 6-9.

TABLE D-6 Package Shipments: Sample Data

Date	Package Shipments (millions) PS	Average Price per Package (dollars) PRICE	Employment in Finance Insurance and Real Estate (millions) EMEFIR	Employment in Services (millions) EMESER	Industrial Production Printing and Publishing (1982 = 100) JIP27J	Industrial Production Chemicals and Drugs (1982 = 100) JIP283	Industrial Production Computers (1982 = 100) JIP357	Industrial Production Electrical Components (1982 = 100) JIP367	Industrial Production Communication Equipment (1982 = 100) JIP366	Industrial Production Scientific Instruments (1982 = 100) JIP38E	Industrial Production Aircraft Parts (1982 = 100) JIP372
1984: I	209,334	19.91	5.606	20.364	75.267	85.433	52.033	103.767	80.833	84.667	70.367
II	231,916	19.27	5.656	20.672	75.900	87.433	59.300	105.400	83.700	86.500	72.400
III	263,089	19.40	5.711	20.915	77.600	86.733	64.433	105.600	87.067	88.400	73.733
IV	281,280	19.21	5.779	21.231	78.500	87.867	65.200	99.900	90.733	89.167	74.733
1985: I	316,963	18.95	5.843	21.555	79.433	87.500	69.533	95.600	92.900	89.867	76.267
II	335,721	18.57	5.914	21.845	82.200	88.533	74.400	96.700	94.467	91.433	78.967
III	355,003	19.36	5.986	22.124	80.633	88.733	75.667	87.767	94.900	91.000	82.133
IV	390,641	17.55	6.078	22.470	81.733	89.267	77.700	94.567	96.500	92.067	84.533
1986: I	412,126	17.40	6.156	22.687	82.133	92.233	81.733	96.533	94.600	92.267	87.467
II	440,710	17.00	6.246	22.920	81.667	97.300	78.900	96.933	95.600	92.067	90.767
III	463,691	17.05	6.330	23.156	83.267	96.600	84.433	98.500	99.000	92.133	93.033
IV	491,257	16.73	6.400	23.446	89.333	100.533	87.133	98.400	99.567	94.033	95.867
1987: I	515,322	16.49	6.468	23.766	93.933	99.000	92.967	99.833	100.700	96.233	97.967
II	550,458	16.17	6.536	24.077	100.100	99.433	97.667	99.467	99.433	98.900	99.600
III	580,064	16.04	6.577	24.394	102.900	101.600	101.633	99.700	99.833	100.433	100.700
IV	602,714	15.64	6.606	24.701	102.100	99.667	107.433	100.667	100.033	104.300	101.733
1988: I	640,823	15.35	6.635	25.079	103.367	104.033	114.433	97.367	101.867	106.833	101.733
II	659,857	15.40	6.658	25.422	102.600	105.800	122.467	100.367	104.067	109.033	102.267
III	698,097	15.55	6.686	25.785	104.500	110.133	124.133	103.733	105.267	112.667	104.667
IV	723,619	15.36	6.727	26.109	105.500	108.333	122.967	99.767	103.300	115.300	104.500
1989: I	746,277	15.19	6.681	26.664	108.767	105.800	133.400	102.933	103.933	117.233	106.567
II	789,503	15.17	6.703	26.962	109.233	107.633	136.900	110.233	106.133	119.467	110.933
III	813,832	15.21	6.739	27.229	107.100	109.033	139.400	105.700	107.133	117.233	112.067
IV	848,380	15.33	6.772	27.526	108.800	109.867	138.833	106.433	107.267	117.900	101.033
1990: I	870,793	15.48	6.811	27.838	112.033	110.067	144.767	106.867	108.200	119.967	111.333
II	859,543	15.95	6.835	28.096	113.167	112.967	149.633	107.833	109.133	119.433	113.133

See example 6-5 and Table 6-9.

TABLE D-7 Final Sales: Sample Data

Date	Final Sales FS	Real Income YD82	Population POP
1970	2,437.97	1,668.12	205.075
1971	2,504.90	1,728.45	207.700
1972	2,636.17	1,797.35	209.900
1973	2,735.62	1,916.27	211.950
1974	2,695.20	1,896.62	213.875
1975	2,688.87	1,931.72	215.975
1976	2,815.52	2,001.00	218.075
1977	2,964.97	2,066.55	220.300
1978	3,105.17	2,167.32	222.625
1979	3,173.77	2,212.65	225.100
1980	3,136.97	2,214.32	227.750
1981	3,175.55	2,248.62	230.175
1982	3,164.17	2,261.52	232.575
1983	3,305.42	2,331.90	234.825
1984	3,523.12	2,469.75	237.025
1985	3,713.87	2,542.77	239.325
1986	3,842.07	2,635.32	241.675
1987	3,945.72	2,676.65	243.975
1988	4,071.37	2,793.20	246.375
1989	4,173.41	2,905.04	248.826
1990	4,262.86	2,974.75	251.258

See equations (6-51) and (6-53).

TABLE D-8   Travel Expenditures: Sample Data

Travel Expenditures (billions of dollars) TE	Income (billions of dollars) Y	Population (millions) POP	Per Capita Travel Expenditures PCTE	Per Capita Income PCY	Reciprocal of Population RPOP
0.899	9.1	0.505	1.780	18.020	1.980
0.778	6.4	0.513	1.517	12.476	1.949
1.181	6.0	0.530	2.228	11.321	1.887
0.555	8.3	0.614	0.904	13.518	1.629
1.138	10.6	0.625	1.821	16.960	1.600
0.628	8.0	0.687	0.914	11.645	1.456
0.551	7.6	0.705	0.782	10.780	1.418
0.725	8.9	0.823	0.881	10.814	1.215
6.455	12.6	0.917	7.039	13.740	1.091
0.429	12.6	0.962	0.446	13.098	1.040
1.502	13.6	0.978	1.536	13.906	1.022
0.934	10.5	0.999	0.935	10.511	1.001
2.517	13.7	1.037	2.427	13.211	0.964
1.531	13.0	1.156	1.324	11.246	0.865
1.724	14.8	1.426	1.209	10.379	0.701
1.250	19.9	1.605	0.779	12.399	0.623
1.757	16.3	1.623	1.083	10.043	0.616
1.270	19.1	1.951	0.651	9.790	0.513
1.821	23.4	2.346	0.776	9.974	0.426
1.729	31.9	2.440	0.709	13.074	0.410
1.252	23.0	2.598	0.482	8.853	0.385
2.297	32.1	2.676	0.858	11.996	0.374
1.766	35.1	2.903	0.608	12.091	0.344
3.836	36.9	3.072	1.249	12.012	0.326
2.415	53.1	3.155	0.765	16.830	0.317
4.628	45.1	3.190	1.451	14.138	0.313
3.016	33.4	3.302	0.913	10.115	0.303
2.784	39.1	3.310	0.841	11.813	0.302
2.222	38.6	3.720	0.597	10.376	0.269
1.720	40.3	3.989	0.431	10.103	0.251
4.933	55.7	4.163	1.185	13.380	0.240
3.797	64.5	4.349	0.873	14.831	0.230
3.415	57.9	4.349	0.785	13.313	0.230
3.731	49.2	4.461	0.836	11.029	0.224
3.327	50.1	4.726	0.704	10.601	0.212
3.850	60.0	4.762	0.808	12.600	0.210
4.692	62.4	5.001	0.938	12.478	0.200
2.770	65.2	5.492	0.504	11.872	0.182
4.418	76.6	5.636	0.784	13.591	0.177
5.212	88.1	5.798	0.899	15.195	0.172
4.851	68.9	5.842	0.830	11.794	0.171
5.246	67.8	6.166	0.851	10.996	0.162
11.416	120.7	7.517	1.519	16.057	0.133
6.273	117.7	9.058	0.693	12.994	0.110
6.420	134.4	10.740	0.598	12.514	0.093
17.645	144.0	11.050	1.597	13.032	0.090
7.754	161.1	11.522	0.673	13.982	0.087
8.352	151.0	11.887	0.703	12.703	0.084
14.979	205.8	16.083	0.931	12.796	0.062
15.653	266.3	17.746	0.882	15.006	0.056
29.012	390.9	25.795	1.125	15.154	0.039

See examples 6-7 and 6-8 and equations (6-55) and (6-59).

TABLE D-9 Interest Rates: Sample Data

Date	Three-Month Treasury Bill Rate (percent) INTRATE	Disposable Personal Income (billions of dollars) (SAAR) YDP	Money Supply, M1 Definition (billions of dollars) (SA)	Percent Change in Money Supply (percent) PMONEY	Consumer Price Index 1982 – 1984 = 100 CPI	Percent Change in CPI (percent) PPRICE
1969: Dec.	7.81	684.5	204.0		37.7	
1970: Jan.	7.87	687.4	206.5	1.23	37.8	0.27
Feb.	7.13	691.2	205.1	−0.68	38.0	0.53
Mar.	6.63	694.8	205.8	0.34	38.2	0.53
Apr.	6.50	712.8	206.7	0.44	38.5	0.79
May	6.83	710.6	207.4	0.34	38.6	0.26
June	6.67	710.0	207.6	0.10	38.8	0.52
July	6.45	721.8	208.1	0.24	39.0	0.52
Aug.	6.41	726.3	210.0	0.91	39.0	0.00
Sept.	6.12	731.3	211.8	0.86	39.2	0.51
Oct.	5.90	731.1	212.9	0.52	39.4	0.51
Nov.	5.28	731.9	213.7	0.38	39.6	0.51
Dec.	4.87	738.0	214.5	0.37	39.8	0.51
1971: Jan.	4.44	750.9	215.9	0.65	39.8	0.00
Feb.	3.69	753.4	217.5	0.74	39.9	0.25
Mar.	3.38	759.0	218.8	0.60	40.0	0.25
Apr.	3.85	763.6	220.1	0.59	40.1	0.25
May	4.13	769.3	222.1	0.91	40.3	0.50
June	4.74	789.4	223.5	0.63	40.6	0.74
July	5.39	779.6	225.0	0.67	40.7	0.25
Aug.	4.93	785.4	225.7	0.31	40.8	0.25
Sept.	4.69	787.6	226.5	0.35	40.8	0.00
Oct.	4.46	788.7	227.3	0.35	40.9	0.25
Nov.	4.22	792.9	227.8	0.22	40.9	0.00
Dec.	4.01	801.4	228.4	0.26	41.1	0.49
1972: Jan.	3.38	801.1	230.4	0.88	41.1	0.00
Feb.	3.20	808.5	232.4	0.87	41.3	0.49
Mar.	3.73	812.1	234.4	0.86	41.4	0.24
Apr.	3.71	817.4	235.6	0.51	41.5	0.24
May	3.69	825.9	235.9	0.13	41.6	0.24
June	3.91	820.3	236.8	0.38	41.7	0.24
July	3.98	835.9	238.8	0.84	41.9	0.48
Aug.	4.02	846.6	240.9	0.88	42.0	0.24
Sept.	4.66	853.5	243.2	0.95	42.1	0.24
Oct.	4.74	872.1	245.0	0.74	42.3	0.48
Nov.	4.78	886.4	246.4	0.57	42.4	0.24
Dec.	5.07	895.4	249.4	1.22	42.5	0.24
1973: Jan.	5.41	899.4	251.7	0.92	42.6	0.24
Feb.	5.60	911.4	252.2	0.20	42.9	0.70
Mar.	6.09	922.3	251.7	−0.20	43.3	0.93
Apr.	6.26	926.1	252.7	0.40	43.6	0.69

Date	Three-Month Treasury Bill Rate (percent) INTRATE	Disposable Personal Income (billions of dollars) (SAAR) YDP	Money Supply, M1 Definition (billions of dollars) (SA)	Percent Change in Money Supply (percent) PMONEY	Consumer Price Index 1982 – 1984 = 100 CPI	Percent Change in CPI (percent) PPRICE
May	6.36	936.2	254.9	0.87	43.9	0.69
June	7.19	945.9	256.9	0.78	44.2	0.68
July	8.01	948.6	257.6	0.27	44.3	0.23
Aug.	8.67	962.6	257.9	0.12	45.1	1.81
Sept.	8.29	968.4	258.0	0.04	45.2	0.22
Oct.	7.22	981.3	259.1	0.43	45.6	0.88
Nov.	7.83	994.4	261.1	0.77	45.9	0.66
Dec.	7.45	1,000.5	263.0	0.73	46.2	0.65
1974: Jan.	7.77	1,006.3	264.1	0.42	46.6	0.87
Feb.	7.12	1,006.6	265.4	0.49	47.2	1.29
Mar.	7.96	1,006.7	266.8	0.53	47.8	1.27
Apr.	8.33	1,012.9	267.1	0.11	48.0	0.42
May	8.23	1,023.1	267.7	0.22	48.6	1.25
June	7.90	1,030.2	268.6	0.34	49.0	0.82
July	7.55	1,044.9	269.4	0.30	49.4	0.82
Aug.	8.96	1,053.0	270.2	0.30	50.0	1.21
Sept.	8.06	1,060.7	271.2	0.37	50.6	1.20
Oct.	7.46	1,071.4	272.4	0.44	51.1	0.99
Nov.	7.47	1,070.1	273.8	0.51	51.5	0.78
Dec.	7.15	1,074.7	274.4	0.22	51.9	0.78
1975: Jan.	6.26	1,076.5	274.1	− 0.11	52.1	0.39
Feb.	5.50	1,080.7	274.8	0.26	52.5	0.77
Mar.	5.49	1,084.0	276.7	0.69	52.7	0.38
Apr.	5.61	1,110.7	276.1	− 0.22	52.9	0.38
May	5.23	1,184.4	278.9	1.01	53.2	0.57
June	5.34	1,149.9	282.7	1.36	53.6	0.75
July	6.13	1,141.7	283.3	0.21	54.2	1.12
Aug.	6.44	1,157.2	284.8	0.53	54.3	0.18
Sept.	6.42	1,168.3	285.6	0.28	54.6	0.55
Oct.	5.96	1,180.1	285.3	− 0.11	54.9	0.55
Nov.	5.48	1,186.3	287.9	0.91	55.3	0.73
Dec.	5.44	1,193.7	287.6	− 0.10	55.5	0.36
1976: Jan.	4.87	1,210.1	288.9	0.45	55.6	0.18
Feb.	4.88	1,219.3	291.1	0.76	55.8	0.36
Mar.	5.00	1,224.8	292.3	0.41	55.9	0.18
Apr.	4.86	1,230.6	294.1	0.62	56.1	0.36
May	5.20	1,236.8	296.1	0.68	56.5	0.71
June	5.41	1,243.0	295.9	− 0.07	56.8	0.53
July	5.23	1,255.8	297.1	0.41	57.1	0.53
Aug.	5.14	1,263.3	299.0	0.64	57.4	0.53
Sept.	5.08	1,270.6	299.6	0.20	57.6	0.35

TABLE D-9 *(Continued)*

Date	Three-Month Treasury Bill Rate (percent) INTRATE	Disposable Personal Income (billions of dollars) (SAAR) YDP	Money Supply, M1 Definition (billions of dollars) (SA)	Percent Change in Money Supply (percent) PMONEY	Consumer Price Index 1982 – 1984 = 100 CPI	Percent Change in CPI (percent) PPRICE
Oct.	4.92	1,276.9	303.0	1.13	57.9	0.52
Nov.	4.75	1,294.4	303.6	0.20	58.0	0.17
Dec.	4.35	1,306.2	306.5	0.96	58.2	0.34
1977: Jan.	4.62	1,310.2	309.3	0.91	58.5	0.52
Feb.	4.67	1,307.6	311.6	0.74	59.1	1.03
Mar.	4.60	1,336.0	313.6	0.64	59.5	0.68
Apr.	4.54	1,347.5	316.1	0.80	60.0	0.84
May	4.96	1,357.2	316.5	0.13	60.3	0.50
June	5.02	1,372.3	318.2	0.54	60.7	0.66
July	5.19	1,391.0	320.6	0.75	61.0	0.49
Aug.	5.49	1,404.7	322.2	0.50	61.2	0.33
Sept.	5.81	1,416.4	324.5	0.71	61.4	0.33
Oct.	6.16	1,425.3	327.6	0.96	61.6	0.33
Nov.	6.10	1,437.6	329.3	0.52	61.9	0.49
Dec.	6.07	1,446.4	331.5	0.67	62.1	0.32
1978: Jan.	6.44	1,453.6	334.9	1.03	62.5	0.64
Feb.	6.45	1,471.7	335.4	0.15	62.9	0.64
Mar.	6.29	1,499.3	337.0	0.48	63.4	0.79
Apr.	6.29	1,521.6	340.4	1.01	63.9	0.79
May	6.41	1,535.8	343.4	0.88	64.5	0.94
June	6.73	1,545.6	345.7	0.67	65.2	1.09
July	7.01	1,561.6	347.7	0.58	65.7	0.77
Aug.	7.08	1,573.3	349.4	0.49	66.0	0.46
Sept.	7.85	1,586.1	353.4	1.14	66.5	0.76
Oct.	7.99	1,607.7	354.5	0.31	67.1	0.90
Nov.	8.64	1,621.3	356.3	0.51	67.4	0.45
Dec.	9.08	1,637.3	358.8	0.70	67.7	0.45
1979: Jan.	9.35	1,650.3	359.4	0.17	68.3	0.89
Feb.	9.32	1,664.8	361.0	0.45	69.1	1.17
Mar.	9.48	1,684.4	361.6	0.17	69.8	1.01
Apr.	9.46	1,690.1	364.8	0.88	70.6	1.15
May	9.61	1,702.2	365.8	0.27	71.5	1.27
June	9.06	1,712.1	371.1	1.45	72.3	1.12
July	9.24	1,740.9	375.8	1.27	73.1	1.11
Aug.	9.52	1,754.2	379.8	1.06	73.8	0.96
Sept.	10.26	1,763.5	384.1	1.13	74.6	1.08
Oct.	11.70	1,781.4	381.9	− 0.57	75.2	0.80
Nov.	11.79	1,797.1	384.2	0.60	75.9	0.93
Dec.	12.04	1,810.3	386.1	0.49	76.7	1.05
1980: Jan.	12.00	1,848.8	386.3	0.05	77.8	1.43
Feb.	12.86	1,857.7	390.5	1.09	78.9	1.41

Date	Three-Month Treasury Bill Rate (percent) *INTRATE*	Disposable Personal Income (billions of dollars) (SAAR) *YDP*	Money Supply, M1 Definition (billions of dollars) (SA)	Percent Change in Money Supply (percent) *PMONEY*	Consumer Price Index 1982 – 1984 = 100 *CPI*	Percent Change in CPI (percent) *PPRICE*
Mar.	15.20	1,866.2	387.7	−0.72	80.1	1.52
Apr.	13.20	1,862.7	379.5	−2.12	81.0	1.12
May	8.58	1,867.0	380.8	0.34	81.8	0.99
June	7.07	1,879.7	386.6	1.52	82.7	1.10
July	8.06	1,913.8	392.2	1.45	82.7	0.00
Aug.	9.13	1,932.9	401.6	2.40	83.3	0.73
Sept.	10.27	1,955.3	409.1	1.87	84.0	0.84
Oct.	11.62	1,985.7	410.5	0.34	84.8	0.95
Nov.	13.73	2,009.7	415.4	1.19	85.5	0.83
Dec.	15.49	2,035.3	412.2	−0.77	86.3	0.94
1981: Jan.	15.02	2,049.2	411.7	−0.12	87.0	0.81
Feb.	14.79	2,065.1	415.5	0.92	87.9	1.03
Mar.	13.36	2,082.4	417.7	0.53	88.5	0.68
Apr.	13.69	2,089.5	422.7	1.20	89.1	0.68
May	16.30	2,091.2	421.6	−0.26	89.8	0.79
June	14.73	2,106.7	421.9	0.07	90.6	0.89
July	14.95	2,143.4	425.5	0.85	91.6	1.10
Aug.	15.51	2,165.9	429.6	0.96	92.3	0.76
Sept.	14.70	2,176.6	432.1	0.58	93.2	0.98
Oct.	13.54	2,187.1	429.5	−0.60	93.4	0.21
Nov.	10.86	2,189.7	434.3	1.12	93.7	0.32
Dec.	10.85	2,184.3	439.1	1.11	94.0	0.32
1982: Jan.	12.28	2,198.0	443.4	0.98	94.3	0.32
Feb.	13.48	2,206.6	442.1	−0.29	94.6	0.32
Mar.	12.68	2,216.9	441.1	−0.23	94.5	−0.11
Apr.	12.70	2,238.4	443.3	0.50	94.9	0.42
May	12.09	2,244.8	444.4	0.25	95.8	0.95
June	12.47	2,242.3	445.6	0.27	97.0	1.25
July	11.35	2,276.9	447.4	0.40	97.5	0.52
Aug.	8.68	2,275.6	453.4	1.34	97.7	0.21
Sept.	7.92	2,283.2	460.9	1.65	97.9	0.20
Oct.	7.71	2,299.8	466.2	1.15	98.2	0.31
Nov.	8.07	2,321.7	473.1	1.48	98.0	−0.20
Dec.	7.94	2,332.7	476.4	0.70	97.6	−0.41
1983: Jan.	7.86	2,344.3	477.3	0.19	97.8	0.20
Feb.	8.11	2,339.2	484.0	1.40	97.9	0.10
Mar.	8.35	2,353.7	489.0	1.03	97.9	0.00
Apr.	8.21	2,382.0	491.4	0.49	98.6	0.72
May	8.19	2,397.4	498.2	1.38	99.2	0.61
June	8.79	2,406.9	502.5	0.86	99.5	0.30
July	9.08	2,438.6	508.5	1.19	99.9	0.40

TABLE D-9 *(Continued)*

Date	Three-Month Treasury Bill Rate (percent) INTRATE	Disposable Personal Income (billions of dollars) (SAAR) YDP	Money Supply, M1 Definition (billions of dollars) (SA)	Percent Change in Money Supply (percent) PMONEY	Consumer Price Index 1982 − 1984 = 100 CPI	Percent Change in CPI (percent) PPRICE
Aug.	9.34	2,433.2	511.9	0.67	100.2	0.30
Sept.	9.00	2,457.7	515.4	0.68	100.7	0.50
Oct.	8.64	2,499.1	518.2	0.54	101.0	0.30
Nov.	8.76	2,528.7	520.0	0.35	101.2	0.20
Dec.	9.00	2,555.9	522.1	0.40	101.3	0.10
1984: Jan.	8.90	2,585.2	524.9	0.54	101.9	0.59
Feb.	9.09	2,614.3	527.3	0.46	102.4	0.49
Mar.	9.52	2,635.9	530.6	0.63	102.6	0.20
Apr.	9.69	2,637.8	533.1	0.47	103.1	0.49
May	9.83	2,637.0	535.7	0.49	103.4	0.29
June	9.87	2,653.5	540.0	0.80	103.7	0.29
July	10.12	2,675.9	540.9	0.17	104.1	0.39
Aug.	10.47	2,688.0	541.5	0.11	104.5	0.38
Sept.	10.37	2,709.4	545.1	0.66	105.0	0.48
Oct.	9.74	2,710.9	543.7	−0.26	105.3	0.29
Nov.	8.61	2,725.5	547.3	0.66	105.3	0.00
Dec.	8.06	2,749.5	551.9	0.84	105.3	0.00
1985: Jan.	7.76	2,771.2	556.0	0.74	105.5	0.19
Feb.	8.27	2,764.6	563.1	1.28	106.0	0.47
Mar.	8.52	2,757.9	566.3	0.57	106.4	0.38
Apr.	7.95	2,832.9	569.8	0.62	106.9	0.47
May	7.48	2,890.2	575.0	0.91	107.3	0.37
June	6.95	2,829.2	583.2	1.43	107.6	0.28
July	7.08	2,835.1	589.0	0.99	107.8	0.19
Aug.	7.14	2,837.4	597.1	1.38	108.0	0.19
Sept.	7.10	2,847.5	604.3	1.21	108.3	0.28
Oct.	7.16	2,877.2	607.4	0.51	108.7	0.37
Nov.	7.24	2,887.5	612.7	0.87	109.0	0.28
Dec.	7.10	2,933.7	620.5	1.27	109.3	0.28
1986: Jan.	7.07	2,944.9	621.3	0.13	109.6	0.27
Feb.	7.06	2,958.1	625.3	0.64	109.3	−0.27
Mar.	6.56	2,974.6	634.2	1.42	108.8	−0.46
Apr.	6.06	3,010.6	641.5	1.15	108.6	−0.18
May	6.15	3,004.5	652.1	1.65	108.9	0.28
June	6.21	3,004.2	660.6	1.30	109.5	0.55
July	5.83	3,013.5	670.1	1.44	109.5	0.00
Aug.	5.53	3,022.2	679.9	1.46	109.7	0.18
Sept.	5.21	3,037.0	687.4	1.10	110.2	0.46
Oct.	5.18	3,047.7	695.3	1.15	110.3	0.09
Nov.	5.35	3,061.2	707.1	1.70	110.4	0.09
Dec.	5.53	3,081.4	725.9	2.66	110.5	0.09

TABLE D-9 *(Continued)*

Date	Three-Month Treasury Bill Rate (percent) INTRATE	Disposable Personal Income (billions of dollars) (SAAR) YDP	Money Supply, M1 Definition (billions of dollars) (SA)	Percent Change in Money Supply (percent) PMONEY	Consumer Price Index 1982 – 1984 = 100 CPI	Percent Change in CPI (percent) PPRICE
1987: Jan.	5.43	3,111.3	730.8	0.68	111.2	0.63
Feb.	5.59	3,152.7	732.0	0.16	111.6	0.36
Mar.	5.59	3,164.4	734.8	0.38	112.1	0.45
Apr.	5.64	3,053.1	745.1	1.40	112.7	0.54
May	5.66	3,176.5	746.6	0.20	113.1	0.35
June	5.67	3,184.6	741.3	−0.71	113.5	0.35
July	5.69	3,205.0	742.8	0.20	113.8	0.26
Aug.	6.04	3,225.4	745.6	0.38	114.4	0.53
Sept.	6.40	3,240.0	747.9	0.31	115.0	0.52
Oct.	6.13	3,312.3	757.3	1.26	115.3	0.26
Nov.	5.69	3,300.3	754.6	−0.36	115.4	0.09
Dec.	5.77	3,345.7	752.3	−0.30	115.4	0.00
1988: Jan.	5.81	3,345.8	758.4	0.81	115.7	0.26
Feb.	5.66	3,377.9	760.1	0.22	116.0	0.26
Mar.	5.70	3,405.4	763.8	0.49	116.5	0.43
Apr.	5.91	3,399.0	771.2	0.97	117.1	0.52
May	6.26	3,438.0	771.1	−0.01	117.5	0.34
June	6.46	3,470.5	776.5	0.70	118.0	0.43
July	6.73	3,495.5	782.5	0.77	118.5	0.42
Aug.	7.06	3,509.9	782.4	−0.01	119.0	0.42
Sept.	7.24	3,529.5	783.7	0.17	119.8	0.67
Oct.	7.35	3,584.2	785.4	0.22	120.2	0.33
Nov.	7.76	3,572.6	786.6	0.15	120.3	0.08
Dec.	8.07	3,605.4	790.3	0.47	120.5	0.17
1989: Jan.	8.27	3,641.9	786.3	−0.51	121.1	0.50
Feb.	8.53	3,697.8	787.5	0.15	121.6	0.41
Mar.	8.82	3,728.8	786.3	−0.15	122.3	0.58
Apr.	8.65	3,718.7	783.2	−0.39	123.1	0.65
May	8.43	3,747.2	773.4	−1.25	123.8	0.57
June	8.15	3,777.2	770.3	−0.40	124.1	0.24
July	7.88	3,798.5	777.2	0.90	124.4	0.24
Aug.	7.90	3,808.6	777.4	0.03	124.6	0.16
Sept.	7.75	3,813.4	781.1	0.48	125.0	0.32
Oct.	7.64	3,842.6	787.7	0.84	125.6	0.48
Nov.	7.69	3,877.9	789.6	0.24	125.9	0.24

See example 6-9 and equations (6-79) and (6-80).

Appendix E

The Durbin-Watson d Statistic

TABLE E-1 Level of Significance α = .025

| | k^a = 1 | | k = 2 | | k = 3 | | k = 4 | | k = 5 | |
n	d_l	d_u	d_l	d_u	d_l	d_u	d_l	d_u	d_l	d_u
15	0.95	1.23	0.83	1.40	0.71	1.61	0.59	1.84	0.48	2.09
16	0.98	1.24	0.86	1.40	0.75	1.59	0.64	1.80	0.53	2.03
17	1.01	1.25	0.90	1.40	0.79	1.58	0.68	1.77	0.57	1.98
18	1.03	1.26	0.93	1.40	0.82	1.56	0.72	1.74	0.62	1.93
19	1.06	1.28	0.96	1.41	0.86	1.55	0.76	1.73	0.66	1.90
20	1.08	1.28	0.99	1.41	0.89	1.55	0.79	1.72	0.70	1.87
21	1.10	1.30	1.01	1.41	0.92	1.54	0.83	1.69	0.73	1.84
22	1.12	1.31	1.04	1.42	0.95	1.54	0.86	1.68	0.77	1.82
23	1.14	1.32	1.06	1.42	0.97	1.54	0.89	1.67	0.80	1.80
24	1.16	1.33	1.08	1.43	1.00	1.54	0.91	1.66	0.83	1.79
25	1.18	1.34	1.10	1.43	1.02	1.54	0.94	1.65	0.86	1.77
26	1.19	1.35	1.12	1.44	1.04	1.54	0.96	1.65	0.88	1.76
27	1.21	1.36	1.13	1.44	1.06	1.54	0.99	1.64	0.91	1.75
28	1.22	1.37	1.15	1.45	1.08	1.54	1.01	1.64	0.93	1.74
29	1.24	1.38	1.17	1.45	1.10	1.54	1.03	1.63	0.96	1.73
30	1.25	1.38	1.18	1.46	1.12	1.54	1.05	1.63	0.98	1.73
31	1.26	1.39	1.20	1.47	1.13	1.55	1.07	1.63	1.00	1.72
32	1.27	1.40	1.21	1.47	1.15	1.55	1.08	1.63	1.02	1.71
33	1.28	1.41	1.22	1.48	1.16	1.55	1.10	1.63	1.04	1.71
34	1.29	1.41	1.24	1.48	1.17	1.55	1.12	1.63	1.06	1.70
35	1.30	1.42	1.25	1.48	1.19	1.55	1.13	1.63	1.07	1.70
36	1.31	1.43	1.26	1.49	1.20	1.56	1.15	1.63	1.09	1.70
37	1.32	1.43	1.27	1.49	1.21	1.56	1.16	1.62	1.10	1.70
38	1.33	1.44	1.28	1.50	1.23	1.56	1.17	1.62	1.12	1.70
39	1.34	1.44	1.29	1.50	1.24	1.56	1.19	1.63	1.13	1.69
40	1.35	1.45	1.30	1.51	1.25	1.57	1.20	1.63	1.15	1.69
45	1.39	1.48	1.34	1.53	1.30	1.58	1.25	1.63	1.21	1.69
50	1.42	1.50	1.38	1.54	1.34	1.59	1.30	1.64	1.26	1.69
55	1.45	1.52	1.41	1.56	1.37	1.60	1.33	1.64	1.30	1.69
60	1.47	1.54	1.44	1.57	1.40	1.61	1.37	1.65	1.33	1.69
65	1.49	1.55	1.46	1.59	1.43	1.63	1.40	1.66	1.36	1.69
70	1.51	1.57	1.48	1.60	1.45	1.63	1.42	1.66	1.39	1.70
75	1.53	1.58	1.50	1.61	1.47	1.64	1.45	1.67	1.42	1.70
80	1.54	1.59	1.52	1.63	1.49	1.65	1.47	1.67	1.44	1.70
85	1.56	1.60	1.53	1.63	1.51	1.66	1.49	1.68	1.46	1.71
90	1.57	1.61	1.55	1.64	1.53	1.66	1.50	1.69	1.48	1.71
95	1.58	1.62	1.56	1.65	1.54	1.67	1.52	1.69	1.50	1.71
100	1.59	1.63	1.57	1.65	1.55	1.67	1.53	1.70	1.51	1.72

[a] k = number of regressors, excluding the constant.

Source: J. Durbin and G. S. Watson, "Testing for Serial Correlation in Least Squares Regression, II," *Biometrika*, vol. 38, 1951, pp. 159–78. Reprinted by permission of the Biometrika Trustees.

TABLE E-2　Level of Significance $\alpha = .01$

n	$k^a = 1$ d_l	d_u	$k = 2$ d_l	d_u	$k = 3$ d_l	d_u	$k = 4$ d_l	d_u	$k = 5$ d_l	d_u
15	0.81	1.07	0.70	1.25	0.59	1.46	0.49	1.70	0.39	1.96
16	0.84	1.09	0.74	1.25	0.63	1.44	0.53	1.66	0.44	1.90
17	0.87	1.10	0.77	1.25	0.67	1.43	0.57	1.63	0.48	1.85
18	0.90	1.12	0.80	1.26	0.71	1.42	0.61	1.60	0.52	1.80
19	0.93	1.13	0.83	1.26	0.74	1.41	0.65	1.58	0.56	1.77
20	0.95	1.15	0.86	1.27	0.77	1.41	0.68	1.57	0.60	1.74
21	0.97	1.16	0.89	1.27	0.80	1.41	0.72	1.55	0.63	1.71
22	1.00	1.17	0.91	1.28	0.83	1.40	0.75	1.54	0.66	1.69
23	1.02	1.19	0.94	1.29	0.86	1.40	0.77	1.53	0.70	1.67
24	1.04	1.20	0.96	1.30	0.88	1.41	0.80	1.53	0.72	1.66
25	1.05	1.21	0.98	1.30	0.90	1.41	0.83	1.52	0.75	1.65
26	1.07	1.22	1.00	1.31	0.93	1.41	0.85	1.52	0.78	1.64
27	1.09	1.23	1.02	1.32	0.95	1.41	0.88	1.51	0.81	1.63
28	1.10	1.24	1.04	1.32	0.97	1.41	0.90	1.51	0.83	1.62
29	1.12	1.25	1.05	1.33	0.99	1.42	0.92	1.51	0.85	1.61
30	1.13	1.26	1.07	1.34	1.01	1.42	0.94	1.51	0.88	1.61
31	1.15	1.27	1.08	1.34	1.02	1.42	0.96	1.51	0.90	1.60
32	1.16	1.28	1.10	1.35	1.04	1.43	0.98	1.51	0.92	1.60
33	1.17	1.29	1.11	1.36	1.05	1.43	1.00	1.51	0.94	1.59
34	1.18	1.30	1.13	1.36	1.07	1.43	1.01	1.51	0.95	1.59
35	1.19	1.31	1.14	1.37	1.08	1.44	1.03	1.51	0.97	1.59
36	1.21	1.32	1.15	1.38	1.10	1.44	1.04	1.51	0.99	1.59
37	1.22	1.32	1.16	1.38	1.11	1.45	1.06	1.51	1.00	1.59
38	1.23	1.33	1.18	1.39	1.12	1.45	1.07	1.52	1.02	1.58
39	1.24	1.34	1.19	1.39	1.14	1.45	1.09	1.52	1.03	1.58
40	1.25	1.34	1.20	1.40	1.15	1.46	1.10	1.52	1.05	1.58
45	1.29	1.38	1.24	1.42	1.20	1.48	1.16	1.53	1.11	1.58
50	1.32	1.40	1.28	1.45	1.24	1.49	1.20	1.54	1.16	1.59
55	1.36	1.43	1.32	1.47	1.28	1.51	1.25	1.55	1.21	1.59
60	1.38	1.45	1.35	1.48	1.32	1.52	1.28	1.56	1.25	1.60
65	1.41	1.47	1.38	1.50	1.35	1.53	1.31	1.57	1.28	1.61
70	1.43	1.49	1.40	1.52	1.37	1.55	1.34	1.58	1.31	1.61
75	1.45	1.50	1.42	1.53	1.39	1.56	1.37	1.59	1.34	1.62
80	1.47	1.52	1.44	1.54	1.42	1.57	1.39	1.60	1.36	1.62
85	1.48	1.53	1.46	1.55	1.43	1.58	1.41	1.60	1.39	1.63
90	1.50	1.54	1.47	1.56	1.45	1.59	1.43	1.61	1.41	1.64
95	1.51	1.55	1.49	1.57	1.47	1.60	1.45	1.62	1.42	1.64
100	1.52	1.56	1.50	1.58	1.48	1.60	1.46	1.63	1.44	1.65

[a] k = number of regressors, excluding the constant.

Source: J. Durbin and G. S. Watson, "Testing for Serial Correlation in Least Squares Regression, II," *Biometrika*, vol. 38, 1951, pp. 159–78. Reprinted by permission of the Biometrika Trustees.

Appendix F

Sample Data Sets for Examples in Chapter 7

TABLE F-1   Gas Consumption: Sample Data

Date	Sales of Natural Gas (millions of cubic feet) GAS	Price per Cubic Foot (1981 = 100.0) PRICE	Price per Kilowatt Hour (1981 = 100.0) ELECT	Nonagricultural Employment (thousands) EMPLOY	Heating Degree Days HDD	Cooling Degree Days CDD
1979	221,559	95.8	96.5	752	3,365	2,164
1980	207,072	98.5	98.9	779	2,993	2,062
1981	204,299	100.0	100.0	810	3,377	1,991
1982	231,871	98.7	100.1	865	2,941	2,235
1983	197,548	101.0	107.5	858	2,643	1,840
1984	244,567	112.6	113.1	875	2,882	2,184
1985	210,892	124.8	114.4	907	3,025	1,800
1986	219,655	140.4	115.4	943	2,956	2,681
1987	245,483	144.3	115.8	989	3,394	2,357
1988	225,052	153.6	114.5	1,016	3,372	2,088
1989	205,216	166.1	120.1	1,018	3,142	2,784
1990	187,112	173.6	127.2	1,043	2,846	2,430

See example 7-1 and equation (7-2).

TABLE F-2 Logarithmic Transformations and Freight Shipments: Sample Data

Date	High-Value Freight Shipments (packages) SHIP	Consumption of Services (billions of 1987 dollars) CES87	Consumption of Durables (billions of 1987 dollars) CED87	Consumption of Nondurables (billions of 1987 dollars) CEN87	LOG(SHIP)	LOG(CES87)	LOG(CED87)	LOG(CEN87)
1982: I	133,038	1,019.2	247.7	764.2	5.1240	3.0083	2.3939	2.8832
II	139,514	1,023.5	249.1	768.3	5.1446	3.0101	2.3964	2.8855
III	149,537	1,027.2	251.8	772.8	5.1747	3.0117	2.4011	2.8881
IV	159,960	1,038.1	262.0	778.6	5.2040	3.0162	2.4183	2.8913
1983: I	175,699	1,044.6	263.3	786.3	5.2448	3.0190	2.4205	2.8956
II	193,110	1,059.4	280.0	795.7	5.2858	3.0251	2.4472	2.9007
III	222,286	1,068.3	288.5	806.2	5.3469	3.0287	2.4601	2.9064
IV	253,695	1,078.6	300.5	812.7	5.4043	3.0329	2.4778	2.9099
1984: I	285,701	1,085.0	312.6	814.5	5.4559	3.0354	2.4950	2.9109
II	320,236	1,096.1	322.5	828.2	5.5055	3.0399	2.5085	2.9181
III	360,310	1,103.5	324.3	829.6	5.5567	3.0428	2.5109	2.9189
IV	387,158	1,116.8	333.1	831.2	5.5879	3.0480	2.5226	2.9197
1985: I	435,145	1,136.2	344.8	838.2	5.6386	3.0555	2.5376	2.9233
II	463,234	1,144.1	350.3	843.0	5.6658	3.0585	2.5444	2.9258
III	486,464	1,156.8	369.1	850.0	5.6871	3.0633	2.5671	2.9294
IV	536,968	1,172.2	356.4	858.3	5.7299	3.0690	2.5519	2.9336
1986: I	565,733	1,177.1	363.7	870.1	5.7526	3.0708	2.5607	2.9396
II	606,696	1,178.0	374.5	878.8	5.7830	3.0711	2.5735	2.9439
III	635,207	1,183.4	401.9	879.1	5.8029	3.0731	2.6041	2.9440
IV	675,493	1,196.8	397.5	883.5	5.8296	3.0780	2.5993	2.9462
1987: I	706,968	1,214.5	376.1	887.7	5.8494	3.0844	2.5753	2.9483
II	756,063	1,229.5	389.3	889.0	5.8786	3.0897	2.5903	2.9489
III	795,432	1,240.9	403.8	891.8	5.9006	3.0937	2.6062	2.9503
IV	827,609	1,250.0	389.4	892.9	5.9178	3.0969	2.5904	2.9508
1988: I	881,379	1,265.9	408.4	896.6	5.9452	3.1024	2.6111	2.9526
II	905,832	1,272.8	414.8	899.2	5.9570	3.1048	2.6178	2.9539
III	954,735	1,287.0	410.7	910.3	5.9799	3.1096	2.6135	2.9592
IV	994,193	1,295.2	420.5	912.0	5.9975	3.1123	2.6238	2.9600
1989: I	1,027,907	1,306.7	419.3	915.0	6.0120	3.1162	2.6225	2.9614
II	1,082,677	1,319.0	424.9	909.7	6.0345	3.1202	2.6283	2.9589
III	1,114,070	1,332.9	436.4	920.8	6.0469	3.1248	2.6399	2.9642
IV	1,167,868	1,350.3	421.6	917.5	6.0674	3.1304	2.6249	2.9626

See example 7-8 and equations (7-22) and (7-23).

TABLE F-3 Logarithmic Transformations and Revenue Forecasts: Sample Data

Date	Personal Income (billions of dollars) INC	Population (millions) POP	Per Capita Personal Income (dollars) PCPI	Sales Tax Revenues (thousands of dollars) REV	Sales Tax Rate (percent) RATE	LOG(INC)	LOG(POP)	LOG(PCPI)	LOG(REV)	LOG(RATE)
1960	5,746	3,575	1,607	107,092	2.0	3.7594	3.5533	3.2060	5.0298	0.3010
1961	6,073	3,622	1,677	108,339	2.0	3.7834	3.5589	3.2245	5.0348	0.3010
1962	6,450	3,673	1,756	117,737	2.3	3.8096	3.5650	3.2445	5.0709	0.3617
1963	6,844	3,718	1,841	133,139	2.5	3.8353	3.5703	3.2651	5.1243	0.3979
1964	7,354	3,771	1,950	153,399	2.5	3.8665	3.5765	3.2900	5.1858	0.3979
1965	8,020	3,798	2,112	169,323	2.5	3.9042	3.5796	3.3247	5.2287	0.3979
1966	8,859	3,822	2,318	184,868	2.5	3.9474	3.5823	3.3651	5.2669	0.3979
1967	9,470	3,859	2,454	194,087	2.8	3.9763	3.5865	3.3899	5.2880	0.4393
1968	10,533	3,878	2,716	216,536	3.0	4.0226	3.5886	3.4339	5.3355	0.4771
1969	11,439	3,897	2,935	234,224	3.0	4.0584	3.5907	3.4676	5.3696	0.4771
1970	12,405	3,937	3,151	247,392	3.0	4.0936	3.5952	3.4984	5.3934	0.4771
1971	13,618	4,010	3,396	305,289	3.3	4.1341	3.6031	3.5310	5.4847	0.5185
1972	15,312	4,088	3,745	374,005	3.5	4.1850	3.6115	3.5735	5.5729	0.5441
1973	17,531	4,138	4,236	427,880	3.5	4.2438	3.6168	3.6270	5.6313	0.5441
1974	19,390	4,202	4,615	466,691	3.5	4.2876	3.6235	3.6642	5.6690	0.5441
1975	20,978	4,261	4,924	493,517	3.5	4.3218	3.6295	3.6923	5.6933	0.5441
1976	23,625	4,329	5,457	650,768	4.3	4.3734	3.6364	3.7370	5.8134	0.6335
1977	26,183	4,402	5,948	784,067	4.5	4.4180	3.6437	3.7744	5.8944	0.6532
1978	29,859	4,462	6,692	890,663	4.5	4.4751	3.6495	3.8256	5.9497	0.6532
1979	33,508	4,533	7,392	965,216	4.5	4.5251	3.6564	3.8688	5.9846	0.6532
1980	36,958	4,603	8,030	993,830	4.5	4.5677	3.6630	3.9047	5.9973	0.6532
1981	40,872	4,639	8,811	1,083,204	4.5	4.6114	3.6664	3.9450	6.0347	0.6532
1982	42,969	4,666	9,208	1,143,883	4.5	4.6332	3.6689	3.9642	6.0584	0.6532
1983	45,745	4,690	9,753	1,225,438	4.5	4.6603	3.6712	3.9891	6.0883	0.6532
1984	50,360	4,728	10,652	1,584,443	5.3	4.7021	3.6747	4.0274	6.1999	0.7243
1985	53,681	4,766	11,263	1,798,533	5.5	4.7298	3.6782	4.0517	6.2549	0.7404
1986	57,523	4,800	11,984	1,928,575	5.5	4.7598	3.6812	4.0786	6.2852	0.7404
1987	62,533	4,855	12,880	2,060,255	5.5	4.7961	3.6862	4.1099	6.3139	0.7404
1988	67,979	4,911	13,842	2,180,559	5.5	4.8324	3.6912	4.1412	6.3386	0.7404
1989	72,600	4,968	14,614	2,308,778	5.5	4.8609	3.6962	4.1648	6.3634	0.7404

TABLE F-4   Housing Sales: Sample Data

Date	Single-Family Home Sales (millions) (SAAR) SALES	Additions to the Available Capital Stock (millions) (SAAR) ADD	Employment in Construc-tion (millions) (SA) EMPCON	Index of Con-sumer Sentiment (1966:QI = 100) JCS	Unemployment Rate (percent) (SA) UNEMP	Number of Households (millions) (SA) HH	Price of Housing (1982 – 1984 = 100) PHOME
1971: I	1.930	0.902	3.576	78.200	5.933	67.082	37.467
II	2.013	0.873	3.684	81.600	5.900	67.482	37.633
III	2.017	0.989	3.727	82.400	6.033	67.914	38.233
IV	2.123	1.051	3.810	82.200	5.933	68.378	38.600
1972: I	2.177	1.117	3.852	87.500	5.767	68.947	38.967
II	2.147	1.136	3.886	89.300	5.700	69.407	39.233
III	2.277	1.155	3.897	94.000	5.567	69.837	39.700
IV	2.417	1.160	3.917	90.800	5.367	70.237	39.933
1973: I	2.450	1.180	4.008	80.800	4.933	70.497	40.233
II	2.347	1.296	4.072	76.000	4.933	70.921	40.667
III	2.287	1.283	4.142	71.800	4.800	71.397	41.333
IV	2.253	1.134	4.153	75.700	4.767	71.921	42.467
1974: I	2.410	1.099	4.216	60.900	5.133	72.633	43.667
II	2.353	1.008	4.105	72.000	5.200	73.133	44.900
III	2.230	0.992	3.951	64.500	5.633	73.563	46.500
IV	2.167	0.911	3.833	58.400	6.600	73.923	48.133
1975: I	2.193	0.871	3.652	58.000	8.267	74.077	49.367
II	2.457	0.840	3.456	72.900	8.867	74.410	50.233
III	2.537	0.831	3.476	75.800	8.467	74.790	51.000
IV	2.733	0.908	3.531	75.400	8.300	75.219	51.933
1976: I	2.880	0.907	3.580	84.500	7.733	75.802	52.767
II	3.003	0.979	3.565	82.200	7.567	76.266	53.267
III	3.140	1.023	3.567	88.800	7.733	76.711	54.100
IV	3.240	1.026	3.592	86.000	7.767	77.137	54.833
1977: I	3.457	1.078	3.649	87.500	7.500	77.469	55.900
II	3.600	1.198	3.841	89.100	7.133	77.911	56.800
III	3.707	1.195	3.917	87.600	6.900	78.390	57.933
IV	3.820	1.334	3.968	83.100	6.667	78.906	59.000
1978: I	3.900	1.277	3.997	82.267	6.333	79.552	60.100
II	4.043	1.301	4.234	81.500	6.000	80.081	61.567
III	3.960	1.395	4.308	80.400	6.033	80.588	63.200
IV	4.043	1.389	4.346	73.467	5.900	81.079	64.867
1979: I	3.937	1.384	4.361	71.467	5.867	81.380	66.400
II	3.960	1.344	4.461	66.633	5.700	81.978	68.467
III	3.867	1.338	4.505	63.867	5.867	82.691	71.167
IV	3.547	1.243	4.508	62.133	5.967	83.506	74.167
1980: I	3.163	1.284	4.526	63.467	6.300	84.650	77.233
II	2.540	1.179	4.325	54.367	7.333	85.447	80.633
III	3.127	0.986	4.262	67.767	7.667	86.122	81.867
IV	3.057	0.857	4.298	72.067	7.400	86.661	84.433
1981: I	2.667	0.858	4.284	68.267	7.433	86.899	86.600
II	2.630	0.916	4.240	73.933	7.400	87.273	88.800
III	2.337	0.893	4.157	74.800	7.400	87.628	92.300
IV	2.040	0.816	4.090	65.700	8.233	87.968	93.767

Rental Price Residential (1982 – 1984 = 100) REN	Housing Affordability Index (Base = 100) HAI	Interest Rate Conventional Home Mortgages (percent) INT	Vacancy Rates of Rental Units (%) RVAC	Real Disposable Income (billions of 1982 dollars) YDP82	Average Selling Price of Existing Houses ($) OLDSP	Median Price New Homes ($) MPNEW	Average Selling Price New Homes (thousands) PNEW	Vacancy Rates for Homes (%) HVAC
47.902	149.000	7.853	5.30	1,708.1	26,433	24,233	35.1	1.0
48.478	150.367	7.477	5.30	1,731.9	27,600	25,800	35.9	0.9
48.904	147.267	7.710	5.60	1,734.2	27,867	25,300	36.8	1.0
49.325	150.267	7.717	5.60	1,739.6	27,633	25,533	37.5	1.0
49.688	152.033	7.530	5.30	1,750.9	28,200	26,200	37.9	1.0
50.112	148.233	7.473	5.50	1,767.6	29,500	26,833	38.3	1.0
50.543	147.533	7.533	5.80	1,801.5	30,033	27,933	38.8	0.9
50.964	151.233	7.593	5.60	1,869.4	29,667	29,233	40.3	1.0
51.642	147.500	7.697	5.70	1,893.2	31,567	30,333	41.0	1.0
52.217	145.067	7.750	5.80	1,907.6	32,900	32,633	41.4	0.9
52.814	139.800	8.037	5.80	1,922.2	33,667	33,533	43.1	1.1
53.430	137.167	8.497	5.80	1,942.1	33,200	34,333	43.9	1.2
54.099	131.800	8.633	6.20	1,907.2	34,700	35,033	44.9	1.2
54.759	127.833	8.737	6.30	1,888.3	36,000	35,500	45.7	1.1
55.483	122.700	9.140	6.20	1,898.6	36,867	36,500	46.8	1.2
56.255	122.200	9.493	6.00	1,892.4	35,800	37,300	47.9	1.3
56.964	120.333	9.363	6.10	1,873.1	37,500	37,967	49.7	1.2
57.603	120.167	9.053	6.30	1,965.7	39,267	38,867	50.4	1.2
58.319	119.300	9.053	6.20	1,935.0	39,867	38,833	51.2	1.4
59.104	121.333	9.180	5.40	1,953.1	39,200	41,300	52.4	1.2
59.902	121.033	9.147	5.50	1,983.1	40,500	42,633	52.8	1.2
60.750	121.000	9.017	5.80	1,992.8	42,167	44,333	54.6	1.2
61.589	119.800	9.067	5.70	2,005.9	43,100	44,500	56.0	1.3
62.309	122.767	9.097	5.30	2,022.2	42,867	45,667	56.4	1.2
63.378	121.200	8.997	5.10	2,026.9	44,867	46,367	58.3	1.3
64.338	117.633	8.957	5.30	2,049.6	47,000	48,900	60.4	1.3
65.290	115.167	9.030	5.40	2,086.9	48,000	48,700	61.3	1.1
66.239	115.533	9.087	5.10	2,102.8	48,333	51,967	64.5	1.0
67.421	112.333	9.193	5.00	2,128.2	50,900	52,900	65.0	1.0
68.734	108.333	9.380	5.10	2,162.7	54,500	55,233	68.4	0.9
69.856	103.733	9.707	5.00	2,176.4	57,233	56,067	71.2	1.0
71.066	102.867	9.950	5.00	2,202.0	57,600	58,967	73.1	1.1
72.128	98.233	10.343	5.10	2,216.6	60,367	60,633	75.7	1.1
73.404	93.433	10.583	5.50	2,206.6	64,267	63,200	79.7	1.1
75.019	89.533	11.043	5.70	2,213.7	66,367	64,600	81.2	1.2
76.795	90.967	11.507	5.40	2,213.7	65,000	62,567	82.8	1.3
78.299	82.467	12.377	5.20	2,225.6	69,000	63,467	85.1	1.3
79.977	73.800	13.537	5.60	2,185.7	71,967	63,700	87.5	1.4
81.743	78.467	12.410	5.70	2,207.2	75,800	65,233	89.4	1.4
83.632	76.867	13.110	5.00	2,238.8	74,100	66,433	90.7	1.4
85.267	72.267	13.920	5.20	2,242.9	76,000	66,833	94.0	1.3
87.067	68.367	14.557	5.00	2,235.0	78,600	69,433	96.2	1.3
88.733	64.467	15.417	5.00	2,262.9	79,733	69,300	97.8	1.5
90.633	64.633	16.080	5.00	2,253.7	77,567	69,733	99.5	1.4

Date	Single-Family Home Sales (millions) (SAAR) SALES	Additions to the Available Capital Stock (millions) (SAAR) ADD	Employment in Construction (millions) (SA) EMPCON	Index of Consumer Sentiment (1966:QI = 100) JCS	Unemployment Rate (percent) (SA) UNEMP	Number of Households (millions) (SA) HH	Price of Housing (1982 – 1984 = 100) PHOME
1982: I	1.967	0.689	3.972	66.500	8.833	88.413	94.567
II	1.907	0.597	3.947	66.233	9.433	88.669	96.600
III	1.907	0.621	3.878	66.700	9.900	88.858	98.233
IV	2.183	0.630	3.837	72.467	10.667	88.992	98.133
1983: I	2.543	0.673	3.823	75.267	10.367	88.918	98.167
II	2.723	0.759	3.853	91.533	10.133	89.104	99.100
III	2.810	0.865	3.999	91.567	9.367	89.393	99.867
IV	2.793	0.996	4.101	91.533	8.533	89.789	100.733
1984: I	2.927	1.020	4.244	99.500	7.867	90.437	101.967
II	2.983	1.027	4.342	96.567	7.433	90.936	103.100
III	2.763	1.033	4.434	98.867	7.433	91.425	104.267
IV	2.800	1.045	4.501	94.967	7.300	91.894	105.100
1985: I	2.987	0.993	4.575	94.467	7.267	92.261	105.967
II	3.060	1.066	4.659	94.300	7.267	92.725	107.267
III	3.357	1.063	4.696	92.833	7.200	93.208	108.233
IV	3.453	1.064	4.756	91.067	7.067	93.703	109.400
1986: I	3.297	1.096	4.799	95.533	7.000	94.296	110.067
II	3.477	1.080	4.810	96.767	7.200	94.743	110.633
III	3.587	1.118	4.812	94.833	6.967	95.131	111.167
IV	3.890	1.105	4.849	92.033	6.867	95.465	111.667
1987: I	3.640	1.162	4.915	90.467	6.567	95.628	112.667
II	3.637	1.153	4.949	91.800	6.300	95.957	113.667
III	3.437	1.152	4.969	93.900	6.000	96.334	114.667
IV	3.390	1.097	5.032	86.400	5.900	96.762	115.600
1988: I	3.300	1.105	5.028	92.333	5.700	97.342	116.800
II	3.643	1.076	5.116	93.567	5.500	97.796	117.833
III	3.663	1.080	5.155	96.033	5.500	98.223	118.900
IV	3.770	1.086	5.189	93.000	5.300	98.619	120.100
1989: I	3.547	1.077	5.263	95.867	5.200	98.917	121.267
II	3.340	1.125	5.282	90.933	5.267	99.233	122.200
III	3.443	1.037	5.320	92.467	5.300	99.673	123.500
IV	3.537	0.988	5.331	91.767	5.300	100.065	124.700

See example 7-10, Figure 7-5, and equation (7-35).

Rental Price Residential (1982 – 1984 = 100) REN	Housing Affordability Index (Base = 100) HAI	Interest Rate Conventional Home Mortgages (percent) INT	Vacancy Rates of Rental Units (%) RVAC	Real Disposable Income (billions of 1982 dollars) YDP82	Average Selling Price of Existing Houses ($) OLDSP	Median Price New Homes ($) MPNEW	Average Selling Price New Homes (thousands) PNEW	Vacancy Rates for Homes (%) HVAC
92.367	66.400	15.653	5.30	2,245.7	79,233	66,367	99.3	1.4
93.767	65.667	15.887	5.10	2,260.9	80,767	69,600	100.9	1.6
95.400	67.933	15.487	5.30	2,263.4	81,333	69,567	100.5	1.5
96.967	74.133	14.310	5.50	2,276.1	80,100	71,633	99.3	1.6
98.433	79.567	13.347	5.70	2,288.4	80,467	73,267	101.4	1.4
99.567	82.033	12.733	5.50	2,311.1	82,567	75,000	101.7	1.5
100.633	81.800	12.693	5.80	2,335.4	83,900	77,667	104.7	1.6
101.700	85.067	12.523	5.50	2,392.7	83,100	75,900	104.0	1.6
102.967	87.167	12.210	5.60	2,446.9	84,500	77,933	104.5	1.6
104.667	87.033	12.153	5.50	2,456.6	86,267	80,500	107.3	1.7
106.067	84.333	12.680	6.00	2,479.2	86,967	81,333	107.7	1.7
107.500	86.167	12.863	6.30	2,496.3	85,733	80,300	108.9	1.7
109.133	88.400	12.357	6.30	2,509.4	88,233	82,900	110.1	1.8
110.967	90.967	11.983	6.20	2,563.5	90,667	84,000	109.4	1.9
112.533	95.467	11.320	6.80	2,535.4	92,433	83,367	110.2	1.8
114.467	99.867	11.187	6.70	2,562.8	91,100	86,833	110.8	1.6
115.800	99.933	10.747	6.90	2,609.2	94,300	88,333	111.4	1.5
117.867	100.567	10.243	7.30	2,648.6	100,633	91,933	114.9	1.7
119.133	103.800	10.207	7.50	2,637.3	99,233	93,533	114.4	1.6
120.367	109.267	9.840	7.70	2,646.2	99,000	95,133	111.6	1.6
121.633	111.067	9.290	7.40	2,672.3	103,367	97,367	115.5	1.7
122.433	111.033	9.267	7.50	2,632.5	106,933	103,467	116.9	1.7
123.733	110.067	9.370	8.10	2,675.6	107,900	106,100	118.4	1.7
124.867	114.767	9.257	7.80	2,726.2	106,600	111,767	116.3	1.6
126.233	111.633	9.180	8.00	2,757.2	110,667	112,933	117.2	1.6
127.200	111.400	9.227	7.70	2,773.3	112,767	110,833	116.8	1.6
128.433	110.633	9.290	7.80	2,806.4	114,233	114,867	116.7	1.6
129.500	112.100	9.463	7.30	2,835.9	112,233	114,767	116.4	1.6
130.767	107.600	9.790	7.30	2,881.7	115,933	118,000	120.6	1.5
132.100	101.400	10.350	7.30	2,887.6	118,300	119,500	119.0	1.5
133.500	101.467	10.237	7.30	2,919.2	120,300	119,300	120.4	1.8
134.867	105.767	10.097	7.25	2,936.9	117,567	124,333	119.2	1.6

TABLE F-5 Cash Collections and Time Lags: Sample Data

Date	Cash Collections (thousands of dollars) CF	Sales (thousands of dollars) S	Sales Lagged One Month	Sales Lagged Two Months	Sales Lagged Three Months
1985: 4	92,564	98,174	100,361	86,408	83,903
5	84,719	100,892	98,174	100,361	86,408
6	99,057	106,962	100,892	98,174	100,361
7	95,524	105,964	106,962	100,892	98,174
8	109,131	107,022	105,964	106,962	100,892
9	95,297	108,839	107,022	105,964	106,962
10	108,336	105,655	108,839	107,022	105,964
11	106,585	106,388	105,655	108,839	107,022
12	110,826	127,490	106,388	105,655	108,839
1986: 1	87,782	96,655	127,490	106,388	105,655
2	92,215	100,434	96,655	127,490	106,388
3	118,246	115,494	100,434	96,655	127,490
4	114,985	129,436	115,494	100,434	96,655
5	128,817	139,519	129,436	115,494	100,434
6	141,441	150,074	139,519	129,436	115,494
7	137,192	142,112	150,074	139,519	129,436
8	121,515	145,581	142,112	150,074	139,519
9	123,447	147,755	145,581	142,112	150,074
10	126,713	143,698	147,755	145,581	142,112
11	116,736	146,195	143,698	147,755	145,581
12	156,437	169,677	146,195	143,698	147,755
1987: 1	124,701	119,297	169,677	146,195	143,698
2	117,175	125,063	119,297	169,677	146,195
3	123,971	145,334	125,063	119,297	169,677
4	138,842	149,721	145,334	125,063	119,297
5	143,493	153,859	149,721	145,334	125,063
6	130,583	158,145	153,859	149,721	145,334
7	148,164	151,709	158,145	153,859	149,721
8	131,449	161,755	151,709	158,145	153,859
9	148,304	157,236	161,755	151,709	158,145
10	131,171	153,798	157,236	161,755	151,709
11	150,378	152,939	153,798	157,236	161,755
12	157,568	178,183	152,939	153,798	157,236

TABLE F-5 *(Continued)*

Date	Cash Collections (thousands of dollars) CF	Sales (thousands of dollars) S	Sales Lagged One Month	Sales Lagged Two Months	Sales Lagged Three Months
1988: 1	133,919	135,938	178,183	152,939	153,798
2	134,554	130,618	135,938	178,183	152,939
3	135,311	152,292	130,618	135,938	178,183
4	133,024	160,377	152,292	130,618	135,938
5	138,379	165,179	160,377	152,292	130,618
6	161,493	165,050	165,179	160,377	152,292
7	140,314	163,241	165,050	165,179	160,377
8	165,775	177,278	163,241	165,050	165,179
9	163,186	170,054	177,278	163,241	165,050
10	166,580	171,125	170,054	177,278	163,241
11	150,385	159,240	171,125	170,054	177,278
12	183,349	198,022	159,240	171,125	170,054
1989: 1	138,298	139,540	198,022	159,240	171,125
2	142,160	137,774	139,540	198,022	159,240
3	141,032	165,134	137,774	139,540	198,022
4	158,067	166,142	165,134	137,774	139,540
5	150,430	174,090	166,142	165,134	137,774
6	171,681	181,730	174,090	166,142	165,134
7	180,557	178,310	181,730	174,090	166,142
8	160,180	184,848	178,310	181,730	174,090
9	162,017	181,630	184,848	178,310	181,730
10	179,947	184,996	181,630	184,848	178,310
11	171,998	168,038	184,996	181,630	184,848
12	164,467	209,286	168,038	184,996	181,630
1990: 1	149,645	146,812	209,286	168,038	184,996
2	133,105	153,082	146,812	209,286	168,038
3	163,898	180,341	153,082	146,812	209,286
4	155,537	180,342	180,341	153,082	146,812
5	169,730	185,437	180,342	180,341	153,082
6	198,771	197,506	185,437	180,342	180,341
7	180,214	184,074	197,506	185,437	180,342
8	172,882	188,988	184,074	197,506	185,437
9	160,609	191,349	188,988	184,074	197,506
10	148,961	181,850	191,349	188,988	184,074
11	173,973	181,492	181,850	191,349	188,988
12	187,528	218,698	181,492	181,850	191,349

See example 7-11 and equation (7-42).

TABLE F-6 Consumption and Adaptive Expectations

Date	Consumption Expenditures (billions of dollars) C	Disposable Personal Income (billions of Y dollars)	Three-Month Treasury Bill Rate (percent) r
1969: I	581.7	631.5	6.087
II	592.7	647.0	6.190
III	602.7	667.7	7.010
IV	614.3	680.5	7.347
1970: I	625.1	691.1	7.210
II	635.1	711.1	6.667
III	646.8	726.5	6.327
IV	653.0	733.7	5.350
1971: I	671.7	754.5	3.837
II	685.2	774.1	4.240
III	696.8	784.2	5.003
IV	712.4	794.4	4.230
1972: I	729.3	807.2	3.437
II	747.0	821.2	3.770
III	764.8	845.3	4.220
IV	789.2	884.6	4.863
1973: I	813.2	911.0	5.700
II	827.9	936.1	6.603
III	846.2	959.9	8.323
IV	861.6	992.1	7.500
1974: I	880.0	1,006.5	7.617
II	907.8	1,022.1	8.153
III	935.3	1,052.8	8.190
IV	943.0	1,072.0	7.360
1975: I	967.4	1,080.4	5.750
II	996.6	1,148.3	5.393
III	1,029.6	1,155.7	6.330
IV	1,057.5	1,186.7	5.627
1976: I	1,091.8	1,218.0	4.917
II	1,111.2	1,236.8	5.157
III	1,139.8	1,263.2	5.150
IV	1,174.6	1,292.5	4.673
1977: I	1,211.8	1,317.9	4.630
II	1,239.2	1,359.0	4.840
III	1,270.2	1,404.0	5.497
IV	1,307.6	1,436.4	6.110
1978: I	1,332.6	1,474.9	6.393
II	1,391.1	1,534.3	6.477
III	1,424.6	1,573.6	7.313
IV	1,465.7	1,622.1	8.570
1979: I	1,501.8	1,666.6	9.383
II	1,537.6	1,701.5	9.377
III	1,590.0	1,752.9	9.673
IV	1,637.5	1,796.3	11.843

TABLE F-6 *(Continued)*

Date	Consumption Expenditures (billions of dollars) C	Disposable Personal Income (billions of Y dollars)	Three-Month Treasury Bill Rate (percent) r
1980: I	1,682.2	1,857.6	13.353
II	1,688.9	1,869.8	9.617
III	1,749.3	1,934.1	9.153
IV	1,810.0	2,010.3	13.613
1981: I	1,862.9	2,065.6	14.390
II	1,896.4	2,095.8	14.907
III	1,940.9	2,162.0	15.053
IV	1,960.2	2,187.0	11.750
1982: I	1,996.3	2,207.2	12.813
II	2,023.8	2,241.8	12.420
III	2,065.6	2,278.6	9.317
IV	2,117.0	2,318.1	7.907
1983: I	2,146.6	2,345.7	8.107
II	2,213.0	2,395.4	8.397
III	2,262.8	2,443.2	9.140
IV	2,315.8	2,527.9	8.880
1984: I	2,361.1	2,611.8	9.170
II	2,417.0	2,642.8	9.797
III	2,450.3	2,691.1	10.320
IV	1,493.4	2,728.6	8.803
1985: I	2,554.9	2,764.6	8.183
II	2,599.3	2,850.7	7.460
III	2,661.4	2,840.0	7.107
IV	2,700.4	2,899.5	7.167
1986: I	2,734.3	2,959.2	6.897
II	2,761.0	3,006.5	6.140
III	2,826.0	3,024.3	5.523
IV	2,868.5	3,063.4	5.353
1987: I	2,914.7	3,142.8	5.537
II	2,989.4	3,138.1	5.657
III	3,055.9	3,223.5	6.043
IV	3,083.3	3,319.4	5.863
1988: I	3,148.1	3,376.4	5.723
II	3,204.9	3,435.9	6.210
III	3,263.4	3,511.7	7.010
IV	3,324.0	3,587.4	7.727
1989: I	3,381.4	3,689.5	8.540
II	3,444.1	3,747.7	8.410
III	3,508.1	3,806.8	7.843
IV	3,550.6	3,871.3	7.653

See example 7-12 and equation (7-57).

TABLE F-7 Fuel Prices and Partial Adjustment Model

Date	Natural Gas Consumption (millions of cubic feet) GAS	Price per Cubic Foot (1982 = 100) P	Natural Gas Consumption Lagged One Period	Date	Natural Gas Consumption (millions of cubic feet) GAS	Price per Cubic Foot (1982 = 100) P	Natural Gas Consumption Lagged One Period
1975: 1	1,003	35.4	1,014	1979: 1	1,121	49.0	1,149
2	966	35.5	1,003	2	1,084	50.5	1,121
3	955	35.3	966	3	1,178	52.6	1,084
4	964	35.5	955	4	1,174	54.2	1,178
5	946	35.6	964	5	1,179	56.4	1,174
6	945	35.7	946	6	1,166	60.6	1,179
7	952	36.2	945	7	1,200	63.9	1,166
8	949	36.5	952	8	1,199	67.9	1,200
9	1,037	37.0	949	9	1,194	71.5	1,199
10	985	37.7	1,037	10	1,154	72.9	1,194
11	975	38.2	985	11	1,126	73.9	1,154
12	964	38.5	975	12	1,100	75.6	1,126
1976: 1	970	38.5	964	1980: 1	1,099	79.6	1,100
2	1,079	38.6	970	2	1,034	83.5	1,099
3	1,056	38.3	1,079	3	1,001	85.7	1,034
4	1,048	38.2	1,056	4	979	86.1	1,001
5	1,063	38.1	1,048	5	949	86.1	979
6	1,067	38.3	1,063	6	976	86.5	949
7	1,087	38.4	1,067	7	979	86.8	976
8	1,083	38.6	1,087	8	897	86.9	979
9	1,077	38.8	1,083	9	960	86.9	897
10	1,068	39.2	1,077	10	923	86.5	960
11	1,114	39.9	1,068	11	942	87.8	923
12	1,129	40.9	1,114	12	985	90.6	942
1977: 1	1,240	42.1	1,129	1981: 1	1,080	96.9	985
2	1,378	43.1	1,240	2	1,048	104.6	1,080
3	1,223	43.6	1,378	3	975	107.4	1,048
4	1,194	43.7	1,223	4	958	106.9	975
5	1,208	43.8	1,194	5	935	106.2	958
6	1,192	43.8	1,208	6	915	105.6	935
7	1,170	43.9	1,192	7	873	105.0	915
8	1,178	44.0	1,170	8	978	104.4	873
9	1,179	44.1	1,178	9	937	104.3	978
10	1,189	44.5	1,179	10	889	104.1	937
11	1,163	44.9	1,189	11	948	104.7	889
12	1,141	45.2	1,163	12	972	105.7	948
1978: 1	1,140	45.7	1,141	1982: 1	932	106.2	972
2	1,109	46.0	1,140	2	903	105.8	932
3	1,171	46.0	1,109	3	899	102.8	903
4	1,181	45.9	1,171	4	929	99.3	899
5	1,252	45.8	1,181	5	991	99.8	929
6	1,153	45.7	1,252	6	996	101.7	991
7	1,135	45.6	1,153	7	1,004	102.2	996
8	1,181	45.5	1,135	8	932	102.2	1,004
9	1,128	45.8	1,181	9	957	102.6	932
10	1,165	46.5	1,128	10	1,016	104.8	957
11	1,168	47.4	1,165	11	996	107.0	1,016
12	1,149	48.3	1,168	12	903	106.6	996

TABLE F-7 *(Continued)*

Date	Natural Gas Consumption (millions of cubic feet) GAS	Price per Cubic Foot (1982 = 100) P	Natural Gas Consumption Lagged One Period	Date	Natural Gas Consumption (millions of cubic feet) GAS	Price per Cubic Foot (1982 = 100) P	Natural Gas Consumption Lagged One Period
1983: 1	835	103.9	903	1987: 1	989	75.5	983
2	797	101.3	835	2	974	77.9	989
3	785	96.8	797	3	960	77.5	974
4	848	94.5	785	4	973	77.5	960
5	915	96.1	848	5	942	77.1	973
6	928	96.0	915	6	998	77.2	942
7	963	95.9	928	7	1,013	77.1	998
8	978	95.8	963	8	998	77.8	1,013
9	994	96.5	978	9	1,005	77.6	998
10	960	96.7	994	10	1,004	78.5	1,005
11	930	96.6	960	11	1,049	80.3	1,004
12	857	96.6	930	12	1,079	80.5	1,049
1984: 1	934	99.5	857	1988: 1	1,075	80.8	1,079
2	1,073	106.6	934	2	1,025	80.9	1,075
3	976	102.2	1,073	3	1,080	80.5	1,025
4	907	100.7	976	4	1,092	80.2	1,080
5	974	100.5	907	5	1,078	80.0	1,092
6	1,054	100.0	974	6	1,078	79.1	1,078
7	1,012	98.7	1,054	7	1,046	76.9	1,078
8	994	96.8	1,012	8	1,046	76.3	1,046
9	983	96.3	994	9	1,016	75.9	1,046
10	964	97.0	983	10	1,022	74.6	1,016
11	977	97.1	964	11	1,006	75.0	1,022
12	947	96.9	977	12	1,019	76.8	1,006
1985: 1	948	96.2	947	1989: 1	1,063	80.5	1,019
2	943	96.5	948	2	1,069	81.4	1,063
3	894	96.1	943	3	1,078	81.5	1,069
4	956	96.5	894	4	1,062	82.5	1,078
5	992	96.1	956	5	1,011	81.5	1,062
6	972	94.7	992	6	1,047	80.2	1,011
7	987	93.2	972	7	1,070	79.7	1,047
8	965	92.1	987	8	1,068	78.9	1,070
9	943	93.2	965	9	1,079	79.3	1,068
10	1,043	95.3	943	10	1,050	82.0	1,079
11	1,072	99.3	1,043	11	1,066	83.9	1,050
12	1,069	101.8	1,072	12	1,085	88.7	1,066
1986: 1	1,041	100.7	1,069				
2	970	91.5	1,041				
3	1,046	85.1	970				
4	1,067	80.2	1,046				
5	1,054	76.9	1,067				
6	1,010	75.3	1,054				
7	1,016	71.1	1,010				
8	1,084	69.3	1,016				
9	1,045	70.2	1,084				
10	980	70.0	1,045				
11	1,007	70.0	980				
12	983	71.3	1,007				

See example 7-14 and equation (7-63).

Appendix G

Sample Data Sets for Examples in Chapter 9

TABLE G-1: Automobile Sales (millions; annualized rate)

Date	Sales	First Differences	Date	Sales	First Differences
1967: I	7.993		1979: I	11.201	0.009
II	8.883	0.890	II	10.434	−0.767
III	8.485	−0.398	III	10.711	0.277
IV	8.057	−0.428	IV	9.889	−0.822
1968: I	9.420	1.363	1980: I	10.442	0.553
II	9.401	−0.019	II	7.802	−2.640
III	9.980	0.579	III	8.769	0.967
IV	9.816	−0.164	IV	8.915	0.146
1969: I	9.697	−0.119	1981: I	9.759	0.844
II	9.629	−0.068	II	8.079	−1.680
III	9.615	−0.014	III	9.035	0.956
IV	9.386	−0.229	IV	7.265	−1.770
1970: I	8.750	−0.635	1982: I	8.001	0.736
II	9.077	0.327	II	7.683	−0.318
III	8.921	−0.156	III	7.789	0.106
IV	6.861	−2.060	IV	8.446	0.657
1971: I	9.974	3.113	1983: I	8.244	−0.202
II	9.943	−0.031	II	9.194	0.950
III	10.360	0.417	III	9.236	0.042
IV	10.634	0.274	IV	10.041	0.805
1972: I	10.471	−0.163	1984: I	10.412	0.371
II	10.651	0.180	II	10.500	0.088
III	10.806	0.155	III	10.264	−0.236
IV	11.564	0.758	IV	10.384	0.120
1973: I	12.304	0.740	1985: I	10.844	0.460
II	12.126	−0.178	II	10.879	0.035
III	11.133	−0.993	III	12.314	1.435
IV	9.837	−1.296	IV	10.113	−2.201
1974: I	9.300	−0.537	1986: I	10.755	0.642
II	8.988	−0.312	II	11.204	0.449
III	9.412	0.424	III	12.685	1.481
IV	7.396	−2.016	IV	11.155	−1.530
1975: I	8.227	0.831	1987: I	9.665	−1.490
II	7.685	−0.542	II	10.284	0.619
III	8.933	1.248	III	11.307	1.023
IV	9.308	0.375	IV	9.857	−1.450
1976: I	10.024	0.716	1988: I	10.907	1.050
II	9.848	−0.176	II	10.702	−0.205
III	9.880	0.032	III	10.462	−0.240
IV	10.225	0.345	IV	10.485	0.023
1977: I	10.966	0.741	1989: I	9.820	−0.665
II	11.269	0.303	II	10.332	0.512
III	11.000	−0.269	III	10.783	0.451
IV	10.948	−0.052	IV	9.300	−1.483
1978: I	10.491		1990: I	9.900	0.600
II	11.800	1.309	II	10.150	0.250
III	11.172	−0.628			
IV	11.192	0.020			

TABLE G-2: Daily Ridership

DOW*	Riders	DOW	Riders	DOW	Riders
Wednesday	108,014	Wednesday	103,009	Wednesday	154,037
Thursday	109,954	Thursday	106,222	Thursday	154,742
Friday	103,058	Friday	105,483	Friday	154,082
Saturday	18,231	Saturday	22,471	Saturday	25,632
Sunday	2,396	Sunday	3,366	Sunday	4,053
Monday	107,332	Monday	107,500	Monday	109,095
Tuesday	107,482	Tuesday	106,869	Tuesday	139,347
Wednesday	109,388	Wednesday	108,521	Wednesday	141,592
Thursday	114,060	Thursday	109,603	Thursday	147,891
Friday	106,900	Friday	105,455	Friday	150,259
Saturday	19,587	Saturday	25,200	Saturday	20,648
Sunday	2,824	Sunday	4,796	Sunday	3,380
Monday	112,029	Monday	115,910	Monday	173,548
Tuesday	116,931	Tuesday	115,073	Tuesday	163,737
Wednesday	110,636	Wednesday	105,683	Wednesday	162,015
Thursday	112,075	Thursday	3,117	Thursday	175,872
Friday	106,284	Friday	45,367	Friday	149,639
Saturday	17,533	Saturday	15,856	Saturday	29,249
Sunday	2,903	Sunday	2,468	Sunday	36,341
Monday	105,426	Monday	112,580	Monday	155,478
Tuesday	103,142	Tuesday	111,767	Tuesday	148,292
Wednesday	104,769	Wednesday	118,087	Wednesday	140,387
Thursday	106,087	Thursday	129,561	Thursday	147,442
Friday	103,443	Friday	115,799	Friday	142,675
Saturday	18,630	Saturday	28,021	Saturday	27,467
Sunday	2,837	Sunday	3,406	Sunday	3,450
Monday	111,310	Monday	155,825	Monday	152,394
Tuesday	111,881	Tuesday	136,763	Tuesday	143,096
Wednesday	114,568	Wednesday	134,686	Wednesday	144,531
Thursday	129,223	Thursday	140,182	Thursday	153,201
Friday	109,316	Friday	138,005	Friday	143,510
Saturday	22,586	Saturday	26,671	Saturday	27,828
Sunday	2,758	Sunday	3,810	Sunday	3,592
Monday	4,342	Monday	148,340	Monday	149,084
Tuesday	113,050	Tuesday	145,056	Tuesday	143,486
Wednesday	115,692	Wednesday	147,791	Wednesday	141,537
Thursday	123,445	Thursday	158,594	Thursday	147,228
Friday	117,443	Friday	151,063	Friday	145,417
Saturday	21,851	Saturday	32,889	Saturday	30,046
Sunday	3,155 ·	Sunday	4,753	Sunday	27,868
Monday	118,941	Monday	172,768	Monday	156,646
Tuesday	119,187	Tuesday	167,242	Tuesday	149,737
Wednesday	118,488	Wednesday	183,625	Wednesday	156,051
Thursday	121,661	Thursday	208,390	Thursday	169,838
Friday	113,739	Friday	188,462	Friday	163,849
Saturday	23,720	Saturday	59,489	Saturday	32,264
Sunday	2,942	Sunday	8,022	Sunday	3,876
Monday	116,485	Monday	63,837	Monday	172,337
Tuesday	109,402	Tuesday	1,407	Tuesday	148,972
Wednesday	111,154	Wednesday	116,120	Wednesday	145,673
Thursday	118,151	Thursday	132,054	Thursday	147,825
Friday	111,034	Friday	133,438	Friday	104,829

TABLE G-2: *(Continued)*

DOW*	Riders	DOW	Riders	DOW	Riders
Saturday	21,355	Saturday	32,024	Saturday	20,064
Sunday	2,544	Sunday	4,293	Sunday	1,931
Monday	118,541	Monday	80,568	Monday	141,493
Tuesday	116,361	Tuesday	2,453	Tuesday	143,618
Wednesday	120,322	Wednesday	125,177	Wednesday	149,781
Thursday	119,355	Thursday	140,998	Thursday	163,400
Friday	118,623	Friday	144,108	Friday	166,076
Saturday	23,596	Saturday	28,622	Saturday	37,775
Sunday	3,288	Sunday	2,836	Sunday	3,740
Monday	148,577	Monday	138,252	Monday	164,688
Tuesday	129,687	Tuesday	144,019	Tuesday	140,468
Wednesday	122,885	Wednesday	133,906	Wednesday	137,478
Thursday	132,642	Thursday	137,246	Thursday	142,162
Friday	127,570	Friday	135,422	Friday	14,729
Saturday	21,197	Saturday	25,743	Saturday	25,263
Sunday	2,917	Sunday	3,740	Sunday	3,099
Monday	121,891	Monday	147,571	Monday	141,518
Tuesday	132,362	Tuesday	133,926	Tuesday	138,013
Wednesday	131,497	Wednesday	133,937	Wednesday	137,998
Thursday	135,958	Thursday	138,572	Thursday	146,034
Friday	147,233	Friday	133,765	Friday	142,892
Saturday	27,740	Saturday	24,067	Saturday	27,317
Sunday	3,293	Sunday	2,742	Sunday	2,468
Monday	140,495	Monday	124,322	Monday	157,449
Tuesday	130,906	Tuesday	131,018	Tuesday	147,074
Wednesday	125,511	Wednesday	136,164	Wednesday	141,578
Thursday	127,808	Thursday	137,661	Thursday	145,164
Friday	126,445	Friday	134,661	Friday	135,244
Saturday	21,400	Saturday	28,169	Saturday	25,066
Sunday	2,741	Sunday	3,400	Sunday	3,139
Monday	129,317	Monday	145,128	Monday	142,645
Tuesday	126,409	Tuesday	144,442	Tuesday	137,591
Wednesday	129,842	Wednesday	150,367	Wednesday	136,022
Thursday	131,856	Thursday	152,346	Thursday	145,402
Friday	126,531	Friday	153,599	Friday	140,515
Saturday	23,906	Saturday	18,274	Saturday	25,682
Sunday	2,901	Sunday	3,269	Sunday	2,639
Monday	167,913	Monday	152,258	Monday	150,703
Tuesday	159,420	Tuesday	138,955	Tuesday	147,388
Wednesday	139,034	Wednesday	138,694	Wednesday	140,227
Thursday	129,131	Thursday	143,947	Thursday	142,539
Friday	121,254	Friday	138,224	Friday	139,531
Saturday	22,575	Saturday	20,508	Saturday	24,868
Sunday	2,901	Sunday	4,007	Sunday	3,025
Monday	132,185	Monday	150,600	Monday	143,566
Tuesday	117,885	Tuesday	145,407	Tuesday	137,684
				Wednesday	141,543
				Thursday	151,540
				Friday	140,458
				Saturday	24,641
				Sunday	1,820

* DOW = day of week.

TABLE G-3: Monthly Sales Figures
(thousands of dollars)

Date	Sales	Date	Sales
1985: February	1,023	1989: January	34,154
March	1,254	February	35,396
April	1,500	March	36,660
May	1,769	April	37,944
June	2,052	May	39,247
July	2,366	June	40,581
August	2,691	July	41,928
September	3,040	August	43,299
October	3,405	September	44,695
November	3,795	October	46,116
December	4,196	November	47,554
1986: January	4,607	December	49,025
February	5,048	1990: January	50,522
March	5,505	February	52,036
April	5,979	March	53,586
May	6,483	April	55,155
June	6,995	May	56,750
July	7,523	June	58,357
August	8,068	July	59,987
September	8,639	August	61,634
October	9,236	September	63,304
November	9,864	October	64,996
December	10,518	November	66,718
1987: January	11,197	December	68,456
February	11,899	1991: January	70,208
March	12,629	February	71,796
April	13,384	March	73,756
May	14,151	April	75,568
June	14,935	May	77,412
July	15,744	June	79,281
August	16,578	July	81,181
September	17,434	August	83,103
October	18,315	September	35,048
November	19,223	October	87,021
December	20,150	November	89,023
1988: January	21,100	December	91,051
February	22,069		
March	23,064		
April	24,074		
May	25,100		
June	26,153		
July	27,224		
August	28,319		
September	29,440		
October	30,588		
November	31,754		
December	32,945		

Appendix H

Critical Values of Chi-Square Statistic

TABLE H-1 Critical Values of Chi Square

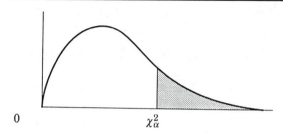

df	$\chi^2_{.995}$	$\chi^2_{.990}$	$\chi^2_{.975}$	$\chi^2_{.950}$	$\chi^2_{.900}$
1	0.0000393	0.0001571	0.0009821	0.0039321	0.0157908
2	0.0100251	0.0201007	0.0506356	0.102587	0.210720
3	0.0717212	0.114832	0.215795	0.351846	0.584375
4	0.206990	0.297110	0.484419	0.710721	1.063623
5	0.411740	0.554300	0.831211	1.145476	1.61031
6	0.675727	0.872085	1.237347	1.63539	2.20413
7	0.989265	1.239043	1.68987	2.16735	2.83311
8	1.344419	1.646482	2.17973	2.73264	3.48954
9	1.734926	2.087912	2.70039	3.32511	4.168216
10	2.15585	2.55821	3.24697	3.94030	4.86518
11	2.60321	3.05347	3.81575	4.57481	5.57779
12	3.07382	3.57056	4.40379	5.22603	6.30380
13	3.56503	4.10691	5.00874	5.89186	7.04150
14	4.07468	4.66043	5.62872	6.57063	7.78953
15	4.60094	5.22935	6.26214	7.26094	8.54675
16	5.14224	5.81221	6.90766	7.96164	9.31223
17	5.69724	6.40776	7.56418	8.67176	10.0852
18	6.26481	7.01491	8.23075	9.39046	10.8649
19	6.84398	7.63273	8.90655	10.1170	11.6509
20	7.43386	8.26040	9.59083	10.8508	12.4426
21	8.03366	8.89720	10.28293	11.5913	13.2396
22	8.64272	9.54249	10.9823	12.3380	14.0415
23	9.26042	10.19567	11.6885	13.0905	14.8479
24	9.88623	10.8564	12.4011	13.8484	15.6587
25	10.5197	11.5240	13.1197	14.6114	16.4734
26	11.1603	12.1981	13.8439	15.3791	17.2919
27	11.8076	12.8786	14.5733	16.1513	18.1138
28	12.4613	13.5648	15.3079	16.9279	18.9302
29	13.1211	14.2565	16.0471	17.7083	19.7677
30	13.7867	14.9535	16.7908	18.4926	20.5992
40	20.7065	22.1643	24.4331	26.5093	29.0505
50	27.9907	29.7067	32.3574	34.7642	37.6886
60	35.5347	37.4848	40.4817	43.1879	46.4589
70	43.2752	45.4418	48.7576	51.7393	55.3290
80	51.1720	53.5400	57.1532	60.3915	64.2778
90	59.1963	61.7541	65.6466	69.1260	73.2912
100	67.3276	70.0648	74.2219	77.9295	82.3581

TABLE H-1 *(Continued)*

df	$\chi^2_{.100}$	$\chi^2_{.050}$	$\chi^2_{.025}$	$\chi^2_{.010}$	$\chi^2_{.005}$
1	2.70554	3.84146	5.02389	6.63490	7.87944
2	4.60517	5.99147	7.37776	9.21034	10.5966
3	6.25139	7.81473	9.34840	11.3449	12.8381
4	7.77944	9.48773	11.1433	13.2767	14.8602
5	9.23635	11.0705	12.8325	15.0863	16.7496
6	10.6446	12.5916	14.4494	16.8119	18.5476
7	12.0170	14.0671	16.0128	18.4753	20.2777
8	13.3616	15.5073	17.5346	20.0902	21.9550
9	14.6837	16.9190	19.0228	21.6660	23.5893
10	15.9871	18.3070	20.4831	23.2093	25.1882
11	17.2750	19.6751	21.9200	24.7250	26.7569
12	18.5494	21.0261	23.3367	26.2170	28.2995
13	19.8119	22.3621	24.7356	27.6883	29.8194
14	21.0642	23.6848	26.1190	29.1413	31.3193
15	22.3072	24.9958	27.4884	30.5779	32.8013
16	23.5418	26.2962	28.8454	31.9999	34.2672
17	24.7690	27.5871	30.1910	33.4087	35.7185
18	25.9894	28.8693	31.5264	34.8053	37.1564
19	27.2036	30.1435	32.8523	36.1908	38.5822
20	28.4120	31.4104	34.1696	37.5662	39.9968
21	29.6151	32.6705	35.4789	38.9321	41.4010
22	30.8133	33.9244	36.7807	40.2894	42.7956
23	32.0069	35.1725	38.0757	41.6384	44.1813
24	33.1963	36.4151	39.3641	42.9798	45.5585
25	34.3816	37.6525	40.6465	44.3141	46.9278
26	35.5631	38.8852	41.9232	45.6417	48.2899
27	36.7412	40.1133	43.1944	46.9630	49.6449
28	37.9159	41.3372	44.4607	48.2782	50.9933
29	39.0875	42.5569	45.7222	49.5879	52.3356
30	40.2560	43.7729	46.9792	50.8922	53.6720
40	51.8050	55.7585	59.3417	63.6907	66.7659
50	63.1671	67.5048	71.4202	76.1539	79.4900
60	74.3970	79.0819	83.2976	88.3794	91.9517
70	85.5271	90.5312	95.0231	100.425	104.215
80	96.5782	101.879	106.629	112.329	116.321
90	107.565	113.145	118.136	124.116	128.299
100	118.498	124.342	129.561	135.807	140.169

Source: "Tables of the Percentage Points of the χ^2-Distribution," *Biometrika,* vol. 32, 1941, pp. 188–89, by Catherine M. Thompson. Reproduced by permission of Professor D. V. Lindley and the Biometrika Trustees.

Appendix I

Sample Data Sets for Examples in Chapter 10

TABLE I-1 **Historical Monthly Attendance Figures**

1989: Jan.	124,410
Feb.	126,582
Mar.	129,809
Apr.	134,070
May	138,952
June	144,045
July	148,782
Aug.	152,800
Sept.	156,491
Oct.	161,058
Nov.	166,277
Dec.	171,531
1990: Jan.	176,707
Feb.	180,820
Mar.	183,393
Apr.	185,603
May	188,600
June	192,930
July	198,587
Aug.	204,371
Sept.	208,976
Oct.	212,060
Nov.	215,430
Dec.	218,855
1991: Jan.	221,526
Feb.	223,316
Mar.	224,082

See example 10-2.

Author Index

Subject Index